Most Comprehensive Origins of (
Expressions Volume II

Most Comprehensive Origins of Clichés, Proverbs, and Figurative Expressions

Volume II Revised and Expanded

CLICHÉS, OLD SAYINGS, PROVERBS, IDIOMS, AXIOMS, SIMILES, METAPHORIC EXPRESSIONS, CATCH PHRASES, CURIOUS WORDS AND SELECTED OXYMORONS IN THE ENGLISH LANGUAGE WITH DEFINITIONS AND EARLY CITATIONS

Many British & Aussie Expressions
PlUS Lots More American Sayings

1200 + Entries in this version

Stanley J. St. Clair

Edited by Kathy Ann Barney

StCP

ISBN **978-1-947514-20-1**

Printed in the United States of America by

St. Clair Publications
PO Box 726
McMinnville, TN 37111-0726

http://stclairpublications.com/

Cover Design

Kent Grey-Hesselbein Design Studio
www.kghdesignstudio.com

Major Acknowledgement and Dedication

I wish to express my deepest gratitude to my two dear friends, **Niven Sinclair**, of Surry, U.K., who purchased several copies of my first volume of ***Most Comprehensive Origins of Clichés, Proverbs and Figurative Expressions*** for friends and was relentless in providing me new expressions to research, many of which are British and a few, Scottish; and radio talk show host **Kelly Marlow**, of McMinnville, Tennessee, who has had me on the air as a guest on several occasions, and has utilized that first book since its original release, as a means for callers to learn the origins of sayings as found therein, and as a result, has sold many copies to members of his audience. It is to these two amazing friends that I dedicate this second large volume.

Also, I give special thanks to Rondo B B Me of Queensland, Australia, for contributing a great number of sayings from "Down Under" for this volume. Kent Hessselbein is also a big part of my success, and I thank him from the bottom of my heart for the great job on this and all of the **St. Clair Publications** covers which he has done. And last but not least, a big 'thank you' to **Kathy Ann Barney** of Greenville, South Carolina, for her splendid work on editing and proofing this volume.

Author's Introduction

Back in 2010 when I began researching phrase origins, I had no idea how far this exciting journey would lead me. I originally published two smaller volumes of ***On the Origin of the Clichés and Evolution of Idioms*** which I used in the composition of the first book of ***Most Comprehensive Origins of Clichés, Proverbs and Figurative Expressions.*** That original tome was a huge hit and was selected to be placed in libraries, both public and private, across America, and has sold in at least seven countries. It received high critical praise from individuals with degrees far above my own. I was humbled and grateful.

I thought publication of that work would be the last of my research; however, the two friends, mentioned earlier in my acknowledgement and dedication, who had contributed to this effort and actively promoted the book, continued to send me additional expressions, or ask me about ones I had not been able to include. Thus, I knew that my effort must eventually continue.

As noted in the first volume of ***Most Comprehensive Origins***, when researching for my original cliché origin books, I discovered that much of the information already in print, even by major publishers, and even more so online, is incomplete, often undocumented, or in some cases, *inaccurate*. A lot of it was based on what is commonly called, 'folk etymology,' which makes for interesting anecdotes, but may not hold up under solid research. This has continued to hold true. Also, none of the other major publications carry detailed early citations, as I have included in these volumes.

In combing through ancient works of this type, novels, and periodicals, as well as modern volumes of etymology and phrase origins and definitions, I have found more than ever, that every tongue on earth is ever-evolving, and that we often take for granted the words and expressions that have become as natural to us and the breath we breathe.

In these two books I not only included the time-worn sayings and clichés which we have so freely inserted into our vocabularies over the past centuries in America, the U.K., Australia (hundreds in this book are decidedly British; many, Aussie), and other countries where English is spoken in a fair capacity, but I am using more fresh phrases which are coming of age as I am typing these words. I have even included several regional colloquialisms and slang expressions while avoiding offensive obscenities.

Since my mother was a public school and business college teacher once included in '*Who's Who in North Carolina Education*' who would remove printed works from the shelves and systematically edit the typos as she read, writing and editing just came to be engrained into my makeup. When I gave up art (something which I dearly love, and for which I received early recognition) as 'not my strongest talent,' I adopted writing and have found its pursuit irresistible. Words have become my paint and the computer, my brush. It is my fondest hope that these books will become standard-bearers for future authoritative reference. They include clichés, old sayings, metaphoric idioms, axioms, proverbs, similes, curious words, and a few common short rhymes and acronyms. Since my degree is in Religious Education, rather than English, I have expended many thousands of hours in self-education and research. While coming to understand etymology and practical lexicography as they apply to expressions in order to be effective and knowledgeable in this realm, I have strayed to the extent of being more in-depth in the explanations than an average dictionary. It has continued to be my objective to always burst myths about phrase origins when applicable. Even with all of this massive effort, which has literally taken years, there is no possible way to include all English phrases in even these two volumes. All entries, regardless of origin, are in American spellings except when direct quotes from British or Australian publications. I have striven to make this volume even better organized and cross-referenced than the original.

Note: Quotations from books, periodicals, etc. herein are printed as in the original document; spelling and punctuations will reflect the period, country of publication, and authors' misspellings when applicable.

Note: On entries which have proven to have origins different than what is popularly believed or printed in other dictionaries or authoritative sources, the entry will be followed by ^.

Note: Phrases used primarily in the U.K. have ^{2} after the main entry; those Used primarily in Asutralia are followed by a ^{3}. Those known to be used in more than one country may have multiple digits. One with a ^{4} is for Scottish origin.(Several others are noted as having either Scottish or Irish origins, but are now in common usage in other countries.) A rare ^{1} beside any of these indicates that it is used in America as well. Those with no digit are primarily Americanisms.

In addition, in this volume, the more modern method of ascribing dates is utilized: instead of BC and AD, BCE and CE are noted which may mean Before Current (or Christian) Era and Current (or Christian) Era.

New entries found only in the Revised Expanded version are followed by a plus sign +.

Definitions

Acronym – a word formed from the initial letters or groups of letters of words in a set phrase or series of words

Aphorism – a tersely phrased statement of a truth or opinion; an adage

Aussie Expressions – slang words or phrases used in Australia which are likely unrecognizable in other cultures

Axiom – a self-evident truth that requires no proof

Cliché – a trite, stereotyped expression; a sentence or a phrase usually expressing a popular or common thought or idea that has lost originality, ingenuity and impact by long overuse

Corruptive derivative – This is a newly coined phrase in the first volume (obviously not the 'proverb' mentioned in the introduction) which is a combination of corruption and derivative. A corruption of a word is a misspelling or change which later becomes an accepted word. A derivative is a new word or phrase derived from the same original base word, often from another language. Therefore, a corruptive derivative, as used in this book, is a newly formed phrase based on previously accepted words which, though deemed incorrect, became an accepted expression.

Curious words and catch-phrases – expressions which are often used, whether as a single word or a phrase, which seem strange as to their exact origin or meaning and need clarification

Earliest known citation – as used herein means earliest dated printed reference found during extensive research for this dictionary

Etymology – the derivation of a word

Euphemism – a mild or indirect word or expression substituted for one considered to be too harsh or blunt when referring to something unpleasant or embarrassing

Hyperbolic – relating to hyperbole; exaggerated

Idiom – an expression, the meaning of which is not predictable from the usual definitions of its constituent elements or from the general grammatical rules of a language, and that is not a constituent of a larger expression of like characteristics

Metaphoric phrase – a cliché or expression which applies in a broader sense to a comparison or resemblance of a literal image to a figurative one; an idiom

Metonymic adage – aka 'metonymy' is a figure of speech used in rhetoric in which a thing or concept is not called by its own name, but by the name of something intimately associated with that thing or concept

Old saying – a phrase of obscure origin which has become a part of popular jargon

Oxymoron – a figure of speech in which apparently contradictory terms appear in conjunction

Platitude – a remark, usually of moral content, that has become cliché

Practical Lexicography –- the craft of compiling dictionaries

Proverb – a short popular saying, usually of unknown and ancient origin, that expresses effectively some commonplace truth or USeful thought; adage

Simile – A figure of speech in which two unlike things are explicitly compared

A

Above one's pay grade

This expression means that that person does not know the answer to a question or the solution to some problem, or is not authorized to deal with it, and that someone else more knowledgeable or higher up the chain of command needs to be consulted. It began being used in the mid-1990s, and the origin is most likely military, as the earliest citations are from books relating stories from the American Armed Forces. The very first known example in print is from *Tail of the Storm: Flying Missions in the Gulf War* by Alan Cockrell, 1995, page 43:

> "We said so many times, but the response was always 'that's **above my pay grade'** or something similar."

ace up one's sleeve, An (See: **Have an ace up one's sleeve**)

Aching for a breaking+

This is but one of a number of rhyming phrases, most popular from the 1960s, meaning that a person was asking for trouble by his or her actions. Other such terms include 'Cruising for a bruising,' 'Strolling for a rolling,' 'Angling for a mangling,' and 'Aiming for a maiming'. 'Aching for a breaking' is the oldest known of these, going back as far as Wednesday, February 5, 1947, when it appeared in Montreal's ***The McGill Daily*** in a poem titled ***Fell, Fell, Fell*** on page 4, column 3:

> "Fast you're **aching for a breaking**, which you're going to get!"

Afraid of one's own shadow

This hyperbolic expression is used to describe a person's extreme timidity. It refers to someone who is easily alarmed and the least bit of noise or disturbance is enough to fill him or her with gripping fear. The basis of this is traced back to William Shakespeare's *Merchant of Venice*, I, ii:

> ***Por***: "… Palentine, he is every man in no man, if a Trassell sing he fals straight a capring she will fence with **his own shadow**."

The earliest known citation in print of the actual saying, however, is from *Atlas Japannensis, Being Remarkable Addresses by Way of Embassy from the East India Company of the United Provinces to the Emperor of Japan certified in several Writings and Journals* by Arnoldis Montanis English'd and Adom'd by John Ogilby published in London in 1670:

> "…and when he goes to drink, he first stirs the Water with his Snout, that he may not swallow any hurtful Creature; which is more credible than what Theophilaétus Simocatus faith, That the Beast stirs the Water because he is **afraid of his own Shadow**."

After the fact

From the Latin *ex post facto,* this term is used in law for an accessory to a crime, called 'accessory after the fact.' It was in use as early as 1676 when Thomas Tomkinson used it in *Truth's Triumph, or; A Witness to the Two Witnesses,* published in 1690, and later by subscription in 1823, at that time 'after the fact was done' on page 297:

> "Now if the law had been as visible to Cain and his fury, before the murder of his brother, as it was to him **after the fact** was done, surely he could not have done it; but that could not be, for sin is not known to be sin till it be cemented."

It has come to be used in any situation where something has taken place after the actual occurrence of important events. In 1982 James West Davidson and Mark Hamilton Lytle released a book titled ***After the Fact**: The Art of Historical Detection*. There have been several other additions by Mark H. Lytle. The books are designed to show students how historians go about interpreting the past.

Agree to disagree+

This is an old common phrase meaning that all parties in a conflict or dispute are willing to resolve their differences by tolerating the opposing views while maintaining their own position. It first appeared in print in 1770 in John

Wesley's sermon, *On the Death of Rev. Mr. George Whitefield,* preached November 18, 1770, in which he acknowledges their doctrinal differences:

> "There are many doctrines of a less essential nature ... In these we may think and let think; we may 'agree to disagree.' But, meantime, let us hold fast the essentials"

Wesley enclosed the phrase in quotation marks indicating that he was not the originator of it. Wesley's brother, Charles, deemed to be the founder of the Methodist Church, attributed the expression to Whitefield himself, who had used it in a letter to "Mr. B." twenty years earlier, dated June 29, 1750:

> "After all, those who will live in peace must **agree to disagree** in many things with their fellow-labourers, and not let little things part or disunite them."

But the gist of the saying came earlier; also first used by a minister, John Piggott, in *Sermon on Union and Peace, preach'd to several Congregations, April 17, 1704*:

"And now why should we not **agree to differ**, without either enmity or scorn?"

All bark and no bite

Often said of someone who makes cutting remarks, this means full of big talk but lacking action, power, or substance. It was inspired by the fact that many dogs which bark a lot are actually afraid of people. This is a form of the saying 'His bark is worse than his bite' from Anglican priest, George Herbert in his 1651 book of proverbs. This saying, per se, however, began popping up in the mid-nineteenth century. The earliest available reference is from *The African Repository and Colonial Journal*, Volume 23, page 41, February, 1847:

> "When the zeal of theories rises to the height of non-resistance, the danger to the nation is small. It is **all bark and no bite**. But a political parly implies the shedding of blood if deemed necessary; and when men set out with theories which cannot always be reduced to practice, as they could wish, they may find in the end that their theories."

All good things must come to an end^

This old proverb is widely claimed to be based on a line from Geoffrey Chaucer in his tragic epic poem, *Troilus and Criseyde*, circa 1374. Many even use it as a quote. But these words *never* appear in the poem. The closest found is in Stanza 140, "I hope of this to maken a good ende."

The earliest known citation in print of a close form of this comes in July, 1839 from *Bentley's Miscellany, Volume 4*, in 'Some Passages in the Literary Life of Olinthus Jenkinson' on page 74:

> "**All things must come to an end**, and so did our dinner."

The first printed reference available to the actual proverb comes 20 years later from Henry Martyn Field in *Summer Pictures - From Copenhagen to Venice*, 1859, page 21, still referring to eating a meal:

> "But **all good things must come to an end**, even the best of breakfasts, and that source of happiness being at length exhausted; we sailed forth to find the coach for Plymouth."

All hat and no cattle

This metaphoric idiom means the same as "all bark and no bite," or "all wax and no wick." It implies that something is pretentious, lacking in substance, action or power. The earliest known printed reference is found in *Ural-Altaische Jahrbücher*, Volumes 51-53, page 87, 1979:

> "As they say in Texas, **all hat and no cattle**. To be retained from those pages is just the proposal that the Yiddish verb base davn- could come from Kipchak — and that's not a fact but a suggestion."

A form of the saying is the title of a 1981 report by Harvard Business Review: *Big Hat, No Cattle; Managing Human Resources*.

Several publications of the middle 1980s state that this is a Texas saying. *The Regis Touch*: *Million Dollar Advice from America's Top Marketing Consultant,* by Regis McKenna on page 27 says:

> "There's an old Texas saying about a cowboy who was '**all hat and no cattle**.' That is, he was all show and no substance."

The British also have a saying, "all froth and no substance."

All or nothing

This common idiom means not allowing for qualifying or compromise; either fully in or out in a particular situation. It has been with us since the 17th century. The earliest citation in a similar usage is from *Strange Histories Consisting of Ballads and Other Poems Principally* by Thomas Deloney, 1607:

> "Sith I am king, thus did he say,
> Why should I not both rule and Raigne?
> My heart disdaines for to obey;
> Yea, **all or nothing** will I gaine.
> Hereon he raiseth armies great,
> and drawes a number to his part.
> His fathers force downe right to beat,
> and by his speare to pierce his heart."

Then in 1637, this appeared in *A Voyager to the Lavant*; *A Brief Relation of a Journey, Lately Preformed by Mafter H.P. Gentleman*:

> "...he still defigns one, or both, for his taske; that not as other Princes, for counterpeyfe with intent of Peace; but with a resolution irrevocably engaged, to bee **all, or nothing;"**

This example from 1645 may be even a bit closer to today's interpretation of the saying. It is from *The Sound Believer, A Treatise of Evangelicall Conversion* by Thomas Shepphard:

> "...when the Lord calls to the soule to come and take all with nothing, take **all or nothing**."

All smoke and mirrors

This idiomatic expression means that someone's actions are all trickery or deceit. It is often used regarding political efforts. It has its origin in illUSions which use actual smoke and mirrors to make something appear different than it actually is; i.e., making something disappear in a magic show. The figurative use was gleaned from the writings of Jimmy Breslin, an American journalist in *How the Good Guys Finally Won Notes from an Impeachment Summer*, 1975:

> "All political power is primarily an illusion... Mirrors and blue smoke, beautiful blue smoke rolling over the surface of highly polished mirrors... If somebody tells you how to look, there can be seen in the smoke great, magnificent shapes, castles and kingdoms, and maybe they can be yours."

"The ability to create the illusion of power, to use mirrors and blue smoke, is one found in unusual people."

The earliest verifiable usage of the exact expression in print is found in *InfoWorld*, Volume 6, Issue 23, June 9, 1986:

"Thurow was talking about integrating economics into the social sciences. Talk about subjects like that is usually **all smoke and mirrors**, but he got right down to specific cases, namely, why has American productivity been growing so slowly?"

All that jazz

This cliché means the same as the Latin phrase, *et cetera*, or 'all those type things.' It comes from the title of a rousing song in the 1975 hit Broadway play, *Chicago,* later a high-grossing film in 2002, based on the 'Roaring '20s' when jazz music was king.

All the bases covered (See: **Cover all the bases**)

All wax and no wick[2]

This parallel for 'all bark and no bite' was coined by Garrison Keillor in *Wobegon Boy* in 1996:

"This guy is all foam and no beer**. All wax and no wick**. A rocket without a payload."

Along for the ride

This idiom means to participate in an activity or event without playing an active part in it. The expression was being used in what might be considered a literal context as early as July, 1911, when it appeared in *Rollins Magazine* in a futuristic article on page 10 by Richard Maxwell Winans titled "Unburied Treasures:"

"'...Now, son,' interposed the old man, rising from his chair, 'the men have finished loading those crates. I must go. Come **along for the ride**.'"

An explicitly figurative citation showed up in the November 6, 1920 edition of *Our Paper* published by the Massachusetts Reformatory in an article titled 'They Risk Their Lives Taking Pictures in the Air' on page 2, in quotes:

> "It occurred to me that I was like the young man at the funeral who 'just went **along for the ride**.' And immediately thereupon I wished that the thought had not occurred to me."

Ambulance chasers

This term was coined to refer to lawyers who gained a reputation of seeking out accident victims and encouraging them to sue, often promising large settlements. The earliest known citation is from an 1897 newspaper article about these attorneys soliciting clients through the mail. Over the next few years the term became very well known through journals, speeches and books. In *Accident and Injury, Their Relations to Disease of the Nervous System*, by Pierce Bailey, AM, MD, 1898, we find the following on page 343:

> "In New York city the value of information regarding an accident is so generally recognized that witnesses carry the news voluntarily to the offices of '**ambulance chasers**,' ..."

Then, in *Contingent Fees, an Address to the Graduating Class of 1905, Being One of the Lectures of the Hubbard Course of Legal Ethics* by Irving G. Vann, LLD, Associate Judge of the Court of Appeals, Delivered at the Commencement of Albany Law School (NY) a clear definition is given of what had already by then become a smear on the legal profession:

> "There are other evils, which in my judgment, are distinctly traceable to the statute which gives attorneys pecuniary interests in the results of the action. Who has not heard of **ambulance chasers**? If a definition is necessary, let me quote from the language used by the President of the Medical Society of the State of New York in his late annual address to the members of that representative body of learned men: 'There are lawyers,' he said, 'who have runners constantly on watch for accident cases of which they learn through the daily papers...'"

Amp up+

This is a modern idiomatic expression for exciting arouse or energizing something or someone's emotions. It may be used to mean increasing the force of anything. Amp was used as a short form noun for an amplifier as early as

1882. According to a popular online dictionary amp was first recorded as a verb in 1960-1965. Amp(ed) up was first used as a phrase, according to *Merriam Webster*, in 1972.

Apple pie order[2]

This primarily British idiom means tidy and well organized; in good order. It most likely originated from the French *cap-a-pie* (from head to foot). Admiral Sir Thomas Pasley first recorded it in English in his *Private Sea Journals*, 1780:

> "Their Persons Clean and in **apple-Pie order** on Sundays."

Are we having fun yet?

This comical cliché is a famous quote of the bizarre comic-strip character Zippy the Pinhead coined in 1979 by cartoonist Bill Griffith, who published a Zippy storybook book by that title in 1985. It was later used by superstar rocker and best-selling author Sammy Hagar on his cooking and partying website featuring receipts and stories, as well as on TV. It has caught on with the public as a favorite saying.

Arm's length

This very old expression now means that a transaction has no particular link as between a buyer and seller. It may infer that any two entities have no known connection; independent and on equal footing. It may be used after the words 'kept at' when making certain that such a condition remains intact. The term was in use from the 17th century, and seems to be figurative in this snippet from page 26 of *The Christian in Combat Armour* by William Gurnall, 5th Edition, 1669:

> "But to come to deal with one who prays and hears, one that is a Pretender to Hope and Faith in God, here is a man in glistering Armour, he hath his Weapon in his hand, with which he will keep the Preacher, and the Word he chargeth him with, at **arms length**. Who can say, I am not a Saint?"

Another spiritual analogy which is surely metaphoric is found in London's *The Monthly Magazine*, published by Sir Richard Phillips February, 1798, in a letter to the editor, Dr. John Aiken:

> "...whilst the wretched patient, to escape from the flames which threaten to devour him, and to keep his tormentor, the devil, at **arms' length**, wastes his whole fortune in daily, weekly, monthly, and annual obits, and, at length, dies stupefied and distracted..."

By the mid-19th century, the term was being used in its modern application, even in court cases. Multiple references were made to it in *Session Cases: Cases Decided in the Court of Session, &c* Volume 3. One clear example from June 13, 1865 from the House of Lords, on page 53 is:

> "But we must ascertain whether, when the notice ought to have been given, the parties were at **arms-length**."

As American as apple pie

The intro, 'as American as,' means that a person, product or item is essentially typical of the United States and does not owe its origin or qualities to any other country. Americans as a whole love apple pie and it can usually be found at Independence Day celebrations as well as Thanksgiving dinners. Apples are abundant in America, and it is a dessert of choice for so many that it is considered a quintessential American dish. Apple pie, however, does not fit the bill for the simile, because it was not invented in the U.S. It was enjoyed by the English for hundreds of years prior to colonization of New England. In 1902, soon after a British author suggested that apple pie should only be eaten twice weekly, The *New York Times* editor shot back in a most defiant manner, placing pie in the position of a patriotic American icon:

> "[Eating only twice per week] is utterly insufficient, as anyone who knows the secret of our strength as a nation and the foundation of our industrial supremacy must admit. Pie is the American synonym of prosperity, and its varying contents the calendar of changing seasons. Pie is the food of the heroic. No pie eating people can be permanently vanquished."

In March, 1920, the earliest reference known in print came in *World Outlook*, on page 45 in "The Town that Got Acquainted with Itself" (Chester Pennsylvania) by Margaret Widdemer:

> "Baths are **as** characteristically **American as apple pie**. Chester started Americanizing its foreigners by letting them use the shower baths in the school houses."

\

As bald as a coot[2]

Coots are water birds which have the appearance of having bald heads, though they do not in fact. It is because of the streaked markings on their white heads.

This is one of the very oldest British similes, first expressed in John Lydgate's *Chronicle of Troy*, 1430:

> "And yet he was as **balde as is a coote**."

As brave as a lion

This simile, which is self-explanatory, was first known to be printed in 1790 in *The Haunted Tower, a Comic Opera in Three Acts* by James Cobb in Act III, Scene ii:

> "Bar. Alarmed, my lord? ''hy, though I am naturally **as brave as a lion**, yet, I do not like to be taken thus by surprise; it is that which alarms me; and Sir Palamede, I am sure is at the bottom of this.'"

As cheap as chips[2]

This British simile refers to an item which may be purchased inexpensively and is a very good deal. It is taken from potatoes which are cut into long narrow strips and deep-fried which are commonly sold with fish. The saying popped up in the mid-19th century, and the first known printed reference is on page 326 of *Knights and Their Days* by Dr. Doran, 1854:

> "He was actor of all work, wrote thousands of songs, which he sold **as cheap as chips**, and composed four pieces for Astley's Theatre, for which he received fourteen pounds — hardly the price of a couple of arm-chairs."

As cold as charity[2]^

This British simile is the equivalent 'as cold as ice.' It is meant to express the irony of something which should be seen as warm being just the opposite, such as institutional charity given grudgingly. Contrary to popular beliefs that this saying originated in the Victorian Age, it is much, much older; from the mid-17th century. The earliest verifiable citation is from the play *A Virgin Widow: A*

Comedy in Five Acts, in Prose and Verse, by Fra. Quarles, Second Edition, 1656:

> "Art. I find by her Water, there has been too fudden Alterations: in her constitution: Is she not fometimes very hot, and fometimes very cold? * * . . ; - Page. Yes Sir, fometimes **as cold as Charity**, fometimes as hot as Zeale. - .* Art. I find obnoxious."

There are numerous usages of the phrase in books from that period on.

As dead as a dodo[2]

This has reference to someone who, or something which, for all practical purposes, is as dead as the long extinct bird. The dodo was native to Mauritius, a volcanic island nation in the Indian Ocean, and was last seen alive by Dutch explorers in 1662 and thought to have died out completely by 1690.

In November, 1890 *The Cornhill Magazine* first printed an article titled 'Big Birds' which used the following analogy, later reprinted in *Littell's Living Age*, which apparently triggered the advent of the simile.

> "The cats and pigs helped in the slaughter by eating the defenceless eggs and callow young; and half a century after the Dutchman came the **dodo** was as **dead** as Julius Caesar."

Then, on December 6, 1899, the actual simile was cited in an article titled 'Small Talk of the Week' in *The Sketch, a Journal of Art and Actuality*:

> "Whether such an apparently Utopian association will ever exist depends upon the revival, under strong leadership, of an esprit de corps among playwrights which at the present time is **as dead as the dodo**."

As different as chalk and cheese[2]

This common British simile refers to two things which could not be more variant from one another. One of the oldest of all comparative statements, the earliest citation of the first form is found in John Gower's Middle English text *Confessio Amantis*, 1390:

> "Lo, how they feignen **chalk** for **chese**."

In September, 1704 the London literary magazine, *The History of the Works of the Learned,* had the following:

> "But there is another fort of Syncretists who would reconcile those different Opinions. It's true, that Opinions, which seem **as different as Chalk** is from **Cheese**, are oftentimes [only **different** in the Terms us'd to explain them."

As different as day and night

Comparisons of night and day and use of them in dialogue go back as far as the Genesis creation story in the Bible, thought to have been written circa 1,440 to 1,400 BCE. But actually making an analogy using 'different as' in English is not to be found in any known printed sources until the 17th century. In 1663,*Another Collection of Philosophical Conferences of the French Virtuosi, upon Questions of all Sorts for the Improving of Natural Knowledg. Render'd into English by G. Havers, Gent and J. Davies of Kidwelly, Gent* contains the following forerunner:

> "Add to this, that darkness, filence, and the coldness of the **night** being fit to recruit the Spirits, and promcte their retirement ... who turn **night** to **day**, and **day** to **night**, a course of life much **different** from that which is observ'd by the Superiours **...**"

In 1685 we find a near-perfect citation in *The Famous Romance of Tarsis and Zell* by Roland Le Vayer de Boutigny, translated into English by Charles Williams, in Book III, page 247:

> "First Celemante tell me little the difference, that you pretend there is between a Gallant and a Lover; it is fo great, replyed he, as the **day** is **different** from the **night**, for a Lover is one that sleeps not, that eats not, laughs not, who seems nothing ..."

As dull as a fro (See: **Dull as a fro**)+

As easy as falling off a log+

This simile has reference to the inability of a person to stay on a log, particularly one which has fallen into a stream or body of water. It originated in the United States in the early 20th century when logs were cut in the forest and floated down the rivers to the saw mills. It is much easier to fall off than to stay on. It is used of some job or needed action which requires no skill and is very simple to perform.

As green as grass

This simile can be used in more than one sense. It can just apply to the true hue of an object. Someone who is green is ignorant about a subject. If one is 'green as grass,' then he or she is a true novice. William Shakespeare coined the phrase in a literal sense in *Two Gentlemen of Verona*, believed to have been written between 1589 and 1592, Act IV, Scene iv:

> "Her eyes are **green as grass** and so are mine."

In a figurative usage it was found as early as 1842 in *The Royal Rake: and the Adventures of Albert Chesterton* by William Leman Rede, page 149:

> "All the knowing ones now agreed that the Duke was **as green as grass**. 'What should he know about poultry? —why didn't he stick to horses, dogs, and fighting cocks?'"

As mad as a March hare

This analogy derives from the strange behavior of hares during March which is their mating season. It was in used as early as the mid sixteenth century and a version of it was first cited in *The Works of Thomas More, Knyght, Sometyme Lorde*, 1557, printed in Old English, now difficult to render:

> "If that mä wer not for malice **as mad** not **as a march hare**, but as a madde dogge y runneth forthe ..."

It was listed verbatim in *The Proverbs, Epigrams and Miscellanies of John Heywood* in 1562:

> "95. 'Of the March Hare.' **As mad as a March hare**: where madness compares, [hares? Are not Midsummer hares as mad as March?"

As much fun as ants at a picnic

'Ants at picnics' has long been a topic of jovial conversation. Obviously, the last thing anyone wants at an outing is ants invading them, which is one of the most likely things to occur. This comical metaphor was first used by staff writer Kevin Thomas in a *Los Angeles Times* article on 17 June 1988 in regard to the comedy flick, *The Great Outdoors,* starring John Candy and Dan Aykroyd. Since then it has been used by numerous bloggers, and even best-selling author, David S. Brody in his 2015 novel, *The Isaac Question* in chapter 4, page 95.

> "He nodded and sighed. 'You're right. I'm about **as much fun as ants at a picnic.**'"

As much use as a chocolate teapot[2]

This means something is of no use whatsoever. Again, it is from the U.K., and was first cited in the British National Newspaper, *The Guardian*, July 17, 1978 in an article by Michael Parkin, "Barnsley Bashers Face the Chop:"

> "Tourists that go to the home games of Barnsley Town will hear some of the finest football wit and repartee in the land. Players are accused of being 'as nimble as a stone trough,' or '**as much use as a chocolate teapot**.'"

Obviously Barnsley didn't originate the saying, as he is quoting others using it, but he repeated it in another similar article in the February 13, 1980 issue of *The Guardian*. Desmond Morris used it in *The Soccer Tribe* in 1981, again in a sports context:

> "If the referee gives the opponents a penalty, he yells, 'When they circumcised you they threw away the wrong part.' If a player is not trying hard enough, he bellows, 'You are **as much use as a chocolate teapot**.'"

As rare as edelweiss[2]

Edelweiss is a small alpine plant with silver grey leaves and a tiny white flower which grows in remote areas of the Alpines, so it is rarely seen. This simile is similar in meaning to "As rare as hen's teeth" but a more colorful expression for something which is rare and beautiful. This species was brought to international attention in a song in the 1965 hit musical film, *Sound of Music.*

In July, 1895 the earliest known reference in print to this comparative expression appeared in *Lippincott's Monthly Magazine* in an article titled 'The New Womanhood:'

> "But, you will object, if conjugal happiness belongs only to the few who are highly developed, it is indeed **as rare** a plant as the **edelweiss**, and grows in the same inaccessible altitudes."

As sick as a dog

This analogy, referring to someone who is extremely ill, thought to have originated in the early 1700s when it was common to call something unclean or unwell a dog, actually began much earlier. Germs and disease were often spread by animals throughout history. This phrase was cited in print as early as 1592, when *Four Letters and Certain Sonnets Especially Touching Robert Greene* by Gabrielle Harvey contained the following in a poem titled 'A Due Consideration of the Quipping Author' on page 2:

> "Now **sick as a dog**, and ever brain-sick,
> Where such a raving and desperate Dick?"

As sick as a parrot[2]^

This is a British expression. A doctor in Liverpool stated that the phrase originated from 1926 when the previously obscure disease of bird psittacosis became a pandemic of clinical importance, involving humans in twelve countries with more than 800 cases. This could have popularized the simile in the 20th century. But actually, this doesn't seem to ring true. Here's why.

First, the thought is actually much older. It was first coined by the dramatist Aphra Behn in her 1681 comedy, *The False Count*, in which the maid Jacinta says of her mistress Julia (Iii1),

> "Lord, Madam, you are **as melancholy as a sick Parrot**."

This simile is used to expresses a feeling of disappointment rather than one of nausea because of the meaning in the play and its reference to Julia, who is deprived of liberty by her jealous husband.

Still, it doesn't appear much in books. In 1975 the following was on page 13 of *Imprisoned Tongues* by Robert Roberts where an illiterate speaks of his inability to learn:

> "It's knocked me **sick as a parrot."**

As tough as nails (See: **Tough as nails**)+

As we speak

This cliché, sometimes prefaced with 'even,' means right at this very moment in time, and is often used in an exaggerated manner, or comically to make a point. Pinning down the exact origin of this is difficult, but 'even as we speak' was used as early as June, 1839, in *The Monthly Magazine*, in Library Monologue:

> **"Even as we speak**, returns the vision of rusty curtains, tarnished brass wires, armless chairs, cushion-less stools, and rent carpeting."

Ate up (with)+

This is a slang expression meaning strange, stupid or weird. Though it is widely reported to have originated in the United States military, this expression has been in use in a slightly different connotation for hundreds of years in print. In *Bell's Edition: The Poets of Great Britain complete from Chaucer to Churchill* by John Bell, 1777, a poem by Charles Churchill contains:

> "With the small-pox, his body maim'd and mat'd, **Ate up with** the king's evil, and his blood tainted therewith.

At someone's beck and call^

This metaphoric phrase means that a person is totally subservient to someone else, meeting his or her every whim. The word 'beck' is what sets the expression apart. It is actually a shortening of the word 'beckon,' meaning to silently signal for someone with a motion of one's hand or finger. Though it originated in Middle English between 1325 and 1375, in modern English it is never used without being attached to the word 'call.' Contrary to a major source which states that the first printed reference to 'beck and call' is from *Salve Deus Rex Judaeorum*, by Amelia Lanyer, in 1611, John Heywood had already used it in his 1562 book titled *The Proverbs, Epigrams and Miscellanies*:

> "(c) 'I have been common Jack to all that whole flock' (d), in disparagement; i.e. at everyone's **beck and call**: cf. 'a twangling jack…'"

At the getting place+

This has been used, particularly in the American South, for over 100 years, as a euphemism in answer to the question, "Where did you get that?" and means roughly, "Mind your own business." The earliest available citation of the phrase in this connotation is found in ***Bulletin of the University of Texas, A Word-List from East Alabama,*** May 1, 1909, on page 314:

> "**getting place**: used in evasive answers: 'Where did you get that?' '**At the getting place**.'"

At the stroke of a pen[2]

This British expression, and its American counterpart, 'with the stroke of a pen' mean that something is done swiftly and easily. The earliest verifiable citation to a figurative use of it is found on page 211 of *The Grand Essay: Or, A Vindication or Reason and Religion against Impostures of Philosophy*, by W.C. M.D. C.M. L.C., 1704:

> "In answering things you needed not have troubled your felf to have answered, or Playing Booty (as we fometimes fay), with your felf, either by contradicting your felf, or writing on my Side, tho you defign'd **the Stroke of your Pen** to be against me..."

At the top of one's game^

This old expression means to do the very best one is capable of doing. A major dictionary places the origin of this phrase in the 1930s. It was actually in use much earlier as seen in this citation on page 7 of *Golf Illustrated*, June 16, 1899:

> "Varden, after all, is the only man who always plays, **at the top of his game**."

At the top of the food chain

Food chain, in a more literal implication, is a series of organisms interrelated by their eating habits. Smaller or lesser aggressive creatures are eaten by larger and better equipped ones. In spite of sources stating that the term originated between 1925 and 1930, it was used earlier in this sense. In *The Principles of Human Psychology,* July to December, 1918, page 1156, we find this reference:

> "As a result the **food chain** would be converted to carbon dioxide and an affinity left unsaturated until it could take up another food-molecule."

Then, in *Scientific Monthly*, page 295, July, 1920, the following clear reference appears:

> "Each such fish has its "**food-chain"** or series of alternative chains, leading back from the food of man to the invertebrates upon which it preys and then to the food of these, and so down to the smallest and simplest organisms in the sea..."

References to the top or bottom of the food chain have long been in use in the same literal relevance. However, the figurative usage applying strictly to persons is a modern term. In the 21st century jargon, being 'at the top of the food chain' means that a person is considered better than everyone else around him or her in every single way: faster, better looking, and more intelligent. An early example is from *Leadership: Lessons from the Coyote, Volume One* by Johnny R. Purvis and John W. Smith, 2008:

> "Furthermore, organizations often thrive in spite of the leadership provided **at the 'top of the food chain'**. Fact is, the organization would even thrive more if the individual(s) **at the top of the food chain** would simply disappear from the scene."

Attitude of gratitude

This universal cliché is an admonition to think positive and be grateful for all one has. These two words have been used in relation to one another for hundreds of years, but the earliest citation known of them in a very similar connection is from *Historical Sketches of the Ten Miles Square Forming the District of Columbia* by Jonathan Elliott, 1830, on page 116 under 'Landing of the Pilgrims on Plymouth Rock,' in regard to the carving over the door leading to the Eastern Portico on the Capitol Rotundo:

> "Behind, in the boat, looking towards heaven, with an eye and **attitude** of devotional **gratitude**, for deliverance from the sufferings and hardships of the voyage, stands his wife..."

In *The Science of Getting Rich*, 1910, by Wallace D. Wattles, page 29, he wrote what may be the earliest exact citation of the current saying:

> "The more gratefully we fix our minds on the Supreme when good things come to U.S., the more good things we will receive, and the more rapidly they will come; and the reason simply is that the mental **attitude of gratitude** draws the mind into ..."

B

Baby daddy / baby mama

Since early in the 21st century these terms have been popularized by the gossip media, and were originally intended to mean the father of mother of a baby who was not married to the other parent, and not the current 'significant other.' However, since about 2014 the lines have been blurred with the media even referring to the engaged partner in this manner.

The origin of these terms, according to Julia Turner, editor-in-chief of the online magazine, *Slate,* is from Jamaican Creole. The earliest known citation of 'baby-mother' is from *The Daily Gleaner* in Kingston, December 20, 1966:

> "Two girls have three children for him. One **baby-mother** is in America and the other is in the country."

But the most interesting, though possibly controversial, thought on the root of the saying is author and Columbia Associate Professor John McWhorter's theory is that it came from the Antebellum slaves who picked it up from British plantation owners who whose dialect left off the 's' on the end of many words, thus using terms in line with, and possibly even, 'Baby father' and 'Baby mother.' McWhorter notes that 'Even today you might hear someone in Yorkshire say among friends, 'my sister husband' rather than 'my sister's husband.

Baby on board+

This began as a message on a small sign which was placed, usually in the rear window of an automobile to let other drivers know that an infant was riding in the vehicle. The first signs were found in Germany in the early 1980s by a lady in Medford, Massachusetts, who partnered with her sister to start a company to market them in the United States. After they became a fad in the U.S., in 1985, a rash of alternative humorous signs was spawned, causing a sharp decline in sales in the U.S. but is still somewhat popular in the U.K. 'Baby on board' is now used as a saying for other instances, such as a pregnancy, and the birth of a baby in an unusual place, such as a plane or taxi.

Back o' Bourke[3^]

This Australian cliché means at or to an extremely remote place. It was taken from the town of Bourke, in northwestern New South Wales. This place is remote, but being back of there is metaphorically the most remote place a person may visit. In spite of a major dictionary's claim that this saying originated between 1915 and 1920, it has been in Aussie dialect longer. The earliest known citation is found in *Fair Girls and Grey Horses; With Other Verses* by Scottish poet Will H. Oglivie, first published in 1898, who seems to have actually coined it in the title of a six-verse poem. Here is the first verse:

"AT THE BACK O' BOURKE!

"WHERE the mulga paddocks are wild and wide,
That's where the pick of the stockmen ride —
At the **Back o' Bourke**!
Under the dust-clouds dense and brown,
Moving Southward by tank and town,
That's where the Queensland mobs come down —
Out at the **Back o' Bourke!"**

By 1902 this hyperbolic metaphor was in common usage in Aussie books and speech.

Backstairs deal[2]

This means goes to the meaning of backstairs, and is an arrangement between two parties which is secretive or scandalous, use with 'deal' coming into play in the early 20th century. A good early example is found in *The World Court, Volume 4*, page 8, 1918:

> "At Brest-Litovsk the inexperienced Russian delegation was confronted by well-known diplomats of the old school, Dr. Kiihlmann, Germany's Foreign Minister, presiding. Fortunately, however, there can now be no **backstairs deal** with a Czar..."

Backstairs gossip[2]

Backstairs was used from the 18th century in relating scandalous activity, and most often, with gossip. This first available close citation is from *The Letters of Hon. Horace Walpole, to George Montagu, Esq. from the year 1736 to the year 1770*, as published in June 1818 in *The British Critic*:

> "He must content himself with the obsolete scandal and antiquated **gossip** of generations which now rest from their ... beauty, where we may listen to the **back-stairs** tittle-tattle of our great-grandfathers, and the tea-table whispers of their reviving ..."

In 1834 the exact expression was used in Adam Waldie's *Select Circuit Library, Part 1*, page 178:

> "...as you may have been enabled to pick up in your station; both **backstairs gossip**, and firestairs gazelles, for even political movements do much depend on the private foibles of loading persons, and I know of old your talent for making observations on the manners of the quality."

Bad day at the office?+

This is a question asked jovially and often facetiously, in modern times, when the person being addressed is in a grouchy mood for no apparent reason. It actually has nothing to do with an office. It is used frequently in both the U.S. and the U.K., where it is used in sporting commentary. In football, the cliché, 'A bad day at the office' means that 'a team has had a poor result or that a manager has made some big mistakes' according to the languagecaster.com website. This phrase originated in the 21st century.

Bad egg

This has reference to a person who turns out to be undesirable. The use of this term in a metaphoric manner didn't take place until the mid-19th century. The earliest example in print is found in 'The Landlord Abroad,' published in *Stories of Irish Pleasantry* by Mrs. S. C. Hall, 1840:

> "'Didn't Macmurray himself say—' 'Don't name Macmurray,' interrupted Peggy, speaking for the first time; '**he's bad**, **egg** and bird, and no fit companion for you at all at all, Paul; his character's blasted this many a day, and he always had a spite ...'"

Then the definition is found in *The Athenaeum*, October 29, 1864:

> "A **bad egg** ... a fellow who had not proved to be as good as his promise."

Bad news travels fast

This old adage means that information about trouble or misfortune is likely to reach others more quickly than news about good fortune. This proverb was first recorded by Thomas Kyd in his Elizabethan play, *The Spanish Tragedy* in 1592:

> "**Euill (evil) newes flie faster still than good**."

bad penny keeps showing up, A+

This proverb means a person or thing which is unpleasant or unwanted tends to reappear at the most inopportune times. It is derived in the Middle Ages, before the standardization of coins, from the debased or counterfeit coins which showed up in trade and were difficult to detect. The term 'bad penny' was established in English by the late 14th century. William Langland used it metaphorically in his well-known prose poem, *Piers Plowman* (1730-1790):

> "Men may lynke letterid men… to **a badde peny**."

As a metaphor a bad penny was in use by 1742 when it was mentioned by Henry Fielding in his English translation of *Aristophanes Platus*. Long before August 21, 1890, the actual proverb was certainly in use as it appeared in the sports publication, *Forest and Stream,* called an old adage:

"…yet the old adage '**a bad penny always turns up**' proved its truthfulness…"

bad workman always blames his tools, A

This very old proverb illustrates the fact that it's not the tools which determine the result of our work, but how they are employed. Many times a person who has performed poorly will look for something to blame other than his or her lack of skill. The oldest form of this seems to be French from the 13th century: *Mauves ovriers ne trovera ja bon hostill.* Loosely translated, this means 'A bad workman will never find a good tool.'

A French and English Dictionary compiled by M. Randle Cotgrave, published in London in 1611, and reprinted in 1673, lists the proverb as "**A bungler cannot find (or fit himself with) good tools**."

Bag of bones

This ancient analogy applies to a person or animal which is extremely thin. The earliest reference known in print is from 1650 in *Solomonis Panaretos: Commentary upon the books of Proverbs, Ecclesiastes and the Song of Solomon*, by John Trapp:

> "he was a very **bag of bones**, and those also burnt as an hearth. Psal. 102"

The part which Trapp interpreted as a very **bag of bones** is from *Psalm 102:5*. This was a description of David, according to Trapp. In the *King James Version* (1611) this reads "By reason of the voice of my groaning, my bones cleave to my skin."

In a 1708 play, *The British Apollo; Or Curious Amusements for the Ingenious* in a section titled Poems, we find (letters altered to be readable):

> "Q. Apollo, I'm a Plump and Jolly brown Went by Love Mirth, when on Lewdness it does not Intrench; I'm Courted by one is so lean, you would swear, That with Flesh and Blood he at Enmity were; A mere **Bag of Bones**, from his Feet to his Crown, ..."

Bag of tricks

This common idiom refers to all of one's resources; every possible stratagem at one's command. The thought for this came from the fable of the Fox and the Cat, the earlier version attributed to Aesop (620-564 BCE), in which the Fox says to the Cat, "I have a sack full of sciences and wiles," (William Claxton translation, 1484) The earliest known actual citation of 'bag *of tricks'* is from another book of fables: *The Manuel of Youth, Containing Sixty Fables*, 1807 by J. Ouiseau, A.M., in a similar fable called the Fox and the Crow, also in a statement by the Fox, who wished to fly into the tree and eat the crow:

> "Let's see in my **bag of tricks**; let me see if I cannot there find something which will answer the purpose of wings."

In 1839 came the earliest known reference in print of "bag of tricks" outside a fable in *Bentley's Miscellany, American Edition; Volume III* in 'Handy Andy' by Samuel Lover:

> "'I've pump'd you, sir — all your electioneering **bag of tricks**, bribery, and all, exposed; and, now go off to O'Grady, and tell him how the poor ignorant Irish have done you: and see, Mr. Johnstone,' added Dick, in a quiet undertone, 'if there's anything that he or you don't like about the business, you shall have any satisfaction you like, and as often as you please.'"

Bag of wind

This expression has been around in American slang since about the early 19th century. It refers to a loquacious person who has nothing of substance to communicate. The first known citation for 'bag of wind' in a figurative context is found in *The Monthly Law Reporter*, November, 1838:

> *They will also bring fictitious suits in order to "give themselves an opportunity to 'cut a great swath,' in a distant court, and appear more like a disgusting '* **bag of wind**, *' than any thing that is just, liberal and manly."*

Balance the books

This term, in a literal sense, means adding up the debits and credits of an account to reconcile any differences. It has been used in a similar manner in English since at least 1643, when this citation was printed in the *Journal of the House of Lords,* London, Volume 6, page 694:

> "That the Commissioners and the faid Auditors may be the better enabled to go forward in their feveral Places and Trusts, according to the Directions herein prescribed, the Commissioners of Excise shall **balance** and make up their **Books** on the 11th of September next for the year."

In the more figurative meaning of settling with someone, it has been used since at least the late 1800s. In *Ninth Session, 1877, The Acts and Resolutions Adopted by the Legislature of Florida,* on February 17, 1877, we find:

> "Sec. 3. That the Collector shall make reports to the Comptroller and County Judge, as now required by law, and pay over to the officer sworn to receive the same so much thereof as shall be sufficient to **settle and balance the books** of the said George W. Allen..."

Bamboo curtain

This archaic, colorful expression was used during the Cold War of the 1950s to represent the political demarcation between the Communist states of East Asia, particularly the People's Republic of China, and the capitalist and non-Communist states of the region. It was derived from the term 'Iron Curtain' (see) used in Europe from the late 1940s to the early 1990s to designate the area of the Union of Soviet Socialist Republics. 'Bamboo Curtain' was also sometimes, though rarely, used for the DMZ dividing North and South Korea.

Though in use slightly earlier, the first verifiable printed reference is found on page 60 of *The Rotarian*, August, 1951:

> "While their fellow Chinese in Formosa are prospering under Nationalist reforms, the people back of the **bamboo curtain** have been bitterly disappointed."

Banana-bender[3]

This common Aussie colloquialism refers to a Queenslander, who according to local badgering by denizens of other southern states, spends his or her time putting the bends in bananas. The term was first coined jovially in an article in the *Queenslander* on August 15, 1837, which included the following about a man who was asked his occupation by the Queen:

> "'I'm a **banana-bender'**. Further to enlighten her Majesty he explained that bananas grew straight on the trees, and so just before they ripened, his was the job to mount the ladder, and with a specialised twist of the wrist, put into the fruit the Grecian bend that was half its charm."

Queensland is widely known for its extensive banana crops. In 1964, Douglas Lockwood, in his best-seller, *Up the Track,* wrote:

> "We are so close to Queensland that I think we should hop over the border. What do you say to a quick look at the **banana-benders**?"

Banger – sausage[3, 2^]

This colloquialism is often attributed to the fact that during World War II, under rationing, in the U.K. that there was very little meat in sausages. This term, however, was in use since World War I. The pun came about because such sausages were much more likely to pop if not cooked at the right heat level due to pressure of steam. Some say 1919, but there is an earlier reference in a novel published in the U.S., *The Long Trick*, by 'Bartimeus,' in Chapter IV, War Babies, 1917, on page 79:

> "Too good to waste onboard. The footer ground's bagged — let's have a picnic in one of the cutters. Have tea ashore, an' fry **bangers** over a fire."

The phrase is also currently used in Australia.

Bare-knuckle ride, A[2,3]

In a literal sense, bare-knuckle means without gloves, bandages or any other protection. Bare-knuckle boxing, of course, from which the basic term was derived, is boxing with no gloves. In 1921 Fox released a film titled *Bare Knuckles* starring William Russell, Mary Thurman and Correan Kirkham written by A. Channing Edington and directed by James P. Hogan. Very little seems to be known about the film now, which likely is no longer available.

'Bare-knuckle ride' is a modern term used in the U.K. and Australia to indicate a traumatic situation, particularly as it applies to the economy of a country or even the world. It was used by Alex Wright in the book, *Who Governs Scotland,* on page 168, when quoting R. Wilford and R. Wilson: "A Bare Knuckle Ride: Northern Ireland," the *Irish Times* article by Donald Clarke, Wednesday, August 3, 2011 titled 'Taking a Bare Knuckle Ride' and in an August, 2015 Australian article in *The Sunday Mail* (Queensland) by Terry McCrann, titled 'Bare Knuckle Ride as Markets Tumble Worldwide'.

Bat one's eyes+

This is an idiom referring to fluttering the eyelids flirtatiously and is almost always is used when speaking of a female. According to the *OED*, from the 19th century 'without batting an eye' was used in the negative to indicate lack of emotion. Presumably, the word 'bat' in this sense derived from a fluttering of wings like a bat, and was used early in falconry to describe how the birds repeatedly flapped their wings.

Battering ram[2]

A battering ram from ancient times was a heavy beam swung or rammed against doors of enemies to bash them down. In the medieval age they were used on castles, and even into the 19th century they were still being used to forcibly destroy property. Originally they were so named because the end of it was carved in the shape of a ram's head, though this changed with time.

Figuratively, this has come to refer to something or someone used to crush opposing views. It was being used in this respect as early as 1890 in a commentary of *II Kings 10:18-31* about the biblical Jehu in *The Sunday School Journal*, April 12, a book of International Bible Lessons:

> "He is the champion of rights of an oppressed people… He is the iron head of the **battering ram** driven against the royal sham and shattering it."

Battler[3]

In Australian jargon, this expression refers to a person with few to no natural advantages who is not willing to give up, and works with all due diligence even with no promise of reward to make ends meet, displaying remarkable courage.

The earliest citation known is from *While the Billy Boils* by Henry Lawson, 1896:

> "I sat on him pretty hard for his pretensions, and paid him out for all the patronage he'd worked off on me, and called him a mug straight, and walked round him, so to speak, and blowed, and told him never to pretend to me again that he was a **battler**."

Today in Australia this may also be used of people struggling with everyday bills and attempting to pay down a large mortgage. It also may refer to an unemployed person or itinerant worker. On April 2, 1898 it was used in the *Sydney Bulletin,* on page 14, in this manner for the first time:

> "I found patch after patch destroyed. Almost everyone I met blamed the unfortunate '**battler**,' and I put it down to some of the Sydney 'talent' until ... I caught two Chows vigorously destroying melon-vines."

Be a canary in a coal mine

The modern idiomatic expression, 'be a canary in a coal mine' means to be chosen as the individual in a company or group who acts as a test person to uncover a dangerous situation, thereby clearing the way for others. It is derived from the era in the late 19th and 20th centuries when miners took a caged canary into a coal mine to detect if there were dangerous levels of carbon monoxide in the mine, in which case, the canary would die. If the canary lived, it was then considered safe to send in miners. An early figurative example is found in *The Millitarizarion of South African Politics* by Kenneth W Grundy, 1986, page 85:

> "Although it may be Pretoria's policy to regard the homeland security forces as part of a collaborative regional defense system to fight together against the Marxist onslaught, their anticipated role may be little more than the **canary in the coal mine** — to signal to the SADF that larger-scale action must be taken to stem the tide of opposition to a homeland government..."

Beat a hen a pecking / a rootin'+

The earliest known reference in print to this American slang expression, referring to something highly unusual, is in the *Winchester Journal*, an Indiana newspaper, on October 25, 1876:

> "Peter Reinheimer thought it **beat a hen a-pecking**."

The hen a-rootin' version, which prevailed throughout the 1950s in the South, was first attested in 1939, according to The University of Wisconsin-Madison's *Dictionary of Regional English.*

Beat a path to someone's door+

This idiom is most usually used to mean that a large number of people are anxious to discover or obtain something, and will come in droves. It also can mean that anyone who wants something badly enough will not let anything stop him or her from going to a particular place. The earliest known usage is in the saying about building a better mousetrap found in the original volume on page 80, and is attributed to Ralph Waldo Emerson (1803-1882). Since at least the early 20th century, however, beating a path to someone's door (or other locale) has been commonly used for numerous other things. The September 26, 1916 edition of Kentucky newspaper, *The Mount Sterling Advocate,* carries the following citation in 'Merchants Try This,' on page 6, column 1:

> "Advertising will get the people to a store that is worth going to, but the merchant and his own goods must do the selling. Step up gentlemen. What merchant in this town wants the people to **beat a path to his store**?"

Beat oneself up

This is used figuratively meaning to harshly criticize oneself. It came into common usage in the late 20th century. The earliest verifiable citation is from *The Washington Post,* November 12, 1989, in 'The Oxford House Experiment:'

> "'Don't **beat yourself up**, man,' Big Mike tells him. 'It doesn't help.' 'What will help,' says John, is going to NA meetings every day and avoiding anybody still doing dope.'"

Beats me^

This old idiom means "I have no idea." Edgar Rice Burroughs is often credited for first using it in *The Land That Time Forgot*, Chapter 4, 1918:

> "'Flowering shrubs don't thrive in the subterranean caverns from which geysers spring,' suggested Bradley. Olson shook his head. 'It **beats me**,' he said."

Again, wrong! It was in use figuratively as early as 1824 on page 57, in *Douglas, A Tragedy, by John Home, Reduced to Scottish Rhyme, Chiefly the Broad Buchan Dialect*:

> "**Norv**. Weel, I am in a primonirie now--- 'Completely **beats me** how I'm to get through.'"

Beautiful inside and out+

This is a popular phrase used to describe a person who has desirable personal qualities such as intelligence, kindness, thoughtfulness and friendliness, while also having a natural beauty which is easily seen by others. The expression is not new, and goes back at least until 1878 when it appeared in ***The New Idea of***

Astronomy and the Sight of the Eye by D. Woodwell Hunt who used it in regard to an observatory tower, not a person:

> "The tower was **beautiful inside and out** with every convenience and observation of the planets and stars…"

Through the 20th century it was used to describe buildings, cars, etc. Only in modern times has it begun to be used in regard to people**.** An early example is found in the ***Wall Street Journal***, June 1, 1987 in the article, 'What do you like about your kid?' on page 3:

"Leslie Dean's Dad: She's **beautiful inside and out**, she shows what's real, and she's very dependable."

Beck and call (See: **At someone's beck and call**)

Become a three-ring circus

Literally, a three-ring circus is self-explanatory—a circus with three separate rings for simultaneous performances, used since the late 1800s. The earliest example known in print is from *Gaillard's Medical Journal*, New York; August, 1881:

> "COUP'S **Three-Ring Circus** will endeavor to secure Dr. F. D. Weisse, of N. Y., in his feat of firing at a cadavar, in illustration of the performance of Guiteau, in his assault upon the President."

Figuratively, in modern times, becoming a three-ring circus has come to mean a public display of show and put-on with no real value. The earliest available citation is from page 9 of *Black Belt Magazine*, March, 1997:

> "UFC Needs a Credibility Check The Ultimate Fighting Championship (UFC) **has become a three-ring circus**."

Before you embark on a journey of revenge, dig two graves (Update from entry in first book, **He who seeks revenge should remember to dig two graves)**

This proverb is attributed to famed Chinese philosopher Confucius (551-479 BCE). Actually, it is a mis-translation of his teaching which meant something quite different. According to a modern student of Chinese, 'Aero Windmaker,' what he said literally meant 'a gentleman who does not take revenge is not a gentleman'. Confucius further added that even when one does not take revenge right away because of circumstances, he will think about it every day, and do it when the timing is right, even if it costs him his life. According to 'Windmaker,' this was the source of this proverb framed after Confucius' teaching. Revenge, to Confucius, was a part of human dignity.

Strangely enough, in 2004 this saying was even attributed to Booker T. Washington in Performance *Appraisals Made Easy* by Lisbeth S. Margulus and Jaquelyn Ann Melin:

> "**Before you embark on a journey of revenge, dig two graves**." —Booker T. Washington

Beginning in 2005 it became popular to use quotes attributed to Confucius, and numerous books began including this one.

Behind bars+

This is a popular slang term for being imprisoned. The word 'bar' came into Middle English in the late 12th century as *barre* from the Old French derivative of the Latin *barra*, meaning rod. As an idiom, being 'caged' has been referred to as being 'behind bars' since at least the late 19th century. A poem titled 'Behind Bars' about a bird in a cage was included in a book by Mary McNeil Fenollosa titled *Out of the Nest; A Flight of Verses*, on page 77, in 1899. In 1902, Leslie Hamilton French used the phrase 'behind bars' in *Hezekiah's Wives,* a book about canaries, to describe all 'imprisoned animals' in the preface on page vi.

Very soon thereafter incarcerating people began to be referred to as putting them behind bars. Paul H. Drake used it in *Democracy Made Safe* in 1918, on page 55:

> "If those desires still remain (*lording it over others*), it will be considered doing the possessor of such 'ambitions' a favor to put him **behind bars** where he can no longer injure and defraud the common good."

Being in someone else's shoes (See: **Fill someone's shoes)+**

Bellwether[2]

This unusual term, used since at least the early 1700s, literally refers to the leading male sheep of a flock, usually with a bell around his neck. Figuratively, it has come to mean a person or thing that assumes leadership; sometimes a ringleader in a mutiny or conspiracy; or may even mean a predictor or harbinger of something certain to come.

As early as 1891, the person in charge of a church was referred to as a bellwether on page 174 of *Historical Connections of Ohio: An Encyclopedia of the State, Volume II* by Henry Howe:

> "He was for forty years clerk of court, was prosperous, had excellent sense, and some sheep-raising man—it must have been—told me he was in his day the '**bellwether'** of the Methodist church here."

In the context of a trendsetter or predictor of things to come it was in use by 1937, as seen in this snippet from an ad for Buick from *Life Magazine* on March 27:

> "So you set the pace— keep up front without fatigue or effort— because you're driving the **bellwether** car of the year."

Belt and braces[2] (U.K.) or **Belt and Suspenders** (U.S.)

Belts and braces or suspenders are tools used to keep trousers from falling off, and using both is a double protection against losing one's pants. Hence, the term belt and braces came to be widely used in a figurative connotation before the mid-20th century. Belt and braces was cited in the following context in *Maid of the Mist* by John Oxenham, 1914:

> "However, he peeled also, and by careful contrivance with **belt and braces** they bound their bundles on to their heads and stepped into the water."

The earliest figurative use of belt and suspenders known is from *The Rotarian,* March, 1929, page 29:

> "A pessimist may wear both **belt and suspenders**, and he may look through a glass but darkly, yet when it comes to rushing into danger he is usually on the side of the angels. Optimism that is akin to faith we need."

Bend the rules

This metaphor means to ignore or change the accepted standards to suit one's own preferences or whims. This expression is very old and was in use by the late 17th century, when the earliest available citation is found in, *An Enquiry into the Power of Dispensing with Penal Statutes* by Sir Robert Atkyns, 1689:

,

> "Let us not (says he) approve of all Things, though delivered by Authors of greatest Name; for they often serve the Times, or their Affections, and **bend the Rules** as Occasion requires."

This was used again in 1734 in Atkyns' *Parliamentary and Political Tracts, etc.* on page 262.

best time to plant a tree was twenty years ago (The). The second best time is today (or now)

Regardless of the true origin of this proverb, it is a truism which bears repeating. In the late twentieth century it became fashionable to throw out this type of statement and label it as 'an old Chinese Proverb'. Two sources even referred to it as an African proverb. No record was found in print of this in English prior to 1989. In his business strategy book, *Guerilla Marketing Attack*, that year, Jay Carrad Levinson cites the axiom on page 178 in A MOTTO: DO IT NOW:

> "An old Chinese proverb suggests that **the best time to plant a tree was twenty years ago. The second best time is today.** Reading about the guerrilla marketing attack may be fun, but it won't hurt your competitors,..."

In 1993, another book called it simply, 'an old adage'. After the turn of this century, it began appearing in numerous books as a Chinese proverb. The earliest was *Effective Men's Ministry: The Indispensable Toolkit for Your Church*, Phil Downer, editor, page 13, 2001:

> "A Chinese proverb says, '**The best time to plant a tree was twenty years ago. The second best time is now.**'"

Apparently 'ancient Chinese wisdom' is a must in building Christian churches! Nevertheless, the popularity of the saying abounded in the 21st century, as well as the fame of the mythical Chinese philosophers. It was applied in a literal sense, and figuratively in relation to monetary, religious and philosophical causes.

Champ Zumbrun, in *A History of Green Ridge Forest* (2010) attributed the quote to Fred W. Besley (1872-1960), Maryland's first State Forester, who retired just prior to World War II, after devoting 60 years to the cause of scientific forest management. If anyone was worthy of coining this, surely it was he. Perhaps, however, the best fit was the origin claimed in *500 of the Most Witty, Acerbic, and Erudite Things Ever Said about Money* by Philip Jenks and Stephen Eckett, 2006: 'Anonymous'.

Better half (See: **My better half**)+

Better than a poke in the eye with a burnt stick[3]

This is now primarily used in Australia, but is very similar to the American metaphor listed in the first volume, 'Better than a poke in the eye with a sharp stick;' even there, Australia was mentioned as the possible origin. Strangely enough, the first citation available is actually from *Belgravia, A London Magazine* in September, 1875 in an anonymous serial, 'His Second Inheritance,' chapter VIII:

> "'Ah, yes, the legacy!' said Petworth, taking up the document and looking at it again. 'Five thousand, eh? **Better than a poke in the eye with a burnt stick**, as we used to say as boys.'"

It was used again in March, 1885, also in a London journal, *The Taylorian,* in Pleasant Hours:

> "It is not a reprieve truly — but a respite is better than **a poke in the eye with a burnt stick**."

Citations continued in the U.K. In one it was said to be used in Lancaster. In November of 1897 it appeared in an American Magazine, *Current Literature*, which is after the earliest citation of the similar American phrase. It was in 'The Sketch Book: Character in Outline,' an Irish Election by Stephen Gwyan reprinted from *Cornhill Magazine*:

> "Again there was a long silence: at last Termater Bill rose and stretched himself. 'Spose,' he exclaimed, 'I was ter give yer a fifteen years' lease, wi' a half share in the profits, twud be a blanky sight better than **a poke in the eye with a burnt stick** ...'"

In the very early 20th century, the burnt stick version was still cited in both the U.S. and U.K., but died out by the early 1920s. We find the following snippet from the short story, *The Windmill,* by M.T. Shanley, of Brisbane, Australia, first published in *The National Times*, January 25, 1985:

> "'Yair. Get inside, Mum's got something for you. Got any horses Mr. Cadwillicker?'
>
> "'Ah, no.'
>
> "'Pity. Here, get this into you. Better than **a poke in the eye with a burnt stick**.' Fullarton splashed three tin mugs to the rim while the Cadwalladers stared."

It is possible that 'burnt stick' was misunderstood for 'blunt stick' (sometimes used) in America, and changed to sharp stick as a more practical weapon.

better the fruit (The), the more wasps to eat it[2]

Proverbs, Maxims and Phrases of All Ages, Volume One, compiled by Robert Christy, published by G.P. Putnam and Sons, New York and London, 1893, lists this as a German proverb on page 420. This is the earliest printed reference known to this saying. It means that the better something is, the more it will be attacked by those who wish to kill its virtues.

Beware Greeks bearing gifts

The thought behind this was first recorded by Socrates who lived from 496 to 406 BCE, which attributed the idea of being weary of gifts from enemies to an even more ancient proverb:

> "Nought from the **Greeks** towards me hath sped well.
> So now I find that ancient proverb true,
> Foes' **gifts** are no gifts: profit bring they none."

But the saying is more commonly associated with the tale of the "Trojan horse" used by the Greeks who stowed away inside it to sneak into the city and conquer it which was related by Virgil in *Aeneid, Book II* in 19 BCE:

> "Do not trust the horse, Trojans. Whatever it is, **I fear the Greeks even when they bring gifts**."

This actual phrase was used in near exact verbiage in the late 1800s, the first such reference in print coming from the *Journal of the Proceedings of the Missouri State Convention*, page 188, 1862:

> "I wonder how he would have felt when he knocked for admission into the Democratic church, if some old patriarch had got up and said, 'My brethren, beware of this new convert! **beware** of the **Greeks bearing gifts**!'"

During a copyright dispute during the mid 1990s, the saying was resurrected online. A company named Compuserve owned the copyright to the GIF image format, and some who were using them without permission were in fear of being sued. Thereafter it began being used frequently by others to express fear over deception from adversaries.

Beyond the black stump[3]

This Australian idiom means going past an imaginary point at which the country is considered remote and uncivilized. The origin of the expression is contested. It seems most likely that it derived from the use of fire-blackened tree stumps around a settlement, and the saying likely developed in the late 19th or early 20th century. It is used much like Americans might use the expression 'In the middle of nowhere' (see). In is assumed that even going as far as you can, the black stump is a little farther. The term 'Black stump' was used as land markers on surveyors plans, first cited in a New South Wales court case involving a land law dispute on October 12, 1831 (R v West [1831] NSWSupC 66). It referred to 'a black stump beyond the line,' which was said to have been marked.

Robbery Under Arms, a work of fiction by Rolf Boldrewood first published in 1888, refers to the **Black Stump** as an actual place 'within a reasonable distance of Bathurst' well known to all in the area. Boldrewood further stated that it 'had been a tremendous old Ironbark tree—nobody knew how old, but it had had its top blown off in a thunderstorm, and the carriers had lighted so many fires against the roots of it that it had been killed at last, and the sides were as black as a steamer's funnel.'

In 1956, a young American engineer visiting Australia prospecting for oil in the sheep-raising country there became educated in the ways of Australia and fell in love with a delightful local girl. Under the pseudonym Nevil Shute he wrote a book titled ***Beyond the Black Stump*** which was published by Morrow in New York.

BFF^

The *Oxford English Dictionary* (OED) dates the origin of this acronym, meaning best friends forever, at 1996. It is often used in text messages, social media and other online communications. However, once again, this has proven incorrect. It was cited twice *in Dear Judy, Did You Ever Like a Boy (who Didn't Like You?)* by Judy Baer in 1993; first on page 9:

> "...a best friend may suddenly refuse to speak to you or find a new **BFF** (That's Best Friend Forever!)"

Then on page 40:

> "You are traveling through a very unstable, unpredictable time in life. Though a friend would be a great help, you might not find the ***BFF*** (Best Friend Forever) you've been looking for."

Baer's book may actually be the earliest printed source.

Billy[3] (See under '**Bluey**')

Bird-brained

This slang metaphoric expression means lacking in seriousness or maturity; foolish or scatterbrained. The earliest known citation of this expression is found in *The Century Illustrated Magazine*, August, 1910 in a story titled 'Mrs. Northmere's Treasure' by Gertrude Hall:

> "She was burdened with overstanding debts of her son's, with the support of a **bird-brained**, extravagant, indirigible daughter-in-law, with doctors and luxuries and changes of air to furnish for Innesley."

Bit between one's teeth[2] (See: **Take the bit between your teeth**)

Bite one's nails^

This old metaphoric idiom means to exhibit signs of anxiety. *The American Heritage Dictionary*, 2013, dates the saying at 1870. Of course, in a literal sense, biting one's nails was referred to in numerous books much earlier. But in *The*

Pilgrim's Progress, 1743, John Bunyon, on page 79, used the following possible figurative citation:

> "...he is by reason of Age, and also of the many showed Brushes that he met with in his younger Days, grown so crazy and stiff in his joints, that he can now do a little more than sit in the Cave's Mouth grinning at Pilgrims as they go by, and **biting his Nails** because he cannot come at them."

Bite someone's head off

This metaphoric cliché means to speak to someone in a harsh, angry or impatient tone or manner with no apparent reason, usually in response to that person's statement or action. The phrase came into play in the 18th century. It was first used in a figurative sense in Colley Ciber's play, *The Refusal, Or, The Ladies Philosophy,* Act V, published in 1721:

> "...I'll let him fee (see) prefently that I know how to pay a handsome Compliment to a fair Lady, as well as himself: I-gad, I'll **bite his Head off**."

Black look

This American idiom refers to a sullen expression on someone's face denoting that the person is full of anger and hate. The principle of this saying came from *King Lear*, Act II, by William Shakespeare, 1605-1606:

> "***Lear.*** She hath abated me of half my train; **Look'**d **black** upon me; struck me with her tongue, Mast serpent-like, upon the very heart."

By the late 1800s the current phrase was in use as seen in *On Board the "Rocket"* by American author, Robert Chamblett Adams, about adventures on a cargo ship, page 128, 1879:

> "All this was said in a loud tone for the benefit of the men, and the second mate was so much encouraged by this endorsement, that the same day he broke a deck-bucket against another sailor's head, who gave him a **'black look**,' and as a boy was coiling up a rope that he fancied..."

Blame game

This idiom refers to people trying to blame other individuals or groups for something bad that has happened. The earliest known citation is from *The U.S. at 200*, Compiled by Sharifah Abdulah, 1978, page 201, where quotes are used:

> "You must remember that in Washington today, the Democrats now have all the levels of power. They have the House, they have the Senate, and they have the White House. For eight years we have played in Washington what has been called a '**blame game**'."

Bleeding heart+

It is believed that images of a literal bleeding heart used to depict the suffering of Jesus on the cross is the origin. From the Middle Ages to the 19th century, a religious group was called The Order of the Bleeding Heart, which prayed to the Virgin Mary, was depicted with a heart pierced with swords. London has a Bleeding Heart Yard, which was featured prominently (22 mentions) in Charles Dickens' 1857 novel, *Little Dorrit.*

This is a pejorative idiom for someone who is overly emotional about something. It was not coined as a metaphor, however, until 1937, when syndicated American newspaper columnist Westbrook Pegler (1894-1969), in an article protesting a bill proposed by Washington liberals against lynchings, which he no longer saw as a major problem, first used the term in this respect:

> "I question the humanitarianism of any professional or semi-pro **bleeding heart** who clamors that not a single person must be allowed to hunger but would stall the entire legislative program in a fight to ham through a law intended, at the most optimistic figure, to save fourteen lives a year."

One of Pegler's favorite targets was Eleanor Roosevelt. It has since been used politically in the U.S. by conservatives in this regard since then.

Bleed over into…

This idiom derived from fabrics being dyed with pigments that are not color-fast. When the fabrics are washed the colors bleed over into the other colors. At one time Madras shirts were popular for the very reason that the colors bleed and created a different effect. Figuratively, this has come to mean that a principle or idea 'bleeds over into' another area of thought or practice. The earliest known reference to the literal use is in *The Dyestuffs of the Berlin Aniline Works*, page 12, 1904:

> "Unfortunately however, very few are so fast that they do not **bleed over into** white material."

By the early 1980s this was being used metaphorically, as evidenced in *Preaching with Purpose: The Urgent Task of Homiletics,* a seminary textbook by Jay Edward Adams, 1982, page 95:

> "They will love it, and, as your storytelling powers increase and **bleed over into** your sermons, your congregations will love it too."

Bless your heart!^

Also, 'bless your little heart,' and 'bless your pea-pickin' heart,' this is a favorite Southern American saying going back generations. It is used more frequently by women, but men also say it on occasion. It can fit in various contexts, but most likely in gratitude for a deed thought well-done, or for, "how could you be expected to understand?" However, it is not meant to be hurtful, only accommodating or appreciative. But the use of this phrase goes back much further than most would expect, or have revealed in origins, and did not originate in the United States. The earliest known citation of the exact phrase is in the British play *The Padlock, A Comic Opera* written in 1766 by Charles Dibdin, performed in the Royal Theater in 1768. The use is obviously by a black servant in Act I Scene vi:

> "***Mung***: Ah, Massa, **bless your heart**."

Then in *He Would Be a Soldier, a Comedy in Five Acts* by Frederick Pilon, 1787; Act III. Scene ii:

> **"*Cal.* Bless your heart**! no master of any kind for me to-day: I never put on a new suit of clothes in my life, that I did not make holyday."

It continued to be used in numerous comedies throughout the late 18th century and 19th century, such as Oliver Goldsmith's *Stoop to Conquer*, 1771, in which it was a bit contemptuous, and even in other books published in England, Scotland, Ireland and even France and Italy. Charles Dickens used it in *A Christmas Carol* in 1858. In the February 26, 1826 issue of *Religious Intelligencer*, published in New Haven, Connecticut carried the first reference found in print in the U.S.

> "She was then asked, if she understood all that she read? "**Bless your heart**," answered she, "I am a poor ignorant creature, and have no book of knowledge…"

Many other examples followed, all printed in the Northern states. In fact, the earliest known Southern American publication with reference to this saying is the February, 1857 issue of *The Southern Literary Messenger*, Richmond, Virginia, in Laurence Neville's Lilias, Chapter XXIII, also spoken by a black slave 'mammy:'

> "Oh, bless his heart! Come to your mammy, my darling boy! **Bless your heart**! **Bless your heart**! Where has mammy's baby been?"

In novels this continued to be cited through the 20th century. As far as the Southern tradition, it is quite likely that it was first popularized by slaves in antebellum times, and carried forth into the general population afterward.

In the April 6, 1946 issue of Billboard *Bless Your Little Heart*, was listed as Number One on the WMMN (Fairmont, WV) country music hit parade.

During country music star Tennessee Ernie Ford's stint as a disc jockey at XKLA AM radio in Los Angeles in the late 1940s he began using '**Bless your pea pickin' heart'** as a catch phrase, and earned the nickname Ol' Pea-Picker. In 1966 he released a song on Pickwick Label titled *Bless Your Pea Pickin' Heart* which became one of his signature songs and solidified the saying even more in the American South.

Blind rage

This expression refers to lashing out without thinking about the consequences. It is very old, going back as far as the *Works of John Knox* in 'A Godly Letter to the Faithful in London,' written in 1548, on page 170 of the 1853 publication:

> "And that is the cause why Germanie and England hes bene plaguit thir yeiris bypast; whilk may be an ansueir to the **blind rage** of ignorantis, who never will knaw the verie cause of God's plagues."

Blood money

This idiom can mean any one of several things: a fee paid to a hired hit person; compensation paid to the family of a murdered person; money paid to someone who gives information leading to the arrest and conviction of a killer; or likely more common today, money obtained at the cost and senseless suffering of others. Some Bible scholars believe that the saying is based on the statement of Judas Iscariot following his paid betrayal of Jesus recorded in *Matthew 7:24 (NIV)*:

> "'I have sinned,' he said, 'for I have betrayed innocent blood.'"

However, the earliest known citation known in print of the actual phrase is in *A Classic Dictionary of the Vulgar Tongue,* 1785:

> "**Thief takers**, fellows who associate with all kinds of villains, in order to betray them, when they have committed any of those crimes, which entitles the persons taking them to a handsome reward, called **blood money**."

After that date other references began appearing in books, all with this basic connotation, which makes this the most likely original meaning.

Blood on someone's hands (See: **Have blood on someone's hands**)

Blow a gasket

This idiom means to become very angry and 'fly off the handle' (see first volume). It comes from gaskets in engines which are seals between metal, as in the engine head, used to keep in the pressure of combustion. There is no warning when a gasket blows, so this is a suitable likeness. The earliest known figurative citation is from *On with Torchy* by Sewell Ford, 1914, page 251:

> "'Might **blow a gasket**, eh?' says I. 'And you want me to go up and scout around. But what if I'm caught at it — am I peddlin' soap, or what?'"

Blow a kiss

This is done by kissing one's fingertips, flinging them forward and blowing into the air. According to author Marcel Danesi in his popular 2013 book, *The History of the Kiss* (Palgrave McMillan), "The act of blowing kisses originated in Mesopotamia as a means to gain favor with the gods." This civilization existed around 3,000 BCE.

Actual use of the term in English goes back to 1680 when it was cited in *The Wits Paraphrased: Or, Paragrafe upon Paragrafe in a Berlesque on the Several late Translations of Ovids Epistles,* page 76:

> “When you the Bantling chuck I take
> And hug the Bratt for th' Mothers fake,
> Sometimes I take the Pot to pifs
> And from my Bawble **blow a kiss**.
> Sometimes I try to Bribe your woman:
> She tells me I'm a fot, and no man;"

The composition of this poetry was done by Publius Ovidius Naso who lived in Sulmo, Italia, Roman Republic from March 20, 43 BCE to CE 17/18, placing the use of the term in Latin before this.

Blow (or **toot) your own horn**

This is most often stated as a negative: “Don't blow your own horn, or trumpet,” or “Don't toot your own horn.” The thought which formed this metaphor is originally from the *Bible*. In *Matthew 6:2*, (New Testament), in the Sermon on the Mount, Jesus warns against the practice of proclaiming our own virtues to be praised by others for our charitable gifts using strikingly similar phraseology. The *New World Translation* is closest on this:

> "...When you go making gifts of mercy, **do not blow a trumpet ahead of you**, just as the hypocrites do in the synagogues and in the streets, that they may be glorified by men..."

Remember that the original text on this was written in the early 1st century CE, so naturally the wording would be slightly different, but the meaning is the same.

In the “Warren-Adams Letters” (letters between U.S. President John Adams, Samuel Adams and James Warren, 1743-1814) the following more modern wording is found, in a humorous positive connotation:

> “I think modesty is highly overrated as a virtue — my motto is ‘**Toot your own horn** lest the same never be tooted.’”

Blue[3]

This expression is used in Australia for a fight or heated argument. Citations are 21st century. A good example is from *Monsoon* by Di Morrissey, 2007:

> "'Bit of **a blue going on** near the base. They've sent a platoon out to check. She'll be right.' One of the soldiers tried to ask Col for an autograph but the lanky singer was belting out popular songs from the hit parade."

A redheaded male in Australia is also customarily called a blue or bluey. (See also: She'll be right)

Bluey[3]

The most common use of this Australian slang term is a swag used by foot-travelers, particularly in the bush, to carry daily necessities, so called because the outer covering of the swag was traditionally a blue blanket, also called a bluey. The earliest available citation where it is used in this manner is from *The West Australian Settler's Guide and Farmer's Handbook*, published in Perth in 1897:

> "There are many men who have lived for years under the genial sun of Australia who have never owned anything more than a '**bluey**,' a 'billy,' and a thirst."

A billy is a vessel, usually made of tin or aluminum, used for boiling water or making tea over an open fire. It comes from the Scottish word *billy-pot,* meaning a cooking utensil. They have been in use in Australia since the mid-19th century. From the 1770 Australia was colonized by the British, but famine and epidemics in Scotland brought the first significant Scottish emigration to Australia in the 1820s and 1830s.

As noted above, bluey is also used as a nickname for red-headed males.

Boatload of trouble

Metaphorically, this modern expression, used in both the U.S. and the U.K., means so much trouble that you could fill a boat with it. The earliest citation known is from *P.C. Magazine*, June 15, 1996, in an article titled 'File Management for Windows 95' on page 18:

> "So stay organized with Navigator Because as we all know, a misplaced file or two can bring you a **boatload of trouble**."

It seems ironic that an article in a computer magazine about staying organized would go to print with an obvious error like capitalization of the word 'because' in the middle of a sentence.

Body language

This refers to non-verbal communication whereby thoughts, intentions and feelings are expressed through various physical behaviors. Among these are facial expressions, body posture, gestures, eye movements and touch. This exists both in humans and animals. The earliest known citation of the term 'body-language' is in reference to communication of early man in *A History of Music, Volume One,* by John Frederick Rowbotham, 1885, on page 72:

> "The first language, then, that man spoke was a language of gestures and cries, these gestures and cries being in the ... old **body-language** grew daily less and less able to render with due precision the thought which struggled for expression."

Then in 1919 John B. Watson, professor of Psychology at Johns Hopkins University, published a book titled *Psychology from the Standpoint of a Behaviorist* in which he stated the following on page 14:

> "Implicit habit responses: 'thinking,' by which we mean sub vocal talking, general **body language** habits, bodily sets or attitudes which are not easily observable without instrumentation or experimental aid; the system of conditioned reflexes in the various glands and unstrapped muscular mechanisms…"

By 1931, the term was in common usage outside medical circles as evidenced in popular feminist novelist Faith Baldwin's *Skyscraper*, page 265:

> "Like any accomplished wordsmith, she details the business girls' clothing, cosmetics, facial expressions, and **body language**."

Noted Harvard Business Administration Professor, psychologist and speaker, Amy Cuddy, maintains that our body language determines how we see ourselves, and how others view us.

Bog standard[2]

This thoroughly modern British slang expression means completely, utterly and absolutely ordinary in every way. Bog is a slang word for toilet in the U.K., but that's not believed to be this term's root. The origin is obscure but likely was derived from a literal bog which is a muddy area rural section of land, never more than a plain and tasteless parcel of real estate. It has been suggested that it could have been a form of the obsolete term, 'box-standard.' According to etymologists, the first usage comes from the early 1960s. However, the earliest *verifiable* citation available is from page 57 of *Cycle World Magazine*, January – May, 1984:

> "The bore-and-stroke dimensions are unfashionably undersquare (67mm by 70mm, respectively), the cylinder head is of a **bog-standard** two-valve design, and valve adjustment is via the same type of shim-and-bucket arrangement that has been bumping poppet valves for decades."

Though numerous other references, unverifiable as to time frame, are definitely from British sources, *Cycle World* is published in Los Angeles, California.

Bombing back into the Stone Age

This now common saying for causing great devastation through war was first spoken by U.S. Air Force General Curtis LeMay (1906-1990), who ran with George Wallace on the American Independent Party for Vice President in the 1968 campaign. In his memoir he reportedly suggested that rather than negotiating with Hanoi the U.S. should **"bomb them back to the Stone Age"** by taking out their factories, harbors and bridges, 'until we have destroyed every work of man in North Vietnam.' Later, in a *Washington Post* interview, LeMay said that "I never said we *should* **bomb them back to the Stone Age**. I said we had the capability to do it."

Right after 9/11 there were reports that the U.S. threatened to 'bomb Pakistan back into the Stone Age" unless it joined the war on terror.

Bone dry (See: **Dry as a bone**)

Bone idle[2]

Another British-ism, this term refers to an absolute state: absolutely and totally lazy. A forerunner of it was found in *The Vocabulary of East Anglia*, an 1830 glossary by Robert Forby. It certainly came close:

> "Bone-lazy, bone-sore, bone-tired, adj. so lazy, sore, or tired, that the laziness, the soreness, or the fatigue, seem to have penetrated the very bones."

Thomas Carlyle 'hit the nail on the head' in *New Letters*, 1836:

> "For the last three weeks I have been going what you call **bone-idle**."

Boob tube+

This is an antiquated American colloquialism for a television set. Early models had a vacuum picture tube. This basic principle persisted until the advent of, first projection models, then present day thin, flat screen monitors. This term was in use by 1965, according to *Etymology Online*. This time frame was validated through further research.

Boots on the ground

This phrase refers to military ground forces actually taking part in fighting a conflict or war rather than taking part in air strikes or other types of warfare. It is attributed to Commander in Chief of U.S. Readiness Command, General Volney Warner, first cited in an article by John K. Cooley in the *Christian Science Monitor* on April 11, 1980 referring to the Iranian Hostage Crisis.

> "U.S. options grow more difficult as the chance of a Soviet response increases. However, many American strategists now argue that even light, token U.S. land forces – 'getting U.S. combat **boots on the ground**,' as General Warner puts it – would signal to an enemy that the U.S. is physically guarding the area and can only be dislodged at the risk of war."

Booyah

This 21st century term is used to express immediate great joy, usually brought on by a sudden accomplishment or victory. It is often used in military or sports settings. A major dictionary states first use at 1990. Prior to this usage, the word existed as far back as the early 20th century, meaning 'to be beaten up'. Other meanings followed. The earliest citation available of this meaning, and giving its stated origin, appears in *Hoops Nation: A Guide to America's Best Pick-Up Basketball*, by Chris Ballard, 1998:

> "**Boo-yah!** exclamatory term used after an impressive play, deriving from the Latin phrase 'boolis ad yahseum' meaning damn that was nasty."

Booze it and lose it

This saying comes from the title of a Governor's Highway Safety Campaign which first began in North Carolina in 1994, and means that someone caught drinking and driving would lose his or her driver's license. *The Presidential Incentive for Making .08 BAC the National Legal Limit* (1998) states the following:

> "Programs such as... North Carolina's '**Booze It and Lose It'** campaign, result in a large number of criminal apprehensions and recoveries of stolen property."

The campaign is also credited with saving many lives and later was also adopted by the State of Tennessee.

Bored to tears

This common hyperbolic metaphor is popular all over the English speaking world. It means being so extremely bored that one is at the point of frustration or irritation. The earliest known citation is from *Sinister Street*, a British novel by Compton Mackenzie, Volume II, 1914, chapter 3:

> "'Well, I'm getting rather fed up with it,' said Michael. 'I feel more like a tourist than a Varsity man. Every day we lunch and dine and take coffee and tea in great masses of people. I'm **bored to tears** by half the men I go about with, and I'm sure they're bored to tears with me.'"

Similar expressions are 'bored to death' and 'bored stiff'.

Borrowing trouble (See: **Don't borrow trouble,** original volume)

Boston strong

This is a slogan created in honor of the reaction to the Boston Marathon bombings on April 15, 2013. It started immediately, within hours, as a hashtag on Twitter which grew extremely popular worldwide within days. Two students at Emerson College, Christopher Dobens and Nicholas Reynolds began a tee-shirt campaign using the slogan printed on them. It was painted on what is called the 'Green Monsters Wall' at the famous Red Sox home field, Fenway Park. At the first Red Sox game after the bombings the announcer told the fans, 'We are one. We are strong. We are Boston. We are **Boston strong**.' Only two days after the bombings, the Boston Bruins hockey team had the slogan placed on their helmets. Trademark patent requests for the slogan were denied. The slogan belongs to all who call Boston home.

Actually, the roots of the saying run deeper. It can be traced back to Livestrong, 2003, Army strong, and Jersey strong, other similar mottos and slogans which all predated Boston strong.

Bottler[3]

In Aussie slang, this term means something excellent, or may be used to express delight for something that has gone the way you want it. It is dated to the 1960s. It is said by etymologists to have started in New Zealand and come to Australia a few years later. It is listed in John Blackman's *Aussie Slang Dictionary*, 2012, with the example used often, 'you little bottler!' The term however, may also be used of a prostitute, so caution in use is advised by visitors.

Bouncing off the walls+

This is a colloquial expression for being active and energetic in a hyperactive, uncontrolled or excited manner. It was first used in this connotation in *Trumbull Park* the debut novel of Frank London Brown in 1959 about the first black families to integrate that public housing project in Chicago. The only known earlier use of the phrase was as the title of a blues tune by Marion "Little Walter" Jacobs in 1953. It is believed to have originated from some sport such as squash, in which a ball is bounced off a wall.

Bound and determined

The question of the origin of this phrase has heretofore been unresolved. It simply means that one is firmly resolved not to change their will on an issue no matter what others think or regardless of the consequences. Bound has been in use in English since 1387 to mean 'tied or fastened'. The person is bound or obliged to follow through.

The earliest known reference in print to this actual expression is in Sir Walter Raleigh's *History of the World, the Second Book of the First Part*, page 552, 1614:

> "…as it were in a dreame) that he entered Jerusalem, and layed (laid) hands on Jehoiakim: whom he first **bound and determined** to fend (send) to Babylon, but changing befell he caused him to be flane (slain) in the place, and gaue (gave) him the Sepulcher of an Asse, to be deuoured (devoured) by beasts and ravenous birds..."

This reference, likely the actual first, may give us a clue to how it came to be used as it is; likely a misinterpretation of the author's intended usage. A slight variation in this meaning comes in 1658, just a few years later, in *To Diapheronta, or Divine Characters, in Two Parts* by Samuel Crook and Christopher Barker, chapter XI, Part 1, on page 105.

> "Sinne hath now **bound and determined** it to sinne, not to sin by compulsion, but of choice; not in the nature, but in the use of it; not in this, that it actually willeth; but, in that it cannot now of it self will what in duty it should. So it freely willeth…"

From this we can clearly understand how this saying could have come to mean what it does today. By the Christian teaching that all are bound by sin at birth, the analogy was used here "sin(ne) hath **bound and determined** it..."

In 1776, in the *Acts of the General Assembly of the Province of New Jersey,* by Samuel Allison, at the bottom of page 264 and top of page 265 we read:

> "Title, Interest and Property of the said Messuages, Lands, Tenements and Hereditaments so held and claimed as aforesaid, as lying and being within this Colony, or any Part or Parcel thereof, shall be intended to be **bound and determined**, shall be fully and completely and absolutely bind, and for-ever

determine the Right, Title, Interest and Property of the said Lands, Messuages, Lands, Tenements and Hereditaments, to all Intents, Constructions and Purposes in the Law, whatsoever:"

In Great Britain's *Parliamentary Register*, recorded by John Almond and John Debrett, 1787, the term is used to describe legal obligations of the court.

"The sense of the court is to be **bound and determined** by a majority of votes…"

By the 20th century, the phrase had evolved to the common use of today. Jean Stratton-Porter, in her novel, *Keeper of the Bees*, 1930, on page 266, wrote the following:

"He just seemed **bound and determined** to do everything in the world except the thing she wanted to do."

Bound hand and foot

Naturally this may have a literal meaning. Figuratively, however, it means that one is bound by legal, moral of social obligations. *The American Heritage Idioms Dictionary* dates this to the 10th century CE. This likely refers to the *Lindisfarne Gospels*, the first translation of the *New Testament Gospels* into English. The phrase appears in the New Testament book of *John, Chapter 11, verse 44,* when it relates the story of Jesus raising Lazarus from the dead, believed to have been written near the end of the 1st century, it says in the *KJV* (1611):

"And he that was dead came forth, **bound hand and foot** with graveclothes: and his face was bound about with a napkin."

This is the obvious origin of the phrase. However, figurative usage in English began in the 19th century. *Proceedings of the Parliament of South Australia: Volume 2*, 1872, page 67 has several references referring to this, the plainest example being:

"He had told them plainly that he was **bound hand and foot** to support the Ministry in their position as long as the session lasted."

Brave the elements+

This is an idiom for facing inclement forces of nature to achieve a desired result or goal. According to *Merriam Webster*, the use of 'elements' to refer to atmospheric conditions dates to the early 16th century. This expression is mostly used today hyperbolically. 'Brave the weather' was used more commonly from at least 1900. Eugeanie Hibbard, Supervising Sister of the American Hospital Ship Maine, used it on the first page of her Journal, *With the Maine to South America,* that year:

> "Those of our friends and of the cause to **brave the weather**—and they were many—bade us farewell, God-speed, and safe return."

'Brave the storm' was cited as early as 1861 in *The Book of Popular Songs* published by G.G. Evans in Philadelphia.

Breadcrumb trail (See: **Leave a trail of breadcrumbs**)+

Break the mold

This means to do something entirely different after it has been done the same way for a long time; to defy convention. A mold is a pattern by which many products are mass produced. The earliest available figurative reference in print to this idiom is in *Social Darwinism in American Thought* by Richard Hofstadter, 1944, comparing William Graham Sumner with Edmond Burke:

> "As thinkers the two, of course, have something in common: both show the same resistance to attempts to **break the mold** of society and accelerate change…"

(see also: They broke the mold when they made someone or something)

Breathing down someone's neck

This common idiom means to watch someone's activities too closely or intently; so much so as to make it uncomfortable for that person.

The expression was first used in Toronto's *The Grip* on 3 March 1882 in an article titled 'Give Us Fair Play,' in a near-literal connotation:

> "Irsacible major to head waiter, who has for some time been sputtering and: **breathing down his neck** in his endeavor to whisper some confidential communication..."

Then in 1899, novelist Robert William Chambers used it in a truly figurative sense on page 270 of *Outsiders: An Outline*:

> "A lady with short hair who had been **breathing down his neck**, asked Weyward to present Oliver, and Oliver learned that he was facing the famous Miss Evelina Ballington Bogle, editor of the *Iron Quill*."

Bricks without straw[2] (See: **You can't make bricks without straw**)

Bring a plate[3]

This Aussie instruction on an invitation to a picnic or barbeque means that you should bring some food to be shared. In America it would be saying to bring your favorite dish to a church social event or family dinner. It was coined with western social gatherings in Australia which usually consist of meat being barbecued, beer and a possible salad. It was first recorded in the1920s. In the early days when welcoming new arrivals to the country, ladies were asked to bring a plate; sometimes gentlemen were requested to bring a donation. The earliest available citation is from March 22, 1951 in Victoria's *Sunshine Advocate*:

> "Mrs. Gum has kindly offered her home on Saturday, 14th of April for a social evening. Ladies **bring a plate**."

It is also used in New Zealand. A good example of usage is found in *The Common Purse: Income Sharing in New Zealand Families* by Robin Fleming and Susan Kell Easting, 1997, page 106:

> "She told us that she thought the '**bring a plate**' approach of Brian's family was a custom specific to New Zealand."

Bring something to the table

This expression refers to a negotiating table. 'Bringing something' means an idea or solution to a problem to be discussed.

This saying evolved from the early modern German phrase *etw aufs Tapet bringen* which means 'to bring something up.' A *tapet* had reference to the covering of a conference table. It is actually from the Medieval Latin *tapeta*, and originally referred to a wall covering. The first reference to a form it is found in Peter Dasypodius in his German dictionary, *Dictionarium latinogermanicon* published in Strasbourg, France in 1536:

> "to lay s. th. (something) On the tapet"

The saying was in use figuratively in the English language by 1680 when it showed up in *The Tryal of Thomas, Earl of Stafford, Lord Lieutenant of Ireland, upon Impeachment of High Treason,* page 229:

> "That all subscribed the Orders, as well those against them, as those for them, and appealed therein to my Lord of *Cork* The Course being, when an order is made, to **bring it to the Table** another day, and take all the Hands of them present; and he added, That their Lordships that are Counsellors know that Course to be used here."

Bromance

This ultra-modern term reflects new attitudes toward male bonding on a highly emotional level, in both non-sexual friendships, and homosexual relationships transcending gender lines. It is derived from a combination of the words brother and romance, though obviously having nothing to do with an actual romantic feeling. According to Michael DeAngelis, in *Reading the Bromance Homosocial Relationships in Film and Television* (2014), the saying is attributed to Dave Carnie, editor of the skateboarding magazine, *Big Brother* in the late 1990s to refer to the relationship which develops between two male skaters who spend a lot of time together. However, a 1992 *Seinfeld* episode titled 'The Boyfriend' (Season 3, Episode 15) had the principle of a 'bromance' several years earlier.

This term was used by Stephen Elliott in 2004 in *Looking Forward to It*, a book about the American electoral process, on page 267:

> "'**Bromance**, remember?' We lean in together, separated by two coffees and two doughnuts, and touch our cheeks."

But it didn't receive broad usage until about 2005 when it began to be used in film and on television.

Brothers in arms

This common phrase is defined as close associates, especially those who served together in military service during war. It has been popularized by both a pop culture song and a TV miniseries. The song, *Brothers in Arms*, originally written by Mark Knopfler in 1982, the year of the Falklands War, was released by Dire Straits in 1985 as the closing track on an album by the same name. It was re-released in 2007 to commemorate the 25th anniversary of the conflict as a disabled veterans' fund raiser. *Bikie-Wars: Brothers in Arms* (2012) was a six-part Australian miniseries about bikers' gang violence.

This is, however, a very old expression some say dates to the Middle Ages. The earliest available citations in print in English are from the late 18th century, when usage became common in British literature. The first of these is in 1784 on pp 213-214 of *Memoirs of Ancient Chivalry from the Romance Writers and Historians of Those Ages* translated from the French by Monsieur de Sainte-Palaye, but it is attributed to a quote from 110 years earlier:

> "And Madam de Sevigne, who wrote in 1674, fays, 'I esteem Barbantanne very much; he is one of the bravest men in the world; of a valour almost romantic: I have a thousand times heard Buffi speak of him; they were **brothers in arms**.'"

Brought to heel

This figurative idiom means to cause someone, to act in a more disciplined fashion. It derives from teaching a dog to 'heel' or walk close behind his or her master, as a part of obedience training. It dates from the late 19th century, and the earliest known reference in print is from 'Janice Meredith' by Paul Leicester Ford on page 325 of *The Bookman, a Journal of Literature and Life* Volume 9, 1899:

> "Then the only man we can **bring to heel** is this bond-servant of thine."

Brush up on+

Originally, as far back as circa 1600, 'brush up' meant to clean something up. Beginning in the early 18th century, it referred to refurbishing something such as suede shoes, a top hat or a woolen coat. Metaphorically it came to be applied to reviving a skill, such as a second language, or reviewing information by 1788, according to Etymology Online. It was then expanded with 'on' to state what was being revived or reviewed. It is now becoming an antiquated expression.

Buckley's chance[3]

This in Australia is much like a 'Chinaman's chance' in America (see entry in first volume). It means having no hope whatsoever, and sometimes is shortened to simply 'Buckley's'. It is said by many to have come from the name of William Buckley, a convict who escaped from Fort Phillip in Sydney in 1803, living 32 years afterward with Aboriginals in southern Victoria. Others claim that it is from the name of a firm in Melbourne established in 1851, Buckley and Nunn. Proponents of this theory suggest that it evolved from a pun on the name Nun with none. The phrase, they say, spawned the saying, "There are just two chances, Buckley's and none."

The earliest known citation is from the *Melbourne Punch*, 22 September 1887:

> "In our sporting columns, in the Fitzroy team appears the name of *Bracken*. It should have been *Buckley*. *Olympus* explains that he altered it because he didn't want the Fitzroy men to have '**Buckley's chance**'."

In *Parliamentary Debates*, New South Wales Parliament, 1899, page 1113, we find the following:

> "He never had **Buckley's chance** of getting it. He is a man who is absolutely impossible as a leader, and let me tell him that it was out of a fine consideration by the members of the party that he was possible as a minister for some time…"

Budgie-smugglers[3]

This odd-sounding term in Australia refers to a pair of tight-fitting male swimming trunks made of stretchy fabric. Internationally these may be called grape smugglers. *Budgie* is short for *budgerigar,* a Kamilaroi word (an

Aboriginal language of northern New South Wales and southern Queensland) for a small green and yellow parrot which is now a popular caged bird. The term is a jocular allusion to the way the garment looks. The term '**Budgie smugglers' wa**s first recorded in the late 1990s. *The Online Slang Dictionary* listed the term under 'grape smugglers' on April 10, 1998.

On November 23, 2002 the *Herald Sun* in Melbourne had the following clip:

> "Nothing stands between you and a continent made entirely of icebergs except the Southern Ocean. That, and a thin pair of Speedos so figure-hugging you can see every goosebump - flimsy togs that are known not-all-that-affectionately by us Brown boys as **budgie smugglers**!"

Build bridges

This common idiom refers to improving relationships between people who are very different and do not like each other. It may be used for individuals, groups or nations. This term began to be adapted in the late 20th century, as cited in this very early example from *Computerworld*, July 30, 1990, in an article titled 'The Hotel Welcome Mat Is Out' by Helen Pike:

> "They're also relying on large databases to build customer **relationships**. ... be looking for people who understand different systems and can help **build bridges** between them, says Peter Salazar."

Bum deal^

This idiom refers to a misfortunate happening or turn of events which most likely was unpredictable beforehand. Though origin has been attributed to the 1960's, it was already in use by February, 1908, when it appeared in Chicago's *Opportunities of To-day* in an article on page 31, titled 'Fifty Million Steers in the U.S. Should Rejoice for Coming Changes:'

> "Beef critters from the range have always got a **bum deal**, ever since we began getting this expensive breeding stock."

Then on March 25, 1909, in Detroit's *Hardwood Record*, it appeared twice in a story on page 29 titled 'Cupid and Inspection.' The first of these is:

"My goodness he has certainly given me **a bum deal**. Mr. Becker I am glad I got you to do this. You----"

A similar expression, 'bummer,' is featured in the original volume.

Bump in the road

This idiom refers to a minor problem or setback which can be solved. The saying began to be used in a literal sense in the early 1900s when automobiles were becoming more plentiful. The following citation is from *The Auto: The Motorist's Pictorial*, October 17, 1908 published by Stanley Spooner in an article titled 'Effects of Road Surface on Cars:'

> "These parts, if reduced in weight, would respond more readily to any slight unevenness, whereas at present their inertia is such that when travelling fast, they have not time to respond to each **'bump' in the road**, with the result that they simply bound up and down in a manner suitable to the 'period' of the springs…"

In the mid 1960s it began to be used as a metaphor, as seen in this example from Norman Spinrad's novel, *The Men in the Jungle*, 1967:

> "The man was always five steps ahead of every political and economic **bump in the road**—even the ones that Vanderling didn't feel when he went over 'em."

Bum's rush

Interestingly, *The Wall Street Journal* published an article on August 22, 2014 by Ben Zimmer on the origin of this comical metaphor. Zimmer stated that the origin 'goes back to the turn of the 20th century,' and mentioned that 'bum' had then come to mean a tramp, a shortened form of bummer, and was likely from the German *bummler*, meaning loafer. He went on to relate the explanation given in a dictionary of slang terms, which is correct. A bum's rush is what would likely occur should a vagrant enter a saloon in hopes of taking advantage of free lunch counters meant for paying customers ordering drinks.

The earliest known citation of the expression is from New York's *Green Book Album Magazine* September, 1911, in the story, 'Broadway Gossip' by Donald Morris Jones:

> "You see, I sort of distracted his attention and when he wasn't looking, gave him a **bum's rush**, and introduced his face to the sidewalk."

The phrase has evolved through the 1960's, '70s and '80's, and a form of it is now is 'bum rush'. In 1987 Public Enemy's debut album was titled, "*Yo! Bum Rush the Show*," making reference to crowds rushing a club to attend a concert. Thereafter bum rushing evolved to mean different things to different groups from hitting from behind to frontal attacks. Bum's rush, per se, however, still may refer to rushing someone away to get rid of him or her.

Bum steer^

This idiom means a piece of false information, whether given on purpose or not. Actually it is attributed to 19th century American maritime humor. 'Steer' in this connotation does not refer to male cattle, but rather to steering a ship in reverse.

It is currently admittedly used more in Australia and New Zealand, but in spite of claims by other researchers that it had only been known in America since the 1920s, *The Foundry*, a publication printed in Cleveland, Ohio, in the issue for April, 1901, has the following in the feature 'Chimmie Powers Answers to Correspondents,' on page 18 in an entry by S.E. Attle:

> "Give de gaffer a **bum steer** de first chanst yu get."

Over the next several years it was cited in numerous U.S. publications including the *Anamosa Prison Press*, Anamosa, Iowa; Saturday, October 24, 1903:

> "Somebody's been giving the P. P. man a **bum steer**."

Then, in the *Saturday Evening Post*, April 22, 1905 in 'A Meteorological Misadventure,' a humorous story by Kenneth Harris on page 7:

> "I studied on it as we plowed along through the dust, and I couldn't help thinking that the Professor had got what is technically known as a **bum steer**."

American citations over the next few decades seem limitless and it was mentioned in *The American Language* by Henry Louis Mencken, first published in 1919, in the 1936 edition.

> "Bum as an adjective (as in **bum steer** and bum food), bum's-rush" (see Bum's rush)

Previous researchers appear to be more accurate as to its appearance in the U.K. around the end of World War II.

Bundle of nerves

This figure of speech means extremely nervous, fidgety and worried to the point that it is impossible to function properly. It is used both in America and Australia. The British normally call it a 'bag of nerves.' The term was used in numerous anatomy and medical text books and papers entirely to refer to the actual bundles containing nerves in the human brain and body from the 17th century. The earliest figurative reference in print known is from is found on page 120 of *A Bunch of Everlastings or Texts that Made History, a Volume of Sermons* assembled by F.W. Boreham published in 1920 in New York, This is in William Cowper's Text (1721-1800) so it is **much older** than this:

> "He is a quivering little **bundle of nerves**; slight of figure; with pale, pinched face, and eyes swollen with chronic inflammation."

Bun in the oven (See: **She's got a bun in the oven**)

Bursting at the seams

This expression has a both literal and hyperbolical uses. Of course, literally it means breaking open or flying apart with sudden violence, such as a garment which is too tight. Often, in a figurative connotation it has reference to sudden expression, pride, laughter, excitement or emotion. It may also be used when a person or animal is so full of food that they feel or appear terribly uncomfortable, even when there is no real danger of bursting seams. It can actually denote anything that is *filled beyond capacity*.

Literal usage began before the middle of the 19th century, and the earliest known citation is from *Ainsworth Magazine: A Miscellany of Romance*, Vol. 7, in Hints on Servants, 1845:

> "The consequence is, he must either have another rig out, or go with his great red hands staring a mile through his sleeves, and his late baggy breeches all but **bursting at the seams**. But the failure in clothes is not half the evil."

By November, 1889 it was in slightly metaphoric application in Chicago's *American Poultry Journal* referring to a Thanksgiving turkey full of juices and dressing:

> "First—Turkey, crisp and crackling of skin, **bursting at the seams** with luscious juices and savory dressing, white of ample breast, and dark as to sturdy drumsticks, lying in lordly unconcern on his broad back like the monarch of the board as he is in calm and restful superiority."

Then, within 20 years the meaning was broadening to refer to purely figurative usage, as seen in the June 17, 1909 *Life Magazine* in 'The Matter with Montaigne:'

> "The inventor and most brilliant exemplar of the essay has had a horde of indifferent imitators–many of them rejoicing in robust physical health, and **bursting at the seams** with optimism."

Burst into tears

This very old expression, with us since the early 17th century, means to begin to cry suddenly, unexpectedly, with no warning. In 1623, *A Shakespeare Dictionary: Part One, Julius Caesar* was published by Arthur E. Baker, Borough Librarian in Taunton, England, which contained the following comments on Scene II act i on page 26:

> "When Brutus and Portia parted for the last time in the island of Nisida, Plutarch relates that she restrained all outward expressions of grief in order not to shake the fortitude of her husband, but in passing a picture of Hector and Andromache she at length **burst into** a passion of **tears**:"

Obviously this dialogue is not found in Shakespeare's 1599 play, but only in this commentary some 24 years later when speaking of the writings of Plutarch, who must have been writing from first-hand viewing of the play in London.

In *A Compleat History of the Lives and Reigns of Mary Queen of Scotland and of her Son and Successor, James the Sixth, King of Scotland; And (After Queen Elizabeth) King of Great Britain, France and Ireland, The First (of evre Blessed Memory)* by William Sanderson, 1656, the following exact citation appears on page 123:

> "But, being denied, She **burst into tears** and scorn, I am, faid fhe, Cofin to your Queen, descended from that Royal King Henry the Seaventh; a married Queen of France; and anointed Queen of Scotland."

Business is business+

This is a very old idiomatic cliché used to mean that in order for a business to succeed, it is sometimes necessary to do things that are hurtful or upsetting to other people. It has been in use since at least the early 19th century. English playwright Douglas William Jerrold used it several times in his 1834 two-act drama, *The Rent Day*. The first is found in Act I, Scene iv:

> "BULL. I'm going. **Business is business**."

Butter someone up

This common idiom means to flatter or be overly nice to someone to gain their favor or get something in return. The most common belief as to the origin of the metaphor is that it came from spreading butter on a biscuit or bun to make it more appealing to the taste buds. Another belief is that it came from ancient India where balls of butter were thrown at statues of gods to gain their favor. The former seems more likely. The earliest known citation of this use is from 1798 in *A New Dictionary of the Spanish and English Languages*, (*Dictionario Nueva de las dos Lenguas, Español e Englesa*) by Thomas Connelly. The English version on page 413 reads under LAVAR LA CARA Á ALGUNA COSA:

> "To flatter a perfon; to **butter him up"**

In 1827, we find the following example in *Elizabeth Evanshaw,* a novel by William Pitt Scargill, on page 115:

> "And besides, you have no palaver at the beginning about their 'honourable lordships,' and your 'respect,' and all that. I would first **butter them up**, and then make use of my grandfather, and my father, and my uncles, by telling that they did for their country..."

Butt heads

This metaphor means to argue uncompromisingly. It comes from horned animals, like rams or goats, becoming involved in a fight in which their horns are used constantly clanging together. The saying is actually adapted from Shakespeare's *The Taming of the Shrew*; Act V, Scene xii, 1590:

> ***"Bap.*** How likes Gremis these quickwitted folks?

> ***Gre.*** Believe me, Sir, they **butt heads** together well.
> ***Bian.*** Head and butt? an hasty-witted body Would say, your head and butt were head and horn."

Button up^

As a figurative term, this can have two meanings. It may mean to stop talking and keep one's mouth shut. It may also refer to conclude business by finalizing a deal, completing all details. A major dictionary of slang lists it from 1925 "to refrain from admitting loss; 1890 'Ec U.S. Stockbroking;' 1841, button up your lip." It is actually used as early as 1839 in a figurative sense meaning 'concluding an activity,' from which either of these meanings could have easily evolved. It is found in *Essays Moral and Humorous* by Joseph Addison, on page 87 in 'The Life and Opinions of Thistram Shandy:'

> "What is the life of man! Is it not to shift from side to side; from sorrow to sorrow; — to **button up** one cause of vexation, — and unbutton another!"

By no stretch of the imagination (See: **Not by any stretch of the imagination**)

By the same token

In this idiom, 'token' refers to evidence. The tokens purchased for public transportation, for example, are the evidence that the fare was paid. Throughout history tokens were sent as proof of loyalty and gratitude, as early as Old Testament days. The earliest actual known reference in print of the exact term in English is in *The Bee Hive of the Romishe Church*, 'translated out of the Dutch to the Englishe by George Gilpin the Elder,' 1579:

> "…but the holie father the Pope is in possession, and both enjoy the landes which S. Peter left unto him by testament: **by the same token** it is called Pattimonium S. Peter..."

By the scruff of the neck (See: **Take by the scruff of the neck**)

By the way+

By the way is a connective phrase used to introduce a different idea which has most likely just occurred to the speaker or writer. When this phrase first came into use in the 900s CE, according to the *OED*, it was literal, meaning along the side of a road (then called a 'way'). The first change came about 1000, when it came to mean 'while going along, in the course of one's journey.'

It wasn't until the mid-to-late16th century when it evolved to figuratively mean, 'incidentally', 'in passing.' The earliest such example available in print seems to be by Shakespeare in *A Midsummer Night's Dream*, 1590:

> "Lets follow him, and **by the way** let us recount our dreames."

Shakespeare used a similar example was used in *The Merry Wives of Windsor*, 1598, but as time went on the metaphoric meaning became clearer, as in Edward Burt's *Letters from a Gentleman in the North of Scotland*, circa 1730:

> "**By the Way**, altho' the Weather was not warm, he was without Shoes, Stockings, or Breeches."

C

Call a spade a spade

•

One could think that this derived from the derogatory term for blacks. Sadly, some have used it this way; but, thankfully, this is not the original intent. It means that anything should be called exactly what it is, and one should not try to hide the truth about a person or subject, or 'beat around the bush' (see in first volume). The coining of it goes back much further, coming from Nicholas Udall's *Apophthgmes, that is to saie prompte saiynges First gathered by Erasmus*, translated into English in 1542:

> "Philippus aunswered, that the Macedonians wer feloes of no fyne witte in their termes but altogether grosse, clubbyshe, and rusticall, as they whiche had not the witte to **calle a spade by any other name then a spade**."

This citation actually refers all the way back to Plutarch's *Apophthegmata* which were the sayings of Spartan kings and commanders. Plutarch was a Greek historian and biographer who lived from 45 to 120 CE. *Apophthgmes* seemingly had replaced the earlier version, using words more common to the day.

The modern version appeared in John Ray's *A compleat Collection of English Proverbs,* 1737, on page 210:

> "To **call a spade a spade**"

It became popular among English writers as far back as John Dryden, in his letters. The following appears in *The Works of John Dryden, Volume XVII*, Letter II, published in London, 1808:

> "Two of the verses I remember:
> I **call a spade, a spade**; Eaton,* a bully;
> Frampton a pimp; and brother John, a cully."

Call in one's markers

This idiom refers to turning to people who owe one favors because of some need to do so. It came from gambling. When a player ran out of money he would ask another player or the 'house' for a 'marker,' or loan in order to stay in the game. The earliest known reference to this type marker in print is from *The Road of the Rough* by Maurice M. Minton, 1893, page 74:

> "At last his money and his chips are gone.
> "'Give me a hundred and put up **a marker**,' he says."

Metaphorically, calling in markers began appearing in print by the mid-1980s. The earliest available reference, certainly not the origin, was in *A Third Story* by Carole Taylor, 1986, page 11:

> "He never turned down an opportunity and only **called in** his own **markers** when his pride or his job was at stake."

Call it a day^

This idiomatic expression means to stop or terminate something; declare one has had enough. A major online reference source states that it is from the 1840s. Another states that 'call it half a day' was first recorded in 1838 meaning to leave the work place before the end of the work day. This site states that the actual expression didn't come until 1919. Neither gives citations. The accurate first reference in print of 'call it a day' in this sense is from *Secret Service Old and Young King Brady Detectives*, Number 415, a weekly magazine published in New York, January 4, 1907:

> "'Oh, forget it,' cried Harry. 'What you have spent on the girl didn't amount to much anyway. Now, then, since you can't find Alice, what are you going to do? **Call it a day** and go home?'"

Call the shots^

This cliché refers to making all relevant decisions. A major English dictionary places the phrase as originating in 1967. But the saying was in use since the 1940s. The earliest citations are a bit literal, like the one from *Popular Mechanics,* October, 1943 on page 69 in 'Television...The New War Baby:'

> "He watches a cathode ray oscillograph to keep track of the wave shape patterns, and switches the transmitter feed from one camera to the other as the director **calls the shots**."

But within three years it was definitely being used figuratively. On October 7, 1946, the following citation appears in *Life Magazine* in an editorial with the heading 'Shall We Have a Depression' on page 69:

> "Sometimes Wall Street **calls the shots** and sometimes it miscalls them, but it never turns sharply without reasons."

Call the tune (See: **He who pays the piper calls the tune**)

Calm before the storm

Derived from a literal anomaly in weather patterns, this figuratively refers to a lull in activity just before a period of great excitement or activity. The earliest known reference to a form of this in literature is from a play titled *Love Triumphant or Nature Will Prevail,* Act V Scene i, published in 'Don Sebastian, King of Portugal, Or, The Two Socias,' 1725:

> "Speak, Mother, speak: My Father gives you time, He stands amaz'd, irresolute and dumb; Like the still Face of Heav'n **before** a **Storm**: Speak, and arrest the Thunder 'ere it rolls."

Then in 1730 the following precise example appeared in *The History of the Principality of Wales: In Three Parts*;

> "...he eased them on several Taxes of his predecessor, and was affable and kind to all. But this was a fhort **Calm before a great Storm**; for foon after Duke William fent his Ambaffadors to him to mind him of his Oath;"

Canary in a coal mine (See: **Be a canary in a coal mine**)

Can't do something to save one's life^

This idiom means that the person is extremely bad at doing a certain thing and believes doing it properly is entirely impossible. It is, of course, another bit of hyperbole. In spite of an online source from a well-known academic 'Royal Academy' stating that the first usage of this is from Anthony Trollope in *Kellys and O' Kellys*, 1848, it was cited 21 years earlier in Rev. C. Weller's *Church Register*, in 'The Young Midshipman,' published in Philadelphia on November 17, 1827:

> "...it has never been freighted with a thinking mind, or soul, or heart, or whatever else you choose to call it, and now in this awful tempest of adversity, when all is gloom and horror around me, I **can't, to save my life**, recollect one word of prayer."

Cardinal rule^

Here we need to take a peek at the etymology of the word 'cardinal'. It comes from the Latin *cardo*, meaning hinge. A cardinal rule, according to etymologists, is a fundamental principle upon which everything related hinges. That is true, but its use in print did not begin quite that way. The first mention known in print, however, uses 'cardinals Rule'. It is found in *Relique Wottenianie: Or a Collection of Lives* by Sir Henry Wotton, 1672:

> "...which (I faithfully vow unto your Honour) was never yet utter'd, but in this Letter, and may far. hinder me, if others hear it; I hope the Merchants are in that mind yet, or otherwise I will trust the old **cardinals Rule** no more, The Occurreuces are thus: victuals are arisen in price at Vienna penny in the pound, flesh; and after the like rate in ..."

The expression was also used in a reflection to one of Aesops Fables, The Dog and His Master written between 620 and 560 BCE, when translated to English also as 'cardinal's rule' in 1692 by Roger L. Estrange in *Fables of Aesop and Other Mythologists with Morals and Reflections*, thus linking it to the 'princes of Rome:'

> "The **Cardinal's Rule** to one of his Laquayes that had lost his Coat, comes very well to our present Purpose, The Boy said that his Eminence told him they were all so Holy at Rome, that he thought there had been no Thieves there."

In *The Works of Mons. de la Bruyere* by Jean de la Bruyere, a Translation from the last Paris Edition by N. Rowe, Esq., 1752, it is first used as 'cardinal rule' which would prevail to this present day.

> "One would think it was the **cardinal Rule** of Place-men and Directors to throw in the Way of those who depend on them for the Care of their Affairs, all the Obstacles they might apprehend."

Notice that all the way through, the word 'rule' was capitalized.

Cash is king^

This saying is self-explanatory. It is better (and often much cheaper) to be able to buy something with cash rather than on credit. The buyer with cash will always be given precedence over someone who needs to resort to deferred payments or to a mortgage.

A major online source, though stating that the origin of the phrase is unclear, place its coining at around 1988. This is, however, 149 years off first use in print. In the *London Saturday Journal, November, 1839*, in an article titled 'Social and Political Economy,' under the heading 'Cash,' we find the following citation:

> "All powerful as it is, cash is the mere creature and servant of men's wants and wishes; it enables one man to give his brains for bread, and another to exchange bread for beef. **Cash is king** of the Exchange, but exchange rules cash…"

Then in April, 1893, in the *Southern Cultivator and Dixie Farmer* has the following clear example of the expression:

> "The South thinks cotton is king, the West believes that corn is, but the managers of the world's commerce and exchanges know that **cash is king**."

William A. Reed, London, wrote a novel titled ***'Cash Is King'*** first highlighted in *The Saturday Review* on September 21, 1901, which seemed to popularize the saying during the early 20th century. After remaining dormant for some years, it made another comeback in the last quarter of the century.

Cast a long shadow

This idiom refers to something or someone which or who has considerable influence on people or events. A figurative reference to death casting a long shadow is first recorded in a letter to Cardoness, elder, dated April, 1637, signed S.R. (Samuel Rutherford), published in *Mr. Rutherford's Letters, Now Divided into Three Parts,* first published in Edinburg, Scotland in 1761:

> "Now when ye are drinking the grounds of your cup, and ye are upon the utmost ends of the last link of time, and old age, like death's **long shadow**, is **casting** a covering upon your days; ..."

Catch some Zs

This humorous idiom means to get some sleep. It comes from comic strips in which sleep is portrayed by Zs flowing from someone's head. In British English it is sometimes 'cop (or get) some Zs'. A major idiom dictionary states that it is from 'the second half of the 1900s'. They are correct. Though not the coining, the earliest citation available in print is Tom Clancy's *Clear and Present Danger*, 1989, page 210:

> "'How do things look, Sergeant?' Captain Ramirez asked quietly.
>
> "Nothing moving at all, sir. Why don't you **catch some Zs**?'"

Cat head, cat-head or cathead biscuits

Biscuits, a type of which, known as the soft biscuit, was common in Scotland, came to be a viable type of bread in the Southern U.S. before the Civil War. In 1875, Alexander Ashbourne invented and patented the first biscuit cutter. A cathead biscuit, however, is a name applied to a large buttermilk biscuit, usually between six and eight inches around, made almost exclusively in the South, served with either gravy or butter (or margarine) and jelly, preserves or jam. They are crisp on the outside and fluffy inside. The term is believed to have originated in the Carolinas, and comes from the fact that they are normally about the size of a cat's head. The earliest known reference in print to these being called 'cat-head biscuits' is found in *Speaking to Persuade*, by LeRoy Brown, 1960, on page 74:

> "I shore like them **cat-head biscuits** and I want to sop gravy with you."

Cat nap

Forms of this metaphoric expression have been used for 200 years to describe a short period of sleep during the day. Cats sleep long periods at a time, so it may seem strange to call it by this name. Some researchers say that it started in Ancient Egypt when cats were sacred and Pharaohs began to emulate the way cats sleep. But there are no records to indicate that. When cats sleep, they are sound asleep one minute and awake the next; there is no drowsy period trying to wake up; hence, the cat nap. The first use was actually 'cat's nap.' The earliest known citation is from *The Pioneers, or the Sources of the Susquehanna; a Descriptive Tale* by James Fenimore Cooper, 1823, on page 156:

> "Why d'ye see, Squire, the parson was very solemn, and I just closed my eyes in order to think the better with myself, just the same as you'd put in the dead lights to make all snug, and when I opened them ag'in I found the congregation were getting under weigh for home, so I calculated the ten minutes would cover the lee-way after the glass was out. It was only some such matter as a **cat's nap**."

Cooper used it the same way 2 years later in *Lionel Lincoln*, on page 111, 1825:

> "Wine should never slumber on its lees until it has been well rolled in the trough of a sea for a few months; then, indeed, you may set it asleep and yourself by the side of it, if you like a **cat's nap**. As orthodox a direction for the ripening of wine ..."

It continued to be cited in books as cat's nap for the next ten years, then in 1835, Harper and Brothers in New York published Matilda Douglas' *Blackbeard: A Page from the Colonial History of Philadelphia* in which contained the following at the beginning of Chapter XIX, on page 225:

> "Towards two of the morning, not long after the moon had gone down, Nero, who was sitting up for his master, was aroused from a **cat-nap**, into which

he had insensibly fallen, by a subdued murmur of rough voices, and a heavy tramp of many men passing along Penn-street ..."

In the late 19th century three dictionaries were published listing 'cat-nap'. The first was *Americanisms, Old and New*, 1889, by John Stephen Farmer.

"**Cat-nap**. — This is given by Lowell as a short doze"

(Presumably famed American writer-poet John Russell Lowell)

Caught in the act +

In use since at least the 19th century, this common phrase means to witness someone actually doing something, and normally carries a negative connotation. It is most often refers to someone committing a crime. In 1888 Chrisnell Newton published a play with this title with Ames Publishing Company in Clyde, Ohio.

A similar expression is 'caught red handed' (See original volume, p 96).

change is as good as a rest, A

This old English proverb means that one can be refreshed as much from changing his or her occupation or locale as from a time of relaxation. A major online source for phrase origins dates this to '100 years ago,' however, it comes from at least the early to mid-1800s, which would place it at more like 150 years ago, plus. In more than one publication in the late 19th century it is referred to as an 'old saying.' The earliest available citation is from November, 1882, in the *Wesleyan-Methodist Magazine* in 'Gobo, and the War in Egypt: A Letter from the Reverend John Leverack,' dated 8 September that year:

"The old saying is '**a change is as good as a rest**;' and not finding much time for rest, last evening we decided on a change in the shape of a trip to Gozo."

changing of the guard, The

This phrase is now used idiomatically to refer to any dramatic or large change, especially when new people are replacing others in positions of importance, but in subtle cases as well. It is inspired by the actual ceremony in which soldiers or other government officials guarding a major government facility or state house are replaced by a new shift. It was made popular by the event at Buckingham

Palace in London, and later, in Washington, DC, by the ceremony at the Tomb of the Unknown Soldier. Both are elaborate ceremonies which attract many visitors each day. But the practice predates both of these. Soldiers have guarded Royal Palaces since 1660.

The first mention of 'the changing of the guard' in print was *The White Rose of York, A Midsummer Annual* 1834, by George Hogarth, pages 30-31:

> "Still the stranger passed on apparently uninterested in all he had observed, until he came to the outer gate where he merely paused for a few moments as though to observe the movement of the soldiers, and **the changing of the guard**."

By 1918, it was being used metaphorically. Here it is stated regarding birds. In *From the First Shot: A Picture History of the Great War* by Hannah White published by Independent Corporation, New York, in the story, 'Paris with a Difference' by Harold Howland:

> "It is **the changing of the guard**. Each hour of the day — and night as well, as you shall see — four faithful birds like these mount guard above the city, and sail and dart and skim about, and watch and watch and watch."

Chapter and verse! Chapter and verse!

This idiom infers that the person being addressed has not given enough specific, provable information about his or her assessment of a particular matter in the statements made and much more specific proof is needed to be convincing. It is derived by quotations from the *Bible* made by priests, ministers or teachers to support a sermon, written statement or lecture. The *Bible* has long been regarded in Christian circles as the absolute authority, thus, this analogy.

By the mid-to-late 19th century it was becoming customary to demand chapter and verse for proof in biblical arguments. *The Evangelical Repository and United Presbyterian Review*, February, 1868, gives us a good example of this in the first article, titled 'Church Union' by the Rev. D.F. Bonner:

> *"And no man has a right to say I shall sing any thing without giving a 'Thus saith the Lord.' If he cannot give the* **chapter and verse** *for the exclusive use of the Psalms, I tell him I am a Protestant." Show me "the* **chapter and verse"** *directing women to eat of the Lord's supper? Show me "the* **chapter and verse"** *defining Christian baptism ...*

The earliest known example of this being used in the current manner in print is from *New Theories and the Old Faith* by James Allison Picton, 1870, on page 112:

> "I remember a debate, somewhat celebrated at the time, in which an evangelical clergyman persisted in interrupting his opponent by calling out **"chapter and verse! chapter and verse!"**

This became a standard practice in biblical matters during the late 19th century, and by the early 20th century it had bled over into secular usage. The earliest known reference in print is from *Proceedings for Phychical Research*, published in 1906 by A.W. Verrall, in an entry from page 403 in the Appendix dated Augsut 21, 1904, questioning the author:

> "When he has read the papers he will see what I mean. **Chapter and verse, chapter and verse**, tell him that. AWV I mean."

Check all the boxes (See: **Tick all the boxes**)+

Cheeky monkey[2]

This British slang expression, though peaking in television and media offerings in the 1970s and 1980s is still in use today by folks in the British Isles and Australia. It is used to chide someone in a playful, good-natured fashion, though it also may be used dismissively. It was common on such comedy TV series as 'Doctor in the House,' 'Open All Hours' and 'Are You Being Served.' It has been used referring to men who made advances on ladies as well as to refer to rambunctious or mischievous children. The phrase is never used in America. The earliest known printed reference is from 1962 in *Granada Manchester's Plays*, in 'Independent Means' by Stanley Haughton, Act II, page 118:

> ***"Sam:...*** [To Mac] Oh, bring in an extra cup, will you?
> ***Mac:*** Aye, sir. Do you want one, Mr. Watling?
> ***Watling:*** **Cheeky monkey**. *I* put the kettle on."

Chicken-livered

This metaphor means easily frightened, timid, fearful or cowardly. It derives from the fact that chickens are easily spooked and run at the slightest noise. The first example we have of 'chicken' meaning a coward comes in 1595 in *An Humble Supplication to Her Maistie* on pages 22 and 23:

"John Savage, likewise when he came vnto the Court, was soe well knowne to be **a Chicken** of that fether, that two Pinsioners were charged to have a spetiall eye on him, and to watch him soe long as he stayed there…"

The first mention of 'chicken-livered' as a separate idiom was in the British novel, *Old Bachelors, Their Varieties Characters and Conditions* (by the Author of *Old Maids*) 1835, page 103-104:

"Talk of a hen-pecked husband, forsooth! — a wife's authority may be excused or tolerated, as in nine cases out of ten, she governs for the benefit of her family and her faint-hearted spouse: but the authority of a housekeeper — the hen-pecked Old Bachelor! — truly this is pushed to extremities that would make the veriest **chicken-livered** husband in existence rebel."

A similar expression is lily-livered.

Chill out

This means to relax, especially after a period of hard work of a stressful situation. Tracking the origin is difficult, but it was said to be started as an African American expression in the late 20th century, and became very popular in the 1980's and '90s. A variation was 'take a chill pill' (a popular nickname for Ritalin and other ADD medications). The earliest available citation is from *New York Magazine*, July 5-12, 1982 in a story titled 'Central Park,' on page 49:

"'**Chill out**,' he says, almost gently. 'Why don't you **chill out**.'"

The phrase 'chill out music' was applied to songs which were relaxing. This is the opposite of 'hot under the collar' (see).

Chook / Clever chook[3]

In Australia, a chook is either a chicken or a woman (chick). It comes from old British dialect (chuck or chucky) for a chicken. It has been used Down Under since the mid-19th century. The earliest available citation is from the *Melbourne Punch,* August 22, 1867, in a poem titled 'The Old Hen's Lament' on page 57:

"Oh! listen gentlefolks, I beg,
To my **chook**-a-chooky, **chook**-a-chooky,**chook**, **chook**, **chook**;
Not long ago I laid an egg.
With a **chook**-a-chooky,**chook**-a-chooky, **chook**, **chook**, **chook**.
'Twas but a small one I must own,
Yet that was better far than none,

> And proud I was of this here one,
> Of my **chook**-a-chooky,**chook**-a-chooky, **chook**, **chook**, **chook"**

Clever chook now is a common slang expression for a skillful, quick-thinking young Aussie girl, but the earliest available reference in print for this expression in found in *Hey, It's O.K.!* By Jane E. SKILLICORN, 2013, page 37:

> "She was one very **clever chook**!"

Chuck it in

This means to quit or give up, similar to 'throw in the towel' (see first volume). Chuck, used in this matter, seems to be a variant of chock, from the French choc, meaning to throw or toss. The earliest available citation in this usage is from *Buffet for Unwelcome Guests* by Christianna Brand, on page 200, 1983:

> "'I suppose I shall just have to **chuck it in**,' he said. '**Chuck it in**!'"

Chunk of change; good or handsome chunk of change

This idiom means a large sum of money. The earliest known citation if from *Sunset Magazine, the Pacific Monthly*, February, 1915 in a story titled Alien Pearls by Edward H. Hurlbut:

> "'And the girl might kick through with a good **chunk of change** even to talk to him over the phone!' Lanagan, strolling from the telephone office, caught a glimpse of Maggart hurrying through the lobby."

Strangely enough, it seems to go dormant until the 1990s when it came back 'with a vengeance.' (See)

clash of the Titans, A

As an idiom this phrase means a battle for acceptance of theories or struggle and competition between two intellectuals with opposing viewpoints. In Greek mythology, the Titans were the original gods who gave birth to the Olympian gods, and were cast down by their offspring. The 'clash of the titans' was their war which spawned the two movies by that name in 1981 and its remake in 2010. The latter inspired a video game by the same name. But as an idiom it only started being used around the turn of this century. The earliest example in print available if from *British Corruption to the Europe of the Twenty-first Century* by Prof. Basil S. Markesinis, 2002 on page 78:

> "It was also quick to re-affirm its established case law in a quick succession of judgments, thus preventing the creation of a parallel but different jurisprudence. But the **clash of the Titans** was not over yet."

Clean house

This is a figure of speech for getting rid of anything unwanted and / or undesirable, particularly in an organization or business. It often refers to illuminating corruption. Exact origin is unknown, but it came into use in the early to mid 20th century. A good early example is from *Investigation of Un-American Propaganda Activities in the United States Congress*, 1947, page 272:

> "**The CHAIRMAN**. You say, Mrs. Talmadge, that we should **clean house**. Of course, it is very easy to say that, and we have been saying it for a long time, but the Communist Party in the past few years, even though we have been saying it, has made progress."

Clean someone's clock

This means to trounce one's opponents in a game or inflict severe reverse in any competition, match, election, etc. Though cleaning someone, the root of the saying, goes back to the early 1800s. The earliest known citation of this actual figurative phrase is found in *The Trenton Evening Times* (New Jersey) on 28 July, 1908:

> "It took the Thistles just one inning to **clean the clocks** of the Times boys."

Clean up your own back yard

This popular Southern American platitude has various endings: before you barge into someone else's; before you go knocking on your neighbor's door; before you clean up your neighbors; before you come over to mine and start running your mouth, etc. This saying originated in the May, 1915 *Child Labor Bulletin, Annual Labor Bulletin, Proceedings of the Eleventh Conference*, page 47, and is in a quote from David Clark, Editor of the Southern Textile Bulletin, who likely coined it:

> "I do not think your organization has been granted any commission to enforce the laws of North Carolina, and coming from states whose violations

of laws, including those of child labor, are in excess of those of my state, I say that you should **clean up your own backyard** before you attend to ours."

In 1969, Elvis Presley recorded a song written by Mac Davis and Billy Strange titled *Clean up Your Own Backyard* which came out as a single, but wasn't featured on any album. It was from the soundtrack of the movie *The Trouble with Girls*, and reached number 35 on the *Billboard* Hot 100 Chart and 22 in the U.K. Singles Chart.

Clear as crystal

This very old cliché means transparent, very clear or easy to understand. It is both a simile and a metaphor, in that it is almost always used in a figurative context. It was first cited in *Four Letters and Certain Sonnets* by Gabriel Harvey in 1592:

"Where should I find that I seek, a person **clear** as a **crystal**?"

Cloud-cuckoo-land[2]

This is a metaphoric British expression used to mean a fanciful or ideal realm; and one of the oldest. It was coined in the 4th century BCE by Greek playwright Aristophanes in his fanciful play, *The Birds*.

"Chorus leader: So what name shall we give our city?
Pisthetairos: Well, do you want to use that mighty name from Lacedaimon - shall we call it Sparta?
Euelpides: By Hercules, would I use that name Sparta for my city? No. I wouldn't even try esparto grass to make my bed, not if I could use cords of linen.
Pisthetairos: All right then, what name shall we provide?
Chorus leader: Some name from around here - to do with clouds, with high places full of air, something really extra grand.
Pisthetairos: Well, then, how do you like this: **Cloudcuckooland**?"

When this play was first translated into English in 1824 by Henry Carey, the term was entered into British English. The entire play may be found in *The Acharnians, Knights, Wasps and Birds or Aristophanes; Translated into English Prose* published by Harry Slatter at Oxford, 1830.

Cock and bull story^

This old idiom is applied to a tale which seems so fanciful that it is entirely unbelievable to anyone who is not extremely naïve. The story has been well circulated that the phrase was coined at Stony Stratford in Milton Keynes, a market town in Buckinghamshire, England. The name Stony Stratford stood for 'the stony ford on the Roman Road' of Watling Street, now called the 5A. In the 18th and 19th centuries at the height of the coaching era, this was a vital mail and passenger stop between London and the North of England. The Cock and Bull were two of the main inns in town, and rivalry between the guests frequenting the two establishments is claimed to have reached fever pitch, resulting in exaggerated fantastic tales, which became known as 'cock and bull stories'. Both inns still exist. This, however, is not the true origin of the phrase. Versions of it actually predate this period.

Old folk tales featured magical animals. The first actual citation in English of 'cock and bull' is from John Day's 1603 play, *Law Trickes*, Act IV, page 66:

> "Didst marke what a **tale of a cock and a bull** he tolde my father whilst I made then and the rest away."

The early 17th century French term, from which this more likely derived, is *coq-a-l'âne.* Randle Cotgrave's *A Dictionary of the French and English Tongues*, 1611, referenced elsewhere in this book, listed the saying with the definition;

> "An incoherent story passing from one subject to another."

The literal translation of the French is 'from rooster to jackass'. Later the Scots used this saying as 'cockalayne'. Another way of saying this is the term we in America have heard, 'cockamayme' (also spelled cockamamie). Either way, the meaning fits well with 'cock and bull.' Bull was being used as a term for silly stories even earlier.

Then in *The Anatomy of Melancholy* by Robert Burton, 1621:

> "Some mens whole delight is, to take Tobacco, and drink all day long in a Tavern or Ale-house, to discourse, sing, jest, roar, talk of a **Cock and Bull** over a pot, &c."

Though a tavern is mentioned in the one above, the context of these citations do not jive with the story of the infamous British inns. A cock and bull indicated tales of farm denizens. Both hotels were there before the 17th century, but the story that the derivation of the phrase was from there was apparently not 'hatched up' (see) until the 20th century, and seems a bit cockamamie.

Cocksure

In today's world, this term means presumptuously or arrogantly confident. It dates to the early 16th century. The earliest known citation is from *Vulgaria* by Robert Whittington, 1520:

> "I haue knowen a man or nowe that thought him selfe **cocke sure** of his intent."

At that time it meant 'absolutely safe and free from danger,' so the definition as altered greatly with time.

In Francis Grose's *Dictionary of the Vulgar Tongue*, 1811, he stated an opinion of origin which is not correct due to the fact that it pre-dates the musket:

> "**COCK-SURE**. Certain: a metaphor borrowed front the cock of a firelock, as being much more certain to fire than the match."

Guesses as to the actual origin include being 'as sure as a cock's crow at daybreak,' and one that seems much more likely; that it came from the archaic euphemism for God, 'cocke,' plus sure. This euphemism appeared in numerous medieval oaths down through the 16th century, including cockes bones, cockes passions and cockes wounds. Thus, it originally represented the security of rightfulness equal to that of God. One example is in the play, *The Tyde tarryeth No Man* by John Payne Collier, compiled by George Wapull, 1576:

> ***"Corage:*** **'Cockes passion**! this is the gentlemans man, [Sþeahing to GREEDINES. Which at home doth tarry for thee. Syr, Welthinesse is not hence far away.'"

Cocky[3]

This is a term applied to farmers or land owners in Australia, often now classified according to their interests; cow cockies, cane cockies, wheat cockies, etc. The term began being used in the 1870s as an abbreviation of 'cockatoo farmer,' which was a disparaging term for a small-scale farmer. It came from the fact that these farmers in the 19th century would often use a small tract of land for a short term, then move on to another area, in the manner which was perceived of someone feeding cockatoos. The earliest mention in print available is from an article in *Once a Month: An Illustrated Australian Magazine*, 1 March 1886 titled 'Scalping Extraordinary:'

> *In speaking about squatting life I forgot that I was conversing with a new chum, and said,*
> *"At any rate the squatters here are not so much annoyed by* **'cockies'** *as they are in New South Wales."*
> **"Cockies***?" inquired Jones.*
> *"It is the short for Cockatoo," said I. "They settle on the runs by the dozens, and have ruined many a fine station."*

Coin a phrase

The verb 'to coin' was first used for the actual minting of money. Around the 14th century, as a noun, coin referred to the cutting dies used in this process. Within the next 200 years persons in the public eye were constantly 'coining' new words and phrases. Though we don't know who 'coined' this phrase, the earliest known citation of a form of it was in *The Art of English Poesie* by George Puttenham, 1589, chapter XXII:

> "Young schollers not halfe well studied before they come from the Vniuersitie or fchooles, and when they come to their friends, or happen to get fome benefice or other promotion in their countreys, will seeme to **coigne fine wordes** out of the Latin."

Learned people were not kind in their views of new words in those days. Shakespeare was a chief offender; creating os many of our current fabulous expressions. He also used this circa 1607 in *Coriolanus,* Act III, Scene i*:*

> "So shall my lungs **Coin words** till their decay."

The earliest printed reference available to coining a *phrase* is from *The Veterinarian*, a monthly journal of veterinary science, July, 1830:

> "'The all-fitting shoe' (if I may **coin** such a **phrase**) would be more proper than the expansion."

Coin flip (See: **Heads or tails**)

Coin of the realm+

This colloquial figurative term is used for the legal currency of a country or something valued or used in the same manner as money in a particular civilization or society. Then word coin originally derived from the Latin word *cuneus*, meaning corner or wedge. Coins were originally struck with a wedge-shaped device holding a die that pressed an image or inscription on a blank disc. Over time, the word *cuneus* came to be used for the money itself instead of the device and die. An early citation of this term came on page 2 of the *Bill for Provision of Gradual Resumption of Payments in Cash by Bank Ireland*, 1821, in speaking of gold:

> "...payable on demand, and which the said governor and company shall not purpose or offer to pay on demand, in the current lawful **coin of the realm**..."

In modern times anything from books to latte, to information has all been referred to as the 'coin of the realm' by reporters and other writers.

Cold as Kraut^

Kraut was a derogatory name that American soldiers called Germans during World War I and II. Many, therefore, believed that saying something was 'cold as kraut' referred to the 'cold-hearts' of Nazis. However, this simile actually developed in Appalachia, and it referred to sauerkraut which was kept in smokehouses or root cellars in vats during the winter before the days of refrigeration. The earliest available reference in print is from *Three Lives for Mississippi*, by William Bradford Huie, 1965, page 81:

> "The winter was '**cold as kraut**.' And 'folks yah met on the street just didn't care whether yah lived or died.'"

Cold comfort[2]

This British metaphor means a nominal consolation at the time of severe circumstances. A form of it was coined back in the 14th century in the poem *Patience*, by 'The Gawain Poet,' an allegory on the biblical Jonah.

> "Lorde! **colde** watz his **comfort**, and his care huge."

It was used by Shakespeare more than once. The earliest example being from *King John*, 1595, Act V, Scene iv, in dialogue from the King:

> "I beg **cold comfort;** and you are so strait, And **so** ingrateful, **you** deny me that."

Cold, hard facts^

This means facts that are dependable and verifiable. A major dictionary of American slang puts 'hard facts' at being coined circa 1887+. But that is not based on 'hard facts' because it is almost 100 years too late. *The History of the Trial of Warren Hastings, Esq., Late Governor General of Bengal* (Including Impeachment by the Commons of Great Britain), published in 1796, London, includes the following citation:

> "He complained of the hard language which had been used against him in the course of the prosecution. Hard language was a mode of accusation which would do him no harm; for, unless supported by **hard facts**, abusive words would recoil on him who used them..."

Numerous other printed references occurred in the years following, long before 1887. Even the later term, cold hard facts, came earlier. In *Older England*, a Course of Seven Lectures, by J. Frederick Hodgetts, published in London in 1884 we have the first known citation of this phrase:

> **"Cold, hard facts** have to be learnt. A discriminating power has to be acquired, and the lesson taught by the mystic number two has to be mastered."

Comeback kid

This expression is used frequently to describe a person who has fallen from popularity or 'grace' and made an unlikely comeback in the eye of the public. It has been used in regard to sports figures, entertainers, clergy and politicians. It was often a descriptive phrase for former U.S. President, Bill Clinton. The earliest available reference in print is from *The Typographical Journal*, July, 1913, page 46, under the heading 'Syracuse, New York' in speaking of the president of the local typographical union:

> "The toastmaster was Thomas XL Gafney, who, in introducing President Connolly, referred to him as the 'original **comeback kid**,' owing to the fact that Mr. Connolly had just been elected for the third time as president of No. 55 (being the first to have that distinction)."

The context would indicate that the term was already in use.

Comedy of errors

A comedy of errors is situation made amusing by bungling and incompetence. It comes from *The Comedy of Errors,* the title of one of William Shakespeare's early plays—a farcical comedy about the wars of secession in France, thought to have been written in the latter part of 1594, first published in 1595.

The earliest known reference to a comedy of errors in the current sense is from *The Political and Miscellaneous Works of Thomas Paine, Volume II*, in 'Speech on the Constitution,' the translation of which was read Citizen Lanthera, in the Convention, July 7, 1775, published in London, 1819,

> "Judging by their own foolish ideas of Government, they ascribed appearances to causes, between which there was no connection. Every thing on their part has been **a comedy of errors**, and the actors have been chased from the stage."

Come off the grass[3]^

This now primarily Australian slang expression means that the person is not thinking rationally and needs to think about what they have said more realistically. A major phrase origin dictionary put the first date of use at 1890. It was correct in that it did not originate in Australia. The earliest known citation is from Charles Dickens' *The Life and Adventures of Martin Chuzzlewit* first serialized in 1843, then published as a book in London in 1844:

> "'Hallo!' cried the gentleman.
>
> "'Sir, your servant!' said Mr. Pecksniff, taking off his hat. 'I am proud to make your acquaintance.'
>
> "'**Come off the grass**, will you!' roared the gentleman."

Comes with the territory^

Metaphorically this means that what has happened is to be expected under the circumstances. It comes from a territory or area that is assigned to someone accepting a position, such as a sales area or a job in law enforcement. A major online source places the origin at the second half of the 20th century. This is close, but the earliest known reference in print is actually from *Life Magazine*, February 21, 1949, in a caption under a picture from Arthur Miller's Pulitzer Prize and Best Drama Tony winning play, 'Death of a Salesman' on page 118:

> "A salesman has got to dream, boys; it **comes with the territory**."

The first performance had been on February 10th, and this is likely the coining of the saying.

Come unraveled

In a literal sense, unraveled, meaning separation of threads in a woven fabric, has been in our vocabulary since the late 16th century. Metaphorically, however, coming unraveled refers to a situation which was thought to be well in hand now becoming out of control. Perhaps a plan or agreement. In this connotation, it first began usage in the late 1700s. The earliest known citations in print are from 1791. In July, *The Gentleman's Magazine* had the following in a letter to the editor concerning relief granted to Roman Catholics:

> "Soon after, However, the mystery was **unraveled** by the bill introduced into the Upper House by the aforesaid Noble Earl…"

That same year, in *Rights of Man*, Thomas Paine used unraveled in the following figurative statement on page 45:

> "But as fome management was necessary to keep this plan, concealed till the moment it fhould be ready for execution,... But in a few days from this time the plot **unraveled** itself."

Common denominator

In a literal scenario, in mathematics, a common denominator is a number by which two or more larger numbers may be divided evenly. It may also be defined as a number that is a multiple of all the denominators of a set of fractions. Figuratively, it is a trait, characteristic or belief which is shared by all members of a group. The word 'denominator' derives from Medieval Latin, 1535-1545. The earliest known reference in print of common denominator, in a literal connotation is from *The Gvnner Shewing the Whole Practise of Artillery*, by Robert Norton, 1628, page 23:

> "But if all the Denominators be alike, adde all the Denominaters together, and fet (set) their **common Denominator** vnder the sums of them…"

It was not until about 1930 that common denominator began to be used in a figurative sense. The earliest example known in print is from the *U.S. Department of Agriculture Technical Bulletin 206*, November, 1930, page 106:

"It may not be possible to define the environmental complex except in terms of individual factors which are themselves not reducible to a **common denominator**."

Common thread

This metaphoric expression refers to a theme, idea or characteristic found in a variety of stories or situations. It began to be used in this sense in the last half of the 19th century. The earliest verifiable citation is from the *Edinburgh Review*, October, 1871 in Professor Jowell's Translation of Plato:

"Though the sequence of Dialogues cannot be absolutely fixed, we see them broadly falling into divisions which mark successive periods of Plato's mind. We see also a **common thread** of connexion running through them all, from 'Charmides' or 'Lysis' to 'Laws.'"

Conjure up

The word 'conjure' means to make something appear or seem to appear by using magic. It came into Middle English from the Anglo-French *conjurer*, which in turn was derived from the Latin *conjurare*. The expression '**conjure up** the dead' is used of the practice known as divination, said to used by seers or 'mediums' who claim to have contact with the spirits of the dead. The craft has been practiced for thousands of years. It is mentioned in the *Bible* in *I Samuel 28:8* when King Saul, the first King of Israel, (c 1025 to 1018 BCE.) against Jewish law, disguised himself and consulted the 'witch of Endor' in an effort to bring up the spirit of Samuel the prophet *(KJV):*

"**Conjure up** for me, please, and bring up for me whom I shall name to you."

The first, *Wycliffe Translation*, 1384, used 'raise thou up for me' rather than conjure up'. 'Conjure up' became a familiar figurative expression in English, however, for preparing something so quickly that it would seem magical, as early as 1588, even before the *King James Bible* version of the Endor witch story was published in 1611. *Perimedes the Blacke-smith* by John Payne Collier has the following on page 40:

"Hee made no account of winning credite by his workes, as thou doft, that dost no good workes, but thinkes to bee famosed by a strong faith of thine owne worthines: his onely care was to have a spel in his purse, to **conjure up** a good cup of wine with at all times."

Contrary to popular opinion

This cliché refers to something, usually to follow, which is the opposite of what is commonly believed. 'Popular opinion' was used in Shakespeare's *The Merry Wives of Windsor*, circa 1597 and many times thereafter; however, the earliest known example in print of a close form of this using 'contrary to' was found in *The Scott's Magazine*, November, 1745 in 'The Speech of Q. Marcius Philippus, in the Character of the Marquis of Tweeddale:'

> "...where every thing meets with due consideration it encourages me to deliver my sentiments freely, tho' they may perhaps be **contrary** to what is the **popular opinion** without doors."

The actual expression is used in September, 1788 in *The English Review, Or, An Abstract of English and Foreign Literature*:

> "Though it is certain that this representation is **contrary to popular opinion**, and neither accords with the latitude of the country, or the fondness of the Athenians for a country life, yet the authorities he quotes are so respectable,"

Convince a man against his will and he's of the same opinion still^

This great proverbial piece of wisdom is usually attributed to Dale Carnegie in his remarkable 1936 best-seller, *How to Win Friends and influence People*, which has helped millions along their way to understanding how positive relationships enable us to live better and more productive lives. It was in the section headed, "You Can't Win an Argument." However, he did not originate it. British writer and feminist Mary Wollstonecraft (1759-1797), included this proverb verbatim in the notes to Chapter 5 of her 1792 treatise, *A Vindication of the Rights of Woman*. But she did not coin it either. It is in quotes in her book. The earliest known citation of a form of it is from Samuel Butler's 17th century poem, *Hudibras*. Part III, Canto iii, lines 547-550.

> "**He that complies against his will**
> **Is of his own opinion still**
> Which he may adhere to, yet disown,
> For reasons to himself best known"

It is very possible that Butler was the originator of this profound thought.

Cooked enough for an army+

This hyperbolic Southern expression was often used in the 20th century when someone had prepared far too much food for those being served. The origin of the term goes a bit further back, and is not from the South. It originated with American reformer and eccentric Joseph Sechler Coxey (1854 – 1951), and was first stated as "Enough (grub) to feed Coxey's army" in reference to the protest march by unemployed workers Coxey led from Massillon, Ohio to Washington, DC in March, 1894. Then first article about his march was published on page 7 of the Maine newspaper, *Lewiston Evening Journal*, April 16 of that year; several others followed. The earliest actual printing of the expression came in the May 16, 1920 edition of *The American Magazine* in an article by Scottish-born American financial journalist B.C. Forbes, actually referring to another cavalcade in which he had participated, through Utah:

"We pitched our tents in Red Canyon, three miles distant from the town site. We had thirty-one horses, five wranglers, two cooks, six Japanese waters and ***enough*** grub ***to feed Coxey's army*** going and coming.

Cook the books

This metaphor refers to changing financial records of a business with fraudulent intent. A minor definition of 'cook' in the Oxford English Dictionary is 'present in a surreptitiously altered form.' The use in this manner dates back to 17th century England. The earliest known usage of cook in this intent was by the Earl of Stratford in his 1636 *Letters and Dispatches*:

> "The Proof was once clear, however, they have **cook'd** it sense."

'Cooked up' was used by the mid-16th century. The earliest citation available, however, of 'cook the books' is from 1940 in *Purbeck Shop: A Stonecutter's Story of Stone* by Eric Benfield, 'Mushroom Merchants,' pp 137,138:

> "Yet although all men died or finished work in debt, all merchants made big money. I am not arguing that they did **cook the books**, though the temptation to do so must have been great, but the fact is that since those days no more fortunes have been made".

Correct me if I'm wrong+

This statement literally means, "I believe this to be true," and implies that the other person may see the situation in a different light. It has likely been in verbal use longer, but it gained popularity in print in the 1960s.

An alternative would be, "If I'm not mistaken."

Cot case[3]

In Australia and New Zealand, this term literally refers to a person too ill to leave his or her bed. Figuratively it has come to mean someone incapacitated by alcohol or an eccentric or mad individual, or someone perceived to be so. It is actually used, however, in *Case Histories in Abnormal Psychiatry* published by Stanford University Press in 1940 in this snippet from page 12, Case 8 'Paraplegia:'

> "On December 31st the patient was dressed, waiting in the hospital grounds for embarkation to England, as a **cot case**, the left leg being useless."

The earliest citation from Australia in a figurative usage of today in a play by Greg McGee, a New Zealander, titled *Tooth and Claw,* published by Victoria University Press in 1984; Act I, Scene ii:

> ***"Kelly*:** Jesus, you'd be a **cot case**. Want to pour some concrete tomorrow, rehabilitate yourself?"

Coulda, shoulda, woulda+

This idiom has been arranged in all possible ways, but has the same meaning. It is a rhyming catchphrase used to dismiss another person's regrets over past experiences gone awry. It means that we can't do anything about the past; therefore we must let it go. It is fairly recent in origin. The earliest known citation in print (arranged in this way) is from is an advertisement in the *New York Times* for Halpert, Oberst and Company, a municipal bond company, June 19, 1977. However, the previous year, in the American *Catalogue of Copyright Entries*, July through December, the following appeared:

> "12 Aug 1976, EP357U93, E35740 it. I but **woulda, coulda, shoulda**, w E m, Curtis Emerson."

A precursor to the saying, however, appeared much earlier, in American novelist Theodore Drieser's *An American Tragedy* in 1925:

> "I **coulda** chucked my job, and I **woulda**."

Cover all the bases

This figurative expression means to prepare for any possible situation. The absolute origin of this metaphor has not been established. It came into use early in the 20th century and is likely American, though it is also used frequently in Australia. It also is thought by some to have derived from baseball where having men on all bases during play is mandatory to defensive play; but this is taken for granted. Another thought is that it could have been coined in the military, referring to having military bases manned well. This actually makes more sense. The earliest known figurative reference to a form of it is in *Partners in Providence* by Charles D. Stewart, in the title to chapter XXIX on page 488:

> "Clancy Gets **All Bases Covered**"

Actual use of cover all the bases started showing up in print in the mid-1900s, and the first known example is in an article titled 'Oh for Halcyon Days, Film Work Belongs to Strong' by Jess Oppenheimer on page 13 in *Billboard Magazine* on June 14, 1952:

> "Desi Arnaz and I work awfully hard on all of the production phases of I Love Lucy and we still don't have enough time in a week to **cover all the bases**."

Cozzie[3]

In Sydney and all over New South Wales, Australia, this is slang for a swim suit or ladies' bikini. Sometimes spelled 'cossie' or cosale, it is actually short for 'costume,' and showed up there between 1915 and 1920 according to major sources. The earliest available citation is from New Zealand-British Lexicographer, Eric Partridge, in *A Dictionary of Slang and Unconventional English, Eighth Edition*, 1984:

"Y. & B. cosale (pron. **cozzie**). A swimming costume: Aus., from ca. 1919"

Crapshoot

This slang expression refers to anything which is risky or problematic. Derived from tossing dice, often called shooting Craps, it means that something is a gamble at best. A major online dictionary places its origin as a metaphoric idiom at around 1970. The earliest available figurative citation, though a bit removed from the current use, is actually from an article in the *Austin Chronicle* by Margaret Mosser written on December 31, 1969, titled 'Janice Joplin, Texas and the Big Beat:'

> "The Cosmic Giggle must have been in full-tilt hysterics on January 19, 1943 when the oil refinery seaport of Port Arthur, Texas, won the heavenly **crapshoot** as the birthplace of rock & roll's first female superstar, Janis Joplin."

This term became widely used in the late 1970s and 1980s. An early period printed reference is in *New York Magazine*, July 4, 1977 in the article "The Raise of the Year from a 'Board of Robots'" by Dan Dorfman:

> "'People will think it's a **crap-shoot** business when it's really not,' he complained repeatedly throughout a three-hour interview last week at his posh executive offices in the Warner building at 75 Rockefeller Plaza."

Crash and burn

This metaphoric idiom means to have an utter failure. It is derived from an automobile wreck or plane crash, particularly in the movies, in which the car or aircraft explodes and is engulfed in flames upon impact. It was used in a literal sense in *Life Magazine*, December 26, 1938, on page 35, in a caption under a picture from the 1930 WW I Errol Flynn war movie, *The Dawn Patrol* being rescreened:

> "Niven, in plane nearby, helplessly sees him **crash and burn."**

The phrase was used in a somewhat figurative connotation in *Life Magazine* as early as February 2, 1959 in relation to a skier meeting with a serious out-of - control tumble, but certainly not actually 'burning,' on page 70, in 'The Scary Sappy Life of the Nation's Ski Maniacs' by Sports Editor Marshall Smith:

> "The transition from slope to flat at the bottom, where the skier feels safer than in church, is the place where he is most likely to **crash and burn**. Overconfidence is the most grievous of the sins which lead to skiing accidents."

A similar citation appeared in *Skiing Magazine* in November, 1966, showing that the metaphor had caught on.

> "That skiers occasionally **crash and burn** makes us wince, but we accept the fact philosophically, just as we accept our own painful bruises."

The earliest known citation of this phrase in its current explicit meaning is in *Billboard*, 15 December 1973, on page 40, in 'Snuff's Philosophy:'

> "Snuff's routine in those days was weeks of such grueling work then off for a while when he'd "**crash and burn"** then back into the studio for more."

Here the expression is in quotes indicating that it was already known, but likely fairly new in this vein of use. The phrase has been the title of several books and a song written by Jesse Frasure and Chris Stapleton released to digital by Country artist, Thomas Rhett in 2015.

Crime doesn't pay+

This proverbial truism means that sooner or later those perpetrating crimes will be apprehended and punished. It was cited numerous times by American author, Nick Harris in his book, *In the Shadows: Thirty Detective Stories Showing Why Crime Doesn't Pay, A Series of Famous Cases*, 1923. It was then popularized by the serialized radio drama, *The Shadow,* based on a character developed by Walter B. Gibson, first appearing on CBS on July 31, 1930.

Crook as a dog[3]

In Australia, this means the same as sick as a dog in America; extremely unwell. The earliest citation is from Alan Marshall in children's classic, *I Can Jump Puddles*, 1955, page 186:

> "'Sore as a boil,' muttered Peter, looking round him as if for direction. He suddenly leaned wearily on the rail of the fence. 'I'm **crook as a** mangy **dog** this morning.'"

Crooked as a dog's hind leg^

This metaphor implies that a dog's hind leg is more crooked than other animal's limbs. That is likely because the knee turns backward, therefore it is thought unnatural. Someone about whom this expression is used then is unusually corrupt. Mark Twain sometimes gets credit for this in his *Letters from Hawaii*, 1866, and it is possible that he used it earlier in a speech; however, there is an earlier citation in *The Amateur's Magazine*, November, 1859 in The Mammoth Grub, Part II:

> "'Well, I can only say if it was the best, it didn't speak much for his mode of training 'em, for it was as **crooked**, sir, as a **dog's hind leg**. It was as **crooked**, sir,' lowering his voice to a confidential whisper, 'as some of his ways in business, and they're tortuous enough, I can tell you.'"

Crucify someone

This idiom is based upon the Roman means of execution by which Jesus of Nazareth was put to death, nailing the person to a cross. When used figuratively it means to treat someone cruelly, torment someone, or criticize a person or persons harshly. It was in use in this way by the mid-19th century when it was used by author Thomas Hall in *Rowland Bradshaw: His Struggles and Adventures on the Way to Fame*, 1848, page 104:

> "'I think, Bob, he'll lose his temper.'
>
> "'You are **crucifying him**; he'd not give a sovereign, but he would one of the best stumps in his mouth, to be off that bench.'

"Here the Attorney-general for the petty-sessions of Frescoth rose, and in a very whirlwind of bluster, said he would not submit to such conduct..."

crying shame, A

For hundreds of years people have expressed their emotional feelings of disappointment, disapproval or censure over an extremely unfortunate situation by calling it 'a crying shame.' 'Crying,' here denotes sadness. The earliest verifiable citation is from *The Fortunate Country Maid*, written in French by an anonymous author credited as L_____ V_____, translated by Charles de Fieux Mouhy, published in London in 1758, Volume One, on page 290:

> "Good God! said he, turning to the Count, after embracing me, how young this Lady must have been married! She is an Infant, exceeding handsome; it's a **crying Shame** she should be a Widow at these years!"

On February 1, 1994 the country band The Mavericks released a studio album titled, *What a Crying Shame!* containing a single by the same name on MCA in Nashville.

Cry me a river!

This wisecrack is a common putdown to someone attempting to gain sympathy by unleashing his or her burdens on another person. It was almost certainly taken from the title for a novelty song written by Arthur Hamilton in the 1920s for Ella Fitzgerald, but not published or recorded by her until 1953, and made popular by Julie London in 1955. It has since been recorded by numerous others including Barbara Streisand and Joe Cocker, and attained 'classic' status. The earliest known figurative citation outside the song for the expression is from *Life Magazine*, September 20, 1963, on page 86 in 'A Famous Novelist's Look inside Hollywood' by Bud Schulberg:

> "He didn't have the tact and despot like Irving Thalberg, or the literary background like B.P. Schulberg who drank, gambled, winched and read Conrad, Galsworthy, Dickens and Melville aloud to his children… or the old vaudevillian staying power of Jack Warner, or the whip-snapping cutting-room energies of Darryl Zanuck or the **cry-me-a-river** statesmanship of L.B. Mayer."

It didn't pick up its current usage until the 1980s. The earliest known citation of this in print is from *To Keera with Love: Abortion, Adoption or Keeping the Baby* by Kayla M. Becker with Connie K Heckert, 1987:

> "He stuffed my letter back into an envelope with a sheet of typing paper. On it, he wrote a one-line response: '**Cry me a river**, Kayla. I was only trying to be nice.'"

Curses come home to roost+

This exact saying comes from Margaret Mitchell's *Gone With the Wind,* 1936. But as a proverbial expression, the thought is over 600 years old. The fuller form was 'Curses are like chickens, they always come home to roost.' It was used to express the fact that one's offensive words or actions are likely to come back to them at some point. This appeared in *Roughing it in the Bush, Or. Life in Canada* by Susanna Moodie, 1852:

"The nest time the old woman commences her reprobate conduct, tell her to hold her tongue, and mind her own business, for **curses, like chickens, come home to roost**."

The idea, however, goes back to Chaucer in *The Parson's Tale*, circa 1390 in which he said curses are "**like a bird that returns again to its own nest**."
change is as good as a rest, A^

cut of one's jib, The[2]

This British cliché refers to the general appearance and demeanor of a person. It is derived from the jib of a sailing ship, which is a triangular sail between the foretopmast head and the 'jib boom.' Each country had a different style of sails in the old days, and sailors' opinions of ships were determined by their jibs. This expression came into usage in its current idiomatic form the late 18th century. The earliest known citation is from *The Musical Banquet of Choice Songs* published in Glasgow in 1790 by A. MacGoun in 'The Forecastle Sailor,' page 95:

> "The boatswain pip'd all hands to bale her, And I came down the back-stay so glib; For I am a forecastle failor, You may see by **the cut of my jib**."

Cut the crap

This is a rude expression used to tell someone to stop saying things which are untrue or not applicable, and to get to the real heart of a matter. It has been around since the late 18th century, and likely was Scottish in origin. The earliest printed reference known is from *Scots Poems* by William Taylor of Currie, 1787, in a Gaelic poem 'To one who got a Girl with child…' on page 164:

> "How cou'd you herry virtue's nest, O' female graces far the best: Tho' ye hae sown in pleasure's lap, In har'st o' pain ye'll **cut the crap…"**

In this case it was a call to follow through with a promise of marriage.

Cutting edge+

This is a figurative phrase used in relation to technology, meaning that some idea or product is bigger or better than any other of its type and is likely to revolutionize the industry or market. It has been in use in a literal since 1825 when it was used of plows. Later In the 19th century it began to be used of other technology which had 'an edge over' previous products.

Cut to the quick

This means that something caused deep emotional pain. It is commonly thought to have been derived from the 'quick' under the fingernail that relies upon the nail for protection. When a fingernail is cut too short, the cut goes into this tender area, causing lasting pain which takes time to heal. Some etymologists, however, have suggested that this 'quick' may have come from a word related to death, as in 'the quick and the dead,' from the Old English *cwicu,* which could actually be correct due to early usage. The term is very old, and was in use by 1652, when it was used in a poem on the tomb of the Reverend Mr. John Cotton, teacher of the Church of Boston, Massachusetts, recorded in the book *New-England's Memorial*, by Nathanial Morton; William Bradford and Thomas Prince, editors, published in 1669, on page 169:

> "Here lies magnanimous humility
> Majesty, meekness, Christian apathy…
> Could wound at argument without division
> **Cut to the quick**, and yet make no incision"

Another early reference in *Sylva, Discourse of Forest-Trees and Propagation of Timber in His Majesties Dominions* by John Evelyn, fellow of the Royal Society in London, 1670, also linked the term with death of plants.

> "…accompanied with cruel Frosts and cold blasts, for the space 'of more then two months: night and day, did not amongst neer a thousand cypresses: (growing in my Garden) kill above three or four, which for being very late **cut to the quick…"**

D

Damaged goods

In a literal sense, this means items which were expected to be in good condition which are discovered to be defective because of accidental means. Figuratively, it refers to a person who was once vibrant and healthy is now considered by others to be inadequate or impaired because of unfortunate or traumatic events in his or her life; usually due to drug or alcohol abuse, or abuse by others of a physical, emotional or sexual nature.

The literal use in English goes back to at least 1701, when *An Exact Abridgement of All the Statutes of King William and Queen Mary and of King William III in Force and Use,* published in London, had the following under 'Customs:'

> "Monies shall be paid of which Receiver General shall separate (The whole in four to be divided) which shall remain from time to time after Payments made thereout, by virtue of any Laws now in force upon Debentures for Goods received, or Corn exported, or discounts upon Bonds, and of Allowances for **damaged Goods**, ..."

In 1901 Eugene Brieux, a French playwright, wrote an intensely emotional play called *Les Avaries*, translated into English by Upton Sinclair as ***Damaged Goods,*** about a young couple who contacted syphilis. It was intended to drive home a powerful message of the effects of venereal disease. In 1913 this was made into an American silent short film directed by Tom Rickets and Richard Bennett, starring the latter. In 1919 a British silent version was filmed; then in 1937, an American sound film came out directed by Phil Gladstone, which was a closer look at premarital sex without mentioning venereal disease.

This play and the earliest of these films spawned the use of damaged goods meaning a person not accepted by society because of careless sexual activity outside of marriage. In 1917, Sinclair Lewis, in *The Job: An American Novel* wrote (page 257):

> "She had reason to suppose that her husband was **damaged goods**. She crept to an old family doctor and had a fainting joy to find that she had escaped contamination.
>
> "'Though,' said the doctor, 'I doubt if it would be wise to have a child of his.'"

As time went on, this definition began to broaden. *Popular Science Magazine*, January, 1921, had the following under the heading, "Are You a Reject?" on page 102, in an ad:

> "Like a damaged product of the factory? Look in the glass. See if what you see there is a full fledged man, or a piece of **damaged goods** — a reject of society — nerves gone, vitality sapped, energy- lacking, ambition lost — a weakened, trembling, hopeless, joyless mortal…"

Dance the night away

Whether this is used entirely figuratively is a matter of debate, but it is certainly a very old cliché, going back to 1701. The first use was in regard to fairies when it was coined by Charles Smith in *An Antient and Present State of the Country and City of Cork*: *In Four Books* in Book II, 'The Natural and Civil History of Cork,' Chapter VI, in a poetical description of the area of Burton:

> "Where Sylvan gods disport the live long day
> And wanton fairies **dance the night away**."

The extensive poem became very popular and was reprinted in many books and magazines over the next 150 years, no doubt engraining the line into the hearts on the Irish, including those who immigrated to America.

It was also about fairies in 'The Young Widow,' a poem printed in *Graham's American Monthly Magazine of Literature* (lines written under a miniature) in March, 1842:

> "When in ev'ry flower cup
> Fairies **dance the night away**,
> When the queenly moon is up,
> Moving on her stately way,
> When the stars upon the shore
> Silence e'en the sounding sea—
> Ever till we part no more,
> I'll think of thee!"

The line then was picked up and entered in 'Cottage and Hall' published in 1873 in *The Last Poems of Alice and Phoebe Cary*:

> "And beyond the good green piece of wood,
> And the field of flowers so gay,
> Among its ancient oaks there stood,
> With gables high and gray,

A lofty hall, where mistress of all
She might **dance the night away**."

Even here, it represented a carefree existence with no thought of a serious side of life. It has remained to this day an expression of letting oneself go; fairy-like, escaping the cares of reality.

Darken someone's door

This means to arrive at the door of a home or other building seeking entry. Usually the expression is used in the case where one is either unwelcome or has no desire to go. It is derived from the idea that when a person enters an open door his or her body makes the entrance dark, or that that person's very presence may cause darkness. Like many other very old lines, the earliest available is from a poem, *The Manners of the Age in Thirteen Moral Satirs*, Sat VII, by Thomas Newcomb, 1733.

"Unskill'd, the sovereign secret to reveal,
With physick to work off a hand and *seal*;
When duns each morning **darken** *Philo's* **door**,
His strange disease will pills or bleeding cure?
Will strong *ematicks* his distemper kill,
Or a kind bolus sweat away a bill?"

In 1742 it was used in a sense that we fully understand today in *The True Anti-Pamela* by James Parry, on page 115 (letters modified to modern shape):

"'Madam, says I, 'you've already given me a great deal of Uneasiness, without any just Reason for your so doing: I have made a firm Resolution, never more to **darken** your **Doors**.' With that I made her a Bow, and instantly left her…"

Dead and gone / Dead and buried^

Figuratively, these phrases mean long forgotten; no longer in use. They have been used of laws, patterns of thought, etc. A major online dictionary placed the coining at 'late 1800s'. However, in 1831, Charles Kingsley, in *Wayward the Wake, "Last of the English,"* on page 97, wrote this clear metaphoric example:

"What cares an outlaw for law, in a land where **law is dead and gone**?"

In the same relative time frame, 1842, on page 459 of *The French Revolution: a History, Volume II,* Thomas Carlyle made a reference to Sansculottism, the ideals of the French common people who became radical militant partisans in the French Revolution, as being "Dead and Buried."

> "But as for the body of Sansculottism, that is **dead and buried**, — and, one hopes, need not reappear, in primary amorphous shape, for another thousand years!"

Deadbeat

Previously dead beat and dead-beat, this term is applied to a person who has proven to have no regard to obligations, particularly repaying money loaned or for items purchased on credit. The following is the earliest English citation of the term, and comes from an original printing of the *King James Bible*, translated in 1611, printed in 1612, *Exodus 21:34*:

> "The owner of the pit hall shall make it good, and giue money vnto the owner of them, and the **dead beat** shall be his."

Dead certain

This expression means leaving no shadow of doubt that something is true. It is very old and the earliest known citation, in John Fletcher's play *Women Pleased,* Act I, Scene iii, a 'Tragi-Comedy, 1750, places it in a bit different light, which may just explain how it became what it is today:

> "***Soto***. I'm slain, I'm slain.
> "***Sil***. He's down and dead, **dead certain**,"

Originally it actually meant, 'certain to be dead.' It was over 100 years before the term began to be used like we know it today. In 1881, Jonathan R. Taylor used it in the novel *Macon Moore, the Southern Detective*, on page 113:

> "'It is **dead certain** that we traced our man to this house!' said Rogers. "'And it is **dead certain** that I saw the momentary flash of a light in one of the upper rooms.'"

Dead duck

In America we now call a politician who has lost his or her effectiveness a 'lame duck,' though that term was not initially necessarily political (see this entry, original volume). Actually, historically 'dead duck' has also been used in the U.S. as well as in the U.K. and Ireland. These terms both were dreamed up in the same era. 1829 seems to be the applicable year that 'dead duck' was brought to light on both sides of the pond. Early that year *The New Monthly Magazine* printed this attributed to John Bull:

> "CXCII. A **dead duck** is not a duck in law, after Judge Littledale; a dead rabbit is a rabbit, after Judge Burroughs; sheep are not sheep if any of them are rams, nor horses horses if any of them are mares: — such is the law;..."

On May 15, *The Glasgow Herald* reported that the following was first in the *Glasgow Morning Register*:

> "In opposition to the dictum of Judge Littledale, that a **dead duck** was **not** a duck, Mr. Serjeant Adams has decided that a dead rabbit ***is*** a rabbit. The vitality of a duck is one vitality, and the vitality of a rabbit is another vitality."

Whatever paper first reported this; it seems to have been aimed as a political arrow at the said Judge and possibly began the term to apply in that manner. One month later, the *New York Currier* printed this:

> "There is an old saying 'never waste powder on a **dead duck;'** but we cannot avoid flashing away a few grains upon an old friend, Henry Clay."

Without doubt, this quip was aimed at Clay. Then a letter to the Editor of the *Hartford Courant* (Connecticut), on August 29, 1839 describes accusations made by another party with regards to the next General Election by saying:

> "Respecting this accusation, he let off his popgun at the **dead duck**."

Obviously, by this time the definition was established.

Dead letter[3]

Usually applied to a letter which is undeliverable as addressed, this term, in England, is applied figuratively to a law or ordinance that has lost its force but not yet been appealed or abolished. It is likely that this began with the Christian teaching that the *New Testament* portrayed the Law of Moses as being 'dead.' The 'letter of the law' came to be in opposition to the 'spirit of the law.' The expression was used in this manner as early as 1730. One explicit example that year is in *A Collection of Miscellanies – The Ninth Edition* by John Norris, MA, printed in London:

> "And how should it be expected that men should be more forward than they are to yield obedience to the King, who have found Out an expedient to slip their necks out of Christ's yoke, and have made the Gospel in a worse sense, a **dead letter** than the law?"

That same year the term was being applied to the laws of England as in *A Complete Collection of State Trials and Proceedings for High Treason from the Reign of Richard II Vol. 1*, in the Preface on page vii:

> "The Law itself is a **dead Letter**, Judges are the Interpreters of it, and if they prove Men of no Conscience nor Integrity…"

Dead meat

This hyperbolic idiom is used to drive home a warning to someone, many times an empty threat, indicating that if the person does not abandon his or her direction of actions they are in serious trouble. The earliest known citation in print is from *Leni Leoti Or, Adventures in the Far West* by Emerson Bennett, 1849:

> "'O the infarnals!' sez Ben, jumpin up and showin blood on his noddle. 'I'm **dead meat**, sartin…'"

Dead simple[2]

Much like other similar expressions using 'dead' [dead drunk, dead on, dead right, dead set against (see first volume) etc.] this means extremely simple. Using dead in this manner goes back to the 1590s when 'dead drunk' was coined. The earliest known reference in print is from *The Frauds and Villanies of the Common Practice of Physicke* by Rob Pitt, 1705, in the Preface;

> "They muft prefcribe the Juleps of the **dead Simple** and Compound Brandy Waters."

Dead slow

Here, we go back to the reasoning in the entry above. This means at a crawl, so to speak. It is also used even more figuratively in reference to emotions, etc. The earliest available use in print of this idiom is from *Sporting Magazine*, December, 1826 in 'Second Letter from Ant. Arab on Our Breed of Horses and Other Subjects' on page 82:

> "…but humility is none of their virtues; for they think themselves, their ill put together horses, weather-beaten harness, and clumsy coaches, not cleaned out once a week, the most finished turns out. Their pace too is **dead slow**."

Dead wrong+

This is a common idiomatic expression meaning *completely* wrong. It has been in use for over 130 years in verbal conversation and literature. It is likely that 'dead' refers to being the complete opposite of the living and viable truth. It has been used in print since at least the late 19th century. *The Evening Bulletin*, Maysville, Kentucky, May 19, 1887, carried this citation in an article titled 'Buckner on Finance' in column 1, page 3, about politician Joe Blackburn:

> "Our Joe is companionable and witty and lovable, but **dead wrong**—dangerously erratic on the silver question."

Another connotation came early in the century. Carleton Everett Knox utilized it three times in his 1922 book of poetry, *The Human Touch* referring to things going wrong, rather than a theory being incorrect. One example is in 'Whistle an Old Time Tune' on page 29:

> "When blue and discouraged, when business is bad,
> When everything goes **dead wrong**,
> It's yourself that's to blame—Just get in the game,
> And whistle an old time song!"

Deal-breaker+

This is an idiom used in business, politics and now, relationships, for any factor or situation, which if not resolved, could result in one of the parties involved withdrawing from an agreement, either written or verbal. According to *Etymology Online* it was attested by 1975. Use of the word, however, picked up in publications during the late 1980s and 1990s and is more common today that ever before because of it adaptation to romantic relationships.

Decisions, decisions, decisions!

This expression, meaning that there always seems to be an endless stream of decisions which have to be made, causing frustration and confusion, began to pop up in the late 1950s. Though not the origin, the earliest available citation is from *The Michigan Technic*, May, 1958, under the heading 'Engineering Management Decisions' by Bryan Whipple:

> "**Decisions, decisions, decisions** . . . every engineer should be familiar with the scientific way of tackling those problems which lie outside the realm of formulas."

Depend on a broken stick

Often used as an old adage, 'You can't depend on a broken stick,' this goes back to at least 1900 when it appeared in Maurice Thompson's novel, *A Banker in Bankersville,* on page 17:

> "'You must trust me, or I must go; and to trust me,' he hurriedly exclaimed, 'is to **depend on a broken stick**!'"

Almost a half-century prior to that, the intent was conveyed in *Genevra: Or, The History of the Portrait* by Geneviere Genevra Fairfield, 1851, page 143:

> "I feel it my duty to tell you, that you lean upon a **broken stick** if you **depend** on him for faith."

Devilishly handsome (See: **Handsome devil**)+

devil is in the detail, The

This refers to a mysterious element hidden away in the intent of something. The original catchphrase was actually "God is in the detail," which stressed the importance of doing any job well. The original phrase has been attributed to various individuals. The most notable of these is German-born architect Ludwig van der Rohe (1886-1969), who was credited for it in his obituary in the *New York Times,* just after his death on August 17, 1969 in Chicago. He is also said to have coined 'less is more' (see), though it was first used by Robert Browning. He is not likely the originator of this aphorism, either. An even earlier form 'The good God is in the detail' is most often attributed to French novelist Gustave Flaubert (1821-1880). Still, no originator is certain.

The earliest available citation of 'the devil in the detail' is from Investigating *Accidents with Step* by Kingsley Hendrick and Ludwig Benner, page 19, 1986:

> "The saying among Europeans that '**the Devil is in the detail'** is required to implement such ideas. Details such as the scope of the accident to investigate, investigation methods, analysis and 'truth testing' methods, and work product evaluation..."

devil made me do it, The+

This comical statement became cliché and part of entertainment lore after repeated use by Flip Wilson on the NBC comedy variety show, *Rowan and Martin's Laugh In,* during the 1960s, and *The Flip Wilson Show*, also on NBC, which ran from 1970-1974. It was used as an excuse for anything done which was thought to be bad. For another example of Wilson's lines see "What you see is what you get," *Volume II*, pp 441-442.

In December, 1990, militant Black Nationalist rapper, Paris, used the line as the title for his debut album on Tommy Boy Records. Then, in 2008, Georgina Spelvin used it as the title of her book based on her bawdy memoirs of how she became cast in the lead role of *The Devil and Miss Jones* in 1973, an erotic film which would come to define the era of the Porn Chic.

Die trying

This bit of hyperbole indicates that someone will do everything in his or her power to accomplish a task or reach a goal, regardless of the perceived dangers involved. The earliest known citation, though not likely its coining, is from *Niles Weekly Register*, March 29, 1828 in 'Tennessee Militiamen' and seems a bit more literal:

> "William Oxtrcn, a private of captain Mcbane's company, a witness, being sworn, states: That he heard the prisoner say, sometime in September, that he would go home at the end of three mouths, or **die trying**."

Difficult to swallow (See: **Bitter pill to swallow,** original volume)

Digging up bones

This applies to drudging up old memories, now particularly those of love gone awry, and stressing over things which are better left 'buried.' A song title, *Diggin' Up Bones*, by Country music artist, Randy Travis, written by Nat Stuckey, Paul Overstreet and a bit of credit given to Al Gore, in 1986 brought this expression to the forefront and lent credence to its current meaning. But it certainly was not its origin. The phrase can actually refer to anything that is hidden being revealed. A form of this was used figuratively as early as May,

1916 in: *Sunset: The Pacific Monthly* in 'The Vision of the Ram and He-Goat' by Peter B. Kyne, on page 66:

> "He told himself he would— Old man Hickman proceeded to **dig up** his **bone** of inside information."

In 1968, François Mauriac made this metaphoric reference to digging up a bone in *A Mauriac Reeder*, page 178:

> "No sooner had he signed a prescription and found himself on the way downstairs from his patient's room, than he was back, once more, like a dog **digging up** a buried **bone**, with his fond imagined reveries…"

Digital footprints

This modern metaphoric term refers to a person, company or group's unique trail of activities, actions and communications left online which may lead to motive or intent; examined particularly in criminal cases. This includes emails, social media posts, searches and any interests or communications. The earliest available references in print are from the mid-1990s. A very early reference is from *InfoWorld*, October 21, 1996 on page 32:

> "With the announcement AT&T is essentially integrating its existing cellular network with its forthcoming PCS network to offer a larger **digital footprint** to its customers, said Michael King, a research analyst with Meta Group Inc., in Stamford, Conn."

Dig one's heels in

This means to be unwilling to change one's ideas or plans; to resist stubbornly, refusing to give in. It started being used in the latter part of the 20th century. The earliest available citation, though not its origin, of course, is from *Life Magazine,* May 6, 1969, page 3 in 'You Can Stop Snapping at My Heels, Now:'

> "It was only when the session was over and we were relaxing with a drink that the novelist **dug in his heels**. 'No, gentlemen, I am sorry,' he said, puffing thoughtfully at his pipe."

dime a dozen, A+

This is an old metaphoric saying referring something which is so plentiful that it is inexpensive. A dime was first minted in 1796, and during the 1800s numerous commodities, especially food items such as eggs and various fruit, were sold by the dozen, and advertised for a dime in the United States. An early reference in print is found in the Texas newspaper, *The Galveston Daily News*, in 1866:

> "The San Antonio Ledger says the city is well-stocked with peaches at **a dime a dozen.**"

By the 1930s it was being used figuratively. In 1931 *The Northern Miner* newspaper, Toronto, Ontario, Canada, carried the following citation about boxers:

> "'Carners,' the old-timer said, 'is just an overgrown clown. As for the others—Schaof, Baer, Paulino, Risko, Campolo—they're nothing but '**dime a dozen** fighters.'"

Dipping one's toe(s) into the water

This means to begin something new and unfamiliar in an effort to determine whether it will work or not. [see: Test the waters, (much earlier origin), first volume] This expression came to be used in the late 20th century in this manner. A good early figurative example is from 1998, found in *The Chameleon Manager* by Brian Clegg, page 28:

> "If you currently have a conventional job, it makes a lot of sense to **dip your toe in the water** of flexibility, to expand your portfolio without actually cutting adrift from your old job."

Divide and conquer

This old expression means to formulate a winning strategy by getting one's opponents to fight amongst themselves. Also, retaining power and authority by this unorthodox means. It goes back to the ancient Latin phrase: *Divide et impera,* literally meaning, 'Divide and rule.' The earliest known citation in English is from *The Reign of Henry II,* in the epic poem, *The Battaile of Crescey*, by Charles Aleyn, page 43, 1633:

> "**Divide**, **and** then you **conquer**: For though none Can breake a sheafe of darts, he may breake one…"

DNA doesn't lie+

This modern truism is used to express the fact that the best and most scientific proof of who committed a crime, one's true parentage or ancestry, etc. is a DNA test. It is uncertain who first said this, but a 2011 non-fiction book by Anna Prokos titled *DNA Doesn't Lie: Is the Real Criminal Behind Bars* seems to be the earliest citation in print. A 2015 self-published Sue Swanson adventure novel by Trudy N. Wassenaar with this basic phrase as its title certainly also helped to popularize the saying. The premise started in 1984 when scientist Alec Jeffreys figured out how to identify a person's unique DNA profile. It likely evolved from an old saying, 'statistics don't lie,' popular since the 19th century.

Do a one-eighty

This is a figure of speech for metaphorically making a 'U Turn' in one's attitude, plans or mode of thinking. In a literal sense it has been used since the 1920s, but figuratively it started showing up in print in the early 1990s. The earliest available clear example is from *Skiing Magazine*, March, 1992, on page 58, in a citation in quotes, indicating a recent coining, and with a reference ironically aimed at the automotive industry:

> "When the new Audi 100 was unveiled in Europe, automotive experts there **'did a 180'**— reversing their perception of Audi vis-a-vis the competition."

Do double duty

This idiom usually means that the same person does two jobs, or plays two roles, at the same time. It can also refer to a facility or even a piece of furniture being used for two different purposes, and even other things acting in a dual capacity. The earliest use of 'double duty' known is from *The Workes of that Late Learned Minister of God's Holy Word, William Pemble*, 1659, page 69:

> "In the Issue of this work, there is a **double duty**: 1. If it succed well, Thankfull humility opposed to pride; that when men are converted by his misistery, he ascribe all to God, nothing to himself… 2. If it succeed ill, contented practice opposed to repining thought; as Why should not my Ministery be effectual as another's is? "

An actual example of 'does double duty,' somewhat closer to the fashion of today's meaning, is from 1704, on page 45 of *The Works: Containing His Plays and Poems* by George Etherege, in 'Love in a Tub,' Act III, Scene vii. Here it refers to Graciana's heart mourning for two men.

> "My Heart **does double Duty**; it does mourn
> For you brave *Bruce*; for you brave *Beaufort* burn."

Dog in the manger[2^]

This popular British expression means 'spiteful and mean spirited,' and is especially applied to people who prevent others from having something that they themselves have no use for. Like so many old sayings, it is often credited to acclaimed fable-teller, Aesop (c. 620-564 BCE). However, since some of these fables date back further than his lifetime, much doubt has been cast on the authenticity of his authorship. Actually, we now realize that the first version of *Aesop's Fables* were assembled and printed in German by printer Heinrick Steinhowel in 1480, then printed in English by William Claxton shortly thereafter, in 1484. *Dog in the Manger* was one of these fables, which portrayed a dog laying in a manger, not, of course, because he wanted to eat the hay, but, like the proverbial hog laying in the trough, wanted to prevent other animals from feeding on the hay. The fable of the dog in the manger was used twice by the 2nd century CE Greek writer Lucian of Samosata; first, in *Remarks addressed to an illiterate book fancier* and secondly in his play, *Timon the Misanthrope*.

John Gower, however, had published a version of this fable in English before Claxton, in *Confesso Amantis*, c. 1390:

> "Though it be not the hound's habit
> To eat chaff, yet will he warn off
> An ox that commeth to the barn
> Thereof to take up any food." (Book II, 1.84)

It was used by at least one other Greek storyteller in the 3rd century CE, Straton of Sardis. A likeness of the basic tale was also cited in the apocryphal Gnostic *Gospel of Thomas*, discovered in Nag Hammadi, Egypt in 1945, where Jesus is quoted as having said:

> "Woe to the Pharisees, for they are like a **dog** sleeping **in the manger** of oxen, for neither does he eat nor does he let the oxen eat."

All we can say for sure is that the story is around 2,000 years old.

Dogsbody[2]

In America, this term would likely be 'gofer' or 'lackey.' In the Queen's English, a dogsbody, sometimes referred to as a dog robber, is a junior officer in the Royal Navy who does 'drudge work.'

In the early 19th century the Royal Navy used dried peas and eggs boiled in a bag, known as pease pudding or pease porridge, as one of their staple foods. Sailors called this 'dog's body.' In the early 20th century junior officers who performed tasks that senior officers didn't want to do became known as 'dogsbodies.' Likely this was because the pease porridge was something they didn't want to eat (see: Like two peas in a pod, first volume). About 1930, the term became somewhat common in non-naval situations. An early citation of this type is from *The Nine Tailors* by Dorothy Lee Sayors, 1934, page 196:

> "The Englishman, in his bluff, hearty way is content that under such circumstances the post-office should validate his seals, peruse his correspondence, extract his signature and address from the surrounding verbiage, supply a fresh envelope and return the whole to him under the blushing pseudonym of 'Hubbykins' or '**Dogsbody**' for the entertainment of his local postman."

Dog's breaakfast[2,3]

This chiefly British slang phrase, also common in Australia, has meant 'a complete mess' since early in the 20th century. This could have been derived from a botched attempt at making a decent breakfast which turned out to be something only a canine would consider fit for consumption, but the earliest known form seems to indicate that it had to do with appearance. It can be applied to any situation or project which has turned into an utter disaster. This appeared in *The English Dialect Dictionary* in 1902:

> Phr. (1) all in a lump like **a dog's breakfast**, said of a heterogeneous heap of things"

Then in May, 1907, in the publication *Railroad Men*, published by the Railroad Branch of the YMCA in New York, under 'Railroad Hash' we find:

> "The passenger train which went East the other morning looked like **a dog's breakfast**."

A similar expression is 'dog's dinner.'

Dog-tired

Another way to say this is 'worn out.' It is very old, and refers to physical exhaustion, and is said to come from a tale of Alfred the Great, who reportedly sent his sons, Athelbrod and Edwin, out daily with his extensive kennels of hunting dogs. Whichever son was able to capture more of the hounds won the right to be seated at his father's right hand that evening at the Royal dinner table. Both sons came in 'dog-tired,' but happy in their accomplishment. It is recorded in Bede's *Historia Ecclesiastica Gentis Anglorum* (Ecclesiastical History of the English People, 8th century) that the tradition carried on for the next few generations.

Doing a number on someone

This metaphoric expression refers to doing damage to a person, usually through abuse, and most times used in a physiological implication. It may also apply to swindling someone out of money or property. The expression dates back to the 1970s. A copyright entry was made in January-June 1971 for a song titled *You Really Did a Number on Me* by Keith Colley. Thereafter, the saying took off. It appeared in numerous publications throughout the decade. One such entry is from *Billboard*, November 23, 1974, in Vox Jox by Claude Hall on page 38:

> "So, I **did a number on** Jim Duncan, program director of KSON-AM in San Diego and so this week he's no longer program director, honestly, the two events had nothing to do with each other. . ."

Done and dusted[2]

In British English, this idiom means that a deal has been successfully completed and nothing remains to be done. Before the advent of lead pencils and ball-point pens everyone used quill pens, then metal fountain pens, to write, which had to be dipped into a bottle of ink. The ink took a while to dry, and the paper had to absorb the ink properly before it could be touched and filed away. In order to hasten the process, many people would sprinkle an absorbent powder on the paper. Once it was dry, the powder would be dusted off. The letter or document was 'done and dusted.' As time went on, the phrase began to be applied in the way it is used today in the U.K. A good example is from *Cat's Cradle*, a play by Leslie Sands, 1983, Act I, Scene i:

> "***Merton***: All **done and dusted**. Only two or three very minor mistakes — oh. Company?"

Done like a dinner[2,3]

This primarily Aussie / British expression means comprehensively outwitted or defeated. It has been in common use since at least the mid-19th century. The origin is not clear but a common variation is 'done like a dog's dinner,' The phrase certainly implies that the person completely through with the stated activity; 'washed up.' The earliest citation on record is from *The Love Match* by British novelist Henry Cockton, published in 1845, on page 172:

> "We did him then, and I'm glad he's done now: such a man as that ought to be **done like a dinner**."

In 1853 an early Australian citation may be found in Thomas Francis McBride's *Letters from Victorian Pioneers*:

> "The horse swam for a quarter of a mile down the river with the cart after him ... the driver, who remained till then on his seat on the hurdle up to his neck in water, calling out to me 'he was **done like a dinner'**."

Don't be a (stupid or silly) galah[3]

In Australia, a 'galah' is a label for a 'loud-mouthed idiot.' This expression is common for telling someone off who you think fits the bill. The galah is actually a native bird that makes a disgusting funny-sounding call. Calling such a person a stupid or silly galah became popular in Aussie slang in the 1980s. An early example is found in *Water Ski Magazine*, March, 1987 in 'Oz Speak, How They Say it in Australia,' on page 70, where the term is defined as someone who is gullible to brainless, and it gives the following example of use:

> "However, if you see an unthinking boat driver carving up your slalom course, you would call that person a 'stupid, bloody **galah**,' and then threaten to endanger his physical well-being."

A modern example of admonition to refrain from being one is found in *Among the Fans* by Patrick Collins, 2011 on page 148:

> "In Brisbane, a stern warning was emblazoned across the front of a stand: '**Don't be a galah**. Set a limit and stick to it. Gamble responsibly.'"

Don't call us, we'll call you+

This is a sarcastic cliché response to an application, call or request for work, indicating that there is no need for the applicant to follow up. The earliest known citation in print in is March, 1944, in a syndicated column in the Ohio newspaper, *The Toledo Blade*, in a column by Dorothy Kilgallen titled 'The Voice of Broadway;' this one featuring a fictional heroine:

> "Audition after audition left her with nothing but 'Sorry' and '**Don't call us, we'll call you**' and a heart that was close to breaking."

Don't flatter yourself+

This is a sophomoric catchphrase said by someone attempting to downplay something someone else claims to be true about himself or herself. It was used in numerous plays, both British and American, throughout the 19th century. The earliest known citation in print is in *Turn Out!* A musical farce by English playwright Matthew P. King, 1812:

> "**Mar**. Oh! **Don't flatter yourself**—you have no reason to imagine the contrary."

Don't give up your day job^

This modern sarcastic punch means that the person being addressed has great plans, but perhaps non-attainable ones. It is advising him or her to reconsider plunging into an uncertain field of endeavor. A major dictionary of American slang places its coining circa the 1990s. However, on April 22, 1973, *The Chicago Tribune* printed the following in a column titled 'In the Wake of the News' by David Condon, on page A3:

> "Arthur Rubioff also appeared in the production and could be nominated for best costume. Way to go, Arthur, but **don't give up your day job**."

This must have 'gotten the ball rolling,' because in 1973 the bluegrass band, Country Gazette, recorded an album on the United Artists label with the phrase as its title.

Don't go away mad, just go away!

A lot of people probably think this originated with the 1989 Mötley Crüe Glam metal single released May 28, 1990 by this title, but far from it! In January-June, 1956, a copyright was obtained by Milt Story for use of this phrase, along with a few others on 'silly signs' to be produced by Norwick Mills. Then in the April

14, 1958 issue of *Life Magazine*, in the article 'Gang War' on page 137 we read the following:

> "However, they included all the officers and lieutenants, enough for a conference. We trooped into the Ritz Bar and pushed two tables together in the rear. Over the bar was the usual sign: "If you are under 18, **don't go away mad, just go away**."

Perhaps one of the signs from the copyright was spotted. At any rate, this became a popular snide remark when someone was trying to tell someone else that his or her company was unwanted.

Don't go there

When someone says, 'Don't go there,' it means that he or she doesn't want to discuss the matter in no uncertain terms. It emerged in the 1990s in America. Of course the saying had been used literally for over 100 years earlier, but the earliest known figurative citation in print, though not the coining of the phrase is in *The Gettysburg Times* (Pennsylvania) in January, 1997, in the Question and Answer Column, 'Ask the Chief' by George T. Keeney:

> "Q: My biscuits seldom turn out thick and light. Most of the time they are like a hockey puck. Hey?
> "A: It is a good thing I am a food service professional or I may be inclined to make a reference to the National Hockey League (**Don't go there**)."

The saying has developed alternatives such as 'don't even go there' and 'you don't want to think of even going there.' It is often used by comedians to indicate that they will not be saying anything further about a particular topic. Actually, according to Barry Popik of the American Dialect Society, comedian Martin Lawrence, when talking to *Entertainment Weekly* in 1994 about his Fox sitcom, said:

> "We started using the expressions 'You go, girl!' (see first volume) and 'Don't go there!''" Lawrence said, "'and no one in television was doing that. No one. Now a lot of Fox shows are using the same stuff.'"

Don't hold your breath (See: **Hold one's breath**)

Don't knock it till you've tried it+

This is an idiomatic statement used to let someone know that before criticizing something he or she should experienced it. 'Knock,' as a word for criticism, originated in the 1890s, but this phrase didn't come into use until the mid-20th century. 'Don't knock it' is found as early as May 26, 1916 in *The Bee*, a newspaper in Earlington, Kentucky, in 'Back to Principles' in column 2, page 3:

"If you can't boost your home paper, **don't knock it**."

It likely started among the youth. The earliest available citation in *Emerson*, the Emerson College Yearbook, 1961; at the top of page 40 in the sayings of a Senior male student:

"Europe left its mark...**don't knock it till you've tried it**."

Don't mention it^+

Used as a response to 'Thank you,' this is an idiomatic expression meaning 'You're welcome, I was glad to help.' It simply implies that no thanks was needed. There are similar expressions in French, German and Swedish; so this concept is not exclusive to English. A popular online idiom site states that it has been cited in English since the early 1900s. It was actually being used earlier, in more than one play. *The Passing Regiment, A Comedy of the Day in Five Acts* printed in manuscript only by the author, Augustin Daly, in New York in 1884, cited it five times, the first being in Act I on page 12:

'Bun. (Warmly) **Don't mention it**.'

A Limb O' the Law, A Comedy in Two Acts by Martha Russell Orne, more widely distributed in 1892, has two citations, the first of which is in Act I on page 7:

"Gus. **Don't mention it**, ma'am. It's all in the way of business, you know."

Don't rock the boat

Rocking or swaying a boat can certainly cause it to overturn. This metaphorically means not to do anything which will cause havoc and make something dysfunctional. Use of the phrase in a literal sense goes back to at least 1867. In *Our Young Folks Illustrated Magazine for Boys and Girls*, September issue, in 'A Deer Hunt in the Adirondacks,' we find:

> "'Sit quiet in the stern and **don't rock the boat**. Now be off.' Dan gave the boat a shove, and, as she moved from the shore, sprang into the bows himself,"

It was in use figuratively by at least 1914 when several sources quoted a *Chicago Herald* article, including the August 7 edition of *Chicago Commerce,* which reprinted it on page 7:

> "Sit Tight! **Don't Rock the Boat**! (Chicago Herald) Sit tight! **Don't rock the boat**! That's the watchword today. That's the first duty of every American at this moment. That's what this country needs to keep it straight and safe and true to its course ..."

Don't try this at home!

This admonition is used as a cliché by the media to advise the public, particularly children, against imitating a dangerous activity being pictured or demonstrated. It was popularized on television in the 1990s. But the warning was around before this! The earliest citation available in print is from *Black Belt Magazine*, May, 1980, as a caption under a photo on page 55:

> "Feats of strength are a specialty of Mike Dayton's-**don't try this at home**!"

Do one's block[3]

In Australia, doing one's block means that the person is getting very angry. A major slang dictionary states that this expression was coined in 1907, but gives examples from 1968 and 1971. The earliest example in print available is actually from 1966 in *Australians and the Gold Rush: California and Down Under (1849-1854)* by Jay Monaghan, page 29:

> "People said the Old Man '**did his block**' — a phrase Americans could not understand. Towns immediately decided to send his assembled goods, and more, on his Inchinnan as soon as she came in from New Zealand."

Do or die^

Some claim that this phrase comes from Alfred, Lord Tennyson in his poem *The Charge of the Light Brigade,* which has the lines, "Theirs not to reason why;

theirs but to **do** and **die**." This, however, is not only a mismatch ('do and die'), but the poem was written in 1864.

Others assure us that it comes from Robert Burns' poem *Robert Bruce's March to Bannockburn* about the first War of Scottish Independence. The last stanza of this poem reads: "Lay the profound usurpers low! / Tyrants fall in every foe! / Liberty's in every blow! / Let Us **Do--or Die**!!" Closer, but no cigar (see in first volume). This immortal verse was written in 1793.

In Richard Knolles' *The General Historie of the Turkes from the First Beginning of that Nation to the Rising of the Ottoman Families*, 1610, Second Edition, page 1161, we find a citation near this:

> "...amongst them, most of whom had sometimes serued vnder him, than amongst so many his most mortal enemies: But what remedie, he must now so **do, or die** therefore; for which he was the more to be excused."

The earliest known printed reference, however, comes from 16th century Scottish writer Robert Lindsay of Pitscottie (c. 1532-1580) who wrote in *The Historie and Chronicles of Scotland, 1436–1565*, the first history of the country actually composed by a Scot; Speaking of 'The Earl, seeing that the king was slow in the matter...' (1728 publication version). In the original 16th century text the last of the line read:

> "he knew well thair no remedie but ether to **do or die**."

The use of this term here meant that the time had come when he had to **do** something immediately **or die**. Sounds a bit like the later reference by Knolles, but this was penned first and the intent was 'spot on'(see).

Do someone's dirty work

This old expression refers to doing the unpleasant tasks, legal or illegal, for someone because he or she doesn't want to do them. The earliest known reference in print is from *Felo de se; or, Bishops Condemned out of their own Mouthes,* 1668:

> "Just such a sort of men are we, wallowing in all idleness, pride and filthiness, while our Journey-men do our **dirty work**."

Dot-com companies / Dot-com+

This is an idiom for a company which does most of its business on the Internet, usually through a website that uses the popular up-level domain **.com** (short for commercial). This came into play when the Domain Name System was implemented in January, 1985, initially administered by the U.S. Department of Defense. The first **.com** domain name registered on March 15, 1985, was **symbolics.com,** issued to a now-defunct computer manufacturer. Then in 1993, the first Mosaic web browser made access to the 'World Wide Web' (www) possible, beginning to usher in what was known as the 'dot-com bubble' which lasted until changes came in the year 2000.

Down and dirty

Again, this is an expression with numerous possible meanings, dependent upon context. It can mean unvarnished or unaltered, made or done in haste, given to fierce competition, bawdy, seedy, or even relating to the crudely basic and practical. This saying became popular in the 1980s and spread rapidly through popular culture. Politics and sexual practices rapidly became described as 'down and dirty' in both America and the U.K. It spread through the media and became all or part of the titles of numerous books and articles.

But the phrase was around long before the pop culture blanket was spread. The earliest citations are from the music industry. In 1957 a song named ***Down and Dirty*** by Al Cohen was copyrighted by Planetary Music Publishing Corporation. Later it was recorded as *Hoe Down and Dirty*. Then on February 1, 1964, *Billboard* had an ad on page 27 for an Ella Fitzgerald album:

> "These Are the Blues Ella sings the good old good ones **down and dirty** in a totally new experience in jazz for her. . . and for her legion of fans!"

Down but not out

Like 'down and out' (see first volume), this idiom came from the sport of boxing. A KO, or knock out, means that the victor is clear. When a boxer is knocked down to the canvas, he or she has a ten second call to get back up and resume the match. If the person fails to respond, he or she is declared out. **Down but not out**, used figuratively, means that a person, like a boxer who rises, has been knocked down by life's cruel forces but is able to get up again and continue the game of life. Where the saying 'down and out' is from the late 19th century, 'down but not out,' figuratively, began to be used in the early 20th century. A very early example, the first available in this sense, is from *Paint, Oil and Drug Review,* Chicago, Wednesday, December 14, 1904 on page 10, under 'For Oleomargerine Relief:'

> "Butterine people are '**down' but not 'out**.' They will make at least one more fight for the right to exist. They believe that a moderate tax on butterine would not only allow them to do business, but would be productive of greatly increased revenue ..."

Down memory lane

Often prefaced by a form of 'stroll,' 'walk' or 'trip,' this refers to visiting past pleasurable experiences in one's nostalgic memory. The earliest citation in print is actually, 'down memory's lane,' and is found *in Chained Lighting: A Book of Fun,* by Ike Philkins, 1883, on page 79:

> "You won't have traveled **down memory's lane** over half a mile before something will happen."

It wasn't until after the turn of the century that *Lippincott's Monthly Magazine*, in December, 1906, published a tale by Carolyn Wood Morrison called 'Queen Mary of Memory Lane,' in which this exact phrase first appeared in print:

> "There was a sound of feet hurrying, almost running, **down Memory Lane**. It was Urmson—Urmson driven back by the ghost of two lost years."

But what really popularized the expression were later songs with Memory Lane in the titles. The first, ***Down Memory Lane*** *with You,* was copyrighted on August 5, 1921, had words by Nelle Stratton of Nelsonville, Ohio and music by E.S.S. Huntington. Another song copyright with the title ***Down Memory Lane*** was applied for in 1931, and on December 9, 1932 Universal Pictures copyrighted ***Down Memory Lane*** directed by Monte Bruce. Yet another tune, ***Down Memory Lane*** *with Mollie,* was copyrighted on December 12, 1935 by Abba Warren. Later, famed baritone, big-band leader, Vaughn Monroe, recorded a version of ***Down Memory Lane*** on one of the most popular albums of the mid-1940s. From the 1950s through the 1970s, others followed from country to pop.

But by the late 1930s, the idiom was in use like we know it today. On August 28, 1939, *Life Magazine*, in a Heinz Ketchup ad on page 8, had this:

> "And we cook it the meticulous, old-fashioned way to capture that unforgettable flavor and haunting aroma that take you back **down memory lane** to a farm kitchen at ketchup-making time."

Do you come here often?

This has become the most clichéd pick up line in history; so much so that it is thought nearly antiquated, or at least comical. It has become the title of such creations as novels, a song and a play. But it can be used more realistically in other social situations. It may be spoken in a group setting when everyone suddenly has stopped talking. One of the first, if not *the first* to use the expression in print, though not in the modern connotation, was Charles Dickens in *Master Humphreys Clock* aka *The Old Curiosity Shop*, 1840-1841, page 142:

> “‘**Do you come here often**?’ asked the child.”

In the mid-19th century, the idiom was then taken up by numerous authors in novels as a way to make conversation with strangers. On September 1, 1851, *The Western Literary Messenger* carried a story titled ‘Deacon Whitfield’s Folks’ from the *National Era*. On page 7, the phrase was used by a young man romantically interested in a young lady.

> “‘The flowers of the grass perish,’ said the young man sorrowfully, ‘and our hopes, young damsel, are often like them.’ Then in a livelier tone, he added, as though some sort of hope crossed his mind, ‘**Do you come here often**?’”

Other such citations followed in magazine stories and novels. In August, 1887, *Temple Bar,* a London magazine carried a serial titled ‘Edged Tools: A Romance of Two Summers’ by Ethyl M. Arnold. In chapter 2, a fine example was used as a ‘pick up line,’

> “That night there was a weirdness, a witchery about the scene such as the moon always seems to cast over everything she lights, and, as though under a spell, it was some minutes before either of them spoke.
>
> “‘I’ve never seen it so beautiful as it is tonight,’ he said at length.
>
> **“‘Do you come here often**, then?’ she said quickly, with the faintest tinge of disappointment in her voice.
>
> “Yes; I come here pretty often after dinner. But to-night it wears a new face; it seems as though the sirens had been here and left their influence behind...”

By November, 1891 it seemed that the line was understood as an intended ‘pick up.’ In *The Electric Magazine*, in an article titled, ‘The Abbé’s Repentance,’ the following dialogue appears:

> “‘How grandly the waves roll in,’ she cried, eyeing them with girlish delight. **‘Do you come here often**, M. l’Abbé?’

> "The Abbé gazed at her, astonished. How strange are the ways of these English! He was a priest, to be sure, a celibate by profession; but he was young, he was handsome—he knew he was goodlooking; ..."

Drag one's feet

This idiom means to postpone doing something that needs to be done, usually because of lack of desire to do so. It is derived from the doleful way people walk when they are going toward an unpleasant task. In a literal sense, the term has been in use since the 19th century. As a metaphor, it began to be cited in the 1940s. The earliest known example in print is from *Life Magazine*, May, 1946 in 'The Tragedy of Liberalism' by Joseph and Stewart Alsop, on page 65, where the expression was in quotes, indicating a fairly new coining:

> "Czechoslovakia and Greece are encircled, and the Soviets are frankly **'dragging their feet'** in making the European peace in order to prolong chaos and thus promote the Communist parties in other European nations."

Drag someone's name through the mud

This expression means to badmouth or say bad things about someone, alegedly damaging the person's reputation. It is often associated with character assassination using malicious intent. This may have the same origins as 'your name is mud' (see first volume for complete explanation). Like the other saying, it certainly had nothing to do with Dr. Samuel Mudd who treated John Wilkes Booth in April, 1865, after the assassination of American President Abraham Lincoln. The idiom was already being used as early as 1863 in *The Cost of a Secret,* by British author, Isa Blagden, Volume 3, page 33:

> "She must not **drag** our **name through the mud** — get a divorce; you will be free once more."

Drama queen^

A drama queen is someone who overreacts to minor situations, blowing things out of proportion. A major slang dictionary stated that it originated in the gay community of the 1960s. Actually, it derived from the term 'melodrama,' and was coined much earlier. This person thrives on being the center of attention. The earliest citation of the term in print is from the *Washington Post*, December 10, 1923, 14/ 4:

> "If he is thwarted in his effort to enjoy them, he may either go to the dogs or the **drama queens**, become short-tempered, sullen, grouchy and eventually feel that, in a way he is a failure."

But it really took off in the 1980s. It was in certainly already modern usage by October 17, 1981, when it appeared in *Billboard,* in *Rock 'n' Rolling* on page 16, in a quote from singer Marianne Faithful:

> "This is a bit of affirmation I didn't want to be known as the great **drama queen** of rock'n'roll, though I could have been."

Draw a blank

This is a very old idiom in the English language, stemming from British lotteries set up in Tudor England under Elizabeth I in 1567. Tickets with the names of purchasers were put into a 'lot pot.' Another pot held slips of paper, some with prizes written on them, others blank. A name would be drawn, then a paper from the prize pot. Those who drew the blank papers were said to have 'drawn a blank.'

Lotteries continued and in July, 1786, *The Scotts Magazine*, in 'Parliament: Commons on the Greenland Fishery' uses the term about the lottery:

> "...his lot was equal to a 20,000 L prize in the lottery; whilst another, who chanced to fail of success, was like a man who **drew a blank**."

This usage continued through the 19th century, and into the 20th. The phrase, however, had been in print even earlier, in *A Commentary upon the Fourth Book of Moses, Called Numbers* by Simon, Lord Bishop of Ely, 1699, page 193:

> "Then mixing all these in an Urn, he nad them come and draw: And. to every one who drew a Schedule, that had the Name of Elder in it, he said, God hath sanctified thee but to him that **drew a Blank**, he said, God hath not chosen thee."

In *Glenlonely; or, The Daemon Friend*, Volume 3 by William Henry De Merle, 1839, the phrase is used figuratively of Sir Bruce Crawford's quest for marriage (all marriage being 'a lottery' was voiced by Queen Victoria) on page 171:

> "About three years after his divorce, he once more decided on the lottery of marriage: in England he had **drawn a blank**; in France he was more fortunate. Miss St. Clair was all that could add to the happiness of man; but, alas! how rarely does it happen that they who win the purest gems are allowed to wear them long..."

Note: another metaphor was employed in speaking of women as 'the purest gems,' and being married as 'wearing them.'

It was the 1930s before 'draw a blank' came into common figurative use. In *Princeton Alumni Weekly*, April 20, 1937 in 'The Thumbnail Sketch,' number 130 by H.G. Murray on page 11:

> "This after the college police and town force had **drawn a blank**. Ned simply strolled around the purlieus of the burgh, saw his suit on a mucker, and in the parlance of the local press, 'apprehended the criminal.'"

Draw the short straw (in life) (See also: '**Get the short end of the stick**,' original volume)

In past centuries, people would draw pieces of straw or hay to determine who would do a particular task that no one wanted to do. All pieces were cut in equal lengths except one, which was shorter. The person who drew the short straw was assigned to the unpleasant task. Metaphorically, someone who draws the short straw is the loser in some endeavor, or in life itself. The earliest reference known in print to this practice is found in *The Mirror of Literature, Amusement and Instruction*, December 20, 1828 in 'Memoirs of Vidoco, The French Thief Taker.' This indicates that the practice was common in those days:

> "Seven of us still remained, and we drew straws, as is usual in such circumstances, to determine which of the seven should first pass. I **drew the short straw**, and undressed myself that I might get with greater ease through the hole, which was very narrow; but to the disappointment of all, I stuck fast without the possibility of advancing or receding."

A modern example of 'drew the short straw in life' can be found in *A Jacobean Company and its Playhouse, The Queen's Servants at the Red Bull Theater (c. 1605-1619)* by Eva Griffith, 2013, on page 172, where it is in quotes:

> "On 20 July it was obviously Slatiar who '**drew the short straw' in life**."

Dream on+

This is an expression used to say that one does not believe that something the other person wants will ever happen. The phrase has a long history of being used as the titles of songs. It was originally the name of a song published on page 75 of *The Gem of Song, Part First, Containing a Large Collection of Sentimental and National Songs*, attributed to 'An Amateur' published in Boston, Massachusetts by E. Howe in 1846.

Then it was later the title of a serenade written by Frederic W. Root which was on page 74 of *The New Song Era*, a book of instruction and music for elementary and advanced singing classes, choirs, institutes and conventions published by J. Church in Cincinnati in 1877. Another repeated use in verse occurred in a 1920, in the poem/song 'Your Day Dreams' on page 48 of *Sketches in Lyric Prose and Verse*, by Natalie Whited Price published by Ralph Fletcher Seymour, Chicago, in which it states in a footnote that it was originally published 'with musical accompaniment' by Clayton F. Sammy Company, another Chicago publisher.

In modern times, however, it was popularized as the title of the first single ever released by Aerosmith in 1972. It was written by Steven Tyler over about six years in bits and pieces, and finished with the help of the band. It was not initially a hit, but after the release of their single, *You See me Crying*, in December, 1975, band manager David Crebs convinced Columbia Records to re-release Dream On, and it went to number 6. Later in 1987 and 1993, after a new audience was exposed to their music, their entire first album was re-reissued, bringing Aerosmith to new highs in rock music. *Dream On* has been recorded by numerous groups including the Glee Chorus, and was the title of a book by Tyler's ex-wife, actress Cyrinda Foxe in 1996.

Dream team^

A dream team a group or coupling of persons with the highest ability in any sport or field of endeavor involved in a joint action. The term has been used in regard to many sports teams, and even to a potential political pairing which would seem certain to win an election. A major dictionary places origin at 1935 to1940. Once again, this major source is incorrect, as it was already in use, though likely not for long, in sports by April, 1922, when it was cited in quotes by Philip Lyon in the *Phi Gamma Delta* fraternity publication in praising basketball greats, the 'Iowa State 5' captained by Jack Currie:

> "By June he will have annexed nine major letters and for the third time will have been placed by unanimous choice of Valley experts at premier guard on the '**dream team**.' Captain Currie is fast, clever and hard-working."

dripping roast, A[2]

This term, in Great Britain, is used nowadays in reference to solicitors who stretch their investigations and, thus, increase their costs so it is like a 'dripping roast' or a 'gravy train.' The expression is also used in negotiations, where people 'sweat once' while benefiting greatly from winning an order, especially one resulting in repeat business. It was in use by 1828, when we find an early citation in *Travels in Russia, &c, &c* by William Rae Wilson, Esq. F.S.A., page 316:

> "We proceeded in a steam-boat; for which the proprietor, Mr. Baird, a Scotchman, who has resided here some time, and who, in the language of his native country, has found this concern to be a **'dripping roast'** has obtained a patent for a term of years—a favour that is looked upon with an eye of jealousy by the Russians."

In 1893 Robert Louis Stevenson used it thusly in *David Balfour*, Chapter XVII:

> "And the mere truth is, that they were all in favour of a process which should have remarkable consequences in the Parliament House, and prove for them (in one of their own expressions) a **dripping roast**."

Drongo[3]

In Aussie slang, this means 'moron.' The word, the name of a black bird (some having spots) resembling a crow, thought to have been of Malayan origin, is originally from the indigenous language of Madagascar. Great numbers of them live all around Australasia. They sound their ominous call at the presence of a predator. But this is not the origin of the slang word. It comes from an Australian race horse by the same name which seems to resemble the coloration of the spotted drongo, which was entered in 37 races in the late 1920s, but never won a race; hence the term came to be used as an insult. In September, 1984, *Orange Coast Magazine* listed the word in the column 'Yabber' on page 133, designed to teach people how to 'Speak Australian.'

> "**Drongo**: a born loser"

Drop in the ocean

This is another form of 'a drop in the bucket' (see first volume), meaning a very insignificant amount compared to what is needed. This saying goes back to the 17th century. The earliest known citation as a comparative idiom is from *An*

Elegant and Learned Discourse of the Light of Nature, by Nathanial Culverwel and William Dillingham, 1669, page 87:

> "A single drop is soon dry'd up, and consum'd; I, but a **drop in the Ocean**, when 'tis united to a multitude of other drops."

Drop (or **Fall,** etc.) **off the face of the earth+**

This is a figurative expression used to imply that something will stop existing. Due to the fact that the earth was once viewed by most as being flat, the face of the earth was viewed as ending at a distant point, thus dropping or falling off was a seemingly realistic threat to sailors who dared venture too far. In the *King James Version* of the *Bible* (1611) the phrase 'the face of the earth' was used 33 times. Although this is the obvious source for the idiom, actual references to dropping, falling, disappearing or wiping something off the face of the earth are much more recent, showing up in print only in recent years

Dry as a bone

This ancient simile also goes back to the mid-17th century. The earliest known reference in print is from *Occasional Fac-similie Reprints of Rare English Tracts* by Edmond William Ashbee, 1649, in 'Taylor's Westerne Voyage to the Mount' on page 4:

> "I had the luck twice to have not one dry thread about me, (being wet to the very skin) and yet my cloathes were as **dry as a bone**; the reason is, that l was in the Bathe, and my cloathts out."

Dry as a powder house

This alludes to the fact that gunpowder, which inspired the simile, must be kept extremely dry or it is of no use, and will not fire (see: Keep your powder dry, first volume). This expression came out of the great drought in the U.S. in the 1840s. In 1844 and '45, several publications used the following analogy. One was in the *New England Farmer,* Boston, Wednesday September 25, 1844, when the following appeared on the 2nd page:

"THE DROUGHT

> "We are in the midst of an unparalleled drought. The earth, in city and country, is '**as dry as a powder house**.' Vegetations of all kinds look as though they had been kissed by fire."

The House of Representatives publication stated that the original source was the Rochester (NY) paper.

Dry up and blow away

Thought by some to have originally referred to something shriveling up over time to where it would be so small that it would or could blow away with the wind, it is used hyperbolically for someone losing weight. In the late 19th century there was a hateful command, "Oh, dry up and blow away!" which was like the mid-20th century insult, "Go jump in the lake!" (See first volume) We find an example of this in *How to Gain Health and Long Life* by P.M. Haney, 1899, page 76:

> "The vulgar command — 'Oh, **dry up and blow away**!' contains a truth, which the great majority of us know nothing about. This truth is that there is so much water in the human body that under certain conditions one could **dry up and blow away**."

The earliest citation available, however, is from a book of poetry titled *Whimwhams* by "Four of us," in a piece called "Master Spirits" first published in 1828, This and the one below it, give credence to an application to 'spirits' which were thought to blow about without recognition:

"These poets live — perchance may die-
Though I have heard folks say,
That wond'rous men evaporate-
Ne'er know a closing day:
Perhaps these gifted spirits will
'**Dry up and blow away**!'"

The other one, from this early time frame, is found in *Coburn's New Monthly Magazine,* January, 1835, page 44, in 'The Flying Island,' and also helps us understand why it is used in its current connotation.

> "Year after year he continued to live and dwindle away thinner and thinner, till most people began to cast about for some supernatural cause for this wonderful longevity; and the story at length ran that the last Indian could never be made to die like common mortals, but would **dry up and blow away**."

Duke's mixture

Many have heard of the Duke's Mixture Tobacco, which was loose in a pouch for rolling cigarettes—a best-selling brand in the late 19th century. But the story of the origin of the saying goes back a little further, to the man for whom it was named, Washington Duke of North Carolina, who served in the Confederate Army in the War Between the States, was captured while retreating from Richmond, and released from Libby Prison in 1865. From there he was sent to New Bern, North Carolina, 137 miles from his home. According to Virginia researcher Dave Tabler, who now lives in Dover, Delaware, in a well-documented post on *Appalachian Stories Quotes and Antecdotes* online, he walked the entire distance home with only fifty cents cash he had gotten from a Federal soldier in exchange for a five dollar Confederate note. When he arrived home he found that his farm had been ransacked by the Federals, who left nothing but some Bright tobacco leaf and a small amount of flour. Duke sold his farm, renting back a few acres. After sending for his children, he processed the tobacco in a small barn, bagged it; then loaded it and the flour onto a wagon pulled by a team of blind mules and set out for Raleigh, camping by the road at nght, cooking his own food to survive. After reaching Raleigh, he traded his flour for cotton which was sold there. The tobacco was also marketed, enabling him to buy bacon, and brown sugar for his children. From this humble beginning Duke continued to grow and package granulated tobacco, which he had named Pro Bono Publico, and later renamed 'Duke's Mixture.' Sold by American Tobacco, it became the most important tobacco product between 1896 and 1910. The rumor spread that Duke's Mixture was a 'thrown together stew of odds and ends,' leading to the use of the term for a hodge-posge of something. The earliest known citation of the cliché is from *The Railroad Telegrapher*, December, 1904, in the report from the Illinois Division by M.E. Schooler:

> "This is **a 'Duke's Mixture**,' and I am in hope that some brother on the division will take pity on our readers and myself and relieve me."

Dull as a fro+

This simile is most commonly used without the understood initial 'As'. The original *Dictionary of Phrase and Fable* by E. Cobham Brewster, published in 1894, explains that A fro (or frow) is a type of blunt wedge used for splitting wood which is not sharpened like a chisel is. Since the 19th century the fro has been used as a standard for dull tools.

Dull as ditchwater / dishwater^

This old English simile plays on the dual meaning of 'dull' as both boring and lacking in luster. It goes back to the 18th century. It means, of course, the former, metaphorically. The earliest available citation is from *The Spirit of the Public Journals for 1797*, Volume I, 3rd Edition, printed in book form in London in 1802, in a letter to the editor of the *Morning Chronicle*:

> "It is not heavy as lead, like Mr._____ ; nor **dull as ditch-water**, like Anna 'Matiklaij' nor mad as a March hare, like our present excellent Laureat; nor stupid — — but I should never make an end, if I went on with my comparisons."

This snippet referenced a number of clichés which were obviously in use prior to this date.

The expression carried over into modern English, used in America as well as Great Britain. In spite of those who think it has only been used as 'dishwater' rather than ditchwater since the 1970s in America, there is much evidence to repute this claim. This change was made as early as 1854 in *The Amarnth or Token of Remembrance,* Edited by Emily Percival:

> "Well, when I came down here to meet Poole, as I had promised, — his governor keeps hounds, you know; a capital pack, too, — I was as **dull as dishwater**; I was, I assure you; and whenever there was nothing going on, I used to take out the verses you wrote; and the music you copied for me, to look at;..."

The next year the book was re-released under the title *The Garland or Token of Friendship*. After this book, several American works picked up the 'dishwater' version including Charles G. Leland in *The Egyptian Sketchbook*, 1874, and 'dull as dish-water' was even included in *Roget's Thesaurus* in 1878!

Both ditchwater and dishwater are dirty, dark and foreboding. This change may have been because of the similarity of the two words and the lack of familiarity of Americans of the day with ditchwater.

Dutch courage[2]

Also known as 'liquid courage,' this is valor gained from drinking alcoholic beverages. It is British, and is said to have been coined from English soldiers fighting in the Thirty Years' War (1618-1648), when Dutch Gin was supposed to have been consumed by the British because it was believed to have warming properties. The term, however, didn't show up in print until the 19th century. The meaning comes out in the following early citation from Frederick Marryat's novel of a naval career during the British Mastery of the seas in that era, *Peter Simple*, Volume III, page 227-228, 1834:

> "'I think, Sir,' observed I, 'that it is an injustice to this fine ship's company, to hint at their requiring **Dutch courage**.' (**Dutch courage** is a term for courage screwed up by drinking freely.)"

Dying duck fit+

Alluding to the sound of a squawking duck in the death throws, this is a metaphor for a loud demonstration of anger and frustration. Though having merely a 'duck fit' is known in the U.K., and someone looking like 'a dying duck in a thunderstorm' has been expressed in Australia, this saying is primarily used the Southern U.S. It is similar to a 'hissy fit' (see), but more violent.

Determining the origin is very difficult, but it has been in common use since at least the early 20th century and likely much longer. It is very likely that it came to the South as merely 'duck fit' with early Scots-Irish and English immigrants, and evolved in the Southern Appalachian slang.

E

Eagle-eyed

This nature-based cliché refers to a person's ability to observe closely or pay great attention to detail. The earliest reference in print to this expression is in *Rofallnde Eupheus golden legacie: Memoir of Thomas Lodge* by Edmond W. Gosse, 1590, page 11:

> "Climbe not my fonnes, afpiring pride is a vapour that afcendeth hie, but soone turneth to a fokmaoke: those which ftare at the Starres, stumble vppon stones; and fuch as gaze at the Sunne (vnlesse they bee **Eagle eyed**) fall blinde."

Note here the Early Modern English spellings; v's used for u's and f's for s's in numerous cases. Also, at this stage, the present meaning did not seem to have yet evolved.

By 1619, it appears that the intent of the expression was developing to be observant. The following is from *A Bride-bush, Or, A Direction for Married Persons*, by William Whately, page 166:

> "To be fomewhat purblind in feeing faults, is leffe dangerous, than to be **eagle-eyed**. In such nearenesse and inwardnesse of conuersation, it is impossible, but that diuers wants shall offer themfelues to bee feene."

early bath, An[2,3]

Taking an early bath means that someone was forced to stop an activity before he or she intended. This is most often applied in sports, and may also be used of political ambitions. It is most commonly used in Great Britain and Australia. The earliest reference available in print is American, in reference to baseball, from *Boy's Life*, June, 1964, page 15, in 'A Bad Town for Pull Hitters:'

> "The drive put Cleveland ahead, 6-3, and Walker **took an early bath**."

early bird gets the worm (The), but the second mouse gets the cheese

Pinning down the originator of this 'twisted proverb' has been impossible, but it was brought out online in the early '90s. The first known date ascribed is 07-09-93, which now appears on Instagram posted by subscriber genernow. In December, 1994, a message was posted on Usernet by "Ernst Berg" with the following, with no attribution:

> "Blessed is the second mouse for he shall inherit the cheese."

Then, three months later, February, 1995, a Usernet subscriber called "David Jakovak" posted the following, also with no attribution:

> "The early bird gets the worm, but the second mouse gets the cheese!"

In 1997, a proverb dictionary put out by a major publisher included 'the second mouse gets the cheese'.

On September 13, 1997 the *Sydney Morning Herald*, Section: News and Features "COLUMN 8," Quote Page 1, Sydney, Australia, had the following:.

> "THOUGHT for the weekend, culled by Greg Cocks, of Brooklyn, from the Internet: The early bird may get the worm, but the second mouse gets the cheese."

Obviously this was a little late to be the true origin. At any rate, the saying 'went viral.'

Egg someone on

There is no connection between either 'Egg on someone's face' (see first volume) or 'Over egging the pudding' (see in this volume) and egging someone on, meaning 'urging' or encouraging an action. The etymology of egg, used in this connotation, was taken into the Middle English from the Old Norse word, *eggja*, meaning 'to incite.' The earliest English usage of a form of this, *eggede*, appeared in Trinity College, in *Homer* circa 1200 according to reliable sources. But in its current usage 'egg on' was first cited in Thomas Drqant's translation of *Horace his arte of poetrie, pistles and satyrs englished*, in 1566:

> "Ile **egge them on** to speake some thyng, whiche spoken may repent them."

Elephant in the room^

This idiom refers to an obvious problem or truth that no one wants to talk about. It comes from the fact that if an elephant were in a room, it would be impossible for it to go unnoticed. To show how inaccurate some can get, Derek Paget, in *No Other Way to Tell It*, 1996, attributed the actual coining of phrase to Irish writer, Bernard MacLaverty:

> "Bernard MacLaverty was already a well known Irish writer when he took on the screenplay for *Hostages*…For example, his 1983 novel Cal was filmed in 1984 by David Puttnam's Enigma Company. He is also the likely originator of the popular phrase 'the **elephant in the room'**. He used the idea of an elephant in a room in his 1978 children's book *A Man in Search of a Pet*."

However, the saying had been around much longer. Even the *Oxford English Dictionary* got it wrong by attributing it to *The New York Times* article June 20, 1959 which said:

> "Financing schools has become a problem about equal to having **an elephant in the living room**. It's so big you just can't ignore it."

In 1814, Russian poet and fabulist Ivan Andreevich Krylov wrote a fable titled *The Inquisitive Man*. Its main character went to a museum and noticed the minutest details, but failed to see an elephant. The proverb was born of this tale.

In 1915, *The Journal of Education*, Volume 37, page 288, published in London, had the following:

"Is there **an elephant in the class-room**?"

Empty nester

This expression refers to a parent whose children are grown and have left home. It comes from birds which have taught their young to fly and are now left with an empty nest. 'Empty nest syndrome' refers to the depression felt by some of these parents. The term came into common use in the 1970s, and though certainly not the origin, the earliest known citation of the exact phrase in print is in *Methods of Housing Analysis* by James W. Hughes, 1977, page 119:

> "Compact Family — **Empty Nester** (Move-Down): ..."

Empty nest, applied this way, is found as early as 1960 in *The Minnesota Community: Country and Town in Transition* by Lowry Nelson, page 54:

> "Of course, the family as an institution is an ongoing concern, but the individual family runs its inevitable cycle from marriage through the various stages, dictated by birth and growth of children, to the **empty nest** and the death of the founding ..."

The theme spawned a television citcom, Empty Nest (1988-1995), originally on NBC, starring Richard Mulligan and Dinah Manoff.

Empty promise

This refers to a promise which is worthless or meaningless because it will never be fulfilled. It has been attributed to Thomas Bilson (c. 1547-1616), Bishop of Winchester. The earliest known citation currently available, however, is from *A Treatise of the Passions and Facvlties of the Soul of Man* by Edward Reynolds, 1647, page 237:

> "Philosophers have called Hope the dreams of waking men j like that of the Mufitian whom Dionyfiut deceived with an **empty promise**, of which I spake before:..."

Empty vessels (or **cans) rattle the loudest** (or **make the most sound)**

This old proverb means that people who are always talking are often the ones with the least substance in their repertoire of knowledge. Those with the most to say watch the weight of their words to make each one count. This proverb crosses language and cultural barriers and has been around in various civilizations for hundreds of years. Versions of it have been attributed to 'The

Chinese' but most often, Plato (c. 428-348 BCE). Yet numerous searches of the *Complete Works of Plato* using each word come up blank. Shakespeare used it in *Henry V,* Act IV, Scene iv (1600), but did not take credit:

> "... the saying is true—**The empty vessel makes the greatest sound**."

In 1609 it was included in *A Treasury or Storehouse of Similes: Both Pleasant, Delightful, and Profitable* by Robert Cawdry, which is very near the supposed 'Plato' quote:

> "As **empty vessels make the loudest sound**: so men of least wit are the greatest babblers."

end is nigh, The

The roots of his saying go back to the *Bible*, particularly to the predictions of Jesus in *Matthew 24*. In speaking of the end of the age, or in older translations, the end of the world, verse 33 (*KJV,* 1611) says:

> "So likewise ye, when ye shall see all these things, know that it **is near**, even at the doors."

Throughout history, since that time, there have been several times when the end of the world as we know it has been predicted. The saying "The end is nigh" comes from a man who walked up and down London's Oxford Street in the early 21st century, either wearing a sandwich board, or at times, carrying a placard, bearing the phrase "The end is nigh!" It became a cultural phenomenon.

An annual British fanzine was launched by Michael Molcher at the Bristol Comic Expo in 2005, which has since become a semiannual publication.

Enough already! Alright already! etc.

The consensus among etymologists and lexicographers is that 'enough already' began among New York immigrant Yiddish speakers early in the 20th century, becoming common by the 1930s among younger offspring who spoke only English. 'Already' continued to be used with other exclamations such as 'Alright already!' and 'Shut up already!' These became an excepted part of the urban American dialogue. Composer Emil Stern copyrighted a song titled *Alright Already* in January – June, 1957, and in 1993 Larry Stewart, formerly of Restless Heart recorded as his first solo effort, another tune written by Byron Hill and J.B. Rudd by the same name on RCA. Then from September 7, 1997 to May 4, 1998, The WB network aired a sitcom starring Carol Leifer and Amy Yasbech called *Alright Already*.

Even as we speak (See: **As we speak**)

Everybody and his brother / The world and his brother / The world and his wife+**

All versions of this idiomatic expression have been used to refer to a great many people, or most people. The earliest form is "all the world and his wife", first recorded by Jonathan Swift in *Polite Conversation*, 1738, page 192 in Dialogue III.

> "*Lady Smart*, Why, there was **all the World, and his Wife**; there was Mrs. *Clatter*, Mrs. *Singular*, the Countefs (Countess) of *Talkham* (I should have named her firft;) *Tom Goflin*, and fome others whom I have forgot."

In 1908, *The World and His Wife* was used as the title of a Broadway play written by Charles Frederic Nirdlinger, later released in 1920, as silent film produced by Cosmopolitan Productions and distributed by Paramount Pictures, which has since been lost.

In the U.K it was picked up and later used is as "the world and his brother". By the mid-20th century it was being used in its current form in America, "everybody and his brother" as in *The Great All-Star Animal League Ball Game* by Vincent Starrett, 1950:

"…**everybody and his brother** gathered on the diamond of the Field…"

Everything is relative

Also stated as 'It's all relative,' this idiomatic expression sometimes means that there are various viewpoints on every topic, and different people view things differently. It also is used to mean that circumstances may necessitate dissimilar conclusions for the same person. For instance, what may seem 'expensive' when a person is working for minimum wage may appear much more reasonable after he or she is earning a six figure income. This idea did not originate with Albert Einstein's Theory of Relativity. Einstein wasn't born until 1879. In *Wilhelm Meister's Apprenticeship and Travels*, Volume II, Book VII, a great novel by German author, Johann Wolfgang von Goethe, first published 1795-1796, as translated into English in 1858 by Thomas Carlyle, on page 120, we find the following:

> "Everything is, in the long-run, reduced by them to what they call effect; **everything is relative**, say they; and so indeed it is; everything with them grows relative, except absurdity and platitude, which truly are absolute enough."

Excuse me / Pardon me for living!+

This is an expression used to show annoyance when someone is told that he or she has done something wrong, letting the other person know that the criticism is unreasonably critical or rude. It has been in use since at least the early 20th century. The student newspaper of St. Teresa's Junior College, Windmoor, Kansas City, Missouri, *The Gleam*, Volume Two, Issue One, November, 1923, has the following citation on page 6, in 'College Humor':

All stereotyped expressions such as the following are ruled strictly bad form by the student lady (Isabel Glick):

1. 'Due to the fact'
2. '**Pardon me for living**'
3. I just can't live
4. 'Written anything for *The Gleam*?'
5. 'Prepared your logic?'
6. 'Mail out yet?'

Expect the best and plan for the worst^

This proverb means that a positive attitude is important in life, but even so, one must always have a 'back up plan' in case of an unexpected disaster. It is often attributed to Zig Ziglar, the wonderful motivational speaker who certainly brought this to our attention. The basis of this saying, however, goes all the way back to the late 17th century. *Seneca's Morals Abstracted in Three Parts* by Roger L'Estrange published in London in 1679 has this on page 104-105:

> "I would **hope the Best, but prepare for the Worst**."

Almost 200 years later it was used in *The Day of Rest, An Illustrated Journal of Sunday Reading*, from the Church of England, August 23, 1873, in a column titled, 'The Bright Side:'

> "But he who looks on the bright side in a religious spirit will **prepare for the worst**, though he **hopes for the best**."

Oregon Teachers Monthly, January, 1906, in 'Ashland Normal News' by editor Armilda Daughty said it this way:

> "**Hope for the best**, **prepare for the worst**, and take what comes."

Eye of the storm

This common idiom refers to a false calm at the center of a controversy. In the middle of an actual hurricane, there is a peaceful core, but the twirling mass itself holds encroaching doom. According to *The Century Dictionary and Cyclopedia*, 1911:

> "And there is then observed the peculiar and dreadful calm within the whirl, to which sailors have given the name of '**the eye of the storm**.'"

The first known citation of the metaphoric use of the expression is found in *Narrative Structure in the Novels of Sir Walter Scott*, by Michael H. Cusac, 1969, on page 65:

> "This duty is performed in literature by the ordinary man . . .; [these men] are, so to speak, **the 'eye' of the storm** which rages about them, and serve to measure the departure of the others from virtue, sanity, moderation, or merely normal ..."

Eyes in the back of one's head (See: **Having eyes in the back of one's head**)

F

Fact (or **Truth**) **is stranger than fiction**

This self-explanatory proverb refers to the fact that often things that actually happen are harder to believe and more amazing than stories that are contrived. This goes back to the early 1800s. The earliest notation in print of the exact phrase using 'truth' appears to be in *The Parriana; Or Notices of the Rev. Samuel Parr, LLD*, and in part written by E.S. Barker, Esq., Vol. II, 1829, page 445, where it is attributed to the late Lord Byron (1788-1824):

> "In reply to this, I would quote the maxim of Lord Byron, 'that **truth is stranger than fiction;'**"

Actually the meaning of the proverb was coined in Byron's satirical poem, *Don Juan*, 1823:

> "'Tis strange - but true; **for truth is always strange;**
> **Stranger than fiction**; if it could be told,"

The earliest citation in print with 'fact' is from the *New Monthly Magazine*, London, June, 1935, in 'Scenery and a Scene' on page 9:

> "The awkward thing about all story-telling is transition. Invention you do not need if you have experience; for **fact is stranger than fiction**."

Fair dinkum[3]

This Australian idiom actually originated with a now-extinct dialect word from the East Midlands of England from the late 19th century, where it has long since 'lost its luster.' Dinkum (or dincum) meant hard work or fair work. Fair dinkum, therefore, means honest, genuine, fair play. A fair dinkum Aussie embodies the nation's values.

A report of a political meeting in Lincoln (Lincolnshire, England) in the *Nottingham Evening Post*, February, 1882, tells of Robert Hall, a local magistrate who was complaining about unfair government policies which he believed favored the wealthy:

> "In all of these things he thought there should be **fair 'dinkum'** to all classes of people."

Around this time, numerous criminals and mineworkers were transported from the East Midlands to Australia. Two years later 'fair dinkum' appeared in *The Bulletin*, a Sydney, Australia newspaper. It stuck there!

Fair suck of the sauce bottle[3]

This popular Aussie slang expression is used to protest someone who has taken more than his or her fair share. A June 17, 2009 article in the *New York Times* quoted a *Sky News* interview with Australian Prime Minister Kevin Rudd, who was said to have grinned while speaking.

> "'We've appointed the first woman as governor-general of the Commonwealth of Australia – **fair shake of the sauce bottle,** mate,' Rudd smirked, when grilled about whether his government had done enough to promote women."

It seems that using 'mate' following the expression is very common in Australia, and it's a relatively new phrase. This statement brought it to the public attention and put Rudd in a spotlight he may not have wanted. It is assumed Down Under that this idiom originally referred to a bottle of liquor, and according to *Ozwords*, an Australian publication, it was first recorded in the 1970s.

Falling between two stools[2]

This very old British idiom means that something failed because of the inability to choose between two alternatives. It can be traced back to John Gower's *Confessio Amantis*, 1390.

> "Bot it is seid - **Betwen tuo Stoles** lyth the **fal**..."

The first time it was referenced in modern English is in *Alma; or, The Progress of the Mind*, by Matthew Prior, 1717:

> "Now which were wise, and which were fools?
> Poor Alma sits **between two stools**;
> The more she reads the more perplex'd,
> The comment ruining the text:
> Now fears, now hopes her doubtful fate."

False dawn[2]

This is a thin ambient zodiacal light which proceeds the true dawn—usually by about an hour, but varying in different parts of the globe. It is now primarily British. According to a major dictionary this was coined in between 1825 and 1835.

Metaphorically, it refers to a situation in which one thinks something good will occur, but it does not. The original term was likely Persian Arabic, as the earliest citation is from *A Vocabulary Persian Arabic and English* by William Kirkpatrick, 1785, page 85. Other references would also lead to this conclusion. Then in April, 1800, in *The Atlantic Monthly*, the false dawn is mentioned in 'The North Shore Watch:'

> "The Anecdotes of Siena seem to us to fail in that lark-like unpremeditation which belongs to the lyric — the liquid flow that is here discoverable in only two instances: in The **False Dawn** and Be God's the Hope. The **False Dawn** is one of those fantastic conceptions into whose exact meaning it is not well too curiously to inquire, lest there be no crock of gold at the end of the rainbow."

The earliest known figurative usage is in the form of a true metaphor in *The Oriental Herald* November, 1828, in the poem, 'The First Kiss of Love' by J.A. St. John, Esq., immediately following 'Zalim Kahn, A Tale of Modern Persia,' a third reason to suggest Persian origins:

> "Yet the light that shines over Our youth is, at best, But like the **false dawn** That illumines the east,"

Then in 1849, master storyteller, Charlotte Bronte, writing under the pseudonym Currer Bell, in *Shirley, A Tale, Volume I* brought the metaphor to life on page 138:

> "According to this flattering prophet, she was to know disappointment, to feel chill no more: she had entered on the dawn of a summer day — no **false dawn**, but the true spring of morning — and her sun would quickly rise."

False prophets

This term, in religion, is someone who falsely claims to possess the gift of prophecy of divine inspiration, or who uses such a proclaimed gift to evil means. The test is whether or not a 'prophecy' comes to pass. The holy writings of Judaism, Islam, and especially Christianity, all warn against false prophets.

Metaphorically, outside religion, this term has now come to applied to promoters of scientific, medical or political theories which the person writing of speaking believe to be false. An early example of this is libertarian science writer Ronald Bailey's 1994 book *The False Prophets of Ecological Apocalypse,* in which he applied the term to proponents of global warming, a claim which he later recanted in 2005. Then in 2008 Dr. Paul A. Offit first published a book titled, *Autism's False Prophets: Bad Science, Risky Medicine and the Search for a Cure*.

Fashionably late+

This idiom is used to imply that being a late for events is expected of someone in high society, likely because of the demand on their time, thus making a notable entrance. The earliest available citation is in *Tales of Fashionable Life,* a book containing three novellas by highly successful English writer, Maria Edgeworth, 1800, on page 156, in 'Almeria':

> "She was somewhat surprised, especially as she came **fashionable late**, to find in the drawing-room only old Mrs. Wynn, her nephew and a lady, who from her dress and modest appearance was evidently nobody."

Fast food

This term is applied to foods which are prepared quickly and usually from preheated or precooked ingredients. It was made popular in the United States in the very early 1950s and the term was first recognized in a dictionary in 1951. On December 22, 1951, the first advertisement featuring the expression 'fast food' was printed in *Billboard* on page 61, at the bottom left. It was for the Helman Lacy 'Minute Bar-BQ-Bar' boasting a $48.00 per-hour profit.

> "Perfect for any **fast food** service operation — serves a sandwich a minute per toaster head."

Fat chance

This idiom is an extreme slice of sarcasm. It means that even though it may be thought that something will happen, there is actually little or no probability of it. The saying was likely originally Scottish, as it was in the *Etymological Dictionary of the Scottish Language* by John Jamieson, printed by University Press, Edinburgh, 1825, page 683:

> ***"To Win aff or off*** (1.) To get away] *Add;*
> **Fat chance** he furder had she cud na tell
> but was right fain that she wan aff hersell.
>
> " ***Rosse's Helenore*** p. 40"

This rhyme is taken from the 1778 best known work of Scottish poet Alexander Ross (1699-1784), *Helenore, Or The Fortunate Shepherdess,* not to be confused with the later Scottish writer by the same name. It shows how far back the saying actually goes.

fat's in the fire, The

This idiomatic phrase is used when something that has been done will inevitably result in dire consequences. There is surely trouble ahead. Centuries ago it was very common for meat to be roasted above open fires. When it got very hot, pieces of fat would often fall into the flames, causing popping, and bits of it would be thrown out and burn those around the fire. It was first listed in *The Proverbs, Epigrams and Miscellanies of John Haywood*, 1562, on page 217:

> "243: **'Of Fat in the Fire'**
> ***The fat is in the fire***: that is a shrewd turn;
> Cast the lean after; fat and lean, let all burn!"

Faux pas

This French term is often used in by English speakers and writers to mean a social blunder; literally it means a false step. The earliest known citation of the expression in an English text is from Act V, Scene i of a comedy written in 1674; *The Plain-Dealer* by William Wycherley, performed at the Theater Royal in London and published in 1677:

> ***"Oliv***. How, Coufin? (Cousin) I'd have you to know, before this **faux pas**, this trip of mine, the World cou'd not talk of me."

Feed a cold, starve a fever

The earliest form of this old wives' tale comes from John Withals' *A shorte dictionarie most profitable for yong beginners the second tyme corrected, and augmented, with diverse phrasys, & other thinges necessarie thereunto added*, published in London in 1574:

> "**Fasting is a great remedie of feuer**."

By August, 1785 it was already known that this advice was very errant. That month *The Gentleman's Magazine* carried the following admonishment:

> "The vulgar and absurd proverb, "**Stuff a cold, and starve a fever**,'" has, where-ever it has obtained, been perhaps more destructive to mankind than the plague itself.

This must not have gotten around well, because the saying prevailed for hundreds of years. Modern medical personnel tell us that starving a fever by eating fewer calories may actually make it more difficult for one's body to fight off the flu.

Feet of clay[2]

This is an expression, primarily used in Britain, which refers to a person's weakness or character flaw; especially a person of prominence. It comes from the biblical Book of *Daniel*, chapter *2,* verses *31-33*, in which the Hebrew Daniel interpreted a dream of the Babylonian King, Nebuchadnezzar.

> "Thou, O king, sawest, and behold a great image. This great image, whose brightness was excellent, stood before thee; and the form thereof was terrible. This image's head was of fine gold, his breast and his arms of silver, his belly and his thighs of brass, His legs of iron, his **feet** part of iron and part **of clay**." *(KJV)*

This foretold the decline of the powerful Babylonian empire. Using this analogy means that no matter how strong the rest of a person is, feet of clay would cause him or her to topple.

Fess up!

This Americanism is a directive to someone to 'come clean' and take responsibility for something the person has done. It is a cute way of saying, 'Confess!' The three earliest citations are all from 1884. On March 17, *The Independent,* a New York publication, printed a feature titled *Old Abram's Lament* by Jeanette S. Walworth, a story about an old African American gentleman. In it is the following dialogue:

> "You mus' **fess up** yo' sins—leetle sneaky ones an' small. You mus' ax him furt grant his grace unto us all!"

It seems likely that this expression was taken from a common interpretation of black American speech in the late 19th century. After that, it became an acceptable part of American jargon.

Fifth wheel

A fifth wheel, metaphorically speaking, is an extra, unneeded, unwanted person, place or thing. In a literal sense, the term has been around since at least the mid-1700s when it was used in a comical simile in *The Way to Christ Discovered* by Jacob Boehme, 1752, on page 222:

> "…as useful as a **fifth wheel** in a Waggon…"

Thereafter there are numerous references to the term as a mechanical device, originally on coaches and wagons, often ridiculed, right down to the modern fifth-wheel trailers.

Then in 1892, Herman Melville used the expression figuratively in his classic novel, *Moby Dick*, perhaps for the first time, still with 'a wagon' on page 91:

> "'Oh, perhaps you hav'n't got any,' he said quickly. 'No matter though, I know many chaps that hav'n't got any, — good luck to 'em; and they are all the better off for it. A soul's a sort of a **fifth wheel** to a wagon.'"

The analogy must have taken root, for only six years later, future U.S. President, Woodrow Wilson, used it, without the wagon part, in *The State: Elements of Historical and Practical Politics*, 1898, page 235, obviously popularizing the term, and giving it a prominent place in American expressions:

> "The canton, indeed, is little more than an election district; and the arrondissement is only a **fifth wheel** in the administration of the Department."

File 13+

This is a humorous euphemism for the trash can. 13 is a number which is applied superstitiously to something causing bad luck. The expression is commonly used in the American military, with a similar one, "round file" being used in the British military. The origin is unclear, with some believing that it came from the fact that since there are only twelve months in a year, and many files are stored by the month, the thirteenth month is non-existent, therefore represents items which should be trashed. According to *Random House Historical Dictionary of American Slang*, Volume 1, A-G by J.E. Lighter, the first citation was as U.S. military slang for a wastebasket in 1941; so it is likely that it was coined in the during World War II.

Fill someone's shoes / Being in someone else's shoes+

A previous entry in the Original Volume, page 63, **Big shoes to fill**, deals with this premise, and goes back to a quote from U.S. President Andrew Jackson in 1829, referring to his replacing popular president, John Quincy Adams. Metaphors about being in someone else's shoes, however originated much earlier, in the Middle Ages. In those days journeymen traveled around Germany, often spending the night in communal dormitories. Sometimes they would be tempted to steal something. To avoid getting caught, the items were slipped down into the boots of a fellow traveler. This way if they were stopped the other man would be blamed for the theft. The term evolved into not wanting to be in someone else's shoes.

Finger-pointing

This refers to actions or words that bring unfair attention to a particular person, group of persons or issue, blaming the person or persons for that problem. This expression has been used since at least 1875 when it appeared in *Ancient History from the Monuments. Assyria from the Earliest Times to the Fall of Nineveh* by George Smith, page 19:

> "…the evil invocation, the **finger pointing**, the marking, the cursing, the sinning…"

There could be some shadow of doubt as to the exact meaning of this, based upon other citations of that day. In the early 20th century there were mentions of 'accusing fingers pointing' at people. Then in *Life Magazine*, December 6, 1943, in an article headed "Never mind 'who done it'—pitch in and help get it done!" the following statement on page 120 was 'crystal clear:'

> "So there's been a lot of **finger pointing** and hollering for the OTHER FELLOW to do something—QUICK."

First past the post

Also known as 'winner takes all;' this is a term referring to an election that is won by the candidate receiving more votes than any others. It is common, but not universal. It is used in the U.S., India, the U.K, and Canada.

The term originally came from horse racing where the winner of the race was decided by the horse's head which first went past the post at the end of the race course. An early example is in *The Sporting Magazine*, London; August, 1831:

> "…interest was excited between Tommy Tickle and Post Captain, they having met two or three times before, and each having ... managed to make a good race of it to the end, when Tommy's rider contrived to get his horse's head **first past the post**, ..."

Fish or cut bait+

This is a common metaphor which means that a person needs to either do take immediate action on an issue or step aside so someone else can. It dates to the mid-19th century, and derived from the commercial fishing industry in the United States when "cutting bait" was cutting up a small fish to use for bait to catch larger ones. The earliest known citation in print comes from *The Opal, A Monthly Periodical of the Lunatic Asylum*, Utica, New York, 1852:

> "But delicacy is attacked with Epilepsy in depicting so faithfully the results of sane life; the truth needs no commentary; farther, the moral turpitude of such customs, among those who profess so loud, and long, their fortunate position among folks; and hence, their infallibility bids him who indulges his time to pass in their narration, to **fish or cut bait**."

The meaning is rather obscure here, though obviously figurative. The following year, in a highly publicized court case presided over by American judge, Levi Hubble, concerning a legal dispute over land ownership between U.S. Attorney General Caleb Cushing and William Hungerford, it was brought to national attention. Cushing was displeased with Hubble's handling of the case and threatened to have him impeached. Hubble responded by saying:

> "Judge Cushing has commenced a suit in the United States Court. Judge Cushing must either **fish or cut bait**."

Several newspapers printed the story, but all seemed to be confused as to Hubble's intent. In an article in August, 1853, *The Milwaukee Daily Sentinel* stated, "There was some discussion among council, without any conclusion, as to the meaning of this phrase."

After this, the expression began to be used and understood to have the connotation we know today.

Fit (or **Fill**) **the bill**

This means to be suitable for some particular purpose. It is used in America, Britain and Australia ('fit' being primarily British). It was derived by a legal document, a bill of fare or playbill requiring certain conditions to be made to be suitable. 'Fill the bill' was used as early as 1889 in the *Full Musical Score of The Oolah*: as Played by Francis Wilson and Company at the Broadway Theater by Charles Lecocq and Sydney Rosenfeld in 'The March and Entrance of the Prince' on page 45:

> "…she does not seem to **fill the bill**, no, not at all."

The earliest available citation of 'fit the bill' is from *Bill Drafting*, by James McKirdy 1912, page 12:

"Some constitutions require that it state clearly the purport of the bill. It is essential, then, that the title be drafted last to **fit the bill**; and not, as is often the case, the bill to fit the title."

Five o'clock shadow

This old expression refers to a thin re-growth of beard which shows up on a man's face in the late afternoon after he has shaved that morning. There is a theory that the reason it was called 'five o'clock shadow,' rather than choosing another hour, is because of the British custom of having teas at five o'clock. Perhaps. However, the earliest known reference in print is from the American *Life Magazine*, January 9, 1939. An article under 'Speaking of Pictures,' headed 'This is how celebrities see themselves in their shaving mirrors,' featuring numerous photos, states:

"A razor company tries to plant a sense of guilt about '**five o'clock shadow**.'"

The company was Gem Safety Razor Company; they were coining a phrase to sell their 'Micromatic' Blades.

Then in the 1940s, the topic received wide publicity. Jazz great Elliott Lawrence even recorded a song on Columbia Records by that title in 1946.

Flat-out^

This can apply to being 'flat out wrong,' telling the 'flat out truth,' or anything absolute or performed with all-out effort. A major online dictionary puts the origin at 1925-1930. Miriam Webster dictionary places the earliest use at 1906. They are both 'flat-out' wrong.

However, let's go back and look at how this came to be what it is today. Before we used the term this way, it had a bit different connotation. For example in 1847, in *Shakespeare and His Friends*, Robert Folkestone Williams used it this way:

"But in conclusion, upon this dispute they fell **flat out** to outrageous choleric words, with straining and struggling at the doors, that all lameness was forgotten, and, in the fury of the conflict, the jailer had his new perwig torn off his crown; and yet here the battle ended not, ..."

That same year the phrase was used in the August issue of *Knickerbacker, OR, New York Monthly Magazine* in 'A Question in Single Rule of Three' in this manner, in quotes:

"'The rolling spheres' may roll out of sight and out of existence; solids may melt to liquids, and liquids '**flat out'** into plane surfaces, and then evaporate into thin air; but Euclid and Company will survive the general dissolution, and flourish in immortal greenness."

By 1851 the term had even another meaning as a verb, according to *The English Language in Elements and Forms* by William Chauncer Fowler, page 125:

"To **flat out**= to prove a failure."

In 1860, a dictionary of Americanisms, *A Glossary of Words and Phrases* by John Russell Bartlett (page 165) enlarges upon that definition to include, 'to collapse'.

But 1876, a new meaning was developing. The midsummer issue of *Good Things: A Picturesque Magazine for Boys and Girl*s carried the following citation of the term unmistakably as it is used today in 'Up A Tree; Or, A Very Queer Breakfast Party' by 'An Idle Voyager,' on page 115:

"Then he took to botherin' our boss (master) to send his men up to strengthen it; but the old sinner kep' puttin' it off and off, jist like them lazy beggars alius does, till at last Bob up and told him, **flat out**, that if he didn't do the right thing, he might look out for another 'help' for he wouldn't sarve him any longer."

This obvious perception of ignorant dialogue stuck in American jargon, and is still around to this day.

Flattery will get you nowhere/everywhere

This saying is used to let someone know that flowery praise will not persuade you to do anything you do not want to do already. Though historically flattery has been practiced to achieve favor of others, most times it is an insincere ruse. The first available citation in print, however, of this popular expression is a copyright entry for a musical composition by this name in the 'last half' of 1944 in the *Catalogue of the U.S. Library of Congress*. Then, *Billboard Magazine,* on December 7, 1946, makes this statement about the song, which had been recorded by Gordon MacRae:

"It's a bouncy and attractive rhythm ditty in **Flattery Will Get You Nowhere** and a more promising slow ballad in Oh, But I Do."

In the 1950s the phrase picked up popularity in American daily speech and was used by numerous writers. One example is from *Flying Magazine*, November, 1954 in 'The Gremlin Corner' by Weyman C. Carver on page 58:

> "'Where've you side show escapees been?' I asked.
> "'**Flattery will get you nowhere**,' Dopey cracked.
> "'Yeh,' Sludge said, as he reached for my coveralls to wipe his greasy hands on."

Strangely enough, it was another song which brought the coining of the converse saying as well. The first time this one showed up in *Billboard* was in the November 30, 1968 issue, on page 50, when it debuted on the country chart at number 60. *Flattery Will Get You Everywhere* was by Lynn Anderson.

Both expressions have remained with us in America into the 21st century.

Flex one's muscles

Figuratively this means to demonstrate one's power or superiority over others, especially in a threatening way. In a national or organizational scope this is used in relation to military or financial strength. A major online source states origin at early 1900s, which is feasible. Though certainly not the origin, the earliest available reference in print is in *Life Magazine*, May 14, 1945, in an article titled 'Argentine Crisis Spotlights Rivalry of America and Russia' by John K. Jessup:

> "The Americans, who at the moment are a good deal more powerful than the Russians, chose the occasion of April 30 to **flex their muscles**."

Flight of stairs

The odd term, 'flight of stairs,' means a set of steps between two floors or levels in a building. The term goes back to the early 18th century. In this case, the word 'flight' refers to getting away, or possibly going up higher, as in the case of the stairs. The earliest verifiable citation, but obviously not the origin, is from *An Accurate Description of Newgate: With the Rights, Privileges, Allowances, fees, Dues and Customs Thereof* by Betty Langley, 1724: page 34:

> "The Stone Hall is the Firft, into which you enter at the Head of **a Flight of Stairs**, fituated on the Left-Hand fide of the Gate going out of the City, being over the Gateway facing Newgate Street."

Flip one's lid / Flip one's wig+

Both of these comedic hyperbolic metaphors mean suddenly become deranged or lose one's self control; react to something with strong emotion. They allude to a person losing the top of his or her head and date to the 1930s to 1940s according to a popular online dictionary. Etymology online states 'flip (one's) lid was first attested in 1949. Billboard, September 17, 1949 has this citation of a form of it with wig:

> "Talking Boogie. Not quite as **wig-flipping** as reverse style—but a **wig-flipper**."

There are also examples in print in the '50s and '60s. Today just plain 'flip' or 'flip out' is more common.

Float a loan

This old term refers to borrowing money. A floating interest rate is a term in home loans going back centuries, and means that the rate is not fixed for the term of the loan, and may vary with changes in the market. In this respect, this was in use as early as 1781 when the following was printed *in The Parliamentary Register; Or, History of the Proceedings and Debates of the House of Commons* in London, page 207:

> "Nothing he had heard that day struck him as sufficient force to render it neceffary that the terms of the **loan** fhould be altered, and the whole let on **float** again."

The actual use of the term, 'float a loan' didn't come till just over 100 years later. This is in *Victoria Parliamentary Debates Session 1872* (Australia):

> "If that be so, why should we for the accommodation of persons who desire to loan money to the Government and not from any necessity on the part of the Government, seek to **float a loan** at 4 per cent?"

Flush out something

This is an idiom meaning to cause something previously obscure to become obvious. It came from 'flushing' a person or animal out of hiding. It came into general usage in the third quarter of the 20th century. A good early example is in *The Foundation of Education for Librarianship* by Jesse Hauk Shera, 1972, page 433:

> "The first two are largely acquired and can be learned, though native ability is, of course, not to be ruled out; the last are ... to pursue truth through the jungle of distortion, misrepresentation, ideology, and special interest, and to **flush out** the lies ..."

Fly solo

This, when used metaphorically, means to do something totally on one's own, with no help whatsoever from any outside source. The use of the term in this connotation came in the latter half of the 20th century. The earliest available citation is from *New York Magazine*, December 28, 1981, in an article headed 'The Learning Annex,' on page 58, where the following appeared in reference to a course being offered:

> "**Flying Solo**: The Art of Being Single"

Follow in someone's footsteps

This idiomatic phrase means to imitate another person, especially in a career choice. Footsteps, originally 'foote steppes,' has been around since Middle English, circa 1200 CE. This saying has been in use at least the late 16th century, as seen in *A Suruey of the Popes Supremacie* by Francis Bunny, published in London in 1595:

> "As did Christ and his apostles, (whose **footsteps** he should not be afhamed to **follow)** but he will teach by his owne leffons, and believe by his owne doctrines…"

Follow the money

This catchphrase, popularized by the dramatic 1976 documentary film, *All the President's Men,* refers to discovering conspiracies and illegal activities by investigating the 'trail of money' distributed during the corrupt activities. But the phrase was used in this sense prior to the film's release. In 1974, American folk-legend Henry 'Ole Pete' Peterson used it at the Senate Judiciary hearings when Earl Siebert was nominated as a U.S. Attorney. Then in 1975, *Crime in Britain Today*, a book by Clive Borrell and Brian Cashinella included the phrase. But the term was around even before these citations. In 1971, New Zealander L.S. Sealy in *Cases and Materials in Company Law* wrote the following on page 170:

> "It would be entitled, on the principles of *In re Hallett's Estate*, to **follow the money** as long as it or any property acquired by its means could be identified."

Even back in 1942, following the money was discussed in regard to legal cases, per the following quote from the *New York Court of Appeals, Records and Briefs,* page 44

> ".. it may perhaps be inferred that the parties intended that such withdrawal might be made without accountability, and so no right to **follow the money** withdrawn would arise, even though the parties might be regarded as joint tenants, or tenants ..."

Food chain (See: **At the top of the food chain**)

For a song

Getting something, or something going for, a mere 'song' is another creation of William Shakespeare, 1604, in *All's Well That Ends Well*, Act III, Scene ii.9:

> "I know a man that had this tricke of melancholy hold a goodly Mannor **for a song**."

Thereafter it was cited by many authors, poets, and writers, and became a part of our popular culture.

For crying out loud!

Like many other illogical exclamations, several of which are found in the first volume, this is what is known as a 'minced oath,' or something coined in Christian culture of the past to keep from saying something viewed as swearing. This one replaces, 'For Christ's sake.' The earliest available use of it in print is from *The Union Postal Clerk*, January, 1921, under 'Famous Sayings of Clerks of the Mailing Division.'

Forked tongue (See: **Speak with a forked tongue**)

Fork in the road

This metaphor is based on a place in a literal road where one must turn one of two ways, and means a point in life at which a decision must be made as to which direction must be taken. The phrase is found in biblical text in *Ezekiel 21:19-23, NIV*:

> "For the king of Babylon will stop at the **fork in the road**, at the junction of the two roads, to seek an omen: He will cast lots with arrows, he will consult his idols, he will examine the liver."

Earliest translations used 'the parting of the ways.' Robert Frost's classic 1916 poem, *The Road Not Taken*, which speaks of a crossroad, is often mentioned in relation to this term; however, the poem does not actually contain this phrase. The earliest verifiable citation available is much earlier anyway: from *The Rural Carolinian* published in Charleston, South Carolina, April, 1873, in 'Blue and Grey: The Story of the Late Civil War:'

> "We had a long ride of seven or eight miles, when, coming to a **fork in the road**, the Major took one company and myself the other, and pushed up the forks."

Fortune favors the bold

This is one popular translation of various similar Latin Proverbs, likely the nearest one being, *Fortuna Audaces Iuvat,* literally translated 'Fortune helps the bold.' The earliest reference in print in Latin now available is from *Symbola divina et humana Pontificum, Imperatorum, Regum*, printed in 1601 in Rome. The earliest English reference is found in *Zingis, A Tragedy in Five Acts* by Alexander Dow, 1769:

> "Art thou only **bold** When **fortune favors** in the gloom of night?"

Then in 1799, E. F. Lantier, in the English translation from the French of author Étienne-François de Lantie, used the proverb in *The Travels of Antenor in Greece and Asia* on page 46:

> "Love, like **Fortune**, **favors the bold**."

Fountain of youth

Literally, the 'fountain of youth' is a mythical spring that supposedly restores youthful vibrance to anyone who drinks from it or bathes in its magical waters. Tales of such a fountain date back to as early as the 5th century BCE in the writings of Heroditus, the ancient Greek contemporary of Socrates, continuing in the Romance of Alexander the Great in Legend originally written in the 3rd century CE, and revived in the Early Crusades 11th and 12th century stories of Prester John and found to also be prevalent in the legends of the Indigenous peoples of the Caribbean in the Early 16th century age of New World

Exploration, It was propitiated by Spanish Explorer, Ponce de Leon, the first Governor of Puerto Rico. Figuratively, it has come to be used of any longed-for paradise of escape, where time seems to stand still. In the July, 1887 issue of *School Education*, in 'A Workman's Hints on Teaching Work,' we find the earliest available reference to 'a fountain of youth' used metaphorically:

> "For there is **a fountain of youth** in teaching at all events."

Fraidy cat / Scardey cat+

This is a colloquial Americanism for someone who is easily and unduly frightened; a coward. It comes from the fact that when a cat hears an unrecognizable sound or voice, it becomes immediately alert. It likely evolved from the pronunciation of "afraid" as early as 1816 in Africa and the East Indies, and according to etymology.com goes back to 1871. The earliest available citation, however, comes from a poem on page 17 in *A Boy's Book of Rhyme* by Clinton Scollard, 1896:

> "**FRAIDIE-CAT**
>
> "I Shan't-tell you what's his name!
> When we want to play a game,
> Always thinks that he'll be hurt,
> Soil his jacket in the dirt,
> Tear his trousers, spoil his hat—
> **Fraidie-cat! Fraidie-cat!**"

This poem later appeared in numerous poetry books, and was highly publicized, and was certainly the vehicle which popularized the term, if not the actual origin.

A later expression with the same meaning is "scaredy-cat". In spite of conflicting sources, including a popular online dictionary which states origin at 1930-1935 and *Merriam Webster* which cites 1948 as earliest known usage, this term was in print as early as 1906 in the book, *Billy Bounce* by American author, William Wallace Denslow:

> "'That is **Scaredy Cat**, and she will never come back.'"

French leave

In the military service this would be called AWOL (Absent Without Leave), as it means leaving a place without permission or announcing that one is departing. The term was coined in the mid-18th century and was said to derive from the French custom of leaving a dinner or ball without saying goodbye to the host or hostess. This expression was first recorded prior to the Seven Years' War (1756–63); and supposedly came from the French *filer à l'Anglaise*, literally translated, ironically, 'to escape in the style of the English.' There was much disdain at the time between the feuding nations.

The earliest citation known is from *A Choice Collection of Original Essays on Various and Entertaining Subjects* published in London in 1748:

> "***French Leave***, as now taken in Braiant and Flanders, By the polish'd French troops, and politer command- Is still more resin'd: For tho' nothing they pay, as, They strip all their hosts — to bear something away. **French Leave** is so courteous, twill cut a man's throat..."

frog does not drink up the pond in which he lives, The

This proverb serves as a reminder that the creatures of nature know better than to destroy their environment and know by nature how to protect their habitat. Man constantly has been his own worst enemy in the destruction of the earth and its precious resources. It is attributed in a number of modern sources as an Oglala Sioux Tribe Native American saying.

From stem to stern

Originally a nautical term referring to going 'from the front to the back of a ship,' this came to mean from one end of something to the other, or entirely and fully. The earliest verifiable citation of the expression is found in *A Select Collection of Novels, Volume the Second*, published for John Watts in London in 1720, in 'The History of the Captive,' on page 365:

> "...as he stood amoung them on the Gang-board, roaring and bawlmg out to them to pull away, toss'd him about from Hand to Hand, **from Stem to Stern**, and gave him such Knocks and Gripes, as they toss'd him, that before he reach'd the Mast, his Soul was in Hell."

Fuddy duddy+

This is an old idiomatic expression used for a person who is fussy while being an old-fashioned, likely conservative traditionalist, possibly to the point of eccentricity. It is one of many rhyming fused phrases. *Online Etymology*'s statement that it was first attested in America in 1871. William Dickinson's *A Glossary of Words and Phrases Pertaining to the Dialect of the Cumberland*, 1899, has a definition of a similar phrase from which it likely originated:

> "**Duddy fuddle**, a raged fellow"

An even earlier usage of these words occurred in 1833 in *The Wee Raggit Laddie,* a poem by Scottish poet, James Ballantyne:

> "Wee stuffy, dtumpy, dumpie laddie,
> Thou urchin, bare an' **duddy**,
> Are fairly baggit,
> Although the breekums on thy **fuddy**,
> Are e'en right raggit."

Full of beans / prunes^+

Originally "full of beans" referred to being peppy or energetic. It was first a term used for horses after a feeding of horse beans. Beans were raised for fodder for horses as far back as Roman times, but this expression only came into use in the early-to-mid 20th century. A good example is found on page 3 of printed proceedings of the *CIA Career Service Board Meeting* dated Monday, November 23, 1953:

> "You do a job, and that doesn't make a hell of a lot of sense with a fellow 21 or 22 years old and who is **full of beans**, and feeling the world is his oyster..."

In spite of a popular phrase origin book stating that "full of prunes" came later, there is actually a citation in a poem "You and Me Both" by Strickland W. Gillian, in a book titled *Including You and Me* published in 1916:

> **"You and Me Both**

> "I have my grievous faults.
> My pilgrim way is filled with halts
> And limps and stoppings by the road.
> When discipline applies her goad I wince. I often note (with grief
> That holds no prospect of relief
> Through future mornings, nights and noons)
> That everyone is **full of prunes**,
> Including me. But I cheer up
> And feel joy brimming in my cup
> When I look closer still and see
> How patient I have been with me!"

Though it can be a used as substitute for "full of beans", full of prunes often refers to someone thought to be a bit goofy, as seems to be the case in this early citation.

G

Game changer^

This idiom is applied to a new element or factor which significantly changes a situation. Miriam Webster dictionary stated the earliest known usage as 1993. The earliest reference in print known is from *Why Time Begins on Opening Day* by Thomas Boswell, 1984, page 168:

> "Find the 6-2, 200-pound super jock, put him at third and you've got the **game changer**."

game is up, The

This very old idiom has, like many others, evolved during the centuries. Originally meaning "All is lost," the earliest citation is from Shakespeare in *Cymbeline*, Act III. Scene iii, Exit, written circa 1611, originally published in 1623:

> "Euriphile, Thou wast their nurse; they took thee for their mother,
> And every day do honour to her grave:
> Myself, Belarius, that am Morgan call'd,
> They take for natural father. **The game is up**."

Today is means the same as 'the gig is up,' you can't fool me any more by your tricks and deceit. This is illustrated well in *New Outlook*, December, 1953, in an article by A.S. Pearce titled Success on page 83:

> "Such means of securing a living are dangerous, because animals employing them are led to depend more and more on special means, and if deception is discovered, **the game is up**."

gentleman and a scholar, A

This old cliché praise was intended to mean that a man held notable qualities which invoked the respect and high regard of his fellow man. It was usually because of his achievements as a caring human being or statements made which showed forth great knowledge and wisdom. It was popularized by J.D. Salinger in his controversial Pulitzer nominated 1951 novel, *The Catcher in the Rye*. The earliest known citation of the phrase in an entirely different connotation, as two separate people, is in *New Double Grammar: English-French, French-English*, 1696, page 109:

> "The third Dialogue between **a Gentleman and a Scholar** who learns French."

The current meaning, however, comes very quickly afterward, in 1709 in *The Golden Spy: Or, a Political Journal of the British Nights Entertainments of War and Peace and Love and Politics* by Charles Gildon, page 140:

> "I am, Madam, **a Gentleman and a Scholar**, my Friends who oblig'd me to take Orders, could not divest me of Humane Nature and Humane Passions;..."

Get a bad rap

This refers to getting blamed for acts for which one is not guilty, possibly getting an erroneous conviction or sentence. It may also refer to any unjust condemnation. 'Rap,' in a legal connotation, may refer to arrests, detentions or sentencing, as in the case of a 'rap sheet.' 'Bad rap' started coming into use in early 1970s. The earliest available citation is from *Public Papers of the Presidents of the United States, "A Conversation with the President" Interview with Howard K. Smith of the American Broadcasting Network*, March 22, 1971:

> "Yes, as a matter of fact, I think President Johnson did **get a bad rap** from the press and for the wrong reasons—on his style, for example." (Richard Nixon)

Get a handle on something^

This expression means to find a way to understand something well enough to take control of it or use it effectively. Other sources put 'get a handle' at mid-to-late 1800s; however, a figurative use comes as early as 1809 in *Works of Fisher Ames* in Letters on page 515:

> "The chiefs of party, of course, cannot **get a handle** to turn him out; and their inducement to do it is always least, when the squad of the party that is secretly opposed to him is the most clearly convinced of his imbecility."

This obviously refers to being able to control the person in question. The first verifiable reference to metaphorically getting a handle *on something* actually doesn't come till 1967 in *The Logic of Decisions and Actions* by Nicholas Rescher, page 67:

> "...and the system B looks like a way to **get a handle on** this condition, without sacrificing V to A."

Get an eyeful

This idiom means to get a long steady look at something, especially when being surprised by it. It can also mean to see more of something than one wants to, and is used both in Great Britain and America. It came into usage in the early 20th century. The earliest citation available is from *Electric Railway Journal*, Daily Edition, Chicago, Tuesday October 9, 1912 in 'Conventionalities,' on page 2:

> "Come on around to space 200," said W. E. Keily, of the Electrical World, "and **get an eyeful** of a lightning display being arrested for disorderly conduct."

Get back on one's feet

This idiom comes from being able to stand up after sitting down. It means, figuratively, recovering from a period of illness or financial problems. It began to be used in this way in the early 20th century. The first verifiable citation is in *The Southern Pharmacutical Journal*, May, 1914, in 'Principle Success Qualities, Article III:"

> "When a man has lost his money and his friends, and is without a good character, how can he ever **get back on his feet** again?"

Get bad/good press

This old expression refers to getting criticized or praised in the media, particularly newspapers or magazines, but may also apply to television or radio. Also 'get **a** bad/good press'. The earliest known reference in print is from *The Rattle of the Theta Chi,* Norwich University, New York, May-June 1936 in 'An Audit of Fraternity Experience' by Dr. Henry M. Wriston:

> "Let's take some chances. Security is no ideal for a nation. And I don't like the fact that the fraternities, being under fire and gaining a **bad press**, as you have gained a **bad press** at Yale and Dartmouth and elsewhere, have taken a defensive line ..."

Get crackin'^

This humorous saying means 'get busy! Get going! Originally Scottish, it is widely used in the U.K., and has been popular in the U.S. since at least the mid-20th century, but in spite an online research source stating that a major dictionary places origin at 1936, and no usage noted before the late 19th century, it has been around since at least 1824, when it appeared in a delightful poetical book printed in Sterling titled *Tak Your Auld Cloak about Ye; To which are Added, Tom Bowling. Thou art gan awa.* Auld Saunders M'Craghan. Lady Onlie, on page 15:

> "I'd hurry them all off to **get crackin'** wi' thee."

The earliest American printing available is from a University of Mississippi publication, 1947, *The Comics*, by Coulton Waugh, on page 259:

> **"Get crackin,'** kid; sock that Japanazi in his yellow slats…"

Get down to the nitty-gritty^+

This is a figurative expression meaning to focus on the most important aspects of a situation; the basic facts. Folk etymology has alleged that this expression had its origins with the slave trade in 18th century. It was claimed in newspaper reports in the U.K. in the early 21st century that getting down to the bottom of something, (nitty gritty) came from the debris left in the bottom of ships after the slaves had been removed, and perhaps even referred to the slaves themselves. There is no evidence whatsoever, however, that this was the origin of this colloquialism. Nitty- gritty didn't even appear in print until the 1930s.

The earliest known citation was in the New York *Catalog of Copyright Entries, Part 3 - Musical Compositions*, 1937 that listed a song titled '*That Nitty Gritty Dance*' which was copyrighted by Arthur Harrington Gibbs. "Down to the nitty-gritty" isn't found until 1956 when Alice Childress used it in her novel, *Like One of the Family*:

> "You'll find nobody comes **down to the nitty-gritty** when it calls for namin' things for what they are."

Get in on the action / Get into the act+

This is a colloquial expression meaning to begin to take part in an activity already in progress in order to gain an advantage from it. "Get in on the action," per se, began appearing in print in the mid-1970s. A good early example appeared in *The Ottawa Jewish Bulletin and Review*, January, 1975, on page 3, in "Teams Invited to Join J.C.Y."

> "To **get in on the action**, come to any meeting of the group held each and every Sunday afternoon at the Jewish Centre, 2:00 PM."

According to a popular online English forum, "get into the act" dates to the mid-1900s. This appears accurate, as *The Instructor*, published by the Mormon "Deseret Sunday School Union", in the April, 1963 issue had the following citation in an article by that name by Hazel West Lewis on page 103, in which it was already called "a saying":

> "More likely he goes to participate, or as the saying goes, 'he wants to **get into the act**.'"

Get into high gear

Getting or moving into high gear means to speed up one's actions or efforts to maximum ability. Much like 'get crackin,' it is a way to say 'get the move on!' or announce that something is going great. It comes from the gears of an automobile in which 'high gear' represents the fastest speed. It has been used in a literal since the early days of automobiles, particularly in regard to racing, as seen in *The Automobile*, published in New York and Chicago, April 9, 1908, in the article 'Rapid Growth of Automobiling in the South:'

"The course is about a mile long, and the start is made from what is practically a standstill, only 100 feet being allowed for the driver to **get into high-gear** before crossing the line."

Figurative use came just a few years later. This early example is from *The Metal Worker, Plummer and Steam Fitter*, September 26, 1919, in 'News of the Trade Associates:'

"We have had a long vacation and now it is time to **get into high gear** and boost the association some more. At this meeting one of the attorneys of the Fidelity Trust Co. will speak to us on the subject of 'Wills'."

Get more than one bargained for+

This is an idiomatic expression for receiving a different outcome than a person expected, particularly more unfavorable or difficult to deal with. The earliest known citation of a form of it is found on page 227 in *Stories of the Sea* by Frederick Marryat in 1835:

"Well, we hoisted our jib, drew aft our foresheet, and were soon clear of the harbor; but we found that there was a devil of a sea running, and **more wind than we bargained for**."

Get nowhere fast^

This means to work at something but make little or no progress in completing the task. A major slang dictionary placed origin at 1920s+. Getting nowhere was cited as early as 1899 in *The American Journal of Dental Science*, edited by FJS Georges, MD. DDS and Richard Grady, MD, DDS, Vol. XXXII, printed in both Baltimore and London, on page 430:

"He floundered about tor quite a time saying nothing and **getting nowhere**."

Nineteen years later the full expression was in *Go, Get 'em!: The True Adventures of an American Aviator of the Lafayette*, by William A, Wellman, 1918:

"...although the daily task was one highly conducive to the use of profanity, for it seemed as though I were **getting nowhere fast**, three weeks after my maiden trip I actually heard my teacher say the heart-gladdening words..."

Get one's ears lowered+

This is an American idiomatic expression meaning "get a haircut" made popular in the 1940s and 1950s. The earliest available citation is found in *The Current Sauce* published by Louisiana State Normal College, Natchitoches, Louisiana, Monday, January 25, 1942, in "Freshman Class Makes Study of Slang Words on Campus" by Annette Alderman and Carolyn Russell on page 2:

> "**He got his ears lowered**."

It derived from the fact that boys at the time were thought to be "shaggy" when their hair grew down below the tops of their ears. Getting a haircut would make their ears appear lower on their heads.

Get one's foot in the door

This idiomatic expression means to complete the initial step in a process. It comes from the outdated practice of sales persons sticking their foot in a door to gain admittance to someone's home. Later, getting one's foot in the door meant that one had obtained admittance in a logical manner. The uncouth practice of literally putting a foot in a door to prevent it from being closed was cited in *The Law Times Reports* (London), June 1, 1867, in the case of Weltzar V Zachariah:

> "Merely putting your **foot in the door**, or putting a pair of shears in to prevent its being closed, will not constitute a 'possession' in that sense — i.e., in the sense of a peaceable possession."

Foot in the door was first used metaphorically by the great J. M. Barrie, author of Peter Pan, in *Margaret Ogilvy*, page 156, 1896:

> "He is not opaque of set purpose, often it is against his will—it is certainly against mine, I try to keep my shutters open and my **foot in the door** but they will bang to."

The earliest known reference to getting one's foot in the door, in the modern application is in *Supreme Court Appellate Division – Fourth Department*, New York, 1934. Page 185:

> "**The Court**: It seems to me your examination opened the door, I think you got your **foot in the door** and I think the record shows you have not taken it out."

Get one's hands dirty

Figuratively, this expression can have a double meaning. First, it can refer to doing manual labor; secondly, it also may refer to becoming involved in dishonest dealings. Numerous literal references are made prior to this, throughout the 19th century; however, an early figurative reference occurs in October 25, 1921 in the publication, *Power,* in 'Engineering or Engineman by E. L. Jessup:'

> "…he is a man who has brains, uses them and knows how to **get his hands dirty**."

Obviously this is a reference to doing whatever work is necessary to get the job done. In *Kiplinger's Personal Finance*, June, 1974, page 12, we find an early example of the other meaning just coming into play, in 'Ways They Cheat You When Servicing Your Car:'

> "But there are certain ploys that unscrupulous operators can get away with more easily than others— and the cost to you can be pretty substantial. ... They can cheat you without **getting their hands dirty** by 'kiting' your credit card invoice."

Get outta (or **out of**) **town!+**

This is figurative expression of disbelief used to mean, "That is unbelievable!", "That is ridiculous!" or "You've got to be kidding!" Origin is difficult to pin down, but the expression in this connotation became popular among young people in America in the 1980s. A good example is found in the 1985 Minnechaug Regional High School yearbook, *The Falcon*, Wilbraham, Massachusetts, in expressions used by the soccer team:

> "**Get outta town**, you kill me!"

Get some air (See: **Need some air**)

Get something for a song (See: **For a song**)

Get something straight^+

This is an idiom for making certain that there is a clear understanding of what is meant by something someone has said or written. According to a popular online idiom site, it dates to approximately 1920. It was actually in use at least five years earlier. American playwright Kenneth Sawyer Goodman used it in his one act comedy play, *Dancing Dolls*, 1915:

> "**BUFFO**. Wait a minute! Let me **get this straight**."

Get the monkey off one's back+

This is an old colloquial expression for removing or solving a problem or situation that has been difficult or has made someone unhappy. It is most often used of addictions.

In John Bunyan's classic, *Pilgrim's Progress* (1678), in the migration from Turmoil to the City of Light, there is an analogy of everyone having burdens clutching to their backs with "claw-like arms", which is a precursor of this saying.

Early on in the 1800s, the earliest citations appeared in books about piggy-backing monkeys. The first figurative reference to someone having a monkey on his back, however, was in *The Parterre of Poetry and Historical Romance: With Essays, Sketches and Anecdotes,* Volume Five, by Effingham Wilson, Junior, published in London in 1836, page 218, under the heading "The Philosophy of Fairs":

> "The abridged retires from society with a ***monkey on his back,*** and bequeathing a cordial benediction to the author of this diabolical "Essay on Man."

Get the picture

Getting the picture refers to understanding the situation or comprehending the meaning of something. It's been used figuratively since the 1930s. The earliest citation known, though not the origin, is from *The Rotartian*, August, 1937, in an article titled 'There's Always a New Crowd' by George T. Eager, on page 20:

"Some of his friends had heard my remark and he had been laughed at by the crowd. Do you **get the picture**?"

Get the show on the road^

This universal English idiom means to start an undertaking or enterprise. In spite of a major dictionary of phrases stating the origin at 'perhaps as early as c. 1910,' and an online reference dictionary starting '1949s+,' this was used in 1889 in *Pioneers of Beverly: Series of Sketches* by Canadian author, John A. Cornell, in which it was called 'an expression of the day,' on page 354:

"One Mr. Tory Gregg who has appeared many times at Rockton Show seems to have that special quality, creating good audience participation and to use an expression of the day, '**get the show on the road** and keep it running.'"

Get (or **take) the upper hand**

This idiom refers to gaining a dominate position. Some have suggested that this originated in baseball on playgrounds where team captains grab the bat and potential team members each place hand over hand until the top of the bat is reached, thus selecting who will be on each team. This comes much too late to be the origin. At least as far back as the 19th century, when holding hands the dominant partner took the 'upper hand,' symbolizing the position in the relationship. *History of England*, 1848, by Thomas Macaulay says this:

"Then several meetings were spent in settling how many carriages, how many horses, how many lacqueys, how many pages, each minister should be titled to bring to Ryswick; whether the serving men should carry canes; whether they should wear swords; whether they should have pistols in their holsters; who should **take the upper hand** in the public walks, and whose carriage should break the way in the streets."

But that is not the earliest citation, so still not its origin, though it well may give us insight into its intent. The earliest known citation is from *An Open Letter to the Christian Nobility of the German Nation Concerning the Reform of the Christian Estate*, 1520 by Martin Luther and Charles Michael Jacobs, pp 57, 58:

"Oh, the pity, that kings and princes have so little reverence for Christ, and His honor concerns them so little that they allow such heinous abominations to gain **the upper hand**, and look on, while at Rome they think of nothing but to continue in their madness and increase the abounding misery, until no hope is left on earth except in the temporal authorities."

Other 16th century citations were similar in meaning, with no hint as to why it was used that way.

Get with the program

This is used to mean 'Keep up with the current trends of thinking, priorities, etc. Your thinking or behavior is out of date.' It can also mean to work productively toward a shared objective. The earliest citation known in print is from *Ebony Magazine*, October, 1965, in a letter to the editor from James Lopez on page 11:

> "It's people like Simeon Booker that give conservatives a bad name by implying that they are against civil rights, by lumping them with such radical organizations as the Ku Klux Klan, American Nazis, etc. I protest this, and the sooner you people **get with the program** and realize this, the sooner we can get together to work out things."

ghost of a chance, A

This idiom means even the slightest hope of success, and is usually preceded by a negative. It came into common usage in the first half of the 19th century. The earliest known reference in print is from *The Mirror of Literature, Amusement and Instruction,* July 19, 1828, on page 45, in 'The Sketch-Book:'

> "From this fatal moment the sailors were kept constantly at the pumps, although so instantaneous was the rush of water into the hold, that they did little or no good; there seemed, in fact, not the **ghost of a chance** left us; even the mate had ceased whistling, and the captain's oaths began to assume thee nature of a compromise between penitence and hardihood."

Give a man a fish and you'll feed him for a day; teach a man how to fish and you'll feed him for a lifetime

This old proverb has at times been attributed to 'a Native American saying,' 12th century Rabbi Moshe ben Maimon, and even the *Bible*! But it is most often attributed to ancient Chinese philosopher, Lao Tse (circa 599 CE). No verifiable evidence has been found for any of this. The earliest citation in print of a form of it in English, however, and most like the true origin, is from the 1885 novel, *Mrs. Dymond*, by British author Anne Isabella Thackeray Ritchie (the daughter of William Makepiece Thackery):

> "'I don't suppose even Caron could tell you the difference between material and spiritual,' said Max, shrugging his shoulders. 'He certainly doesn't practise his precepts, but I suppose *the Patron* meant that **if you give a man**

> **a fish he is hungry again in an hour. If you teach him to catch a fish you do him a good turn**. But these very elementary principles are apt to clash with the leisure of the cultivated classes. Will Mr. Bagginal now produce his ticket—the result of favour and the unjust sub-division of spiritual environments?' said Du Parc, with a smile."

Give away the farm

Originally this expression referred to revealing strategic secrets in the U.S. military, and there seems to be no evidence that it was in use before the second half of the 20th century. The earliest available reference in print is in the book, *United States Army in Vietnam 1965-1973* by Jeffery J. Clark, published by the Center of Military History in Washington, DC in 1988, page 499:

> "Lt. Gen. Ralph E. Haines, the U.S. Army component commander in the Pacific (1968-70), called Vietnamization 'a race against time,' adding that, 'although each passing day works in our favor,' he feared 'that we might **give away the farm** precipitiously…'"

In addition to its original meaning, it is used to refer to giving too much of a product or service for the price.

Give instruction to a wise man, and he will yet be wiser

Sometimes used as 'give wisdom,' this proverb actually comes from the biblical book of *Proverbs*, attributed to King Solomon, often hailed as 'the wisest man who ever lived'. It is found in the 9th chapter and the first part of the 9th verse and is word for word in the *King James Version* of 1611. The entire verse reads:

> **"Give instruction to a wise man, and he will be yet wiser**: teach a just man, and he will increase in learning."

Give it to me straight

This expression means that the speaker wants another person to stop 'hedging' and be open, honest and direct with his or her statements. The earliest known verifiable citation is from a New York detective story magazine called *Secret Service, Old and Young King Brady Detectives*, June 30, 1899, in 'The Opium King,' chapter 5, page 9:

> *"Up town to Madame La Vine's gambling house," replied Harry. "Ever been there ?"*
> *"No," said Ben, turning red. –*

"It won't do," said Young King Brady quietly.
""What won't do?"
"You must **give it to me straight**.*"*

Give it up for^

This expression, meaning give applause for, or don't hold anything back, was coined in the late 20th century to show appreciation for celebrities and entertainers, and is still commonly used by media and live shows. Again, a major dictionary placed origin too late, at 1990. The earliest known usage in this connotation was on the live album, *Waiting for Columbus,* recorded at London's Rainbow Theater in August, 1977 by Little Feat, and released by Warner Brothers in 1978. The emcee starts out by saying to the audience:

"**Give it up for** Little Feat!"

The phrase was later popularized by Arsenio Hall, who used it as a catch phrase on his television show which began on CBS in January, 1989. Reportedly, he had used it before, as early as 1980, not long after the Little Feat album release.

Give lip service (See: **Pay lip service**)

Give me five! / High five

Originally this was "gimme five!" and originated in the 1950s. It meant to shake hands then, but now it would be followed by a 'high five' hands slapped together. The high five most likely was started by Dusty Baker and Glenn Burke of the Los Angeles Dodgers, who first used the words accompanied with the hand action on 2 October 1977. Later it was picked up by other professional athletes, then it caught on with the general public, according to Jon Mooallem in the ESPN article, *The History and the Mystery of the High Five* which showed up online July 39, 2011.

The earliest usage of 'gimme five' in print is found in *Simply Heavenly* a play with music by Langston Hughes, with earliest copyright date in 1953, first presented by Stella Hall at 85th Street Playhouse in New York on May 32, 1957 and published in current form in 1959:

"**Gimme five**, Miss Mamie, **gimme five**! (They shake hands.)"

Give someone a black eye

The literal meaning is clear, but figuratively, it means to harm someone's reputation or character. The earliest known reference in print of giving someone a black eye, metaphorically, is in *The Epoch*, a weekly New York publication, June 21, 1889, on the 3rd page:

> "Massachusetts **gave them a black eye** and now Pennsylvania knocks them into a cocked hat!"

Give someone a heads up

This idiom means to give someone new information, making the person or persons aware of a situation or impending action. The expression has been used in a lot of ways over the past 100 years, including a heads up game, a heads up attitude, a heads up industry, a heads up sport, a heads up battle, etc. Heads up seemed to represent a positive in any area. But there appears to be no evidence of its present usage of 'giving a heads up' until the late 20th century. In *Washington's War on Nicaragua* by Holly Sklar, 1988, page 333 we find:

> "[Jensen] is giving **a heads up** to the N.S.C. He would like us to watch over it. Call Kellner, find out what is up…"

Give someone a piece of one's mind

This metaphor means to tell someone angrily, in no uncertain terms, the way you feel about something he or she has done or something about the person that you believe is very wrong. The basic idea has been around since at least 1667, when British playwright John Dryden used the earliest form of it in his tragic comedy *The Maiden Queen*, Act II, Scene iii:

> "***Cel.*** By fate she shan'not love me: I have told her **a piece of my mind** already."

Telling someone a piece of one's mind continued to be the standard phrase until 1836, when writers changed to 'giving a piece of one's mind.' One of these first examples came in *Metropolitan Magazine*, May, 1836 in the syndicated novel, 'Snarlleyyow, or the Dog Fiend' by Capt. Marryat, Chapter XII:

> "I'll **give you a piece of my mind**, old Turk…"

Give someone the boot

The boot here has a reference to kicking. It means to figuratively 'kick' someone out of a job, position, club, group or organization. Prior to its current connotation, the phrase was often used for kicking someone, either literally or figuratively. Since at least 1920 when Lindley Grant Long used it in *Farmer Hiram on the World's War* it has been used hyperbolically for kicking on page 171:

> "They 'lowed he'd cam down, and be half way a man;
> But hinted, if not, they wud give him the can.
> It didn't result ez they reckoned it shud;
> And so they decided 'twuz time to make good.
> They **give him the boot** and sent him sky-high,
> And landed him up where the weather wuz dry."

Then on April 1, 1931, *Princeton Alumni Weekly* printed a statement in Refutation by Mr. Casement that showed that as a figure of speech the meaning of the phrase was expanding:

> "When Princeton men shall be satisfied merely 'to instill content into catch-words and ideas into phrases,' then life will brutally give **them the boot**."

Give someone the slip

From the early 14th century, slip was used to mean 'to escape, to move softly and swiftly.' The expression to give someone the slip has been used in English since at least the late 1600s. The earliest known printed reference is in Roger L. Estrange's translation of *Aesop's Fables*, in 'A Daw with a String at's Foot,' 1692, page 152:

> "A Country Fellow took a Daw and ty'd a String to his Leg, and so gave him to a Little Boy to Play withal. The Daw did not much like his Companion, and upon the First Opportunity **gave him the Slip**, and away into the Woods again, where he was Shackled and Starv'd. When he came to Die, he Reflected upon the Folly of Exposing his Life in the Woods, rather than Live in an Easy Servitude among Men."

Give something a go

This means to attempt to do something. The first known use in print has it a bit different, as 'a go-by.' It is found in *Decisions of the Court Sessions*, 1781-

1822, in the session from June 9, 1803. It was published by David Hume in Edinburgh, Scotland in 1839:

> "Armstrong, because writing would put off time, and interfere with the drinking; Robson, because he meant to **give it a go**-by, and did not wish to be a witness to any drunken bargain."

The earliest verifiable printed reference to 'give it a go' is from *Boy's Life*, November, 1948 in Tropical Snow Climb by James W. English on page 47:

> "'What do you say? Go on despite the weather, or turn back?'
> Mike started up the trail. 'Let's **give it a go**,' he said."

Glass is either half full or half empty depending on your view

Originally a rhetorical question: "Is the glass half empty or half full?" this is an illustration commonly used to illustrate the difference between pessimism and optimism. It is sometimes used by motivational speakers to encourage optimism. Comparisons of half empty, half full go back as far as 1664, when the following appeared in *A Copious Dictionary in Three Parts* by Francis Gouldman, printed in London:

> **"Half empty**, **half full**, as the moon in the first quarter..."

Then in *The Honest Thieves, A Farce in Two Acts*, by T. Knight, first preformed at the Theater-Royale in London on 9 May 1797, Act II Scene iv, we have a clearer view of the comparison being unveiled:

> "Man. Then take the bottles with thee.
> Tea. [Takes the bottles.] One is **half full**, and t'other **half empty**."

It wasn't until the 1960s that the philosophical question arose. It showed up in a Peace Corp Ad on page 8 of *Boys' Life Magazine* on January 5, 1968 on a picture of a glass:

> **"Is the glass half empty or half full**? If you think its half empty,
> maybe the Peace Corps is not for you.
> If you think it's half full,
> you've got the first thing we look for in Peace Corps people
> Optimism.
> If you want to know more about what it takes
> to pass muster in the Peace Corps, write U.S."

Gloves are off

This is used to mean that two persons are factions of people have begun to argue or fight in a more serious manner. It comes from the fact that if boxers remove their gloves during a fight they will inflict more serious injuries. The earliest available citation is in *Once a Week* by Enheas Sweetland Dallas under the heading 'The Casual Observer,' November 20, 1875:

> "You see, it was like this: Crawling along in Piccadilly, on one of the most sultry August days, we met Dick Reece, and languidly complained of our state, which was one of constantly melting away, our **gloves were off**, and they would not go on again; big drops bedewed our brow; and there was a feeling existent that nature had turned us into a peripatetic machine for the purpose of distilling all the fluids we could possibly imbibe;…"

Go ape

This hyperbolic expression means to become violently emotional or extremely enthusiastic about something (go ape over). It is, of course, derived from the high strung antics of primates. A major dictionary of idioms states 'second half of the 1900s' as era of origin. Ape, as used to mean 'imitate' goes back at least to the 1630s, and 'playing ape,' even further. The actual expression, 'go ape,' was in use by January 1, 1942 when John Button, as Franklin W. Dixon published the Hardy Boys mystery, *The Clue of the Broken Blade*:

> "She's very beautiful, but we're not going to **go ape** over her."

Early in 1959, Neil Sedaka released a song on RCA titled ***I Go Ape***, with only minor success in the U.S., but reaching number nine in the U.K.

Gobbledygook+

This nonsensical expression has reference to language that is meaningless or is made unintelligible by excessive use of abstruse technical terms. According to *Merriam Webster*, the first known use was in 1944. U.S. Congressman Murray Maverick of Texas disliked drawn out dialogue and rebelled against the pompous way in which information was being presented in Washington, coining this word to describe it, "based on the meaningless 'gobbling' noise of turkeys when made by human gook."

Go in, come in or **move in for the kill**

This means to prepare to ruthlessly and completely defeat someone in an argument or competition when they are already in a weak condition. The earliest known reference in print is from *The Coursing Calendar for the Autumn Season 1868, Containing Results of All the Public Courses Run in Great Britain and Ireland*, Edited by 'Stonehenge,' published in London, 1869, on page 243:

> "Dunkeld made a miserable exhibition of Folly, who, however, **came in for the kill**, leaving Dunkeld winner by at least a score of points."

Going rogue

Though this term may be used as a euphemism, in the normal sense, this idiom means coming away from the rest of the people or animals in an expected group and doing things totally differently with no warning. It first started appearing in print in 1997. An early citation is found in *Political Science Fiction,* edited by Donald M. Hassler and Clyde Wilcox, in 'Governing the Alien Nation,' on page 168:

> "These elephant-like creatures have a herd mentality, and need constant social interaction to prevent them from **going 'rogue**.'"

In 2009, Republican Vice Presidential candidate, Sarah Palin, popularized the term as the title of her best-selling autobiographical book.

Going the extra mile

This idea came from the words of Jesus in his famed 'Sermon on the Mount, in *Matthew 5:41*. Jesus is quoted as saying:

> "Whoever forces you to **go one mile, go with him two**." *(NASB)*

Here he was referring to the Roman practice of 'impressment,' which allowed a Roman soldier to require a Jewish citizen to carry his backpack, weighing upwards of 100 pounds, for one Roman mile, consisting of 1,000 paces. The expression has been used as the title for everything from books to films, songs and music albums.

Good cop, bad cop

This refers to a physiological tactic used in negotiations and interrogations of suspects. The two officers may either alternately of jointly conduct an interview.

The term is also used figuratively to apply to two people taking opposite views in dealing with others about any matter to be decided. It came into use in the last quarter of the 20th century. The earliest citation in print is from *The Whole World is Watching, Mass Media in the Making*, by Todd Gitlin, 1980, page 224:

> "**Good cop, bad cop**: the roles were divided up all fall, sometimes sharing speechwriters, as the White House consistently refused to disavow Agnew. Thanks to Jeb Magruder's post-Watergate memoir, we know something of the secret tactics."

Good egg^

This saying refers to a person who is pleasant, agreeable and trustworthy. A major dictionary places its origin at 1915-1920. Actually, it was used in this respect over half a century earlier. In *Supplements to the Connecticut Couramt for the year 1855,* printed that year in Hartford by Thomas M. Day, on page 24 we find that it was on a gravestone even then:

> "In a flourishing city on the line of the New Jersey Railroad, a grave-yard, in which stood a tombstone on which was inscribed by weeping friends the following touching and simple, yet exquisitely poetic epitaph: — '**He was a good egg**'."

The expression did not become popularized, however, until the 1930s. In the May 13, 1932 issue of *The Michigan Alumnus*, in 'Confessions of a Pseudo-Quadrangler,' Arthur G. Brown wrote:

> "I knew he would slip me the credit, for he was a '**good egg**'."

Here it is in quotes. After that date, the term began appearing in numerous publications.

Goodness gracious sakes alive (See: **Sakes alive!**)+

Good things come in small packages

This proverb is used to illustrate the fact that the size is not what matters; it's the quality. It is sometimes said of people of small stature. This has been around since at least February, 1879, when *Demorest's Monthly Magazine* in New York printed a story titled 'A Painful Lift' by 'Madge,' in which the following appeared on page 63:

> "'You, darling,' said her lover, as he clasped her to his breast, 'little women are and have always been my admiration; I should not have loved you should you have been one inch taller; do I not know that the choicest goods **come in small packages**?'"

The exact saying then was featured in *Wines and Vines of California* by Frona Eunice Wait in 1889, on page 214:

> "A quiet unpretentious place is that of Mr. Joseph Fetz, on the corner of Third and Mission Streets, but on the assumption that **good things come in small packages**, it will be well worth while to examine and sample the old stock..."

The Scottish version of this is '**Guid gear gangs aye i' sma' parcels'** which predated the English rendering. In *Peasant Life: Sketches of the Villagers and Field Laborers in Glenaldie* by Malcolm McLennan, 1872, page 230 we find:

> "...she thought; and she thought, moreover, that wisdom did not go by bulk of body. "Ye may ca' me little, gif ye plaise, Sally; but am nae witless. **Guid gear gangs aye i' sma' parcels**."

Good things come to those who wait (See: **All things come to he who waits**, original volume

good time was had by all, A^

This is a very old expression meaning that at a particular social gathering, the guests all were pleased and entertained. A major phrase origin dictionary stated that it was coined by immortal actress Bette Davis in 1908 to 1909, but credited it to poet Stevie Smith who acquired it as the title from a parish magazine. Ms. Davis undoubtedly popularized it; however, this was in numerous publications in the latter years of the 19th century. The earliest known printed reference is in *A Souvenir of the Anchor Line Agents Excursion on the Steamer California*, August 14, 1872:

> "After dinner several toasts were drank and responded to in happy style, and a general **good time was had by all** on board. There were about 400 persons on the excursion, many of whom were ladies."

In the 1890's the saying became popular. It is impossible to pin down who actually coined this phrase.

Good to go

This saying means completely prepared and ready to proceed to whatever is next. A major etymology dictionary places its origin at 1989. This time frame is logical. It was popularized during the first Persian Gulf War in 1990, and a good example of it is in the U.S. Marine Corp publication *Humanitarian Operations in Northern Iraq*, 1991, by Ronald J. Brown, in The Mission of MSSG-24 on page 44, where it was in quotes, suggesting recent introduction:

> "Planning was hampered by incomplete intelligence, constantly changing information, and lack of specific instructions. Despite these problems, MSSG-24 completed many alternative plans and was **'good to go'** when the Charleston closed Iskenderun Harbor."

Go out in a blaze of glory

This expression is referring to making a choice to fight back against a foe which is much better prepared and very likely to win, usually because of strong convictions against that foe. "A blaze of Glory' has been around in English since at least 1735, when it was cited in the play, *The Fatal Secret*, Act IV, Scene i, page 37

> ***"Fcrd***. 'This Darkness suits, and pictures **out** your Fortune.' From what a **Blaze of Glory**, where your fate Inshrin'd a wonder ..."

Then in December, 1853, in *The Southern Literary Messenger*, in 'The Duke of Wellington' by Asher Clarkson, we find it coupled with 'go out:'

> "...and from the first deeds of each rose that long **blaze of glory**, destined to **go out** only in the cold damps of the grave."

The exact phrase came out in 1877, in *The Proceedings of the Annual Conclave of the Great Commandery Knights Templar of the State of Mississippi* Held at Natchez, Thursday and Friday, May 10th and 11th, on page 74:

> "Well, this bubble must burst some time, and it might as well **go out in a blaze of glory** at Chicago as anywhere else."

Got 'em or **gotem**

This is a 21st century interjection when someone has succeeded in pranking someone else. It sometimes appears on Twitter with a hashtag (#). It has become so popular among the younger generations that there are even a 'Gotem' board game, toys and other paraphernalia. Though the phrase could be found for hundreds of years, this expression was used in this sense as early as 1992 with things like the following from the novel *Steelwork* by Gilbert Sorentino, page 5:

> "Yeah. We sure **got em**, Artie! We **got em**, Red, we **got em** all right. Yeah, Red said. We **got em**. We **got em** good!"

Go the distance+

This figurative expression means to persist with some activity or goal until it is completed. It derived from sports, particularly in running races and boxing, in which it means completion of a match without being knocked out. In baseball it means pitch and entire game. It was already in use in running as early as circa 1912 when it was used three times by American-Irish sports official, James Edward Sullivan (1862-1914) in *How to Become an Athlete*, which was published posthumously in 1916; the first being on page 23:

"To succeed as a quarter-mile runner to-day, a man not only needs to be a sprinter, but he must be as game as a pebble, and well able to **go the distance**, and in training for this event his preliminary work must be diversified."

Go through channels^+

This is a common metaphor which alludes to a hierarchy in which decisions are made by offices which tend to important matters. It means going through the proper procedures to insure that things are handled right. According to an online idiom site, the phrase has been used since the early 1900s. Another popular dictionary states that it has been used as a conduit since the mid-1900s. Strangely, this phrase was used figuratively as early as 1882 in *Inez, A Drama in Three Acts* by American playwright Irene Ackerman, Act II, Scene iv, where the script is talking of keeping people safe and promoting great ideals:

> "Who can I trust? Oh! happy thought! My country, I trust it all to you!—In your bonds it will all be safe from tire and from thieves. In your bonds it will yearly bear good fruit. There I will plant this golden tree, and its rich fruit **shall go through channels** safe and sure."

Go to bat for

When someone goes to bat for someone or something, he or she takes a firm stand in defense of that person or cause. It comes from baseball in which players go to bat for their teams in order to help win the game. A major idiom dictionary places the phrase's origin at 'early 1900s'. In a literal way, it was use as early as July, 1887 in print in *Puck's Library* on page 20 in 'Base-ball Mechanism-Two Prophecies:'

> "It made me feel sad and lonely to see the club that had the last innings **go to the bat for** the final time without saying confidently: 'We have got to make 22 to tie, and 23 to win.'"

The earliest figurative use available is from *The Mixer and Server*, official journal of hotel and restaurant employees, in the January 15, 1919 issue, page 40, in an article titled 'Why Not Dissolve Congress:'

> "Speed the day when the American Legion and the American Federation of Labor **go to bat for** the benefit of the people."

Go to the mat

This idiom, derived from wrestling, refers to a person supporting a person or cause in unyielding way regardless of the struggles which may be involves. A major dictionary of idioms places figurative use at circa 1900. The earliest use in this manner available is actually from *The Rotarian*, August, 1913 under the heading **A Quarrel with Galveston** "in which San Diego attempts to **go to the mat** with Galveston…"

Gracious sakes alive (See: **Sakes alive!**)+

Grandfathered in

This term is now applied to any provisions which are covered under a 'grandfather clause' in a contact or constitution which exempts an activity or item from new regulations that would otherwise prevent activity or use of that item or license. 'Grandfathered' became a regular part of our American jargon after the American Civil War. The government made a literacy requirement for voting. In the early 1890s, the 'Grandfather Clause' was enacted to the law to allow poor Southern Whites to vote if their grandfathers could vote. Because of the 15th Amendment, blacks could not be refused the right to vote because of race. However, former slaves had to pay poll taxes and pass literacy tests in order to vote, because their grandfathers did not have a right to vote.

In the latter part of the 20th century, the term 'grandfathered in' began to be used freely for other provisions. In *America, Inc. Who Owns and Operated the United States* by Morton Mintz and Jerry Cohen, 1971, In Chapter 6, The Congress, there is a good example of our modern conception of this phrase on page 211:

> "The bill was inadequate, because it '**grandfathered in**' most of the major one-bank holding company acquisitions that already had occurred."

Green-eyed monster

Green as a color is often associated with both sickness and jealousy. Shakespeare is likely most responsible for this. He mentions 'green-eyed jealousy' in *The Merchant of Venice*, 1596. Then in 1604, in *Othello* he coined the phrase, 'green-eyed monster:'

> "**Iago**:
> O, beware, my lord, of jealousy;
> It is the **green-eyed monster** which doth mock
> The meat it feeds on; that cuckold lives in bliss
> Who, certain of his fate, loves not his wronger;
> But, O, what damned minutes tells he o'er
> Who dotes, yet doubts, suspects, yet strongly loves!"

Greetings and salutations+

This is an idiom formed by combining two fairly interchangeable words of greeting. Known as a 'pleasantry,' It actually means something like 'greetings and good wishes,' and is used when meeting someone on friendly terms. It was popularized as a saying in the 1988 comedy movie *Heathers* which starred Winona Ryder and Christian Slater, in which it is used by Slater's character, Jason Dean. But the term goes back to at least the early 20th century. A book titled *The Art of Translation with Special Reference to English Dramas of Gerhart Hautpmann and Hermann Sudermann* by Karl Schotz published in 1918 has it as the title of one of the sections in Setting of the Drama.

Grey nomad[3]

This Aussie expression was coined by documentary filmmakers Catherine Marciniak and Steve Westh for the 1997 documentary *Grey Nomads* screened on the Australian public broadcaster ABC at 8:30pm on September 23rd that year. It refers to a retired person, 55 or older, who travels extensively within his or her own country, particularly in a caravan or motor home. Grey, of course, is taken from the natural hair color when it fades with age.

Grinning from ear to ear

This hyperbolic expression is used to describe a very wide, beaming smile. It was likely coined by poet Edward Thompson in *Trinculo's Trip to the Jubilee,* published in London in 1769:

> "Some on the gay Rotundo star'd,
> Compos'd of wood and paper;
> **Grinning from ear to ear**, declar'd,
> They long'd to cut a'caper."

Grow a pair

This vulgar hyperbolic metaphor is inferring that the person being addressed, presumably a male, has no manly courage and needs to develop some in order to survive. "A pair" refers to testicles. This saying has become popular on television during the past few years in the absence of once-stringent censorship, as have been many other crude expressions. In 2006 the term began appearing in print. One example is from *The G.A.P.P., Great American Pity Party and Social Musings* by Lee Cain, on page 19:

> "Look, **grow a pair** and the next time someone tells your wife to do certain things to him then do like Woody Harrelson...ask him how much he's paying."

Growing by leaps and bounds

This refers to something which becomes larger very quickly. It comes from running, in which a sprinter gains speed by taking leaps and bounding over the course. Shakespeare first paired the words 'leaps and bounds' in *Venus and Adonis* in 1593:

> "Imperiously he **leaps**, he neighs, he **bounds**,
> And now his woven girths he breaks asunder;
> The bearing earth with his hard hoof he wounds,
> Whose hollow womb resounds like heaven's thunder:"

In *Pindarick Poem on the Happy Coronation of His Most Sacred Majesty, James II and His Illustrious Consort, Queen Mary* by Mrs. Behn, 1685, we find:

> "Proud of his Glorious load, he **leaps, and bounds"**

It is not until after the turn of the 18th century, however, that 'by leaps and bounds' appears in John Drydon's *The Annual Miscellany for the Year of 1694*, published in 1708, in Boileau's 'Art of Peotry,' Cant III:

> "And boldly take the Trumpet in their hand;
> Their fustian Muse each Accident confounds;
> Nor can me fly, but rife **by leaps and bounds**,
> 'Till their small stock of Learning quickly spent,
> Their Poem dies for want of Nourishment."

But it was almost another 200 years before 'growing by leaps and bounds' came into use. The earliest citation known is from *The Outlook, A Family Paper,* 13 April, 1895, in 'Bimetallism in City and County:'

> "In America they are **growing by leaps and bounds**. The consequence is that the value of most property, except during the last two years, has more than held its own. Outside such cities, on the other hand, population is increasing but slowly…"

Grubby little hands / paws / mitts+

Usually used nowadays in the hateful idiomatic statement, "Keep your grubby little hands (paws or mitts) to yourself," it is a warning for someone to stay away, not touch, or become involved with, someone or something. It has most often been used by children or youth who are at odds with their peers. It implies that the other person is inferior, contemptible and unclean. It seems to allude to an infestation with grubs, also known as grub worms, a most vexsome lawn pest in the United States, which live under the soil, and can remain undetected until significant damage is done. But "Grubby little" has been used contemptuously since at least the early 20th century, and not just in the U.S. It appears in *Songs of*

London: A Melody Grave and Gay by Herbert Furst, 1908, in the poem 'A Dance of the Muses in Princes Road, Notting Hill' on page 24:

> "Nine little girls, **grubby little** girls,
> In dirty frocks; tattered frocks;"

In 1921, it was used with 'hand' in the poem 'Johnnie' credited to 'B.A.A.' published in *Melodies and Mountaineers* by Isabel McMeekin. But here it is in an entirely different connotation, regarding a delightful small child:

> "And a soft way of patting your cheek with his **grubby little hand,**"

Current usage came in the mid-20th century. A good early example is found in the University of Toronto publication, *The Varsity*, Friday October 9, 1959, in a quote in 'Big Ben Tolls Knell as Western Face Hell' on page 11, column 2:

> "Just for once, why don't you **keep your grubby little pinkies** out of everything and let things happen as they may."

Guardian Angel

In the literal interpretation of this term, it is applied to a heavenly messenger thought to guard a person, thereby keeping him or her from harm. In the Judeo/ Christian scriptures a reference is in *Exodus 32:4* where God says to Moses:

> "My **angel** shall go before thee." *(KJV)*

Another is in *Psalm 91:11*:

> "For he will command his **angels** concerning you to **guard** you in all your ways;" *(NIV)*

The *New Testament* concept of guardian angels comes from the Parable of the Wandering Sheep in *Matthew 18:10,* where Jesus said:

> "See that you do not despise one of these little ones. For I tell you that **their angels in heaven** always see the face of my Father in heaven…" *(NIV)*

The word translated 'angel' in the *Bible* actually means 'messenger.' The term has also come to be used, figuratively, of individual human being who watches over someone in a special way. The earliest known reference to this use is in *The London Magazine and Monthly Chronologer*, September, 1742:

> "She, in the most explicit Terms, professed the greatest Gratitude and Respect for him, who had been **a Guardian Angel** to her; ..."

Guilty as charged

This colloquialism means that the person speaking admits to having done the deed or taken the action of which the other person has accused him or her. It came from verdicts in courts of law where the accused subjects were found guilty of crimes for which they were charged. Often it is said jovially. It started being used this way in about the 1970s, and though not its origin, an early example is in *The Magic Journey, A Novel* by John Nichols, 1978, on page 241:

> "Okay, I'm **guilty as charged**, I'll admit that. Now come on, love, back to the car. Let's go home, have a soda—we'll make a black cow, okay? Please—"

H

Hail and Farewell+

This is the term used in the U.S. military for the traditional formal ceremony when dining in to celebrate a change of command. It formally welcomes the new commander while honoring the one leaving. The name comes from the final line of the energetic, yet tender, Roman poem *Catullus 101* by Gaius Valerius Catullus, originally in Latin as *ave atque vale*. The poem, written c. 57 BCE, was addressed to his the 'mute ashes' of dead brother.

Hail Mary, A

A Hail Mary, literally, is a prayer to 'the Virgin Mary' made by a Catholic, based on the biblical greetings of Gabriel (*Luke 1:28*) and Elizabeth (*Luke 1:42*). In a figurative sense, it is a 'last ditch effort' (see) made in a football game, usually unsuccessful, to change the outcome of the game. It was coined in the late 20th century, and the earliest available citation in print is from *Texas Monthly*, October, 1983, page 244:

> "Taking the ball with 2:13 left on the clock, on a fourth-and-21 play from his own 18-yard line, Sterling quarterback John Tomjack lofted **a Hail Mary** pass that was answered by the official's flag."

Hair of the dog

This colloquialism refers to alcohol consumed to lessen the effects of a hangover. In the late 19th century, it referred to a method used to treat a rabid dog bite by placing hair from the dog on the bite area, but also was used for drinking. *Brewer's Dictionary of Phrase and Fable* by Ebenezer Cobham Brewer, published in 1898, page 570, contains the following:

> "In Scotland it is a popular belief that a few hairs of the dog that bit you applied to the wound will prevent evil consequences. Applied to drinks, it means, if overnight you have indulged too freely, take a glass of the same wine within 24 hours to soothe the nerves. 'If this **dog** do you bite, soon as out of your bed, take a **hair** of the tail the next day.'"

Brewer goes on to quote a poem to this effect attributed to Aristophanes, who lived circa 446 – circa 386 BCE. However, 'hair of the dog' was applied as a cure to drunkenness in an even earlier ancient text from the city of Ugarit, now in Northern Syria, dating to the late second millennium BCE, in which the Canaanite god Ilu becomes hung-over at a feast. In the text, as a cure, goddesses place the 'hairs of a dog' on Ilu's head and serve him a beverage made of parts of an unknown plant mixed with olive oil. The text was translated and published by Dennis Pardee in *Ritual and Cult at Ugarit*, 2002. This is very likely the true origin of the saying, which may have been passed down through the generations, as the Scottish have a legend that the ancestors of the Celts were Nomadic and originally came from the Middle East. Interestingly enough, this expression also is known to exist in Hungarian. Translated literally it applies to curing a dog bite with its fur.

Another citation of interest which ties the two practices together is found in *The Life and Adventures of Obadiah Benjamin Franklin Bloomfield...Written by Himself*, published in Philadelphia in 1818, page 138:

> "And what do you think they came for? Why truly to initiate their *dupe* in the art of mysteries of dram-drinking; or to speak more fashionably, to teach him how to cure his headache by a repetition of the *indiscretion* which had occasioned it. 'A **hair of the dog** is good for his bite' — is a phrase in high repute, and well understood, amongst topers."

Half a loaf is better than none

This old English proverb means that possession or attainment of a partial possession or achievement is preferable to not having attained any of it at all. It was first listed in John Haywood's 1546 book of proverbs, *A dialogue containing the number in effect of all the proverbs in the English Tongue*:

> "Throw no gift again at the giver's head; For, **better is half a loaf than no bread**."

Half-hearted

This idiom means having one's attention divided in such a way that zeal is lacking in one's efforts. It actually was around nearly 200 years before its converse form, whole-hearted. The earliest citation of a similar expression is actually faint-hearted which first appeared in print in the English-Latin dictionary, *The Promptorum Parvulorum Sive Clericorum,* 1440, page 153:

> "**Feynt hertyd**, *Vecors*"

Half-hearted, per se, was first cited in John Florio's Italian-English dictionary, *Queen Anne's New Words*, 1611:

> "Semicorde, a coward, **halfe-hearted**"

Whole-hearted didn't come until February, 1801 in *The Missionary Magazine*:

> "I abhor the practice of those **whole-hearted** men, who throw out the terrors of hell and damnation in a light and impudent way."

Hands are tied

This cliché refers to a person being restricted by circumstances in such a way that he or she is unable to help someone else in the way that is needed. It has been in use in English since at least the late 17th century. The earliest record known in print is found in *A Collection of State Tracts, Publifh'd on the Occasion of the Late Revolution in 1688 and During the Reign of King William III, Volume I*, printed in London in 1705, on page 367:

> "But then, though I am bound not to refift (resist), I am equally bound to affift (assist), my **hands may be tied** both ways."

Handsome devil+

This is a figurative expression referring to a man who is so uncommonly good-looking that women swoon over him in large numbers. He is very charming and has an aura which women find him irresistible, and is a bit of a scoundrel, thus, the use of 'devil.' In the Bible, Lucifer, who became the devil, was originally a very good-looking angel. He may also be called 'devilishly handsome.' The expression has been in use for over 100 years. Though certainly not the first printed reference, Rupert Hughes used it in his 1917 novel, *In a Little Town,* on page 51;

> "…no **handsome devil** with any kind of eyes tried to lure her away."

Happy as Larry[3]

This expression, popular in Australia and New Zealand, means 'extremely gleeful.' The actual origin is unknown, but *The Dictionary of New Zealand English* suggests a Scottish origin (from the Clydesdale area) *larrie* being a Gaelic-derived word for 'joking, jesting, gibing.' The phrase is first recorded in Australia on January 10, 1896 in the *Alexandra & Yea Standard* in Victoria, formerly the *Alexandra Times*:

> "The guests one and all appeared as **happy as Larry**, and they sang and danced - and danced and sang - with a vim that did our heart good to look upon."

Happy little Vegemite[3]

Down Under, this means a very happy, satisfied person. It derived from a jingle in the 1950s for a yeast-based spread called Vegemite:

> "We're **happy little Vegemites**, as bright as bright can be we. We all enjoy our Vegemite for breakfast, lunch, and tea."

On 14 April 1981 the Sydney, New South Wales *Bulletin* carried the following:

> "Expatriate Australians living in Italy have to pay dearly to be '**happy little Vegemites**.'".

Hard-core^

The meaning of this term, like so many, has evolved through the years. The earliest use of hard core was as far back as the early 17th century when it was used to describe the center of fruit. By the late 19th century it was being applied to the interior or foundation of a structure, such as a dike as in the *Geological Society of America Bulletin*, March 30, 1985 in an article on Buttes:

> "Cabezon butte, New Mexico, resembles the tepee in that it is occasioned by a hard, cylindrical core. It differs in the material of the core. The dike butte also has a **hard core**..."

As roads and highways began to be developed it was used to describe the surface materials comprised of gravel, etc. By early in the 20th century it was being applied as an adjective to unrelenting factors, as in this citation from *Engineering News* editorial, 'Rail Troubles Not Ended,' August 24, 1916:

> "The **hard-core** hypothesis was employed previously by others in a different way."

Contrary to reports from a major Internet source that it came to be used regarding pornography first in the 1970s, we see an earlier citation in this quip from 'The Fight Against Filth,' *American Legion Magazine*, May, 1961:

> "Obscenity, Pornography and Censorship In [**hard-core**] pornography the main purpose is to stimulate erotic. ren, we shall greatly reduce our frightening sex crime rate."

Hard facts (See: **Cold hard facts**)

Hard-nosed^

Again, this is an evolving term. The earliest known printed reference is in *The Sportsman's Directory or Park and Groundkeeper's Companion*, 3rd Edition, by John Meyer, published in London in 1819, on page 16, regarding a dog:

> "He must neither skulk, skirt, break field, follow, watch, blink, hug, labour, nor point at sight, not he **hard-nosed**, or near-scented; but wind his game at long distances, keep his points fast, back the same without jealousy, crouch to dog, bird, and gun…"

Later references also referred to bullets. However, contrary to a report by the most often quoted online etymology site which points to 1927 as the first usage as stubborn, stern, tough, and practical. James John Garth Williamson used it this way in *On Human Science and Its Works and On Divine Revelation and Its Works and Sciences* published in 1876, on page 33:

> "...although these consequences may deceive coarse observation by appearing at a distance from their causes, just as the influence of sewers and their connection with fevers was scarcely appreciated by our **hard-nosed** ancestors."

Hard pressed^

This figurative expression means heavily burdened or distressed, as by financial obligations or an overload of work. A major online dictionary places date of origin at 1815-1825. It was, however, in use much earlier. The first verifiable citation is from *Calendar of State Papers, Foreign Series, of the Reign of Elizabeth,* Public Records, Great Britain, 1589, page 56:

> "Has been so **hard pressed** by the King here since Colonel Simple left that he has had to subscribe to their confession of faith."

The exact meaning of this and other earlier citations is cloudy, but this reference from *A Defense of Natural and Unrevealed Religion* by Robert Boyle in 1737, on page 104, clearly indicates distress:

> "Mr. Hobbs being aware of this Difficulty, therefore in Café (case) he should be too **hard pressed**, he gives us a Hint, that possibly Sensation may be something more, viz. a Power of Perception naturally inherent in all Matter;..."

Hard Yakka[3]

In Aussie dialect, this expression refers to very strenuous labor, and comes from yaga in the Yagara indigenous language of the Brisbane area, which means work. Yakka became a part of the country's jargon before the middle of the 19th century, and was first recorded in 1847, according to the authoritative Australian National University Dictionary Center. Strangely enough, the word Yakka, spelled the same way, is used in South Africa and Ceylon with different meanings (a dance and an ancient tribe, respectively). In the Hindustani tongue of India it can mean 'single, solitary,' and refer to a one-horse vehicle or a solitary soldier.

Has a nice ring to it+

This old adage means that something sounds good. It was originally used to express the quality sound of a bell. It was in use earlier in relation to other things, but oddly didn't start showing up in print until the 1970s and did not become popularized until the 1980s. The earliest verifiable examples are found in the *Kansas State Collegian*, Wednesday April 30, 1972, in which it appears four times, the first being in an advertisement on page 13, where they are focusing on engagement rings:

> "Say '*HOLIDAY JEWELERS*' IT **HAS A NICE RING TO IT**"

Hatched up

To hatch something up means to invent a plan, usually erroneously, to accomplish something of one's own desire and making. It comes from hatching eggs to raise chickens or other fowl, and is native to the Appalachian region in the Southern U.S. The following is the earliest known reference in print, and comes from the September, 1888 issue of *The Century Illustrated Magazine* in a story titled 'The Mountaineers about Monteagle:'

> "But 'thout a pertendin' ur a lettin'on ter counterdick 'em, I thes up an 'lowed ter the feller ez hed done the main chance er the praincin' roun,' how 't them all was mighty fine p'ints fer showin' off an like's not they growed naiterlez chinkipins whur that cuntrivance wus **hatched up**, but how ez I'd hyern tell 't outsiders had ter do some monsturs tall tradin' afore they'd git a hold er 'em."

Have a look-see

Having started in Britain, this idiom is also popular in the U.S., particularly in the Southeast. It simply is a comical, informal way to say, 'Take a quick look.' A major dictionary places origin at 1883. It had made its way to the U.S. by September, 1918 when it was used in *Boy's Life* on page 14 in Ralph Henry Barber's serialized novel 'For the Freedom of the Seas,' Chapter VI:

> "The papers had a piece about a German raider off Great Abaco last week and I reckon we're sent down to **have a look-see**."

Have an ace up one's sleeve

This metaphoric cliché refers to someone having some secret knowledge or skill which will give him or her advantage in a given area or situation. It comes from the game of poker in which a dishonest player may hide a high-value card in his or her sleeve to be slipped out when others players are unaware. The earliest known mention of the practice in print is from *The Mysteries of London*, by George W. M. Reynolds, 1845, Volume I, Chapter LXVII, page 210:

> "There—all that there is to do is to secrete a particular card under the palm and partially **up** the **sleeve** till it is required. When your opponent is well primed, you can easily introduce a fifth king, or fifth **ace**, in this way."

The earliest known figurative use is from Australia in *Parliamentary Debates*, New South Wales Parliament, 1862, page 728:

> "It will be remembered that when the hon. Colonel opened his debate he assumed a very defiant attitude towards hon. gentlemen opposite. So apparent was this that the hon. Gentleman who sat behind me exclaimed, 'Isn't he cocky! He must have an **ace up his sleeve**.'"

Have a pity party (See: **Pity party**)+

Have a shot at

The expression is used metaphorically in Britain, America and Australia for trying to do something, usually for the first time. It comes from the obvious, shooting at something, usually game, or someone, with a gun. The earliest figurative citations are from 1912, one of which is in the November issue of *Boy's Life* in "'Meramec Dan' McDonald," on page 14:

> "'You ought to have a fire, and our matches are wet.'
> "'Well,' said Harry, 'we'll **have a shot at** first aid to begin with. Here, take this and cut the laces of my shoe.'"

There is another meaning of this idiom which is only used in Australia. That is to criticize someone.

Have as many notions as a dog has fleas+

This is an antiquated American expression used in the mid-twentieth century for a person who is unable unsettled and not able to stick to one path of action. It may have been coined by Jeanette Covert Nolan in her biographical book, *O. Henry, the Story of William Sidney Porter*, 1943, but was likely in use in rural America before this:

"…at age eight, and soon to be nine, **had as many notions as a dog has fleas**."

Have a wild hair+

Not to be confused with "wild hare" which refers to a rabbit called by that name in *Alice's Adventures in Wonderland*, which showed up at the Mad Hatter's tea party, having or getting a "wild hair" is often used in a bit of a vulgar connotation, mildly put, "get a wild hair up one's butt". It has to do with having a fixation on something which causes erratic behavior. In this respect, it was first used in 1954 by Nobel Prize winning American author, John Steinbeck, in his sequel to *Cannery Row*, *Sweet Thursday*, on page 69:

> "Wide Ida shook herself out of a mountainous lethargy. 'He used to be the easygoingest guy in the world. Now he's **got a wild hair**.'"

Have bigger or **other fish to fry^**

Versions of this are popular in several languages including French, German and Spanish. It means that there are more pressing matters at hand. The first appearance of this term in English, in spite of the claim by another popular cliché origin book that it was coined in *Memoirs* the diary of John Evelyn, written in the early 1700s but first published in 1818, it appeared much earlier, in *The Works of Francis Rabelias* published by the Navarre Society in London in 1653:

> "Do'st thou think, continu'd my Lord, thou 'rt in the Wilderness of your foolish University, wrangling and bawling among the idle, wandring Searchers and Hunters after Truth? By Gold, we have here **other Fish to fry**, we go another-gat's way to work, that we do…"

Have it made in the shade+

This American idiomatic expression means to have a very easy life or be in an enviable position. Some feel that it have originated with the old children's rhyme, "Ice cold lemonade, **made in the shade**, stirred with a spade, by an old maid." This, however, does not seem likely, as this saying has an entirely different meaning. It came into popular use in the 1950s. The earliest available citation is in the student newspaper of Susquehanna University, Selinsgrove, Pennsylvania; Tuesday, September 6, 1956, on page 4, in 'Orange and Maroon End Road Jinx,' where it is obvious that it is already a known phrase:

> "If the judges are watching this game, he **has it made in the shade**."

Have one's head in the clouds

This idiom refers to a person being unaware of what is going on around him or her because of being caught up in fantasies or daydreams. It has been in use since the 1600s. The earliest available printed reference in English is found in Francis Bacon's *The Essays or Counsels, Civil and Moral*, 1680, page 211, in 'A Fragment of an Essay of Fame:'

> There is a *flourish*: There follow excellent Parables; as that she gathereth strength in going; that she goeth upon the ground, and yet hideth her **head in the Clouds**."

Though a bit variant usage than today, it is clearly figurative. In Alexander Pope's 1715 English translation of Homer's *Iliad* written circa 1200 BCE, we find much the same usage in XXXII, 503:

> "Fame (he says) is properly feign'd to hide her **Head in the Clouds**, because the Grounds and Authors of Rumours are commonly unknown."

In April, 1819 the phrase was recognized as a metaphorical expression in London's *Quarterly Review* in speaking of Aristophanes in 'View of Grecian Philosophy-The Clouds &c:'

> "As a person given to abstraction and solitary speculation is proverbially said to have his **head in the clouds**, it was but another step, therefore, in the poet's creative mind to make the clouds the chorus of his piece."

Have one's mind in the gutter

This slang phrase means that a person has his or her mind occupied with crude or obscene subject matter. 'Gutter' has been used in a figurative sense since the late 19th century. One such example is from *Phrenological Journal and Science and Health,* March, 1890, in 'Thoughts and Things:'

> "That man's spirit wants to **get out of the gutter**..."

The present usage began in the 1940s. In the February 20, 1943 issue of *Billboard*, 'The Crossroads' by Nat Green, Chicago, on page 43 he writes:

> *Says Maclver: "'Joe Millers' may not be entertaining according to your views, which, to my* ***mind, are in the gutter****. You evidently get a belly laugh out of dirty gags..."*

In *The Comics*, a pop culture book by Coulton Waugh, 1947, we find a clear example on page 320:

> "One day he was leaning, depressed, on his broom when a sergeant spotted him. 'What do you think you're doing?'
> "'Trying to lift my **mind** out of **the gutter**.'"

Have someone or something in the crosshairs (See: **In the cro**sshairs)

Have someone's back

This idiomatic expression means to be willing to support or defend someone in any situation. Origin is unclear, but it came into common use late in the 20th century. The earliest verifiable citation is from the crime novel *Down in the Zero* by Andrew Vachss, 1994:

> "'I'm going in,' I said into the phone. 'Tonight. Nine o'clock.'
> "'**I've got your back**,' Blankenship replied."

Have tickets on yourself[3]

In Aussie slang, this expression means to have a high opinion of yourself. According to the Australian National University's Dictionary Center, the original meaning of ticket in this sense is obscure, but it could refer to betting or raffle tickets; meaning that a person is so conceited that he bets on himself. The saying started in the 20th century, but has become much more popular in recent years. A good example is in *The Last Magician* by Jeanette Turner Hospital, 2003, page 184:

> "...boys on the corner, who are much older than Charlie, who are in Grade 8 in fact, tell Charlie he **has tickets on himself**,..."

Having a laugh at someone else's expense

Joking, laughing or pulling a prank at someone else's expense means to make someone the victim in a way which hurts the person's feelings, damages his or her reputation or causes harm to the person in any way. This has been used figuratively since at least the 1760s, when it was cited in *The Life of Mr. James Quin, Comedian, with the History of the Stage*, printed in London in 1766, page 95:

> "Much has been said about Quin's love of good living, and not a few jokes were uttered **at his expense** with regard to his character."

Having blood on someone's hands

This idiom means to be responsible for someone's death. The principle is taught in the Hebrew *Bible*, in *Ezekiel 3:18* written from 571/70 BCE to 562 BCE:

> "When I say to the wicked, 'You will surely die,' and you do not warn him or speak out to warn the wicked from his wicked way that he may live, that wicked man shall die in his iniquity, but his **blood** I will require at **your hand**." *(NASB)*

The *NIV* and some other versions say, "I will hold you accountable for their blood." Also, seeing blood on the hands of someone at a murder scene is telltale evidence of guilt in most cases. In Shakespeare's *Macbeth*, written between 1599 and 1606; Act II Scene ii, 721, the blood on his hands could not be washed off, metaphorically representing his guilt in murdering the King:

> "What hands are here? ha! they pluck out mine eyes.
> Will all Neptune's ocean wash this **blood**; Clean from my **hand**?
> No, this my hand will rather
> The multitudinous seas in incarnadine,
> Making the green one red."

Having eyes in the back of one's head

This hyperbolic cliché is used in both Britain and the U.S., and means that the person seems to know everything that is happening around him or her, even when unable to physically see it. The earliest known citation for this saying is found in *The Polar Star or Entertainment and Popular Science,* Vol. II, published in London in 1830, in a story titled 'Prosers of all Kinds,' on page 148:

> "Now, if the enemy should look back; — nay, hath he not **eyes in the back of his head**? — cannot his pig-tail see? — or can he not snuff his prey a mile off?"

Head in the clouds (See: **Having one's head in the clouds**)

Heads or tails?

This cliché comes from the practice of flipping a coin to decide the outcome of some decision in which one of two parties benefits from the correct choice. The practice began in ancient Rome, and was originally called *navia aut caput* (ship or head), because some coins had a ship on one side and the head of the emperor on the other. Later, in England, according to a December 31, 2009 article in *The Telegraph* by Richard Allenune titled 'Coin tossing through the ages' it was referred to as 'cross and pile.' The term 'heads or tails' evolved because of heads and tails being considered opposite body parts.

The earliest reference to this term known in print is from Act II of *The Atheist: Or the Second Part of The Soldier's Fortune* by Thomas Otway, 1684:

> "Now may I do by my Mistresses as the Boys do by their Farthings hustle 'em in a hat together, and go to **Heads or Tails** for 'em."

Heads up (See: **Give someone a heads up**)

Heart of stone

This is a metaphor for being cruel and lacking sympathy for others. It has its origin in the *Bible*, in *Job 41:24*:

"His **heart** is as firm as a **stone**; yea, as hard as a piece of the nether millstone." (*KJV,* 1611)

Helicopter parent

This metaphoric expression refers to a parent who 'hovers over' one or more of his or her children, like a helicopter. In other words, pays perhaps too close attention to every move the child makes, particularly in institutions of learning. Another name for this type parent is a 'cosseter'. Parents cling to the term 'helicopter parents' even though it is almost always used pejoratively by the media. The earliest known reference in print to the practice comes from a best-selling 1969 book by Dr. Haaim Gennot titled *Between Parent and Teenager,* in which a youth complains:

"Mother hovers over me like a **helicopter**.."

But the actual term was coined by Foster W. Cline and Jim Fay, co-founders of the Fay/Cline Institute in Golden, Colorado, in 1990 in *Parenting with Love and Logic: Teaching Children Responsibility.* One reference is on page 25:

"They're dependent on their parents when they enter the real world as the kids of **helicopter parents**."

Hellfire and brimstone

This idiomatic expression has been used to describe the sermons of ministers who preached scary messages to urge members of their audiences to repent and turn to God. It comes from various scriptures in the book of *Revelation* at the end of the Christian *New Testament.* One is from *Revelation 21: 8, King James Version,* 1611:

"But the fearful, and unbelieving, and the abominable, and murderers, and whoremongers, and sorcerers, and idolaters, and all liars, shall have their part in the lake which burneth with **fire and brimstone**: which is the second death."

The earliest known reference in print outside the *Bible* is from *An Exposition Vpon the Prophet Ionah Contained in Certain Sermons, Preached in S. Maries Church in Oxford* by George Abbot, Professor of Divinitie, 1613:

"Saule may haue a spirit of Prophecic, Maker, wherewith he had embraced him, should be utterly taken from him, and now nothing but **hellfire and brimstone** should remaine..."

Hell on wheels+

This is a metaphor for a disastrous situation. It is also used for a person or animal that is tough, aggressive and hard to handle. This expression was coined in 1869 in the Springfield, Massachusetts newspaper, *Republican*, by its editor, Samuel Bowles to describe the itinerant collection of flimsily assembled gambling houses, dance halls, saloons, and brothels that followed the army of Union Pacific railroad workers westward as they constructed the First Transcontinental Railroad in North America.

Hell's bells

This is a rhyming cliché used to show dissatisfaction with something someone has just said, or, in most cases, an answer which was disappointing. The earliest use of the expression in this meaning in print is found in *Cycle and Automobile Trade Journal*, April 1, 1920, in 'How Pete Put One Over:'

> **"Hells bells,** Pete, if it wasn't that he was a customer of mine I'd write him a letter that he could use for an anti-freezing solution…"

An interesting anecdote: during World War II the U.S. Navy began using a new sonar recognition device to help detect underwater mines. A ping went forth from a submarine which could detect a mine up to 300 yards away. When it reached a mine a bell sound came back. At that point, the captain of the submarine would begin turning the sub immediately away from the bell to avoid being blown up. The bell sounds became known as 'hells bells.'

But long before either of these, hells and bells were rhymed in *The Works of Thomas Moore* (not the earlier Thomas More) in the poem, 'Tom Cribs Memorial to Congress,' on page 515, 1826 (actually written in 1818);

> "Seeing as how, I say, these Sicells
> "Are soon to meet, by special summons,
> "To chime together, like '**hells bells**,'
> "And laugh at all mankind, as rum ones"

He puts on his pants one leg at a time like everybody else

This popular saying means that the person being referred to is just an ordinary person, no different than anyone else. According to the Ohio State University football website, here is how the saying originated:

> "(Francis) Schmidt also introduced the tradition of the 'gold pants.' After accepting the coaching position (1934), he was asked how he expected to cope with the OSU nemesis from Ann Arbor. His matter-of-fact answer developed into a cliché: '**They put their pants on one leg at a time same as everybody else**.' Schmidt's comment led to the formation of the 'Golden Pants Club,' which awarded miniature gold football pants to all players who had a hand in a victory over the Wolverines."

Here's to mud in your eye!+

This old expression is one which seems to have a negative connotation, but is just the reverse. It is used to wish someone good health, good fortune or cheer them up when they are down. It derives from the biblical story in *John 9:6* when Jesus spat on dirt and rubbed it in the eyes of a blind man, restoring his sight.

He who hesitates is lost

This proverb means that delay or vacillation may have disastrous consequences. Throughout the ages versions of this proverb have been used by poets and writers. The present wording is a misquotation or an adaptation from English essayist and poet Joseph Addison's play, Cato, 1712:

> "**The woman that deliberates is lost**."

An earlier similar thought is found in *The Act of Preaching*, 1685, by a French author, made English by 'F. B., Esquire,' in Cant. III, on page 44:

> "Once Benson preach'd (where I devoutly went)
> Bespoke his *Congregation* to Augment;
> Scarce had **He** whining, with a School-Boys Tone,
> And quaking Limbs, his whole *Exordium* done,
> But Stammers, **Hesitates**, and is quite out;
> Which having, at a Time so fatal, **lost**
> Says any Thing next that comes uppermost:
> Like *Marriner*, having his compass lost,
> At all Adventures up and down is tost,

He who pays the piper calls the tune[2]^

This simply means whoever bears the cost of a venture or enterprise should have the authority over it. A major cliché dictionary places the coining of this expression at late 1800s. The earliest known citation is actually from October

13, 1864 in *The Official Report of the Annual Meeting of the Church Congress,* in 'Middle Class Education and the Bristol Diocesan Trade School' by the Rev. Preb. Brereton:

> "Such conditions are inevitable in the system. **He who pays the piper calls** for the **tune** — and there is no limit to the exclusion of important truths that may be enforced, when the State collects in one hand the payments (not ancient and customary)…"

Here it is safe to say from the context that the saying was known by the readers. On November 1, 1889, in *The Fortnightly Review* it was referred to as an *old proverb*:

> "The old proverb expresses the fact crudely enough, but truly: 'He **who pays the piper calls the tune**.' Speaking roughly, economic dependence means personal subservience; and economic independence means personal freedom."

Hiccup

Besides the obvious literal meaning, a hiccup is a problem that delays or interrupts something on a temporary basis without causing serious long-term difficulties. It is derived from the fact that physical hiccups are only temporary, but can cause delays in our activities. A metaphoric precursor to the present usage comes in *The Day's Work, Part I*, 'The Devil and the Deep Sea' by Rudyard Kipling, 1909, pp 186-187:

> "There was nothing more that could be made to move, the engines brought up, all standing, with a **hiccup** that seemed to lift the *Halliotis* a foot out of the water;"

By 1942 it was being used in the current figurative form, as seen in *Billboard*, September 12th, in 'Now Play on Broadway' Reviewed by Eugene Burr on page 10:

> "The first sigh of the new season— if we except the brief **hiccup** that marked the beginning and end of the Saroyan Repertory Theater—came to the Cort Theater Thursday night in the form of a military melodrama *titled I Killed the Count*."

Hidden in plain sight

This cliché means that something is actually out in the open but not easy to detect if one doesn't know where to look and is not expecting it to be there. It can also refer to facts which have esoteric meanings, or is possibly coded. Jesus, for example, spoke in parables. His messages were spoken freely, but those who didn't understand them were oblivious to their true meanings. The expression came to be in the early 1920s. The earliest citation known is refers to a school game and is from *Primary Education*, November, 1920:

> "A ball is **hidden (in plain sight)** while several pupils leave the room or are blindfolded."

Then in June, 1922 we find much the same connotation as we know today in *The Century Illustrated Monthly Magazine*, in 'A Vagabond in the Sun' by Harry A. Franck:

> "Sharp-eyed with appetite, I came near, nevertheless, to passing unseen early in the afternoon a village **hidden in plain sight** along the flank of a reddish, barren hill."

High dollar^+

This is a popular expression for something which is very expensive. It is, of course, of American origin and according to the *OED*, was first known to have been cited in *Popular Mechanics Magazine* in the 1960s. Long before that, however, it was already in common usage in a little different connotation, meaning the top bid. As early as August 13, 1915, the Kentucky newspaper, *The Stanford Interior Journal* had the following citation in an auction ad on page 6:

> "This property will positively be sold for the **high dollar** regardless of price."

A specific early reference in print to the modern meaning comes in *Marine Corps Stock Fund* 1953-1967, page 214, published January 1, 1968:

> "Typically, such items are long-lived in use, of **high dollar** unit value, reputable, and subject to control report…"

High five (See: **Give me five!**)

High-wire act

This is a modern metaphor for a risky job or occupation, taken from the extreme danger of high wire acrobats and tight rope walking. The origin is obscure, but it began to appear in the 1990s. An early example comes from *Cruise Travel*, May, 1993, in *Interview at Sea: Lady Maitre D'* by Beverly Shaver on page 55:

> "Women in management positions have to walk a tightrope, 'Thelma & Louise'-style. They've got to be tough but sweet, hard-driving but sensitive. It's a **high-wire act** more suited to circus acrobats than a cruise-ship manager."

Hissy fit+

It is popularly believed that this expression is either an allusion to the hissing or sputtering sound made during an outburst; or most likely a contraction for hysterical. Another theory is that it derived from the Japanese word Romanized as 'hisshi' or hissi,' meaning desperate. But there are two problems with this train of thought. First, the American origin before U.S. major involvement with Japan in WW II, secondly, the actual Japanese pronunciation is he-she. At any rate, it is an erratic display of temperamental emotion in reaction to something which triggers a person's negative aggressive feelings. It originated in the United States, and is first attested as simply 'hissy' in the 1934 edition of *American Speech*:

"**Hissy** is probably provincial slang. I have heard it for eight or ten years. He threw a hissy or He had a **hissy** means that a person in question was very disturbed and very angry."

Hit the deck

This is an idiom which may be used for either for getting out of bed or falling to the ground for protection. It has been in use metaphorically since the early 20th century. It was originally a nautical term for getting out of bed. In January, 1919, *Country Life Magazine* carried a Navy story called 'You'll Like It' by Frances Buzzell with the following on page 33:

> "'**Hit the deck'** was his war cry, and he chanted it at intervals of ten seconds. Jim, hearing thuds and much shouting, decided that the deck was being hit considerably, and he needn't bother about it himself. Why should the deck be hit anyway?"

Hit the hay

Being just the reverse of hit the deck, this means 'go to bed'. It has been used in America since the dawn of the 20th century. Many mattresses in that era were actually stuffed with hay. In *People You Know*, by American author George Ade, published in 1902 we find:

> "After Dinner he smoked one Perfecto and then, when he had put in a frolicsome Hour or so with the North American Review, he crawled into **the Hay** at 9.30 P.M."

The earliest known example of the phrase 'hit the hay' was in the *The Oakland Tribune*, Oakland California in July, 1903:

> "'Sam' Berger, the Olympic heavyweight ... was sleepy and he announced that 'he was going to **hit the hay**.'"

Hit the jackpot^

Hit the jackpot, in a literal sense, refers to winning a large amount of money, as in gaming or a lottery. Figuratively, it means to be exactly right in a conclusion made about some matter. One online dictionary places the coining of the word jackpot to early 1900s, while another frequently sought source places the actual term 'hit the jackpot' and others 'any use outside poker' at 1944. The reason 'pot' is used is because it refers to an amount of money put up to win. Jack came from the fact that face cards in poker carry higher points, and the lowest of them is the jack. Some more accurate sources place use of the term in poker at late 19th century. But all are inaccurate on the first usage outside poker being 1944. In June, 1887, *Lippincott's Monthly Magazine* carried an article which signaled the expanding of the definition, titled Book-Talk:

> "Like most writers on the subject, Mr. Keller has only hard words for the **jackpot**, which somebody declares to be as irrelevant to poker as a raffle for a turkey injected into a game of whist."

Still, 'hit the jackpot' was not used here. However, contrary to numerous other sources, that expression came in 1910 in Florence Land May's novel, *The Broken Wheel,* page 355:

> "'The trouble is,' piped a Scotchman of athletic proclivities, 'that each mother's son of us wants to reform the other fellow.'

> "'Well,' said McKenzie, 'you've **hit the jackpot**.'"

Hog heaven^

This figurative expression means a very happy or satisfied state in which one has no worries or concerns. It comes from contented swine wallowing in mud. A major dictionary places first usage at 1944. The term was in use, however, by 1863, when it was cited in the *Report of the Commissioner of Agriculture* in Washington, DC, page 204, where it is in quotes, likely indicating that it was recently coined:

> "In the height of the hog season in Chicago, in the neighborhood of the yards, it would sometimes seem as though we had almost got into a '**hog heaven**,' for, turn which way you will, in the cars, in the yards, in the streets, all is hog, hog; and their cowardly, pointed heads all turned eastward, running, grunting, squealing, and all showing a disposition to travel anyway but the direction wanted."

The above citation was actually related to hogs, though the use of 'heaven' was figurative. A very clearly metaphoric example, as used today, comes by 1904 in Elizabeth Robins' (C.E. Raimond) novel. *The Magnetic North* page 42:

> "'Oh, let him alone. He's got a flask in his bunk, swillin' and gruntin;' he's just in **hog-heaven**.'"

Hold all the cards

This again, has an obvious origin in playing cards, in which one player has a distinct controlling advantage, and refers, metaphorically, to the same situation in a true-life scenario. Though not the origin, the earliest known reference in print to the figurative use of the term is in the *Bulletin of the Atomic Scientists*, June, 1956, in 'Can We Halt the Race for Atomic Arms?' by Clinton Anderson on page 226:

> "Nations rushed to hold press conferences and attend activities. Isn't it possible that there might be a similar pattern in weapons, and that no one nation **holds all the cards**?"

Hold down the fort^

Originally 'Hold the Fort,' this comes from the days when forts were the defense of a nation, and an enemy attack must be prevented or fought off at any cost.

This expression means to keep an eye on things while the person in charge is away. It did not originate with General Sherman in the American Civil War as suggested on a major online etymology site. It had been used in the following manner in 1736 in *A History of the Life of James Duke of Ormonde*, Volume I, by Thomas Carte, page 461:

> "The officers and soldiers in garrison had already suffered much extremity through want, that it was not possible for him to **hold the fort** above ten or fourteen days longer, and therefore earnestly desired, either immediate supplies,..."

Soldiers through the ages before the American Civil War were instructed to 'hold the fort' as in *History of the New Netherlands, Province of New York and State of New York* by William Dunlap and Adriaen van Donck, 1839, page 154:

> "They call the commandant 'noble and loyal Captain Leisler.' They repeat the advice to **hold the fort** and disarm papists, and promise assistance, if required, from Connecticut. —"

The first known printed reference to the figurative expression, 'hold down the fort' is found in *Princeton Alumni Weekly*, January 19, 1940,' in an entry by the secretary of Alexander Hall at the Theological Seminary there:

> "Outhwite and I continue to **hold down the fort** here with little excitement."

Hold one's breath

This idiom means to be excited or nervous in anticipation of a hoped for outcome like winning an election or awaiting the result of a competition. Literal use of the term, meaning to stop breathing temporarily dates back to the 18th century. The earliest known figurative use of 'don't hold your breath' comes in 1919, in Julie M. Lippmann's novel, *Flexible Ferdinand*, page 32:

> "You're a team, you two, but mother'll make you walk Spanish and don't you forget it! And take my tip! **Don't hold your breath** till you get those studs."

Hold (or **hang) on to your hat!**

This idiom means 'Get ready for a big shock!' It is derived from going into a harsh wind or on a rollercoaster ride where one's hat is sure to be blown away if it is not well in hand. It was used in a literal sense in writing as far back as the early 20th century. In *Four Boys in Mississippi* by Frank Eugene Kellogg, 1909, it was used on page 38 in jest:

> "'**Hang onto your hat**, Commodore. We're going pretty fast,' remarked Dick facetiously, poking his head out of the door."

It wasn't until the 1950s when it began to be used in the manner we know now. Don Appell used it in *Lullaby: A Comedy*, 1953, Act II, Scene ii, on page 58:

> " **JOHNNY**: She don't have to tell me, I know!
>
> "**EADIE:** You do, huh? "**Hold onto your hat**! Mrs. Collins' boy ain't on furlough. He's been discharged. He's got what they call a Section Eight, and that means he ain't never goin' back"!

Hold someone's feet to the fire

This figurative phrase refers to pressuring someone to consent to something to which he or she is opposed. This derived from torture exacted by the Roman Catholic Church during the Crusades between 1096 and 1291 CE to extract a confession of heresy. A modern example might be offering a plea bargain in a criminal case in return for a testimony against a worse offender. In the earliest verifiable citation, from the *Reformatory Press*, Anamosa, Iowa, Saturday October 10, 1909, it is used jovially in 'The Silent School Hours' by 'Sonny Jim,' on page 6:

> "Fosha is away in the lead of us all in history and geography, but we will **hold his feet to the fire** for a while with grammar and arithmetic."

Holed below the water line[2]

This British idiom came from the fact that when a ship is badly damaged 'below the water line' it takes on huge amounts of water and is in serious danger of sinking. Figuratively, it has come to apply to organizations or projects which are likely to be closed or abandoned, or fail to achieve its purpose, putting its future survival in doubt. The origin is obscure but it was in use by the late 20th century as seen in *Strategic Project Management* by Michael J. Termini, 1999, page 47.

"Who on the project team is capable, comfortable, and willing to make those **below-the-waterline** decisions?"

Hole up^

This idiom means to hide out, and is taken from hiding in a hole or cave. A major dictionary and the most-quoted online etymology site both place origin at 1875. In spite of this, it was used in 1839 by Daniel Pierce Thompson in *The Green Mountain Boys: A Historical Tale of the Early Settlement of Vermont,* on page 232:

> "To be cribbed and **holed up** here like so many hunted foxes, with forty divils over our heads, who may be preparing to send down one of those great hemlocks to smush us like migets, for any thing we know, or fixing some other contrivance for us not much better, and all without allowing us the least chance to know the how, when and whereabouts, is a thing I don't fancy."

Holy mackerel!

This exclamation indicated surprise. Like so many other such slang expressions, this is believed a euphemism for 'Holy Mary.' The origin is uncertain, but mackerel became a nickname for Catholics because they ate fish on Fridays. Another suggested origin is that mackerel was sold on Sundays in the 17th century because it spoils rapidly, and it became known as a 'holy' fish. This seems too early. It has been claimed to have first appeared in 1803, but no evidence of this was found. It only became popular in the 1870s, and the earliest citation available is in *Ballou's Monthly Magazine*, December, 1875, in a story titled, 'One Thousand Dollars Reward: The Woman Chief' by Patent Coupler:

> "'By the **holy mackerel**,' he exclaimed, 'it's the she devil!'"

Home and hosed/dried[3,2]

This idiom, which is fairly common in Australia and New Zealand, but also used in the U.K., originated from a horse when he had finished a race and was back home in his box and had been hosed down. It came to mean that a horse which was 'home and hosed' was a sure winner, being back before and the rest of the horses. Figuratively it means that one has safely reached his or her destination, or been successful in a venture. Also, home and dried, now used more often in the U.K., as cited in Australian Vance Palmer's novel *The Passage*, 1930:

> "...**home and dried** on the pig's back..."

Cobbers, Thomas Wood's story about his journey from Essex to Australia, published in 1934, has another version:

> "…**home in the stall** with a rag on…"

Earlier examples of 'home and hosed' are illusive, and actual origin is obscure. It was being used figuratively by 1984, when it appeared in *Picket* by the Australian author, Renfrey Clark, page 11:

> "I knew then that was it. From here on we were **home and hosed**."

hoot, A (See: **That's a hoot/ real hoot**)+

Hope springs eternal+

This is a common proverb meaning that positive people will keep on hoping, no matter what the odds. It was coined by Alexander Pope in his epic poem, *An Essay on Man,* first published in 1734.

hop, skip and a jump, A

This idiom has long been used to mean a short distance, and has been around since 1760 according to a major dictionary. It originally referred to an exercize or game involving these three movements. Figurative use came by the mid-to-late 1800s. The earliest verifiable reference in print of this as an exercize is from *The Life and Opinions of Tristam Shandy, Gentleman*, Volume I, by Laurance Sterne, 1792, on page 33:

> "To which Yorick, with his usual carelessness of heart, would often answer with a pshaw!—and if the subject was started in the fields,—with a **hop, skip, and a jump** at the end of it…"

An early example of figurative use is *Loch Creran, Notes from the West Highlands*, 1887 by Scottish author William Anderson Smith, page 279, in the events of February, 1883:

> "Just **a hop, skip, and jump**, and the storm demon passed over us, sending three blinding flashes at intervals as his heels struck fire from the granite of Ardchattan, the trap of the Scaur, and the white quartz rock of Appin."

Hot button issue^

This term applies to a number of types of issues: social, economic, spiritual, theological, scientific, legal, etc, which are highly politicized, igniting passionate responses, needing to be settled. In spite of a claim by a major political dictionary that 'hot button' has been used of political issues 'since 1981' it appeared in quotes in the 1974 reprint of William R. Carson's *Consequences of Failure,* on page 156:

> "There will be lower and lower voter turnout in almost all elections except local ones where the **'hot button' issue** of the moment coincides with election day. Issues will become more and more transitory; the problem of today that can't be solved ..."

Hot date

Properly defined, this idiom means a social outing with a current or potential lover which holds the possibility of a romantic encounter developing. Many times, however, the term is used when the person speaking only wishes this were the case. The use of hot, meaning 'exciting lust' goes back to at least 1450-1460 in *Merlin, Or, the Early History of King Arthur: A Prose Romance*, in Chapter XXVI, 'Gawein's Request to the Queen' as edited by Henry Benjamin Wheatley and published in London in 1869:

> "But she was the moste **hotest** woman of all Breteigne, and moste luxurious…"

The term 'hot date' seems to have been introduced to American popular culture in the mid-20th century. In the *Catalogue of Copyright Entries for Musical Compositions*, 1942, Washington, DC, on 1-12-1942, there is an entry for 'You Have a **Hot Date** with the Mikado' 34679. But it was the early 1950s before the phrase became popular. Originally copyrighted in 1939, the 1950 edition of Nelson Bond's *Lancelot Biggs, Spaceman* had the following on page 86:

> "The V-I unit continued to work like a dream, our erstwhile lumbering old crate went flashing through space like a quantum with a **hot date**, and me — I was in seventh heaven…"

In Joyce R. Ingalls' *Teen Talk: Sixteen Character Sketches for Teen-Aged Boys and Girls*, 1953, the meaning is very clear:

> "Boy, you must have **a hot date**. I never saw such action. Someone really special, eh?"

Hot mess

This idiom has evolved a lot over the past 150+ years. During the American Civil War it would have meant food for soldiers, and in military situations, it may still have that connotation. Today this most usually means either a situation which is in a pitiful shape or a disheveled or unbalanced person, yet remains somehow attractive.

The former is the case in *I Think We Should Go into the Jungle* by New Zealand author, Barbara Anderson, 1989, page 38:

> "I thought it a mess, and a **hot mess** and I wished to be gone, especially when Mildred turned to me with a smile and said — Beth?"

In 2003, in a book titled *Criminal Slang: The Vernacular of the Underground Lingo* by Capt. Vincent Joseph Monteleone also listed the following definition:

> **"HOT MESS** (N) A stolen object; trouble."

Hot minute (See: **It's been a minute/ hot minute**)+

Hot off the press

This cliché means that some publication is so new that it has barely been printed. It applies primarily to newspapers which were originally printed by a process known as hot metal printing which involved molten led being poured into a mould to form a printing block. Figuratively, it came to mean anything which is newly printed. This expression didn't appear in print, however, until the early 20th century, and the first verifiable citation is from the March 15, 1904 edition of *The Mixer and Server* printed in Cincinnati, Ohio, on page 75, in a letter from the Nashville, Tennessee Local 517 President, T. L. Bradshaw in speaking of this very issue:

> "Will you let us have next issue of the Mixer and Server **hot off the press**, that copy of same will reach members before March 17? No expense has been spared to make this entertainment the social event of the year."

Hot on someone's trail / tail

This colloquialism means to be very close to finding or catching up with someone. The earliest citation known is from *The Forayers: or, The Raid of the Dog-days* by William Gilmore Simms, 1855, page 377:

"'And we was sworn, both me and the Trailer, to hev' this same Willie Sinclair.'

"'Why were you so hot on his trail, Dick?'"

A similar idiom 'hot on someone's tail' means following a person closely. The earliest citation available for this is in *Boy's Life*, October, 1943, in 'High Jinx,' on page 34:

"Two Bits fled down the sideline, Buzz **hot on his tail**."

Hotshot

In our modern English vernacular, a hotshot is a brash, flashy and successful male. This meaning has prevailed in America since 1927, when J. Frank Dobie used it in *Texas and Southwestern Lore*:

"Men who are either slow or lazy are given such names as...**'Hot Shot**'... 'Lightning,'...and 'Speedy.'"

But ages before that, in Britain, it meant a reckless person; overeager trouble-maker (in a slightly different spelling), as evidenced in *The Famous Chronicle of King Edward the First* by George Peale, 1593:

"O maister doubt you not but your Nouice will prooue a **whot shot**, with a bottle of Metheglin."

Then a few years later, in *Father Hubburds Tales or the Ant and the Nightingal,* 1604, showing similar sentiment, Thomas Middleton wrote:

"To the warres I betooke me, ranckt my selfe amongst desperate **Hot-shots**."

Though entirely separate meanings, the saying in both cases originated from bullets which are hot from being fired.

Hot under the collar

This old idiom means to become angry, upset or aggressive. It is derived from the fast that when one is angry their face and neck usually turn red. Since the color covers the neck, this expression came to be used. A much-consulted online dictionary places origin at 1900. However…in the *Ohio State Bar Association Reports, Volume 4, Proceedings of the Annual Meeting of the Association held at the City of Dayton, Ohio, December 29 and 30, 1885*, printed in Columbus in 1886, on page 26, we read:

> "If he is defeated in both courts everything conspires to make him **hot under the collar**, time suddenly becomes either immaterial to him, or he may think that the more of it he can get in the supreme court the better…"

Houston, we have a problem!

This statement has become a humorous cliché to denote any situation that needs attention. It came from a solemn statement made by U.S. Astronaut John 'Jack' Swigert during the Apollo 13 moon mission at 21:18 on April 13, 1970. The actual statement was 'Houston, we've had a problem here.' This, however, in the 1995 movie made about the flight, was misquoted as, 'Houston, we have a problem.' It was used in print as early as 1997 when Bryce Ragland cited it in *The Year 2000 Problem Solver: A Five Step Disaster Prevention Plan*, page 11:

> "The calculations would indicate that a tracking station in the Indian Ocean is the one that can communicate with the shuttle, when in reality the shuttle is somewhere over North America.
>
> "'**Houston, we have a problem**.' But Houston doesn't even hear the message."

How 'bout them ________!^

When Coach Jimmy Johnson went into the Dallas Cowboys locker room at Candlestick Park after their 30-20 NFC Championship Victory over the San Francisco 49ers on January 17, 1993, he made history, and made famous his resounding proclamation, 'How 'bout them Cowboys!' After that the expression was taken up by anyone wanting to make a fuss over their favorite team following a remarkable win. But that was not the origin of the expression, 'How 'bout them______!' Some have tried to equate it to the one about apples, but that was really 'How do you like them apples!' (see first volume) and it came long after this one was popular. The earliest known citation comes from *Coupon Bonds: A Play in Four Acts* by John Townsend Towbridge, 1876, Act III:

> "**Mr. D**. Yes. I got talkin' with him and led to the subject of Gov'ment bonds. 'What do you think of them as an investment,' says I. 'Excellent,' says he. 'So I thought,' says I. 'But **how 'bout them** air cowpon bonds? Ain't they ruther ticklish property to have in the house?' says I."

The main characters in the play were the Ducklows, a 'well-to-do' American farm family whose dialect reflects their obvious lack of formal education. The expression was undoubtedly one in use in rural America in the late 19th century. Following this, it became a popular expression among authors.

How now, brown cow?+

This is a rhyming phrase sometimes said jovially as a greeting. It was originally used in elocution teaching to demonstrate rounded vowel sounds. Each 'ow' sound represents the diphthong/au/ in the International Phonetic Association's phonetic alphabet. Use of this phrase dates back to at least January 1, 1926 when it appeared in *Elocution Do's and Don'ts* by Louie Bagley.

By 1942 it was being used in jest. It was cited in the Maryland newspaper, *The Capital*, in February that year:

> "Laird Cregar, now contributing his booming voice to 'Ten Gentlemen from West Point,' explains how he got it. When first tried out for the Pasadena Community Playhouse his voice wouldn't carry past the front rows. Coach Belle Kennedy has him declaim **How Now, Brown Cow** and The Rain in Spain Still Stains over and over."

Brown Cow, as a term, however, goes back as far as the early 18th century, when it was in use in Scotland as a jocular name for a bear barrel. Alan Ramsey used it in *The Gentle Shepherd, A Scotts Pastoral Comedy*, in 1725:

> "The auld anes think it best With the **brown cow** to clear their een.

How's that working for you?/ out for you?

This is a 21st century, somewhat sarcastic, cliché used to chide a person who is trying to solve a problem he or she has failed to resolve in the past. Talk show host, Dr. Phil, was using the first version by 2003, in a different light, as he states that he actually means it. It is uncertain, but the good Doctor may have actually originated common use of the phrase; but the intent changed when others picked it up. In 2005, on page 26 of *The Endless Moment* by Wayne C. Allen, it is obvious that the other meaning had taken hold:

> "To which we ask, '**How's that working for you**?' The only way anything will ever change in your life is to do something differently."

How sweet it is!+

This exclamatory catchphrase means that something is very special in a person's way of thinking. It was the title of a 1964 Marvin Gay hit, and a 1968 film starring James Garner and Debbie Reynolds. Even earlier, Jackie Gleason popularized it as a saying on *The Jackie Gleason Show* (CBS, 1952-1957). But it has been in use much longer. A poem by that title, in which each verse begun with these words, was published in *Australian Poems* by Emma Styles in 1883.

Humdrum

This very old term, now somewhat archaic, means dull and boring. The earliest verifiable example in an English publication is from *The Craftsman: Being a Critique on the Times, Volume 6* by Caleb Danvers at Britain's famous Grey's Inn, published in 1731, page 235:

> "It might have been reasonably expected that the great Encouragement, which hath been lately given to *these Writers* by a *certain Gentleman at the piblick Expenee,* would have animated their Genius, and added a little Vivacity to their Dissertations, but They still continue plodding on in their old **humdrum** Way…".

Hump day+

This slang expression refers to Wednesday, the middle of the average work week. It became used in this connotation because of 'getting over the hump' and heading down the other side toward Friday. *Dictionary of American Regional English* (DARE) in 1965 has the earliest known printed reference to hump day, per se, as Wednesday. But the idea had been around much longer, and evolved from the use of hump as the half-way point as early as the late 1800s. 'Hump' as the middle, or beyond the most difficult point, was first in print in 1914 in *A Vocabulary of Criminal Slang* by Louis E. Jackson, page 46:

"**Hump,** **N**oun…The middle of the term: the half-way point in a prison sentence."

Then in 1955, the academic journal, *American Speech,* cited the earliest known use of Wednesday in this respect:

"**Hump night**, Wednesday night, which is over the hump of the week."

Hunky-dory

This odd expression, meaning very satisfactory, has its origins in the Dutch word '*hunk'* from the Middle Dutch, *honc* meaning base, refuge or safe position, plus the English word dory, which has varied meanings. It dates back to the mid- to late 19th century. The expression was popularized by a song by the black-face group, Christy Minstrels, written in 1862. *Hunkey* with an e was also being used for fit and healthy, and is the spelling in the original song.

"Hunkey Dorey
"'Air—Limerick Races'

"One of the boys am I,
That always am in clover;
With spirits light and high,
'Tis well I'm known all over.
I am always to be found,
A singing in my glory;
With your smiling faces round,
'Tis then I'm **hunkey dorey**."

A complete 6 verse version of the song spelled **Hunky-Dory** was published in 1866 **in** *Harry Pell's Ebony Songster* on page 7, which said it was sung at the Opera House by Tony Pastor.

An 1872 *Americanisms, the English of the New World* by Maximilian Schele de Vere, however, tells a very interesting story about the origin of this phrase on page 482:

"Hunk, not unknown in the provinces abroad, means here a large piece of bread, butter or cheese. It occurs occasionally in the sense of a place of refuge, a homestead; and is used by boys in play, when they have reached

> their 'base;' they call it 'being *honk.*' This term is derived from the Dutch honk, a place, a home, and has led to the practical slang term of *Old Hunkers,* which means persons clinging to their homestead, and opposed to innovators. Hence, also, the familiar ***Hunky Dory***, a term originating among the Virginia mountaineers, who used it to express very empathetically that they were 'well and in good spirits.'"

Hush money+

This is a colloquial term for bribery in which one party offers another an attractive sum of money to remain silent about illegal or inappropriate behavior or actions taken by the party offering the bribe. According to the *EOD*, the term was first put into print by Irish writer Sir Richard Steele in 1709, who published his first journal, *The Tatler* on April 12 that year; later founding the daily publication, *The Spectator*, in 1711. It was greatly popularized as the title of a two-act farce written by British playwright George Dance, first published in London in 1825.

I

I beg your pardon? Or, **pardon me**

'I beg your pardon' is now most usually a cliché question which means that the speaker has not heard what has just been said and would like it repeated. But it did not originate that way. This phrase was around as a statement for hundreds of years in much the same usage as 'pardon me'. The earliest citation in print is found in *The Ideal of a Gentleman* by Abram Smith Palmer, DD, originally published in 1586, on page 353:

> "'**I beg your pardon,'** and with a smile and a touch of his cap Harry Edmond handed to an old man, against whom he had accidentally stumbled, the staff which he had knocked from his hand."

There are countless citations in books and magazines through the past 400 plus years of this connotation. Like 'pardon me,' it may still be used in the same situations. I beg your pardon may also indicate disagreement with someone. It is derived from 'I beg you to pardon me.' 'Pardon me' is still usually a statement.

The earliest known example of using this as a question comes in 1942 in *Court of Appeals, State of New York Notice of Motions, Affidavit, Exhibits A, B &C*, Gaspere Puccio versus Metropolitan Jockey Club, page 32:

"Q. 'And for what period of time did you do that?'
"A. '**I beg your pardon**?'"

I can resist anything except temptation

The original quote was 'I can resist everything except temptation.' It is an oxymoron-type sentence and comes from Oscar Wilde in his acclaimed play, *Lady Windermere's Fan*, 1893, Act I, Scene i:

***"Lord D.* I can resist everything except temptation."**

I could count on my fingers the number of times…

This old adage means that something has not happened many times or is rare. It is now often used as 'the fingers of one hand,' but the earliest citation did not read that way. It is from *Transactions of the Section on Laryngology, Otology and Rhinology of the American Medical Association…May 22-26, 1822;*

"**I can count on my fingers the men** of the 'Old Guard' who are grounded in otolaryngology and micropathology."

Then in *Miriam Copley* by John Cody Jeaftreson, 1859, page 154, we see this exact phrase:

"I **could count on my fingers the number of times** I had been to church during the whole course of **my** life…"

But by 1846, the idea of counting something rare on only one hand had been written in a story titled 'Three Friends,' printed in more than one magazine including *Littell's Living Age,* July 18 issue:

"That I **could count**, upon the **fingers of one hand,** with whom I know such bonds might be…"

I could no more do that than I can fly+

This now antiquated saying means that a person is totally and unequivocally unable to do something. It was in popular use throughout the 17th, 18th, 19th and most of the 20th centuries. The earliest available citation, originally in French, is in *Letters of Madame Guyon* (1645-1717), *Being Selections of her Religious Thoughts and Experiences*, in Letter XV written to her by Froncois de Salignac Fenelon (1651- 1715) to Madame Guyon, on page 203 of the English version translated by Mrs. P.L. Upham, published in New York in 1870:

> "And I could no more dissapate these thoughts, and the grief attending them, than I could fly."

This citation, originally in English, is found in *Sixteen String Jack*, a romantic drama in three acts by Leman Rede (1802-1847) preformed at the Theater Royal in London, Act I, Scene ii:

> "***Kit***....**I could no more swell about and do as you do than I could fly**; and whether I could fly or not, I ask any reasonable creature to answer."

I couldn't do that again if I tried (or 'You, He or She...)

The earliest known citation in print of this old cliché actually is the 'you' version and comes from New York's *The Dollar Magazine* (so called because the annual subscription was one whole dollar), November, 1842 in 'The Commencement Vision,' by Mrs. E Rockwell:

> "...whereupon he raised his head over the breast work and sung out—'Oh, you lubber, **you couldn't do that again if you tried** forty times.'"

I didn't recognize you with your clothes on^

This passé statement is sometimes used in jest by a male attempting to appear macho and make others laugh, at the expense of a lady. It is credited as a quote from James Bond (played by Roger Moore) in *The Man with the Golden Gun,* 1974:

> "Miss Anders! **I didn't recognize you with your clothes on**."

Few, however, realize that the creators of Bond did not originate the line. It is from a joke included in *The Medical Pickwick, a Monthly Magazine of Wit and Humor,* Julian W. Brandis, Editor, January, 1918, on page 1:

> "A famous surgeon met a prominent society woman several months after having preformed a serious operation on her. He did not recognize her at first, but suddenly his face took on a look of intelligence and he exclaimed

loudly: 'Oh yes, Mrs. Rivers, **I didn't recognize you with your clothes on**.'—Nebraska Angnan."

I didn't see that coming

This is a common response made by a person who has just been totally blind-sided by something unexpected. In *The Conscience of Coralie* by F. Frankfort Moore, 1900, on page 410 we find the earliest citation known of a form of this phrase:

"Coralie's dress was made to withstand even a sudden immersion in a salmon-pool — she had subjected it to this test the day before. **'I didn't see that coming** on,' said Bertie, 'but I might have known that it was on its way to us.'"

But it was late in the 20th century before the saying became popular. We find a good example in *Drawing Blood* by Poppy Z. Brite, 1993, page 261:

"I have to admit I **didn't see that coming**."

I (or **someone**) **don't** (or **doesn't**) **know someone** (or **something**) **from Adam's off ox**

Not knowing someone from Adam goes back further, to at least 1830, when it was used in *The Follies of Fashion, A Comedy in Five Acts* by Richard Butler, Earl of Glengail in Act III, Scene i:

"***Major***…'By all the powers I **don't know him from Adam'"**

But the earliest known citation in print of the 'Adam's off ox" version is found in *The American Bee Journal,* published in Chicago, February 16, 1881, on the first page under Correspondence in an entry called 'A General Law is Needed' written by G.W. Demekee where it is in quotes, indicating that it is likely recently coined:

"The Commonwealth of Kentucky, in order to make good a charge of violation of her laws, must prove the charge against the accused, and he must be tried before a jury of his countrymen, and not one juryman in a hundred (however intelligent he might be in other matters) would **know** glucose **from 'Adam's off ox**.'"

I'd rather take a beating

This old cliché had its beginnings in the mid-19th century when beatings were common punishment for youth gone astray. Though not its coining, the earliest example available in print is from the novel, *Totemwell*, by American author, George Payson, 1854, page 166:

> "'I'd **rather take a beating** myself,' replied Ben, with a glance at the black eye Philip had received in his defense, 'I'm used to it!'"

If I'd known you were coming I would have baked you a cake

The earliest known citation of this sometimes insincere greeting comes from *Munsey's Magazine*, January, 1912, in a story titled 'Paddling Sam' by J.E. Rath:

> **"If I'd** only **known you were coming**,' Beek apologized, **'I'd have had** a **cake**.'"

If wishes were horses, beggars would ride+

This is an old proverb meaning that if wishing could make things happen even the most destitute people could have anything they wanted. It is based on a line from a old nursery rhyme, the first version of which was published in 1605 in *Remaines of a Greater Worke, Concerning Britaine*:

> "If wishes were thrushes beggars would eat birds."

The earliest version with horses was printed in James Carmichael's *Proverbs in Scots* in 1628:

> "**And wishes were horses, pure (poor) men would wald ride**."

After appearing only a bit differently in John Ray's *Collection of English Proverbs* in 1670, the modern version appeared in James Kelly's *Scottish Proverbs* in 1771.

If you can live with it, I can live without it

In 1973, Bill Anderson released a song with this title on his RCA album, *'Bill.'* It hit number two on the country charts. In 1975 Jean Shephard covered it. The saying became popular as a cliché for people who had loaned money which others did not return.

If you can't run with the big dogs, you'd better stay on the porch

This saying means that if a person is unable to do what others are already doing then it is best not to try. This is a proverb which has only become popular in recent years. Origin is obscure, but the earliest known citation is in *And the Sun Stood Still* by Guy Parish, 2002, page 101:

> "They run like a scared Chihuahua back to the porch yelling, 'Oh, God, oh, God, oh, God!' **If you can't run with the big dogs, you'd better stay on the porch.**

If you don't like it, you can lump it

This old idiom means that the result obtained or the incident which has occurred is the best that can be expected and regardless of whether one approves or not, it is unchangeable. Lumping something is of Irish origin and goes back to the 16th century. The earliest example in print of 'like it or lump it,' however, comes in September, 1807, in *The Monthly Mirror,* a London magazine, in 'Rules for Punning:'

> "Mrs.—purposely sends a dish of tea to a lady, without sugar, of which she complains.
> Mr.—(Handing the sugar basin.) — Well, ma'am, **if you don't like it, you may lump it."**

If you don't stop crying I'll give you something to cry about

This shocking parental warning, or versions of it, go back to at least 1935, when it was used by American novelist Ellen Glasgow in her excellent work about a stalwart Appalachian woman, *Vein of Iron*, page 381:

> "'You can't go back. Don't you hear me? **Stop crying**. I'll get you another the next time we go back to Queenborough.' . . . 'But we ain't goin' ... out of the window. **If you don't keep quiet, I'll give you something to cry about** as soon as we get home.'"

If you pay peanuts, you get monkeys^

This brainy saying means that if an employer isn't willing to pay very much, the persons who work for him or her are going to be poor workers who will deliver poor results. It is often credited to flamboyant European Industrialist and author, Sir James Goldsmith. The earliest citation of a form of this proverb, however, is from a classified ad for a sales person in the *New York Times*, February 16, 1953:

> "ONLY **MONKEYS WORK FOR PEANUTS**, but YOU will be working and making BIG MONEY with US."

According to several normally reliable sources, though this citation was not found, the actual statement was made in *Director* by Leslie Coulthard, in speaking of directors' pay, August, 1966:

> "Shareholders want the best available businessmen to lead the companies and recognize that you get what you pay for. **If you pay in peanuts, you must expect to get monkeys**."

This was followed by two others who obviously 'borrowed' it in 1979.

If you're not living on the edge, you're taking up too much space^

On Wednesday morning, January 27, 2016, on NBC's *Today Show*, a man fighting an evacuation order in a costal apartment complex in Pacifica, California because of erosion used this 'old saying' to justify his position. This proverb has been credited to Canadian author Stephen Hunt (used in *The Court of the Air*, 2007), and famed American mountain climber, Jim Whitaker, the first American to reach the summit of Mount Everest and author of *A Life on the Edge: Memoirs of Everest and Beyond*, 1999. That same year it was used as the title of a book by Will Willis. It is also the title of a YouTube **Film Courage** film by Tiffany Shlain. The saying, however, predates all these books, and certainly the video. Jim Whitaker didn't even claim to have coined the proverb. In his acclaimed book he says:

> "I heard a phrase not too long ago that pretty much captures my philosophy of life: '**If you're not living on the edge, you're taking up too much space**.' It has nothing to do with thrill-seeking. It's about making the most of every moment, about stretching your own boundaries, about being willing to learn constantly and putting yourself in situations where learning is possible – sometimes even critical – to your survival. Being out on the edge, with everything at risk, is where you learn – and grow – the most."

The first citation known in print actually came in November, 1997, in *American Motorcyclist Magazine*, in an article titled 'A Common Road, Celebrating Women and Motorcycling,' in a quote from Kelly Friend. But she didn't claim to originate the saying, either, so the actual origin seems illusive. One website actually lists it as 'anonymous.'

Jim Whitaker defined it well. It may be stated that by 'pushing the envelope' (see in original volume), not being satisfied with the status quo; always searching for new answers, one discovers things about themselves and the Universe that others have never imagined. Some, however, see this philosophy as demeaning to the majority of humanity who wish only to 'live and let live' (see in original volume).

If you see something, say something

Originally, this saying was coined by Allen Kay, the Chairman and CEO of a major Manhattan advertising agency who has written about half of the 80 slogans that his agency has come up with since its beginning in 1982. This one was for the Metropolitan Transportation Authority. The day after the 9-11 tragedy in 2001, he jotted it down in his office on one of the 3X5 index cards he carries around just for this purpose. Though the MTA was already a client, he wrote this one without being asked to help prevent a new attack, but didn't present it until they asked him in 2002 for a security awareness campaign. By January, 2003, the slogan was on posters, subway cars, buses, etc.

Soon, it was broadcast around the world and became a 'global phenomenon'. It was taken as the name of a song by the alternative rock group, Taking Black Sunday, a book about French photographer, Touhami Ennadre, a monologue by Mike Daisey.

In July, 2010, Homeland Security launched the campaign by this name in conjunction with the U.S. Department of Justice's nationwide Suspicious Activity Reporting Institute. The slogan has been posted on billboards throughout Ohio by Homeland Security there. It is all over the Internet and it seems there is no end as to where it will appear.

If you want to go fast, go alone; if you want to go far, go together+

This proverb, like many others, is likely wrongly credited; this one taunted as an 'African Proverb.' It has been said to be thus in a modern work of Christian fiction (noted below), as well as in memes posted on Social Media. *30 Rock* (Season 4, Episode 6; November, 2009) famously quoted former U.S. Vice

President Al Gore as saying 'There's an old African proverb that I made up,' then using this exact wording. This 'quote' was obviously a joke. There is no concrete evidence that it was ever used in Africa. This is reminiscent of 'It takes a village to raise a child.' (See also in Volume II) The earliest use available in print is from novelist Robin Jones Gunn who used it in her book, *Coming Attractions,* published a few months before the episode aired (June 2009), in which a white missionary named Eli said to a white girl named Katie Weldon:

> "In Africa we having a saying, '**If you want to go fast, go alone. If you want to go far, go together**.'"

Ignite a firestorm+

In the literal sense, according to the *EOD*, a firestorm is a very intense and destructive fire; one usually caused by bombing (or during a wildfire), in which strong currents of air are drawn into it enabling it to create and sustain its own wind system. During the late 20th century, figuratively, igniting a firestorm came to refer to starting a fierce controversy. A very early reference in print is found in *Maryland Historical Magazine*, Fall 1975 issue, on pp 243-244:

> "For most Baltimoreans war had become an acceptable policy in 1807 when the British frigate *Leopard* attacked the American warship *Chesapeake* and impressed several sailors. This national indignity had **ignited a firestorm** of military patriotism in Baltimore."

Ignore him and he will go away

Though this statement is not always true, it's often been voiced. The idea of ignoring someone in hopes that they will leave goes back to at least 1920 when Edgar Rice Burrows used it in *Tarzan the Untamed,* page 273:

> "The best thing to do is simply to **ignore him**. Make no advances, but be sure to give no indication of fear and, if possible always keep me between you and him. **He will go away** presently I am sure and the chances are that we shall not see him again,"

After this, other authors began using the saying regularly, such as William Dudley Pelley, in *The Fog* the next year, page 319:

> "Let's just **ignore him**. Maybe **he'll go away."**

I hear you loud and clear! (See: **Loud and clear**)

I'll be John Brown!

Though most often this Southern American term is used today as only, "I'll be John Brown!" it was originally, 'I'll be John Browned.' John Brown was a staunch abolitionist during the American Civil War who and led slave revolts, helping many escape. He was convinced that God had called him to this mission, and would stop at nothing, including killing those opposed to his extreme tactics. He was captured after his raid on Harper's Ferry, Virginia in 1859 and hanged at Charles Town. To be 'John Browned' presumably meant 'damned' or hanged. It is used in the South now simply to indicate amazement or surprise. The earliest citation of being 'John Browned' is from *Overland Monthly*, May, 1870, in an article titled 'A Piney-Woods Character:'

> "He'll **be John-Browned** fust. But come, set up, stranger, and take a snook."

I'll have you know+

This is an idiomatic expression used to angrily emphasize a point, especially following a statement from someone else which seemed to be a personal put down. It was in use by at least the early 20th century. British authors Agnes and Egerton Castle used it in *Incomparable Bellairs* in 1907:

> "'**I'll have you know**, Miss Kitty,' pursued Mr. Stafford…"

I'll see you in the funny paper (See: **See you in the funny paper**)

I'm game if you are

This common idiom means that one is up for the challenge presented, or 'that sounds good to me.' It comes from being willing to take a risk even when some danger may be present. The earliest known citation of 'I'm game' is from *The Submissions of Dependence, A Novel, Interspersed with Poetry*, 1797, page 89:

> "You know **I'm game** to the back-bone; 'At her again, my buck!' says I.— In a word, sighs, agonies, poisons, pistols, and mock priests, did the business."

It wasn't until Saturday, April 2, 1870, in *Chambers Journal* in an article beginning on the first page titled 'The Suez Canal' that the expression 'I'm game if you are' first appeared:

> "'Let's have a bathe,' cries Smith, with his coat off, 'just for the fun of the thing. **I'm game, if you are**—only, look out for the sharks: I'm told that lots come up here, to get away from the noise of the docks.'"

Immediately, if not sooner

This comical expression for getting to something in the quickest possible time originated in the first half of the 19th century. The earliest known example is from the August, 1833 issue of *Frasers Magazine*, London, in 'The Last Duel I Had a Hand In' by C. O'Donoghue:

> "He was determined to fight; right or wrong, fight he must, and fight he Would—— **immediately, if not sooner**."

I'm too old for this

Forms of this saying have been popular since the 19th century. The earliest citation known in print is from *Parliamentary Papers, House of Commons and Command, Volume 22*, Reports of Commissioners, Army, Military Punishment, Session, February 4 to August 20, 1836, page 218, London, 1836:

> "…and when the old soldiers find themselves disappointed in not getting the lot, they say, '**I am getting too old for this**, I should like to take my discharge now, I cannot do so well as I used to do.'"

In the 1990s the saying became commonplace and cliché, and was often accompanied by profanity.

In a bubble (See: **Living in a bubble**)

In any way, shape or form

In other words, you can look at a problem from any angle but the outcome will be the same. This rhetorical idiom is used in places in which a less flamboyant term would have sufficed, but emphasis is intended. The origin is obscure, but the exact phrase was in use by Friday, July 28, 1826, when *Colonial Times*, Hobart Town, Tasmania, Australia, printed this on the Communications page:

> "And secondly, that permission to marry be obtained exactly as it is in Britain, upon the application of the parties, without subjecting them to Mr. Bedford's interference in **any way, shape, or form** whatever;..."

In 1747, the following forerunner of the expression appeared in the religious publication, *A Treatise on Miracles* by Abraham Lemoine, Chaplin to His Grace the Duke of Portland:

> "...Falshood, and Vice in **any Shape or Form**, or **any** thing contrary to the Attributes of God, or any thing idle, useless, or absurd, or in any wise prejudicial to me."

In a pickle

This truly ancient cliché expression is another way of saying 'in a quandary' or difficulty. Though literal pickles changed through the ages, 'pickle' comes from the Low German word *pekel* which translates to 'something piquant' The idiom, however, came from the idea of being mixed up like the stewed vegetables which were made into pickles by the mid-15th century. The earliest English rendition of the word later to become 'pickle' in English was in *The Morte Arthure*, published circa 1440, wherein were the supposed ingredients of King Arthur's diet:

> "He soupes all this sesoun with seuen knaue childre, Choppid in a chargour of chalke-whytt syluer, With **pekill** & powdyre of precious spycez."

In modern vernacular this would read: "He dines all season on seven rascal children, chopped, in a bowl of white silver, with **pickle** and precious spices."

Then, in 1573, first figurative use appears in Thomas Tusser's *Five Hundreth Pointes of Good Husbandrie*:

> "Reape barlie with sickle, that lies **in ill pickle**."

Though this usage is a bit offbeat, using 'ill pickle,' Shakespeare brought us to a version of the understandable term, 'in a pickle' in Act V, Scene i of *The Tempest*, 1610:

> "ALONSO:
> And Trinculo is reeling ripe: where should they

Find this grand liquor that hath gilded 'em?
How camest thou **in this pickle**?

"TRINCULO:
I have been **in such a pickle** since I
saw you last that, I fear me, will never out of
my bones: I shall not fear fly-blowing."

In a world of trouble

Having kindred to 'in a pickle' its origins are in much the same time frame. In the anonymous Elizabethan history play, *The Trve Tragedie of Richard III*, entered into the Stationer's Register June 19, 1594, we find:

> "Vnto whose gouernment, I commit to my brother the Protector, But to thee Elizabeth my Daughter, I leaue the **in a World of trouble**…"

Strangely enough, the next citation of this now familiar idiom does not occur until 1693, when it shows up in *The Present State of Europe* (for the month of January, 1693), *Volume IV*, published in London, page 332:

> "The Intendant of that Province is **in a world of Trouble**."

In cahoots

This became a trite expression in Western movies during the golden age of Hollywood. But it was around much earlier. The first known reference in print is in Pennsylvania Supreme Court Justice Hugh Henry Brackenridge's immortal historic classic, *Modern Chivalry*, the first two parts initially published in 1792, as it was in the 1846 version, Volume I, on page 98:

> "This fellar that calls himself capting, is the head of a gang of horse thieves, and t'other fellar goes **in cahoots** with him…"

It means that two or more persons are or were involved in a partnership or shared equally in a venture. It has often been used in negative connotations as in a conspiracy.

In clover

To live, be or roll 'in clover' means in a state of luxury; having good financial fortune. A major Internet dictionary lists origin at 'about 1700.' That is close;

however, it was in use by at least 1677, as it was utilized in *Depositio cornuti typographici: that is, A Comical or Mirthful Play* by John Rist published in Frankfurt-On-the-Main that year, on page 49:

> "When of my 'prenticeship the term was gone and over
> I was exceeding proud, as Grandee I would pose,
> Who in his vain conceit could always live **in clover**;
> Altho' no man did more all goodness to oppose."

Clover is excellent grazing for cattle, and grows thick and heavy, likely attributing to the expression. Rare four-leaf clovers are thought of as good luck charms; but this only came to be much later. The earliest reference in print available is from *Margaret: A Tale of the Real and Ideal, Blight and Bloom*, by Sylvester Judd, 1845:

> "Wal, now I want you should tell me if you ever found a **four-leaf clover**? Speak low; walls have ears."

In cold blood

This line dredges up memories of Truman Capote's classic award-winning 1965 non-fiction book about the rural Kansas murders of four members of the Herbert Clutter family in 1959 by that name, later made into a popular film. It means 'deliberately or ruthlessly' and with no emotion. It is derived from a person acting like a cold-blooded animal. The term has been used in English since at least 1601, when it appeared in *Civill Considerations Vpon Many and Svndrie Histories, as Well Ancient and Modern* by Lord Leme of Florence, French by Remigio Nannini, Gabriel Chappuys, English by W.T., page 190:

> "And for this cause men say that counsels and enterprises are to be taken in hand **in 'cold blood,'** and the execution thereof to be done in hot blood."

Then in 1609, in *A General History of the Netherlands* by Jean François Le Petit and Ed Grimeston, page 1244, the citation is more obvious, speaking of being 'slain:'

> "...were at their coming out of the fort, slaine **in cold blood**, and almost all their souldiers, except some who beeing stript into their shirts saued themselues by their heeles."

Indian summer

In its literal application, this term refers to a period of unusually dry, warm weather in autumn in the Northern Hemisphere. Figuratively, it means a time of happiness or success late in one's life. According to a lengthy article in *Monthly Weather Review*, February, 1902, titled 'The Term Indian Summer' by lexicographer Albert Matthews of Boston, he had done an in depth study in an attempt to discover who coined the term, uncovering a treasure trove of citations going back as far as the late 18th century, but not being able to pinpoint the precise origin. It was first recorded in 1778 in *Letters from an American Farmer* by a former French American military man named J. H. St. John de Crèvecoeur (known as. Michel-Guillaume-Jean de Crèvecoeur):

> "Then a severe frost succeeds which prepares it to receive the voluminous coat of snow which is soon to follow; though it is often preceded by a short interval of smoke and mildness, called the **Indian Summer**."

Matthews had one theory that it may have been derived from a term once in use, 'Indian harvest,' which he felt could have referred to Indian corn, or maize, harvested in the late fall when it was dry. Yet, he had problems with this derivation because it had become obsolete long before the term Indian summer came into use. Another, possibly more plausible, theory had to do with Indian mythology about an old Native American named Shadowdance, who kept his eyes steady on the North, and when he sighed in the fall, it caused balmy Southern airs, giving us Indian summer.

It was in the 1830s that this idiom began to be cited metaphorically. In 1834, famed American Quaker poet, John Greenleaf Whitaker, in *Memories,* made reference to that late-life renewal:

> "Thus, while at times before our eyes
> The shadows melt, and fall apart,
> And, smiling through them, round us lies
> The warm light of our morning skies,--
> The **Indian Summer** of the heart!"

Then in 1867, in his gripping novel, *The Guardian Angel,* Oliver Wendell Holmes, wrote:

> "An **Indian summer** crept stealthily over his closing days."

Other common theories as to how the name came about include the phenomenon being noticed by early European settlers who gave it the name because of the 'Indians' living on the North American continent; the belief that haziness of the

Indian summer was caused by prairie fires deliberately set by Natives, and the fact that it was during this time that the First Families harvested their crops.

In for a penny, in for a pound[2]

This primarily British proverb means that once a person has gotten started on a project, he or she should see it through to completion even if it has proved to be more difficult than first imagined. The origin was in reference to the thought that if one owed a penny, it might as well have been a pound. In 1695, playwright Edward Ravenscroft first cited it in *Canterberry Guests*, Act V, Scene i;

> "Sir *Bar.*
>
> "Well than, *O'er shooes, o'er boots.* And *In for a Penny, in for a Pound.* Whee—ho— *Toby.*"

Americanization of the term, 'In for a dime, in for a dollar,' was used by Timothy M. Bracy with folk rock band, The Mendoza Line, in the lyrics to *Settle Down Zelda.*

In it to win it

This now common idiom means that a person is serious about a competition, and didn't just enter because someone asked him or her to do so, but has every intention of giving the competition his or her full effort in hopes of being a winner. The saying was popularized by Randy Jackson on NBC TV's *American Idol* which premiered June 11, 2002. But Jackson didn't coin the phrase. The late Illinois professor and political author, David Kenney, published a book in 1998 titled *In It, to Win It: A Personal Memoir*. Since then, two other books have had this phrase at the first of their title.

In mothballs+

To 'put something in mothballs' or 'mothball something,' is an idiom used metaphorically to mean that a product or idea is being 'shelved,' or not developed, for a period of time. It comes from the outmoded practice of packing out-of-use clothing in mothballs (small naphthalene balls) from the late 19th century to the mid-20th century, to keep them from being destroyed by moths. The figurative expression was first used circa 1946 as a naval term regarding ships not being put out of service after World War II.

In my book

This hyperbolic American expression refers to a mythical book kept mentally by a person, reflecting that individual's opinions and beliefs. It simply means 'in my opinion.' The actual genesis of this is illusive, but it may have been derived from comments by authors through the ages beginning as early as the late 17th century about opinions presented in a literal book which the person had written. For instance, in 1680, John Humphreys, in *Vindiciæ veritatis: a narrative vindicating the truth,* included the following on page 12:

> "... which he in Scorn called Heresie, and me a Papist, being himself both ignorant of the Truth and of Popery, he charged me then that I said Christ was filthy— let all sober Persons judge that, if **in my Book** such an Expression is — but we may say Christ was guilty..."

But it was the mid-20th century before the figurative saying really caught on. The expression was obviously already in use, but *Billboard*, in January 17, 1942, carries the following early citation under the Editor's Desk on page 43:

> "This manager is **okay in my book**. He has been furnishing shade, smokes, cold drinks, sandwiches and an electric fan for us players all afternoon."

In my humble opinion / IMHO+

This is a humorous expression indicating that one feels that he or she is right about something. This phrase has been used throughout history back at least as far as the late 17th century. It was used six times in *Two Proposals Humbly Offer'd to the Honorable Houfe of Commons, Now Assembled in Parliament*, presented and published in London in 1696. The first citation appears on page 9:

> "...there needs nothing more, **in my Humble Opinion**, to induce a compliance to fuch (such) a Propofal (proposal);"

Only in modern times, since the early 1990s, has the acronym IMHO come into usage, and the exact origin and meaning, whether humble or honest, has come into question, though the consensus deems to stick to humble.

In nothing flat

This curious idiom means 'in very little time.' The word 'flat' has long been used to mean precisely. It came from measurement of volume, not time. For example, a flat bushel of grain or some other substance once measured in this way. In 1882, In the English Dialect Society's Publication, *A Glossary, The Lancaster Dialect, Part II, F – Z*, under 'Skip,' we find:

> "In Sussex it means **a flat bushel**, a vessel for yeast, a bee-hackle, a bee-hive (as in Norfolk), and even a hat." *Survival of Early Eng. Words*

The earliest known reference to 'in nothing flat' comes not long afterward, in *The Petroleum Gazette,* Titusville, Pennsylvania, January, 1910, in 'An Easy Finishing Job,' on page 9:

> "It is said by bystanders that Driller G. B. Primmer and Tool Dresser W. White made the first hundred yards **in nothing flat**, but at the end of the hundred yards, when rocks, some of them weighing at least 10 pounds, commenced to rain down that their time was increased for the second hundred, at the end of which distance they only had a good start."

In one's own backyard^

This idiom refers to something being very close to a person's domain; closer than hoped. A major online dictionary lists its origin as mid-1900s. This expression, however, was around over half a century earlier. In *The Overland Monthly*, July, 1890, in a story titled 'A Set of Born Fools,' on page 62, we read:

> "The home will have to be changed before the school can do much for them, and under the most favorable surroundings there can never be progress beyond the rudest decency. It's a case of heathen **in our own backyard**, instead of in Hawaii or Japan and I feel called upon to labor with them."

In over one's head

This metaphoric expression has to do with a person or group being involved with someone who, or in something which, has more problems that he, she or they is or are able to handle. The saying is often applied to heavy indebtedness or financial decline. It is derived from persons who have trouble swimming wading out into deep water. The origin is unclear, but the saying came into use by the late 19th century. A fine early example is from *Twenty Years in Wall Street* by Henry Clews, 1888

> "They were really an over-issue by the Company. It was a Waterloo in a double sense for Jerome and his fellow bulls. **They were in over their heads**."

Insanity is doing the same thing over and over expecting different results^

This definition of insanity (used by Alchoholics Annonymous) is most often attributed to Albert Einstein and second most frequently to Benjamin Franklin (there have also been others including Zig Ziglar and Oscar Wilde). None of these originated this thought. The first *verifiable* attribution of this astute proverbial saying being credited to Einstein was in 1998, and earliest *verifiable* source attributing this quote to Framklin was in an article in 2004. The problem with direct attribution is that usually a prolific idea undergoes alterations down through time, and is transferred to another great thinker who states it in his or her own way. Another on-line source says that the earliest form was in French, and coined by author and philosopher, François-Marie Arouet, known

professionally by the psudynm Voltaire (1694-1788), a friend of Benjamin Franklin when he was U.S. Ambassador to France. Again, not a true source, but a likely hoax. In a book titled *The Great Secret*, by Osho, an Indian mystic guru, published in 1975, chapter 10, page 181, he wrote:

> "To be mad is to keep repeating something that has already been seen as useless, as worthless."

This is certainly on the track of the saying. Feminist Rita Mae Brown included the actual proverb in her book, *Sudden Death*, in 1983. It has also been claimed that this version originated in AA, and that it appeared in their textbooks as early as 1981, but verification is not available.

In spades

Though other card related idioms, even 'call a spade a spade' (see) had been in use for centuries, this one didn't show up in its figurative use until the 20th century, and was coined in America. The fact that the saying represented a maximum was most likely relevant to the fact that spades are the highest ranking suit in Contact Bridge, a very popular game in the U.S. when the term came to be. The term was in constant usage in the game at the time. But in October, 1929, American journalist Damon Runyon, said this in an article printed in *Hearst's International* magazine:

> "I always hear the same thing about every bum on Broadway, male and female, including some I know are bums, **in spades**, right from taw."

The term may mean, to a very high degree, or achieved with a good margin.

In the cold light of day[2]

This old idiom is used more frequently in British English, yet is also known in America, and refers to facing or thinking about a matter clearly and calmly, as it really is, with no emotion related to an actual event, but often with remorse. It is derived from light revealing truth, and cold representing the lack of passion. The term developed in the mid-19th century, and the earliest citation, though with some variation of connotation, is from *An Art Student in Munich* by Anna Mary Watts, Volume II, page 178, 1853:

> "And above the crowd of living figures rise colossal forms of armed warriors, and peaceful poets, and sceptred monarchs; these glowing crimson; those standing calm and pale **in the cold light of day**."

By the close of the century, the term was taking on a bit different color. In *To-day,* November 5, 1898, in Chapter 2 of John Buchan's 'A Lost Lady of Old Years,' on page 8 he writes:

> "Even the rhetorical parting did not comfort him. Seen **in the cold light of day**, it seemed crude and boyish."

In the crosshairs

Someone or some cause 'in the crosshairs' is in the position to be attacked. Crosshairs are lines which intersect in a rifle scope, zeroing in on a target. A similar expression is 'Target on someone's back' (see). It is unknown who coined it, but this term did not begin figurative usage until around the turn of this century. A very early example is in *What the Best CEOs Know* by Jeffery E, Krames, 2003, in a heading on page 6:

> "CEOs **IN THE CROSSHAIRS**"

Within the next few years it became commonplace.

In the dark about something+

This is a metaphoric expression for being ignorant or uninformed about a particular subject or development, and is most usually used when someone deliberately withholds information from someone else. According to a popular online dictionary the saying dates back to the 1670s. Three actual references are found in *The Building of the Tower of Salvation: Being a Preparation Sermon* by Scottish minister, James Simson, who died c 1694. From the 3rd Edition published in 1723. The first one is on page 14:

> "Secondly you may be at this Disadvantage, **to be in the Dark about Thy duty**,"

In the eye of the storm (See: **Eye of the storm**)

In the heat of the moment

This refers to something said or done without thinking about the results because of anger or excitement. 'In the heat of the battle' was in use as early as the late 16th century. Two hundred years later, this expression took root. The earliest known citation is found in *The Critical Review; Or Annals of Literature, Extended and Improved* by A Society of Gentlemen, Volume II, in 'William's Letters from France' on page 66, 1792:

> "...and the little influences of these partial disturbances on the whole: to which may be added, that accounts transmitted **in the heat of the moment** are always exaggerated, because they are dictated while the resentment is warm, and while fear adds imaginary evils to the real ones."

In the lap of luxury

This ancient cliché refers to living in plush comfort and lavish conditions because 'money in no object' (see). The earliest known citation is in *Lord Beilhaven's Speech to the Scotch Parliament Saturday the 2nd of November on the Subject Matter of the Union of Scotland and England*, 1706:

> "For the disasters of that shameful year, awaked the nation that had been laid asleep so long **in the lap of luxury**, and heaven directed the voice of the people to raise a man to power, who was born to restore a falling state."

In / Out of the loop

These related idioms refer to keeping a person included or excluded from a group which is informed and up-to-date about a particular matter. 'Loop,' in this sense, comes from the definition; 'a sequence of control activities in which each depends upon the previous one.' 'Out of the loop' is a converse variation. Both are American in origin and began to be used in the 1970s. Out of the loop was cited by January, 1973, when the following was printed in *The Educational Technology Reviews Series Number Ten: Using Programed Instruction* on page 128:

> "...simple punch card maintenance of a child attendance audit puts the teachers almost entirely **out of the loop**."

Early citations of 'in the loop' are illusive. Both really took of in the 21st century. A good example in print of 'in the loop' is in *Store Manager: The Professional Experience* by Larry Frazio, 2000, page 20:

> "Nonetheless, the musical director is usually present for each rehearsal, and needs to be **kept in the loop** of information and have workspace in the rehearsal hall."

In the middle of nowhere

This means in an extremely remote place, away from civilization, now often referred to as 'off the grid' (see). The saying was in use in America by the late 19th century. The earliest example available in print is from *The Annals and Magazine of Natural History*, July, 1893, in 'Notes on the Mexican Coccidae' by T.D.A. Cockarell, on page 47:

> "It proved that the engine and freight cars in front had left the rails, owing to a 'wash-out,' and consequently we had to spend many hours **in the middle of nowhere**, six miles north of Montezuma R. R. Station, in the State of Chihuahua."

In the mind's eye

This figure of speech refers to a person's memory or imagination. The idea is ancient, going back to at least the late 14th century. Geoffrey Chaucer brought it to light in circa 1387 in the 5th of *his Canterberry Tales*, *The Man of Law's Tale*:

> "It were with thilke **eyen of his mynde**, With whiche men seen, after that they been blynde."

The more modern English version came in a letter written by Hubert Languet in 1577 which was published in *The Correspondence of Sir Philip Sidney and Hubert Languet* in 1845:

"What will not these golden mountains effect ... which I dare say stand before your **mind's eye** day and night?"

But the term was popularized by none other that Shakespeare in his immortal play of plays, *Hamlet*, Act I, Scent ii, in 1602:

"HAMLET:
Thrift, thrift, Horatio! the funeral baked meats
Did coldly furnish forth the marriage tables.
Would I had met my dearest foe in heaven
Or ever I had seen that day, Horatio!
My father! - methinks I see my father.

"HORATIO:
Where, my lord?

"HAMLET:
In my mind's eye, Horatio."

In the shadow of (See also: **Walking in someone's shadow**)

This can now mean either near in position or close events, or being in *someone's shadow* may refer to receiving attention because of your relationship physically or relationally. 'Shadow,' in essence, has been used figuratively for over 3,000 years (pre-dating English). Through the ages this phrase has been shaped into numerous metaphoric symbols. It was used by King David when he wrote the *23rd Psalm, verse 4*:

"Yea, though I walk through the valley of **the shadow of death** I will fear no evil, for thou art with me..." *(KJV)*

In Christian literature this term was being used in other ways than in relation to death by 1567, when the following appeared in *A Rejoindre to M. Jewels Replie against the Sacrifice of the Masse,* in the Preface to the Catholic Reader:

"The sacrifice hath come in the place of all those sacrifices of the Old Testament, whiche were sacrificed **in the shadow of** the sacrifice to come."

The term 'in the shadow of' continued to be popular in various metaphors in Christian writings throughout history. But, in *The Jew of Malta,* Act II, Scene i, Christopher Marlow used this brilliant line in 1633:

> ***"Barabas***
> "Thus like the sad presaging Raven that tolls
> The sicke mans passeport in her hollow beake,
> And **in the shadow of** the silent night
> Doth shake contagion from her sable wings;"

Here, though absence of light prevails in night, 'shadow' is used metaphorically to represent the ominous presence of overall darkness.

In 1906, J. Henry Harris used the idiom in his novel, *Cornish Saints and Sinners* in chapter two, in respect of 'walking in the shadow of' in a secular format:

> "It was one of those towns in which you seem to be always **walking in the shadow of** a long yesterday."

In the soup

This idiom is used to mean in trouble, or in a bad situation. The phrase was popularized in New York City in the late 1800s. One theory is that it started at a Polo Grounds basketball game in June, 1888. Another story is that when the fighter Kilrain's ship was not allowed to enter New York Harbor, a few ruffians took a tugboat out to meet him. One, it is told, fell into the Hudson, 'into the soup.' All of these seem a bit iffy. On September 1, 1888, *The New York Times* printed this on page 8:

> "McLaughlin won with King Crab in the easiest possible fashion, and Speedwell finished **'in the soup'**."

The following, however, sounds more like the source was 'in the know.' In the November 8, 1888 issue, a lady wrote to the editor of the *Trenton Times* in Trenton, New Jersey, asking about the origin of two then popular idioms. One was 'in the soup.' Here's the editor's answer on page 3, column 2:

> "In answer to the above...we would say that '**In the soup**' had its first appearance in the vernacular slang at the Hoffman House in New York when an awkward waiter stumbled and fell while carrying an urn of soup through the dining room. As he fell the scalding liquid flew over his head and face, and he ran from the room in great pain. A gentleman turning to Tom Ochiltree, who was dining with him, asked what was the matter with the waiter, and the wit replied, 'He's **in the soup**.' The waiter, of course, lost his position, and grumbled because he thought he had not received proper

> treatment. The politicians took the phrase up and have applied it to defeated candidates, and the parallel is easily seen."

In tow

This means following or going along under someone's control. It is taken from automobiles being towed when enroute to a garage, or behind a motor home, etc.; or vessels being towed by tugs on waterways. Figurative use is modern and began in the late 20th century. An early citation is in *A Searching Heart*, by Jeanette Oak, 1998, page 165:

> "He was almost to the bedside before Virginia realized that he had her **in tow**,"

I rest my case

This cliché is a statement made after the person being addressed has realized that the speaker is right in a disagreement. It is based upon the statement made by an attorney after closing statements are made in court. In a literal sense, it has been in use since at least the late 18th century. In the 'Trial of Renwick Williams' printed in *The Lawyers and Magistrates Magazine*, July, 1790, the earliest known example in print appears:

> **"I rest my case** to the decision of an English Jury; and, in hopes of being able to establish my innocence in your opinion, I most furiously appeal to the Great Author of Truth, that I have the strongest affection for the happiness and comfort of the superior part of this creation..."

The figurative use goes back to at least the 1960s. In *The Impossible Years, A Comedy in Two Acts*, Act I, Scene ii, 1964, Arthur Marx uses the following non-legal example:

> "**Alice**. It certainly looks like your signature.
> **Miss Hammer**. But it isn't?
> **Alice**. No.
> **Miss Hammer**. **I rest my case**."

Iron curtain

This figurative term was used for the physical boundary which divided Europe between the close of World War II and the end of what was known as the 'Cold

War' in 1881. It was a symbol of the Soviet Union's block of it and satellite states from free contact with Western non-communist states. Though this term had been used infrequently in other connotations since the 19th century, it was popularized for this meaning by British Prime Minister Winston Churchill in a speech on March 5, 1946 made in Fulton, Missouri when a guest of the U.S. Government, containing this statement:

> "From Stettin in the Baltic to Trieste in the Atlantic, an **iron curtain** has descended across the continent."

Iron fist (See: **Rule with an iron fist**)

It ain't over till it's over

This Yogi-ism (attributed to the late famed Yankee catcher, manager, Lawrence Peter "Yogi" Berra), means not to give up too soon, before the final result is in.

But this phrase *may* have been in use in a different context before Barra brought it to popularity. In *Who Gave Pinta to the Santa Maria*, by Robert S. Desowitz, 1980, the following citation appeared:

> "With yellow fever **it's not over till it's over**; the vast sylvatic reservoir remains, and outbreaks, although not on the grand scale of yesteryear, still occur."

Itching palm

This is an idiom meaning that a person is greedy, as having an itchy palm has long been a superstition for about to receive money. In reality, this is a sign of a skin problem; possibly eczema. This saying goes back to Shakespeare in *Julius Caesar*, Act IV, Scene iii, 1599:

> ***"Bru.*** Yet let me tell you, Cassius, you yourself Are much condemned to have an **itching palm**, To sell and mart your ossices for gold, To undeservers."

It is better that ten guilty men go free than for one innocent man to be imprisoned

There have been numerous versions of this proverb since William Blackstone famously wrote it in *Commandments on the Laws of England* in 1769. Here is his declaration:

> "**The law holds that it is better that ten guilty persons escape, than that one innocent suffer**."

Another British scholar, Thomas Starkie, in his 1824 book on *Evidence* wrote:

> "**That it is better that ninety-nine ... offenders shall escape than that one innocent man be condemned**."

In a letter to Benjamin Vaughn dated March 14, 1785, published in the *Writings of Benjamin Franklin*, edited by Albert H. Smyth, Volume 9, page 293, published in 1906, we see:

> "**That it is better 100 guilty Persons should escape than that one innocent Person should suffer,** is a Maxim that has been long and generally approved."

But the person who actually coined the saying was Voltaire in his 1749 philosophical novel, *Zadig: The Book of Fate, An Oriental History*, on page 53, where he credits it to the protagonist of his tale, a fictional Babylonian philosopher:

> "It was to him, the Nations round about were indebted for that generous Maxim; that **'tis much**, **more Prudence** to **acquit two Persons**, **tho' actually guilty**, **than** to **pass Sentence** of **Condemnation** on **one** that is **virtuous** and **innocent**."

It is better to have loved and lost than to have never loved at all

This proverbial saying comes from a poem by Alfred Lord Tennyson completed in 1847: *In Memorium, A.H.H.*, Cantro 21:

> "I hold it true, whate'er befall;
> I feel it when I sorrow most;
> **'Tis better to have loved and lost**
> **Than never to have loved at all**."

It never rains but it pours+

This is a very old proverb meaning that troubles and trials often come in rapid succession, like heavy downpours of rain. It has been in use since at least the early 18th century, when it was recorded in a book (actually a pamphlet) said to have been written by Queen Anne's physician, John Arbuthnot, in 1726 titled *It Cannot Rain but it Pours; or In London Strow'd with Rarities.*

That same year, Jonathan Swift published an article using the same title as Arbuthnot's book. In 1766, twenty-one years after Swift's death, however, it was included in *The Works of Dr. Jonathan Swift*, Volume V, on page 165, where it is attributed to Arbuthnot. But it is curious why it was in Swift's works. Another twist in the 1892 publication *The Life and Works of John Arbuthnot, MD, Fellow of the Royal Court of Physicians* compiled by George Atherton Aitken. On page 107/108, may give us the answer:

> "Another piece, *It Never Rains but it Pours*, is probably Swift's, though it's sometimes attributed to Arbuthnot. It refers to a wild boy named Peter, who was found in Hanover in 1725, brought to England, and committed for some time to Arbuthnot's care. He died in 1785. Another pamphlet on the same subject, published in 1726, and reprinted in *Arbuthnot's Miscellaneous Works*, may also be Swift's. It was called *The Most Wonderful Wonder that ever Appeared to the Wonder of the British Nation* and contained a satirical dialogue upon the ways of civilised society between the wild boy and his foster mother, an old bear which had been brought to London by Mynheer Veteranus. It was described as 'written by the Copper-Farthing Dean,' in allusion to the controversy over Wood's halfpence, in which Swift had taken so active a part."

At the time of the writing of this pamphlet, according to this author, Arbuthnot was seriously ill. Swift, a close lifelong friend of Arbuthnot, was believed to have taken over writing for his friend.

A similar expression came much later, "When it rains it pours." (See original volume, page 599)

It's a dog's life

This saying was coined and popularized in past centuries when dogs guarded the homes in small communities. Winters were especially rough and the dogs slept outside. Life for them was not good, and was often short. The phrase meant that life was very bad. It is still used to mean that the tasks which have become one's lot in life are unpleasant but necessary. The earliest citation in print available is found in *Blackwood's Magazine*, October, 1847, in an article titled 'Hounds and Houses at Rome:'

> "A **'dog's life'** has become a synonym for suffering; nor does the associating him with another domestic animal (If a second proverbial expression may be trusted) appear to mend his condition…"

It's a woman's prerogative (or **privilege) to change her mind**

Bibliotheca scholastica instructissima, or, A treasury of ancient adagies and sententious proverbs selected out of the English, Greeke, Latine, French, Italian, and Spanish, by Thomas Draxe, published first in London in 1616, is the earliest source in print, and lists this as a Berman proverb. It is sometime used by females when males object to a statement or opinion she states which is very different from the one which she previously made or held.

It's been a minute/ a hot minute+

This is a modern saying, like so many other current idioms, which means just the opposite. It means it has been quite a while since something has happened, particularly since seeing another person. Though the term 'hot minute' dates to the mid-19th century, it was used entirely differently. In numerous references between 1932 and 1984 a hot minute was used to mean a short time. Then the Red Hot Chile Peppers had a hit song in the 1990s, *One Hot Minute*. Beginning around the turn of the century, it became the in thing to reverse the meaning, increasing use of such expressions as 'bad threads' for nice clothes, and more recently, 'that's so dope!' (See) reversing the way Americans speak.

It's curtains for (you, him, her, us, them, etc.)**!**

This metaphor came from theater curtains going down at the end of a play. It soon began to be used for something coming to an end. Telling someone 'it's curtains' means that whatever 'game or part they have been playing' is coming to a sudden hault. It came into use in the early 20th century, and a great early example is from the *San Francisco Daily Times*, February 23, 1918 in 'Social Profile,' by Tantalus under 'Zoloags and Fraser,' page 12, where 'curtains' is in quotes:

> "The picador stoops forward in the saddle, the most dejected, woe-begone, beaten old seriocomic **you** ever saw. There is no doubt about it, **it's 'curtains'** for him."

It's easier to get forgiveness than permission

This proverb means that when a person has already done something questionable, asking those hurt by it is easier than if permission had been asked. The indiscretion may be forgiven, but permission would likely have never been granted. This is a quote from U.S. Naval Rear Admiral Grace Murray Hopper (1906-1992), who was well known for her wit and wisdom, that was published in *Chips Ahoy* magazine, July, 1996. After that it became very popular.

But the saying was around before that. In February, 1984 it was listed in *Mother Jones Magazine* as number 262, along with hundreds of other witty sayings to be printed on tee shirts. Then in *The Rotarian* magazine, April, 1986, we find:

> "You've heard of Murphy's Law: if anything can go wrong, it will. Here are a few others: Stewart's Law: It is **easier to get forgiveness than permission**..."

This is because it actually appeared in a book titled *Murphy's Law Book Two* by Arthur Bloch published in 1980.

It's five o'clock somewhere

This saying is used comically as an excuse to drink and party at any time of the day. It is the title of a song recorded on the Arista label by Alan Jackson and Jimmy Buffett in May, 2003, released June 2nd. It was a hit on both the country and pop charts; the first since the 1970s for Buffett. The song was written by Jim 'Moose' Brown and Don Rollins.

It's like riding a bicycle / bike

This universal axiom is used to relate to an activity that once learned is easy to remember, even though it hasn't been performed in a long time. The exact origin is obscure. There is an early example in which, before this analogy became popular, the opposite was stated. In *First Person Singular* by Florence Ryerson and Colin Clements, 1937, in reference to doing math in one's head, on page 12 we read:

> "I didn't say I could do it now. **It's** something you get out of practice of. **Like riding a bicycle**. Or roller skating."

Then about 20 years later, the modern saying had taken root. In *Popular Mechanics*, January, 1958, in 'The Army Adopts a New Rifle,' on page 150, we see the following:

> "Firing the Ml must be **like riding a bicycle** — once learned, it'**s** not forgotten."

It's lonely at the top

This means that those who are most successful sometimes have the fewest true friends. An online source states that a German philosopher made a statement similar to this in the 19th century, but no proof of this has been found. This *principle* was stated in English as early as July 12, 1909 in *American Druggist and Pharmaceutical Record* in the Business Building section on page 12:

> "There may be a few who are still working for glory, but they must feel sort of **lonely** at times."

The idea of high places, in a literal sense, being lonely, was expressed in *The Diaries of Paul Klee* (1898-1918) later published in 1964. In Diary 11, on page 102 we find:

> "It had become high and **lonely**. A mountain **top** is much more **lonely** when a vast sea is below."

This exact saying was popularized by Randy Newman's 1972 soft rock hit titled *It's Lonely at the Top,* making light of the self-pity of the successful.

It's no skin off my teeth (or **nose**)

Both expressions are used to mean that something is not much of a concern to the person saying it. Both are used at times in the U.S., and only 'teeth' seems to be prevalent in the U.K. The 'nose' version appeared as early as June, 1910, when *Cosmopolitan* the following citation appeared in 'Propriety Pratt, Hypnotist' by Alfred Henry Lewis, on page 18, where it appears to be already a known expression:

> "Your romancin' 'round single that a-way **ain't no skin off my nose**."

The earliest known citation for 'no skin off my teeth' in in *Atlantic Monthly*, Vol. 162, (July-December) 1938:

> "'Cap'm,' he said, looking at the ground, 'I'm a man doesn't never kick in no other man's stall.'
> "Well, maybe you do and maybe you don't. **That ain't no skin off my teeth**, and if you get killed messin' around here that won't be nothin' new.'"

It's your funeral

This is an expression used to show lack of sympathy for another person's intended foolish actions, when he or she knows that the personal consequences will be catastrophic. This saying came into being in the mid-to-late 1800s, and the earliest example available in print is from A. Frank Pinkerton's detective novel, *Marked for Life*, 1887, page 75:

> "Carlos gave a slight shiver as the Jew spoke of murder, but feeling that Simon was looking at him with searching eyes, he laughed, and saying, 'Well, I don't care, **it's your funeral**, not mine, and if—'"

It takes a village to raise a child

This proverbial saying was popularized by a 1996 book credited to Hillary Rodham Clinton, actually primarily written by ghostwriter Barbara Feinman, titled *It Takes a Village and Other Lessons Children Teach Us*. The title is credited to 'an African proverb,' but there is no solid evidence of this or the other popular source claimed, 'a Native American saying.' In fact, a previous children's book also had the title, *It Takes a Village*, which was written by Jane Cowan-Fletcher, published in January, 1994.

The idea that this was an African proverb was introduced by Roscoe Pound in *An Introduction to the Philosophy Law*, first copyrighted in 1922, then 1954 by Yale University Press, page 58. Note that it was already a cliché in the U.S.:

> "The African proverb '**It takes a village to raise a child**' has become a cliché in current discussions about education in the United States."

Since Clinton's book came out numerous sources have claimed various tribes originated the proverb. An online group did extensive research on the subject and came up 'empty-handed.' The actual origin remains a mystery.

I've been around the block a few times

This expression is used in Australia, as well as America, to let someone know that you are not a novice, and that you understand a situation, either good or bad, from firsthand experience. Using the idea in the third person is often derogatory, meaning that the person is immoral or lacks discipline. It became a part of regular American jargon in the last half of the 20th century. The earliest example known in print of a form of it is from *Billboard*, page 56, October 10, 1970, in 'Nashville's Gospel Apple Corporation;' here in a favorable setting:

> "Steve Singleton heard them sing, and Steve has **been around the block a few times** in the record business, having learned it first hand at home and in the studio. He felt he had something. So he and the kids went to work."

Tom Clancy used the first-person version in his best seller, *Clear and Present Danger*, 1989, on page 111:

> "But **I've been around the block a few times**, just like you people..."

I've (you've) got to hand it to you (or someone)+

This idiomatic expression means that one feels compelled to give another person credit for something, likely an ability or attribute at which he or she excels. It has been in use since at least the early 20th century and likely longer. In *Baseball Ballads* by American poet Grantland Rice, 1910, it appeared in several verses, including In 'Rooter's Row,' page 102:

> "**You've got to hand it to him**, Bo, and dat's no foolish tip,
> he makes bloomin' batters look like chickens wid de pip;"

I've slept since then+

This is a modern cliché response to a question about which the one being asked does not remember how to respond. It implies that since it has been a while since the subject has been in his or her mind, the answer is uncertain or has been forgotten. Though it has come to the forefront in the 21st century, it has been around for over 100 years. *The International*. A New York monthly magazine edited by George Sylvester Verreck, published by Moods Publications, cited it in a rhyme in January, 1917:

> "Although for long elsewhere, **I've slept since then**;
> And elsewhere been busy with my pen."

I was just in the neighborhood+

This is a phrase used as an obvious ruse for suddenly showing up at someone's door unannounced. Origin is unknown, but it became popular in plays and television shows in the last quarter of the 20th century.

I wasn't born yesterday^

This is a classic response to someone who has just said something indicating you know nothing about a matter, or have no experience in something. It means you are not naïve or gullible, and do not need his or her advice. In spite of a major slang dictionary stating the origin as late 19th to early 20th century, the saying was already in use as early as 1840, when it appeared in *The Life and Adventures of Valentine Vox, Ventriloquist* by Henry Cockton, on page 508:

> "'Do you think,' he added, with an ironical grin, 'that you'll go for to gammon me into that air! I'm hinnocent, I know, but **I wasn't born yesterday** exactly.'"

I wish I could buy him for what he is worth and sell him for what he thinks he is worth

There are variations of this popular thought, often called an old saying, but its origin is illusive. One version is 'If I could buy him for what he is worth and sell him for what he thinks he is worth, I'd be a rich man.' Of course gender is optional on either side. The earliest available citation is from radio minister J. Vernan McGee's 1984 biblical study book, *Genesis through Revelation*, Chapter 5, The Healing of Naaman:

> "Have you ever heard it said, "**I wish I could buy** that **man for what he is worth and sell him for what he thinks he is worth**?"

J

Jailbird

This term refers to a person who has been incarcerated on more than one occasion. The word jail was originally spelled 'goal;' thus, the word was first, 'goal bird.' The earliest reference in print comes from *The Scotch Rogue, or Life and Actions of Donald MacDonald,* page 66, 1706:

> "But as luck wou'd have it, I quickly after met with my **Goal-Bird**-Companions; who had promis'd me such mighty things in Prison; he Was over-joy'd to see me, and especially at such a time when he told me he cou'd serve me…"

Jiminy Cricket!

This is what is known as a minced oath or euphemism for Jesus Christ. Most people likely believe the saying came about as a result of the jolly conscience of Pinocchio in the 1940 Disney movie; however, this is certainly not the case, but the opposite is true. The talking cricket in Italian author Carlo Collodi's 1883 *The Adventures of Pinocchio*, which first appeared as a serial in 1881 and 1882, was an unnamed minor character, changed to a green grasshopper-like smiling character in Disney's ever-popular cartoon film, was named so because the expression was already in common usage. In 1864, in Charles Reed's *Very Hard Cash*: *A Novel*, page 42, after several statements about the sport of cricket, we find the following:

> "'Woman, indeed!' said a treble at the door; 'no more than I am; it's for a young lady. O, **jiminy'**!"

In *Cricket at the Seashore*, 1896, by Elizabeth Westin Timlow, page 315, this snippet uses a 'jiminy' expression close to the word Cricket:

> "'Goes down hard enough. Seems to want ilin' or suthin.' Land o' **Jiminy**!' He chanced to turn his head and saw **Cricket** calmly ascending as the pole went higher and higher."

'By Jiminy' was also used around the turn of the century. *A Bunch of Roses and Other Parlor Plays*, 1903, a play called *His Lordship*, by Mollie Evelyn Moore Davis, has the following on page 65, first published in 1899:

> "An' all takin' on over me as if I was--- **Jiminy cricket**!"

Then in 1906 Seymore Seldon Tibbles used the exact expression on page 5 in Act One of another play, *At the Village Post Office: A Musical Play in Two Acts:*

> "**Jiminy cricket**, what was that stung me? Must have been a wasp."

The euphemism was well established in movies before Jiminy debuted as a Disney Character, being used in 1937 in the Disney cartoon predecessor of *Pinocchio, Snow White and the Seven Dwarfs*. The saying was spoken by Judy Garland in both *Listen Darling*, 1938, and as Dorothy in the 1939 Classic, *The Wizard of Oz,* when she cried out, "Oh! Oh! **Jiminy Crickets**!" when she was startled by the Wizard's pyrotechnics.

Ward Kimball who worked on *Snow White* actually designed the character.

Jump out of one's skin

This idiom means to be extremely shocked or surprised by something. It is derived from the fact that a person often jumps suddenly when this happens. It was originally used for jumping for joy. The earliest available reference for that is found in *Blue-Beard*, a play by George Coleman, the Younger, 1798, page 18:

> "O Mahomet!—If ever I get away safe from this gentleman who has **jumped out of his Skin**, I shall **jump out of my** own, for joy!"

This same meaning was later used by Mark Twain. But in 1841, Eliza Leslie used the more common, modern terminology in *A Gift; A Christmas and New Year's Present for 1812,* page 104:

> "'In your father's birth, did you?' says he, and he give me a look and spoke so sharp, 'I **jumped** as if I was going **out of my skin.'"**

Jury rigging+

This is a slang expression for doing makeshift repairs with whatever tools and materials are readily available rather than having them done professionally. It has no reference to a legal jury. The saying originated on boats and ships which were sail powered. After dismasting, a replacement mast was put together and stayed to allow the craft to continue toward its destination. 'Jury' for makeshift or temporary has been in use since at least 1616 according to the *Oxford English*

Dictionary, 1933 edition, when it was used in John Smith's *A Description of New-England* and also appeared in his more extensive work, *The General Historie of Virginia, New England and the Summer Isles* in 1624. 'Jury rigged' was first known to be cited in 1788 according to the same edition of the OED, in their corrected printing in 1967.

Just do it!

Just do it! is a trademark of the Nike shoe company and a highly successful campaign started by them in 1988. Though the term has been used occasionally throughout history, it never took over as an idiom until after the Nike campaign. Now it commonly used as an urge to get all sorts of things going. One example is in G. Robert Jacks' *Just Say the Word; Writing for the Ear*, 1996, page 175:

> "I bent at the waist, hearing the great cloud of witnesses urging me on: Mom was saying, 'OK now, **just do it**!' My swimming teacher was saying, 'OK now, **just do it**!' Ned was saying, 'OK now, **just do it**!'

K

Kangaroo court^

This term dates back to at least the mid-19th century, and refers to any mock court which disregards ethical and legal means to bring about what the members feel is swift justice, whether within or outside the legal system. The exact origin is unknown, and so numerous unsubstantiated theories have surfaced as to its coining, including that because kangaroos are native to Australia, it was started there, and 'claim jumping' during the 1849 California Gold Rush. The earliest citation is American, but in spite of a major dictionary placing the first publication of this article in 1853 in Philip Paxton's 'A Stray Yankee in Texas,' it was actually printed earlier, on July 20, 1850, in *The Literary World*, a New York publication, in 'Drafts at Sight in the Southwest:'

> "By an unanimous vote, Judge G. — the fattest and funniest of the assembly — was elected to the bench, and the 'Mestang' or '**Kangaroo Court**' regularly organized. Impossible as it would be for one to convey to the reader a correct idea of the ludicrous and supremely ridiculous scene which occurred, I will yet attempt it."

Though here spelled 'mestang,' the alternative term for such a proceeding is mustang court. Notice both are in quotes, indicating a term already coined. Obviously there is an insinuation that this type hastily assembled group is 'jumping to conclusions' (see in first volume).

Keep mum[2] (See: **Mum's the word, first volume**)

Keep one's ear to the ground+

This old idiomatic expression means to try to be well informed about current trends or opinions, and can apply to a certain subject. It originated in the late 1800s, and comes from the practice of putting one's ear to the ground in order to detect the sounds of distant horses' hoof beats or people's footsteps approaching. The idea was used in print in a literal sense as early as 1861 in *Instructions for Officers and Non-commissioned Officers of Cavalry by Lieut. Colonel Von Arentschildt, First Hussars German Legion*, on page 56:

> "Sometimes a man should dismount and **listen with his ear to the ground**, by which means he will hear the march of Troops at a great distance."

A good early figurative example of this exact verbiage is found in *The Bisbee Daily Review*, Bisbee, Arizona, Sunday, February 26, 1922, in an article by Harry Hunt in Section Two titled "I'll Leave Congress with Friends of Both Sides," Says "Uncle Joe" Cannon, where it is in quotes indicating a known saying, likely recent:

> "To be successful, he insists, a candidate must know his people and what they are thinking and wanting. He must '**keep his ear to the ground**.'"

Keep someone in the dark

This refers to deliberately withholding known information or facts about a situation or subject from someone desiring to be kept informed. The earliest form of this cliché was written by Roman playwright Titus Maccius Plautus in *The Pot of Gold*, Act II, circa 210 BCE. The following is from the 1916 English translation by Paul Nixon:

> "We can't conceal it, **we can't keep it dark any longer** now. But I must go in and do what master ordered me before he gets back."

In *All's Well that Ends Well*, Act IV, Scene i, 1604-1605, Shakespeare used the following similar connotation:

> ***Lord.*** "Till then I'll **keep him dark**."

Keep someone on a short leash

This means to maintain control over someone. It is taken from having a dog on a leash in order to restrain and train it to obey commands. Figurative use came in the third quarter of the 20th century. An early example is in *Life Magazine*, November 10, 1961, in a caption under a photo on page 95:

> "The U.S.S.R. made concessions to Polish nationalism but holds Gomulka and country **on a short leash**."

Keep/ Put something on ice+

This idiomatic term means delay taking action on a plan or idea. It is derived from putting food in an icebox before refrigeration was available to keep it from spoiling until it was needed. It came into figurative use in the early-to-mid 20th century. A good early figurative example in print is found in the Twin Falls, Idaho newspaper, *The Times News*, Tuesday, June 24, 1947, in an article on page 1 titled 'New Tax Cut Bill Bobs up in Committee.' It quotes Minnesota Congressman Knutson as saying about the bill:

> "If there's a big enough demand we'll take it up; if not, we'll **keep it on ice**."

Keep the champagne on ice

This popular British saying is used when a celebration is expected but there may

be a time of waiting before it begins due to circumstances beyond control. It means to stay ready for an impending victory. The earliest known reference is from April 13, 1990, when independent campaigning organization on environmental problems, Greenpeace U.S.A, released the following statement:

> "'Until we see detailed substantiation of the intentions of Bumble Bee and Chicken of the Sea,' said Greenpeace Dolphin Coordinator Lesley Scheele, 'we'll **keep the champagne on ice**.'"

Kick up one's heels

This idiom in America refers to having a vigorously entertaining time doing things one enjoys. It likely originated from horses, when released from a stall, kicking up their hoofs in seeming celebration. The earliest citation is from the allegorical work, *A Hue and Cry after Conscience or The Pilgrim's Progress* by Candlelight, 1681, written by Father John Dunton, on page 49:

> "Now had they known the remedy, all that had gone beside my pocket, nay, sometimes I have (especially when I have the guilt come fiush) made 'em sick as well as I have found occasion, keepin' 'em on the Rack for my advantage, by perpetual Physics till nature weakned, and the powrs of life decayed, they en'e **kicked up their heels**, and bid good night to ye."

In British English it may also refer to waiting impatiently to be summoned. This apparently is derived from foot tapping that people sometimes resort to when made to wait impatiently for something. The following first reference to this is from Samuel Foote's *The Minor*, 1760, page 56:

> "I suppose, this is a spice of your foreign breeding, to let your uncle **kick up his heels** in your hall, whilst your presence chamber is crowded..."

This version is also used now as 'kick one's heels'.

Killing someone with kindness

This old metaphoric expression refers to being nice to someone when they have not been kind to you, in such a way that it will irritate them because you won't retaliate against their negative attitudes and actions toward you or your beliefs or actions. It likely came from the old proverb about the ape who loved her young to death, popular from the 1500s. It was related and recorded by John Ray in *A Collection of English Proverbs*, 1678, page 254:

> "To **kill with kindness**. So the Ape is said to strangle her young ones by embracing and hugging them..."

Kindred spirit+

This figurative expression refers to another person whose opinions, interests and attitudes are very similar to one's own. 'Kindred' comes from combining the words 'kin' and the Old English word *redden,* meaning condition. Kindred entered English as a noun in the 12th century. It means one's relatives. It began to be used as an adjective in the 14th century. The earliest known use of 'kindred spirit' appeared in the comedy play, *The Open Gate: An Original Domestic Drama in One Act* by Charles Haddon Chambers, published by Samuel French in New York in 1887, where it is cited multiple times. After repeated use of the term by Jessie in regard to Ada, a cousin of Garth, Garth explains:

> "By **kindred spirit** she only means that we are fond of the same things—poetry, and—"

King of the swingers[2]

This saying, used primarily in Britain, actually is based on the song, '*I Wanna Be Like You*' written by Robert and Richard Sherman, crooned by King Louie, king of apes, in Disney's 1967 classic movie, *Jungle Book*. Kenny Ball and his Jazzmen released a single of the ditty in 1968, and featured it on their 1969 album '*King of Swingers.*' Other covers followed. King Louie's gravelly voice was a clear imitation of the King of Jazz, Louis Armstrong. The phrase has come to mean a macho man who is a wild example of manly attractiveness.

Kiss and make up^

This expression, in a literal sense, means that if two (especially romantically involved) individuals have had a spat; they should kiss and forget the problem which initiated the disagreement. Figuratively, it signifies that two individuals who have been friends who have developed a schism should ask forgiveness of one another and renew their bond. In spite of two major online dictionaries citing mid-1900s as the origin date, the earliest known printed reference comes from *The Phrenological Journal,* Samuel R. Wells, Editor and publisher, New York, March, 1870. Kiss and Make Up is the title of a poem by 'H.A.F.' Each verse concludes with the line. This is from the first verse:

> "When the Wrath-king first offers to young lips his cup,
> How quickly they spurn it and **kiss and make up**."

It is possible that this poem actually initiated, or at least popularized, figurative usage of the phrase, because in 1890, in *The Century Dictionary of the English Language*, Volume IV, prepared under the supervision of William Dwight Whitnet, Ph.D., LL.D., we find the following on page 3588:

> "To make up. (a) To effect a reconciliation; settle differences; become friends again: as, **kiss and make up**."

An earlier version of the phrase was 'kiss and be friends,' as used in the *Diary of Samuel Pepys,* 1660, page 2191, in the 1893 Unabridged version edited by H.B.W. Brampton:

> "So from that minute my wife begun to be kind to me, and we to **kiss and be friends**, and so continued all the evening, and fell to talk of other matters, with great comfort, and after supper to bed."

Kiss of life

This term is used to colloquially describe mouth-to-mouth (or mouth to nose) resuscitation in which such action allows the lungs of an unresponsive individual to deflate with each blow, bringing back normal breathing and saving the person's life. It may also refer figuratively to anything that revitalizes or reinvigorates.

The term was actually used figuratively, in a different sense, as early as September 18, 1886 in a poem titled 'Kiss of the Wife that's True' on the Page of Fugitive Verse in *Good Housekeeping:*

> "There's the kiss of youth and the kiss of years,
> And the kiss we lay in the grave;
> The kiss we press in sunshine and tears
> The kiss for the brow of the brave;
> But the kiss that is the **kiss of life**,
> To him who the gamuts run through
> That bring surcease to anguish and strife,
> Is the kiss of the wife that's true."

It was used elsewhere in poetry in the early 20th century, and so beautifully in Alfred de Musset's *Confession of Child of the Century* in 1910, on page 120:

> "The passing wind no longer gives you the **kiss of life**, its benediction on all that lives and breathes; it buffets you and makes you stagger."

This expression did not gain the connotation of mouth-to-mouth (not used in the U.S. until 1956, though the first successful example was in London in 1744) until the mid 20th century, as seen in *Milestones in Midwifery* by Walter Radcliffe, first published in 1947, in its 1967 reprint:

> "Foetal asphyxia was treated, first by slapping the souls of the feet, and if that failed by mouth-to-mouth artificial respiration—the '**kiss of life**' as it is now popularly known."

The name came from a caption to a photo in 1967 taken by Rocco Morabito showing Jacksonville, Florida utility worker J.D. Thompson at the top of a utility pole giving mouth-to-mouth resuscitation to co-worker Randall G. Champion after he came in contact with a high voltage wire. Thompson saved Champion's life and he lived another 35 years. The photo was printed in the *Jacksonville Journal*, and Morabito won the 1968 Pulitzer Prize for Spot News Photography for the remarkable shot.

Knee jerk reaction

This idiomatic expression, used in both the U.S. and U.K., means an automatic immediate reaction to an event or a revelation about something made without examining the circumstances or consideration of the underlying facts. It is derived from what is called the involuntary patellar reflex from someone tapping the knee sharply. Knee jerk reaction was acknoledged as early as the 1840s. In *The Supremity of Mind: A Lecture*, Reverend Samuel W. Fisher in 1845 wrote:

> "The simple reflexes of **reaction** to physical stimuli with their centres in the spinal cord, and typically exemplified in the segments of the earthworm and the **knee jerk** of man."

The earliest known figurative usage in print is from the Ohio newspaper, *The Coshocton Tribune* in the article 'New York Day-By-Day' by syndicated columnist Oscar Odd 'O.O.' McIntyre in October 1921:

> "Itinerant preacher stemming Broadway on a soap box. And gets only an occasional **knee-jerk**."

Knock off

This is another term which has evolved, having numerous meanings throughout the past 400 years. The earliest of these, dating to the 17th century, is to stop or take leave from work, which has continued in use. This is first illustrated in *The Works of William Bridge*, 1654, page 34:

> "I wil presently **knock off** where I am, and I wil strive to love where yon would have me: doth not this Child hear his Father now, in that he knocks off and will go no more to the person that he was in parlay with…"

To dispose of or to complete hastily, and 'to report as disobedient' for the purpose of deprivation or getting rid of, date to the early 19th century. In *Reports of Cases Argued and Determined in the English Courts of Common Law, Volume XIV,* edited by Thomas Sergeant and John Lowber, published in Philadelphia in 1830, we read on page 181, in 'Trane Versus Bennett, T.T.,' 1827:

> "…and the captain said that he would **knock off** several of them, (meaning that he would report them as disobedient, to deprive them of their shares of the cargo)..."

Another meaning used is stealing. This was recorded in the London publication, *The Athenaeum Journal* in August, 1919:

> "A curious term used by a Tommy [British soldier], in 'explaining' his deficiencies of kit, is 'Someone **knocked it off'** for 'Someone pinched (or made away with) it'."

Knock off for a smoko[3]

This humorous variation of 'knock off' is an Aussie expression meaning take a break from work, not only for a smoke, but it is also used for a morning tea break. 'Smoko' has been in use late 19th century, particularly in relation to smoking. An excellent citation, however, using 'knock off' and 'smoko' in the same sentence is in *Parliamentary Papers Volume 3, Queensland Parliament*, 18 November, 1928, page 648,

> "When the men **knock off** they sit down in the shelter and they do not come back until they hear the whistle blow, and it takes some time to get into their stroke again. I am not condemning **smokos**, but that is my experience of them."

A great modern example, in which a tea or snack break is insinuated, is found in Susan Lucas' *Inside My Skin*, 2011, page 384:

> "Through repetitive use and consistency I've taught Tia **'smoko'** and **'knock off'**. True to my word, each time the word **'smoko'** is used we migrate in the direction of the Bungalow to share a snack, food is an easy teaching tool."

Knowledge is power

This proverb has been attributed to both Francis Bacon, who used the Latin equivalent *scientia potentia est* in his *Meditationes Sacrae* in 1597, and Thomas Jefferson, who utilized it twice in correspondence:

From the polygraph copy at the Massachusetts Historical Society, these are lines Jefferson writing to George Ticknor on November 25, 1817:

> "…this last establishment will probably be within a mile of Charlottesville, and four from Monticello, if the system should be adopted at all by our legislature who meet within a week from this time, my hopes however are kept in check by the ordinary character of our state legislatures, the members of which do not generally possess information enough to percieve the important truths, that **knolege is power**, that knolege is safety, and that knolege is happiness."

And from the polygraph copy at the Library of Congress, his letter to Joseph C. Cabell on January 22, 1820:

> "All the states but our own are sensible that **knolege is power**."

Like so many other proverbial sayings, it has likely been picked up by wise men of every age. The earliest documented occurrence of the phrase '**Knowledge is power'** is from Imam Ali (599-661 CE). It was quoted in the 10th-century book *Nahj Al-Balagha*:

> "**Knowledge is power** and it can command obedience. A man of knowledge during his lifetime can make people obey and follow him and he is praised and venerated after his death. Remember that knowledge is a ruler and wealth is its subject.

> *"— Imam Ali, Nahj Al-Balagha, Saying 146"*

L

Lance the boil[2]

This idiom, popular in the U.K., though also used in the U.S., means to get rid of a problem—by whatever means necessary. It came into usage in the mid-to-late 20th century. An early example is from *Test Case: Italy, Ethiopia, and the League of Nations* by George W. Baer, page 276, 1976, here in quotes, showing that it had already, likely recently, been established as an idiom:

> "Mussolini exhorted him to '**lance the boil'** of the putative government at Gore, but Graziani's immediate concern was simply to protect his vulnerable force."

Land (or **Put**) **someone behind bars** (See: **Behind bars**)+

Last ditch effort^

This cliché means the final try at doing something before abandoning the idea. In spite of attributions for first coining by Thomas Jefferson, this has its origin in a speech made by British King William III in the late 17th century, when he made a plea for all Englishmen to fight and "die in the last ditch" to defend their country. In *A History of the English People Volume VIII, 1660-1683* by John Richard Green, published in 1880, page 162, we read:

> "'Do you not see your country is lost?' asked the DU.K.e of Buckingham when he was sent to negotiate at the Hague. 'There is a sure way never to see it lost,' replied William, 'and that is to **die in the last ditch**.' With the spring of 1673 the tide began to turn."

A century and a half later, Thomas Jefferson, who obviously knew the history of England, thus likely had heard this quote, made a similar statement in 1821, recorded in *Memoirs, Correspondence and Private Papers of Thomas Jefferson*, 1829, page 75:

> "For, while laboring under the want of money for even ordinary purposed, in a government which required a million of lives a day, and **driven to the last ditch** by the universal call for liberty, there came a winter of such severe cold, as was without example in the memory of man, or in the written records of history."

But even earlier than Jefferson, the saying 'dying in the last ditch' was called a maxim. In *The Scots Magazine*, January, 1779, on page 28, we read:

> "The maxim of dying in the **last ditch**, after every exertion has been made, is what I avow to be my principle."

The actual term, 'last ditch effort' came into usage after the beginning of the 20th century. The earliest known citation is from *The Midwestern*, April, 1907, page 2, in the political article, 'Bryan in Iowa,' about Presidential Candidate William Jennings Bryan:

> "The Democratic party, the party whose very basic principle is opposition to special privilege, became the handmaiden of Blythe in his **last ditch effort** to stop the progress of the popular movement in the Republican party."

Last hurrah+

The Last Hurrah is the title of a 1956 novel by Edwin O'Connor which was adapted for film in 1958. As a metaphor, it has come to refer to the last occasion on which a person does something, particularly at the end of his or her career; a final attempt.

Laughing stock

This means the subject of ridicule. Despite claims by some that 'stock' here is taken from the stock or butt of a gun, and a laughing stock is like being referred to as the butt of a joke, the term was around for much longer than this might have applied. It was not originated by Shakespeare in *The Merry Wives of Windsor*, even though it did appear there also. It was used in John Firth's 1533 book, *An Other Boke Against Rastel:*

> "Albeit … I be reputed a **laughing stock** in this world."

But another problem to the etymology is that according to experts, stock came into Old English in 862 from the German word meaning 'tree trunk.' At that time it meant, '*something or someone treated as the object of an action, more or less habitually,*' clarifying the origin of the term within the idiom, 'laughing stock.'

Lay down the law

This idiom means to sternly tell people what they must do in no uncertain terms, not caring about their reaction to the command. It comes from legal decisions in which the strict letter of the law was interpreted and carried out. The phrase was recorded in the English version of *The Works of Molière* (1622-1673), Volume X, page 134, first printed in Paris circa 1739, in his Tragedy Ballet, 'Psyche,' written in 1671, Act V, Scene iii:

> "You wish to **lay down the law** to me, you, whom we so often see receive it from me; you, who have a heart as susceptible as any other, you envy mine the delights which your own enjoys!"

Lay eyes on+

This is an idiom for looking at something, especially for the first time. It dates back to the early 13th century according to another popular dictionary of idioms. It was quite different at that time, however; in Old English, eye was *ege*. Similar terms are clap eyes on (popular in the U.K.) and set eyes on, which both came later.

Lazy bones

A close relative of the term 'bone lazy' (see), this one was first listed in 1740 in *New Dictionary, Spanish and English* by Pedro Penida:

> "You **Lazy-bones**, perezoso que eres."

Leave a bad taste in one's mouth

This metaphoric expression is used to refer to something that leaves a bad impression on someone, thus causing a lasting unpleasant memory. It came from food that tasted repulsive. A form of it was used in *The Lady's Magazine*, August, 1775 in 'The Trial of Mrs. Jane Butterfield' on page 3:

> "…at least in the course of long practice, he never had a patient die in his hands; that the deceased never had the **bad taste in his mouth** at Cheame, or after he **left** Woodcote."

This reference, however, is ambiguous, and a bit uncertain as to connotation. The earliest available citation showing a clear figurative meaning is in *The*

Illustrated Magazine, London, 1865, in 'A Peep at the Black Country' by Mrs. Carolyn A. White:

And thus the care of children, home cooking, and home cleanliness are thrown over for weekly wages, to which the man looks for compensation for loss of family love, comfortable meals, neatness, and thrift; and if the coins **leave a bad taste in his mouth**, he has at least what he has bargained for.

Leave a trail of breadcrumbs+

This is a metaphor has been traditionally used for someone intentionally planting items or clues which will lead someone else to their location or, even more figuratively, point of view. On a website, a 'breadcrumb trail' is a navigation tool that allows the user to see where the current page is in relation to the hierarchy of the site. It comes from the famous German fairy tale, *Hansel and Gretel*, by the Brothers Grimm, Jacob and Wilhelm, originally told by the latter's future wife, Dortchen Wild, and first published in 1812 in *Kinder- und Hausmärchen.* In the story, these siblings left a trail of breadcrumbs while walking through the forest so they could find their way home.

Leave no stone unturned

This metaphor means to do everything possible to achieve the desired result. It has been in use in Englsih since at least since the 17th century. According to *Dictionary of Idiomatic English Phrases* by James Main Dixon, Professor of English Literature at the Imperial University of Japan, 1891, page 318:

> "To **leave no stone unturned** — to adopt every possible method of search or inquiry; to take every possible means towards gaining an object. P. A phrase borrowed from the Greek dramatist Euripides. Polycrates asked the Delphic oracle how to find the treasure buried by Mardinius, the General of Xerxes on the field of Platea. The oracle replied, '**Turn every stone**.'*(Paenta kinesai petrin)"*

Mardinius lost the battle to Polycrates (Greco-Persian Wars) and hid the treasure in 477 BCE. According to *A History of Origins*, 1824, legend says that the oracle was to ask the advice of Apollo. The Latin command was actually, *Omnem move lapindem*. Polycrates, the story said, returned to the field and found the treasure.

The earliest available reference in print in English of modern usage is found in *A Ternary of Paradoxes* originally in French by Jean Baptist Van Helmont, translated by Walter Charleton, printed in London, 1650:

> "However, that We may **leave no stone unturned**, under which any the most minute particle of' Truth, to whose Explanation the concernment our praesent Theme doth adlige Us, may be thought to lye neglected..."

Leave someone out in the cold

This expression means to keep someone uninformed, disallow inclusion in activities, neglect a person or deny him or her benefits given to others. The phrase is an 'Americanism' and came into usage in the mid-1800s. The earliest available reference is from Charles Dickens' *All the Year Round*, April 15, 1865, in 'How the Bank Was Wound Up:'

> "...and the unfortunate shareholders be—to use an Americanism—'**left out in the cold**.'"

Less is more

This obvious oxymoron, as a proverb, means that simplicity and clarity lead to good design. It comes from famed 19th century English poet, Robert Browning's poem '*Andrea del Sarto*,' also called 'The Faultless Painter' published in 1855:

> "Who strive - you don't know how the others strive
> To paint a little thing like that you smeared
> Carelessly passing with your robes afloat,
> Yet do much less, so much less, Someone says,
> (I know his name, no matter) - so much less!
> Well, **less is more**, Lucrezia."

In 1947, German-American architect and furniture designer Ludwig Mies van der Roch adopted the concept for Minimalist design and architecture.

Let the games begin

Figuratively, this command means 'let's get started.' It had its beginning as a reference to the Olympic Games, a phrase still used at the start of the games. The earliest known citation in print is in *The Last Night of Pompeii*, Canto III, by Sumner Lincoln Fairfield, published in New York in 1832:

> "And Pompeii's might and affluence await
> The Praetor's voice, and the vast fabric gleams
> With million glances and with million cries
> Echoes, as from the tribune now the word
> Of Power commands—' Lo! **let the games begin**!'"

lie can travel half way around the world (A) while truth is putting on its shoes or boots, or **has a chance to get its pants on**

Versions of this proverb have been attributed to Alexander Pope, Mark Twain, Charles Spurgeon, Fisher Ames, Thomas Jefferson and Winston Churchill. Then of course, someone called it a Chinese Proverb. But let's take a look at the truth. The earliest version is worded somewhat differently; then, over time, the proverb 'evolved. On November 2, 1710, Jonathan Swift, in London's *The Examiner*, wrote:

> **"Falsehood flies, and the Truth comes limping after it."**

In 1716 *A Charge of Error, Heresy, Incharity, Falshood...* by Henry Pickworth had this statement on page 310:

> "**Lies, Falfhood**, &c. even that Spirit of Wickedness, **will** furely **fly…**"

Then in 1787 in *Sermons on Various Subjects, Volume III* by Thomas Francklin in 'On Vigilance,' on page 233, the following appeared:

> **"Falsehood will fly, as it were, on the wings of the wind, and carry its tales to every corner of the earth; whilst truth lags behind; her steps, though sure, are slow and solemn**…"

Seven years afterward, in 1794, *The Confessions of James Baptiste Couteau* by Robert Jephson was published, in which he ascribed the following to Alexander Pope:

> **"Can waft a lie from Indus to the Pole."** The author added: **"Lame Truth limps after too tardily to prevent the winged progress of her adversary."**

This was actually a misquote, supposedly written of a love letter in his poem *Eloisa to Abelard*. What Pope really said as recorded in *Works of British Poets: With Prefaces,* 1795, *Volume Eight*, compiled by Robert Anderson, MD, page 56, was:

> "**And waft a *sigh* from Indus to the Pole**."

On January 16, 1808, *The Boston Times*, in a column titled 'Thoughts' included a similar proverb to the original by Swift:

> "'**Falsehood,**' says one, '**flies, and truth comes limping after it.**'"

On September 5, 1820, *The Portland Gazette* (Maine), in an article about a court case brought the maxim a bit closer to what we have today with no attribution:

> **"for falsehood will fly from Maine to Georgia, while truth is pulling her boots on."**

The following year, 1821, Editor William Tudor attributed this adage to statesman Fisher Ames in Boston's *The North American Review*.

> "…recollecting **Mr. Ames'** remark, that '**a Lie would travel from Maine to Georgia while Truth was getting on his boots;**'"

This attribution was again backed up by *Niles Weekly Register* in Baltimore ten years later, on May 7, 1831. It was in 1834 that Maine to Georgia was replaced by 'half way over the world' in Boston's *New England Magazine*, April issue, book review on Man's Accountability for His Belief by Lysander Spooner:

> "…**error will run half over the world while truth is putting on his boots to pursue her**…"

After another version in 1835, and slight variances in 1844, attributed to John Randolph, and another in January, 1846 erroneously listed as 'a Chinese Proverb' by *Brownson's Quarterly Review,* also in Boston, the saying comes very close to what we hear today. Charles Spurgeon used it in one of his sermons delivered in Exeter Hall, calling it 'an old proverb'. In 1859, it was included in a collection called *Spurgeon's Gems* published in London:

> "**A lie will go round the world while truth is pulling its boots on.**"

Other versions occurred, three being attributed to Mark Twain. In February, 1919, *Standard Player Monthly* in New York printed:

> "Mark Twain once said that **a lie will fly around the whole world while the truth is getting its boots on;** and the statement is hard to contradict successfully."

The other was February 24, 1921 in *The Denver Post*, in Nubbins by Burns Jenkins:

> "'**A lie can travel around the world and back again while the truth is lacing up its boots.**'—Mark Twain."

Then in 1987, the publication *The Wit and Wisdom of Mark Twain*, edited by Alex Ayers, brought it to what we know today:

> "'**A lie can travel halfway around the world while the truth is putting on its shoes.'** —Attributed"

It's possible that Twain actually used the old adage, but he obviously didn't originate it.

Life of the party^

This expression refers to a lively, amusing person who is the center of attention at social gatherings. In spite of claims by online sources that this came into usage metaphorically in the first half of the 1800s, there seems to be no evidence of this. Literal usage of the phrase, meaning the length of life of a person or political party date back to the 1700s, but the earliest figurative usage available in print is from 1919, in a book by that title by Irvin Shrewsberry Cobb. In chapter II we see that this gives us the current meaning:

> "It was fine to have been the **life of the party**. It was not quite so fine to discover that the taxicab to which he must entrust himself for the long ride up to West Eighty-fifth Street was a most shabby appearing vehicle, the driver of which, moreover, ..."

life with love will have some thorns, (A), but a life without love will have no roses

Though this proverbial saying has been attributed to Dr. Seuss, no one knows who first said it. It started showing up in print in the 21st century, so it likely didn't originate sooner. Nevertheless, it is a truism. It means that loving relationships do not come without problems, but they are nevertheless worth the risks involved. A similar proverb is 'It is better to have loved and lost than to have never loved at all' (see).

Lighten up

Though there are obvious literal uses of this term, referring to shade or weight, figuratively it means to be less serious or gloomy about circumstances. It is used to let someone know that he or she needs to relax and be cheerful. A major online dictionary places origin at 1960s. Though ahead of his time, in *Up: A Little Book of Talks on how to Wake Up, Get Up, Think Up, Climb Up* by George Mathew Adams, 1920 he uses it like this in 'Love-Keeps' on page 108:

> "Our Love-keeps make us happy-human. They point us to better things, and help to steer us true. They lessen our sads and **lighten up** our glads. They feed us as we. match steps with things eternal."

Light the blue touch paper[2]

In British colloquial English this means to do something that causes anger or excitement. Touch paper is a strip of paper impregnated with saltpeter which is composed of sodium nitrate and potassium and is used to fuse explosives. In actuality this proverbial saying has to do with igniting a series of events which is impossible to stop, thus usually causing a lot of 'sparks to fly.' In times past there was a standard instruction on fireworks about lighting the blue touch paper, and a warning to stand back or later, 'retire' afterward. The earliest available citation in print to the metaphor in English is in John Mortimer's translation of French playwright Georges Feydeau's *Cat Among the Pigeons*, 1970, page 35-36, Act I:

> "LUCETTE. (*Takes one pace* D.L. to BOIS D'ENGIEN.) 'Yes, Darling?'
> BOIS d'ENG. 'Lucette, we must part…'
>
> "LUCETTE. (Astonished.) 'What?'
> BOIS D'ENG. 'Yes, we must. (Aside.) Now . . . **light the blue touch paper** and stand well clear.'

Like a bad penny that keeps showing up (See: **bad penny always turns up, A**)+

Like a dog with a bone

This vivid expression refers to unwillingness to stop thinking, talking about or dealing with a matter until it is resolved. It is derived from a dog tenaciously continuing to gnaw on a bone until every edible morsel has been consumed, and hoarding it from any animal or person wanting to take it away. Similes of persons acting like a dog with a bone go back to at least 1800, when Joel Chandler Harris used this comparison in his biographical sketch of the famed ambitious Atlanta newspaper magnate, *Life of Henry W. Grady,* page 258:

> "He hid about in the day-time, avoiding everybody, and seeming to carry off his love and his passion, as a **dog with a bone**, seeking an alley. At night he would be seen hanging **like** a guilty thief about the hut in which his treasure was hid."

Like a duck to water

Usually preceded by takes to (something), this simile speaks of someone having a natural tendency or talent toward a particular field of endeavor or subject, and enjoying 'diving into it' immensely, even the first time it is approached. The earliest known reference to it in print is from the July, 1860 issue of *Baily's Magazine of Sports and Pastimes* in 'Our Jockeys:'

> "…he took to a horse **like a duck to water."**

Like a lobster pot[2]

Lobster pots are enticing traps for catching lobsters, and have been in use since at least 1764. They were traditionally made of wood, but now are plastic, and are known for being secure in holding their catch. Lobsters are lured in through a tunnel or 'chamber' of netting into the parlor which holds the bait. In British English, this saying has come to refer to something you can crawl into but cannot get out of or something you have agreed to, only to find that there isn't a cancellation clause. A modern example in print is from *Eternal Fragments* by Francis Castro, 2010, page 29:

> "Irony is **like a lobster pot**. It's a trap only for the lobster's insipience."

Like a red rag to a bull

This has reference to a deliberate provocation intended to bring about an adverse effect. As early as the 17th century, 'red rag' meant someone's tongue, and waving it meant constant prattle. In *The Classic Dictionary of the Vulgar Tongue* by Francis Grose, 1785, he listed this saying:

"Shut your potatoe trap, and give your **redrag** a holiday."

The earliest mention in print of using a literal red rag with creatures is form *A Rich Cabinet with a Variety of Inventions* collected by "J.W." printed in London in 1668. Here it is catching a duck:

> "Presently he getteth about a yard of strong thread, and .finding a little **rag** of **red** cloath, tyeth it to one end of the thiead, and at the other end tyeth a piece of Cheese (some what lesser than a Bean) with part of the rind on, and throweth it amongst the parings to the Fowle."

Then in 1724, there was in reference to trapping a pheasant with a red rag in John Trenchard and John Gordon's religious essays, *Cato's Letters:*

> "Foxes are trapann'd (*trapped)* by Traces, Pheasants by **a red Rag**, and other Birds by a Whistle; and the same is true of Mankind."

After that references were made to other critters such as snakes (to extract venom), and turkeys; but bulls were not recorded as being attracted by red cloths until March, 1836, when the first figurative use of the term appeared in *Tait's Edinburgh Magazine* in 'Sam Pogson's Jealousy:'

> "'Consarn them red coarts!' was Samuel's first exclamation; — 'they catch wimmin's eyes **like a red rag at a bull**.'"

Bulls, however, cannot distinguish color, so the use of red in bull fights is for the advantage of the human audience rather than to distract the bull, who would react the same to any cloth waved before his eyes.

Like a scalded dog / cat

Sometimes preceded by run, take off or go, and with various animals attached, this means to scurry with lightening speed. It goes back to the days when a lot of cooking was done outside, and animals came around looking for morsels of food. Sometimes boiling water would get knocked out of a cauldron and get on a household pet, causing an immediate yelp and dash for safer ground. It is used figuratively to mean someone is running away from unpleasant circumstances. The earliest known reference in print is like a scalded cat, and is from *Corbett's Two Penny Trash or Politics for thee Poor* by John Corbett, 1831, page 257:

> "...I will bet Mr. Attwood just what he likes; that he does not find, between Temple-bar and Bishopsgate, one single shopkeeper who would not **run like**

> **a scalded cat** and hide himself under his counter, if he were in danger of being exposed to endure what Mr. Attwood deemed such an honour."

'Scalded dog' comes 23 years later in *Westminster Abby* by Emma Robinson, 1854, Volume I, page 282:

> "'Nay, nay, we will not **run** the palace **like scalded dogs**! — Master Roodspere, methinks you should have some sense of his grace's condescending, if but — Who is there?' exclaimed Cromwel, breaking off as a tap at the oratory door…"

Like it's going out of style

This comparative expression means to do something continually or rapidly like you will not be able to do it for long, even if there is actually no danger of that. The logic is that if something is going out of style one better use it while it is still available. The simile came into usage in America in the mid-20th century. The earliest printed example known is in the February, 1955 issue of *Jet* magazine in an article about legendary American boxer, Sugar Ray Robinson, titled, 'Sugar Ray's Money,' on page 53:

> "Sugar Ray always had the ego of a King. In an effort to conquer the memory of poverty, he spent money **like it was going out of style**."

Like nobody's business^

Like other similar similes, 'like crazy,' for example, this means that something is happening with a high degree of intensity. The actual origin seems obscure. In spite of a major dictionary listing a first reference in 1938, there is a citation of this expression nine years prior in the 1929 *Michiganenisan*, the yearbook, published by the senior class of the University of Michigan, Ann Harbor, on page 493-494, in the article 'Our Candidate for President' by Dr. Thomas Lovell:

> "Maurice 'George' Lichtenstein
>
> "Because he was the one person who saved the Gargoyle from being a total flop; because he could cartoon and caricature **like nobody's business**, and thereby combined art with futility when he drew for the Gargoyle, because he is about the one person on campus who became famous through ability and not petty political pull."

Like there is / was no tomorrow

This is yet another simile meaning that something is being done rapidly and with express resolve, such as 'like it's going out of style,' above, and not too unlike 'like nobody's business.' This also insinuates lack of careful thought or planning. Though the exact origin is unknown, the earliest available citation is in *Jet*, August 25, 1955, page 42, in Gerri Major's 'Society World:'

> "Herbert Provost solaced whatever unhappiness resulted from his unsuccessful wooing of Houston's Delores Wesley by purchasing a motor boat and sailing **like there was no tomorrow."**

Lion hearted^

This means exceptionally courageous or brave. A lionhearted person continually challenges himself or herself, pushing on toward becoming the best that he or she can be. One major online dictionary cites 1700-1710 as date of origin, while a major dictionary places this at 1616. This is much closer. The earliest reference now available in print is actually in *The History of Great Britaine Under Ye Conquests of Romans, Saxons, Danes and Normans*, dedicated 'To the Most High and Most Potent Monarch, Iames' (James), 1614, page 473:

> "...which (though it were afterward punished by the Lawes) might seeme a presage, that this **Lion-hearted** King (as his by-name Ceur-de-Lion did import) should beea fpeciall destroier of the Enemies of our Sauiour."

This is, of course, in reference to Richard I, the Lionheart (1157-1199). The French equivalent was in print as early as 1553 in *Annales et Chroniques de France, depuis la destruction de Troye ...* (Annals and Chronicles of France During the Destruction of Troy).

> "Antost apres le trefpas dudict roy Henry, qui fut l'anmil cent quatre vingts & neuf fut Roy d'Angleterre ledict Richard, sonsils, parauant Comte de Poitiers, qui fut surnommé coeur de Lion: lequel paísa & accorda auecques ..."

Qui fut surnommé ***coeur de Lion*** translates to 'who was nicknamed Lion Heart'.

Live and learn

This statement indicates that one has just learned a new fact. It can also mean that we grow to be better persons from our mistakes and misfortunes. The earliest printed reference to this term is in *A Survey of the Summe of Church-discipline: Wherein the way of the Churches is Waranted out of the Word,* by Thomas Hooker, page 12, 1648:

> "...desirous to propound things, wherein difficulties yet appear unto us, hoping some further evidence may be given for the manifestation of the truth, which we only seek, if we know what we seek: and therefore would **live and learn...**"

Living in a bubble

This expression was inspired by children who lost all immunity to disease and of necessity were confined to a sterile environment and kept in a 'bubble' of plastic. This problem was brought to a height of public awareness by the 1976 ABC TV movie, *The Boy in the Plastic Bubble* starring John Travolta. A 2001 comedy film, *Bubble Boy,* renewed public interest.

This came metaphorically to refer to persons who stay isolated from society for various reasons. Many are misunderstood victims of society who have developed low self esteem, and feel lonely; others may merely be shy and introverted. One example in print is from *Weekly World News*, March 4, 1994, page 13, in a snippet claimed to be from the *Chicago Tribune* about Bo Derek:

> "'I go through life and when frowning people see me, they smile. I don't have to go into a store and be treated badly. It's like **living in a bubble**,' she says."

It also refers to a bubble of privilege, as in *Minor Characrters: A Young Woman's Coming-of-Age in the Beat Orbit of Jack Kerouvac* by Joyce Johnson, 1983, page xxii:

> "Teena, of course, was white, middle-class, and suburban in spirit if not in fact, **living in a bubble** of privilege amid America's ever poorer and more ethnically diverse cities."

Local rag[2, 3]

In British and Australian colloquialism, this refers to a local newspaper or questionable magazine. It is used almost exclusively in the pejorative sense. Before the development of pulpwood paper in the mid-19th century, rags were commonly used to make paper for printing. However, a rag, as far back as the 16th century, meant any worthless scrap. One such example of this connotation is found in *The Trimming of Thomas Nash, Gentleman* by Ricardo de Medico, 1597, page 17:

> "Ha ha! **a rag** borrowed from your owne dunghill."

It was even used metaphorically to refer to people considered worthless. Noted 19th century author, John Ruskin (*The Works of John Ruskin*, page 187, 1875), in *Fors Cavigera*, used this metaphor:

> "…she could have gone well enough, too, to put herself on his road, and prevented him from looking at **that rubbishy rag of a girl**."

Rag, then, was a word of contempt. The earliest known example of this term as a contemptuous newspaper is found in *The London Magazine*, April, 1840, in 'Charivari:'

> "This nobleman having thought it necessary to enrol a number of constables for the protection of his person and property, in a very disturbed state of the country, a **local rag**, yclept the *Nottingham Mercury*, attacks his Grace in the grossest and most indelicate manner."

Location, location, location

It is frequently stated that in the real estate business the three most important factors in determining desirability of property are 'location, location, location.' A colleague of language expert, William Safire told him that coining of this phrase was attributed to British real estate tycoon Lord Harold Samuel, because it was claimed so in his 1987 obituary. Safire quickly found this to be inaccurate, as he located a citation in the *Chicago Tribune* in 1926 when Samuel was 14 years of age. The context of this reference indicated that it was already in use at that time. The truth is that no one knows who coined it, but it remains a truism.

Lollygagging

This popular term is an Americanism meaning just hanging around doing nothing. Exact origin is unknown, but online sources place its coining at mid-19th century. A variation is lallygag. Etymologists believe it is of dialect origin. The late Middle English word, 'loll' meant to drop or dangle. It actually came from a word for 'tongue.' Today this means to relax and pass time idly. According to some experts in language, 'gag' in this sense could have referred to 'stuffing or filling.' This sounds like a tongue being stuffed down one's throat. Perhaps. An 1868 issue of the *Northern Vendicator*, a weekly Estherville, Iowa newspaper says:

> "...the lascivious **lolly-gagging** lumps of licentiousness who disgrace the common decencies of life by their love-sick fawnings at our public dances."

After the turn of the 20th century, the expression started showing up often in writing. The earliest example available is from *Eshter Damon* by Mrs. Fremont Older, 1911, page 227:

> "The widow menaced him with the poker as she returned fire: 'Quit right there, Bobby. None of your **lolly-gagging**.'"

Lone wolf

This common metaphor had its origin with wolves which leave their pack and strike out on their own in search of prey. It is applied to humans who eschew association with the masses, and particularly to those with rabid agendas such as terrorists and assassins. In *The Poetic Melange*, Volume II, published in Edinburgh in 1828, a literal lone wolf is referenced in print:

> "Midst the towers of thy Salem the **lone wolf** is howling,
> O're the wrecks of thy Temple the wild Arab strays
> 'Mong the tombs of thy fathers the tiger is prowling,
> As a dream we remember the fame of thy days.—"

Lone Wolf was once a popular Native American name. In *Sheridan's Troopers and Borders* by De Benneville Randolph Keim, 1885, page 157, we find one of several references in print about Native Americans by this name:

> "After some parlay Santana and **Lone Wolf**, and a Comanche, joined the column."

The earliest application known in print to the expression 'a lone wolf man' is from *The Clever Magazine,* November, 1903, in 'The Epic of Lone Wolf' by Melville Irvin Arni on page 102:

> "One could never make **a Lone Wolf** man believe that 'Caesar' did not invade New El Dorado with the express purpose of carrying a chip on his shoulder as a challenging gauntlet…"

long and the short of it, The

This idiom refers to a quick summary of a matter, giving the most important parts in the simplest way possible. The earliest form of the expression, 'the short and the long,' was used by Shakespeare four times in his plays, the earliest of which was *A Midsummer Night's Dream*, Act II, Scene ii.59, first performed 1595-1596, printed in 1600:

> "For **the short and the long** is, our play is preferred."

'The long and the short' was first printed in 1603 in *The Essayes of Montaigne*, Vol. 5, translated by John Floro, page 86:

> "…nor other end of the joint, betweene the overmuch and the little; **the long and the short**; the light and the heavie, the neare and the farre…"

The modern usage with definition appears first in *Rules for Spelling and Writing English, Second Edition* by William Baker, 1724, page 79:

> "This is **the long and the short of it**, i.e. this is the Substance of the Matter."

Long arm of the law

This metaphorical cliché originated in the early 19th century. Now scarsely used, except in humorous contexts, it refers to the immense outreach of police departments to work together to apprehend the perpetrators of crimes. The earliest known mention in print comes from *The Monuments and Genii of St. Paul's Cathedral, and of Westminster Abbey*, by George Lewis Smyth, published in London in 1826:

> "A fellow-student prevailing on him to become security for the payment of a tailor's bill, he was soon obliged, in consequence of his inability to keep the engagement, to leave Edinburgh precipitately. But the tailor pursued him in

> his retreat with **the long arm of the law**; he was arrested in Sunderland, and conducted back to the college by bailiffs.

Though this expression is utilized in both the U.S. and U.K., 'strong arm of the law' is also in use in the states.

Long shot

Of course, in a literal sense this phrase can refer to a camera shot taken at a great distance from the subject to allow a broader view, and a gun fired at a vast distance. Metaphorically, it also has two variants, though related meanings, dependent upon connotation. When used alone, it refers to a sports team, a horse, or other entity which has a very slim chance of success in a contest, game, race or other endeavor. This is derived from the distant gunshot, used reputedly by writers since the 18th century, often with a symbolic inferred meaning that it was a difficult try. By the mid-20th century it was being used in other figurative circumstances, such as the example in *Flying* magazine, December, 1950, page 36, in 'I Learned about Flying from That!' by Edna Ungerer:

> "It **was a long shot** but I decided to try to reach home. The cloud was growing bigger and blacker and the sun was sinking lower and lower and I was getting more uneasy all the time."

When prefaced by 'not by' or simply 'by,' it has to do with measurable degrees. 'By a long shot' means a wide margin or large difference in disparity. The following is an early example from *Saratoga: An Indian Tale of Frontier Life* by Daniel Shepherd published in 1877, page 179:

> "His faith wouldn't move mountains by a **long shot**."

Look as black as thunder[2]

This expressive idiom refers to the countenance of a person who is very angry. It can be traced back to an earlier version found in London's *The Literary Gazette*, Volume 2, 1818, page 570, in a story titled *The Hermit in London or Sketches of English Manners No. IX: A Day in the Country*, author uncertain:

> "The eldest daughter, however, claimed the right of primogeniture, whilst the second sister danced with tears in her eyes for disappointment, and Mademoiselle **looked as black** as a **thunder**-cloud."

This wording actually makes more sense. This story was reprinted in a number of publications into the early 1820s. Then in 1824 a book titled *The Gamblers; or a Treacherous Friend, A Moral Tale, Founded on Recent Facts* was published in London, also with ambiguity as to the author, being listed as 'by the author of several popular works.' Thus, it may have been by the same writer. But here the expression was changed to the current strange form:

> "He **looked as black as thunder**, in a minute, but put his hand in his pocket, and I began to chuckle, He drew it out again however empty: 'I have nothing but a ten pound note, Heward; but I'll go and get change, and be back before the kettle ...'"

That same year it appeared in another novel published in London with a similar title by Hannah Maria Jones, *The Forged Note: or Julian and Marianne, A Moral Tale, Founded on Recent Facts*, leaving one to wonder if the authors were not the same. On page 169:

> "The old man **looked as black as thunder**, but he did not say a word, but paid me my wages, and off I came."

After that other authors used the expression freely.

Looking (or **staring) down the barrel of gun**

This vivid metaphor means that a high risk of imminate danger exists and there appears to be no way out. The earliest available citation of someone literally finding himself looking down the barrel of a gun is in *The Stricket Minister: And Some Common Men* by Samuel Rutherford Crockett, 1894, page 62:

> "He applied his eye, and, just as John Howieson was doing at that moment over at the manse, he found himself **looking down the barrel of a gun**."

The first mention in print of a figurative version available is in *The Engineers' Review*, January, 1907, in Lubricators—Valves in Water Columns, page 26:

> "Having valves in the water column connections is something like a man **looking down the barrel of a gun**, as long as he is careful and makes no mistakes he is all right, but there is liable to come a time when there will be 'something doing.'"

Look Ma, no hands!

There are several theories and claims as to the origin of this phrase, but no proof seems to exist of most. They range from a 1937 Marx Brothers movie to James Cagney in *White Heat*, 1946. Then there is the TV commercial in the 1950s or 1960s for Band Aids, toothpaste or laundry detergent. Images of a boy on a bicycle holding out his hands yelling to his mother flutter through our minds. It is safe to say that the saying was around by January, 1949, when it appeared in *Popular Science* magazine on page 113, under the photo of a flying helicopter in which both occupants are holding their hands out the windows.

> **"Look, Ma, no hands!...**For years helicopter pilots have been like Don Quixote, continuingly jousting with their windmills…"

Lose the plot[2,3]

This British and Aussie idiom means to lose sight of a particular objective or cease to behave in a rational manner. It is derived from someone reading a novel or watching a movie, who loses track of, and is unable to comprehend the intended drift or vane in which the plot of the story is headed. Figurative use has been around since the mid-1990s. The earliest available reference in print is from *Kenya National Assembly National Debates, Hansard Official Report*, 15 November, 1994, page 647:

> "The Fund has not explained how they **lost the plot** that was given by the Government and then later went to acquire it from Bright Enterprises at Kshs 25 million, more than its actual value."

Loud and clear

This expressive cliché, meaning that something is clearly understood, came into popular use during WW II, from radio reception and telephone communication that was precise and distinct. The phrase, however, has been employed since at least the 17th century, describing the tolling of bells and the clarity of voices and cries of animals. The earliest citation in print is from *Du Bartas: His Divine Weekes and Workes* by French Huguenot courtier and poet, Guillaume de Salluste Du Bartas, 'The Third Book of Judith,' Lib. 4, 1584, English version translated by Josuah Sylvester, 1641, page 365:

> "There hideous horses, braying **loud and clear**,
> There Pagans fell, with clamour huge to hear,

Made such a din as made the Heav'n resound,
Retented hell, and tore the fixed ground."

Love birds

In reality a lovebird is one of nine species of the genus Agapornis, taken from the Greek words αγάπη *agape* 'love;' and όρνις *ornis* 'bird.' They are small, colorful parrots which are very affectionate. Species of the bird are native to tropical climates such as West Africa and Madagascar, Japan, China, Australia and South America. They make excellent pets. The term is metaphorically applied to lovers. The earliest known verifiable citation of what *seems to be* humans being called love birds is in Charles Dickens' serialized novel, *Bleak House*, 1852-1853:

> "Mr. Guppy, going to the window tumblkes into a pair of **love-birds**, to whom he says in his confusion, 'I beg your pardon, I am sure.'"

There is a more certain example of a love bird simile in 1890 in *Village Verse Stories and Other Poems* by Canadian Crawford Slack, page 43:

> "Talk about the courts of justice bein' cold and lackin' cheer,
> Not an eye in thet whole buildin' but theet day let fall a tear.
> Say the judge, he cried a little, bid us bury bygone strife,
> Said it was his pleasin' duty to pronounce as man on wife,
> Then we started for our home, sir, back to old Ontario,
> En we've never had a jungle, though that's many years ago.
> Sakes, we live just like tew **love birds** tew each other kind en true,
> And I think thet are divorce court was the makin' of us two."

The analogy did not take root and become a part of our popular jargon, however, until after 1921, when Sigmund Romberg opened the musical comedy, *Love Birds* at the Apollo Theater on Broadway. It was only two acts, and sadly, short-lived, playing only 103 performances, from March 15 to June 11. Still, use was not widespread.

Another comedy, published in 1927, first played in 1929, used the figurative term of lovers in the script: *The Royal Family: A Comedy in Three Acts,* by George S. Kaufman and Edna Ferber, Act I:

> ***"Fanny*** (...Descends the last step) Well, what brings you two **love birds** around at the break of day?"

By the 1930s, it began to pick up steam, being used in novels such as feminist Faith Baldwin's *Skyscraper* (1931), and songs, like *Duet for **Lovebirds*** by

Stanley Kauffmann (1937) and in the N.O. Myer lyric, 'We're the lov-in-est **love birds** you ev-er did see' (1938).

Love means never having to say you're sorry+

This is a familiar catchphrase in popular culture based on a line in Erich Segal's bittersweet 1970 novel, *Love Story*, popularized by the screen adaptation that same year starring Ali McGraw and Ryan O'Neal. It is used twice in the film, once in the middle by McGraw's character, Jennifer, and once at the end, by O'Neal's character, Oliver. In the movie script it is worded slightly different, as 'not ever' rather than never. It has since been used in another movie, *What's Up Doc?* and numerous TV shows.

Luck of the devil[2] / Devil's luck

In British English lore, this has to do with the old superstition regarding selling one's soul to, and making a 'pact' with, the devil in exchange for his working magic in your life to bring about good fortune. John Ray first recorded a form of the saying in *A Complete Collection of English Proverbs* in 1737, on page 97:

> "The Devil's child **the Devil's luck"**

Dickens popularized the phrase in *Nicholas Nickelby*, Chapter LIV, 1854:

> "You won't have to pay his annuity very long; you have **the Devil's luck** in bargains, always."

In 1893 it was cited as 'the luck of the devil' in a serialized tale by that name in *The Pall Mall Magazine* one reference is in Chapter III:

> "Why you've the **luck of the devil** to-night, Seymore! See all you've won!"

Luck of the Irish

During the American gold rush in the last half of the 19th century, the majority of those who struck healthy veins of precious metal were either Irish, or Irish Americans, leading other prospectors to start the rumor that they had 'found the pot of gold at the end of the proverbial rainbow' in the gold fields of California. Many said derisively that it was 'pure luck,' rather than brain power; hence the saying, 'luck of the Irish' was born.

Meanwhile, back in Ireland…the history being portrayed took on a less-bright picture. Martin Haverty, in *History of Ireland, Ancient and Modern*, 1860, described their inherent tendency on page 446 as:

> "…the ill-**luck of the Irish…"**

Even in America, the term did not become cliché until well into the 20th century; then some questioned its validity. In *American Insurance Digest and Insurance Monitor*, June 10, 1922 in 'Pluck, Determination and Hard Work Brought Judge Dugan Success,' on page 11, we read:

> "They call it 'the **luck of the Irish**.' But they're wrong.
>
> "Just a few years ago one of our leading authors wrote a book which he called 'The **Luck of the Irish**.' The more of the story one read the more one realized that he, too, was wrong.
>
> "For it isn't the luck of the Irish. It's the pluck of the Irish."

Lucky dip[2]

As a cliché, in Britain, this term, begun in the mid-1800s, means a selection or decision made purely at random. It comes from an old game in which prizes are mixed up and concealed in a container, usually a large bucket, and for a small fee a player can dip his or her hand into the container and select a prize at random. In America, similar children's games are played, and carnival chances are sold yielding much the same result. The earliest known mention of the metopher is in *The Literary World*, March 20, 1852, in 'Literature;'

> "The chance medley of such a book is its attraction; every page is not equally good, and you dip into it with the excitement of a lottery, finding a good thing in the mass to suit your own taste. For a **lucky dip** into its seven hundred pages and three thousand 'leetle anecdotes' take the following…"

Another interesting citation is found in *Some Old Love Stories* by Thomas Power O' Connor, 1895, page 247-248:

> "A woman may be happy in a union that has so inauspicious a beginning by a **lucky dip** in the lottery of marriage; or she may be saved from an awakening by a want of intelligence."

Lucky stiff

This comical cliché refers to someone thought to be an average person who has experienced something bringing great fortune. The impression is that the person is unworthy and undeserving, and was merely lucky. 'Stiff' originally meant a dead person, and was later applied to a ne'er-do-well; thus, the individual was thought to be as deserving as someone who is dead. The phrase started showing up in magazines in 1914, but it was seemingly already known. One of the first is in *Pearson's Magazine*, that June, in 'Getting the Break' by Billy Evans about American League professional baseball:

> "(Ty) Cobb makes his luck; he created the situations that entitle him to the break. Following his entry into the American League, if he hit a slow bounder to an infielder and beat it out because of his speed, or due to its having been badly handled, he was a '**lucky stiff**,' to use the favorite expression of many of the players."

Obviously, history didn't view Cobb in this manner.

Lukewarm

This odd-seeming word, meaning only barely warm, according to etymologists, derived from the Middle English word lew, lewk or leuk, which meant tepid, or slightly warm. The earliest usage of the word lukewarm in a literal sense was in the 14th century, and in about 200 years it also took on the figurative meaning 'lack of enthusiasm.' The earliest citation known is in *Songs and Sonnets written by the ryght honorable Lord Henry Haward late Earle of Surrey*, in the section 'Nicholas Grimald's Poem's,' page 152, in 'A funerall song, upon the deseas of Annes his mother,' 1557:

> "And Nicolas you naamd, and naamd agayn: With other speech, aspiring heauenly raign: When into ayre your sprite departed fled, And left the corps a cold in **lukewarm** bed. Ah, could you thus, deare mother, leave us all?"

Here, of course, it is literal. Just a few years later, in 1579, we find this figurative citation in *Gaping Gulf, with Letters and Other Relevant Documents* by John Stubbs, in a clear reference to the biblical story in *I Kings 18*:

> "Take not the word of God in your mouths, you that breathe such **lukewarm** counsel, halt no more on both sides. If God be God, let him be so honored. If Baal be your god, take you to him altogether."

M

Mad as a hatter [2, 3]

This expression in Great Britain and Australia is used in reference to a person deemed to be insane. In the late 18th and early 19th century, mercury was used in the production of felt used to make hats. People who were employed in the hat trade were exposed to daily trace amounts of metal, which over time led to mercury poisoning, causing dementia. This became known as 'mad hatter's syndrome,' thus creating the saying. The first mention of this term in a book comes from *With Harp and Crown* by Walter Besant and John Rice, 1800, page 106

> "No will would stand a contest with Chauncey as **mad as a hatter**."

Mad (crazy or silly) as a two bob watch / cut snake[3]

This Aussie idiom means stupid, idiotic, unpredictable, or erratic. It dates from the 1950s. A two bob watch was one which only cost 'two bob,' meaning two shillings, and that it was a cheap and badly made timepiece, therefore useless. An earlier related expression, from the 1940s, was a 'two bob' lair, which was someone who dressed flashily but cheaply. Another Aussie saying, 'mad as a cut snake' dates back to at least June 12, 1900 when a version of it was first cited in the *Queensland Times*:

> "A man named John Molloy was brought up at the Police Court ⅆ on suspicion of being of unsound mind ... Molloy was taken to Ipswich, examined (I am informed) by a medical man, and discharged. Some surprise has been expressed at this course, for, according to all accounts, the man was, to use a colloquial expression, **'as mad as a snake'**."

An American synonym is 'madder than a wet hen' (see in original volume).

Made from scratch

'Scratch' has been in use since the 18th century for a line drawn, or 'scratched' on the ground as a starting point in sports; especially cricket and boxing. In *The Muses Mirror: Being a Collection of Poems*, Vol. II, 1783, in a poem on page 180 titled 'The Noble Game of Cricket,' we read:

> "Ye strikers observe when the foe shall draw nigh,
> Mark the bowler advancing with vigilant eye;
> Your skill all depends upon distance and sight,
> Stand firm to your **scratch**, let your bat be upright."

Scratch came to mean 'the basic starting point' for any game, and eventually, *anything*. In 1879, *The Electrical Researches of Henry Cavendish* has the following illustration on page 309:

> "The thickness was then tried in 4 different parts of circumference at 4-4 inc. distance **from scratch**. It was then weighed in water in the same manner as the others."

Then in *The General Magazine and Historical Chronical*, January, 1939 we see an even more marked change in connotation:

> "Again, in order to further accentuate this concept of equality of opportunity, a system of universal 'free' public school education was provided by government so that everyone might begin **from scratch**, as it were, in the competitive struggle."

Preparing foods 'from scratch' came by the mid-20th century. A good early example is from *Life Magazine*, January 31, 1964, in Great Dinners on page 47:

> "Until you eat this, or any other rich broth **made from scratch**, you will never know how good a home-cooked broth can be."

Main squeeze

A main squeeze is the most important girlfriend or boyfriend someone has, especially one who is known to 'play the field.' The word squeeze has been around with numerous meanings, particularly as a verb, for centuries, but the use of main squeeze as a most important person was cited first in *Black and White: A Monthly Magazine of Facts for Insurance Policy Investors*, March, 1896, in 'Miscellany:'

> "I went in and asked the **main squeeze** of the works how much the sack meant to him, and he said I could have it for 400 simoleons."

Make it snappy+

This idiom means 'hurry up,' 'do it quickly.' The word 'snappy' has been in English since the mid-18th century, and as meaning quick or energetic since 1825. Since 1871 is has been used also to mean clever or smart. From the early 20th century 'make it snappy' has meant exactly what it does today. The earliest available example in print is found in *A Scout's Honor*, a one act play by American playwright Clifton Lisle, 1917:

> "**Mr. H.** '...The rest of you fellows work! **Make it snappy**!'"

Make one's mark

Originally this referred to a person who could not read or write making an X for a signature, particularly on a legal document. This is attested in *The Duty of Executors and Administrators* by John Facuhereaud Grimke, 1797:

> "Two witnesses swore, that the testator did not publish it as his will, but that another guided his hand, and that the testator **made his mark**, but said nothing, nor was he capable."

This expression has long meant and still means to do something important and meaningful which makes one famous or successful. This is illustrated as early as August, 1882, in the *Wesleyan-Methodist Magazine,* in the obituary of businessman Henry Farr:

> "From the commencement, by incorruptible integrity and persevering assiduity, he **made his mark** in business; but he used often gratefully to refer to one of his earlier experiences, at a time when the young tradesman's capital was necessarily limited, and yet he had to give long credit."

Making one's hair stand on end

This hyperbolic idiom means to cause someone to be very freightened, and goes back to William Shakespeare, who compared this illusion to quills on a 'fretful' porcupine in *Hamlet*, Act I, Scene v, 1602:

> "I could a tale unfold, whose lightest word would harrow up thy soul, freeze thy young blood, make thy two eyes, like stars, start from their spheres, thy knotted and combined locks to part and each particular **hair to stand an end**, like quills upon the fretful porpentine."

Mama bear about...

Being 'mama bear' metaphorically usually refers to a mother or other female responsible for care of children being excessively protective of a child or children, but may also apply to any subject which someone viciously defends. It is taken from the fierceness of a mother bear when defending her cubs, and only came into popular usage in the 21st century. An early example in print of the alternative use is from *Standing By: The Making of an American Military Family in a Time of War* by Alison Buckholtz, 2009:

> "'That sound is part of our marriage,' she said, firmly. 'I wouldn't give it up for anything.'
> "'I get it,' I said. 'You're very **Mama Bear about** the Navy, aren't you?'
> "'It's just part of my coupon-cuttin,' Spam-eatin' self,' she laughed, dipping a nacho."

Man of straw / Straw man^

The British and American English expression 'man of straw' originated as a q person with weak character, and along with the related term 'straw man' (often interchangeable), refers to an idea which is weak and easy to refute and defeat, thus the principle of 'straw man arguments,' which in essence, contrary to the comments on a major online free encyclopedia, has been around since at least the early 19th century. In *Some Account of the Life, Writings and Speaches of William Pinkney* by Henry Wheaton, 1826, page 593, we find:

> "This is to combat with a **man of straw**, and to put fitters upon a shadow. The gentlemen must, therefore, abandon either their doctrine or their restriction — their argument or their object — for they are directly in conflict, and reciprocally destroy each other."

This soon afterward began showing up with 'straw man,' rather than 'man of straw,' very much involving the word argument for the rest of the 19th and early 20th century. Then in 1935, we read in the *New York Court of Appeals Records and Briefs*, on page 24:

> "Entirely confident in our position as above outlined, we will now in this brief attack the **'straw-man' arguments** of respondents, and at the risk of extending our brief, meet them on the ground of their own choosing."

But these basic terms go back several hundred years. As early as 1677, in *A Vindication of the Ordinations of the Church of England* by Gilbert Beunet, we see this on page 70:

> "That through the form of our Ordination since King Edward the 6th, his days, till his Majesties happy Restauration was invalid…And having set up this **Man of Straw**, he runs unmercifully at him, he stabs him in at the heart, he shoots him through the head, and then to make sure work of him, he cuts him all to pieces that he ſhall never live nor speak again; and an this out of pure chivalry to shew his valour…"

A Compleat Dictionary Dutch and English by Egbert Buys, 1766 has the following entry on page 790:

> "A **straw man**, (an insignificant fellow)"

Man upstairs, The

This humorous cliché is sometimes used to refer to God. It is derived from references in Hebrew and Christian scriptures attributing masculine gender and human characteristics to the Supreme Being, and the statement that man was made in His image (*Genesis 1:27*), coupled with the teaching that he dwells in the heavens (*Psalm 115:3*) above our planet.

In *The Converted Catholic*, January, 1909, in 'Dr. Pentecost's Address,' we find the earliest available record of the term being utilized to alude to God; here in quotes, indicating prior coining:

> "It was to **'the man upstairs'** that he had to render account, and as long as he was satisfied, the gatekeeper cared little for the opinions of others about him or his work. We should do our work for Christ in the same spirit."

Many a mickle makes a muckle[4]

This old Scottish proverb means many little things combined eventually will make something big. Our English word much actually derives from the Middle English *Mikel*, the root of both of these words. The British equivalent was historically, 'Many a little makes a micle,' which appeared earlier in print than the Scottish version, though it may or may not have proceded it in oral usage. The earliest known printed reference is in William Camden's *Remaines of a greater worke concerning Britaine, 1605* printed in 1614:

> "**Many a little makes a micle**."

Printed reference to the Scottish saying came in George Washington's *Writings* in 1793:

> "A Scotch addage, than which nothing in nature is more true 'that **many mickles make a muckle.**'"

Both were popular in 19th century writings.

Many hands make light work

This is a biblically based proverb, which follows principle in *Proverbs 10:4*. The *NIV* reads:

> "Lazy **hands make** for poverty, but diligent hands bring wealth."

But the actual axiom was recorded first in *The Proverbs of John Heywood: Being the 'Proverbes' of that Author Printed 1546.*

Many moons ago+

This metaphoric term has long been used to mean 'a long time ago,' and alludes to months as 'moons' due to the phases of earth's moon. This expression was used by Native Americans who defined days and nights by the sun and moon. Specifically, it is attributed to the sophisticated Kuna people, also known as Cuna Indians who occupied the region now known as Panama and the San Blas Islands in the 16th century. But the word month, itself, derives from the word moon. Old English *menoth* comes from the Old Saxon, *menon*, meaning moon.

Marching orders

This literally refers to military orders to begin a march or troop movement, and in this vein, also figuratively means any order or instructions to move out or proceed; also, a notice of dismissal from a job or position of employment; aka 'walking papers.' The term in its most literal sense originated in the 17th century. The earliest known printed reference is in *The Compleat Body of the Art Military*, the Second Edition by Richard Elton, Leivtenant Collonel, 1659, page xxxi:

> "Their **Marching order**, was a Deep-Herse, produc'd from the former, by moving away (1) the Front (which was followed by the *Tabernacle* and it's Ministers..."

Figurative use began in the late 19th to early 20th century. The earliest available citation is from *Leaves from a Squatter's Note Book* by Australian Government Inspector Thomas Major, published in London in 1900, page 132:

> "If not now in delirium tremens, he was fast approaching it, so **he was given his marching orders**, time being graciously allowed him to roll up his blanket. If he did not then decamp, he would be kicked from off the premises..."

May the force be with you

This is a parting wish invoked many times by various characters in the *Star Wars* series movies, first used in the original *Star Wars* movie, later called *Episode IV, A New Hope,* released May 26, 1977. It was used by General Dodonna, (Alex McCrindle) when he wished Luke Skywalker (Mark Hamill) good luck when preparing to go against the Empire.

> ***Luke**: "It's not impossible. I used to bullseye womp rats in my T-16 back home, they're not much bigger than two meters."*
> ***General Dodonna**: "Then man your ships. And **may the Force be with you.**"*

It came to achieve cult status among fans and has been used as a slogan, particularly in parting, to wish a person or group good luck and fortune.

Mea culpa

This is a somewhat rare type of expression, in that it is one of a limited number of Latin phrases welded into the English language with no alteration. It means literally, 'through my fault.' It comes to us via a prayer of confession of sinfulness called the *Confiteor* (I confess), which is voiced in the Roman rite at the beginning of Mass, or when receiving the sacrament of Penance. As a figurative term, it is used even lightheartedly to admit having made a mistake which should have been avoided. Catholics may, however, accompany this with tapping on the chest as being used in a religioUS context. In the U.S., the slang synonym 'my bad' (see in first volume) may be used instead. It has been active in English since at least 1374 when Chaucer wrote the following in *Troylus*:

> "Now, **mea culpa**, Lord! I me repente."

It is now used most frequently in law legalese as an admission of fault where there is no 'due filligence.'

Meal ticket

In the literal applicatiom this means a ticket or document which may be redeemed at a specific restaurant to provide a meal or meals for an individual, and as such, has been used since the 1800s. In a figurative sense, it refers to a person or thing which provides a living for someone. The earliest citation of this is older than most would think, and comes from *One Thousand Jokes from Vaudville* by various contributors published in 1908, from a joke by comic Jack Hazard on pages 22 & 24:

> "Several times in the presence of the waiter, when she ordered more, she laughingly referred to me as her **'meal ticket**,' and when she had finally finished and the waiter brought me a check for $11.75 I told him I only had two dollars."

Mealy mouthed+

This is an old-fashioned idiom which is now nearly antiquated. It refers individuals who avoid the use of direct and plain language, afraid to say what they really think. It originated in the 1570s, according to *Etymology Online*, and it thought by many to have derived from the Old English word *milisc*, meaning sweet, which came from the Proto-Germanic *meduz*, honey, from which mead, the sweet honey based drink was derived. Both the the French and Spanish word for sweet is *miel*. The thought here is that the person only used sweet words. Another possibility, which seems more likely, is that it came from the German phrase, *Meal in Maule behalten* (to carry meal in the mouth), based on the notion of the softness of ground flour.

Method in one's madness+

This is an old figurative expression meaning that one has a purpose to what he or she is doing. It came originally from Shakespeare's *Hamlet* (1599-1602), Act II, Scene ii:

"POLONIUS *(aside)* Though this be **madness,** yet there is **method in it**."

Mexican standoff

This expression refers to a confrontation between two or more parties in which no participant is able to proceed or retreat, putting someone in danger. As a result, all parties maintain a strategic position until an outside party, usually an arbitrator, intervenes or an event such as an ensuing battle makes resolution possible. Various origins have been claimed, the most feasible of which is an event in the Mexican American War (1846-1848). The earliest known citation in print is in a short story about an American being held up by a bandit in Mexico, published in the weekly paper, *Sunday Mercury*, New York City, March 18, 1876:

> "'Go-!' said he sternly then. 'We will call it a stand-off, a **Mexican stand-off**, you lose your money, but you save your life!'"

Middleman

Originally, this term was used in 15th century late Middle English as a maker of girdles. The current meaning came as early as the mid-17th century. It means either a person between a producer of goods or services and the consumer, or any intermediary or agent between two parties, as in the following early example. In *An Essay toward the Amendment of the last English-Translation of the Bible* by Robert Gel, 1659, page 265, we read:

> "…the Priest is he, whose duty it is to be a **middleman** between God and the people, faith [*saith*] Chryfostom [*Chrysostom*]; and to make intercession for the people as Moses and Aaron often did."

Milk something or **someone (for all it's, he's** or **she's worth)+**

This is a figurative expression for attempting to get as much out of something or someone as possible; take full advantage. Today it is believed to be from continuing to squeeze on a cow's udder until every drop of milk is extracted. There was first, however, an old legal term 'mulct.' The origin of this goes back as far as the early 16th century. David Hume, in his *History of England*, 1529, states that Parliament granted King Henry VIII a discharge of all debts, saying that his creditors 'were well pleased to take the opportunity of mulching them.'

In the context it implies that they were getting back as much as they possibly could. Certainly this could be the origin of the current term 'milking them.'

Mind over matter^

This thought-provoking phrase, popularized during the 1960s and 1970s, is used in various concepts, including mind-centric spiritual doctrines, parapsychology and philosophy. Most often it is used in controlling pain that one may or may not be experiencing. In spite of claims in the most-used online Encyclopedia that this term first appeared in 1863 in *The Geological Evidence of the Antiquity of Man* by Sir Charles Lyell, it actually made its debut in print 110 years earlier in *The Principles of Natural and Revealed Religion Occasionally Opened and Explained in a Course of Sermons Preached before the Honorable Society of Lincolns Inn, in Two Volumes, Volume the First* by the Reverend Mr. Warburtin, Preacher of the Society, printed in London in 1753:

> "Thus Matter carries in it no further marks or notice of a creating Hand, than an aptitude of falling back into nothing on the withdrawing the influence of that power... But besides this obvious superiority of **Mind over Matter** in the nature of their essences; there is as sensible a difference in the ends of their Creation, or in the effects produced by their exertion of their several qualities."

However, the online source was 'on the mark' in bringing attention to the fact that another related saying goes back much farther into the realms of history. '**The mind drives the mass**' was coined between 29 and 19 BCE by none other than the legendary Roman poet, Virgil, in *Aeneid,* Book 6, line 727.

Mind's eye (See: **In the mind's eye**)

Miss one's calling (See: **You missed your calling, original volume**)

mixed bag, A

This idiom refers to a heterogeneous collection of people, things, ideas, activities—or even wintry weather. The earliest known reference in print is from *Blackwood's Edinburg Magazine*, August, 1877, in 'Mine is Thine, Part II:'

> "A little of your unadulterated blamey will soon set matters right for you and your unique **mixed bag**."

Mom-and-pop operation

This Americanism refers to a small business which is primarily owned and operated by members of a family. It came into use in the 1980s and has gained much popularity. The earliest verifiable citation is from *Jane Brody's Good Food Book: Living the High-Carbohydrate Way* by Jane E. Brody, first published January 1, 1980, on page 240. It was already known by that time.

> "I admit to being spoiled by living in a food oriented city (New York)...and where several supermarkets, **mom-and-pop** grocerics, meat and fish markets, and bakeries are within walking or biking distance of my house..."

Mommie dearest+

Today this term is used facetiously to depict an abusive or hateful mother. It comes from the 1981 biographical MGM movie, *Mommie Dearest*, about actress Joan Crawford starring Faye Dunaway and Diana Scarwid. It reveals her abuse of her adopted daughter, Christina, taken from her memoirs published in 1978.

Money for old rope[2]

This common British idiom means doing something simple, exerting very little effort, to earn money. It comes from taking something useless and turning it into something useful. Two primary stories are told about how it came into being. One not so plausible suggestion is that it dates back to the days of executions by hanging in England. The hangman, it is said, was responsible for keeping the rope after the hangings for future re-use. Macabre souvenir hunters, it is claimed, were willing to pay a prime price for pieces of the rope, so it was cut up and sold. Another theory is that it derived from days in the Workhouse, in the mid-1800s, when workers were given damaged rope to pick into strands which would be spun into new rope. Hemp ropes gave out and were picked apart and recycled; then rope fibers, known as oakum, were hammered into the cracks between planks in the ship, and hot pitch poured over it to calk and seal the cracks, waterproofing the ship. The folks who provided the material to workers were getting paid well for the recycled rope. Both of these possibilities were from at least the 19th century. The problem is that the idiom never showed up in print until far into the 20th century, the earliest citation being in British author, James Curtis' novel, *Gilt Kid*, 1936:

> "He would spin her a fanny about the marriage laws, tie the poor kid up. It ought to be **money for old rope**."

It seems that the phrase may have been in use by then, but there is no mention of it in the *Sailor's Word Book* by William Henry Smyth published in 1867, which was the dictionary of the terms used on ships back then, do it likely came into being in the early 20th century. Then in *Recollections of Rifleman Bow* by Allen Bolby, 1969, page 122 we read:

> "'**Money for old rope**,' said the driver.
> "'Don't you believe it!'
> "I laughed. Then I remembered the Company."

Money is no object

This cliché is used when a person seeking to purchase the finest in a product or service has unlimited funds based upon the perceived value of the product he or she is wanting. Like many other much-used phrases, this was first recorded in a play—*Noteriety: A Comedy* by Frederick Reynolds, 1793, first performed in The Theater Royal in London

> ***"Lavish.*** Pshaw!—**money's no object**.
> "***Mist***. No!
> "***Lavish***. No, I've saved a fortune, Mr. Manager, and am so attached to the stage, that I'll not only act gratis, but when there are not expenses in the house, I'll be bound to pay them, I will, if I save it a thousand ways."

Monkey around

This metaphor refers to doing random, unplanned activities; spending time idly. The first known reference in print is from 1881, in *Dick's Reflections and Readings Number Twelve* by Dick Fitzgerald in 'The Language of the Rail' by Bill Nye, on page 117, which became a part of his novel, '*Forty Liars and Other Lies,'* page 31 in 1889:

> "Now you don't want to **monkey around** much, for if you don't loom up like six bits and go out on the tick, the old man'll give you a time check and the Oriental Grand Bounce…"

Monkey on [or **off**] **someone's back** (See: **Get the monkey off one's back**)+

More money than God (See: **Richer than God**)+

More power to you (or **ya**)

This cliché response to the revelation of an effort by another person may take on varying flavors, depending upon voice intonation or an undertone of skepticism by the speaker. It may be a synonym for 'Good for you!' but may also mean 'Good luck with that!' (See in first volume). The earliest known citations have Irish origins, and reflect the sarcastic meaning. The first is found in *Rory O'More: A National Romance* by 'Samuel Lover,' Volume I, page 81, 1837:

> "'Long life to your grace!' says O'Dempsy, taking off his hat; 'you desarve to be an O'Shaughnessy!' '**More power to you**, Paddy!' says Lord Edward as they put spurs to their horses; and away they powdhered down the road, laughin' like mad."

The next reference has a similar origin and flippant intent. It's from *Shaw's Annotated Report, of the Irish State Trials*, Dublin, 1844, page 75:

> "The English newspapers taunted us, and their writers who first laughed us to scourn, now admit that it is impossible to resist the application for repeal (cries of '**more power to you**.') I thought the monster meetings had demonstrated the opinion of Ireland."

More questions than answers

This popular cliché is used to express the belief that a certain philosophy, teaching or revelation has left a lot of unanswered questions about the truth of the matter. It came into usage in by the mid-18th century. The earliest known citation in print is in *A Handbook of Travel-talk: A Collection of Dialogues and vocabularies Intended to Serve as an Interpretor to Travelers in Germany, France or Italy* by John Murray, published in London in 1847, page iv:

> "The Dialogues will of necessity be found to contain **more questions than answers**, as it is not possible to anticipate what may be the different modes of reply to an inquiry."

More than meets the eye^

This means that there is hidden significance or value to something that is apparent at first glance. In spite of a major online dictionary placing origin at mid-1800s, this expression goes back 100 years earlier. The first known citation is in Edmund Spencer's *Faerie Queen, Volume II*, after Canto XII, in notes on page 428, published in 1758:

> "...and always we must look for **more than meets the eye** or ear; the words carrying one meaning with them, and the secret sense another."

There are numerous other references in print before the end of the 18th century.

Mouth-watering^

This term means delicious enough to make one salivate and lick his or her lips. In spite of a wonderful online etymology site placing first usage at mid-1800s, it was cited 150 years earlier, though in different context, in *Plautus's Comedies, Amphitryon, Epidicus, and Rudens*, made English, by Titus Maccious Plautus, 1694, on page 6:

> "It seems, his **Mouth watering** at Alcmena, unknown to her Husband, he borrows her upon Interest, fairly enjoys her, and gets her with Child too."

Then but a few years later we find this clear connotation in *The History of the Renowned Don Quixote de La Mancha* by Miguel de Cervantes Saavedra English translation by 'Several Hands,' Volume II, 1719,

> "...when the Damsel watches lest somebody comes, and stands with her **Mouth watering** all the while..."

In 1821 *The Third American Edition of Nicholson's British Encyclopedia; or Dictionary of the Arts and Sciences* had this in reference under Physiology about use of the term, with regard to food:

> "When any acrid matter is taken into the mouth, an increased flow of saliva is produced; and this may also follow the mere sight of **food**, and hence has arisen the well-known expression of the '**mouth watering**.'"

Move heaven and earth^

This hyperbolic idiom means to do everything in one's power to make something happen. A major online dictionary states that this term was 'first recorded in 1792.' Actually they are almost 150 years late. The earliest citation in print is in *The History of the Government of France: Under the Administration of the Great Armand Du Plesis, Cardinal and Duke of Richlieu and Chief Minister of State of that Kingdome*, 1657:

> "...we are come to wonder at the blindneffe of Grandees, who turmoil

> themfelves in extremity, who **move heaven and earth** by their broils, and all for thofe things, which death, and the inconftancy of humane affairs caufe to vanifh in a moment."

Move the needle

This idiom refers to making a significant difference, or in some cases, improving one's ratings. As a metaphor it has only come into play in the 21st century, and was popularized, if not coined, in a book titled *Moving the Needle: Get Clear, Get Free, and Get Going in Your Career* by Joe Sweeney and Mike Yorkey, 2014.

Much obliged+

This is an old fashioned formal expression, spoken or written when a person wants to indicate gratitude for a kind deed by someone else. It implies being in the other's debt. It came into use in the late 1500s and became popular in the 1600s. It was used extensively in polite letters from that era through the early 1900s. Some great examples occur in *Letters Written by His Excellency Hugh Boulter, D.D.* to several ministers of the State of England, 1672-1742, in which he used the pleasantry 29 times.

Muddy the waters

This means make a situation thought to be understood more complex or confusing. The earliest known citation is found in *Journal of the Senate of the General Assembly of the State of Iowa*, 1929, page 43, here in quotes, indicating that it was in use, though likely recently coined:

> "Charges that the opposition to the proposed $100,000,000 road bond issue has been attempting to 'cloud the issue' and **'muddy the waters'** were made today in a signed statement issued by State Senator J. O. Shaff…"

Mug shot

This slang term usually applies to photographs taken by law enforcement officials of suspects at the time of arrest. It has come also to be applied figuratively to other pictures of people's faces, such as those on photo ID which remind others of these 'shots.' The term 'mug' as slang for face goes back many years. It came from the Scandinavian word '*mugg*' meaning a drinking vessel. In the late 18th and early 19th centuries, toby jugs, or 'mugs' likely named for notorious 18th century English drinker, Toby Filpot, mentioned in the drinking song, *Little Brown Jug*, were beer mugs shaped like seated men drinking, or human faces, many of which now fetch high dollars on the antique market. It was from these that the expression mug came to be used for a person's face. But the term 'mug shot' didn't come into usage until the 20th century. The earliest citation available is from the *Ohio PSI Omegan*, a fraternity newspaper, April, 1920, in Beta Theta, Georgetown University, Stephen C. Hopkins, Editor, and even here, not the way it came to be used:

> "It is rumored that Brother 'Shorty' Conran had his '**mug shot'** twenty-seven times before he got one that pleased his esthetic taste."

In this snippet we can see that 'shot' is used as a verb rather than a part of the compound noun; but still, it seems to mean a photo of his face. It was the mid-1940s before the common usage began. A good example of this is in *Nancy Drew 22: The Clue in the Crumbling Well* by 'Carolyn Keen' (pseudonym).

> "At headquarters the sergeant on duty consulted the files and informed the Drews that Cobb Hooper had a prison record.
> "'Have you a **mug shot** of him?' Carson Drew asked."

Murphy's Law

This is an adage usually stated: 'Anything that can go wrong, will go wrong.' This concept is extremely old, and similar notions are historically stated in other languages. An early proponent of the concept, which pre-dates the coining of the term, was located by Stephen Goranson, a member of the American Dialect Society, which has done complex studies into this theory; in an 1877 report by Victorian engineer Alfred Holt (1829 – 1911) in a meeting of an engineering society:

> "It is found that **anything that can go wrong at sea generally does go wrong** sooner or later, so it is not to be wondered that owners prefer the safe to the scientific .... Sufficient stress can hardly be laid on the advantages of simplicity. The human factor cannot be safely neglected in planning machinery. If attention is to be obtained, the engine must be such that the engineer will be disposed to attend to it."

The actual term, Murphy's Law, was first referenced in a 1951 scientific journal, according to Irish Central News. In 1948 and 1949 tests to find out if humans could tolerate G forces on impact while flying at high speeds were conducted at

Edwards Air Force Base in California. Involved in the process was Recearch and Development chief, Edward Aloysius Murphy, a renowned World War II pilot from New Jersey. Murphy allegedly installed a key sensor backward, failing to check it before it was made operational. To everyone's embarrassment, he test utterly failed. (For a comparison see: Botched up, first volume.) Dr. John Sapp, who was in charge of the tests, used the term **Murphy's Law** in a subsequent conference, stating that they had learned that whatever could go wrong, would. The earliest printing of the phrase now available is from *The Making of a Scientist* by Anne Roe, 1953:

> "There were a number of particularly delightful incidents. There is, for example, the physicist who introduced me to one of my favorite 'laws,' which he described as '**Murphy's law** or the fourth law of thermodynamics' (actually there were only three last I heard) which states: 'If anything can go wrong it will.'"

Music to one's ears

This metaphoric phrase refers to something that is pleasant or gratifying for one to discover; exactly what the person wanted to hear. It is very old, going back to the 17th century. The earliest known printed reference is in *The Diaboliad: a poem. Dedicated to the worst man in His Majesty's dominions* by William Combe, 1677, page 24:

> "What **music to my ears**, to hear him yell,"

Must have killed a Chinaman[3]

Because of the negative connotations of the word 'Chinaman,' this Aussie expression, which has been historically popular since the early 20th century, is no longer thought appropriate. The saying was brought on by the superstition that killing a person of Chinese descent brought bad luck, so if a person were having bad things happen, this must be the reason.

Mutton dressed as lamb[2]

This derogatory British idiom is used to refer to an older woman who is dressed in a style more compatible to a younger woman, and it has been in use in Great Britain since early in the 19th century. Just before the advent of the term, butchers were offering mutton dressed like venison, as seen in *The*

Housekeeper's Instructor, or Universal Family Cook, by W.A. Henderson, London, 1805, page 461:

> "Haunch of **Mutton dressed like** Venison"

The idea of mutton being dressed in a way different than what was normal likely inspired the term. It was first recorded in print in 1811 by Mrs. Frances Calvert in a social gossip journal then related 100 years later in a dialogue involving Mrs. Calvert and her husband in Knox Blake's *An Irish Beauty of the Regency*, on page 177:

> **"**Girl!' answered he, 'Girls are not to my taste. I don't like lamb; **but mutton dressed like lamb**!'"

My main man

'Main man,' for the central figure in a country or group, has been in use in English since at least the 17th century; however, this idiom is a modern colloquial expression referring to a close and trusted male friend. On March 10-11, 1964, saxophonist Sonny Stitt and trombonist Bennie Green recorded an album at the Ter Mar Studio in Chicago, released on the Argo label, titled '*My Main Man*' featuring seven selections, the longest of which was the title cut. Almost immediately the phrase began popular use in the U.S.; at first more frequently in the African American community, then on a broad scale, in television shows and in print. An early exception to this was in *Life of Tom Horn, Government Scout and Interpretor, Written by Himself*, 1964, page 82:

> "Our horses were a little tired and **my main man** of these Indian volunteers, whose name was Tul-pi, said we could start as late as daybreak and yet strike renegades before night."

My better half+

In modern times this refers to one's spouse; in most cases a man's wife. But it did not originally mean this exclusively, but was used to express closeness to a dear friend. The earliest known reference was made by the Roman poet Horace (c 8th century BCE), and later it was used by Statius (45-96 CE). In ancient Rome it meant that a friend was so dear that he or she was more than half of a person's being. That connotation, meaning better in quality, carried through after it came to refer only to life partners, though it is sometimes used sarcastically in our day. The earliest reference in print referring to a spouse is found in *The Countesse of Pembrokes Arcadia* by Sir Phillip Sidney, 1580:

> "My deare, **my better halfe** (sayd hee) I find I must now leaue thee."

My word is my bond+

This is a very old idiomatic expression meaning someone always keeps a promise. For centuries it has been used as the motto of the London Stock Exchange, "An Englishman's word is as good as his bond." Forms of it have been used since at least c. 1482 when it appeared in the Scottish dialect romance, *Lancelot of the Laik*, "**O kingis word shuld be o kingis bonde**." The poem is anonymous and incomplete and survives in only one manuscript, leaving the origin of this phrase a mystery.

N

Nail-biter

This metaphor refers to a tense situation, the outcome of which is uncertain, causing anxiety and nervousness, especially a sports event which gets intense near the end. It is derived from the nervous habit of chewing on one's fingernails, attested from 1570. Origin of this usage is obscure, but it obviously was not in use as an idiom until the last half of the 20th century. The earliest known citation is from *Jet Magazine*, October 14, 1971, in an article titled 'World Series ends Baseball's Hottest' by Ronald Kisner. It is obvious that the phrase was already known.

> "…the Giants shot off to an early hit 17 home runs, drove in 57 runs, season comfortable lead that reduced to a **nail biter** as the Los Angeles Dodgers, the Giants' old rivals…closed in."

Nailing something

As an idiom this means getting something precisely correct or coing something exactly right. This idiom is recent as idioms go, and only came into common use in the 1970s. The earliest clear reference available in print is from *Flying Magazine*, July, 1977 in an article titled 'Westerlies' by George Clarson on page 80:

> "Kraft told me he felt a little rusty, but as the GCA specialist announced her presence, **he nailed it** on his reference 700-fpm descent at 140 knots."

Naked eye+

This is a metaphorical term for unassisted vision, without a telescope, microscope or other devise used to enhance one's vision. The earliest known usage of the phrase is found on page 19 of John Dunton's *The Athenian Oracle*, 3rd Edition, Volume 2, 1728:

> "Q. *Why does the moon appear red and* large in the ***Naked Eye*** *when near the* **Horizon** *and* little *and* pale when it *approaches the* Mid heaven…?"

Nanosecond

Literally meaning a billionth of a second, this is used hyperbolically to mean a very short time. The term only came into use in the late 1970s and was popularized in the 1980s and 1990s. Though not likely the first, the earliest available example in print of hyperbolic use is in *Uneasy Rider* by Mark Bryan, 1997, page 313:

> "…our waitress passed by with the coffee and made a crack I couldn't hear but Jim did, and he taunted her in a **nanosecond**."

Necessary evil

This very old analogy refers to something that is undesirable, but must be accepted for the 'greater good.' A similar expression is the 'lesser of two evils' (see first volume). It has been in use in English since at least the mid-16th century. The first citation known is in *Sir Thomas More, First English Collectivist* by James Leatham, printed in London in 1551, page 53:

> "But the average man would seem to regard Government as a **necessary evil**, the less of it the better."

Neck and neck^

As might be assumed, this phrase, like several others, is taken from horse racing, and in spite of a fine online phrase origin site placing the earliest printed reference at 1825, it goes back to at least 1806, when British playwright, Charles Macklin utilized it in *Love a la Mode*, a farce performed at the Theaters Royal, Drury Lane and Covent Garden, Act II, Scene i:

> "We were **neck and neck**, madam, for three miles, as hard as we could lay leg to ground—made running every inch;—but, at the first loose, I felt for him, found I had the foot—knew my bottom pull'd up—pretended to dig and cut-all fudge, ..."

Nectar of the gods+

In Ancient Greek mythology, ambrosia was thought to be the food of the gods, and was depicted as conferring longevity or even immortality, upon whoever partook of it. Hence it became known as the nectar of the gods. Today it is used for saying that any drink tastes extremely delicious.

Need some air

In a literal sense this means that a person needs to step outside of a building to get some fresh air, especially when the building is stuffy, smoky, hot or the air inside is stale. Figuratively it may refer to putting some space between oneself and another person, especially when one feels pressured in some way by the other person. Origin is obscure, but figurative use is relatively recent. An early example is in *Ransom Unpaid*, a novel by Fred Hunter, 1999, page 163:

> "'**I need some air**. That probably sounds selfish, but … '
> "'Not at all,' Emily said kindly. 'You've had a shock, and you should go home and get some rest.'"

Neighborhood watch

This modern term is applied to a systematic program of vigilance by residents of a community to prevent crime, and particularly, burglary. This, as an organized National effort in the U.S., began in 1972 by the NSA (National Sheriff's Association) through a grant from the Bureau of Justice Assurance, a part of the U.S. Department of Justice. The program works with local law enforcement agencies, private organizations and individual citizens, thus reducing crime and improving local communities. As a part of the effort, street signs and window decals have been posted in communities involved to make potential criminals aware that they are being watched and should not consider any attempts at burglarizing or terrorizing the residents.

Never hear the end of something

This is a common statement meaning that persons who are involved with a thought or project, whether pro or con, will continue to talk about it whether others want to hear it or not usually this refers to something emabarrassing or annoying to those forced to listen. It is very old, going back to the time of the American Revolution. The earliest known citation is from the comical work, *Free Thoughts on Quacks and Their Medicines* by Francis Spilsbury published in London, 1776, page 76:

> "This is undoubtedly a most curious piece of *mountebankism,* and *charlatannery;* if there ever was any; and more worthy of the ultramontane superstitious enthusiasts, than of a people disengaged from the monkish prejudices of old times: and should we, quacks or empiricks (whatever be the appellation by which we may be designed) be guilty of such, or similar, practices and superstitious absurdities, we should **never hear the end of it**."

Never miss a good chance to shut up

TV talk show host, 'Doctor Phil' McGraw wrote a noted article with this as the title, but he did not originate it. This comical, yet practicle, advice comes from American cowboy humorist and columnist, Will Rogers (1879-1935). What Rogers was likely saying is that we learn more from listening than talking. (See: We have two ears and one mouth, so we should listen more than we say.)

Never take candy from a stranger

This was the title of an American film released in 1960, filmed in the U.K., directed by Cyril Frankel, by Hammer Films, released in Britain as *Never Take Sweets from a Stranger*. But it had long been advice to children given by parents and others concerned about improper advances made by adults on unsuspecting young children. In *The Pedagogical Seminary*, June, 1903, an article titled 'Showing off and Bashfulness as Phases of Self Consciousness' by G. Stanley Hall and Theodate L. Smith speaks of children who don't take candy from strangers due to shyness, seeming not to recognize a danger; on page 187:

> "Children **refuse to accept candy from a stranger** because unable to overcome shyness sufficiently to approach."

Only nine years later, among the list of 'Nevers' listed in 'Advice of Evangelist to Girls' on page 22 of *Our Young People*, a Christian magazine published in Milwaukee, Wisconsin, October, 1912, we read:

> **"Never accept candy**, food, a glass of water, or smell flowers **offered by strangers**, nor buy such — they may contain drugs…"

Nickel-and-dime someone^+

This is a metaphoric expression used to mean that someone is charging small fees or prices in excess unnecessarily which add up to a much larger sum collectively, thus exhausting ones resources. It can also be applied to the practice of weakening or defeating someone through a series of small incursions or by giving too much attention to detail. According to *Merriam Webster*, the first known use was in 1879, and it is obviously American in origin. The earliest uses, however, only referred to shops selling articles for five and ten cents. First use as a verb occurred in 1913, according to the same source. Figurative usage came later. One popular online source says 1965-1970. Another says it has been in idiomatic use for 15 years. Both are too late, because the following appeared in *Broadcasting Telecasting*, October – December, 1957, and was obviously a known term at that time:

> "…to take the money in advance we can **nickel-and-dime them** to death and they'll never notice."

Nobody's perfect+

This is an expression used to acknowledge someone's mistakes or flaws, and remind someone that everyone is subject to failure or error. It was first used in the 1959 hit comedy movie *Some Like it Hot* when Jerry, played by Jack Lemon, who is disguised as a female, Daphne, tries to fend off the repeated marriage proposals of Osgood Fielding (played by Joe E. Brown). Finally, Lemon exposed the true Jerry, shouting, "I'm a man!" to which Osgood simply replies. "Well, **nobody's perfect**."

It has since been used as the title of at least five books, and a song by Hannah Montana (Miley Cyrus).

No earthly (idea, means, purpose or reason)

This simply means 'no conceivable…' as it is derived from relating to earthly means of thinking. The earliest known citation to a form of this is in the Dissertation in *The Lusiad; Or, The Discovery of India: An Epic Poem* by Luís de Camões, translated into English by William Julius Mickle, published in London, 1778:

> "In the first book, Jove summons a council of the Gods, which is described at great length, for **no earthly** purpose but to shew that he favoured the Portuguese."

Here it could be said that 'no earthly purpose' was used because the council was said to have taken place in the heavens, thus it may be a literal application. But in 1832, a clearly figurative example showed up in *Trials of the Persons Concerned in the Late Riots, Before Chief Justice of Great Britain*, page 10:

> "…where he (the Mayor) could have **no earthly** idea whether the military assistance was required at that precise time or not…"

No half measures[2]

In British English, this idiom means that a project will not be attempted with anything less than a complete and forceful effort; it will be done enthusiastically, all the way. It has been around since the 18th century. The earliest citation is from *The Gentlemen's or London Magazine*, April 1785, in the proceedings of the House of Commons for Monday December 1, 1784:

> "Sir Grey Cooper, observed, that the language of the house on the first day of meeting was, that something decisive must be done. No palliative, **no half-measures!** But no sooner was there something brought forth, even before its features were hardly seen, than it is reprobated in the gross, as inadequate, implacable, and abortive."

No love lost

This very long-standing term now means that two parties have historically had a dislike for one another, and any new conflict has no effect one way or the other. In centuries past, unrequieted love was viewed as 'lost,' so that is how it was originally denoted, meaning that two individuals or groups either loved or hated each other to the same degree. The earliest known citation in print is from a play attriburted to Shakespeare, though some question his authorship, from 1592, *A Faire Em*, Act V, Scene i:

> "And never could I see a man, methought,
> That equaled Manville in my partial eye.
> **Nor was there any love between us lost**,
> But that I held the same in high regard…"

Then in 1637, this reference was made in another play, *The Miseries of Enforced Marriage* by George Wilkins, Act V:

> ***"Ilf.*** And there shall be **no love lost**, nor service neither, Ile doe thee service at boord, and thou shalt doe me service at bed."

In the 19th century the meaning seemed to alter a bit toward what it is in our day, not necessarily reflecting either intense love or zealous hate; only a common aversion. In describing the feelings between a city polítition and the editor of the London Times, William Hazlitt, in *Political Essays with Sketches of Public Figures,* 1819, writes on page 168:

> "There is **no love lost** between them. He does not leave them the sole benefit of their old motto, *Odia in longum jaciens qua, conderet auctaque promeret.* He makes neither peace nor truce with them."

No man is a failure when he has friends^

This proverb has been wrongly attributed to Mark Twain. It most certainly was used in the classic Christmas movie *It's a Wonderful Life*, 1946, by the angel character, Clarence (Henry Travers), in the note he left for George Bailey (James Stewart) at the end:

> "Dear George, remember **no man is a failure who has friends**. Thanks for the wings. Love, Clarence."

But the earliest known citation of a close form of it comes from *The American Hereford Journal*, December 15, 1916, a publication for cattlemen, in an article titled. 'The Sothams Have Mastered the Business of Handling Public Sales,' in describing the attributes of T.F.B. 'Tom' Sotham, head of a Lansing Michigan sales organization, likely written by Editor, John Hazelton:

> "His enemies didn't think **he** could 'come back,' and they felt more comfortable because of this belief. **No man can be a failure who has friends** who believe in him or enemies who fear him."

No more Mr. Nice Guy!

This exclamatory remark it used when a person who has been considerate of the feelings of others has decided that he or she has not gotten the desired respect and results, and will no longer care about the wishes and feelings of others. Glam rocker Alice Cooper released a top-5 song in April, 1973 by this title on both a single and the album *Billion Dollar Baby* which popularized the phrase; but it was around before his song. In the February, 1972 issue of *Boy's Life*, in a story about canoeing in Wisconsin titled 'High Adventure Ahead' by William B. Mc Morris, on pages 6-8, we read:

> "It's about that time that the Voyager trainer will announce in a loud voice: 'Tomorrow you're really going to work! **No more Mr. Nice Guy**.'"

But Mc Morris didn't originate "Mr. Nice Guy" either. On page 20 of the November, 1967 issue of *Billboard,* in one of a series of articles about crooner Andy Williams, contributor Elliott Tiegel writes:

> "In America he is '**Mr. Nice Guy**.' Behind the scenes he is a sagacious observer of show business, with a somber maturity born of a lifetime in the public spotlight."

Before that it was Perry Como. In the January, 1962 issue of *Life*, on page 14, in an advertisement for his music it says:

> "Easily, gently, once - over-lightly, '**Mr. Nice Guy**' turns every song into a warm and wonderful experience"

From the artists laying claim to the title, one can readily see why Cooper would put out such a song. It was used in quotes in these references, and exactly who coined the phrase seems illusive.

Nook and cranny

This paired set of ancient terms is not nearly as old as the parts. 'Nook,' meaning an out-of-the-way hiding place to tuck something back for safe keeping, according to expert etymologists, has been in use since the 14th century, and 'cranny,' defined as 'a crack or crevice' since the mid-15th century. Shakespeare used the latter in 1597 in *A Midsummer Night's Dream*, Act III, Scene iii: 70:

> "Some man or other must present wall, and let him have some Plaster, or some Lorne, or some rough cast about him, to signifie wall; or let him hold

his fingers thus; and through that **cranny**, shall Piramus and Thishy whisper."

Together they are preceded by either 'every' or 'each,' and represent an effort to search thoroughly in every conceivable tiny spot. The origin of the pairing seems to be Irish, but was used also in England. The earliest printed reference available is in *A Letter to G______W______. Esq. Concerning the Present Condition of the College of Dublin,* published in 1734, contains the following:

> "...appointed fome Years ago, to take particular Care of this Bufiness; that by Means of this Office, and the Provost's Strictness and Resolution herein, great Advances have been made towards Filling every **Nook and Cranny** in the College..."

Then, in *History of Ireland from the Earliest Times to the Present Day* by Edward Alfred D'Alton, Half Volume 3, 1547-1659 published in 1920, we read:

> "In the mountains of Slieve Leuchra, in Kerry every **nook and cranny** was searched; the soldiers were divided into various bands; and the hunted people who escaped one band, were discovered and massacred by another."

No pain, no gain^

This popular saying, often used in workouts, means that if a person wants to improve, he or she must work at it so hard that it hurts. It has been attributed to German philosopher, Freidrich Nietschze (1854-1900), Benjamin Franklin and Jane Fonda. It is true that they all used forms of it. Fonda voiced it in her exercise programs; Nietschze developed a philosophy based on the principle and Franklin stated it in *Poor Richard's Almanac* (1734) which was reprinted in his 1758 essay, *The Way to Wealth*:

> *"Industry need not wish,* as Poor Richard says, *and he that lives upon hope will die fasting.* ***There are no gains, without pains."***

But this truism was with us long, long before this. The earliest known citation was in the early 2nd century CE portion of the Hebrew ethical teachings and maxims of the Rabbis, *Pirkei Avot* (*Ethics of the Fathers*) 5:21:

> "Rabbi Ben Hei Hei says, '**According to the pain is the gain**.'"

Then in the 1650 revised edition of British Cavalier poet Robert Herrick's 1648 book of verse, *Hesperides,* this short poem was added:

"NO PAINS, NO GAINS

"If little labour, little are our gains:
Man's fate is according to his pains."

No pun intended

A pun is defined as 'a joke exploiting the different possible meanings of a word or the fact that there are words that sound alike but have different meanings.' There are varying reasons why this cliché is used, both verbally and in writing. A great deal of the time, it is to merely draw intention to the pun just made. A lesser percentage of the time, when one is speaking, it is used to inform the listener that the speaker realized after the fact that a pun was made and doesn't want it to distract from the intent of what has just been said. The opposite is sometimes voiced when the speaker meant to use it and is emphasizing the joke. The earliest mention of an 'intended pun' was in 'Life of Books Published with Remarks' in *The Gentleman's Magazine,* April, 1756:

> "It is objected, that the cutting listen into list is making shreds of the language, but besides the wretched **pun intended** by the terms of the objection, and the absurdity of confounding list with shreds, it is built upon the grossest ignorance."

It is not until *The Oxford Entertaining Miscellany*, Volume 1, 1894—over 100 years later—that we have the earliest known citation of 'no pun intended:'

> "We have to debit Mr. Buckle Is. for the postage of a highly perfumed letter, addressed to the printer of our paper, who opened it under the impression (**no pun intended**,) that it was a private affair of his own."

No strings attached^

This cliché refers to doing something for someone else without expecting anything in return. There is a story told as to how this metaphor came to be coined in the cloth industry where a small piece of string was attached to a flaw in the fabric to mark it so it could easily be spotted. 'No strings attached,' this theory says, would indicate that it was flawless. Another origin theory goes back to the Babylonian Talmud, the scrolls of which were tied by strings, and it also certainly spoke of strings attached. An example is given by proponents of this origin in which a Babylonian man gives his wife a writ of divorce with a string attached but holds onto the string so he can snatch it back if he decides not to grant the divorce. The saying came into use in English in last half of the 19th century, and a lot of writing spoke of strings being attached to various items to denote being constantly connected, including a modern English version of the

Talmud. One example is found in *Dickenson's Theological Quarterly,* July, 1877, in selections from the Talmud which may give credence to the latter story:

> "'I gave thee,' returned the stranger, 'a beautiful spread, with **strings attached** to it; thou hast hidden it in thy house…'"

Then on March 24, 1883 in the *Pacific Coast Law Journal* published in San Francisco, California, under 'Marriage' we see:

> "In the present century marriage is usually preceded by a betrothment, gifts are usually interchanged (but with **no strings attached**), and a causeless withdrawal therefrom by either party is considered infamous."

It seems highly likely that the term arose from the idea of doing away with strings which represented binding together.

Not a hair out of place

This means excessively neat and tidy in appearance. The earliest form is from *A Narrative of the Adventures and Sufferings of J.R. Jewitt, Only Survivor of the Ship Boston* by John Rogers Jewitt, 1820, page 78:

> "The hair, after being well oiled, is carefully gathered upon the top of the head, and secured by a piece of pine or spruce ...strew all over it down obtained from a species of a large brown eagle, which abounds on this coast, and which they are very particular in arranging so as **not to have a single feather out of place,** occasionally wetting the **hair** to make it adhere."

Then in the *New York Literary Journal*, Saturday March 11, 1826, in 'Men of Pleasure,' on page 1, we find:

> "…whose glossy locks dropped down like the beard of old Aaron, whose boots might have served for his looking-glass; and on whose polished heaver **not a hair** sat **out of place**; who had a brooch for every day, a ring for every week, and a fresh snuff-box for every month."

Not all fun and games+

This is an idiomatic phrase used to indicate that a particular activity is difficult and unpleasant. It has been claimed on various websites to have derived from a statement used in Ancient Rome regarding the rules in wrestling against eye gouging: "It's all fun and games until someone loses an eye." This explanation is likely another far-fetched example of folk etymology.

Origin is unknown. At any rate, statements about things either being or not being 'all fun and games' started showing up in print in the 1960s. A good early example is found in an article about a California luxury spa in the Twin Falls, Idaho Newspaper, *The Times News*, Monday April 2, 1962:

> "…at the Golden Door women find it is **not all fun and games**. No alcoholic beverages are allowed."

Not broke but badly bent

This means that a person is not penniless, but certainly very low on funds. The saying, popular in rural Appalachia in the mid-to-late 20th century, comes from the title to a bluegrass song, *I Ain't Broke but I'm Badly Bent* credited to H. Payne, recorded by Kentucky native Lattie Moore in 1953, on the King Label; Bobby Goldsboro (credited to Fred Carter) in 1967, Del Reeves, on Columbia Records in January, 1968; and later by Old and In the Way (1973), and most recently by Dan Tyminski for mp3 download. The first verse is:

> "**I ain't broke but I'm badly bent**
> I had a little money but that's all been spent
> When I look back I wonder where it went
> It ain't no joke **I ain't broke but I'm badly bent**"

Not by any stretch of the imagination^ (or 'by no stretch…')

This old adage means that no matter how hard one tries, it would be difficult to accept something. A major online dictionary places the origin of 'by any stretch' at late 1700s. The idea of stretching one's imagination, however, goes back many years earlier, to the Friday, April 13, 1729 issue of the London publication, *The Spectator*, in which the following appeared on the fromt page:

> "The Gentleman was as diligent to do Juftice to his fine Parts, as the Lady to her beauteous Form: You might fee his **Imagination** on the **Stretch** to find out fomething uncommon, and what they call bright, to entertain her; while fhe writhed her felf into as many different Poftures to engage him."

In a 1793 publication of *The Plays of William Shakespeare*, a notation from 'The Historical Account from the English Stage, Vol. II' by Malone contains the following with a negative connotation:

"It appears that when *Pericle*s was originally performed, the theatres were furnished with **no** such apparatus as **by any stretch of the imagination** could be suppofed to present either a sea, or a ship…"

notch on someone's bedpost, A or **Another**

This pejorative metaphoric expression refers to one of many casual male sexual conquests, typically a one-night stand for the sake of keeping tally. It came into use in the 1990s. The origin is obscure, but the earliest known citation is from *Honey Moon* by Susan Elizabeth Phillips, 1993, page 182:

"Now if the boy were somebody decent, someone who really cared about her and wasn't just looking to put a celebrity **notch on his bedpost**, he'd feel different."

Not eating enough to keep a bird alive

This saying is used when a person is underweight and seems to eat very little. The earliest example of a form of it in print is from *Harpers New Monthly Magazine*, August, 1858 in 'The Quiet Home:'

"'I never saw children with such indifferent appetites,' said Mr. Bird; 'they **don't eat enough to keep pigeons alive**.'"

Not getting any younger

This cliché means that because a person of necessity continues to decline as years go by, anything that he or she wants to do should be done as soon as possible. The earliest example known is from *The Australian Journal: A Weekly Record of Literature,* November, 1876, in Chapter VII of the serialized novel, *August Travers* by 'Europa:'

"Mr. Castletowers, captivated by Minna's extreme beauty, fell madly in love, lent various sums of money to Mr. Dashwood, and proposed to Miss Dashwood. Minna at once accepted when she reflected that she was **not getting any younger**, and they were married on the following week privately…"

Nothing could be further from the truth+

This is a common statement used to state emphatically that something which has been suggested in completely untrue. It has been used since at least the late 1800s. Nathan Matthews included it in *The Citizen and the State* in 1889. In retaliation against a claim that the private Protestant school group which he is representing before the Massachusetts General Court, Committee on Education, is an enemy of the public school system, he states on page 4:

> "**Nothing could be further from the truth**; there are no people more honestly and honestly devoted to the cause of free elementary education than those who have dedicated their lives to the instruction of the young…"

Not know what hit me, you, us, him, her or **them**

This refers to something, usually bad, happening to someone unexpectedly with no warning, whether planned by another person, or not. It goes back at least to the last half of the 19th century. An early example is from *Border Tales around the Campfire, in the Rocky Mountains* by Chaplain Tuttle, 1878, page 132:

> "'This fellow,' said Bruce, pointing to a stalwart chief, '**did not know what hit him**, I guess, for a chunk of lead carried away the roof of his cranium.'"

Not worth the paper it is written on^

This is applied to documents which are not legally binding because they are not backed by the proper authority, or have authenticity. Contrary to the coining date of 1861 in one of the most popular phrase origin dictionaries, the *earliest form of this* was first printed thirty years earlier in a story titled, 'The Lottery Ticket,' which appeaaredd in numerous publications, including the April, 1831 issue of Boston's *The Monthly Traveller* on page 2:

> "'Well, let me see what it is, Sally. This is a lottery ticket! –a whole Lottery ticket; yet I will venture to say **not worth** more than the rag of **paper** 'tis **printed** on.'"

Numbskull+

This old metaphoric term for a dim-witted or stupid person derived from the idea that such an individual must have a thick or 'numb' skull, and would not feel pain if hit over the head. It was first recorded in 1717 as *numskull*, and was preceded by *numskulled*, first attested in 1706 according to *Etymology Online*. 'Numskulled' certainly appeared in *The History of John Bull* a political satire by Scottish scientist and author John Arbuthnot (1667-1735) originally published in 1712, in the phrase 'clot-plated **numskulled** ninny-hammer' on page 48. The old spelling prevailed into the 20th century. A good example is found in Kenneth S. Goodman's *Dancing Dolls*, a fantastic comedy in one act, 1915:

> "MEZZTIN. What did she want? Why the dolt's fallen in love with that drum-beating **numskull**, that wooden-faced clown, that egg-juggling Giles."

Nuts and bolts^

This means the essential basic facts rather than theories about something. A major online source states origin at 1955-1960. This idiom, however, has been around since at least March, 1949, when it was used in an article in *Popular Science,* on page 103, by Editor Perry Githens, titled, 'Nuts, Bolts and People,' dealing with altering the thread patterns of actual nuts and bolts to synchronize them on both sides of the Atlantic, which may have coined the metaphor:

> "Beginning, understandably, with military equipment, a new 'international' design will match up **the nuts and bolts** of Britain, Canada, and the United States."

A bit further down the figurative use takes shape:

> "Words are only the **nuts and bolts** of ideas. But the world needs unified standards to make the interchangeable parts of peace."

O

Occam's razor

This is a problem-solving principle, originally 'Ockham's razor,' or *lex parsimoniae* in Latin, attributed to English Franciscan friar, scholastic philosopher and theologian, William of Ockham (c 1287-1347 CE). His words in Latin were: ""Numquam ponenda est pluralitas sine necessitate," or "Plurality mUSt never be posited without necessity."

Simply put, it is stated as "Among competing hypotheses, the one with the fewest assumptions should be selected." This tenant is sometimes used to shift the burden of proof in discussion. In science, Occam's razor is utilized as a heuristic technique (employing a practical method sufficient for immediate goals).

The principal has been known for many centuries; and even before Ockham, the basis of it was expressed by such philosophers as Robert Grosseteste (1175-1253) and others as far back as Aristotle (383-322 BCE). But the term was coined in the mid-19th century, and it was largely brought to light through the publication in 1853 of *Philosophy of Sir William Hamilton, Bart*, 9th Baronet and Scottish metaphysical philosopher. On page 40, this footnote appeared:

> "The rule of philosophizing, which Hamilton felicitously calls the law of parcimony, was often keenly applied by the logical Occam; hence it is sometimes designated as '**Occam's razor**'."

'Occam's razor' finally became more widely known to the general public after the 1997 release of the Warner Brothers' sci-fi movie, *Contact,* starring Jodie Foster, based on a novel by Carl Sagan about the first confirmed communication by scientists with Extraterrestrial intelligence, which, in the story, leads to a visit with the alien which creates the first step toward interstellar travel.

Odd man out^

This is a method of selecting or illuminating a person from a group, as by matching coins, especially in preparation for beginning a game, The person illuminated is 'the odd man out.' The term is also used to describe a person who differs from others in a group in some distinctive way.

In looking at the origin of this 'odd' idiom, we must visit the etymological roots of the base of it, odd. This was first spelled *odde* in English in the 14th century and was a derivative of the old Scandinavian word, *oddr*, which meant spear point. The Icelandic word was actually *oddi,* 'triangle, a tongue' of land. From triangle came an 'odd' number, rather than even, came about. The compound word *oddamaðr* (ð has the value of 'th' in Modern English as in the, this, that) meant "the third man; he who gives the casting vote." It was from oddamaðr that the English 'third man (out)' was taken, and other words and compounds containing 'odd.'

The first printed reference available to 'odd man' is found in Thomas Holyoke's *A Large Dictionary: In Three Parts*, English and Latin, 1677:

> "An **odd man**. Homo perverfus."

A popular online dictionary lists coining of the actual phrase, 'odd man out' at '1885-1890.' A much earlier citation, however, is found in *The Adventures of a Carpet Bag* by Ernest Thomson, 1853:

> "Indeed all seemed to pity the unfortunate Dumpey, whom Blazes styled as the 'last man in, and the **odd man out,'...**"

Just two years later a perfectly clear example is in *Campaigning in Kaffirland; Or, Scenes and Adventures in the Kaffir War of 1851-2,* by William Ross King, 1855, also in quotes, on page 230:

> "...as they would only accommodate two each, and there were five of us, we tossed up who should be the **'odd man out,'** ..."

Odds-on favorite

This expression means the most likely one to win, succeed or achieve a worthy goal. To find the origin of the word 'odd(s)' see: Odd man out, above. 'Favorite at high odds' was used decades earlier, but the earliest known citation of this particular saying is in *Forest and Stream*, December 19, 1896, in 'Game Bag and Gun: Where to Go:'

> "As you say a deer is a small mark at thirty or forty rods loping through a runway, and it takes a good marksman and a good rifle to score under these conditions, the deer is generally a good **odds-on favorite**."

In reference to a race, it is found the following year in *Turf, Field and Farm*, November 12, 1897, in 'Racing Notes:'

"Two **favorites** were winners and the sensation of the day was the defeat of Dr. Catlett, the **odds on favorite**, in the last race."

Of all things!+

This is an exclamatory remark used to indicate that out of all the conceivable possibilities something turned out to be the most completely unexpected result or conclusion. The phrase has been used in regard to everything existent since medieval times. In 1921, it was used followed by an exclamation mark a the title of a book by American philosophical author, Robert Benchley, which bemoaned what the author saw as the unexpected misuse of the influence and power of the King of Great Britain (George V) to establish a 'absolute Tyranny' over the United States. The phrase seems to have taken root from this thought as a shocking and unexpected conclusion.

Off one's feed

This old idiom means that a person is reluctant to eat and has a loss of appetite, often also feeling dejected, sad and disoriented. The earliest citations are in relation to horses, as this first one in *Sporting Magazine* in January, 1803, in 'A Fashionable Sportsman and His Friend,' included in the feature 'Feast of Wit or Sportsman's Hall:'

"Poor devil, he's badly, and quite **off his feed**!"

The usage regarding animals, including sheep, continued through the early 19th century. The earliest known reference to a human is found in a humorous tale by Charles Dickens in *Museum of Foreign Literature, Science and Art*, April, 1840, titled 'Master Humphrey's Clock,' Chapter I:

"He wos took wery bad one arternoon, artcr having been **off his feed**, and wery shaky on his legs for some veeks; and he says to the mate, 'Matey,' he says, 'I think I'm goin' the wrong side o' the post, and that my foot's wery near the bucket.'"

Off one's rocker

Some etymologists have theorized that since two similar idioms first appeared around the same time, in the 1890s, 'off one's trolley,' which related to the contact wheel of a trolley car which could be very tricky to realign, and off one's rocker, also having to do with a curved piece of wood upon which a chair rocks, that the two were related, and that the rocker intended had to do with trams rather than chairs. The first printed reference to off someone's trolley was in *Artie* by George Ade, 1896, page 92:

> "Any one that's got his head full o' the girl proposition's liable to go **off his trolley** at the first curve."

This snippet from the London *Daily News*, the next year on June 19, 1897, is the earliest known citation in print:

> "When asked if he swallowed the liniment, he said, 'Yes, I was **off my rocker…**'"

One thing for certain, someone who falls off a rocker of any type is *unbalanced*, hence the meaning of crazy and mentally unstable. A literal example in the New Orleans publication, *The Harlequin*, Wednesday, June 18, 1899, page 12, put it well:

> "He really lost his balance and fell, not from the high platform, however, but simply rolled **off his rocker** on the floor of his front room, where he had fallen asleep."

Off the grid

This modern expression refers to living in an area which does not have access to the electrical interlocking system of power lines and power stations, as well as service from other basic utilities such as water. Communities described as off-the-grid usually have self-sufficient independent systems designed to function outside the infrastructure. This idea has been popularized by some celebrities, including Ed Bagley, Jr., who had an HGTV series called *Living with Ed* from 2007 to 2010. use of the term began in a limited sense as early as the mid-1980s, as seen by this excerpt from *The Code of Federal Regulations of the United States of America*, January 1, 1984:

> "Table— Regional Estimates of Oil/Gas Savings Attributable to Electricity Backed **Off the Grid** by Cogeneration."

In April, 2006 USA Today reported that some 180,000 families in the U.S. were living off the grid at that time. Estimates in 2016 go as high as 1.7 million people worldwide living off the grid.

Off to the races+

This is a phrase long used to mean that someone is heading out to embark on some project or adventure. It implies 'setting off' and could be as simple as going to work or on vacation. It derived from the excitement of going to horse races, and was in use in a literal sense in the Virginia Colony before the Revolution. A little later, *Journal of a Young Lady in Virginia*, 1782, contained this citation:

> "The Gentlemen are just set **off to the races**, and I am preparing to set off for Chantilly."

Metaphoric use eventually came to include any venture or business which showed rapid progress. The Georgia State Women's College, Valdosta State University yearbook, *The Pinecone*, 1935, carried this citation on page 34, praising a student, Dorothy Ogletree, at the end of a long line of credits:

> "…Relations Club, (3,4) Glee Club (2,3,4) '**Off to the races!**' Frankly we don't see how she does it!"

Often imitated; never duplicated^

This popular generic term means that many have tried to copy certain products, talents, actions, services, etc., but none have been able to equal the original.

It was a slogan used Traub Manufacturing Company of Detroit, Michigan in 1927 to advertize their 'Orange Blossom' wedding and engagement rings featured in *Photoplay Magazine* that June. These rings are now pricy as antiques.

But 'hold onto your hats' (see)! They were not the first one to use an almost exact claim, though it is highly publicized that they coined it. Close, more rambling phrases date to the late 1800s, but in the January 19, 1901 issue of *The Saturday Evening Post,* on page 19, an ad for Stewart's Duplex Safety Pins made by Consolidated Safety Pin Co. contained the following:

> "Effective guard. I**mitated but not duplicated** by any other maker."

But they were not the only ones to use it that year, so apparently no one felt the need to copyright the slogan. In *Colliers Weekly*, April 20, 1907, an ad on page 21 for 1847 Rogers Brothers silver plate flatware contains this citation:

> "It has been **imitated but never duplicated**. Refuse imitations. The genuine always has '1847.'" (Reference to the year)

Old chestnut[2]

This British cliché refers to an old joke or story which has become tedious and trite because of constant repetition. The origin story for this has become trite in its own right, and has little to do with actual chestnuts. In 1816, the story goes, *The Broken Sword* by playwright William Dimond was performed in London at the Royal Covenant Garden Theater. Act I, Scene ii contained the following exchange:

> "***Zav***. At the dawn of the fourth day's journey, I entered the wood of Collers, when, suddenly, from the thick boughs of a cork-tree—
>
> " ***Pab.*** *[Jumping up.]* A chestnut, Captain, a **chestnut**!
>
> " ***Zav***. Bah, you booby! I say, a cork!
>
> " ***Pab.*** And I swear, a chestnut. Captain, this is the twenty-seventh time I have heard you relate this story, and you invariably said a chestnut, till now.
>
> " ***Zav***. Did I? Well, a **chestnut** be it then. But take your seat again."

Despite bad reviews, the play was successful, and went on to America. It is said that this story was popularized in American newspapers, hence spawning the saying. There is *one* newspaper story, though the playwright's name is incorrect, that may be the key to the origin. News of this story appeared in *Lippincott's Monthly Magazine*, published in Philadelphia, in January, 1888, and later in other magazines:

> "Mr. Joseph Jefferson is responsible for the latest explanation of the word 'chestnut.' He attributes the introduction of the word in its slang sense to Mr. William Warren, the veteran comedian of Boston. 'There is a melodrama,' Mr. Jefferson said to a reporter of the Philadelphia *Press,* 'but little known to the present generation, written by William Dillon and called *The Broken Sword.* There were two characters in it, — one a Captain Zavier and the other the comedy part of Pablo. ... William Warren, who had often played the part of Pablo, was at a stag dinner two years ago, when one of the gentlemen present told a story of doubtful age and originality. *A **chestnut***, murmured Mr. Warren, quoting from the play. *I have heard you tell the tale these twenty-seven times.* The application of the lines pleased the rest of the table, and when the party broke up each helped to spread the story and Mr. Warren's commentary. And that,' concluded Mr. Jefferson, s what I really believe to be the origin of the word **chestnut**.'"

'Old' was later added at the beginning for effect.

Older than dirt

This is a comical metaphor which refers to something extremely old, perhaps more than previously thought. But this may be a bit of a misnomer, since scientists tell us that though the oldest sedimentary rocks are thought to be about '3.9 billion years old,' most dirt that we are able to find has been around only a few thousand years. Some say up to 2,000,000 years old, but not nearly as ancient as rocks; so perhaps the saying should be 'older than rocks.' And the metaphor is not old at all, only dating back to the 1970s. Like so many phrases, we can trace the earliest known citation to a play, *Every Night the Sun Goes Down* by Philip Hayes Dean, Act I, 1976:

> "**PRETTY EDDIE**. Like the bear… makin' tracks and getting' nowhere, Cockeyed rose! Sittin' over there lookin' older than black pepper. "**CLEAN SAM**. Lookin' **older than dirt**."

Old habits die hard

This proverbial axiom means that people generally find it difficult to change their patterns of behavior. American clergyman and historian Jeremy Belknap (1744-1798) is credited as having coined this saying. However, evidence is lacking. This did not come into common usage until the late 19th century—almost 100 years after his death. The earliest available citation, though not its coining, is from *Tea and Tea Drinking* by Arthur Reed, 1884, pages 11-12:

> "'For instance, at Whitby,' writes the historian of that town, 'tea was very little used a century ago, most of the old men being very much against it; but after the death of the old people it soon came into general use.'
>
> "**Old habits die hard**. The stronger beverage of English ale had been so long in use that the old folks could not be induced to relinquish it for a foreign herb."

Another reference showed up in *The Phonetic Journal* on Saturday, July 11, 1885, in 'Intelligence:'

> "**Old habits die hard**, no matter how bad they are."

Gradually, it came into standard use, both in Britain and America, over the rest of the 19th and the beginning of the 20th century.

oldie but a goodie, An

Used more in the music industry, particularly on the radio, than anywhere else, this cute cliché may refer to, not only a nostalgic long-popular song, record, movie or car, but anything which, or even a person who, has enjoyed either continuous or renewed popularity for a great number of years.

It had its genesis in the most logical field in the early 1960s, likely by disc jockeys. The first known printed reference is found in *Billboard*, August 28, 1961 in a front-page feature article titled, "WB's Conkling Sets 'Plus 2' Singles Plan" by Lee Zhito where it is in quotes probably suggesting a recent coining:

> "The new recording will be on the outside track, followed by a wide, six-second divider, leading into the bonus **'oldie but goodie'** selection shortened to a minute and 15 seconds."

Old salt^

This term originated in the navy to describe a well-experienced seaman. One referred to as such is usually a teller of stories of adventures at sea. History and naval service are passed down from one generation to the next. These tales have a reputation of often being somewhat exaggerated, possibly half-truths (or even falsehoods), though some may be fully truthful. Contrary to the origin date of 1840 in a well-respected online etymology source, this term was already established by April, 1734, when it was used in *The Gentlemen's Magazine, and Historical Chronicle*, London, in 'Death's Promotions &c in April, 1734:'

> "The latter end of last month, — *Mr. Christof. Cole*, at *Bristol*, **an old Salt-**Officer: He was very particular as to his Way of Life; his Bed was never made, or hook up, so that it seemed as if a Cavity had been carved out to fit it, in one Posture; his Room was seldom visited without urgent Necessity, and his Money hid in several Parts of it in fear of Thieves…"

Old school^

This term is long established and refers to people, usually 'of a certain age,' (see: Women of a certain age) noted for conservative viewpoints on political and professional topics. Though some may feel that these persons are 'old-fashioned,' in modern usage it usually commands a sense of respect for those of an earlier era. A popular online site states 1749 as date of first usage. However, this citation from *A Free Discourse Concerning Truth and Error, Especially in Matters of Religion* by John Edwards, DD (1637–1716), page 36, printed in

London in 1701 seems to show that this connotation for the phrase was already well known by then:

> "An Other because he had nothing else to say against these Mental Notices and Ionate Characters of Truth, explodes them as an **old School**-Notion, forgeting in the mean time that it was an old Maxim of the Schools, derived from Aristotle and the Old Philosophy, that there is nothing in the Understanding of Man to Think and not have Thoughts and Conceptions…"

This term has been used as a title for a novel, a movie, an Australian TV series, a singing group and more than one song.

On a fast track

This idiomatic expression means taking the most direct and swiftest route to achieve a goal, especially in a competitive situation and for advancement in a career or qualification for a higher level of competition in sports, etc. It assumes that a slower route exists, and is derived from a racetrack with proper conditions to achieve optimum speed. Literal use of 'fast track' goes back to the 1830s. But figurative use came over 100 years later. Coining is obscure, but the earliest example available is from *Billboard*, August 10, 1959, page 1, in an article titled 'Coin Ride Trade Counts Every Dime' by Ken Knauaf:

> "Smaller operators unable to balance costs with income have fallen behind **on the fast track**. And big operators have not only gotten bigger, but the bigger have bought out the big."

On a short leash (See: **Keep someone on a short leash**)

On edge^

This means tense, nervous, irritable and worried. A primary online dictionary dates this expression to the *late* 1800s. However, this evolved from an earlier term, 'set one's teeth on edge' which goes back to Old Testament times, when a known proverb in Israel used it, as we see in *Ezekiel 19:2, King James Version*, 1611:

> "What mean ye, that ye use this proverb concerning the land of Israel, saying, The fathers have eaten sour grapes, and the children's **teeth are set on edge**?"

And again quoted in *Jeremiah 31:29 (KJV)*:

> "In those days they shall say no more, The fathers have eaten a sour grape, and the children's **teeth are set on edge**."

John Bellenden Ker, in 1837, in *An Essay on the Archeology of Our Popular Phrases*, Vol. I, noted this as being well-known at the time, and wrote about it:

> "So that to **set the teeth on edge**, is to set them in a state of excitement, one of pain, uneasiness; and is as the disturbance of a state of rest and ease to harrassing urgent excitement; to rouse from quiescent ease to a state of disquietude."

This plainly tells us that this has the meaning, and is the origin, of 'on edge' as we know it today. In fact, a Scottish dramatic poem published anonymously in 1818, in play fashion, *Borough Reform and City Deformity* used 'feel on edge' in Act I, Scene i, with no mention of teeth:

> "And hardly has my willing palate learned
> To know the savours of a city-feast,
> And **feel on edge** betwixt the day of bidding
> And its most grateful consummation,
> Ere, like a dream, as sweet, and yet as fading…"

One size fits all^

This cliché, in its strictest application, refers to a product designed to be used by anyone, particularly an item of clothing which adjusts for persons of various shapes and sizes. Figuratively, it has evolved to mean one style or procedure which is suitable for all applications. The major online encyclopedia states that this phrase has been in use since 1975 when jazz great Frank Zappa recorded *One Size Fits All.* So true that Zappa popularized the specific phrase; however, the principle goes back much further. Handcuffs, originally made by the Ancient Greeks in the 4th century BCE, certainly worked on this premise, and even the actual saying is much, much older than 1975. In the February 5, 1897 edition of the weekly Journal, *The L.A.W. Bulletin and Good Roads,* Record Petal Manufacturing Company in Boston advertized what was likely the first such product to use this enticing line:

> "The Clothier offering **one size** suit to **fit all** kinds and conditions of men would in the natural order of things, either seek insolvency proceedings or else set a fire. Well, what shall we say about the pedal manufacturer offering one width of pedals? Feet vary as much as any other part of the human anatomy. WE FIT THEM ALL."

By the early 20th century other industries were following suit in use of the metaphor. In January, 1910, Chicago's *The Inland Printer* carried an ad for the Draper Hall Co. of Connecticut for a ratchet:

> "Price of wrench (**one size fits all** quoins), each, 50c"

Motor cars soon got in on the trend by making many interchangeable parts, such as headlights. There were earlier ads for other generic car parts, but *The Auto Trade Journal*, carried a Crew Levick ad in the January 1, 1917 edition with this headline:

> "Solve the Headlight Problem **One Size Fits All** Lamps"

One-two punch

This figurative expression, often called '**the old one-two**,' came from boxing, in which it is a left hand jab immediately followed by a 'right cross.' When put into practice, this duel power play stuns the opponent in such a way as to improve the position of the one using it. The literal application of the phrase and play goes back to at least the 19th century. Use of the term became popular in the early 20th century, as in *Inside the Ropes* by Charles Emmitt Van Loan, 1913, page 274:

> **"Give** him **the old one-two**; the left to the belly and the right to the jaw. Oh, man, but it's a fine house they have out there!"

As a metaphor, it means hitting an unsuspecting opponent in business, politics or other field with one impressive, powerful move followed by another. This didn't become popular until late in the 20th century. An early example in in William Herrick's novel, *That's Life*, page 57:

> "'Okay, Angie,' I said. 'You win. Well eat Ford up — give him **the old one-two**.'"

only difference between the men and the boys is the price of their toys, The

This saying has long been cliché. The earliest verifiable citation was printed on July 13, 1960, in *Wisconsin State Journal* in Madison, in the column called, 'It Happened Last Night' by Earl Wilson:

> "WISH I'D SAID THAT: **The biggest difference between men and boys is the cost of their toys."**

No attribution was given. In the 1960s and 1970s slight variations of the saying popped up in many newspapers and magazine articles. By 1979 it was being called an 'old saying,' and soon it was put on plaques. Then on November 19, 1982, an article in the *Washington Post* by Hank Burchard, 'TOYS, NOT JUST FOR KIDS,' attributed the adage to Dorothy Parker:

> "It need not be, for the exhibition embodies that great and valuable truth about the Human condition uttered by Dorothy Parker:
>
> "'**The only difference between men and boys is the cost and number of their toys**.'"

only good (bug, cop, goblin, human, Indian, snake, etc. **is a dead** [same]), **The^+**

The origin of this premise is often credited to Theodore Roosevelt, who in a speech in New York in January, 1886, fourteen years before being elected the 26th U.S. President, said:

> "I don't go so far as to think that **the only good Indians are the dead Indians**, but I believe nine out of every ten are."

While this usage did apparently spark this craze, Roosevelt certainly did not coin it. It was already a popular buzz phrase at the time, and was used in an address delivered by request in Philadelphia before the Masonic Veterans of Pennsylvania on February 27, 1885, by noted attorney, I. Layton Register:

> "Western people cruelly assert that **the only good Indians are dead Indians**."

Only human

Saying that someone is 'only human' means that the person is no different than any other human being; all are weak, so he or she should not be blamed or singled out for criticism because of mistakes made. The earliest available clear reference in this connotation in print is *The Land Log-book: a Compilation of Anecdotes and Occurrences Extracted from the Journal of the Author* by Sarah Hoding, 1836, page 15:

> "We are spiteful, I think; well, she has often been spiteful to us; we serve her right: keep this out of the Captain's way; Miss Monday says, 'I can't now, its

down, and we are **only human**, and she is older than we, and we are sure to err sometimes.'"

On someone's dime

This means at that person's expense, not anyone else's. It came from the 1960s cost of ten cents to make a local phone call on a 'pay phone' in the United States. Strangely enough, the term didn't become popular until after that time. The earliest available citation is from *Stay, Carl Stay*, the first play in *Stay Carl Stay; Best Half Foot Forward; Pillow Talk: Three One-act Plays* by Peter Tolan, 1991, page 35:

> "**CARL**. Se be que es una mujer ve buen gusto y estilo extraudinario.
> "**DR. WEISS**. (Chuckling.) Le apuesto que le dice esto a todas las mujeres. (They laugh again.)
> "**CAROLINE.** Excuse me. Tick, tick, tick ... the two of you are españoling **on my dime**."

On, (at or **to) someone's doorstep**

This idiom means very close to where someone lives or where they presently are. It is derived from the doorstep to a home which leads up to the door. 'Doorstep' has been used metaphorically since at least the late 19th century. In 1887, popular American humorist, Marietta Holley, wrote this expression in *Samantha at Saratoga*:

> "And we set and see these silent mysteries a goin' on right **at our doorstep** day by day, and year by year, and think nothin' of it, because it is so common."

On someone's or **something's last legs**

This very old expression means worn out, or beyond help. It goes back at least to *The Old Law* by Thomas Middleton and Philip Massinger, Act V, Scene i; 1599, published 1618:

> "My husband goes upon his last hour now—**on his last legs,** I am sure."

In *An Etymological Dictionary of the Scottish Language,* Supplement, Volume 2, published in Edinburgh, 1825, on page 49 it is defined:

> "LAST LEGS: A man is said to be **on his last legs**, either when his animal

strength is almost entirely exhausted by exertion, age or disease, or when he is supposed to be on the borders of bankruptcy…"

On the blink

This expression is used in all English-speaking countries, and means that something, usually a piece of machinery or an electronic device, has lost its ability to function properly. It has been thought that it may have been derived from the fact that when we blink our eyes it keeps us from seeing for the span of the blink. The earliest citation available does not refer to a piece of machinery, but rather a 'tutor.' It is found in a poem in the 1908 *Michiganensian*, the Year Book of the University of Michigan at Ann Arbor, titled 'Freshman This and Freshman That,' on page XT-28:

> "'The tutor's **on the blink**,' says I, 'the tutor's **on the blink**.'
> O, it was pie for Reginald when the dean begun to wink."

Four years later another poem, 'Tune, Everybody's Doin' It' in *The Colorado School of Mines Magazine,* Golden, Colorado, December, 1912 was similar:

> "Poor old Boulder's **on the blink**, **on the blink**, **on the blink**,
> Don't you hear her Captain think, hear him think, hear him think?"

Then, on May 26, 1914, a creamery is referred to as being on the blink in *Chicago Dairy Produce*, in 'Timely Hints for the Buttermaker,' on page 46.

> "While we do not know why the creamery referred to as being **on the 'blink'** is in that condition, we will make a wager that if the real truth is known, it is on account of poor cream."

Then in 1918 we see a battery is 'going on the blink' in *The Moving Picture Boys on the Warfront* by 'Victor Appleton,' page 84:

> "Like the proverb which says 'blessings brighten as they vanish,' so the light of these lamps sometimes glows very strong just before the battery goes **on the blink** and douses the glim."

A similar expression is 'on the fritz' (see).

On the button

This phrase, very popular in Britain, also used in America, means 'in exactly the right place at the right time.' Contrary to some popular belief, in the U.K., and especially Scotland, hoping to link this to the sport of Curling, which originated there in the 17th century, this expression, in this connotation, is much newer. It actually originated in the States. It started in boxing, as 'button' is slang in that sport for 'chin,' or the point of it, to be more explicit. It began in the latter part of the First World War. The earliest citation known was discovered by researcher Gary Martin, and is from the *Logansport Pharos-Reporter* in Logansport, Indiana, in May, 1917:

> "Moran is a one-punch fighter. He packs a mighty mean crusher in his right hand. If it ever lands **on the button** Morris will prove himself a superman if he doesn't go down."

Figurative use came by the 1930s. In February, 1939, the following appeared in *Flying Magazine,* in an article on page 45 titled, 'Love Birds' by Hamilton Thornquist about Robert and Nancy Love:

> "And he learned a lesson when the railroad took the Earhart offer-—because it hit the directors' figures **right on the button**."

On the cutting edge (See: **Cutting edge**)+

On the edge of one's seat

This hyperbolic idiom means having one's complete attention; in suspense, excitedly awaiting the outcome or conclusion of a performance or event, the next action in a book or film, or the resolution of a situation. The expression was first used by Sir Walter Scott in *The Waverly Novels* in *The Heart of Mid-Lothian*, page 173, published in 1830, but the meaning was not as we see it today:

> "The thin pale-faced man, whom their good-nature had brought into their society, looked out of place, as well as out of spirits; sate **on the edge of his seat**, and kept the chair at two feet distance from the table…"

In May, 1929, a story in *Boys' Life* continued, on page 48, titled, 'The Pilot of the Cloud Patrol' by Irving Crump showed the meaning shaping up to embody excitement:

> "Don was **on the edge of his seat**. Every muscle was tensed. His jaw was squared. His eyes glowed with the light of determination and his lips were compressed into thin straight lines."

On the flip side

In a literal sense, from the early 1950s this referred to the other side of a 45 rpm vinyl recording; usually the less popular side of a hit record. While vinyl records were considered to have 'gone the way of the dodo,' after 30 years they are now set to make a niche market comeback after a Detroit manufacturer decided to begin new production, due to demand, beginning in Spring 2016.

Figuratively, this may mean either of two separate, distinct things. First, it could mean much the same as 'on the other hand' (see first volume); usually though, in a negative sense, as the unpleasant aspect of an otherwise positive situation.

This had come into play by the 1980s. A great early example is found in *New York Magazine,* April 25, 1983, on page 82, in 'McEnroe, a Player for All Courses:'

> "**On the flip side**, Argentina's Guillermo Vilas did not make his name at Wimbledon or Flushing Meadow. Sure, he captured a weakened Australian Open on grass and has numerous carpet titles to his name, but basically he is what the fast court boys refer to as a dirtkicker."

Also, from the same basic timeframe, it was used like 'see you later,' in "Catch you on the flip side." The earliest available citation is found in *Princeton Alumni Weekly,* July 13, 1983, on page 48, in 'Class Notes,' at the close of entry 72 by Larry Kurtz:

> "Have a nice summer . . . **catch you on the flip side**."

On the fritz^

The origin of this common expression, meaning that something is in bad condition or out of order, is embroiled in controversy and shrouded in wonder. Some have suggested that it was based on the common nickname for a German soldier which was coined about 1915, in World War I. Others have related it to a bungling German boy named Fritz in *The Katzenjammer Kids* comic strip—unfortunately also not premiering in the Sunday funnies until 1914. Neither has validity, because it was around by at least 1902 in a poem, 'Suppose,' written by an Auburn, New York prisoner:

> "What would the little acorn do
> If it had no place to grow?
> Would Santa Clause be **on the 'fritz'**
> If we never had any snow?"

On April 5, 1907, it was used in 'The Secret Service Old and Young King Brady Detectives' story, *The Bradys and the "Chink" Smugglers; Or The Hurry Call to Canada:*

> "'What's the trouble?' Old King Brady asked.
> "'Oh, the engine has gone **on the Fritz**, I don't understand just what has happened. I'm not mechanic enough for that.'"

Another, perhaps more viable, theory is that it came from a poetical variation of frozen, *friz,* acknowledged by the OED and other dictionaries. An *Atlanta Constitution* article, April 14, 1896, from Cuthbert, Georgia, where a Confederate Monument was built that year, headlined, 'Refused to be Friz' says:

> "There is an evident desire among the administration followers in Georgia to freeze Flem DuBignon out of the race for senate....But the Hon. Flem prefers not to freeze..."

This idea seems to be enforced by a quote from the *Washington Herald* in the *Trenton Evening Times*, New Jersey, February 5, 1908, page 6, column 3, where **'on the friz'** is utilized:

> ""Deep breathing is the thing for you if you are **on the friz**;
> It drives away the devils blue and sharpens up the wits;...."
>
> --*Washington Herald*

On (or **in) the hot seat**

Being on the hot seat means that a person is in an uncomfortable position of pressure and scrutiny and a lot of attention is being focused on him or her. It can also apply to an organization or group of people. It can be applied to undergoing cross-examination, and is also slang for the electric chair, the ultimate 'hot seat.' A major online dictionary places its coining at 1915-20, while others say it was derived in the 1930s from common use of the electric chair for execution. Still others relate it to police interrogations for the origin. However, the term itself meant something quite different at the time, but the earliest citation comes as early as 1855. Usage to mean a place of pressure, however, came as early as 1904. Dangers of Working Girls or, Dealers in White Women by Grace Miller White based on the play by the same name had one of the earliest known citations, in reference to a man suspected of murder, plainly referring to the electric chair, which was first used there on August 6, 1890:

> "'Are you going to make him out guilty? I mean, well, hang it all, how much do you want to make him sit **in the hot seat**?'
> "'Kane slowly rose to his feet. His face was distorted with passion. 'Do you mean that you wish to corrupt the court of the State of New York with gold?'"

Other early figurative citations (those not referring to a seat which was literally hot because of its nearness to a fire or the heat of the sun) also refer to the electric chair. Later a bench or seat wired for shock was called a 'hot seat.' It was the early 1940s before purely figurative use for a place of pressure became popular. A very early example is in *Life*, October 27, 1941, in 'New York City's Able Mayor,' on page 84:

> "Fiorello H. LaGuardia was perhaps more responsible. During eight years **in the hot seat** of the second most complicated administrative office in the land, he had run New York so well that his electorate virtually forgot the incompetents who preceded him, forgot the shadowy tireless leg-men of Tammany Hall."

On the outs with someone+

This is a modern idiom for being in a mild dispute or sharing ill will with someone, particularly indicating that the parties are not on speaking terms. Preceded by the term 'at outs' first attested in 1824, this term evolved in the early 20th century. A great early example, in quotes likely indicating a recently coined phrase, id found in *Why Read? An Address Delivered before the Insurance Society of New York* by William H. Stevens, President of the Agricultural Insurance Company of Watertown, New York, on Tuesday evening, October 8, 1919:

> "...when we get **'on the outs'** with what is around us we die..."

On the QT

In this term, QT is short for quiet, and means that the information is very confidential and not to be shared. The full version appeared in print first in a pamphlet about the New Zealand gold rush, *Otago; Its Gold-fields & Resources*, published in Melbourne in 1862, in speaking of working in the gold:

> "Unless men can work **on 'the quiet,'** they are not likely to make 'piles' so rapidly as Messrs. Hartley and Riley."

Note that 'the quiet' here is in quotes, likely inferring a recent coining. The present abbreviated form came not long afterward, in the late 19th century, and was picking up steam by 1894, when it was explained by Cornelis Stoffel on page 246 of *Studies in English, Written and Spoken,* where earlier examples are cited:

> "The phrase *do the Q.T.,* in the same quotation is parallel with the phrase 'to do a thing **on the Q.T.,** where ***on the Q.T.*** means on the quiet = on the sly, clandestinely. *Punch*, 1882, Vol. II (Vol.83), 156: 'Emphatically the Sea **on the strict Q. T.** — no bustle at railway station — train glides in noiselessly;' *Judy*, Dec. 22, 1886, 298: 'The fightin' barber in Smithe''s Alley as sells alcoholical drinks **on the Q. T.** of a Sunday mornin'."

On the up and up

This odd expression's origins are a bit fuzzy, but it came into use in the early 20th century. It is believed to have come from betting on horse races, and means open and honest, legitimate or forthright. The earliest known citation is from the American pulp-fiction *Munsey's Magazine,* Volume 85, 1925, page 59:

> "That much of it's on **the up and up**; and this is what we add to it — we tell everybody that you're in the ring to earn enough money to search for your parents, and find out who they are, and if they're alive or not."

On the wrong side of a question/or **history**

The idea of being on the wrong side of an issue or question has had a long and mottled past, and what it actually entails may vary sharply with the opinions of writers and philosophers in different ages, and what each believes to be 'Politically Correct.' The earliest known citation is from *The Rights, powers, and Priviledges, of an English Convocation*, by Francis Atterbury, 1701, in the preface on page xxxvi:

> "And if he will therefore but suspend his Opinion of such a Piece, till he hears what I have to say to it, I will endeavour not to let him continue long under his Suspence: for I think I know what Colours can well be put **on the wrong Side of the Question;...**"

From the statements previous to this, where a challenge was made to 'Dr. W.' to produce evidence for his belief, and the context, here we see the clergyman writing was dogmatically dictating that another was 'on the wrong side' of a particular question.

Then the *New Annual Register or General Repository of History, Politics and Literature for the Year 1804, Part I,* published in London in 1805, contains the following reference to this subject on page 279:

> "Farmer, though in our opinion enlisted on the **wrong side of the question**, was a man of far superior talents to his adversary; and he felt no occasion, therefore, for the deadly weapon of acrimony in his replies."

Here, the matter of the wrong side was admittedly in the writer's opinion. Down through history the concept of being on the wrong or right side of a question has continued to be a matter of opinion, hence, the 20th century term, 'On the wrong side of history' arose. But history, like issues, has been written by those whose ideas and ideals have prevailed; many times large voids or misstatements of actual events have been created that those in power may retain control. Though 'on the wrong side of history' has come up and faded out at intervals over the past century, it made a sharp comeback in the new millennium. A 2015 book by John K. Roth, *The Failures of Ethics: Confronting the Holocaust, Genocide, and Other Mass Atrocities*, has a statement that perhaps no conscientious person could refute on page 208:

> "But who among us would want to say that the Holocaust, genocide, and other mass atrocities are on the right side of history? Surely, they are **on the wrong side of history** or nothing could be."

open book, An^

This idiom refers to something which is explicitly clear; easily understood and not attempting to hide anything. It may apply to a person or a thing. A popular online dictionary lists its origin at 1850-1855. The metaphor, however, is very much older and goes back to at least the late 1600s. The earliest example known is found in the classic Puritan devotion manual, *The Practice of Piety: Directing a Christian How to Walk* by Lewis Bayly, first published in 1611:

> "Walk into the fields and meditate upon the works of God; for in every creature thou mayest read, as in **an open book**, the wisdom, power, providence and goodness of Almighty God."

Open confession is good for the soul^

This is not from the Bible, as many have thought, though the principle is taught there. It is an old Scottish proverb first recorded in James Kelley's *Complete Collection of Scottish Proverbs* in 1721, page 270:

> **"16. *Open Confession is good for the Soul*.** Spoken ironically, to them that boast of their ill Deeds."

Open secret^

This oxymoron refers to something which is 'officially' a secret but is actually quite widely known. Most usually those who are cognizant of it are unwilling to categorically acknowledge its validity. A popular online dictionary notes beginning of usage of the expression at 1875-1880. It goes back to at least January, 1838, when it seems to have been in common usage based on the text in *The Foreign Quarterly Review,* in 'Minch's Studies and Recollections' on page 315:

> "The most opposite emotions were called forth by this work, and, by the singular hieroglyphics veiling **an open secret**, the vital question of the times was brought under discussion."

Open the floodgates

Based on opening the floodgates of a reservoir to allow the water which has been held back to flow freely, this cliché means to make it possible for something to happen which would not have transpired without someone's intervention. The root words date back to Middle English in the 13th century, and literal usage of the term is from the 15th century. *Somewhat* figurative use even goes back to at least 1603, when the earliest known such citation is found in *The General History of the Turkes* by Richard Knolles which leads to the conquests of the Ottoman Empire, on page 31:

> "This river then suddenly rising by night by reason of the great rain that fell in such abundance, **as if the flood-gates of heauen had ben opened**, so ouerflowed the place wherein the armie lay encamped vpon the fide ..."

Then just over half a century later, a totally metaphoric example came in the tale of Cleopatra, *Hyman's Love Praeludia: Or; Love's Masterpiece*, the original French by Gaultier de Coste La Calprenède, in the 1659 English rendition by 'J.D.,' page 354:

> "With thefe words she as if it were **opened the flood-gates** to that grief, which was ready to overrun her, and caft her felf on her bed, after a moft pittifull manner, infomuch that *Marcellus* had never feen her fo unable to command her paffions ..."

Out like a light^

Today, this metaphor refers to a person becoming comatose by either falling asleep or lapsing into unconsciousness; or it may be applied to a person's death. It is easy to see how a person's conscience state would be likened to a light, but contrary to those claiming the phrase was first coined after the advent of the electric light in the 20th century, it was around much longer. The basic idea of a person's substance being like a light goes back at least to 1629 when *The Last Battell of the Soul in Death* was first published by Zacharie Boyd, minister of the Barony Church in Glasgow, Scotland:

> "By this at last, all our **light** dyeth **out like a candle**, so that our hearts that were once enlightned, become like a dampish dungeon."

In the 19th century, the analogy was used on things other than a person, as in London's *The National Temperance Mirror,* December, 1885 in 'Darkness and the Dawn of Another Day' by E. Harcourt Burrage:

> "The joy of the humble home went **out like a light** extinguished."

Other examples, even into the early 20th century, referred to a person's hope, demeanor or the quality of life.

Famed 19th century writer and Boston Globe editor, Maturin Murray Ballou (1820-1895), however, included the following quotation of death in his *Pearls of Thought,* 1881, page 56:

> "What is death? To go **out like a light**, and in a sweet trance to forget ourselves and all the passing phenomena of the day, as we forget the phantoms of a fleeting dream; to form, as in a dream, new connections with God's world; to enter into a more exalted sphere, and to make a new step up man's graduated ascent of creation. —***Zschokke***."

The author of the quip was Johann Heinrich Daniel Zschokke (1741-1848), a German, later Swiss, author and reformer. Obviously this was written before the middle of the 19th century.

The references to becoming unconscious, however, seem to actually begin after electricity made the light bulb a reality, in the 1930s. The April, 1934 edition of *Boys' Life* carries this citation in 'Dynamite for Senor McGonigle,' on page 47:

> "He had a grip on Bugle's windpipe. I don't know what Bugle was doing except gurgle. All of a sudden the Spig and I were flopping around alone, and I yelled, 'Come back you quitter,' at Bugle, and caught the Spig square on the chin. He went **out like a light**. I grabbed at the butt of a gun sticking out of his waistband, and jumped up."

Out of pocket

This idiom, like, some other terms in this and the first volume of this set of books, has more than one application, or meaning. The primary use is to refer to the actual expense involved in a transaction or project. It also may mean something out of reach or unavailable, particularly if avoiding one's duties in a job. In Britain, however, it may also refer to being out of money.

In terms of expense involved, paid out, it is extremely old, dating to the 17th century. The earliest known citation is found in *The Tryal of Nathaniel Reading, Esq. for Attempting to Stifle the King's Evidence as to the Horrid Plot*, April 14, 1679, page 55; at which time the phrase was obviously already known:

> ***"Mr. Reading.*** He hinder'd me of receiving a Fee from the other Side, and I am twenty shillings **out of Pocket**, and yet am thus treated for my kindness. There were three Orders I paid for."

The second definition is a bit obscure, and a lot newer. The earliest known reference is from *Three Elephant Power and Other Stories* by Australian poet and reporter, A. B. "Banjo" Paterson, first published in 1917, page 38:

> "The sports grew painfully anxious as they saw him getting further and further ahead of them. The squatter was the biggest loser by far. All the others were **out of pocket**."

The third meaning is nearly as old as the first. In Thomas Southerne's 1691 5 Act Comedy, *Sir Anthony Love; or The Rambling Lady*, Act I:

> ***"Sir Ant.*** Why, I still say – - - A true bred English man is ever out of humour when he's **out of Pocket**: He knows no more how to want Money, than how to borrow it."

Out of sorts^+

This very old idiomatic expression means that a person is in poor spirits and doesn't want to respond to others' questions or demands, possibly from being very tired or somewhat ill. Some have felt that use of the word 'sorts' leading to this connotation came in 1668 in *Mechanick Exercises, or. The Doctrine of Handy-works*, by Joseph Moxon, first printed in 1683:

> "The letters that lye in every box of the case are separately called **sorts** in printers and founders language; thus a is a sort, c is a sort, c is a sort, etc."

If a typesetter was looking for a particular letter found a set of sorts to empty, he could have felt upset about it, or out of sorts.

This however, is over a century too late to have been its origin. *The Proverbs, Epigrams, and Miscellanies of John Heywood*, 1562, includes this entry, with no mention of typesetting:

> "Fit (adj): disordered, **out of sorts**"

Outsmart oneself

This idiom means that a person's efforts at cunning or cleverness end up working to his or her disadvantage. Origin is unclear, but the earliest known citation is in the February, 1942 issue of *Popular Science* in 'Gus Drives a Bargain' by Martin Bunn, on page 218:

> "He probably thinks that the crankshaft is shot. What is wrong is that there is a little too much end play in it. It isn't bad, and probably it'll never give you any trouble. I can fix it, but it won't cost any fifty dollars. Benny's **outsmarting himself**."

A similar expression is 'shoot oneself in the foot' (see).

Over-egging the pudding (or **custard)**[2]

This primarily British cliché metaphor refers to spoiling something by trying too hard to improve it or make it look more impressive that it really is. Putting too many eggs in a pudding would either make it too rich or cause it to not set correctly. Occasionally 'over-egging' is used alone without specifying a pudding or custard.

A theory has been expressed that this saying came from the Ancient Anglo-Saxon use of 'egg' as in excite. Also that pudding here means sausage, since this word originally applied to something whipped up from the entrails of a hog, so based on this, it would have originally been better expressed as 'don't excite the sausage' and would have meant that whipping it up to much would not create a great sausage. This theory seems problematic, mainly because the expression did not come into general usage until well into the 19th century. The earliest citation available is from *Sporting Magazine*, May, 1828, in 'Nimrod's Yorkshire Tour,' on page 12:

> "'Drive my Lord well, lads,' said the landlord; 'but (by a side wind) mind me— *don't* **over-egg** ***t' pudding***'"

Overplay one's hand

Similar to the previous term, this means to spoil one's chance of success by saying or doing too much. It comes from bluffing too confidently in a game of poker, or other such game, which may 'come back to bite you in the butt' (see, first volume). This came into figurative usage in the last half of the 19th century. The earliest known citation is from *The Money Question* by William A. Berkey, 1876, page 413:

> "Although in June he had issued a lengthy report concerning the alleged evils of Masonry, in the long run his crusade had done more harm than good. Called the inquisitor general, he had **overplayed his hand** by trying to intimidate the widely respected former governor."

Over someone's shoulder

Looking or watching or standing 'over someone's shoulder' is a metaphor used to illustrate paying too close attention to someone's every move, normally looking for something to criticize. This may also be called 'micro-managing.' Though the phrase is used much earlier in casual terms, the earliest available reference to this connotation is in *The Complete Works of Sir Walter Raleigh*, Volume VII, page 139:

> "But a general who is **always looking over his shoulder**, and more intent on saving his own army than on doing the service on which he is sent, will hardly, I fear, be found capable of forming or executing a plan which its very daring character might render successful."

Overstep the bounds

This familiar cliché means doing more than a person or entity is allowed to do or should do under the given circumstances. 'Overstep' is a compound of over and step from the Middle English before 1,000 AD. In fact, this term was in use as early as 1728, when it was cited in the "*Rhode Island Almanack*," being the first printed in that colony, later carefully reproduced from a single copy originally by 'Poor Robin' ('Robin Goodfellow' – James Franklin) in Boston in 1911:

> "In Politics it was against the Administration, which bided its time until the pestering sheet **overstepped the bounds** and laid itself open to discipline."

Over the moon

This hyperbolic expression means extremely excited about something. It is believed that it originally came from the nursery rhyme, Hey, Diddle Diddle, first published in 1765. The following comes from *The Best of Mother Goose and Other Nursery Rhymes* published by St. Clair Publications, 2013, p 20:

> "**HEY, DIDDLE DIDDLE**
>
> "Hey diddle diddle,
> The cat and the fiddle,
> The cow jumped **over the moon**,
> The little dog laughed to see such sport,
> And the dish ran away with the spoon.
>
> "(1765)"

The first known reference to a human being happy using 'over the moon' is in *A Collection of Farces and Other Afterpieces* in David Garrick's two act comedy, 'The Irish Widow,' Act I, Scene iii, 1815, on page 56:

> "…I'm in such good spirits that I have gotten rid of my father, I could fly **over the moon** without wings and back again, before dinner."

Actually *being* 'over the moon' came in *The Diary of Lady Lucy Cavendish*, in the entry for February 7, 1857, published in New York after her death, in regard to her siblings' reaction to the announcement of the birth of her younger brother:

> "…they were at first utterly incredulous and then **over the moon.**"

Over the odds[2]

In British English, this idiom, sometimes 'pay over the odds' means more than something is really worth or more than the expected price. It is a comparably new expression, coming into use in the last quarter of the 20th century. The earliest verifiable citation is in the London publication *Third Way*, June, 1979, page 20, in 'The theological book seller:'

> "Not only does he pay **over the odds** for rent and rates, he also spends more on wages and salaries which must mean either that he is generous to his employees or overstaffed. Whoever gets paid **over the odds**, it is not the working director or proprietor."

Over the top

This means to an excessive degree, beyond any reasonable limits. It is a military phrase derived from trench warfare during World War I. It became standard for orders to be given to British and American Infantry troops, "Over the top, lads, and best of luck." The results were disastrous, losing thousands of soldiers in the process. *The Chicago Commerce,* July 19, 1918, carried a lengthy story titled 'Home and Front as One.' A subtitle on page 20 read, '**Over the Top is Over the Top**,' indicating that this process was already considered beyond reason. It started out talking about the Battle of Ypres which 'started on the 2nd of June, 1916.' Down in the next paragraph it reads:

> "The next morning we were to go **over the top.** We all knew we were going **over the top** at a certain time, at 5 o'clock in the morning. Owing to the delay in getting our reserves and supports up we did not go over until 8 o'clock in the morning. Before going over the top the boys sat there in the trenches smoking and you could hear jokes pass right along the line. Some one would shout out 'No flowers by request.' Another fellow, 'Send word to my girl I didn't come back,' and so on like that joking all the time. They don't think any thing about going **over the top**, whatever. When that order comes to **go over the top** they don't wait for anything. But just **go over the top**."

Obviously these brave soldiers knew their slim chances of survival. Before long the phrase had gone into figurative use for anything going above what was expected, as seen in the American National Women's Temperance Union publication *The Union Signal*, May 8, 1919, page 10, here in quotes:

> "Each local Union with a membership of less than ten, which goes '**Over the Top'** will receive $1.00."

Ultimately this became synonymous with a truly foolhardy venture. *Whose Revolution?: A Study in the Future Course of Liberalism in the United States*, by Roger N. Baldwin and Alfred M. Bingham, 1941, on page 81, included the following quote from *Lincoln Steffen's Letters*, 1835:

> "'I had come,' he wrote to a friend, 'to regard the New Capitalism as an experiment till, in 1929, the whole thing went **over the top** and slid down to an utter collapse.'"

P

Pack one's bags

This idiom, taken from filling suitcases to prepare for a trip, figuratively means to leave a place or job and never return. It came into use in the first quarter of the 20th century. An early example of this use is in *Star Dust* by Fannie Hurst, 1921, page 198:

> "'I'm not what you think I am.'
> "'I don't care what you are and what you ain't. I only want you to **pack your bags** and go!'"

An even clearer one is in *The Best Plays, 1938-39* by Burns Mantle, in 'Kiss the Boys Goodbye,' Act III:

> "LESLIE—You're an ambitious, dangerous, evil-tongued little girl!
> CINDY LOU—I'm a lamb among the wolves.
> LESLIE—**Pack your bags**!"

Pain in the neck (or **butt**)

This metaphor means a source of annoyance; a nuisance. 'Pain in the neck' began being used early in the 20th century. The latter came in the mid-20th century as a euphemism for the more vulgar term. *Popular Science*, September, 1929, in 'How to Time a Rough Riding Car,' uses the 'neck' term in quotes, showing that it was in figurative use, but still fairly new;

> "Evidently the phrase **'pain in the neck'** has a definite physiological origin."

The earliest available citation or 'pain in the butt' is from the 1949 three-act play, *Detective Story* by Sidney Kingsley, Act I:

> "Your moral indignation is beginning to give me a quick **pain in the butt**."

Paint (or **gild) the lily**

This idiom refers to adding extra embellishments unnecessarily to something already beautiful and complete. It is taken from Shakespeare's *King John*, 1595, Act IV, Scene ii:

> "SALISBURY
>
> "Therefore, to be possess'd with double pomp,
> To guard a title that was rich before,
> To **gild** refined gold, to **paint the lily**,
> To throw a perfume on the violet,
> To smooth the ice, or add another hue
> Unto the rainbow, or with taper-light
> To seek the beauteous eye of heaven to garnish,
> Is wasteful and ridiculous excess."

Paint with a broad (or **wide) brush**

This term means to describe a class of things or a type of phenomenon in very vague terms, therefore ignoring the details which make it special. The fear of such generalities is the possibility of igniting prejudices. The actual origin is uncertain, but it came into usage in the early 1980s. The earliest available citation is from *The True and the False: The Domain of the Pragmatic* by Charles Travis, 1981, page 5:

> "To **paint with a broad brush**, the rough idea is this: meaning (in a language) is our notion, and it's up to us to decide what it is for something to do so…"

Palm something off

This very old term means to get rid of something undesirable by persuading someone else to take it or purchase it in a deceptive manner. The earliest known citation is from the English version of *De Rebus Adiaphoris Epistola Concionatorum Hamburgensium Ad D. Philippum Melanthonem et Responsio Ejusdem, An Epistle from the Consistory at Hamburgh to Philip Melancton, with His Answer Concerning the Adiaphora,* published in 1549, page 19:

> "...and to which a certain allegorical beauty can be imparted, so that they may be adapted to some use in the Church,—by which art any trifles whatever may be **palmed off** for Adiaphora,——since many wicked persons take advantage of that lax opinion, that servitude can be endured in the Adiaphora."

Pan out

This expression started in the California gold rush of the 1840s, and meant that when someone was panning for gold in the rivers and creeks they had found some nuggets. On the other hand, if they found nothing their search did not pan out. It came to mean much the same in relation to other things. Something 'pans out' when it turns out favorably, and 'doesn't pan out' when it fails to work well. A phrase sometimes *misapplied* to this time is 'flash in the pan' (see first volume). A good example of the literal use is from *Mining in the Pacific States of North America* by John S. Hittell published in San Francisco in 1861, page 116. By this time lead the gold rush had ended and lead was being mined:

> "If the prospector have no one to show him how to use the pan, it might be well for him to practice beforehand, putting some rough little pieces of lead — not round shot, for they would roll out too easily — into the pan with some dirt, and when he can '**pan out**,' so as to get rid of all the dirt and save every piece of lead, he will have skill enough for ordinary purposes."

By 1866, the phrase was being used figuratively, as seen in *Across the Continent: A Summer's Journey to the Rocky Mountains, the Mormons and the Pacific States* by Samuel Bowles, editor of the Springfield Republican in Massachusetts, published that year in New York, page 368:

> "The mines furnish many new phrases: '**Pan out'** for turning out or amounting to; as, a man will '**pan out'** good or bad, or an enterprise '**pans out**' much or little."

Parting is such sweet sorrow

This oxymoronic statement is another Shakespeare quote; this time from *Romeo and Juliette*, published in 1597; Act II, Scene ii, on the balcony, when Juliette says:

> "Sweet, so would I. Yet I should kill thee with much cherishing. Good night, good night! **Parting is such sweet sorrow**, that I shall say good night till it be morrow."

Partner in crime

This cliché, based on the obvious literal connotation, actually figuratively refers to a person upon whom one can depend, who will be there in any venture. The literal use goes back to Richard Cumberland's 1801 *Poetical Version of Certain Psalms of David,* in Psalm L, verses 23, page 64:

> "P18 The robber's friend, th' adulterer's guest, **Partner in crime** as well as feast;"

The figurative use didn't come into print until the 1970s. The earliest available citation is from a U.S. copyright entry on a song in 1974:

> "Will you be my **partner in crime** (while I steal a little kiss)? w. m. & arr. Jean Ryder. 2 p. © Corrus Music Company, solely owned by Jean Ryder; 23 May 74; EP326154. EP326155"

A clear example comes five years later in *Field and Stream*, February, 1980, in a fishing tale titled 'Hotspot for Brookies' by Ed Zern, which has the following citation on page 86:

> "It was the biggest brookie I had caught until I sat in a canoe one day beside the dock at Haines Landing on Mooselookmeguntic Lake in Maine, waiting for my **partner in crime** to get back from Herby Welch's Tackle Shop…"

Past performance does not predict future earnings

This statement of caution is largely used of the performance of mutual funds and has become cliché in the business world in the past 20 years. The question of judging an investment by past earnings, however, goes back to at least 1920—before the Great Depression knocked the winds out of investors and made all think twice about what could be expected. In the *United States Interstate*

Commerce Commission Valuation Docket, January 7-9, 1920, a rosy picture was painted:

> "You **predict** what it will do in the **future** by its record in the past."

The modern axiom, though, is far from new. The very next year, still pre-depression, the following was printed in *The Journal of Industrial Engineering Chemistry published by the American Chemical Society*, page 390:

> "Past **earnings** have lost their significance. Audits and inventories and balance sheets tell the story of **past performance**. What is now required is the assurance of **future earning** power."

In the 1980s, Wall Street investment firms were again hawking stocks, and particularly mutual funds, based upon their performances, showing glowing prospectuses to entice their attractiveness. In 1985 *The Journal of Business Forecasting Methods & Systems* carried this statement on page 5:

> **"Past performance**, among other factors, provides the basis for **predicting future earnings** of a firm."

But once again, reality hit. In March, 1995, Ken Sheets, a *Kiplinger's Personal Finance Magazine* writer, stated in 'Spell Profits,' on page 129:

> "Most newspapers carry so-called trailing P/Es based on stocks' previous 12 months of earnings. But just as with the market as a whole, **past performance does not** always accurately **predict future** prospects."

Pay lip service

The principle of paying lip service comes from the *Bible*, in *Matthew 15:8*:

> "This people draweth nigh unto me with their mouth, and **honoureth me with their lips**; but their heart is far from me." *(KJV, 1611)*

It alludes to a false verbal show of loyalty and gratitude. Just 50 years after this translation of the *Bible*, in 1661, in *The Grand Debate between the Most Reverend, the Bishops and the Presbyterian Divines, appointed by His Sacred Majesty as Commissioners for the Review and Alterations of the Book of the Common Prayer*, printed in London, we have the following reference specifically to 'lip-service,' on page 74:

> "...but will bear more with me some Incuriosity of words (which yet we plead not for) than with a hypocritical, formal heartless **lip-service**; For he

knoweth the meaning of the' Spirit even in the groans, which are not uttered in words;…"

Pears for your heirs[2]

This British adage is used to encourage others to think about future generations rather than only living for the moment. Pear trees (and walnut trees) planted in England represent thinking ahead because of the length of time before the first fruit is harvested. The complete original proverb included walnut trees, and has been around for hundreds of years. John Stevens' *A New Dictionary of Spanish and English and English and Spanish*, 1726, and *Gnomologia: Adagies and Proverbs; Wise Sentences and Witty Sayings, Ancient and Modern, Foreign and British* collected by Thomas Fuller, MD, published in 1732, both contained this related saying:

"He that plants a Walnut-Tree, expects not to eat the Fruit."

Pear-shapped[2,3]

This term, in the U.S., is normally only used in a literal sense. However, in Britain it has three figurative connotations, and one of them is also used in Ireland and Australasia. In England, since the early 19th century, it is applied to people who are narrow at the shoulders and wide at their hips. A good example of this is in *Comin' Thro' the Rye*, a novel by Helen B. Mathers taken from the title of a classic 1782 poem by Robert Burns, first published in 1875, page 14:

"He is talking to mother now; a stout, sleek, **pear-shaped man**, whose legs always seem to me to have been swallowed up by his body,.."

The second, more distinctly figurative definition, which developed in the 20th century, is of a sonorous, rich voice. The earliest available example, here in quotes, likely recently coined, is from *The Tenth Man* by Edward Francis Murphy, 1937, page 21:

"Emma's melon-shaped **voice**, now diminished to '**pear-shaped** tones,' was being given, very agreeably, to song..."

There have been some citations of this meaning in American publications since the 1940s.

The third usage, more widespread in English speaking regions of the Isles, Australia and New Zealand is expanded to 'going pear-shaped'. It is said of a situation that has gone wrong, perhaps horribly so; all is ruined. How this came into being is disputed. It seems to have been first used in the 1980's, and possibly in the Royal Air Force, which may explain its utilization in other English speaking countries. One theory is that a circular graph went haywire and became pear-shaped. The earliest known citation is from *Air War in the South Atlantic*, by Jeffery L. Ethell and Alfred Price, 1983. In *Jackspeak the Pusser's Rum, Guide to Royal Navy Slanguage,* by Rick Jolly and Tugg Wilson, 1989, on page 210 we see:

> "'It all **went pear-shaped**..' - the scheme collapsed or went wrong; see *rats as an alternative."

Pecking order

This is a colloquialism for a hierarchical system of social organization first described by Norwegian zoologist Thorleif Schjelderup-Ebbe in 1921 in his PHD dissertation. Originally under the German terms *Hackordnung* or *Hackliste,* it was introduced into English in 1927. The initiaal use of the term referred to dominance in chickens asserted by various behaviors including pecking as a means to measure leadership order, especially between males and females, which was extended to other species of fowls (and animals) as described in *Bird Display: An Introduction to the Study of Bird Psychology* by Edward Allworthy Armstrong, 1942, page 171:

> "THE SOCIAL HIERARCHY IN BIRD LIFE Social hierarchy amongst birds and animals — Various types of dominance — Peck-dominance and peck-right — **Pecking-order** between male and female — Mitigation of despotism amongst strongly social birds..."

By the late 1960s it had begun to be applied to the hierarchy within a social group or community of people in which those at the top assume positions of leadership, authority and power. One of the first such citations known is from *Social Theory and Social Structure* by Robert King Merton, 1968, page 249:

> "Formality is manifested by means of a more or less complicated social ritual which symbolizes and supports the **pecking order** of the various offices."

People don't care how much you know until they know how much you care+

This proverbial saying has been utilized by numerous authors and leadership experts. John C. Maxwell, Zig Ziglar, Jack Canfield, Ryan C. Lowe, Anthony Robbins, and numerous others have used it in books. Then there was Coach Vince Lombardi who latched on to it. In fact, it has become one of the most oft-quoted proverbs of modern times. It has been quoted repeatedly by sales organizations to emphasize the importance of knowing one's product or service 'inside out' before attempting to present it to prospective buyers. It has been stressed by teachers and professors to impress upon their students the importance of learning.

The earliest claimed use, however, is allegedly by 26th U.S. President, Theodore Roosevelt, who was said to have coined it in a letter in June, 1900 to Mark Hanna, writing, "Nobody cares how much you know, until they know how much you care." Proof of this has never surfaced, however.

Photo finish

Since the beginning of horse racing, many outcomes were extremely close, and to the naked eye it may have appeared that more than one horse crossed the finish line at the same time. It was very difficult for the judges to determine the winner. In the late 1930s cameras called "Photo finish cameras" began to be installed at horse racetracks to determine the winner of the race. The term 'photo finish' soon began to be used for the photo itself, and also was being used to describe close auto races. Before long, it started to be applied figuratively outside racing altogether, to refer to close finishes in other competitions. In *Life Magazine*, November 8, 1940, under the heading 'The Midwest,' page 32, it described a close political race:

> "In another **photo-finish**, a Democrat nosed out the Republican incumbent for the Governorship of pro- Willkie Kansas."

Pick up (or **take up**) **someone's mantle**

This modern analogy means picking up where someone who had been a good example left off. It is a throw-back to the biblical story in *II Kings 2: 12-13* of the prophets Elijah and Elisha when Elijah was 'taken up into heaven' he dropped his mantle, aka cloak, and Elisha picks it up, as a symbol of succeeding him as God's messenger to Israel. The earliest known figurative use of the modern application is from *Children of the Ghetto: A Study of a Peculiar People* by Israel Zangwill, 1892:

> "Well, she would **take up the mantle** of the dead boy, and fill it as best she might. She clenched her little hands in iron determination."

Pigheaded

This means obstinate and stubborn to the point of stupidity. Earliest references to the word referred to the pig-headed armadillo. The first known citation to the current meaning was in Francis Grose's *A Classical Dictionary of the Vulgar Tongue*, Second Edition, 1788:

> "**Pig-headed.** Obstinate"

Pig-out

This modern idiom means to gorge oneself; grossly overeat. It came into common usage in the mid-1970s. The earliest available example is in *Princeton Alumni Weekly*, November 24, 1975 in 'Class Notes,' on page 35:

> "They came from Cape Cod, from Portland, from Miami, from L.A. to the biggest Italian-Jewish **pig-out** since Marco Polo first tasted chopped liver."

Pin back your ears

This expression was derived from an animal which lays its ears back in submission when frightened or scolded. Dogs do this often. It means to be scolded or disciplined verbally in a forceful manner and tone, or soundly defeated in an argument. Being 'pinned back' probably came from the fact that the scolding seems forceful. It is also used in defensive rushing in football. The earliest citation available referring to a human in this vein comes from the Oregon magazine, *The Northern Monthly,* May, 1864, in 'A Philosopher in a Smock Frock,' page 182, and indicates that it referred to being alert rather than intimidated:

> "He was enabled to do this, he said, by mixing among so many different classes of people, while pursuing his vocation, and keeping his mouth sealed, his **ears pinned back**, his eyes open, and then exercising his own judgment!"

Then the June 30, 1881 issue of University of Michigan's *The Chronicle* had this very different usage, concerning going to Chapel services:

> "We did it amidst violent threats that we should have our **ears pinned back**, and legs sawed on. But alas, the pristine glory of the University was no more."

Pink slip

This refers to the American practice said to have originated in the U.S. in the early 20th century of companies giving an employee a pink piece of paper indicating dismissal; either layoff or firing. It is claimed that this color was chosen because it was a color which would be unnoticeable from any other piece of paper, but this sounds suspect because dismissal notices were given in envelopes along with the paycheck. The actual origin of the practice and the term itself is a mystery. The most commonly related story is that Henry Ford began the practice after evaluation of assembly line employees, and provided cubby holes for each to receive their daily messages. The manager reportedly placed a white slip in the person's cubby hole if work for that day was satisfactory, and a pink slip if it was unsatisfactory. Some say that it began in vaudeville, as the United Booking Office, started in 1906, would issue cancellation notices printed on pink paper ('The Argot of Vaudeville Part I' *New York Times*, Dec. 16, 1917, p. X7). Another theory is that in-office company memos were written on triplicate paper with carbons, one copy of which is pink, to be given to the dismissed individual.

The following poem is also enigmatic in its meaning. It seems that it may be a harbinger of the pink slip as we know it. This is from *Fire Underwriter's Association of the Pacific 1903*, *Proceedings of the 27th Annual Meeting,* San Francisco. California, February 17-18, 1903, on page 198:

"THE AGENT AND THE **PINK SLIP**

"Theme: 'O wad some power the giftie gie us,
To see ourselves and others see us.'

"The agent was sad and dejected, his hopes had all vanished in air,
His plans had been briskly rejected, and his forehead was wrinkled with care.
The **pink slip** is with us, he mumbled, Oh, why don't they take it away!
My clients have everyone sputtered, when I've ventured to ask for my pay.
The **pink slip** spells only damnation, the agent gets cussed every time,
He can't even take a vacation, unless he should own a gold mine. I'll agree,
more water is needed, more reservoirs up in the hills;
The work has been sadly impeded, by councilmen's copious bills.
The G.A.s we've favored with business, have ordered the **pink slip** attached;
But the agents who rustled that business, now sit on themselves where
they're patched.
O, that these great men (barring banter) could be with us only a day,
The **pink slip** would vanish instanter, and I could collect up my pay.
O, that they could hear me called grafter, and highwayman, robber and thief;
Although they are daft, they'd be dafter, until they had granted relief."

Pipped at the post[2, 3]

This idiom, though mostly unknown in America, is freely used in Great Britain, Ireland and Australia in reference to being narrowly defeated in a race, contest or athletic event after being within reach of victory. Being pipped came years before 'at the post' added forming the metaphor. Though it had other meanings, such as an egg being 'pipped' by a hatching chick, which led to getting into something which was sealed, by 1855, it also meant to reject by ballot, and by 1891, 'to defeat in a race' (OED). The earliest known reference in print to a form of this, 'pipped on the post' was in reference to horse racing, the obvious origin, in *Baily's Magazine of Sports and Pastimes*, December, 1901, in a feature titled, 'Our Van.'

> "In the Old Cambridgeshire we saw Sidus and Sonatura fighting it out, nose and nose, the pair being **'pipped' on the post** by First Principal. Verdict: two heads."

It was mid-20th century before the phrase had evolved from 'on the post' to 'at the post' and was being used more figuratively. In *Concluding*, by Henry Green, 1950, page 182, we read:

> "Right before the finish, **pipped at the post**, one minute before the whistle, two seconds left for play, guess what? Liz has hooked him. He's buying the hoop Saturday, and they'll be married in September."

Pity party+

This is an idiomatic term for feeling sorry for one's self, and typically showing it overtly and dramatically, eliciting pity from others. The earliest known use is in a 1978 country song by Barbara Mandrell by that title, in which the lyrics describe a sad metaphoric party she is having because of loneliness over breaking up with a lover. This song and the idea may have been inspired by the 1963 hit, *It's My Party* (and I'll cry if I want to) by Leslie Gore, the chorus of which was in the 2015 Melanie Martinez alternative pop hit, *Pity Party*.

Plain as pikestaff[2]

This purely British simile or the alternate thereof, "clear as pikestaff" (the wooden shaft of a *pike*, a heavy spear used in the Middle Ages) means that it is very clear or similar to "As plain as the nose on one's face" (see first volume) or "As clear as crystal." The first known citation in print is from page 33 in *The String of Beads for the Romanisers* by Peter Plapet (pseudonym), 1844:

> "This makes the matter **plain as pikestaff.**"

Play hard to get^+

This is an idiomatic expression, usually applied to a female, meaning to resist advances of males (presumably to seem more attractive) without totally rejecting them. According to *Cassell's Dictionary of Slang* by Jonathan Green (Wellington House, London, 1998, page 927) it originated in the 1920s. Etymology Online, however, places origin at 1945. It began showing up in print, though, at least by April 5, 1940, when it appeared in *The Kentucky Kernel*, official student paper of The University of Kentucky in Louisville, in Out Of This World by Tommy Rusk on page 2, here in quotes, indicating a known but recently coined expression, and oddly applied to a male student:

> "Kappa Gal Tuttle can't understand why KA Walter Stevenson hasn't called her since the Kappa Dance. What's the matter, Walt? Are you **playing 'hard to get'** or are you going to let KA brother Mead Ferris leave you at the post?"

The December 12, 1946 issue of the Tyler Junior College student newspaper, *The Apache Pow Wow,* Tyler Texas, has a good example as we normally think of it in 'Question Box' on page 3:

> "What do you most dislike in a girl? CHARLIE JACKSON—**Playing hard to get.**"

Playing dirty pool

This is an idiom used for playing by one's own rules, and not necessarily the same as 'playing dirty,' which refers to overtly cheating. It simply means that one might be leery of doing business or entering into a contest, or an agreement or arrangement with a person who does not respect standard practices of honesty, integrity or fairness. It certainly can involve tricky, underhanded actions or creating an unfair advantage. The earliest verifiable citation in print is actually figurative, and comes from *The Cane Mutiny* by Herman Wouk, 1951, page 123:

"Had to talk loud 'n' fast, Steve — **I played pretty dirty pool**, you know, in court — poor Jack Challee."

Playing with fire

Literally, this is taking chances with matches or flames unnecessarily. Figuratively, it means doing something that could be dangerous and cause one a great deal of trouble later. It has been used in a literal sense in print since at least 1648. The earliest known citation of a similar analogy is in *The Rule and Exercise of Holy Dying...Together with Prayers and Acts of Virtue* by Jeremy Taylor, DD, 1812, page 128:

"And counterfeiting sickness is a huge enemy to this: It is an upbraiding the Divine Providence, a **jesting with fire**, a **playing** with a thunderbolt,.."

Play into the hands of

This means inadvertently act in such a way that it gives an advantage to an opponent. The earliest known example of the metaphor in print is in *The Great Duty of Labour and Work, and the Necessity There is at Present for a General Work-house for the Poor of this Place* by John Mickleburgh, 1751, page 22:

"...the advantages accruing from their accommodations are usually **played into the hands of** a few dexterous managers."

Play (hold, or **keep) your cards close to your vest/ chest**

This old adage means to keep one's intended actions secret. The original literal version was 'vest,' derived from poker players who kept their cards low at the table, close to their vests. In spite of a major etymology source on line placing origin at mid-20th century, it came into play figuratively in the first quarter of the twentieth century. The first known citation is found in *The Poultry Item*, Sellersville, Pennsylvania; February, 1921:

"If you are not going to get the ten zen then you better watch **your** step in the egg game, '**play your cards** close to **your vest,'** and go easy."

By February, 1953 it was also used as 'chest,' as seen in this snip from *Popluar Science* in 'How Auto Makers Spy on Each Other' by James Jones, on page 136:

"There's always the hope that you can **play your** own hand **close to your chest** — but divine what **cards** the other guy holds."

Soon the idea was carried across the pond (see in original volume), where it stayed 'close to your chest.' More often, since the 1990s,' it is universally 'play,' rather than keep.

Plus one

This modern idiom refers to a person who accompanies an invited guest to a social function. Such events may be labeled as 'plus one' to let guests know that they may bring an unnamed guest of their choosing. Its origin is obscure but it came into usage early in the last quarter of the 20th century. A modern example of use in print is from *Hottie* by Jonathan Bernstein, 2009, page 126:

> "God, the **Plus One** Party was an incredible idea. It hit every button."

Poetry in motion

This metaphor refers to the gentle, flowing movements of a beautiful person or thing. Johnny Tillotson had a number two hit song in the U.S. in November, 1960; number one in the U.K. in 1961, by this title; but this was by no means the coining of the expression. In spite of two online sites citing later dates for first use, the earliest actual verifiable printed reference to this phrase is in Henry Mercer Graves' *An Essay to the Genius of Shakespeare &c*, 1826, page 112, in 'A Letter on Taste, Judgment and Rhetorical Expression:'

> "I can conceive music in motion; but I never could conceive **poetry in motion**. The legs that could form poetry, must have been cleverer than even Mademoiselle Mercandotti's, which said legs shot the heart of the hospitable…"

Point of view+

According to Etymology Online, this very old idiom predates English, going back to the Latin *punctum verus,* and came into English from the French*, pointe de vue* in 1727. It means the position from which a thing is seen. The phrase was used extensively in English literature in the 1800s.

Poisoned chalice

This figure of speech refers to an honor, award or instrument which proves to be a disadvantage or later source of problems to the recipient. It is taken from

Shakespeare's 1606 play, *Macbeth,* Act I, Scene vii. Unwilling to kill Duncan, as his wife feels is paramount, in his discourse, Macbeth says:

> "We'd jump the life to come. But in these cases
> We still have judgement here, that we but teach
> Bloody instructions which, being taught, return
> To plague th'inventor. This even-handed justice
> Commends th'ingredience of our **poisoned chalice**
> To our own lips."

Poison pen

This metaphor refers to a type of letter, usually anonymous, which viciously attacks another person or group, as well as the writer of the letters. Oxford researchers determined that the term was coined, believe it or not, by an American newspaper in Frederick, Maryland, called *The Evening Post* on September 6, 1911 in a headline which read, "More poison-pen letters." Two years later, on January 10, 1913, it was cited in *The New York Times,* in an article describing how a 'poison pen' writer was sending anonymous post cards to coffee roasters, attempting to disrupt a large volume sale.

Within two years 'poison pen letters' were mentioned in *The American Library Annual,* 1914-1915, page 106:

> **"Pollard, Mrs. Anna**. Mrs. Pollard said to have admitted writing **'poison-pen'** letters."

Poison the well

This metaphor originated from the old military tactic of pouring poison into the water source of an invading army in order to diminish the strength of the troops.

The earliest known example of this practice in print is from *The Confession made on the 15th day of September, in the Year of Our Lord 1348, in the Castle of Chillon by the Jews arrested at Neustadt on Charge of* ***Poisoning the Wells****, Springs and other places; also Food, &c., with the Design of destroying and extirpating all Christians.* This confession was published in a number of sources in the 19th century, starting with the index of *Observations on the Principal Medical Institutions and Practice of France Italy and Germany* by Edwin Lee, page 64, published in Philadelphia in 1837.

It is still used as a political rhetorical devise; preemptively presenting negative information about an opponent ridiculing what he or she is about to say or do in order to discredit the opponent. The term was first used in this figurative connotation by Anglican Cardinal, Dr. John Henry Newman in *Apoligia Pro Vita Sua,* in 1864. In refuting a 'Mr. Kingsley,' who had accused him of 'cunning sleight-of-hand logic,' he writes on page 21:

> "I say it with shame and stern sorrow—He has attempted a great transgression; he has attempted (as I may call it) to ***poison the wells."***

Polar plunge / Polar bear plunge+

Polar bear swims have been practiced for well over 100 years in different countries. The earliest recorded is in Boston in 1904. In many Canadian communities it is a New Year's Day tradition, and Vancouver's Polar Day Swim Club has been active since 1920 and boasts 1000 to 2000 registered participants each year. IN Milwaukee it is called the Polar Plunge and has been practiced for over 100 years. It has long been practiced in the Netherlands, the U.K. and New Zealand, where the seasons are reversed from the Northern Hemisphere, the 'Polar Plunge' happens in June.

Pole position^

In spite of claims by a major online dictionary that this metaphor began in the 1950s, it was already in use in the very early 20th century, and comes from the 19th century practice of using a pole in horse racing to denote the starting position next to the boundary fence. It is used in motorsports and means to be in the best position to win, i.e. the front of the grid at a race like the Indianapolis 500. The earliest available citation is from *The Automobile*, published by The Class Journal Company in New York, Thursday, June 22, 1911, in 'Guttenberg Meet Attracts Thousands:'

> "The first race drew a field of six and the E-M-F entry, **in pole position**, jumped to the front at the gun and tin-canned along in front all the way through the five circuits, winning handily in 6:09 from the Lancia and Paige-Detroit."

Politics ain't beanbag

This, like 'poison the well,' is a political cliché and is used as a response to candidates who complain about the nagging problems arising during campaigning for an office. Among these are unfair media treatment and harsh attacks by opponents. Forms of it have been used by both Newt Gingrich and Ted Cruz.

Syndicated newspaper columnist Finley Peter Dunne (1867-1936) coined the saying. It was first spoken by Dunne's character, Mr. Dooley, an Irish-American who sat around a pub in Chicago making conversation about the issues of the day. The entire quote from the *Salt Lake Tribune* (Salt Lake City, Utah), October 13, 1895, page 15, column 3 is:

> "Sure, **politics ain't bean-bag**. 'Tis a man's game, an' women, childer, cripples an' prohybitionists 'd do well to keep out iv it."

Pony up

This expression, per se, likely originated in America in the early 19th century, but was from English roots. It means 'pay up' and was usually applied to a bill which was overdue, or expected to be 'cash on the barrelhead' (see in original volume). The earliest known use in print is from the May, 1819 edition of *The Rural Magazine,* Connecticut publication:

> "The afternoon, before the evening, the favoured gentlemen are walking rapidly into the merchant-tailors shops, and very slowly out, unless they **ponied up** the Spanish (meaning the money).

The 1859 Second Edition, enlarged, *of Dictionary of Americanisms*, put out by John Russell Bartlett, page 332, has this explicit definition:

> "To **Pony up**. A vulgar phrase, meaning to pay over money. Ex. 'Come, Mr. Brown, **pony up** that account;' that is, pay over the money."

It also gives us a hint as to an earlier version which obviously led to this saying:

> "Grose gives a phrase similar to it: 'Post the pony,' i. e. lay down the money."

'Grose' referred to Englishman Francis Grose who published the well-known *Dictionary of the Vulgar Tongue,* first in 1785; then in 1811 (Vulgar at that time referred to colloquialisms, not obscenities). *The Slang Dictionary, Etymological,*

Historical and Anecdotal, a New Edition, 1873, entry on page 258, sheds a bit more light on the original British origin of 'pony' in this sense:

> "Also a generic term for money. Post, to pay down; ' **POST the pony'** signifies to place the stakes played for on the table."

Pop the Question

For almost 300 years this has been an idiom for proposing marriage; traditionally a male role, but in today's society, it could be used by either sex. The earliest known citation is from *The Palace Miscellany* printed and sold in London by J. Dormer in 1733 for 'one shilling and six pence'. This rhyme is part of Canto II of The Progress of Matrimony, and is found on page 35:

> "Then he began t' accrost and woo her.
> And push the matter home unto her,
> Marriage, cry'd she, I understand
> 'Tis taking a great thing in hand;"

Then further down:

> "The Thing's a Thing to make no Jest on,
> 'Tis therefore thus I **pop the Question**;"

Porch pirates

This 21st century metaphor is used for people who steal packages, even more so around holidays, right off other people's porches, often in broad open daylight. As online sales have increased, the problem has become more frequent. The earliest known use of the phrase in this usage is from December 9, 2013, when Wndu.com news had an article titled "Dealing with 'P**orch Pirates'"** that contained the following statement:

> "Our traditional image of pirates stealing treasure on the high seas is replaced by images of land-based marauders taking holiday treasures off our very doorsteps."

Pound the pavement^

This is an Americanism meaning to diligently walk the streets, looking for a job, or in the case of a sales person, attempting to make sales. A major slang dictionary lists origin at 1960. The term was, however, used as early as June 16,

1941 in the sense of walking the streets, in an ad in *Boys Life* for Florsheim Shoes on page 11:

> "They don't have to be coddled, or saved for Sunday best! They can **pound the pavement** all day and look fit as a fiddle that night! Florsheim quality is the answer; Florsheims are made to look better longer!"

In 1949 the definition was given in *Criminal Slang: the Vernacular of the Underworld Lingo* by Captain Vincent J. Monteleone, page 181:

> **"POUND THE PAVEMENT** (V) To walk the streets."

Then, on December 10, 1949, an article titled 'Best Direct to Location Sales of Venders at NAMA Cigarette Operator Clinic' by Is Horowitz in *Billboard* makes clear the meaning of getting new sales locations:

> "H.C. Crowther, of the Dallas Cigarette Service, whose subject was 'Obtaining New Locations,' stressed that the best method was still to '**pound the pavement** early and late.'"

Pregnant pause

This term primarily refers to a technique in comic timing in which an intentional silence after a humorous or awkward statement accentuates its effect. 'Pregnant' is used in the sense of expectancy for the audience reaction. It has also been used to describe the pause after a sales person makes a closing statement or asks a closing question. It has often been said that whoever speaks first 'looses.' This is only in the meaning of having sold the other person on his or her way of thinking. The earliest known use of the term in print is from the Poem 'An Ode to Frenzy,' printed on page 131 of *The Life of Thomas Dermody Interspersed with Pieces of Original Poetry* by James Grant Raymond, 1806:

> "The hurried step, the **pregnant pause** severe,
> The spectred flash of sense, the hideous smile,
> The frozen stare, Revenge's thrilling tear,
> The awful start, sharp look, and mischief's secret wile;
> These are the proud demoniac marks I claim,
> Since grief and feeling are the same;
> Then all thy racks sublime prepare;
> And free me, Frenzy, from despair!"

In *Dublin University Magazine*, May, 1841, in 'A Leaf from the Fortunes of Mordaunt Mervale,' we see a bit clearer citation, herein where the speaker himself broke the silence:

"'If no legitimate method of relief occur, I will even brace myself to meet the worst, and trust to an honest conscience to console me.' 'And now, sir,' added he, after a brief but **pregnant pause**, 'you have heard my determination — attempt not to alter it, and I may receive your acquiescence and your withdrawal as some requital for the insult you have, I shall suppose unwittingly, inflicted.'"

Prepare for the worst and hope for the best (See: **Expect the best and plan for the worst**)

Press gang

This old, primarily British, idiom means to force a person into military service or coerse a person to take a political stand. It may also refer to a detachment of men under military command authorized to force men into military or naval service. The term has been used since the late 17th century. The earliest available citation, however, is from *A Review of the Affairs of France, with Observations on Transactions at Home,* Saturday, March 12, 1705, in 'Advice from the Scandal Club,' where it is used as a noun:

"Yesterday a **Press Gang** came to the Cock and Rummer in Bow-street, Covent-Garden; where they laid Hands of the Master's Apprentice, who if a Cook by Trade, there was a great Dinner then fending up; upon which, the Master of the House sold these Worthy Judges of Men, who are fit to go to Sea…"

Privileged character- PC

A privileged character, often shortened to the acronym, 'PC,' is a person who is on a higher social statis, often due to nepotistic treatment, or in many cases, a person portrayed that way by those jealous of the individual. Use of the term goes back to at least 1766, where it appeared in *Dodsley's Annual Register for the Year of 1765*, page 200, in 'An Essay on the Ancient English Minstrels, from the Same:'

"From the uniform procedure of both these kings, it is plain that the fame mode of entertainment prevailed among both people, and that the Minstrel was a **privileged character** among both."

A good modern example of the acronym is found in *Leaves of a Stunted Shrub: Genealogy of the Scrogen-Scroggin-Scroggins Family*, Volume 5, compiled by William G. Scroggins, 2009, page 15:

> **"He was a P.C.** and Vice Chamberlain before that last date, when he was appointed Joint Ambassador to receive, in Paris on 14 July, the oath of King Louis XII of France to maintain the peace."

proof is in the pudding, The

The original saying was, "**the proof of the pudding is in the eating**." Through the ages, like many other proverbs, it evolved to what we have today. The intended meaning is that in order to really understand anything, one had to experience it for himself or herself.

As explained under the entry for "Overegging the pudding," in past centuries in England, pudding didn't mean a sweet dessert, it meant sausage, since this word originally applied to something whipped up from the entrails of a hog. The earliest printed example available, in which this seems evident, is from *The History of the Renowned Don Quixote, de la Mancha* by Miguel de Cervantes Saavedras, in the 1719 English translation of Volume II, page 139:

> "But you'll guess at the Meat presently by the Sauce; **the Proof of the Pudding is in the eating**, Master…"

The original version was being used until well into the 20th century. The earliest known example of the current rendition comes in the December, 1927 edition of *Professional Engineer*, page 27:

> **"The Proof Is in the Pudding** Proof that Professional Engineer is one of those publications read from 'kiver to kiver' is found in a newspaper clipping from New Orleans which matches Phoenix Chapter's boast of being served dates…"

Publish or perish

This phrase has become more widely popular in recent years since self-publishing is so much easier to obtain. It was popularized by acedemics researching in order to further their careers. It was first cited in print in a non-academic connotation in a 1932 book, *Archibald Cary Coolidge: Life and Letters,* by Harold Jefferson Coolidge, on page 308. The earliest academic use in print, here in quotes, indicating a recently coined, though known, expression, comes from *The Academic Man* by Logan Wilson, first published in 1942 by Oxford University Press, page 197:

"The prevailing pragmatism forced upon the academic group is that one must write something and get it into print. Situational imperatives dictate a **'publish or perish'** credo within the ranks."

Pull one's socks up[2]

This primarily British term means to make an effort at improvement. It obviously comes from a person having to take the inititive to reach down and pull up his or her socks when they are sagging in order to look one's best. The earliest noting of the saying in print is in *Judy, or The London Serio-Comic Journal,* July 20, 1887, on page 29, in 'Poor Will Bunion:'

"Will's bedroom, too, was tastefully covered with mind-improving wall-paper on which were printed beautiful proverbs and maxims, such as—'It is never too late to mend your umbrella,' 'a short clay pipe is the thief of time, and tobacco is the root of all evil,' '**pull up your socks**,' 'a caterpillar is an extravagant housekeeper because she makes the butter-fly,'…"

Pull out all the stops

This idiom means to make every effort possible to accomplish some goal. This saying derived from the way in which pipe organs were made since ancient times. Stops, in these instruments, are used to control the flow of air. Pulling them out would increase the volume of the music. Even before pipe organs were made, the word stop was used to mean note or key. In *The Steele Glas*, 1567, by George Gascoigne, this use was recorded:

"But sweeter soundes, of concorde, peace, and loue, Are out of tune, and iarre in euery **stoppe**."

Later 'stops' was the word used for the knobs on pipe organs which are pulled out or pushed in to control the air flow, thus the volume, of the music. We see this in 1845 in *J.A. Hamilton's Historical, Descriptive and Practical Catecism of the Organ*, on pages 59 and 60:

"It has three composition pedals, or pedals acting on the great organ, which lay hold of and **pull out the stops…"**

Matthew Arnold, a Professor of Poetry at the University of Oxford, was the first to use pull out stops in a figurative sense in *Essays in Criticism*, 1867, page xiv:

"...I can truly say, that, knowing how unpopular a task one is undertaking when one tries to **pull out a few more stops** in that powerful, but at present

> somewhat narrow-toned organ, the modern Englishman, I have always sought to stand by myself ..."

Pull the plug on something

This is *not* taken from pulling the plug on life supports to terminate a moribund person's life, as some may assume. This does mean, figuratively, to terminate or put an end to something, but early 20th century literal examples of the phrase either refer to electric connections or water plugs, so it most likely derived from one of those. The earliest metaphoric citation known is from a *Saturday Evening Post* article in May, 1918 by Gerald Stanley Lee about German Foreign Secretary Arthur Zimmerman's telegram in January, 1917, to German Mexican Minister, von Eckhardt, which had been deciphered by British cryptographers offering Mexico part of its territory in the U.S. if they would join the German cause against America in World War I:

> "Germany by one telegram **pulled the plug** out of the world and mobilized a world against her."

Pushing at an open door

This refers to being able to continuously achieve one's goals because a lot of people are in favor of them and are eager to be of help. The earliest known use of this idiom is from *The Saturday Review of Politics, Literature, Science and Art,* September 6, 1856, on the first page, in 'Austria and Naples versus England:'

> "There is little use in **pushing at an open door**. The citizens of the United States are equally exempt from galling discipline and control."

Push the boundaries

This modern idiom refers to going beyond one's previous limitations; being willing to boldly experiment with new ideas in order to gain knowledge or reach new horizons. This idea can even be extended to pushing one's luck, or delving into areas in which others may feel uncomfortable. I can be applied in any field of thought or endeavor, such as relationships, gender, design, art, religion or philosophy. It was derived from pushing property boundries, a term which had been used since the early 19th century, but figurative use has been around since the 1950s. An early example is from *Michigan Technic*, January, 1958, in an article advertising Northrup Aircraft on page 37:

> "And yet there is no limit to how far man's inventiveness and imagination can **push the boundaries**. Radical new concepts that would have been unthought of just a few years ago are the drawing-board problems of today."

Put a damper on something+

This idiom means to discourage or dishearten. Damper, in this connotation, refers to dampening one's spirit. The first known metaphoric use in print of 'damper' is from *Clarissa; or, the History of a Young Lady* by Samuel Richardson, 1748:

> "I very early discharged shame, that cold water **damper** to an enterprising spirit."

Figurative use of 'put a damper on' first occurred in John F. Murray's *The World of London*, published in 1843:

> "If the clerk of the weather office is determined to **put a damper** on the festivities, more shame to him.

Put an animal or person out of his or her misery

This cruel-sounding expression has been in use in English since at least the early century. The earliest known citation is in *The Life of James II, the Late King of England* by David Jones, 1705, page 347, in writing of General Mackarty:

> "...and he did not escape wounding in several places, and as one of the Soldiers was going to knock him in the Head with the Stock of his Musquet to **put him out of his Misery**..."

Put-down+

This is an expression used for making a humiliating statement about someone or something. It is very old, going back to circa 1400 according to a popular dictionary of idioms.

Put down roots+

This is a metaphor for settling down, particularly applying to someone with a long history of moving from place to place. According to a popular idiom dictionary, it was first recorded in 1921, when plants putting down roots were compared to human settlement. By the mid-1950s, it was being commonly used as it is today.

Put one's foot down

This refers to taiking a firm stand on an issue and refusing to budge in the face of opposition, much like literally bracing oneself and standing securely in one place. The earliest known figurative example in print is from *A Year in Spain by a Young American,* authored by Alexander Mackenzie, 1831, page 370:

> "Finally he **put his foot down** with an air of resolution, and ordered bacon and eggs, to be followed by a stewed hare and a dessert of olives."

A very clear citation was made by American humorist and Political Satirist, Seba Smith three years later in *The Life and Writings of Major Jack Downing of Downingville*, page 228:

> "And he talked and palavered with the President till he finally brought him over, and then the President **put his foot down**, and said the deposites should be moved whether or no."

Put one's foot in one's mouth^

This refers to committing some embarrassing blunder or indiscretion. In spite of a popular online source which places first attesting at 1887, it was cited in *The Disagreeable Surprise*, Act I, Scene iii, published in 'Cumberland's British Theater: With Remarks, Biographical and Critical' in 1828:

> "'Billy,' said the barber, 'whenever you opens your **mouth**, you're sure to **put your foot in** it.'"

Put pen to paper

This cliché traditionally means to begin writing something. In its modern application it may figuratively refer to beginning to compose something on a computer or create music or artwork. The earliest citation in print is from the introduction to *The Trimming of Thomas Nashe, Gentleman* by Ricardo de Medio campo, 1597, page iv:

> "In the mean time Harvey was enjoying his fancied and temporary triumph; but when Nash heard it, he resolved again to **put pen to paper**, to let Harvey and his friends see that his wit had not been exhausted, nor extinguished…"

This introduction may have actually been written sometime after the original printing, but an unmistakably dated citation came only a few years afterward in *The Petition Apolojeticall of Lay Papists, Calling themselves the Lay Papists, calling themselves the Lay Catholics of England* published in London in 1606, page 70:

> "…any thing that might justly offend your grace, that being by the reasons popish reconci: aforesayd pressed to **put pen to paper**, and to haue recourse to your Batt, and Highnesse by way of intercellion, we seeke not for all that to impotunate such trash?"

Put pressure on/ put under pressure

Coming from applying pressure physically, this is and idiom used to refer to attempting someone to do something that he, she or they oppose or would rather not do. The idea of figuratively putting someone 'under pressure' goes back in English to at least 1630, when noted Anglican cleric John Preston (1587–1628), master of Emmanuel College in Cambridge, included the following in his second Christian work, *The New Covenant, or, the Saints' Portion*, 5th Edition, corrected, page 476:

> "…but God hath promised to be a buckler to shield him and to defend him from it **put** the case thou lye **vnder** any **pressure**, any calamity, any crosse, any disease, ..."

Put something in mothballs (See: **In mothballs**)+

Put something to bed

This simply means to successfully finish dealing with something, often sending it on to the next step in conclusion; used a lot in publishing. Kipling used it in 1888 in his novella, *The Man who Would Be King*:

> "One Saturday night it was my pleasant duty to **put the paper to bed** alone. A King or courtier or a courtesan or a Community was going to die or get a

new Constitution, or do something that was important on the other side of the world,…"

Put the screws to someone

Originally 'put the screws on,' this is a hyperbolic idiom meaning to apply extreme coercive pressure on someone. It is taken from the 17th century torture method where metal screws were used on a prisoner's thumbs, as described in *Bishop Burnet's History of His Own Time; From the Restoration of King Charles II to the Conclusion of the Treaty of Peace at Uthecht in the Reign of Queen Anne* by Gilbert Burnet published in 1809, page 253:

"…little **screws** of steel were made use of, that screwed the thumbs with so exquisite a torment, ... And, upon his refusing to take it, they **put** his thumbs in the **screws**; and drew them so hard, that as they **put him** to extreme torture."

Putting the screws on was used somewhat metaphorically by February, 1842, when it appears in *Dublin University Magazine*, in the serialized novel, 'Gasper the Pirate: A Tale of the Indian Seas,' chapter VIII:

"'Shall we **put the screws on**?' suggested another, as the man remained silent and unmoved."

At the bottom of the page it is noted: 'Putting the screws on is a cant term for applying any kind of torture.'

Use of 'put the screws to' in a purely figurative connotation was around by July, 1870, when it was used in the college paper, *The Dartmouth* in 'Exchanges:'

"I did not mean to insult him. I did mean to **put the screws to him** for his own good. The only way to bring some people out of the depths of ignorance, is to **put the screws to them**, and if a man has a sound foundation it never hurts nor insults him."

Put the wheels in motion (See: **Set the wheels in motion**)+

Put up or shut up

This, like 'poot or get off the pot' (see first volume), means that someone should either take action or stop talking about a problem or situation. It was derived from boxing, when a fighter would challenge an opponent to either 'put up' a stake for a match or stop his threats. The earliest known citation is from *The Maryville Tribune*, Maryville, Ohio; July, 21, 1858:

> "Now, if he means business, let him **put up, or shut up**; for this is the last communication that will come from me in regard to this fellow."

Put words in someone's mouth

This figure of speech refers to insinuating that a person meant one thing when he or she actually meant something entirely different. It is a throwback to a biblical statement in *II Samuel 14:3*:

> "And come to the king, and speak on this manner unto him. So Joab **put the words in her mouth.**" *(KJV, 1611)*

Q

Quick fix^

Also sometimes called a 'Bandaid,' this term applies to a temporary solution to a situation which postpones having to cope with the root of the problem. A major online dictionary cites 1965-1970 as time of origin. The phrase was in use, however, over 100 years before that. *The Book of British Poets* by C. H. Monike, published in Germany in 1858, contains a poem titled 'From the Chase' by William Somerville which has the following lines on page 306:

> "They put him down. See, there he drives along!
> Th' ascending bubbles mark his gloomy way.
>
> **Quick fix** the nets, and cut off his retreat
> Into the sheltering deeps. Ah! there he vents!"

'A quick fix' is attested in *Ladies Home Journal*, March, 1921, in a glue ad:

> "Yes! LePage's Glue for mending eye-glasses! Great in an emergency; for **a quick-fix."**

R

Rabbit hole

This metaphor is used to typify the path to a disorienting, bizarre and difficult situation; going into the unknown, and is usually stated as 'going down the rabbit hole.' It is taken from Lewis Carroll's *Alice's Adventures in Wonderland,* 1866, page 13:

> "...and was just in time to see it pop **down** a large **rabbit-hole** under the hedge. In another moment **down** went Alice after it, never once considering how in the world she was to get out again."

Rack one's brain

This idiom means to struggle to recall something. It comes from the medieval torure device called a rack, which eventually could tare a victim's limbs from his body. Combined with 'brain' it means to cause the mind extreme discomfort. Though 'racke,' as it was originally spelled, was used in earlier literature, the first mention of racking a person's brain, in spite of a great online phrase origin source citing the earliest reference in 1680, came from *The Prerogative of Popular Government* by James Harrington, 1658, page xiii:

> "Is it not a fine piece of folly For private men sitting in their Cabinets to **Rack their brains** about Models of Government?"

Rad / Totally rad+

This term is short for radical. In modern slang vernacular, rad is the word for something that surpasses 'awesome' and 'cool.' Use of the expression as an alternate for cool started in the late 1970s and '80s. It was made popular by the 'Teenaged Mutant Ninja Turtles,' and is believed to have begun in California. Today it is making a comeback, and is used frequently by millennials.

Raise Cain+

This is an American metaphor meaning causing trouble or creating an uproar. 'To raise' has meant 'to conjure up' since the 14th century. Since according to the Bible, the son of Adam and Eve, Cain, was the first murderer, killing his brother, Able, conjuring up Cain would cause quite a stir. This expression was first attested in the early 19th century. It was already in use by May, 1840 when this citation appeared in the *St. Louis Daily Pennant*:

> "Why have we every reason to believe that Adam and Eve were rowdies? Because they both **raised Cain**."

In the remainder of the 1800s and early 1900s it was used repeatedly in all types of publications and by authors in novels, including Mark Twain's *The Adventures of Huckleberry Finn*, near the beginning of Chapter VI, referring to Finn's father:

> "Every time he got money he got drunk; and every time he got drunk he **raised Cain** around town; and every time he **raised Cain** he got jailed."

Raise the bar^

This expression is used to refer to gradually setting a standard of success or quality higher. It is said to be taken from pole vaulting and high jumping where the bar is set higher as the competition gets stiffer and new records are set. The earliest references in print, however, are from a different 'bar.' In the *Proceedings of the Illinois Bar Association, Forty-fifth Annual Meeting at Dixon*, June 9, 10, 11, 1921, page 61. Note that it is talking of raising the 'standard of ethics' but that bar is not capitalized, making it ambiguous:

> "We think that if all of the counties throughout the state would do that, it would tend to raise the standard of ethics, of conduct of the profession; and the reading of those canons by the public at large would tend to **raise the bar** in the public esteem."

The next year in the *Proceedings of the Alabama State Bar Association, Held at Southern Club, Birmingham Alabama, April 28, 29, 1922*, a similar statement was made, on page 42, and bar *is* capitalized, indicating that the origin could indeed be from raising the ideals for attorneys, not the bar used in high jumps;

"And already what we say, if we say is right, goes a long way, but when we **raise the Bar** to that high standard it should occupy, where we make every lawyer feel that he is an officer of the court, that the oath he takes is a solemn obligation, that it is up to him to live up to the obligation."

The next unmistakably figurative use of the phrase also comes in a legal context in 1935, in the *New York Court of Appeals, Records and Briefs*, page 59:

"The validity of an indictment does not ordinarily depend upon the correctness of a date appearing therein, provided the time alleged does not **raise the bar** of the statute of limitations."

A similar citation appears in a New York Court of Appeals record in 1942 in regard to raising the bar of a statute. In fact, the first available reference to raising the bar for high jumping does not come until a *Life Magazine* article on July 13, 1953.

Rake someone over the coals (or **ashes**)

This very old metaphor refers to reprimanding someone severely. It was taken from the medieval Catholic Church practice of punishing 'heritics' by dragging them over hot coals. The OED cites the earliest mention this practice in print is from 1565:

"S. Augustine, that knewe best how to fetche an **heretike ouer the coles**."

Figurative use came in the 19th century, and in Britain it was 'haul' someone over the coals. An early example is from *Home Study for Machinists Steam Engineers, Etc.,* Volume I, July 1897 to July, 1898, page 169:

"And oh! how he **raked him over the coals** for not following directions."

Read the fine (or **small**) **print**

This common idiom means to ask specific questions about a legal contract or loan before signing to make sure that you understand all the conditions. It comes from the fact that many less attractive details are often hidden in parts of an agreement which are less obvious. The earliest mention of small print in a publication was in 1744. The first known caution about reading small print is contracts refers to an insurance policy and is in *James G. Blaine, A Sketch of His Life, with a Brief Record of the Life of John A. Logan* by Charles Wolcott Balestier, 1884, page 73:

> "...to be **sure** my authorized agent said so to you, to **be sure** I got it, and got its full value; but when you come to **read** my note — like **the small print** in an insurance policy that always covers the rascality under which the company escapes its liabilities ..."

Read too much into the tea leaves

This figurative modern saying means that one tries to make too much out of something that is uncertain because it is what is predicted to happen under the circunstances, like a political theory. It comes from the ancient practice of Gypsy readers using tea leaves to make predictions about the future. An example in print is from *The Religion Virus* by Craig A. James, 2010, page 73:

> "We use a strainer to remove the **tea leaves** from our tea, and we might say, 'The strainer lets the tea through and stops the leaves'... we use words which have other connotations, and must be careful not to **read too much into** these terms."

Ready to rumble

Modern use of this, meaning get excited about a sporting match, comes from a trademarked catchphrase, 'Let's get ready to rumble,' coined by American boxing and wrestling announcer Michael Buffer, which he has been using since 1984. But the phrase 'ready to rumble' has appeared in print for hundreds of years before Buffer was born. The earliest known use was by the first Sir Winston Churchill (1620-1688) in *Divi Britannici: Being a Remark Upon the Lives of All the Kings of this Isle from the Year of the World, 3855 unto the Year of Grace 1660*, published in 1675, page 148:

> "...for they only busy'd themselves to Forrifie so by Land, as to keep themselves in an uncertain Condition of defence, like men rowling a stone up a Hill, that is **ready to rumble** down again upon their heads, if they do not continually support it with main strength..."

The earliest citation known of a *person* figuratively being 'ready to rumble' in in *The History of the Most Ingenious Knight, Don Quixote de la Mancha* by Miguel de Cervantes Saavedra, translated by Capt. John Stevens, Volume II, 1706, page 190:

> "When I think sometimes he is **ready to rumble** headlong into the Abyss of Folly, he on a sudden blunders out some pithy Sentence that exalts him to the Clouds."

The first positive reference of 'ready to rumble,' comes on May 28, 1884, in the poem, 'Puckerings' from the publication *Puck:*

"Ready to drum for an honest man;
To do the best and most I can.
Ready to thrill till the drum-heads strain,
Booming the cause of Blaine of Maine;
Ready to rumble and throb and roar,
Telling them Arthur is up once more;..."

Red herring[2]

This metaphor, often used in crime mysteries, refers to something used to distract one from discovering the truth. Perhaps a supposed clue planted to make someone other than the perpetrator appear to be guilty. It derives from the fact that when herrings are smoked it turns them red, and gives them a strong odor. In the past, smoked herrings have been used to teach hunting dogs to follow a trail. They were taken across the path of the animal being followed to distract the hounds; then taught to overcome the distraction and continue in pursuit of the prey. The earliest known reference in print to the literal use is from *Roberts' Semi Monthly Magazine,* April 1, 1841, in 'The Poacher,' a novel being printed as a serial, by 'Captain Marryat,' in Chapter XIV:

"''To trail! I think they're fast enough upon our trail already; but if you want to help them, a **red herring**'s the thing.'"

The first available figurative use is found in *The Public,* Saturday June 30, 1903:

"Maybe he intended vaguely to get pensioned out of land values anyhow, and Mr. Chamberlain has sprung the imperial protection scheme to throw him off the landlord scent. However that may be, the scent is there, and if the British workingman once gets on the trail of it no **red herring** is likely to divert him."

Rest in peace / RIP+

This very old phrase is taken from the Latin *Requiescat in pace*, and is sometimes used in traditional Christian memorials and prayers, including Roman Catholic, Anglican, Lutheran and Methodist, to express wishes for eternal rest for a departed soul.

It became ubiquitous on gravestones in the 18th century. It is also used today by individuals when speaking of someone who has passed away. The following appeared in *Memoirs of the Dead and Tomb's Remembrancer* printed in Baltimore in 1806 in reference to George Washington (1732-1799):

> "To the sight of Jesus go. May he **rest in peace**. Amen."

rest is history, The

This end for a great story is used when there is no need to finish because everyone in the audience presumably knows what happened afterward. The earliest known citation of this is in *British History Chronologically Arranged* by John Wade, 1839, page 739:

> **"The rest is history**, of which Napoleon is now almost as much a portion as Caesar or Hannibal."

Just a few years later, Georgia Congressman Robert Tooms, in his speech on the Admission of California, printed in *The Congressional Globe*, February 27, 1850, used it in an overt manner on page 199:

> "The sight of the flag of England once caused every Anglo-Saxon heart on this continent to leap with joy and gladness...Foolish tyrants made it the emblem of degradation. Loyalty was converted into hate—**the rest is history**."

Revenge is a dish that is best served cold^

This old adage means that one who is determined to get even for an injustice should not seek revenge immediately, but should wait until enough time has passed that the target will not expect it and be caught off guard. No one emphatically claims to know who said it first. Contrary to popular sources expressing that it came from the English translations of the French novel, *Dangerous Liaisons*, the earliest citation of a form of it is actually from the English version of another French novel, *The Orphan, or, Memoirs of Matilda* by Eugene Sue, translated by the Honorable D.G. Osborne, Volume I, published in London in 1846, page 303, in italics, like quotes, indicating being somewhat know at the time:

> "And then ***revenge is very good eaten cold***, as the vulgar say — "

In the novel, *The Angel of the Chimes,* 1886, by French author Fortuné Du Boisgobey it is attributed to Italian nobleman Cesare Borgia (1475-1507).

> "But **revenge is a dish** which must be **eaten cold**, said Caesar Borgia, who was a connoisseur in such matters..."

But London publication, *The Saturday Review of Politics, Literature, Science and Art*, October, 1896, attributed it to the French:

> "**Revenge is a dish that is best eaten cold**, according to the French. The Tsar is evidently in no hurry to begin his meal."

Revolving door

This idiom refers mainly to the frequent movement of people from one organization or activity to another, and especially is used of those moving from government jobs to the jobs in the private sector which they were previously responsible for regulating, thus casting doubts upon the impartiality of their regulation. It is sometimes applied to narrow relationships of mutual interest between two persons or entities. It has been in use since the 1990s, and a good early example is from *Laurel and Hardy: A Bio-Biography* by Wes D. Gehring, page 107:

> "Team lawyer and friend Ben Shipman, who was much better at handling alimony claims than movie contracts, credited Laurel's **revolving door relationship** with Ruth giving him a 'permanent case of the triple conniption fits.'"

Richer than God/ More money than God+

This is a common hyperbolic idiomatic expression for being excessively rich. Since God is a spirit and technically has no need for money, it is a senseless concept. *More Money than God* is the primary title of at least two books. In 2003, Steven Z. Leder published a book by this title with a subtitle of *Living a Rich Life without Losing Your Soul*. Then a financial book by Sebastian Mallaby with this title, published in 2010, was subtitled, *Hedge Funds and the Making of the New Elite*.

But the saying was around long before this. *Worlds of IF*, a science fiction magazine, in January, 1954 carried this citation on page 14, in chapter two of *Malice in Wonderland*, a short novel by Evan Miller:

> "Genius! You're going to be a millionaire... You're going to have **more money than God**."

But 'Richer than God' was much earlier appearing in print. The phrase was used in 1904 in *The Great Gospel*: an address to theological students by Simon Peter Long:

> "...would imagine some people are a great deal **richer than God** is. They have bread to throw away."

Riding high

This idiom often means feeling immensely euphoric, possibly exhibiting an egotistical attitude. It may also apply to such feelings experienced from the effects of drugs. Sometimes it is used to mean enjoying great success, which was the first figurative meaning. The earliest citations of 'riding high' date as far back as the 18th century, many poetical, and refer to heavenly bodies, and later, birds, then ships riding high on waves; giving us a glimpse of how the metaphor developed. The earliest figurative reference comes on Saturday, February 28, 1846 in *Chambers' Edinburgh Journal* in the feature, 'Cromwell in Scotland:'

> "It is touching to hear these moans from the spirit of a man who to the world appeared as **riding high** in a position of great glory."

Riding off into the sunset

This dated pop-culture cliché is derived from the American Western literature and films most popular from the 1920s through the 1970s. In such stories, a hero or heroes came into a small western town in which there were outlaws whom the locals were sorely unequipped to handle. After the heroes captured or killed the villains, they would ride toward they west, disappearing into the sunset; thus the expression came to typify a job well done and the end of the story. Though the term was mostly viewed in movies, rather than printed, an example in print comes from the children's classic, *Seven Day Magic* by Edward Eager, 1962, page 172:

> "And mounting the giant's horse he **rode off into the sunset**."

Riding shotgun^

This term has been used figuratively since at least the mid-20th century to describe sitting in a moving automobile next to the window on the passenger's side. It is derived from the person sitting next to the driver on a stagecoach; then called the 'shotgun messenger,' who watched out for would-be robbers. In spite of the claim on the most used online encyclopedia, which quoted another source, saying that the phrase was 'not coined until 1919, then appeared in print later,' it was first printed in 1905 by Alfred Henry Lewis in *The Sunset Trail,* page 349:

> "Wyatt and Morgan Earp were in the service of the Express Company. They went often as guards — '**riding shotgun**,' it was called — when the stage bore unusual treasure."

Riff-raff

This came into the Old English from the Medieval French words *rifle et rafle*, as 'riff and raff,' then meaning one and all, every bit or scrap. It initially appeared in 1338 in *Manning's Chronicle of English.* It first began to be used of all common people who had no social standing. Then it was abbreviated to riff-raff, and was included in *Gregory's Chronicle of London* in about 1470. It was several decades, at least, before it was used only of the very lowest of humanity. By the early 17th century it was clear in British literature that the meaning had been degraded, as we see in the Roman Catholic publication, *The Overthrow of the Protestants Pulpit-Babels*, by John Floyd, 1612, page 322, 323:

> "The state being so full and swelling as they cannot stand one by another, but find away the **riffraff** and rascality of the Land to be the converters of Nations, seeing some must goe, and Ministers being better provided will not goe."

Right back at ya! (you)

This 21st century expression means 'the same to you!' and can be either in a positive or negative connotation depending upon circumstances and tone of voice. The earliest verifiable reference available in print is in *Trina Wants to be a Duck* by 'C Card,' 2007, page 18:

> "Pleased by her straightforward ability to share, Trina also found it refreshing to be so honest.
> "Fred laughed, 'Trina, you slay me.' Nice payoff, he thought.
> "Interesting. Fred didn't take her seriously. Trina also laughed, '**Right back at ya**, Freddy.'"

Right on the money

This means exactly right, correct, and now has nothing to do with money in definition. There are various thoughts as to how the saying came to be, but it likely was something to do with money. One plausible theory is that surveyors hammered steel rods, called benchmarks, into the ground at known points on a piece of property, all at a set height. When the rods tarnished and the tops were difficult to view in a surveyor's transit, at the time a new survey was made, a shiny coin would be placed on top of each rod in order to make the survey easier to run. When the transit and the coins were sitting in proper level position, they were 'right on the money.' Another one to consider is the claim that it is connected with 'right on target,' and that in a prize competition for archers a coin was would placed at the center of a target, and anyone who hit it was 'right on the money.'

Use of this saying in print, however, is fairly recent, compared to many others. The earliest verifiable reference is from *Boy's Life*, September 1943, in 'Don't Look at the Log Books,' a story by J. Marquis Irwin, page 9:

> "The speck became a tiny yellow airplane pointed at the ground. Now it was a black speck. Now it was a tiny yellow plane. Now a speck. Probably **right on the money**. Nice spin."

The context indicates that the expression was known at the time, but gives no clue to its origin. But strangely enough, the citations throughout the 1950s are all in regard to flying. A similar expression is 'hit the nail on the head' (see original volume).

Right smart

This idiom is used in New England, the lower Midwest and the Southern United States, most frequently in the Appalachian Region of the Southeast, usually to mean "a considerable amount." *The Encyclopedia Britannica,* Volume 1, 1896 lists it in Americanisms on page 95 with a variant of this, meaning 'fairly intelligent:'

> "**Right smart** is a pet Southern phrase, where someone often hears of a 'right smart' lawyer or a 'right smart' preacher."

However, the *Indiana Quarterly Magazine of History, Fourth Quarter*, 1905, under 'Folk Speech in Indiana,' by Paul L. Hawthorne and O.G.S., talks about the variance of the dialects and phrases in the Northern part of the state compared to South Indiana. It offers the following which 'nails' the most common usage, attributing it Southern Indiana residents migrating there from the South:

> "The expression 'right smart' in a sentence: 'He has a **right smart** chance of corn,' is an illustration of the dissimilarity."

But the saying is much older, of course. The earliest printed reference known is from the poem, *Epigram on Mr. Drummond* in *Poems by Allan Ramsey, Volume II* on page 244, first published in Edinburgh in May, 1728:

> "Mov'd back a piece, -- his bow he drew
> Fast throw my breast his arrow flew
> That done, as if he'd found a nest,
> He leugh, and with unfonsy jest,
> Cry'd, " Nibour, I'm right blyth in mind,
> That in good tift my bow I find:
> Did not my arrow flie **right smart**?
> Ye'll find it sticking in your heart."

Many Appalachian residents trace their ancestry to Scotland and Northern Ireland, thus making clear its earlier origin in Scotland.

Ring fenced[2]

This British idiom derived from the centuries old practice of building a fence completely around a piece of property to protect its ownership. It refers, figuratively, to money intended for a particular purpose, which is not to be used for anything else. A synonym would be 'earmark(ed)' (see in first volume). It has been used in this connotation since the 1980s. Prior to that, since the 1930s, it had a more general use for anything being protected. The earliest citation of the phrase is from Great Britain's Parliament document, *An Act for Dividing and Inclosing the Open Fields and Commonable Places*... 1767,

> "Sum of Ten Pounds, towards the Expences of **ring-fencing** their respective Allotments in lieu-of Tythes, within One Month after the fame shall be so fenced."

In *The Mystery of Sacrifice, A Meditation on the Liturgy*, by Evelyn Underhill, 1938, in Chapter One, we have an early figurative example in which 'persons' are portrayed as 'ringfenced:'

> "And at once we are reminded that, moving about the visible world as **ringfenced** persons, jealously guarding the real secret of our hearts, at another level of being we are transparent spirits;..."

Rock one's world

The common usage of this idiom is to make a person's life substantially better. The earliest verifiable reference in print is from *The Magic Journey: A Novel* by John Nichols, 1978, page 248, when it seemed to have a variant meaning:

> "If only to use you to satisfy those base and beautiful needs that have always **rocked my world**, keeping me off-balance."

By the 1990s most reference carried the current connotation, as in the example from *Billboard*, May 30, 1998, in 'First Time,' in the comments by Brent Maher on page 43:

> "I'd written for Ike and Tina Turner titled 'work on Me.' Hearing her voice come through that little speaker **rocked my world**, to say the least, what a buzz."

Roll off the tongue

This refers to words or thoughts expressed in speech which come easily and fluently and are appealing to others. The earliest citation to 'rolling off a person's tongue' is *The History of Sir William Harrington*, Volume I, Second Edition, by Thomas Hull, published in London in 1772, page 226:

> "I thought before I spoke (a rare occurrence for me) and catching the word upon the tip of my **tongue** before it **rolled off**, swallowed it immediately, constituting in its room-determined to do an injury to a poor creature who never offended you."

In the early 19th century the expression became commonplace with every bit of its current feeling, as seen in this citation form *Travels Through the South of France and in the Interior Provinces of Provence and Languedoc*, by Ninian Pinkney, 1809, page 22:

> "She rose from an English piano as I entered, whilst her brother introduced me with a preamble, which, he **rolled off his tongue** in a moment."

Roll out the red carpet

This now is a common metaphor for any special efforts made in the interest of hospitality. Anciently this practice was thought to be reserved for 'gods,' but came to be used for royalty, heads of state and visiting dignitaries, and recently for celebrity events. The earliest mention of walking on a red surface is found in

Agamemnon a play penned by Aeschylus in 458 BCE. When the progenitor returns from Troy, his vengeful wife provides a 'crimson path' for him to trod upon:

> "Now my beloved, step down from your chariot, and let not your foot, my lord, touch the Earth. Servants, let there be spread before the house he never expected to see, where Justice leads him in, a **crimson path**."

Agamemnon, knowing that only gods would then be granted this privilege, smelled a rat, and answered:

> "I am a mortal, a man; I cannot trample upon these tinted splendors without fear thrown in my path."

According to Robert McAllister in *Georgetown's North Island: A History*, (South Carolina), 2015, page 33:

> "In 1819, President James Monroe visited Arcadia Plantation on the Waccamaw River**...** A **red carpet** was spread from the barge landing to the front entrance of the house..."

In *Qanoon-e-Islam or the Customs of the Moosulmans of India*, by Jaffur Shurref published in London in 1832, in the traditional wedding ceremony we see that red carpets were used for all brides, page 97:

> "After that having put some *mulleeda* and *pan-sooparee* into the laps of the ladies, spread a red handkerchief| before her on a **red carpet**, and singing, at the same time, perform *chowk bhurna* thereon, *i. e.* they place a quantity of unboiled rice on it in the form of a hollow square, forming various devices with the rice within it."

Roll with the punches

This idiom means to be able to adjust properly to difficult situations in life. It was derived from a boxer who moves his body away from his opponent's blows in order to lessen the impact. The earliest verifiable figurative example in print is from *Changing Times-Kiplinger's Personal Finance*, August, 1955, in 'Whoa, Take it Easy! You'll Do Better, Live Longer,' page 9:

> "Everyone must **roll with the punches**, particularly in these four most difficult periods of life: Adolescence, when new feelings, new knowledge and new problems crowd in so rapidly. The beginning of the work period, when the first real grasp ..."

roof would cave in if I ever went to church, The

It means that something bad would surely happen because it would be such a rare event. According to *The Mythologizing of Mark Twain* by Sara Davis, 1984, page 65, the saying was used by Twain, who might have coined it.

> "Mark Twain asserted that when he delivered one of his earliest comic lectures, to raise funds for a new **roof** on the Presbyterian church in Carson City in 1864, 'everybody said that **the roof would cave** in…and mash the congregation, because I was one of those sinful newspapermen.'"

Twain could have been inspired by earlier stories like the incident later described in an article in *Church Building Quarterly from the Church Building Society, American Congregational Union*, January, 1901, page 94, when rural church buildings had sod roofs:

> **"Venango, Nebraska**
>
> "This is a typical frontier farming town, 'far out upon the prairie.' In the sod tabernacle, which was the best they could do build for themselves, the audience was small. They were afraid **the roof would cave in** and the building did tumble to pieces soon after the dedication of the new church."

Rotten to the core^+

Something which is rotten is totally ruined and not fit for consumption. This is a figurative expression meaning that something or someone is thoroughly and fundamentally bad; for a person it indicates moral corruption. According to a popular online source, it was first recorded in 1804. It was actually around quite a bit earlier, as it appeared in *An Address from John Zephaniah Holwell, Esq.: to Luke Stanton, Esq.*, 1767, on page 26:

> "…this government, the more is verified your own, just observafion, at your first knowledge of it, that is **rotten to the core**, what can be expected from a system rotten to the very heart."

Rough-and-tumble

This old expression now may refer to anything which ignores the common rules and is fiercely competitive. It is sometimes used to describe boisterous political methods. It was originally a disorderly, unrestricted method of fighting. The earliest verifiable citation is from the time period in which this type of fighting was popular in the U.S. *Travels in America performed in the year 1806 for the purpose of Exploring the Rivers Allegheny, Monongahela, Ohio and Mississippi* by Thomas Ashe, Volume I, 1808, page 225 offers an early view of the sport:

> "A ring was formed, and the mob demanded whether they proposed to fight fair, or to **rough and tumble**. The latter mode was preferred. Perhaps you do not exactly understand the distinction, of these terms. Fight fair, however, is much in the English manner; and here, as there, any thing foul requires interference; but when parties choose to **rough and tumble**, neither the populace nor individuals are to intermeddle or hinder either combatant from tearing or rending the other on the ground, or any other situation."

Rub elbows or **shoulders with**

Both figures of speech refer to mingling or socializing with someone, usually a certain class or group of people, with the illusion of being in close touch with them, though not implying actual physical contact ('shoulders' being more prevalent in Britain). Both idioms date to the same time frame, the 1820s. The earliest verifiable citation of 'elbows' is from 1822, but a more properly figurative one comes in 1825, in *Narrative of a Journey into Khorasan* by James B. Frasier, page 181:

> "The consequences of thus mingling with every common act that which should be held sacred and mysterious, nor approached without a shrinking awe; this meeting and **rubbing shoulders with** the holiest things, in the common paths of life, ..."

That same year, Thomas Carlyle used the 'elbows' version in *The Life of Frederich Schiller,* page 229:

> "Towards midnight of the above-said day, when the Castle of Solitude, with all its surroundings, was beaming in full splendour of illumination, there rolled past, almost **rubbing elbows with** it, the humble Schiller Vehicle from Stuttgart, which bore the fugitive Poet with his true Friend on their way."

Rub someone's nose in something

This idiom refers to drawing someone's attention to a painful fact and unduly harassing him or her about it. It alludes to the practice used in housebreaking pets. The earliest known citation is from *Time Must Have a Stop* by Aldous Huxley, 1944, page 115:

> "The prospect of being treated as a baby in front of Mrs. Thwale was particularly distasteful and humiliating. Frowning to himself, he **rubbed his nose in** perplexed uncertainty."

Rule with an iron fist

This means to rule very sternly, requiring absolute control. It is often used to describe unconscionable management techniques. It goes back to monarchies described in the 19th century. The earliest known citation is from *The Christian Review*, July, 1860, in 'Evil Made Subservience to Good:'

> "The **iron fist** of monarchy has given settledness and stability to government; and the buccaneering commerce of free cities, representing freedom."

Rules are made to be broken^

This proverbial statement is made in defense of not honoring rules which are taken for granted by most people under certain circumstances. In spite of the online claim of a popular answer forum that it was first in print in 1953, it appeared in *The Speaker*, September 10, 1892 in 'Among the Mendips' by Theodore Compton.

> "And in a graver sense, too, **rules were made to be broken**: by exuberance, by life, strength, individuality."

In fact there were *many others* far ahead of 1953, like this one from Theodore Howard Somervell in his classic autobiographical book, *After Everest: The Experiences of a Mountaineer and Medical Missionary,* 1936:

> "In one respect I was a complete renegade. I firmly and conscientiously held that **rules were made to be broken**. St. Paul, if I understand him aright, would agree with me. The strength of sin is the law."

Run for one's money, A

The origin of this common expression came from horse racing. When a horse was withdrawn from a race after bets were placed, those investors did not get a run for their money. Figuratively giving someone a run for their money means 'running a good race,' competing strongly in a competition or trying one's best to meet all challenges and accomplish the task at hand, The earliest verifiable figurative example in print is from *The Albany Law Journal* (New York),

December 17, 1898, in 'Evidence of the Accused,' here in quotes indicating that it was in use, but likely had been coined recently:

> "Then there are those, mostly of the junior bar, who, for interested or merely sporting reasons, prefer that a guilty prisoner should 'have **a run for his money**,'"

Run into someone

This common idiom refers to meeting someone you know when you do not expect to. The expression is used as early as 1800 for meeteing someone on a run. Figurative examples started appearing in print about 100 years later. The earliest verifiable example is in *Van Cleve*, a novel by American author, Mary S. Watts, 1913, page 212:

> "As they were hurrying over the bridge, they **ran into** some men and boys who wildly reported that there had been a battle; there had been fighting at Santiago, and our boys had whipped, of course. In the town the streets were full of hurrahing ..."

Run one's mouth

This means talk inappropriately; talk too much with nothing of any real consequence to say. It came into American slang in the mid-20th century. The earliest verifiable citation is from *Ebony*, September, 1960, in 'The Soul of Ray Charles,' page 106:

> "There are about four basic things: love, somebody **running his mouth** too much, having fun, and jobs are hard to get."

Run out of gas

This idiom refers to losing the energy or interest to continue with an activity. It came into use in this regard late in the 20th century. Exact origin is unknown but an early example is found in *The Red Stockings of Cincinnati: Base Ball's First All-Professional Team* by Stephen D. Guschov, 1998, page 115:

> "By the eighth inning, Harry's hardballers had pushed out to a 25–21 lead, and it appeared that the combative Athletics had **run out of gas** just short of the finish line as they came to bat that inning."

Run out of steam^

This is a similar expression to 'run out of gas,' referring to a person's energy, but much older, as steam-powered engines predated gasoline. Contrary to the claim of a popular online phrase origin site which lists 1898 as the earliest reference found in print, it appeared in a delightlul, largely poetical, book in 1836 titled *The Harmonies of Creation; Or, The Music of the Morning Stars* by American professor and tutor, John C. Newman, in 'An Address to the Ladies and Gentlemen of Baltimore,' delivered on May 28, 1836:

"I am sure to say to myself, 'Quick promisers are generally very slow performers'—Poor man, you will surely **run out of steam**!"

Run ragged

This is applied to a person, and means 'very busy,' overworked, possibly to the point of exhaustion. The word ragged has been used in English since about 1300, in refference to cloth, but its roots go back to the Old Norse word *raggadr,* and Old English *raggig*, meaning shaggy. In the 18th century, it was common to say that children were allowed to 'run ragged in the streets,' meaning that they wore tattered clothing. Gradually the meaning evolved going into the 20th century. In *Illustrated World*, October, 1918, in 'Smashing Machine Gun Nests' by E.T. Bronsdon we find a different, figurative connotation, here in quotes:

> "The story of how one German general was **run 'ragged'** and captured by a 'Whippet' in the recent Picardy drive has been told as proof of the agility of these new and tiny tanks."

Runs like a top

This simile is based on the smooth, balanced rhythm of a spinning top. It is used regarding an engine or machine which operates very efficiently. The earliest known printed reference is from *The Country Gentleman Magazine*, 21 March 1821, in 'Farm Mill' by S. Edwards Todd:

> "I then took the mill to a neighbor's barn, who has one of R. H. Pease's Excelsior two-horse railway powers, which **runs like a top**. His horses will weigh about ten hundred pounds each."

S

Sacrificial lamb

As a metaphor, this refers to someone or something that is given to authorities for the purpose of being harmed or destroyed for the common good. It is derived from the Old Testament religious practice of sacrificing a lamb which is a highly valued possession. *Exodus 12:5* states the requirements under the Law for a sacrificial lamb:

> "Your **lamb** shall be without blemish, a male a year old. You may take it from the sheep or from the goats," *(English Standard Version*)

In Christianity, Jesus is pictured as the final sacrificial lamb, as we see in *I Peter 1:19, NIV:*

> "but with the precious blood of Christ, a **lamb** without blemish or defect."

In politics, this term 'sacrificial lamb candidate' is used of a candidate who is used to contest an election with the foreknowledge that he or she has almost no chance of winning. This meaning is historically recent, and a good example is found in Robert Hardin's 2007 novel, *Paradise Marred*:

> "They have you losing less than five points from your almost thirty point lead over the **sacrificial lamb** candidate the Republicans put up against you."

Saddle with+

This metaphoric term means giving someone a burdensome task or indebtedness; something difficult to deal with. Saddling a horse, or other 'beast of burden,' is putting something on its back. The word saddle came into Old English before 900 C.E. as *sadol,* and derived from Old Norse *sothul* and Old High German *satul*. Figurative usage use of *in the saddle* (in an active position of management) is attested from the 1650s. This particular phrase was in use by the first half of the 1800s. It was already known before it appeared twice in *Biography of Edmond Pendleton Gaines* by 'A Friend' published in 1844 The first citation was on page 6:

> "It is but truth to say, that had General Gaines stipulations with the Sac and Fox chiefs been attended to properly, the country never would have been **saddled with** the expenses of the Black Hawk War."

Sakes alive!^+

Forms of this old expression, including, 'Goodness gracious sakes alive,' were most popular in the American South, according to a popular online source, from the 1930s through the 1950s. It is a minced oath, or euphemism, for 'For God's sake!' Another is 'Lands sake!' for Lord's sake. But it actually goes back much further. In *The Poor White: or, The Rebel Conscript*, a story set in the Antebellum South by Emily Clemens Pearson, 1864, it appears seven times; the first being on page 9:

> "Sakes alive! screamed Mrs. Dean. The goat is commin' all alone, for all the world!"

In this book, slavery is mentioned contemptuously. It seems likely that the saying began with slaves. *The Veteran of 1812* by American playwright T. Trask Woodward written about life on a Western Virginia plantation, published in New York in 1883, it is used 12 times, beginning with a quotation in Act I, Scene i, in which one slave is speaking to another. Here it appears twice:

> "**Sakes alive**! What on airth be you darkeys doing? **Sakes alive**! Playing kerds?

Same difference

This oxymoron is a common idiom used to express the speaker's belief that two entities are escentially the same while appearing different. It has been compared to a Hebrew expression, 'mah nishtana,' a ritual question in the Seder, literally 'what differentiates?' but the meaning is not really the same. The saying has been used in English since the early 20th century, as in this earliest available citation in *The Saturday Evening Post*, August 8, 1914, in a Velvet Tobacco ad on page 41:

> "It's the **same difference** between taking a man to dinner at a hotel, and taking him home to supper with your family."

Same old, same old

This means that what is going on is the same thing as usual; nothing has changed. There are two theories as to how this saying came to be. The first one is that it was taken from Pidgin English spoken in the Japan and Korea before and during the Korean War. American soldiers related stories that the locals said samo, samo, referring to sameness. In fact, this expression greatly predated the 20th century. In *A Collection of Voyages: in Four Volumes: Volume 1: A New Voyage Round the World* by William Dapler, published in London in 1729, on page 359, he wrote:

> "When they came to their Houses they would always be praising the *English,* as declaring that the *English* and *Mindanaians* were all one. This they exprest by putting their two fore-fingers close together, and saying that the *English* and *Mindanaians* were ***samo, samo***, that is, *all one*."

Certainly, our saying could have evolved from this. The other theory is that it derived from 'same old thing.'

Save face^

This is a metaphor meaning taking action to salvage one's reputation and keep or regain the respect of others (see first volume for 'losing face'). In spite of a major online phrase origin source which states the earliest citation being in 1899, it was actually cited five years earlier in *Chinese Characteristics* by Arthur H. Smith, Fourth Edition, 1894, page 18:

> "To be accused of a fault is to 'lose face,' and the fact must be denied, no matter what the evidence, in order to **save face**."

This also has an earlier printing of 'lose face' than in the earlier volume of this book, which was listed as 'an early example,' not the earliest citation.

Save one's bacon[2]

This popular British expression means to save someone's life or reccue someone from serious injury. The saying goes back to Medieval England when 'bacon' meant meat of any kind, and came also to refer to the human body. It was used that way as early as the mid-17th century, as seen in *The Works of Mr. Francis Rabelais, doctor in physick, Volume II,* published in 1653, pages 298 and 299:

> "There is another sort, that is your Jail-birds, who having done some rogue's Trick, or other heinous Villany, and being sought up and down to be truss'd up, and being made to ride the Two or Three-legg'd Mare, that groans for them, warily scower off, and come here to **save their Bacon**; Because all these sorts of Birds are here provided for, and grow in an instant as fat as Hogs, tho' they came as lean as Rakes; For having the Benefit of the Clergy, they are as safe as Thieves in a Mill, within this Sanctuary."

This being the earliest known example in print could be the coining, because it called the 'jail-birds' 'birds' and compared them to fat hogs.

Sawmill gravy

Folk etymology tells the story of numerous sawmills which sprang up in the early years of America, at which lumberjacks would be served gravy at breakfast made from corn meal. It is said that the lumberjacks would accuse the cooks of putting sawdust in the gravy because of its course consistency. There seems to be no evidence of this. Sometimes it was also called sawmill gravy when it was made with sausage. It could certainly be possible that a lot of it was comnsumed by lumberjacks, but it is likely because of the coarse consistency that it became known as sawmill gravy. Sawmill gravy was around long before this, but the earliest available use of the term in print was in October, 1971 when *Field and Stream* in 'Cottontail Hunting, Eastern Style,' on page 91:

> "Maynard's wife Em did the cooking and her cornbread with **sawmill gravy** would win a blue ribbon at any county fair, even without the thick strips of lean bacon, the sunny-side-up eggs and coffee with cream right from the cow."

Scads

This is an American term meaning large amounts, and may be used of anything. It came into use in the mid-19th century. It could have been derived from a fish called 'Scads' which were very abundant around Great Britian at the time. The earliest known printed reference to this use, though, is in *The Overton Monthly,* August, 1869 in 'South-western Slang,' pointing to it as a regional coloquiasm:

> "A Texan never has a great quantity of any thing, but he has **'scads'** of it, or 'oodles,'…"

Scapegoat

A scapegoat is someone who takes the fall for a crime, or for the mistakes of someone else, who is not really to blame at all. The word was first recorded in English in 1611 in the *King James Version of the Bible in Leviticus 16: 8* as seen here (1612 printing); then repeated twice in verse 10:

> "8 And Aaron shall cast lottes upon the two Goates: one lot for the LORD, and the other lot for the **Scape goat**."

Under Mosaic Law, a scapegoat (from the Hebrew *Azazel*, meaning absolute removal) was sent out into the desert as a symbol of removing the sins of the people on the Day of Atonement. In Tyndale's 1530 translation it had been rendered 'escape goat.'

Scared of one's own shadow (See: **Afraid of one's own shadow**)

Scaredy-cat (See: **Fraidy-cat**)+

Schooners and middies[3]

In Australia, as in most of the world other than America, liquids are measured in liters, and when it comes to beer, the size of the drink in milliliters (mLs). A schooner is 425 milliliters (less than a pint, but a huge container), while a middie is 285 mL. But it is also available most places in a glass which is 200 mL. *The Literary Digest* published by Funk and Wagnalls in New York City on July 30, 1892, had this reference to 'a schooner of beer' in 'Sociological, Dr. Rainsford on the Drink Question' by the Rev. John Tunis, under the name of Edward F. Hale:

> "They would say that it is a bad education for a young man to drink intoxicants; that after a man has drunk a **schooner of beer** or a glass of wine, he is less competent to judge it he needs a second **schooner** or a second glass; that the experience of seventy years has taught them that the only safe ground, as a matter of education, is total abstinence…"

Screamer – Two-pot screamer[3]

In Aussie jargon, screamer has two possible meanings. In 'Australian Rules football' (a form of soccer) it is a spectacular overhead mark. In the game the ball may be moved by running, kicking or handballing. A 'mark' is when the ball is caught after being kicked 'more than 15 metres' (meters), allowing the catcher to kick the ball (not usual at this point). A 'screamer' is a mark that results from an especially high leap for the ball. This term was initially recorded in 1953, according to *Meanings and Origins of Australian Words* at the Australian National Dictionary Center. The in 1959, a second use appeared in print. That's where two-pot screamer comes in, which has to do with someone with a low tolerance of alcohol. Though 'two-pot' is most common, also used are two-middy screamers and two schooner screamers (see above). The following was recorded in *The Bulletin,* a Sydney newspaper, 3 June 1972:

> "Sefton said she'd become a **two middy screamer**. He said when she had a few drinks she began to shout and tried to dominate the conversation."

Seal the deal

In ancient times, heads of governments put wax on letters, legal documents and scrolls of parchment upon which a heraldic design, sometimes a ring was pressed, imprinting their legal seal as evidence of authenticity. The practice of using family seals dipped in ink was used early in the Middle Ages in dealings among nobles because a lot of individuals could not read or write. When a contract was so imprinted a deal was 'sealed' between two parties. Since the 1940s, 'sealing a deal' means getting the required signatures on an application or any legal document, indicating acceptance by both parties involved. Who first started using the term is uncertain, but the earliest available citation is from *Billboard*, April 15, 1944, on page 67, in an article titled 'Pubs Edging into Disk and Bank Fields:'

> "They also believe that to clinch their hold on music exploitation they'll have to go whole-hog and **seal the deal** with records."

Seeing red

This means being very angry. The color red has long been associated with fire, heat, and heated emotions, as well as blood and communism. Some have associated this saying with the red rag used in bullfights, to distract the bull (see: Like a red rag to a bull for the explanation of this). The term has been used like this since early in the 20th century. The first citation is from *The History of Sir Richard Calmady* by Lucas Malet (pseudonym for Mary Sty. Leger Harrison), 1901:

> "Happily violence is shortlived, only for a very little while do even the very gentlest persons 'see red'."

An article in the March-April, 1914 issue of the Audubon Society's *Bird Lore Magazine,* 'Notes from Field and Study' may hold the clues as to how it actually came to be used like this.

> "While the male members of a sextette were out for a Christmas Census, a few days after December 25, one of them, Dr. T.G. Haggerty, observed a flutter of red in some willows ten rods ahead of us. The doctor became excited at the sight of the unusual bird, and gave vent to a series of wild yells. His companions, somewhat shocked at the doctor's antics, remarked that **'seeing red'** was common experience with some folk, but for a man of his habits was rather strange. They spoke to him soothingly and cautioned him against the dangers of apoplexy from such uncontrolled excitement."

The story continues when another doctor 'saw red' and had the same uncontrolled excitement. In each of the above cases 'see red' and 'seeing red' were in quotes, indicating a recent coining.

In 1916s *Rhymes with a Red Cross Man* by Robert William Service, in a poem titled 'Wounded,' on page 158, it is clear that the meaning included anger:

> "Your sleeve is dripping blood; you're **seeing red**;
> You're battle-mad; your turn is coming now.
> See! There's the jagged barbed wire straight ahead,
> And there's the trench — you'll get there anyhow."

The above and next instances do not have quotes, as the saying was becoming more commonplace. On April 1, 1922, *The Poster* in 'The Growing use of Poster Reds in Magazine Advertising' by Herbert Graham, on page 34, had this unmistakable statement:

> **"Seeing red** nowadays is not a question of getting unduly angered but of looking through the current magazines."

Seems to be a lot of that going around

This modern idiom is used about things, usually having a negative effect, which seem to be happening more frequently than in the past, but not sickness, of which it was a spinoff. The origin is unknown but the earliest example available in print of a close form is in the Australian publication, *AUUGN Magazine*, April, 1994, in 'An Update on UNIX-Related Standards Activities,' page 75:

> "The Vice Chair was also in absentia because of imminent fatherhood, of which there **seems to a lot going around** lately."

See the light of day

This very old expression refers to coming into existence, being made available or public. The earliest known citation is from *The Mythology and Fables of the Ancients*, by the Abbe Banier, 1739:

> "In the mean Time *Pluto* terrified, even in the Bottom of *Hell*, by the earthquakes in Sicily, occasioned by the Efforts which *Typbeus* used to shake off the cumbrous Load of Mount *Eryx*, under which he was buried, resolved to visit that Country, to see if there was not some Chasm made that penetrated even into his Kingdom, fearing that the affrighted Ghosts might **see the Light of Day,** and after having examined all narrowly, he stopped upon Mt. *Eryx*."

See you in the funny paper

This saying was an off way of saying goodbye, particularly from the 1920s through the end of World War II, but many kept using it longer. It was meant in the best light, and indicated that people's lives took quirky turns like characters in the comics. We each could be the subject of our own comic strip. 'Funny paper' was used for comics since the latter part of the 19th century. In *Harper's Weekly,* September 19, 1857, we find this, near some comical drawings:

> "Moreover, a man who expends four cents for a copy of a **funny paper** wastes an amount of money which, if judiciously expended, would provide him with a ...glass of Lager Beer…"

The earliest example of the actual phrase is from the August, 1920 edition of *Commercial Telegraph's Journal*:

> "So long, boys, **see you in the funny paper**. '30
> "J.N. HANNA"

Sell down the river

This means to betray, disappoint or hurt someone who trusted you. It derived from slave trading in the Southern U.S. prior to the Civil War. Selling a slave down the Mississippi River was typically a method of getting rid of one who was seen as rebellious, thus uprooting the person and separating families, and was a great betrayal to all of the family members. The more Southern plantations were noted for harsher treatment of slaves. The earliest known reference to the phrase in print is from *The Ohio Repository* (later *The Canton Repository*) in May, 1837:

> "One man, in Franklin County has lately realized thirty thousand dollars, in a speculation on slaves, which he bought in Virginia, and **sold down the river**."

After this, numerous other citations appeared in books and periodicals about selling slaves down the river. Mark Twain showed a strong understanding of the meaning of such a practice in *Pudd'nhead Wilson*, first serialized in *The Century Magazine* in 1894:

> "'If at the end of that time you have not confessed, I will not only **sell** all four of you, but— I will **sell** you **Down THE RIVER**!' It was equivalent to condemning them to hell! No Missouri negro doubted this."

It wasn't long before the saying was being used figuratively, as in this early example from *Small Bachelor* by P.G. Wodenhouse, published in both the U.K. and U.S. in 1927:

> "When Sigsbee Waddington married for the second time, he to all intents and purposes **sold himself down the river**."

Send someone up the river

In the 19th century, a person who was convicted of a very serious crime in New York City was sent up the Hudson River to Ossining, to the infamous 'Sing Sing prison.' This separated the hardened criminals from the run of the mill (see in first volume) petty thieves and pick pockets. Eventually this term began to apply to anyone sent to maximum security prisons. The earliest available reference in print is from *The New York Supplement*, Volume 46, 1897, in the case of Dunn et el v. Wehle, Supreme Court, Appellate Term, July 29, 1897:

> "...he told the plaintiff that 'if he recovered a judgment he must be very careful because he had sworn in supplemental proceedings he had nothing, and they might examine him again, and he must be very careful, or they might **send him up the river**.'"

A citation in quotes is found in *Popular Science*, August, 1932, page 16, in 'New Prisons are Proof Against Riot and Outbreak,' indicating that the saying had become a colloquialism:

> "Pallister, once a mason, had been **'sent up the river'** before on a burglary charge and at that time he had actually helped in the construction of the death house in which he was confined."

Set one's teeth on edge (See: **On edge**)

Set the wheels in motion / Set the wheels turning+

This figurative term refers to doing something essential to begin a process. It has been in use since the 19th century. I. E. Smith used it in *A Tariff Talk among Working Men* in 1887:

> "A protective tariff went into effect and that **set the wheels in motion** again."

Shake (or **quake) in one's boots** (or **shoes)^**

This means to tremble with apprehension or fear. Contrary to a popular online dictionary which sets the first usage at *late* 1800s, the earliest version of this appeared in *The Literary Panorama,* Volume XIV published in London in 1813 in the poem Address, on page 1004;

> "Tremble no more, he's **shaking in his shoes**.
> At every blast that brings us More good News."

Shameless hussy

A hussy is defined as an impudent, brazen of immoral woman, and has been in English since 1520. Oddly enough, it derived from the Middle English *huswif* from which housewife came. In 1594, In *The Historie of Ane Nobil and Walieand Sqviel, William Meldrum* by Sir David Lyndesay of the Mont had the following on page 531:

> "A nasty **hussy** puts stale into the mashing- and the ale burns the brains."

Gradually, the definition of hussy was enlarged to apply to any girl, and had lost most of the derogatory connotation by the mid-18th century without prefacing it with an unmistakable nasty word. The earliest use of 'shameless' with it to emphasize the original meaning of the term appeared in 1791 in *The Busy Body*, a Comedy play by Susannah Centlivere, Act V, Scene vii:

> "Hey-day! mighty fine! wife truly! mighty well! kissing, embracing — did ever any thing equal this? — Why, you **shameless hussy!** — But I won't condescend to waste a word upon you."

After this, hussy began to revert to mean an immoral woman, often with Centlivere's 'shameless' before it.

Sharp as a razor

Much like 'sharp as a tack' (see original volume), this means quick-witted or intelligent. The expression was used often in the 19th century to refer to blades and points, such as spears. The earliest figurative use was actually near-literal, as it was a story titled 'Autobiography of a Jack-knife' in *Atkinkin's Casket*, Gems of Literature, Wit and Sentiment; published in Philadelphia, March, 1831, in which a jack-knife personified was speaking:

> "...and lastly to what he called a 'leather whetstone,' until I was pronounced to be as **sharp as a razor**."

The first known citation in reference to a person is from Nelson Algren's 1942 novel, *Never Come Morning*, page 14; here about wit and agility:

> "'I'm **sharp as a razor** right now.' He leaned the broom against the counter and jab-jabbed for her with his right."

Sharpshooter^

A bit of folk etymology has attached itself to this term. The story has been often told that a group called Brendon's sharpshooters, during the American Civil War, who used Sharpe's rifles were originally called Sharpe's shooters, and changed their name to sharpshooters. Like so many old stories, this one has no truth to it. This term goes back much further, to Germanic Europe, at least the early 1700s, according to Civil War historian, Fred Ray. It comes from the German word Scharfschütz, which has the same meaning. A man whose nickname was 'Sharpshooter' published a book in 1829 which is now very rare, as seen in the excerpt from *A Catalogue of Manuscripts and Rare Books* published by Myers and Co. in London about 1900:

> "69 COLOURED CARICATURES A Collection of 87 Caricatures on the Catholic Question by Doyle, '**Sharpshooter**,' Dighton, AND OTHER FAMOUS CARICATURISTS. Published by McLean, 1829."

Shave and a haircut—two bits!

This harmonious chant and response are associated with a piece of music styled from a tune by Charles Hale written in 1899 titled *At a Darktown Cakewalk* (an event described in Volume 1 under 'Piece of Cake'). Shave and a Haircut—Bay Rum appears throughout this piece. An early recording of these seven notes are at both the beginning and the end of *On the 5:15* by Billy Murray in 1915. In 1939, two recordings were made of *Shave and a Haircut*. One was a folk melody by Rosalind Rosenthal and Herbert Halpert. Dan Shapiro, Lester Lee and Milton Berle released one titled *Shave and a Haircut—Shampoo.* But 'Two bits,' now archaic, meaning 25 cents, came later.

In the late 1970s the rhyme picked up great popularity with 'two bits.' It was used on the 1978 recording of *Babes in Toyland* and in *What's for Dinner* by James Schuyler, 1978:

> "Before Norris could answer, if that was his plan, the sun set, the dust vanished, and the doorbell sounded in the pattern of '**Shave and a haircut, two bits**.'"

All of this may have been due to the fact that in the late 1970s fast cars and car horns with programmed tunes were all the rage. One was the *Dukes of Hazard Dixie* horn, another featured '*Shave and a Haircut.'*

She'll be right, mate[3]

This is a common idiom in Australian and New Zealand culture that expresses the belief that no matter what is wrong, it will right itself in time. This philosophy is considered to be either an optimistic or an apathetic outlook. The word 'she' is used to mean anything and everything, including extreme hardships and everyday situations. The expression goes back to the 1960s. The earliest available citation is from *Flying Magazine*, August, 1966, page 93, in 'Aviation Down Under' by Gregory R. Copley:

> "Australians are now scratching their heads, for in aviation—as in everything else Down Under—they don't know whether to think British or American. Perhaps this is why people have adopted a relaxed '**She'll be right**, **mate'** attitude."

Another similar expression meaning basically the same is 'she's apples.'

She's got a bun in the oven

Having a bun in the oven *is* alluding to a baby in the womb. The idea is that it takes time for a bun to cook, and it must stay in the oven a while to be fully cooked. It has been around longer than it has been in our common lexicon. The earliest citation is in the World War II classic, *Cruel Sea*, by Nicholas Monsarrat, 1951:

> "'I bet you left **a bun in the oven**, both of you,' said Bennett thickly... Lockhart explained ... the reference to pregnancy."

By the late 20th century it was very commonly used as in *Charades* by 'Janette Turner Hospital,' page 179, 1988:

> "There! ... You can't **have a bun in the oven** at the Duke. Not proper, is it?"

Ship shape and Bristol fashion[2^]

This primarily British expression a few years back was reported to have derived from an ethnical slur related to the slave trade. Again, this was one that had no basis in fact. It was formed by combining two earlier phrases. In *The New World of English Words, Or, A General Dictionary,* 1663, there is a reference to the term, ship-shapen, already in use, which is the predecessor of ship shape:

> "Walereared, a Term in Navigation, not **ship-shapen,** or when a **ship** is built right up."

Bristol fashion was added in 1803. The first citation is found in *Travels of Four Years and a Half in the United States of America* by John Davis, page 427:

> "'My box of diamonds,' says I to the girl, 'his is neither ship-shape, nor ***Bristol*** **fashion**. It was this fashion that made the people at *Constantinople* turn *Turks*."

Davis had used the two as contrasting terms. Within a few years the saying had emerged as we know it today, as a nautical term, as we see in the September, 1816 issue of the *Prairie Farmer,* in an article titled, 'Household Affairs, Soap Making,' under 'Letters to the Editor:'

> "Now gentlemen, don't laugh at this, unless your own *ashdom* is all **ship-shape and Bristol fashion**;' and, Mr. Editor, don't think this is my experience —I have been more fortunate;..."

Shoot first and ask questions later

Figuratively, this means taking hasty action on a suspicious matter without fully investigating, thus resulting in serious consequences. The actual origin is hazy, but the earliest citation in print to this is actually not from a tale of the American West, but from *Bolshevik Propaganda: Hearings Before a Subcommittee of the Committee on the Judiciary United States Senate, Sixty-Fifth Congress,* 1919, page 929:

> "MR. HATZEL. It was practically murder and death to yourself if you opened your mouth against the Bolsheviki. There is no such thing as a trial there. They **shoot first and ask questions later**. If you open your mouth

against the Bolsheviki and tell something about them you are liable to be shot or arrested right away."

Two years later, however, in September, 1921, a Western story titled 'The Rider of Golden Bar' by William Patterson White appeared in *Everybody's Magazine* which used a reference to the idiom:

> "The punchers would be at the ranch-house in another sixty seconds, and if they should discover him with their bound and unconscious employer and two of his friends, they would **shoot first and ask questions later**."

Shoot off one's mouth

This refers to talking too much in a careless, brash or uncontrolled manner, with no thought of the consequences. The earliest known reference in print is from *The Locomotive Fireman's Monthly Magazine*, April, 1880, in the Editorial Correspondence, where it is obvious that the expression was already known at the time:

> "Another says: 'That Harry is always **shooting off his mouth**.' Well, does he talk sense? If so, you want a few more of that kind to make your meetings interesting and instructive."

Shoot oneself in the foot

This cliché refers to inadvertently making a situation worse for oneself. Though common usage didn't happen till the 1970s, the earliest known figurative use was 10 years earlier in *New Scientist*, November 23, 1961, in W. Holmes' light review of *Mankind in the Making: The Story of Human Evolution* (1959), a humorous book by William Howells, and appears to be from Howells' book:

> "He teaches us to be careful of loaded phrases like 'family tree,' 'ancestor,' and 'missing link:' 'Many a specialist has **shot himself in the foot** when he thought he was only cleaning a paragraph'."

Shoot through[3]

This is an Aussie and New Zealand idiom meaning rushing in and out of a place, particularly when trying to avoid having to do something. The origin is uncertain, but the earliest known actual citation is from *Pix*, an Australian pin-up magazine which was published in Sydney in September, 1947:

"**Shoot through**, escape, abscond."

Shop till you drop

This Americanism literally means buying things until a person is physically exhausted, and is sometimes used with the contraction 'til, rather than the alternative of till. It started as an advertising slogan in the early 1920's and has become cliché. Colloquially it means that you have shopped until you are tired of shopping. Actually, a very similar statement was made in the mid-19th century. In the January 1, 1852 edition of *Michigan Farmer*, published in Detroit, an article titled 'Young and Old England' contained the following statement on page 3:

> "I have been amazed at the ignorance of the shop keepers in London, and throughout England. You might go from shop to **shop till you drop** down, in the city of London, without being able to elicit information upon subjects with which every school boy in America is familiar."

The earliest reference known to the modern usage in found in *American Blacksmith and Motor Shop,* September, 1923, in 'Sam Thomas Plans for Christmas Business,' on page 52, in a negative connotation right after the concept had been introduced:

> "Well, how do you like this then? asked Sam picking up a second card. He read.— 'Don't **Shop 'till you Drop** — We have many Things for his Car.'"

Short change^

Literally meaning to give less than the correct amount of change in a business transaction, it has gained a figurative meaning of being dishonest or cheating in any dealings with other people. According to the leading online dictionary, use of this began in the 1890s. However, *Reports of All the Cases Decided by All the Superior Courts,* London, 1864, contained this clear example on page 488:

> "Charles Mills, One of deft.'s cashiers, said: — Pit. had applied to me many times on account of his alleging I had given him **short change**. He has done so fifty times. I and my brother cashier had conversations about this, and I communicated with my master, the deft."

Shotgun wedding^

Though originally an American colloquialism, this idiom is used all over the English-speaking world, and it well understood to be a nuptial arranged by the bride's parents to avoid embarrassment of an unplanned pregnancy. The major online dictionary states origin at 1925 to 1930. Another cites mid-1900s as the genesis of the colloquialism. Actually, it was coined much earlier. In *The Southwest Reporter,* Volume 75, July 8—October 7, 1903, the earliest recorded citation in the case of *State v Kennedy*, indicated that it was already known and in use:

> "He said, pointing to the article, 'That was a **shotgun wedding**, and you will read something a good deal worse than that.'"

Shot of whiskey^

Again folk etymology strikes a blow at truth. Various sources picked up a tale that this term came from cowboys in the old American West paying for drinks with bullets. The word from which shot, with relation to whisky, derives, is an Old Scandinavian word, which came into Old English as *scéotan*, meaning to pay or contribute, later spelled *scot*. This had to do with a tax or penalty, from which we got 'scot free,' referring to not having to pay the tax (see first volume). Because *scot* was pronounced 'shot' rather than with the sk sound in the 17th century, it became associated with paying entertainment expenses, including drinks, called paying shot. Over time the serving of whisky began to be called a shot. Charles Dickens' *All the Year Round Magazine*, September 13, 1862, carried this citation in 'Picture Words' on page 14:

> "**Paying** scot and lot was **paying** what you were expected to **pay** and allotted to **pay**. **Shot**-free is still often pronounced scot-free, meaning payment free."

It was well into the 20th century before whisky was being measured by 'shots.' *The New York Court of Appeals, Records and Briefs*, 1943, page 17-18 has this citation, showing the modern usage:

> "I, at this time, was trying to get into the room in which I had bought the **shot of whisky**."

Shoulda, coulda, woulda (See: **Coulda, shoulda, woulda**)

Show a clean pair of heels[3]

This figurative, nearly antiquated, mainly British expression means to make a quick escape, or go faster than someone else. Basically, it means to run away from someone at alarming speed. It derived from the bloody 'sport' of cockfighting. Often in ancient times, metal spurs were attached to the participants' feet. Sometimes the roosters, rather than face near certain death, would merely run away, showing a clean pair of heels. Sir Walter Scott was the first known to include the expression in his classic, *Ivanhoe*, 1820, page 367:

> "'Urge me not with violence, Sir Knight,' said the Jester, keeping at a distance from the impatient champion,' or Folly will **show a clean pair of heels**, and leave Valour to find out his way through the wood as best he may.'"

Dickens later used the metaphor in *A Tale of Two Cities*, 1859, page 306:

> "No, gentlemen; he'll always **show 'em a clean pair of heels** very early in the scuffle, and sneak away."

Show-stopper^

This refers to a performance which receives enthusiastic, overwhelming applause. Figuratively it may mean a spectacular, appealing or arresting person or thing. The major online dictionary places origin at 1945-1950. *Billboard,* however, initially brought the term to light, beginning in the January 3, 1942 issue, and kept it hot for years. The initial citation was under 'Ted Lewis,' on page 56:

> "The choice of acts has been good and plenty of personality and do a fair vocal high contraption that is a **show-stopper**."

Shucks! (or **Aw, shucks!**)^

This is an American interjection used to show mild disappointment, irritation or embarrassment. A major dictionary lists first usage as 1951; however, the figurative use of 'shucks' actually came over 100 years earlier. It was derived from the idea that corn shucks had no value. *Dictionary of Americanism* by John Russell Barett, published in New York in 1848 had this notation on page 302:

> **"Not worth shucks**, is a Southern expression meaning good for nothing. *If them thar is all he's got to offer, he aint worth shacks; and if you don't lick him, you aint worth shucks, neither.*—Robb, *Squatter Life*." (John Robb)

The earliest known reference in print to 'shucks' being used alone as an expression comes in 1846 in *A Quarter Race in Kentucky: And Other Sketches* by William Trotter Porter, on page 86:

> **"Oh, Shucks**! give us 'Rocky Mounting,' or 'Misses McCloud !'"

Mark Twain used 'shucks' and 'oh, shucks' as a stand-alone expression several times in *The Advantures of Tom Sawyer* in 1876. **Aw! Shucks!** comes in 1888, in *Snagged and Sunk*, a novel for boys by American author Harry Castlemon (Charles Austin Fosdick), page 354:

> "I was goin' havers with you and mam an' Jake,' began Sam.
> '**Aw**! **Shucks**!' exclaimed Matt.
> 'An' then I was goin' to buy some good clothes an' things for myself.'"

Shut the front door!

This is a modern euphemism (to avoid profanity) meaning that the person can hardly believe what he or she has been told. It is like 'shut the______up!"

The most common usage of this term was by Stacy London, co-host on TLC's *What Not to Wear* (2003-2013), on-air during the show's 10-year run. As a result, it was picked up as a part of modern pop-culture.

Shut up shop

This is a very old idiom meaning to suspend an activity, generally in business, either temporarily or permanently. In the game of cricket, it means to bat defensively in the last innings of a match to force a draw when winning is impossible. The earliest citation in print is from *Remaines Concerning Britaine* by William Camden and John Philpot, 1636, page 278 in 'Wife Speeches:'

> "When the wares are gone, and the tooles taken away, we must **shut up shop**."

Sickie[3]

In America this would be 'calling in sick.' In Australia it is the idiom for a day's sick leave when there is little or no medical reason. It is an abbreviation similar to Tassie for Tasmanian devil, and surfie for a surfer. According to the *Australian National University 'Dictionary Center,'* the first recorded use was in 1953, and the following was in the March 3, 1962 edition of the Sydney *Bulletin* newspaper:

> "I don't feel a bit like work today... I think I'll take a **sickie**."

Sick to the back teeth[2]

This British idiom means that a person is angry or bored because a bad situation has continued too long, or a pesky subject has been discussed far too much. It is a newer version of sick tot the stomach, also common in America. It would imply that one is so sick that the vomit has come up to the back of the mouth and is being felt on one's back teeth, coming into use in the late 20th century. The earliest available verifiable citation is from Sarah Daniels' play, *Gut Girls*, first performed in London, November 2, 1985, Act II, Scene iv:

> "**MAGGIE**. And I'm **sick to the back teeth** of these toffs waltzing through here, saying how awful it is — it's them by calling it awful made it seem so awful."

A similar expression is 'fed up with.'

Sign of the times

This idiom refers to something which would indicate evidence of the vein of thought, belief, nature, quality or mode of living at the current time. Often this is said of unpleasant or unwelcome events and circumstances. It is a phrase which was strongly associated with Roman Catholicism in the era of the Second Vatican Council. The expression is taken from the words of Jesus in the biblical text in *Matthew 16:3, Tyndale Version,* 1526:

> "and in the morninge ye saye to daye shalbe foule wedder and that because the skye is cloudy and reed. O ye ypocrites ye can discerne ye fassion of the skye: and can ye not discerne ye **signes of the tymes**?"

Signs of the Times was a text written by Thomas Carlyle and published in the *Edinburgh Review* in June, 1829, then printed into a book that same year. In it he criticized vehemently the ethos of the Industrial Revolution, which he felt was destroying human individuality.

The earliest known reference outside of biblical text, however, to the phrase, is in the Preface to Hugh Rhodes' *The Boke of Nature, or, School of Good Manners for Men, Servants and Children*, on page xiii, 1577 printing:

> "Some of the alterations from the earlier text are worth notice as **signs of the times:"**

Ministers of Fundamentalist groups throughout the history of the Church Age have referred to various factors in world events as 'signs of the times.' The expression, 'Sign of the times' has been such an integral part of pop culture as to inspire, and become the title of numerous songs, albums and even films. Several magazines and books are named 'Signs of the Times,' as well as a British Left Wing discussion group.

Silence is deafening

This metaphorical oxymoron is used to express the profound belief that what someone does not say, particularly in response to a query, reveals more about his or her feelings than anything he or she may openly express. Origin is uncertain, but the earliest available reference in print to silence being 'deafening' is from *The Forum*, May, 1911, in a story titled 'At the Height' by Russell Herts:

> "Then, by an exercise of will, I kept it low and resounding for a while. A few moments of silence. Absolute silence. **Deafening silence**."

The first citation of 'silence is deafening' in this clear connotation, is also from a magazine, only two years later, August, 1913, in *The West Coast, An Illustrated Monthly* in 'News Notes and Comments:'

> "Do you hear the Editors of Big Pressdom thundering against this debauchery of their profession? Their **silence is deafening**."

Sing for one's supper[2]

This old British idiom alludes to wandering minstrels who performed in 17th century taverns and were paid with a meal. It was popularized by the nursery rhyme, 'Little Tommy Tucker,' 1744, taken from *The Best of Mother Goose and Other Nursery Rhymes*, St. Clair Publications, 2013, page 86:

> **"LITTLE TOMMY TUCKER**
>
> "Little Tommy Tucker,
> **Sing for your supper!**
> What shall I eat?
> White bread and butter.

How shall I cut it
Without my knife?
How shall I marry
Without any wife?

"(c. 1744)"

Singing the blues

This popular idiom means lamenting or complaining about one's circumstances, and was derived from the American musical genre known as blues music, often featuring lyrics about bad luck and difficulties. Blues has its roots in African-American history on Southern plantations in the mid-to-late 19th century. Slaves and ex-slave sahrecroppers sang mournful ballads as they regretfully toiled in the cotton and vegetable fields. Some characteristics of the genre were present even much earlier in African music. Three cities have become popular centers for blues music: New Orleans, Memphis and St. Louis.

The saying *Singing the Blues* first appeared as the title for a song by Aliene Stanley, copyrighted in 1921 by Victor Records, which was recorded on a 78 RPM disc. In 1956 another ballad titled *Singing the Blues*, written by Melvin Endsley, was released by Marty Robbins, which becames a smash hit, later covered by Guy Mitchell, Tommy Steele and others, perpelling the saying into our pop culture. The song clearly indicated a state of being dejected and downcast over lost love.

Sit around collecting dust

This hyperbolic expression may refer to an item or a person. It means not being used or useful; good for nothing or doing nothing. It is often said of books which are not being read. In this sense the idiom became popular in the 1970s. An early example is from an ad in *Billboard*, Christmas Day, 1976, page 51:

> "The needless waste of letting your potential hits **sit** on a shelf **collecting dust** instead of COLLECTING ROYALTIES."

Skeleton crew

This idiomatic term means the minimum amount of personnel required to keep basic operations and maintenance going for a business, ship or organization in time of emergency shutdown of normal procedures. This is derived from the fact that the skeleton is the most basic unit upon which the human body is structured.

The word skeleton itself goes back to the 1570s, and comes from the Greek *skeleton soma* meaning 'dried up body,' The Greek noun *skeletos* came into the Latin *skeletus*, and the English forerunner, *skelet* in the 1560s.

'Skeleton crew' did not enter our lexicon until the 19tth century. The earliest verifiable citation is from *Gales and Seaton's Register of Debates in Congress*, First Session of the 20th Congress, February 7, 1828, page 255:

> "From this view of the subject, it is clear that a rule of distribution properly applicable to a full crew, cannot be justly applied to a **skeleton crew** — filling up none of the classes arranged in the prize acts."

Skimming cash

The word 'skimming' is used to mean taking the cream from whole milk before processing it for human consumption. This expression refers to the illegal practice of taking funds off the top (thus skimming) of daily business receipts for personal use. In 1880, According to *Transitions of the Department of Agriculture of the State of Illinois,* it was thought that skimming milk was fraud, which may have led to this term being used as it is.

> "G. P. Lord said the plan, or habit, of **skimming** milk was a fraud, and should be stopped: if every patron should **skim** his milk it would bankrupt any factory."

The first reference available for 'skimming cash,' though not in sync with the current connotation, is from *Agricultural Innovation: The Process of Ecological Change in Indonesia* by Clifford Geertz, 1968, page 62:

> "The Company established the Dutch presence in the archipelago, introduced a few new cultivations (mainly coffee; pepper, spices, and sugar preceded it) and devised, in rough form, most of the techniques for **skimming cash** crops off the surface of an Immobilized subsistence economy which later became so useful when Java filled up with peasants."

Reference to the current meaning came by October 18, 1980 when it appeared in *Billboard,* in 'BOOK REVIEW: Radcliff Joe Probes '70s Disco Evolution:'

> "The latter subject provides just one example of the timeliness of Joe's approach to covering the scene and the insider knowledge he lends to the book. '**This Business of Disco**' was barely off the presses before the Internal Revenue Service charged several operators with **skimming cash** from the till in order to beat income taxes."

sky's the limit, The^

This old idiom means that there seems to be no maximum to something. Like many other expressions, this has erroneously been attributed to Miguel de Cervantes Saavedra in *Don Quixote*. Something close was used in '*The Ghost of Napoleon,*' translated from the French of Theophole Gautier, which told of 'Don Juan.' It is possible that this is the source of this confusion. It appeared in The Oxford Magazine, October 29, 1884:

> "So spoke Don Juan 'neath the chilly skies,
> Weary but fixed to follow my emprise,
> Onward once more I fared.
> Behold! a wide plain stern with solitude,
> And at **the sky's** far **limit**, blood-imbrued..."

Other such phrases were common in the late 19th century. Another good researcher placed the actual origin at 1911; however, it appeared in two sources in 1908. One was *Zollenstein*, a novel by W.M.B. Ferguson, page 7:

> "Gentlemen, **the sky's the limit**," announced Greystone, shuffling the cards with his long, prehensile fingers. '**The Sky's the limit**.'"

The other is from *Proceedings of the American Street and Interurban Railway Association,* published in New York City, 1908, in 'Publicity Symposium Paper' by G.H. Gall of Washington, DC, on page 227, here in quotes:

> "Theoretically, as to possibilities, '**the sky's the limit**.'"

slap in the face, A

This means an action that insults or upsets someone. The earliest known figurative citation is from *The Civil Engineer and Architect's Journal*, July, 1845 in 'Candidus's Note-book:'

> "'Think of august powers and principalities,' continues the audacious Titmarsh, 'ordering the works of such a man as Etty to be backed out of the wall, — that **was a slap in the face** to every artist in England!'"

Slap on the wrist

This hyperbolic metaphor is used to mean receiving only a light punishment or a reprimand for an infraction which called for much more stringent punishment.

The earliest reference in print to the phrase is in *The Life of the Reverend Jonathan Swift* by Thomas Sheridan, Second Edition, 1787:

> "One time he held out his plate with both his hands, stretching it in the most ridiculous posture quite across the table, which provoked Gibbons to call him fool! dunce! and even to give him a **slap on the wrist** with the flat of his knife at the same time showing him how he ought to hold his plate…"

The earliest available clear example of figurative less-than-adequate punishment is from the July 25, 1904 issue of William Jennings Bryan's *The Commoner*, published in Lincoln, Nebraska, on page 4:

> "If 'Hell Roaring Jake' Smith had been but a little bit more brutal he might have received **a slap on the wrist** from the administration."

Sleeping partner[2]

This decidedly British idiom dates back to the 18th century, and means a silent partner in business. It likely inspired the sayings also popular in America, 'sleeping with the enemy' (see original volume) and 'get in bed with' in relation to business arrangements. The earliest known citation is in the English translation of German playwright Johann Henri Samuel Formey's 1748 French language play, *La Logique des Vraisemblences*, where a business arrangement was being discussed:

> ***"Leon***. I guess you were not a **sleeping partner** here."

Sleep like a log

This old saying means to enjoy very sound slumber. Comparisons of people to logs go back as far as the late 1600s. In *A Reviving Cordial for a Sin-sick Despairing Soul in the Time of Temptation*, Rev. James Barry used this analogy in 1699, page 62:

> "I found myself **like a** dead **log**, as if I had neither life nor soul left in me."

Such metaphoric statements were common during the 18th century; then in 1833, Asa Greene took it to the next level in *The Life and Adventures of Dr. Dodimus Duckworth*, page 196:

> "'I declare,' said he, as he came down stairs; 'I **slept like a log** last night.'"

Many picked it up soon, and in 1883, Robert Lewis Stephenson used it in *Treasure Island*, chapter 19:

"I was dead tired, as you may fancy; and when I got to sleep, which was not till after a great deal of tossing, I **slept like a log** of wood."

Sleight of hand

This term refers to motor skills used by performing artists in entertaining or manipulation. It has often been associated with cheating at card games and what is called 'close-up magic.' Because of this, many have confused it as a branch of magic, which is not factual. The word 'sleight' actually means 'dexterity' or 'cunning,' especially so in deception. The synonyms *prestidigitation* and *legerdemain* are Latin derivations. The English phrase goes back to 1562, when it was listed in *The Proverbs, Epigrams and Miscellany of John Heywood*:

"Liger de maine (143a), **sleight of hand**, jugglery, legerdemain."

The introductory term 'liger de maine' here is the Middle French, which came into English as 'legerdemain.' It refers to dexterity, and literally mean 'light of hand,' altered to 'sleight' a Middle English word which has stuck with us.

Slippery slope^

This modern term means a dangerous and irreversible course. Often applied to an argument in logic, critical thinking or political rhetoric, it asserts that a particular result will likely follow a certain seemingly innocent or small action, decision or circumstance. In spite of numerous online sources declaring origin at 1985-1990, the expression was in use over thirty years before that. In *Bulletin of the Atomic Scientists,* June, 1954, and article by Edward Shills on page 242 was titled '**A Slippery Slope.**' In his opening remarks, the expression, which was likely coined here, is in quotes, probably referring back to his title:

"The report of the majority of the Personnel Security Board is one more step down the '**slippery slope**' which leads away from a free society."

In relation to an argument, it was in use by at least 1977, when it appeared in *Feminism and Philosophy,* edited by Mary Vetterling-Braggin, Frederick Elliston and Jane English, page 355:

"Every American girl, be she philosopher-to-be or not, is well acquainted with the **slippery-slope** argument by the time she is ten."

Slow and steady wins the race

This ancient proverb means working at a slower pace will enable a person to continue making progress when others wear out from fast-paced overworking. It comes from the ancient fable of the tortoise and the hare. It is number 226 in the fables attributed to Aesop, who was a slave said to live in Greece between 620 and 560 BCE. The earliest citation available of the proverb in English is found at the end of the fable in *Select British Classics, Volume 29*, page 101, 1803:

> "You may deride my awkward pace,
> But **slow and steady wins the race**."

Slow coach / Slowcoach[2]

This is a British version of 'slowpoke' and reverts back to the coaches of old, before autos, which were often late, and were slow to get to the destination. The earliest mention of the term is in the poem, *The Pastime and Recreation of the Queen of Fairies in Fairyland, the Centre of the Earth* found on page 209, in *Poems by Eminent Ladies Volume II,* published in London in 1755:

> "But if she will a hunting go,
> Then she the lizzard makes the doe,
> Which is so swift and fleet in chafe,
> As her **slow coach** cannot keep pace:
> Then on a grashopper she'l ride,
> And gallop in the sorest wide;"

The first clear reference to slow coach as a person is found in Dickens' first novel, *The Posthumous Papers of the Pickwick Club*, 1837, page 62:

> "For aught I know, it may be a reference to Pickwick himself, who has most unquestionably been a criminally **slow coach** during the whole of this transaction, but whose speed will now be very unexpectedly accelerated…"

Slush fund+

This is an idiomatic expression, most often used in the political arena, for a secret reserve of money which is not properly accounted for, used for corrupt or illegal purposes, especially bribery. The word 'slush' was coined in 17th century England as the name applied to half-melted snow, and first appeared in print in Rural Economy in Yorkshire in 1651.

It was 100 years later when it was first used alternatively for the fat or grease from meat boiled on board ships. It appeared initially in *The Gentleman's Magazine* in 1756:

> "He used much **slush** (the rancid fat of pork) among the victuals."

After it was firmly established in this meaning, appearing in various publications, and being seen as a non-appetizing part of the food, ships cooks began selling the fat garnered from their cooked meat whenever they reached ports. The funds were pooled and became known as a 'slush fund.' William McNally explained the term in *Evils & Abuses in Naval & Merchant Service* in 1839:

> "The sailors in the navy are allowed salt beef. From this provision, when cooked nearly all the fat boils off, this is carefully skimmed and put into empty beef or pork barrels, and sold, and the money received is called the **slush fund**."

Smack dab in the middle^

This old idiom means exactly in the middle. A major dictionary list earliest use of 'smack dab' meaning exactly or directly as 1892 in *Dialect Notes* I, 232. It was, however, in print much earlier in *The Investigator*, January, 1846, on page 27, in 'Mr. Rathbun's Report':

> "If I have to pay an additional dollar for myself and wife, there's fifty-two dollars, at the end of the year, **smack dab**, off of the hundred that I thought was saved."

'Smack' was used even earlier, in 1832, to indicate 'directly,' as seen in *Pierce Egan's Book of Sports*, page 158:

> "Lalla's right mauley was doubled up to his right ear, whilst his left, stiff and straight, pointed **smack** at his opponent's naval."

The earliest known actual example in print of 'smack dab in the middle' is found in Will Nathaniel Harben's *Pole Baker*: a novel published in 1905, page 23:

> "That night fer the fust time sence my marriage I woke **smack dab in the middle** o' the night, an' as I laid thar in the room filled with moonlight I couldn't see a blessed thing but that row o' bottles, an' then my mouth set in to waterin' at sech a rate that I got afeared I'd ketch my death from sleepin' on a wet pillow."

The variants, slap-dab and slap-bang, which had slightly different meanings, date to the mid-18th century.

Small potatoes^

This, like 'small fry,' refers to something or someone deemed as insignificant. It has been erroneously claimed this phrase derived from the fact that during the potato famine in Ireland in 1845-1849, at a time when potatoes were the main source of food, only small potatoes survived, and had to provide food for the hungry. A Chicago newspaper in 1849 called it 'a Southern phrase.' A major slang dictionary places origin at 1836. Actually, the earliest known reference is before the potato famine and after the last date, and was first used in England. On 20 July 1844, the London publication *The Athenaeum: Journal of Literature, Science, the Fine Arts,* under 'Reviews' carried the following figurative quote from 'High Life in New York' by Jonathan Slick:

> "If they've got their lords, and dukes, and princes, haint we no military captins, and ginerals, and deacons, and squires,—— rather **small potatoes** compared to the English, but yet it shows a sort of native notion we've got arter sich things, and don't know no sort of harm one way or t'other."

Smidgen+

This curious word refers to a very small amount of something. It has been in use in English since at least the 19th century. There is more than one theory about which word it evolved from, but either way, it was almost certainly a Scottish word. Originally came into Confer Northumbrian dialectal English as *smiddum.* This was used for a small particle of lead. Some say it came from the Scots *smitch* (*Etymological Dictionary of the Scottish Language*, John Jamieson, Edinburgh,1825), meaning a speck and the Old English derivative, *smitan*, used to mean meaning to smear or smudge. It seems very possible, however, that it derived from the Scottish Gaelic word *smidin*, which meant small syllable.

By the early 20th century it was appearing in print in English publications. An early citation appears in *Greene Brothers Clinical Course in Dental Prosthesis* by Jacob W. Greene, 1910, page 75:

> "Then with the blade of our knife we'll trace on a **smidgen** from same batch along the roof center from front to rear."

smile costs nothing, A

There is an anonymous poem which has made this saying popular, but the thought goes back hundreds of years. The earliest known reference is in *Objects Interesting to the English Nation:* by Elias Habesci, 1793, page 186:

> "A look, a kind **smile**, a word, any other trisle, of that nature, **costs nothing**, even to a great lord, a rich man, and a vise one: And those trisles, generally retain these simpletons, in submission, and attachment."

The New Monthly Magazine and Literary Journal, Part the Third, in 'The Devorcee Devote,' 1833, on page 25, has the first known actual citation of the proverbial statement:

> "Occasionally, I won smiles from the women, and occasionally frowns from the men — the latter, however, not as often as the former. **A smile costs nothing**, you know, and it may show good teeth and dimples, as well as good humour, and needs lead to nothing, for after all, 'tis but a smile…"

Snowball effect

Based upon a small snowball being rolled down a snow-covered hill and getting larger and larger, metaphorically this refers to a tiny or insignificant problem or situation building up and growing larger and more dangerous as time passes until it becomes impossible to control or stop. The earliest reference in print is from Western Union's *Telegraph Age*, December 16, 1919, in 'To Everybody Everywhere' by John F. Skirrow:

> "In a majority of such cases and investigation of the correspondence of the complainant would reveal a lot of useless work, and a rolling **snowball effect** built up by unnecessary questions which have yielded a crop of further unnecessary questions and answers."

So-and-so+

This colloquialism may apply either to someone whose name the speaker does not remember, or may be used as a euphemism for a person who is disliked or has unfavorable characteristics. The first meaning has been in use in English since the 13th century, and though initially written in Hebrew, the phrase was used several times in the Original Text of the *Babylonian Talmud*, the Jewish

Rabbinical texts compiled in the 4th century C.E. in Galilee. The second connotation was first attested in 1595 according to *Merriam Webster.*

Sober as a judge

This ancient simile means completely clear headed and able to function normally. Presumably the most apt person to personify sobriety in 16th century London would have been a judge. The earliest verifiable reference in print is from *A Rod for Turnbridge Beaus, Bundl'd up at the Request of Turnbridge Ladies,* a Burlesque poem published in London in 1701, page 19:

> "Whilst he with very fear alone,
> As **sober as a Judge** was grown,
> And humbly beg'd the Damsel's goodness,
> To pardon all his drunken rudness,.."

Sod's law[2]

This is another British term for 'Murphy's Law' (see). The only slight difference here is that it will happen at the very worst possible time. It is derived from the earlier expression 'unlucky sod' and described as a sort of ironic fate. This earlier idiom apparently was derived from this part of the serialized 'A Winter in a Tipperary Household Fourteen Years Ago,' chapter II, which appeared in London's *Once a Week* on March 22, 1862:

> "We pushed the door out, hoping to have it bolted before he could reach it, but unfortunately a sod of turf had fallen from a basketful which the girl had brought in some minutes previously, and, as our ill-fortune would have it, this **unlucky sod** got between the door and the jamb, so that as we dared not open wider to push it away, there it stayed, and we felt our assailant's strong shoulder opposed to our trembling."

Sod's law is a modern expression, not coming into common use until the late 20th century. The earliest verifiable citation is from *Bully for Brontosaurus: Reflections in Natural History* by Stephen Jay Gould, 1991, page 240-241 in the 1992 paperback version, where it is in quotes as somewhat known to the reader:

> "Every profession has its version: Some speak of '**Sod's law;'** others of 'Murphy's law.' The formulations vary, but all make the same point — if anything bad can happen, it will."

So far, so good

This is a self-explanatory idiom meaning that progress made to this point is satisfactory. Far, in this phrase, of course, refers to length of time, not distance. It can also infer a tad of skepticism; in that future progress in uncertain. It is a very old expression, going back to the first half of the 18th century. The earliest verifiable citation is from *Miss in her Teens, A Farce in Two Acts*, performed in the Theater Royal in London's Covenant Garden and printed in the Fourth Edition in 1747 by S. Powell in Dublin, Ireland, Act I, Scene i:

> "***Tag.*** **So far so good**; and since I have got you to wet your Feet, souse over Head at once, and the Pain will be over."

Soldier on

This military origin metaphor means to steadfastly persist in one's work or in one's mission; to persevere, especially through adversity. Though not quite the full meaning of today's expression, the May, 1959 issue of *Michigan Business Review* had this citation in 'Achieving Administrative Confidence—The Supervisor' by Robert Hilkert on page 6:

> "Would you **soldier on** the job, or would you try to out-do yourself?"

It took ten years before the saying had evolved to what we now know. In *Life,* July 11, 1969, in 'The New Arithmetic of Vietnam,' on page 24, we read:

> "Another line of argument is that we are committed to our 'commitment,' and that the U.S. **must soldier on** in Vietnam until a non-Communist government in Saigon is secured, for to do otherwise would destroy the credibility of U.S. commitments all over the world."

So long+

This is an old expression meaning 'farewell.' There are three possible origins for the phrase. It is thought by some to have come from the Irish Gaelic word for goodbye, *slan*, pronounced 'slawn.' Since it is primarily used in the U.S., those with this belief attribute it to the high influx of Irish and Scots-Irish Gaelic speakers into the U.S. in the 19th century.

Others claim that it was initially imported into Britain by soldiers serving in Malayan-speaking countries. These people believe that it is derived from the

Malayan salutation, *salang*, which was a corruption of the Arabic *salaam*, or the Hebrew *shalom*, meaning peace. *Salaam*, Arabic, is a greeting, therefore an unlikely origin.

The third possible origin, favored by *Etymology Online*, is that it comes from the German, *adieu so lange* which appeared about 1850.

Earliest use in print seems to be in Walt Whitman's poem, '*So Long!*' published in the 1860 edition of his book of poetry, *Leaves of Grass*:

> "While my pleasure is yet at the full, I whisper, ***So long!*** And take the young woman's hand, and the young man's hand for the last time.
>
> "***So long!*** Remember the words –I may again return I love you –I depart from materials; I am as one disembodied, triumphant, dead."

It seems that Whitman's American contemporaries did not yet fully understand the meaning of the expression. A friend who his had never heard it before reading the poem, and asked Whitman to define it. He told him it was a '*salutation of departure, greatly used among sailors, sports and prostitutes—the sense of it is till we meet again—conveying an inference somewhere, some how [sic.] they will doubtless so meet—sooner or later.*"

Some people are born great, some achieve greatness, and some have greatness thrust upon them+

This proverbial axiom comes from Shakespeare's *Twelfth Night*, Act II, Scene v, and is found in the words of Malvolio in an answer to Fabian.

> "It falls into thy hand, resolve in my stars I am above thee, but be not afraid of greatness. Some are born great, some achieve greatness, and some have greatness thrust upon 'em. Thy Fates upon thy hands. Let thy blood and spirit embrace them."

Song and dance^

This refers to trying to 'pull the wool over someone's eyes' (see first volume) by telling a long and complicated story to save face (see). It is derived from the theatrical stage performances which were colloquially called by this name in the 18th, 19th and early 20th centuries in America and Britain. In this respect, the expression dates to the early 1700s. The earliest known reference in print is from *Wit and Mirth or Pills to Purge Melancholy*, a collection of songs printed in London in 1719 in 'A Prologue Spoken like A Scotch Highlander' on page 348:

> "What 'tis we Play is **Song and Dance**, and Shew,
> The Theme, the Devil take me if I knew;..."

In spite of a claim by a great online source that this figurative use began in the 1870s, this metaphoric citation appeared in *The Tattler*, by Isaac Bickerstaff, in 'Memoirs of Sir Richard Steele,' 1794, page 74, which may shed some light on how it means what it does:

> "When the seat of wit was thus mortgaged, without equity of redemption, an architect arose who has built the muse a new palace, but secured her no retinue; so that instead of action there, we have been put off by **song and dance**."

Son, in the race of life always back self interest, at least you know it is trying[3]

According to Australian author, Gerald Sinclair, this proverb comes from Sir William Mc Kell's day (1891 – 1985). Quoting Sinclair, McKell was a 'boilermaker, premier of NSW and Governor General, when horse racing was even more prevalent in the cultural consciousness than it is now (i.e every day of the year apart from Sunday, not just Melbourne Cup Week) and with all sorts of shady results being par for the course), when a young aspiring politician asked one of McKells's hard headed advisers about how he should approach his career got this advice.' Apparently that advisor was Jack Lang (1876-1925), an Australian Labor politician. The saying has become a part of Australian wisdom.

Sorry, Charlie

Charlie is the tuna mascot of the StarKist brand and was created by Tom Rogers of the Leo Burnett Agency in 1961. In cartoon ads, Charlie (voice of Herschel Bernard) tries to get caught by the company to be used in their product. When he is rejected, he says that is cultured and has 'good taste.' He is given a note attached to a fish hook which reads, 'Sorry, Charlie.' Then the announcer (Danny Dark) says, 'We don't want tuna with good taste. Only *good tasting* tuna go into StarKist Tuna.'

'Sorry, Charlie' became a catchphrase complaint response meaning, 'Get over it. I won't help you.'

Sound as a bell

This means in perfect condition, or in excellent health when applied to a person. It goes back to Shakespeare's *Much Ado About Nothing*, 1598-1599, Act I, Scene i, first performed in 1612:

> "I will onely bee bold with *Benidicke* for his companie, for from the crown of his head to the sole of his foot, he is all mirth, he hath twice or thrice cut Cupids bow-string, and the little hang-man dare not shoot at him, he hath a heart **as sound as a bell**, and his tongue is the clapper, for what his heart thinkes, his tongue speakes."

Sounds like a plan

This late 20th century cliché means, 'I like your idea and I believe it will work.' An early example is in *The Eye of the Sibyl* by Philip K. Dick, 1992, page 289:

> "'**Sounds like a plan**,' Cynthia's voice came to him dimly; she had heard."

Soup to nuts

This American idiom means from beginning to end. It is derived from a description of a full-course meal beginning with soup and ending with nuts for desert. The earliest known citation in print is from *Dublin Magazine*, October, 1852, in an article titled 'A Flying Shot at the United States,' here actually referring to preparing a meal:

> "I have heard of a boast being made by a veteran in the art 'that he could get from **soup to nuts** in ten minutes.'"

Many examples of literal use of the term came in the following years. The earliest known figurative example in print, here in quotes, came in *Baily's Magazine of Sports and Pastimes,* in the feature 'Our Van,' November, 1874:

> "…an American parson dined on board an English man-of-war, and on being asked how he had been treated replied in the most glowing terms, and said what struck him most was, that from '**soup to nuts'** he never heard a single G-d d — n."

Southpaw^

This is a colloquialism meaning 'left-hand' or 'left-handed.' Since 1885 this has been baseball slang for left-handed pitchers. It has been claimed that the term was coined by Finley Peter Dunne called 'Mr. Dooley,' Chicago sports journalist and humorist, when baseball diamonds regularly were laid out with home plate to the west. However, it was used earlier in *The Proceedings of the Regular Conclave of the Grand Commandery of Knights Templar of the State of Michigan Held in Detroit Held in Detroit 4th and 5th of June, 1867*, page 75:

> "We, of New Jersey, don't want to have our 'desperate widows' and 'helpless orphans' defended by a valiant Knight who wields his sword in his '**southpaw**,' or who has to hobble upon a crutch to punish some scamp who has insulted some of our 'innocent maidens.'"

It is in quotes, indicating that the meaning was at least somewhat understood and known. Here, as in older times, a left-hander seems to be looked upon contemptuously.

Speaks with a forked tongue

This metaphoric phrase means to deliberately say one thing and mean another. It is traditionally associated with the accusations of Native Americans against white men in the days of treaties which were broken by the United States government. This distrust also bled over into the efforts of white missionaries. In *The United States Catholic Magazine,* August, 1846, 'Peré Jean, Or, The Jesuit Missionary, A Catholic Story Founded on Facts,' Chapter IX, tells of the reaction of a Mohawk tribe to the sermon of a missionary:

> "'He **speaks with a forked tongue**,' said Kiohba; 'he is a liar!'
> 'We are satisfied with our own God,' exclaimed another—'the war-god—Wacondah. The God of the great medicine has made cowards of the Hurons; the God of the Mohawks strengthens the arm of his children in battle.'"

'Forked tongue' was used much earlier by Shakespeare in *Henry VI*, Part II, Act I, Scene i, (1591) referring to a snake, the obvious origin:

> "In pain of your Dislike, or pain of Death; Yet notwithstanding such a strange Edict, Were there a Serpent seen with **forked Tongue**, That slyly glided towards your Majesty, It were but necessary you were wak'd…"

The *Bible* pictures the devil as a 'serpent' and a liar. *Psalm 58, verses 3 and 4* speak of lies as being like the poison of a deadly snake.

> "The wicked are estranged from the womb; they go astray as soon as they be born, speaking lies. Their poison is like the poison of a serpent." (*KJV,* 1611).

It is no wonder that throughout history lying and forked tongues have been linked.

Spill one's guts

This means to reveal all of one's history, especially one's problems and faults. It comes from giving up everything inside a person. The earliest available verifiable citation is from *The Southwest Reporter*, April 14 - May 5, 1920 in the Texas case of Casanova v State:

> "When I met him there at the door, I told him that Will Martin and Tom had **spilled their guts**; then he immediately said, 'Well, if any of us get into trouble, we will all go together…'"

Spin a yarn

This is an idiom meaning to tell a tale, especially one which is long, drawn out, fanciful and deceitful. Literally, a yarn is a heavy string spun from a fiber. This metaphor dates back to the early 19th century. The earliest available citation is from *Greenwich Hospital, A Series of Naval Sketches Descriptive of Life of a Man-of-War's Man* by 'An Old Sailor,' 1826, page 181:

> "I can remember — but, avast, avast; here I am going to **spin** you **a yarn** that's got nothing at all to do with it."

Spineless

This figurative term means lacking courage; cowardly. It infers that because a person lacks a spine he or she can't 'stand up' to problems. Origin is unknown, but the earliest available reference in print is from *The Texas Medical Journal,* January, 1909, in the feature article, 'Medical Politics in Epigram and Otherwise' by G. Frank Lydston, MD, Chicago:

> "Why did this gentleman push onward his grievance and thus propitiate the star-eyed goddess of medical reform? Surely he must have known that the crumb of comfort thrown so grudgingly to him was merely a sop thrown to the Cerberus of growing dissatisfaction among the rank and file. And yet, he may be as egotistic as **he is spineless**."

spirit is willing but the flesh is weak, The

This cliché is taken directly from the *Bible*, from the words of Jesus in the Garden of Gethsemane the night of his arrest when he found the disciples sleeping when he had told them to sit and wait while he went to pray. The passage appears in the parallel Gospels in *Matthew 26:41* and *Mark 14:36*, the latter being an exact quote of the last portion in the *King James Version,* 1611:

> "Watch and pray so that you will not fall into temptation. **The spirit is willing, but the flesh is weak."**

It is used when someone has expressed good intentions and failed to follow through. A good modern secular example is in *The Ignorance Explosion: Understanding Industrial Civilization* by Julius Lukasiewicz, 1994, page 136:

> "A computer translation of 'out of sight, out of mind' may read 'a blind fool;' '**The spirit is willing but the flesh is weak'** could come out as 'The vodka is strong but the meat is rotten.'"

Spit the dummy[3]

In Australia, a 'dummy' is a baby's pacifier. This is an idiom inferring that the person being addressed is having a childish tantrum (spitting out the pacifier), and needs to act like an adult. It has been in use since the 1980s, but the earliest citation available is from the *Sydney Morning Herald* 2 November 1992:

> "With most games, of course, I'd simply **spit the dummy**, hit the switch and give up."

Split hairs

This has reference to quibbling over very small details or insignificant differences of opinion. The origin has been 'hotly debated.' There is one source, *Philosophical Transactions of the Royal Society of London, Volume 10*, published in 1675, page 1366, which speaks of having a hair split, but it doesn't seem to constitute a true form of the idiom:

> "Upon a modest Estimate their thickness is not the 100th part of an **hairs** breadth, and consequently is you imagine an **hair** of your Head **split** into above 7800 equal fibers…"

Another mention comes in 1712, in *John Bull and His Senses, Being the Third Part of Law is a Bottomless Pit,* by John Arbuthnot, page 14. This has a continuous list of insignificant items, a few of which are here, which may serve to be a basis of how 'splitting hairs' came to mean what it does:

> "…making Chains for fleas, Nets for Flies and Instruments to unravel Cobwebs and **split Hairs.**"

The earliest clear printed example of the current connotation comes in *The Works of the Most Reverend John Tillotson, Late Lord Archbishop of Canterbury* (1630-1694), published in 1757, page 1417:

> "In the mean time, the consciences of men are like to be well directed, when instead of giving men plain rules for government of their hearts and lives, and clear resolutions of the material doubts, which frequently occur in human life, they intangle them in niceties and endless scrupulosities, teaching them to **split hairs** in divinity, and how with great art and cunning they may avoid the committing of sin and yet come as near to it as possible."

Because Anglican Archbishop Tillotson died in 1694, it appears that the phrase was known and understood before the end of the 17th century.

Spoon-feed someone

Deriving from the need to place food directly into the mouth of a baby, this is a figurative expression for giving information to someone in a manner which requires no effort on the part of the person receiving it, thus destroying initiative and independent thought. In 1791, the thought of feeding an adult with a spoon was used by James Boswell in *The Life of Samuel Johnson, LLD*, on page 390:

> "Sir, Dr. Goldsmith would no more have asked me to write such a thing as that for him, than he would have asked me to **feed** him with a **spoon**, or to do any thing else that denoted his imbecillity."

The earliest citation available of the expression in a purely metaphoric setting is from *Reports from Commissioners in the British Parliament and House of Commons*, 1866, page 77:

> "Schools do not **spoon-feed** pupils — they must learn themselves."

Spot on[2]

Spot on is a modern expression generally identified as being British. It means exactly correct or completely accurate. According to *Fraser's Phrases*, BBC America website, in the game of Billiards, which came from Colonial India, once the red ball has been potted, it must be returned to its starting position, which is the spot where the black ball goes in snooker. This is how, according to Fraser McAlpine, the term spot on evolved to mean extreme accuracy. The earliest clear example available is actually from Australia, from *Parliamentary Debates, House of Representatives*, 1983, page 3350:

> "The Prime Minister knows that the Deputy Prime Minister (Mr. Lionel Bowen) was right when on 30 May 1978 he said: Anybody who misleads Parliament should not remain in Cabinet and should not remain in ministerial office. **That is spot on**."

The term is also becoming accepted in America.

Spring up

This is a metaphor for appearing to be produced suddenly and quickly. The expression was used as early as 1611 in the *King James Version* of the *Bible, Isaiah 44: 4*, speaking of blessings from God:

> "And they shall **spring up** *as* among the grass, as willows by the water courses."

Spur-of-the-moment+

Something done, 'on the spur of the moment,' means spontaneously, on impulse, with no advance planning. This is an idiomatic adjective phrase describing such impulsive action. The first recorded usage of 'spur' in this connotation, meaning in haste, was in 1801 according to the *OED*. In 1875 in *A Review of the 'Great' Speech of Senator John P. Jones on the Banking and Currency Bill, delivered in the United States Senate, April 1st. 1874,* by Henry S. Fitch, we find 'on the spur of the moment' in quotes, indicating a known expression, likely coined recently:

> "…Mr. Jones, to have been delivered "on the **spur of the moment**."

Squatter[3]

Similar to the term in America, this is Aussie slang for a person who illegally occupies a vacant building. But when it was coined there, in the early 19th century, it was a person who occupied land belonging to the Crown (British government) without legal title. From the 1840s it was used for any person who grazed a herd of livestock without reference to the title on the land, and referred to them as being of an elevated socio-economic status. Such squatters became a force in the Australian economy because of the wealth they obtained; so much do that the term ***squattocracy*** was coined to describe them. In 1867, *Life's Work As It Is; or, The Emigrant's Home in Australia* by 'A Colonist,' published in London, had this statement:

> "Talking of wealth, no men have made wealth faster in this colony than '**squatters**;' that is, in plain English, sheep and cattle owners."

Squeaky clean

When hair is washed, especially long hair, when it is truly clean, pulling it with the fingers will produce a squeaky sound. The earliest citation is from *Motion Picture,* February, 1936, 'The Talkies,' published by Macfadden-Bartel, page 56:

> "Brighten Your Hair with Duart Rinse Choose from 12 beautiful shades. No dye — no bleach. Rinses the hair '**squeaky clean**' and adds a touch of sunlight. Send 10 cents for 2 full-rinse purchase…"

Stag night / party[2]

In America the bachelor's last night of being unmarried is often celebrated by a 'bachelor party.' In Britain this is known as 'stag night' or 'party.' The practice of holding a celebratory party in the groom's honor that night goes all the way back to the Ancient Spartans, who were the first to do this. A huge feast was held in his honor with his men friends gathered around to toast him in gallant style. In France and other French-speaking lands it is called '*enterrement de vie de garcon*' which means 'the burial of the life of the boy.' They both celebrate the groom's new life and mourn the loss of his boyhood. The night is observed with large amounts of alcohol and much festivity.

It is believed that it may be called a 'stag party' because of the Horned god in Wiccon religions who represents hunting, sexuality and the life cycle. Wiccons believed in the male/female deities. The earliest reference to a 'stag party' in print known is from *Littell's Living Age*, February, 1853, in 'The Rooster Pecked Wife' by Eliza L. Sproat, Scene First:

> "***Mrs. Penfeather***…[Is interrupted by the sudden appearance of C, Esq., who has just returned from a **stag party.**]"

Stalking horse

As a metaphor, this refers to a person or entity that tests a concept or mounts a challenge with someone on behalf of an anonymous third party. In politics, it is a candidate who runs in order to provoke the election and allow a stronger candidate to come forward. The term originally derived from hunting wild foul, in which the birds were known to ignore the presence of horses and cattle. Hunters would cautiously approach their prey walking beside their horses, lurking behind them until the flock was within firing range. The animals trained for this were known as stalking horses. Surprisingly, the figurative use of the term dates to the mid-17th century. The earliest known citation is from *Relations and observations historical and political upon the Parliament begun Ano Dom. 1640,* a book including an Appendix Touching the Proceedings against the Independent Faction in Scotland, published in 1648, page 17:

> "Let us no longer make Religion a **stalking-horse**; God, who is all Wisdome and all Truth, will not be deceived. If we talk like Christians, and walk like Turkes, Christ will not own us."

Standing room only (SRO)

This refers to an event in which all seats are filled and the overflow attendees are forced to stand. The phrase 'only standing room' was recorded in 1811, but the earliest citation known for 'standing room only' comes in 1827 in *Authentic Memoir of His Late Royal Highness, Frederick, Duke of York* by Robert Huish, page 53:

> "But in every other place, **standing room only** was afforded. At the time when the public were admitted, the two barriers along the nave were lined on the outside by a single file of the blue horse guards, dismounted."

The acronym, SRO came early in the 20th century. The earliest verifiable reference in print is found in *McClure's Magazine*, August, 1905, in 'The Property Man' by Booth Tarkington:

> "It **was 'S. R. O.**,' that night, chairs in the orchestra and the music under the stage, for Gertrude Lemist was, and is, and deserves to be, one of the great pets of the Golden Gate."

Star-studded cast

This is a much used idiom meaning that a production features a large percentage of well-known personalities. The use of star-studded was common in the 18th century, usually referring to the heavens. The use of it referring to the cast of a play first occurred in April, 1905 in *Munsey's Magazine*, on page 85, as a heading in a feature titled 'The Stage:'

> **"A REALLY STAR-STUDDED CAST**
>
> "Mr. Willard's New York season was but little more successful than Mr. Terry's. Both of these English stars suffered from their lack of good plays and of capable support."

Start World War III

World War III is a term used for a hypothetical future worldwide conflict. The term is also used figuratively when someone is accused of 'making a mountain out of a molehill' (see first volume). It is a modern metaphor, and a good example is found in *Legions of Space* by Keith Laumer, 2004:

> "'Don't touch 'em,' I said. 'Unless **you want to start World War III**.'"

Steal a march on someone[2]

In British slang, this means getting an advantage on someone by taking action before the other person or persons do. The term originated from a military maneuver in which troops are secretly moved in order to gain an advantage over the enemy forces. The earliest known citation is in regard to the Scottish conflict at Sterling in December, 1715, from the *London Gazette,* March 16, 1716:

> "We saw him with incredible Celerity **steal a March** for our Preservation."

The above was later reprinted in *History of Edinburgh from its Foundation to the Present* by William Maitland in 1753. In *An Apology for the Life of Mr. Colley Cibber*, *Comedian,* (written by himself), 1746, on page 117 is another excellent early example of the idiom:

> "...Hamlet was intended to be acted at the other House, where it had not been yet seen (for they were now in a manner left to govern themselves) resolv'd, at any rate, to **steal a March** upon the Enemy, and take Possession

> of the same Play the Day before them: Accordingly, Hamlet was given out that Night, to be acted with us on Monday."

Steal the show

This means capture all of the attention and praise at an event or performance, especially when another performer was the headline act. The earliest known citation was in May, 1938, in *Public Safety*, on page 44, in an article titled 'An Award Dinner Packs 'Em In:'

> "Frankly frightened, Tom literally **stole the show** with a straight-forward plea for adult cooperation in the safety program."

The very next month the expression appeared in the book, *We Too Are the People* by Louise V. Armstrong, pages 441-442:

> "She was unique, and far more effective than any 'blond queen with teeth.' The city newspapers gave her enthusiastic publicity. She spoke in Ottawa over the radio, with her young husband interpreting. Everywhere she went she **stole the show."**

Stepping stone

In the literal sense, this is a rock upon which one steps to aid with crossing a stream, river or pond, or ascend to a higher level. Metaphorically, it refers to something which acts as a means to advancement or improvement. The earliest known figurative citation in print is found in *Good News for Evil Times for Fainting Believers or, the Summ of a Lecture upon Jeremiah 45 Chapter together with another Lecture on the 28 Chapter of Matthew throughout* by Mr. Michael Bruce, Minister of the Gospel, written in 1671, published in 1708:

> "And however Duty is ours, and the Event is the Lords, there is such Love-warm exercise in their Bosoms, that Difficulties are so far from retarding of them to Visit Christs Grave, that they make use of them all as **stepping-stones**, and Causeys to walk upon, they make all Difficulties as light and easie as they can..."

Step up to the plate

Derived from the game of baseball, moving into position at home plate to hit the ball, this means take decisive action in response to an opportunity or crisis, or take responsibility for something. The earliest known figurative usage in print is in the September, 1919 edition of *Textile Worker* in 'Straightening Out the Fade Away:'

> "The place to KEEP such a fund is in some safe, sound profitable security like War Savings Stamps or Savings Certificates... With such a confidence fund behind you, you are prepared for anything. You can **step up to the plate** in a pinch, knowing that YOU HAVE IT ON THE PITCHER."

Stick in the mud

This is another example of a phrase which seemed to evolve with the passage of the ages. Today it refers to a dull, unadventurous person who does not attempt to make progress or improvements in life. It derived from someone whose feet were stuck in the mud and could make no progress. Prior to this expression, other alternatives were used rather than mud, including clay, mire and even briars, as seen in Thomas Cooper's 1565 *Thesaurus*;

> "They beyng accused of extortion and pillage were in muche trouble, or **stacke in the bryars**."

Various British sources in 1733 mention two criminals with the alias 'Stick in the Mud.' Obviously, this was a derogatory expression reflecting their inability to stay out of trouble. Through nearly 100 years thereafter, the phrase doesn't appear in print as a noun, only a verb phrase. Then in the early 1830s' it returns in literature as a noun proceeded by 'old.' The earliest of these comes in *Fraser's Magazine* in William Ellis's 'Miru and the Man Spirit,' 1831:

> "Spirit! pray what are mortals about?
> Are kings hunting conquest, or lame with the gout?
> Do they see in their subjects their own flesh and blood?
> Answer me quickly, old **Stick-in-the-Mud**!"

This usage persists over several years, most using it as a nickname. Then in 1881, an entry was made for it in Thomas Davies' *A Supplementary English Glossary,* which seemed to show an altered meaning:

> "**STICK-IN-THE-MUD,** a slow fellow or bungler. [Example:] This nasty-coloured one is that respectable old **stick-in-the-mud**, Nicias Hughes, Tom Brown at Oxford, ch. x."

Tom Brown at Oxford was a novel, a sequel to Hugh's popular Tom Brown's School Days, published in 1861 by Macmillan in New York.

Stick one's oar in[2]

This largely British idiom means to nosily express one's opinion or try to become involved in a matter that is none of that person's business. A similar Americanism is 'stick one's nose into someone's business' (see in original volume). This phrase has become less common in England than it was at one time. It goes back at least to the 17th century, and originally was 'have an oar.' The earliest available verifiable reference is Thomas Holyoake's *A Large Dictionary in Three Parts,* 1677:

> "To **have an oar** in another man's oar, to meddle with other folks matters."

Put one's oar in was also used. Sticking one's oar in came around the early 20th century, as in this early citation from the American publication, *Poultry Success*, November, 1909, page 34:

> "Right here is where the other fellow will **stick his oar** in, and say they have black legs and white meat."

Sticky fingers^

This common idiom means to have a propensity to steal. It comes from fingers which are coated with a sticky substance picking up items easily. A major online dictionary lists origin at 1930-1935. It was in use figuratively, however, by at least 1902, when Charles Kennett Burrow used it in *Patricia of the Hills,* page 30:

> "One has a personal grudge, and he'll work it off if he hangs for it; another has **sticky fingers**, and will pick up money that should have gone to feed the poor."

Sticky wicket[2]

This figurative term for a difficult situation was derived from the sport of cricket, from difficulties caused by a damp, soft pitch (a wicket being the playing surface), thus it is British. The earliest know literal citation comes from *The Newtonton*, May, 1877, in 'Cricket: Tigenmouth C. C. *v*. Newton College:'

> "These peculiars were very low, straight, and uncommonly hard to get away on the **sticky wicket** so we were all out for 55…"

By early in the 20th century, wicket was being used idiomatically as mentioned in this snippet from the *Encyclopedia Britannica, A Dictionary of Arts, Sciences, Literature and General Information, Eleventh Edition, Volume VII,* 1910:

> "…extended sense applied to that portion of the ground, also called the 'pitch,' on which the stumps are pitched, as when it is described as being 'a fast wicket,' a **'sticky wicket'** and so forth. It also in several idiomatic expressions…"

Sting in the tail[2,3]

This idiom, popular in both England and Australia, means an unexpected, unpleasant end to something which began on a pleasant note; especially a story, a joke or a suggestion. The earliest mention known in print goes all the way back to *Truth's Triumph: Or, A Witness to the Two Witnesses from that Unfolded* by Thomas Tomkinson, written in 1676, published in 1690, Chapter VII, page 315:

> "Those that pretend religion, and yet persecute by laws of restraint, is a synagogue of Satan, a church with a **sting in her tail."**

Historical Collections, Volume III, by John Rushworth, published only a few years later, in 1706, may indicate the origin of the saying:

> "That of the many Complaints brought to the House, there were scarce any wherein they found not him engag'd, having like an angry Wasp, **his Sting in the Tail** of every thing…"

Stir crazy

This idiomatic phrase came from the slang word 'stir' for prison which dates to 1851 according to the *OED* (Oxford English Dictionary). Stir crazy referred originally to inmates which became mentally unbalanced due to prolonged incarceration, and came to mean anyone who felt like he or she was losing sanity because of prolonged unpleasant circumstances. The earliest verifiable reference in print is from *Collier's*, June 20, 1953 in 'The Soldier who went AWOL: U.S. to Korea:'

> "We bought a car and went somewhere almost every week end, for fear of becoming what local slang called Hillhappy, which was the same as loco, or **stir-crazy**."

Stone deaf^

This means unable to hear anything or someone who doesn't want to listen too reason. A major online dictionary dates it to 1830-1840. The term is a bit antiquated and may be offensive to some, especially with those able to hear some sounds. Profoundly deaf is a better choice of words. The term actually dates to the 18th century, the oldest verifiable reference being in *A Description of Millennium Hall and the Country Adjacent, the Fourth Edition* by Barbara Montagu, pseudonym 'A Gentleman on His Travels,' 1768.

> "Thus neighbour Jane, who poor woman is almost **stone deaf**, they thought would have a melancholy life if she was to be always spinning and knitting, seeing other people around her talking, and not be able to hear a word they said, so the ladies busy her in making broths and caudles…"

Stone the crows[3^]

In Australia, and to some extent in Britain, this is an exclamation of disbelief and a feeling of annoyance. British folk etymology attempts to link the origin to a croze, which was a groove at the end of a wooden barrel which holds the end plate in place. If, like this claims, it was originally 'stone the croze,' it would have meant to break open the barrel. There seems no evidence of this at all. It seems to have actually referred to literal crows, and started Down Under. Sheep farms are common in Australia, and crows are common pests, even to attacking young lambs. Seeing them hanging about the farm was great cause for alarm and annoyance when this phrase was coined, so throwing stones at them was a natural way of killing them, or at least driving them away. The earliest known citation is from *Here's Luck* by Australian author, Lennie Lower, 1930:

> "'I told Stanley that you had been thrown out and asked him to pull up, but he merely laughed and refused,' he explained. '**Stone the crows**!' exclaimed Stanley indignantly."

Stool pigeon

Most commonly, this applies to a person acting as an informer. When the phrase was first coined, in the 1820s, in the United States, it referred to someone acting as a decoy to draw outlaws into a trap—and it still may be used that way. The earliest available citation comes from *The Telegraph*, published in New York City on Saturday June 20, 1825, on the first page, under the heading 'Anniversaries,' but it had nothing to do with criminals:

"Indeed this popular preacher, having been countenanced and caressed by the Presbyterians, appears to have sold himself to them for a tool, or rather a **stool-pigeon** to decoy other Methodists into the snare designed to entrap them for the benefit of the Presbyterian clergy."

Many dictionaries state that this derived from a pigeon which was nailed to a stool, or a stump, to be used as a decoy. There seems to be no evidence of this use in a dictionary until the late 19th century. It is believed by some that the origin actually goes to the etymology of the words. Stool, in this sense, however, likely came from the French *estale* which was applied to a pigeon used to entice a hawk into a net. This word appeared in French from the early 1600s, and by the end of the 1700s, according to etymologists, stool pigeon was being used for a person used as a decoy. 'Pigeon' is also applied to someone who allows himself to be swindled.

Stop at nothing+

This figurative, seemingly hyperbolic, expression is used to state that someone will do whatever it takes to achieve a goal or purpose. It was first recorded in English poet and playwright, John Dryden's rhyming Restoration drama, *Aureng-zebe* in 1676:

"The World is made for the bold impious man;
Who **stops at nothing**, seizes all he can."

Stop dead

This means to halt suddenly; come to a complete standstill. It came into use early in the 19th century. An early example is from Henry Cockton's *The Life and Adventures of Valentine Vox, the Ventriloquist,* 1840, page 280:

"This practice at first annoyed Valentine exceedingly, for although his uncle never **stopped dead** in the road, but flew over every crossing with as much of the facility of a greyhound as he comfortably could, whether carriages were or were not within view; he would frequently would do so in the midst of a mortal stream…"

Storm in a tea cup[2]/ aka **tempest in a teacup**

This British idiom means a small event that has been exaggerated, and is out of proportion with reality. It came into usage in the mid-19th century, and the earliest examples are from 1853, including this one from *A Latin-English and English-Latin Dictionary for the use of Schools* by Charles Anthon:

> *"Prov.* excitare fluctue in eimpulo, to raise a **storm in a teacup**; to make much ado about nothing."

The next year, on March 25, 1854, *The Athenaeum* had this in an article on Literature and Drama in its play reviews:

> "This piece has been successful; but less so than the more recent novelty, 'A **Storm in a Teacup'** by Mr. Bayle Bernard; — a little drama possessing the vivacity and neatness of a French plot, with the robust manners and humours of the English..."

But this was only the beginning of productions to use the expression as a title. A 1937 film bore this name, as well as a few albums and songs.

Straighten up and fly right

This idiom, used as more or less an ultimatum, means to make a change in behavior and/or attitude for the better. The earliest use in print of a form of it was in Lewis John Carlino's play, *The Exercise,* which he wrote in 1963 and published in 1968:

> "You're gonna **straighten up**. Hear? Yer gonna toe the mark, hold ranks, stay on the ball and **fly right**! That's my orders and them's yours."

In 1998, Richard Spears used these examples in *NTC's Thematic Dictionary of American Slang* on page 40:

> "It's time for you to **straighten up and fly right**! **Straighten up and fly right** before you get into difficulty."

stranger is just a friend you haven't met yet, A

This proverbial saying has been attributed to both Irish poet William Butler Yates (1865-1938) and American humorist Will Rogers (1879-1935). It is very interesting that these two notable gentlemen lived during the same era, the Victorian Age. Then there is famed American Ad Exec, Leo Burnett (1891-1971). One online source even attributes it to modern British author, Roy R. Stoleworthy. More than one version of this principle exists, and it is most likely that all of these fine gentlemen used it. It is extremely difficult to determine who actually put these thoughts together for the first time. A lot of sources call it anonymous. *The London Medical and Physical Journal, July to December, 1822,* made this statement:

> "…although the proportion is less than half of that of the scholars of Paris, and that **there are no strangers** here."

But if one of these did originate this, it would likely be Yates. The version attributed to him is 'There are no strangers here, only friends you haven't met yet.'

Strapped for

This means 'In need of,' and began in the mid-19th century as simply 'strapped,' which meant 'in need of money.' It evolved rapidly to include other necessities, such as time, food, etc. A very early example in quotes indicating in early use is from *The Fourteenth Ohio National Guard* by Sergt. Maj. Chas. E. Creager, 1899:

> "On September 26th Major Jones arrived at the island with money with which to pay the men, but money to them was 'as filthy lucre,' for although they were **'strapped'** for the most part, they could get almost anything they wanted without paying."

The earliest available citation for 'strapped for,' here involving time, is from *The Hoosier Volunteer*, 1914, by Kate and Virgil D. Boyles, on page 49:

> "…for that matter, and I've thought a many an unkind thing about her for that — but I notice that she has time to take care of my babies when I'm **strapped for time**, and to comb their hair ..."

Straw boss

This colloquialism applies to a person who assists a foreman in overseeing a small group of workers, and still has his or her own work to do. It derived from the idea that straw is never the main product of any farm or business, but only a by-product, thus a straw boss is never the main person in charge. It is seen as a belittling term, mostly used by subordinates. It has been around since the Industrial Revolution of the 1890s, and there are various theories as to how it started; one being that it was originally applied to the person in a mill who took the straw out of the thresher after the wheat had been removed. 'Straw boss' was actually used in print as early as 1833, when it appeared in *The Library of Romance, Volume I, The Ghost Hunter and His Family* by 'The O'Hara Family:'

"There was some clumsy contrivance for a fire-place in another corner; and a three-legged stool, and a **straw boss**, completed the catalogue of her furniture."

From this and later citations throughout the mid-to-late 19th century, it can be ascertained that this definitely referred to a piece of furniture. It wasn't until near the end of the century that the meaning made a clear change, though the other connotation still applied at times. A very vivid example comes in 1895, in *Cases Determined by the St. Louis and Kansas City Court of Appeals for the State of Missouri*, Volume LXII, page 196; here in quotes, likely indicating a recently coined, yet familiar, phrase:

"Witness Hiner, at each examination, detailed a conversation had with plaintiff before his fall from the ladder to the effect that plaintiff's shoulder had been injured by wrestling; but at the last trial the same witness further testified that plaintiff, while at work at the coal chute, acted as a foreman or '**straw boss**,' and was in the habit of changing the boards on the platform, etc."

Straw man[2] (See: **Man of straw**)

Strength in numbers^

This idiomatic expression refers to an emotional and moral strength drawn from a group of people, sometimes called synergy. It has often been attributed to both American wrestler, actor and political commentator, Jesse Ventura (1951-), who criticized organized religion for drawing off the strength in numbers, and American political columnist and commentator Mark Shields (1937-) who said:

"There is always **strength in numbers**. The more individuals or organizations that you can rally to your cause the better."

But this proverbial phrase has been around for hundreds of years. In *The Principles of Population and Production as They are Affected by the Progress of Society* by John Weyland, published in London in 1816, on page 172 we see:

"We must not indeed carry this comparison so far as to forget that man is a moral agent, and that he is never worth his country's having, unless he be both good in bodily health and also in moral quality; and that strength in virtue is as necessary to the preservation of a state as **strength in numbers**."

Strike a chord

This means to bring something to memory in such a clear way that it reminds the person of something or someone familiar and of significance, evoking an emotional response. It may have either positive or negative consequences. It is taken from hitting musical chords which bring about images in the mind. The earliest known reference in print is from *The Boston Examiner*, August 6, 1803:

> "I am now in perfect humour with all the world, and I will not, by peeping into these letters, run the risk of **striking a chord**, which not being in unison with my present feelings, might put the whole machine out of time."

Strike out

Coming from the game of baseball, in which three strikes at bat without making a base hit result in an out, this idiom now most commonly means to fail at an endeavor. A good modern example of this is in *America Taken Hostage* by Hayden Lee Hinton, 2010, page 142:

> **"…he tried** talking to a couple of nice looking young single women at the bar, but **struck out**."

The initial meaning, before baseball, was to draw a line through something which had been written down, which still may be used. It was cited in this manner as early as 1537, when it was recorded in *Criminal Trials and Other Proceedings before the High Court of Justiciary in Scotland during the Reigns of King James the Fourth and Fifth,* Part IX:

> "…and finally, the latter was **struck out**, and 'Bannitus' inserted…"

It may also apply to going out on one's own in a venture, such as a business. A good figurative citation of this is from *Out of the Night: Memoir of Richard Julius Herman Krebs alias Jan Valtin* by Jan Valtin, 1941:

> "I **struck out** on my career of an underground worker on the Pacific Coast."

Stubby[3]

In Australia, this is a short, squat beer bottle, usually one with a capacity of 375 mL. The name comes from the fact that the bottle is short and thick when compared the tall, slender 750 ml bottles of beer. The earliest verifiable citation is from *Summer's Tales, Volume III* by John Iggulden, 1966, page 123:

"Green trees intruded in the pub yard where they rested, drinking beer from small, cold **stubbies**."

Stumble upon something

This means to discover something by chance, not looking for it or expecting to find it. The earliest known reference in print is from *An Easy and Compendious Introdvction for Reading All Sorts of Histories* by Mathias Prideaux, 1664:

"There he **stumbled upon** an Oracle (which in great devotion he consulted with) in this Poetical Rapture."

Sucker punch

Also known as a coward punch or one hit punch in America, and a 'king punch' in Australia, this is a hit made without warning or allowing the other person to prepare for defense. This is usually deemed to be unfair and unethical, and often comes from behind. In boxing, a sucker punch delivered outside the rules is illegal. The expression is very recent, and the earliest known citation in print is from *Paul's Case: The Kingston Letters* by Lynn Crosbie, 1997, page 127:

"Sex killer Paul Bernardo can barely see out of a cut and bruised left eye after he was **'sucker punched'** yesterday."

Sugar-coat something

This is a metaphor for talking about something unpleasant in a way which makes it more acceptable. It comes from putting a sweet glaze on bitter pills to make them easier to swallow. It came into use by the mid-19th century. The earliest verifiable citation comes from *A Memoir of the Rev. Richard Sluyter, Late Pastor of the Ref. Prot. Dutch Church of Claverace New York* by R. Ormaston Currie, 1846, page 79, here in quotes, as a recent but known expression:

"...he seemed to realize that he was preaching for eternity, and had no time **to 'sugarcoat' the truth**, to render it more palatable to the fastidious and vitiated taste of some of his hearers."

The following quote from *Primitive Monitor and Church Advocate,* May, 1892, reprinted 1n 1904, defines it perfectly:

> "To **sugar-coat** a pill, is to make it appear outwardly to be sugar, something that it is not. To **sugar-coat** the truth is to put something on the surface to make it seem to be something else."

Swallow one's pride

This cliché idiom means humbling oneself and admitting wrongdoing. The principle goes back to the days of King Solomon and the biblical *Proverbs (16:18-19, 29:23). The Arethusa: A Naval Story*, Volume 1 by Frederick Chamier, 1837, had the following lines on page 41:

> "The last remark of Hammerton stung him to the quick, ***must*** — here's a word for **pride** to **swallow**; — it nearly choked him; and when his throat relaxed its efforts to keep down his rage, ..."

In 1853, the saying had come to what we know, as seen in *Caroline Mordaunt; or, the Governess* by Mrs. Sherwood (Mary Martha), page 17:

> "...and all these things only on condition that you will **swallow your pride**, and bear with some little uncomfortablenesses of manner."

Swan song

This figurative term refers to a final gesture or performance given before someone's death or retirement. It is derived from the ancient legend that swans are mute during their entire lives, but emit a beautiful, though mournful song, just before they die. Neither is true. Swans are not mute, as they have a variety of sounds which they make, and they do not sing just before death. This legend was noted as being false as early as the first century by Pliny the Elder, in *Natural Historie*, before 79 CE:

> "Observation shows that the story that the dying **swan sings** is false."

The term, per se, appears first in print in English long afterward, in the 18th century when Scottish cleric John Wilson used it in *Scripture Songs for Zion's Travelers*, first published in 1767, in Song VI, page 242:

> "Being a Prophecy of Christ, and King David's **Swan Song** in views of death."

Swear on a stack of Bibles

This is a hyperbolic way to state vehemently that one is telling the absolute 'gospel truth' (see first volume). It is derived from the practice of taking an oath in court by laying one's hand on a Bible. The earliest known citation is from *Investigation into the Alleged Official Misconduct of the Late Superintendent of the Philadelphia, Wilmington and Baltimore Railroad Co. Volume I*, photographed and reprinted by Arthur Cannon, Philadelphia, 1854, page 542:

> "*A*. I'd **swear on a stack of bibles** as high as the house that they didn't."

Swear up and down+

This idiomatic expression is used to emphasize that something is indeed true. It has no reference to actually using swear words. It has been in use since at least the late 19th century. *Good Health Magazine*, May 1, 1883, carried the following citation:

> "Most of the persons or corporations which practice adulteration upon a large scale are rich, and will fight the matter in courts, employing experts of their own who will **swear up and down** that alum is rather beneficial to bread than otherwise…"

Sweet as a nut[2]

According to some, this British simile was started in London and Northward in Newcastle among working class Brits. It is a way of expressing one's satisfaction with the way life has treated him or her, and the present state of things. In America 'everything is peachy' might be a similar expression. Though nuts seem an unlikely item to be called 'sweet,' they have long been used as a dessert item in England, often dipped in honey or sugar (see: Soup to nuts). Almonds, along with small fruit like raisons, currants and figs were sweetened for dessert as early as the Middle Ages. For certain, the expression goes all the way back 1760, when noted English novelist Sarah Fielding used it in *The History of Ophelia, Volume II*, page 11:

> "If Madam's Lips are chapped and her Eyes sore, what's the Matter of that, it is no Body's Business but her own, sure! such fine Tallow as we burn, would not disgrace the Mouth of the first Dutchess in the Land; it is as **sweet as a Nut**, and much more healinger than all their curous salves."

Sweet nothings (See: **Whisper sweet nothings**)

Sweet smell of success

This idiom means that being successful gives one a pleasant feeling. It came into use due to a 1957 melodramatic film by that name, brilliantly directed by Alexander Mackendrick, starring Burt Lancaster, Tony Curtis, Susan Harrison and Martin Milner, chronicling the dominance system of the 1950's. Lancaster's character, a columnist based on Walter Winchell, uses his connections to ruin his sister's relationship with a jazz musician (Curtis), whom he feels is unworthy of her.

Switch gears

Coined when many automobiles still came with 'straight' transmissions, and gears had to be changed manually, this became a metaphor for suddenly altering what one was doing, especially in regard to thinking about a particular activity or subject. Changing gears could literally refer to going faster, slower, or even backward rather than forward. The actual origin is unclear, but the earliest verifiable citation of figurative use is from *Frontiers of American Culture* by Ray B. Browne, 1968, page 192:

> "I remember Russel Nye once saying that when on occasion he teaches a history course he must **shift gears** from his usual critical analysis of a written work to a chronological consideration of events."

T

Take a bite out of one's wallet

Taking a bite out of anything is reducing the size of it. When used with the wallet, it means that something is or was costly, likely more than anticipated. The earliest known reference to a bite being taken from someone's wallet was in an oft-reprinted article titled 'The Mormons, a Discourse Delivered before the Historical Society of Pennsylvania,' March 26, 1850 by Thomas L. Kane, initially appearing in *The Latter Day Saints' Millennial Star*, May 1, 1861:

"Their character was disclosed by their eager request of **a bite from my wallet**; in default of which, after a somewhat superfluous scriptural grace, they made an imperfect lunch before me off the softer of their corn ears, eating the grains as horses do from the cob."

Take a hike

This is an expression of annoyance used in the U.S. and Canada meaning, 'Go away! I've had enough of you.' The word hike is from the English dialectal *hyke*, 'to walk vigorously,' and has been used since the 19th century for taking walks, particularly in settings of nature, for pleasure and exercise. The idiom, however, is much more recent, dating to the last half of the 20th century. Though true origin is uncertain, a good example in print is from *The Wharton's Sketch Book* by Jim and Phil Wharton, 1996, in 'Coaches' Notes' on page 139:

"More than one surly New Yorker has told us to '**Take a hike**, pal!'"

Take aim at

From sighting a target and preparing to shoot, either with an arrow, a gun, other weapon or missile, this is figuratively used to refer to focusing on a problem or situation in order to accomplish a goal. It was being used as a metaphor by the early 20th century, as evidenced in *Collot's French-English and English-French Dictionary* by A. S. Collot, 1910:

"***MIRER***; to aim, to **take one's aim**; — *le but*,- to aim at the place. *une place*; **to aim at** a situation."

Take by the scruff of the neck

This figurative term means to take complete control of something or someone. It is derived from a mother cat grasping her young to move them from place to place. The earliest literal citation available actually references a dog. It is from Thomas Hood's *The Comic Annual*, 1834, in 'The Rope Dancer,' page 2:

"However in they went, with a crash and a dash, and a grip and a grapple, and if they did not **take him by the scruff of the neck**, like a dog, there is no truth in St. Winifred's Well."

Figurative use came by the early 20th century. The first known example is from *Addresses Before the Eleventh Annual Convention of the Navy League of the United States* by Robert Means, 1916, page 43:

> "…these two nations is reported to have once said, while we were engaged in war with Spain, 'If I had a larger fleet, I would have taken Uncle Sam **by the scruff of the neck**.'"

It has also been repeatedly used for taking charge of oneself; the earliest such example being only two years later in *The Outlook*, April 17, 1818, in 'After a Year at War,' page 8:

> "The Happy Eremite, philosophizing amid the jubilant blades, recalled with an effort that he had work to do, took himself **by the scruff of the neck** and proceeded to his study."

Take center stage

This means to be at the center of attention. It is taken from the main stage in classic theater, in which the major scenes in a play are acted out. It was used figuratively as early as 1869 when Sir Norman Lockyer used it in *Nature*, Volume 315, page 9, published by Macmillan Journals Ltd. in London:

> "Science and technology are now central to many foreign policy issues, said Sir Robin, in the way that international trade **took centre stage** 25 years ago."

Take it in stride

This idiom refers to calmly dealing with all situations, accepting both advances and setbacks as normal events in the course of business or life. It came into use during the second quarter of the 20th century. The earliest available verifiable citation is from *Public Safety*, December, 1938, in Editor Paul Jones' column, 'It Did Happen Here,' on page 18, and concerns an animal rather than a person:

> "Dr. Verne Scott, a veterinarian at John Tarleton College, Stephenville, Texas, was feeling very sorry for the calf, as he performed a delicate operation on the animal's eye. The calf **took it in stride**, but a 200-pound student watching the operation keeled over in a faint, jostled Dr. Scott and caused the vet to cut his hand severely with the operating knife."

Take it from the top

Colloquially, this is used mostly in music, and means 'start over at the beginning.' The earliest known citation of the phrase, possibly how it was coined, is from the London publication, *Grammophone*, first published in 1923 by the Mark Allen Group, in the November, 1940 edition, there was a song titled ***Take it from the Top.*** It was later before it came into common usage. A good example is found in the Howard Fast novel, *Phyllis*, 1962, page 204:

> "Then Bingham would say, 'Let's **take it from the top**, Clancy.'

Take it lying down

Usually stated in a negative sense, it refers to accepting an insult, rebuke or setback without complaining or attempting to get revenge. It came into use in 1903, and though it is difficult to tell which citation was first, there are several that year, one of which is in *All Sides of the Fiscal Controversy*, in 'Mr. Chamberlin at Tynemouth, 21st October, 1903:'

> "My second question is — how long do you intend to Retaliation **take this lying down**? I believe, myself, that a policy of and retaliation under such circumstances, the policy, in fact, Negotiation."

Take it on the chin

This means to be brave and endure or accept misfortune well. It derived from boxing, in which getting hit on the chin causes quite a jolt, and being able to rebound easily is quite an accomplishment. The earliest known figurative use in print is in *Traffic Safety*, June, 1938 in 'One of us is Nuts,' by Paul Jones, where it is obvious that the saying was already in use:

> "What WILL they say? Boy! Will I have to **take it on the chin** now from that gang of wolves! And especially after that little episode when I was driving 'em to the club the other afternoon! It just can't happen!"

Take it to the next level

This metaphor is a popular one which has become a cliché. It refers to taking something which has already proven to be good to a higher level of excellence. It seems that more than one group would likely stand in line to claim origin of the saying. Anything from a clockworks company in Switzerland to students at Atlanta's Georgia Tech campus in 2011. With all due respect, the phrase was in use, though no quite on 'the same level,' in 1857, when the following appeared in *An Elementary Course in Civil Engineering for the use of Cadets in the United States Military Academy* by Professor Dennis H. Mahan, page 319:

"Now, in descending on the other side, the boat will require one prism of lift to **take it to the next level**, and this prism of lift will carry it through all the successive locks…"

Though it is hard to pin down the first person to use the idiom as we know it, it seems that it originated in the 1980s, and it was certainly in common use by 1989 when Kate Ferguson Ellis employed it in *The Contested Castle: Gothic Novels and the Subversion of Domestic Ideology* in her Acknowledgements at the front of the book:

"Gene Brown's careful editing of an earlier version of the manuscript provided encouragement when it was needed, and at crucial moments Michael Kimmel defined the project for me in a way that enabled me to **take it to the next level**."

Take leave of one's senses

On a basic level, this is applied to loosing rational judgment. Hyperbolically, in a more formal sense, it means 'going insane.' The earliest verifiable citation of the phrase is in *The Keepsake*, by Frederick A. Heath, 1850, page 2:

"My dear Miss Capel, have you actually **taken leave of your senses**?"

Take off one's hat to

This idiom is used for paying honor or respect to someone, especially for an achievement. The practice of taking off one's hat out of respect began in medieval days. It was practiced later when entering a church. The first known example of a hat being removed, supposedly in respect (here by someone else), is from *A Journal or Historical Account in the Life and Ministry of George Fox, Volume I*, originally published in 1694, in an entry of October 13, 1657, Edinburgh Scotland:

"When the time came I appeared and was in a great room, where many great persons came and looked at me. After a while the door-keeper came and had me into the council-chamber; and as I was going in he **took off my hat**. I asked him why he did so… I was moved by the Lord to say Peace be unto you."

In a French military, this gesture has been a show of honor since the 1700s. *Memoirs, Historical and Military*, 1735 by Antoine de Pas marquis de Feuquières, translated from the French, page 453, has this statement:

"As soon as they have saluted, they are **to** pull **off** their **Hats** without bowing, but standing upright."

The custom was also for a man showing respect to a lady. In Burnett's Travels by Gilbert Burnett, 1738, we read on page 40:

> "...for it is only strangers that **put off their hats to women,** but they make no courtesies: and here, as in all Switzerland, women are not saluted, but the civility is expressed by taking them by the hand."

As a figure of speech, it became prevalent in the 19th century. In the humorous story book with a variety of contributors titled *Funny Dogs with Funny Tales*, illustrated by Harrison Weir, 1852, in 'The Good Natured Dog' by James Hannay, on page 80 we find:

> **"We take our hats off to** such people of course, but **we** keep our love for others,—just as in literature the world will always prefer Goldsmith, Dryden and Felding to Pope and Grey and even Addison."

Take one's eye off the ball

This refers to diverting one's attention from the task at hand, thus losing focus of what is most important. It is derived from sports (particularly golf) in which keeping one's eye on the ball in play is imperative to the game. It has been used in a literal sense for hundreds of years, but figurative use is very recent. The earliest available references are from 2006, when it appeared in *Millionaire Republican* by Wayne Alyn Root, in 'Secret #18:'

> "You can't afford drugs, alcohol, or other negative addictions. You can't afford to be sick (people with positive attitudes have been shown to be much healthier than those with negative attitudes). You can't afford to **take your eye off the ball** for a second."

Take someone to the cleaners

This is used to mean obtaining all of someone's possessions, particularly in a dishonest or unfair way. It derived from dry cleaners which made their appearance in the late 19th century. The metaphoric saying didn't come until early in the 20th century. The earliest known citation is from *The Electrical Worker,* April, 1914, in a letter from Portland Oregon member W.H. Emrick to the Editor:

> "At present we are not in a position to say what the outcome will be but have high hopes of **taking the Employers' Association to the cleaners**."

Take the bit between one's teeth

This ancient saying means to take control of the situation. A bit is the metal part of a horse's bridle placed in the mouth to control the horse's movements when the reins are pulled to one side. By biting down on the bit, a horse can take back control from a person.

The earliest known citation of this figurative expression is under expressions having to do with 'dents' (teeth) in *A Dictionary of the French and English Tongues Composed by. Randle Cotgrave,* 1611:

> "Prendre le frein aux dents. To **take the bit between** his **teeth;"**

The above shows that it was already in use in both French and English at that date. It was utilized in *The Metal* by John Dryden, 1682:

> "But this new Jehu spurs the hot-mounted horse, Instructs the beast to know his native force, To **take the bit between his teeth** and fly To the next headlong steep of anarchy."

Take the fall

This refers to taking the blame and responsibility, and possibly the punishment for something that someone else did. The word, 'fall' originated in Old English, but this connotation came much later. A predecessor of the idiom came as early as 1815, when the following citation appeared in *A Collection of Letters on the Most Interesting and Important Subjects and on Several Occasions* by William Law, published in London, on page 159, in Letter XVI, which referred to 'taking the fall' as taking the curse. This would serve to explain how it came to mean taking the blame:

> "That alone can **take the fall** or curse out of the body which can take it out of the soul. For the curse through all nature and creature is but one and the same thing, viz."

The earliest uses of 'fall guy' in this sense, are from 1906, including one in *A Man Without Principle?* by Retsel Terreve, pseudonym for Lester Everett Broyles, page 84:

> "Well, me conscience don't stand fer makin' er **fall guy** out of no man wot says, 'Mac, help yerself and pay when youse ready.'"

Popular use in print of 'take the fall' didn't begin until late in the 20th century.

Take the heat

This idiom is similar to the previous one, 'take the fall,' but different in that it may not refer to taking the blame *for something perpetrated by another*. It is actually a bit more similar to 'face the music' (see original volume). It is also used in a negative context when someone is said to not be able to take the heat, or endure under the pressure of blame. Figurative use of the phrase did not come about until the third quarter of the 20th century. The earliest citation available is from *Reading Myself and Others* by Philip Roth, 1975, page 61:

> "…yes, President Nixon is quitting because he can't **take the heat**, well, that to my mind would constitute a direct violation of my oath of Office, and I would in fact voluntarily step down from the Presidency, out of a sense of having profoundly failed you, the American people…"

Talk a glass eye to sleep [3,2]

This Aussie and British Naval term refers to a person who is very loquacious, boring and repetitive. Glass eyes were mentioned in literature since the time of Shakespeare. This saying, however, is very recent, and not common outside the mentioned areas, yet it is interesting. In 2000 it was cited in *The Hopeless and Helpless Manager* by Adrian Furnam professor of psychology at ULC, also a consultant and writer for business magazines, the London Sunday Times and Daily Telegraph, and *Rick Jolly*, a Surgeon Captain in the British Royal Navy, published in 2000, page 173:

> "He is such a motormouth that he could **talk a glass eye to sleep** is a Grandmaster of the inappropriate remark."

It also appeared in *Jackspeak: A guide to British Naval slang & usage* by the same Rick Jolly, 2014, first published in 1989 as *Pusser's Rum Guide to British Naval Sang,* in an example on the definition to gob-shite on page 199.

> "**Gob-shite** A loudmouth who is always gobbing-off: 'He's so gobby, he could **talk a glass eye to sleep**!'"

Jolly, aka 'the Doc' was born in Hong Kong and served in the 1982 Falkland War. His work on *Jackspeak* was considered authoritative.

Talk in circles

This means to speak in a confusing or roundabout manner, or argue a point repetitiously. The earliest known reference in print is from *The Galaxy*, June, 1870, in 'Two Women,' Chapter One:

> "If you left Joe to follow his own lead, he was sure to **talk in circles**, and you could take him up half an hour hence at precisely the same place and have lost nothing."

Talk the hind legs off a donkey[2]

In British English, this represents the height of persuasive ability. It means that a person can chatter endlessly without stopping or becoming boring. The story has been told that expression originated in Ireland and is a literal translation of the Gaelic phrase actually meaning 'make a donkey sit down on its rear end,' something a donkey very rarely does. If a person can achieve this impossible feat by talking, they are an extraordinary and influential orator. It is a bit uncertain if the Gaelic origin is true, however, the rest seems to 'hold water' (see original volume). The following is from *The Alpine Journal*, May, 1887, in 'The Ascent of Tetnuld Tau' by Clinton Dent:

> "In addition to the customary halts—about every quarter of an hour—for conversation, innumerable other delays were occasioned. Three or four times the small donkey was flattened down by his burden, and his little legs spread out sideways, so that he looked like a tortoise. This disaster, as might be supposed, set up much chatter; as if they thought that because they could **talk the hind legs off a jackass**, they could talk them on again. Then, all assisting, we propped the donkey up."

There is one slightly earlier citation in print, however, from *The Chaplin of the Fleet: A Novel,* Volume 1, by Sir Walter Besnant and James Rice, 1881, page 92:

> "'I believe,' said Mrs. Gambit, 'that this man would **talk the hind legs off a donkey**. Keep close to me, Miss Kitty. Here may be villainy; and if there is, there's one at least that shall feel the weight of my ten nails.'"

Talk trash

This idiom, also trash-talk refers to saying disparaging things; criticizing other people unfairly. It goes back to at least the mid-19th century. The earliest known citation is from 'The Emerald Studs,' a novel anonymously penned by William

E. Ayetoun, first published in London's *Blackwood Magazine*, in Chapter 1, August, 1847:

> "'Don't **talk trash**! It was the weakest cold-without in the creation.' 'And then ye had a sair fecht on politics wi'anither man in the coffee room.'"

Tall tale

This old term refers to a fanciful story, which is generally greatly exaggerated, told purely for the enjoyment of the listeners. 'Tall,' in this connotation, means embellished, or blown out of proportion. A popular online etymology site lists 'by 1846' as approximate date of origin, and though others say that it goes back about much further, that may not be true. It has been contended that term was even used in the 1714 printing of *The Works of William Shakespeare, The Life and Death of Richard III,* Act IV, Scene iii, written circa 1592:

> "Let not the Heav'ns hear these **Tall-tale** Women Rail on the Lord's Anointed- Strike, I fay."

It is probable that this should have read 'tell-tale' as it does in Julius Caesar, also thought by some to have had reference to tall tale. The hyphen gives it away.

The first unmistakable reference in print of tall tale is found in *The Ladies' Repository*, November, 1873, in Gentle Hortense; Or, The Maiden's Leap by Emma E.H. Specht:

> "Edward came in soon after, telling **tall tales** of the *gentilhomme*, who had been so kind to him."

target on someone's back, A

Often preceded by 'put' or 'paint,' this means that the person has become 'open game' for the attacks of others because of comments made against them or the way they have become perceived by the public. It was used in a literal sense since the 19th century, but the earliest known figurative reference is from *The Balloon* by British economist, Sir Henry Phelps Brown, 1853, page 184, and here it is a metaphor for feeling the target:

> "He knew that from some hole in the wall the sights of the carbine would be trained on him, and he could feel the concentric circles of **a target on his back.**"

A clear cut citation in true harmony with current meaning comes in 1975 in the John Birch Society publication, *American Opinion*, Volume 18, page 86:

> "The name of the electoral game is now divide and conquer. Meanwhile Nelson Rockefeller can continue as the de facto President, letting Gerald Ford walk around with **a target on his back**."

Tea and sympathy[2^]

In British colloquial English this means, instead of receiving real help at a time of need, all one gets is kindness and a listening ear. The popularity of the phrase goes back to a play with explicit and risky themes, especially in that day, written by *American* playwright Robert Anderson (1917-2009) starring Deborah Kerr which debuted at New York City's Barrymore Theater on September 30, 1953. The line by the male lead, husband, which gave the play its name and spawned the saying, was:

> "All you're supposed to do is every once in a while give the boys a little **tea and sympathy**."

MGM later adapted it to a movie in 1956, also starring Deborah Kerr and John Kerr. But because of the codes for morality, the sexually explicit themes were toned down.

But this was not the genesis of the term 'tea and sympathy'! Since it is a British idiom one may have surmised that it was in use in England earlier. In *The Casquet of Literature*, Volume III, edited by Charles Gibbon, 1873, in a feature titled *Chanet* by J.W. De Forest on page 107 we see:

> "Of course it would be impossible to explain that here was a gentleman whom she had caught trying to commit suicide, and whom she had undertaken to cure of his self-destroying propensities by means of **tea and sympathy**."

Tell that (or **it) to the marines!^**

This catchphrase originally had reference to Britain's Royal Marines, and was a bit of a smear, in that the person to whom it was being said was not to be believed. In other words 'the navy won't believe that, so go tell it to the marines and maybe they will.' In spite of what was later admittedly a fabricated tale by William B. Drury, Royal Marine Light Infantry, Lt. Col, Ret., attributing it to

Britain's King Charles II (1660-1685), the earliest publication of the expression is in *The Post Captain; or, the Wooden Walls Well Manned; Comprehending a View of Naval Society and Manners* by John Davis, published in 1804. In fact, it is in the book on four separate occasions, the first being:

> "You may tell that to the marines, but I'll be d----d if the sailors will believe it."

The statement has become a pop-culture phenomenon, appearing in numerous American books, movies and other media. The 1926 movie, starring Lon Chaney, *Tell It to the Marines* reversed the meaning, picturing the Marines more realistically, as tough fighters, not gullible wimps. It even became the focus of a World War II propaganda poster for the U.S. Marines:

> "If you must talk, **tell it to the marines**!"

Ten hut!+

This term is an abbreviation of the word attention, and supposedly originated in the American military. It is actually a shortening of a-ten-hut, which is easier to say than 'come to attention,' which is implied. The command is yelled, particularly in movies and television shows by a drill sergeant in a choppy, authoritative manner.

The January16, 1951 issue of *The Text*, Lowell Textile Institute in Massachusetts, has this on page 1, in 'Military Discipline in Girls Sanctuary':

> "**Ten-hut!** In-spec-SHUN! This has been the order of the day in the most popular terms of these trying times."

Thanks, but no thanks

This is meant to be a nice way to tell someone that the person speaking has no interest in what has been offered. The earliest citation known to a close form of this is from *The Saturday Review of Politics, Literature, Science and Art,* August 31, 1872:

> "In Mr. Layard's time the Secretary was directed to acknowledge the receipt of the letter 'with his **thanks,' but no thanks** are to be found in the formula dictated by Mr. Ayrton."

Still the actual saying did not come into use until about 100 years later. The earliest verifiable reference in print is in *Congressional Record: Proceedings and Debates of the 92nd Congress, Second Session*, Washington, DC, 1974:

> "Over the years, the beef industry has operated clearly under the law of supply and demand. Please let us continue to operate without government interference. **Thanks, but no thanks**.
> Yours Sincerely,
> LEON MILLER,
> President, Alta Verde Industries, Inc."

That'll put hair on your chest

This is applied to something to eat or drink which will be very invigorating or make one healthy, particularly spoken to a male, except when joking. Sometimes this refers to strong coffee or alcohol, or hot chili. It is also used to imply that something will make a 'real man' out of a youth or young man who may feel less than manly. The earliest known citation is from *The Red Dawn* by Stewart Edward White, 1920, page 141:

> "**That'll put hair on your chest**. And if you like the pretties read The Meadow Lark."

That's about the long and short of it (See: **long and the short of it, The**)

That's about the size of it

This statement is made to confirm someone's assessment of a situation, particularly one less than perfect. The earliest verifiable example in print is from Thomas Peckett Prest's Romance novel, *The Jew and the Foundling*, 1847, page 139:

> "You are going to commit a robbery, then?"
> "Ay—**that's about the size** of it."

That's a hoot! / real hoot+

This is a metaphor for something that is fun or funny. Use of the word *huten* as a cry of dissatisfaction or contempt appeared in Middle English in the mid-15th century, and became 'hoot' circa 1600 according to *Etymology Online*. See Volume III, page 209 for use as giving or not giving a hoot. As something funny, it was first attested in 1942 according to this website. By December 13, 1961 it was coupled with 'real,' and it stuck. The Tyler Junior College (Tyler Texas) student newspaper, *TJC Pow Wow* that month had it recorded in 'Band, 'Belles Plan White Christmas for Sunset Home':

> "The band within a band… even Santa gets a real hoot out of Christmas."

That ship has sailed

This popular saying means simply, 'That opportunity has already passed.' Literal use is very old and comes from ships being missed by those who did not make it to the port of departure in time, and in some cases, missed their only opportunity at a new beginning, particularly in the New World. *Saved by a Smile* by James Siree, 1886, has an interesting citation of the phrase on page 39:

> "Another has, and apparently without the faintest reason, decided on a sudden not to sail. **That ship has sailed**, and never again been heard of."

Purely figurative use only became popular in the 21st century. Several early examples came in 2006, including the following example from the biographical sketch of Olympic discus champion, Lemuel Clarence 'Bud' **Houser** (1901 – 1994), *Houser: Pride of America* by Robert Dunn, on page 213, chapter 51:

> "'Maybe you should try out for the 1932 Olympics.'
> "'I'm afraid **that ship has sailed**. I'll be 30 years old by then.'"

That's why I make the big bucks

American pro volleyball player Gabrielle Reece is quoted as having said, "I'm a natural. **That's why I make the big bucks**." The 'big bucks,' of course, means a great deal of money. This comical statement has become cliché, and may be used in jest by people who are near poverty level. Reece was born in 1970, and the first known citation in print of the saying is when she was 12 years old, so obviously she didn't coin it, but she certainly popularized it. *Star Trek II Distress Call* by William Rotsler, 1982, had the following lines on page 125:

> "'A lack of faith?' exclaimed ensign Gottlieb incredulously.
> "Kirk nodded. '**That's why they pay me the big bucks**.'"

It is possible that Reece saw the Star Trek movies, or perhaps read the books.

That's so dope!

This very modern expression means something was so awesome, fantastic and amazing that it surpassed any expectations. It has been around in American slang since the late 20th century, and has been used in movies and TV shows.

The earliest known citation is from *The New Yorker Magazine*, Volume 67, 1991, issue 11, page 43:

> "**That's so dope**! I should get a dog. It would look fly to walk down the street with twin dogs."

That's the way the cookie crumbles

This means, 'that is just the way things usually turn out, and we may as well be resigned to accept it.' This one goes back to the mid-20th century, and one of the earliest citations is from the fraternity paper *Phi Delta Kappa*, January, 1959 in a play titled 'Mad Avenue Aids the School Crisis,' on page 173:

> "GRAY: Too bad, McFlannel, that's the way the ball bounces. MILLTOWN: **That's the way the cookie crumbles** . . . that's the way the banana splits. Say, that reminds me, I'm hungry, let's eat."

Older similar expressions are 'that's the way the ball bounces' and 'C'est la vie,' both in the first volume.

There are no atheists in fox holes

This is a common aphorism used to argue that in times of extreme stress or fear, and especially during war, all people will believe in, or hope for, a higher power. Still there are some who refute this logic. It was first written around the experiences of World War II. The earliest known citation holds no clue as to who coined it, and is found in *Xi Psi Phi Quarterly*, October, 1941, page 1:

> "Some one has rightly said that **there are no atheists in foxholes**, and no atheists in rubber rafts."

U.S. Military Chaplain William Thomas Cummings is said to have used it in a field sermon during the Battle of Bataan in 1942, and it was subsequently repeated by numerous dignitaries and printed in several publications throughout the war and thereafter.

There are no strangers here, only friends you haven't met yet (See: **stranger is only a friend you haven't met yet, A**)

There is a thin line between genius and insanity

This proverbial statement has been attributed to Einstein and others. Of course, it refers to the theory that, as in other areas, there seems to be a 'full circle' from which venturing just a bit further could reach the opposite extreme, like the orb of the globe in which east essentially ***does*** meet west. 'There is a fine line' always means that two entities are actually very closely connected. As far back as the late 17th century, the thought was expressed poetically by John Dryden (1631-1700) in *Absalom and Achitophel*:

> **"Great wits are sure to madness near alli'd And thin partitions do their bounds divide."**

In March, 1846, a close example emerged in *Literary Garland and Canadian Magazine*, on page 46, in 'Notices of New Works' by Valentine Slyboots:

> "The partition which, in his case, Nature had made **thin between genius and derangement**, at length burst asunder."

Then the December 7, 1872 edition of *The Medical Times and Gazette* published Lectures on Insanity by Edgar Shepherd, M.D., Professor of Psychological Medicine at Kings College in London, in which he made the following statements:

> "The groove in which they run has a border-**line** on either side, mapping off the land of **genius and** the land of **insanity**. ... Having no capacity to establish an equilibrium **between** them and external conditions,.."

Twelve years later, on October 9, 1884, *The Nation*, from New York's *The Evening Post Publishing*, in a column by Dr. Paul Radestock titled 'Genius and Insanity,' citing a recent news story, made the following declaration; then pointed to the quote from Dryden given above:

> "The news did not create much surprise, as the **close relationship between genius and insanity is proverbial**, and not only in the sense that extremes meet."

There is many a good tune played on an old fiddle^

This proverb refers to the truism that a person's ability does not depend upon his or her being young. In fact, it may be just the opposite, because wisdom often increases with age. In spite of a major dictionary of American Slang which stated 1903 as the earliest citation, *Fibre and Fabric*, Saturday, December 31, 1898 had reference this in the feature, 'The Woolen Factory,' under "Observations of Peter:'

> "It may be old, but **there is many a good tune played on an old fiddle**."

Another version is: 'The older the violin, the sweeter the music,' which was the title for a hit country single from Hank Thompson written by Curley Putnam, from his album *Kindly Keep it Country,* released in 1973.

There is nothing in a caterpillar that tells you it's going to be a butterfly

This is a quote from noted American architect, author, environmentalist activist and inventor Richard Buckminster Fuller (1895-1983) which has become proverbial. It is closely related to 'You can't judge a book by its cover' (see first volume) and means that you can't tell a person's potential just by looking at him or her. We must allow each person to change with time, and become the individual that he or she is destined to become. Fuller, who was noted for unorthodox ideas on global issues, invented the 'goedesic dome,' the only large dome that can be set directly on the ground as a complete structure and has no limiting dimensions.

There's a lid for every pot / Every pot has a cover[2]

This British proverb was originally in French. It refers to every person having a mate. It's from *The Maid of Thilouse* by Honoré de Balzac, a part of *The Huguenot: A Tale of the French Protestants* (Volumes I, II and III) originally published from 1832-1837, English translation by George Payne Rainsford James, in 1874:

> "So every beast finds a mate, and from the same fact comes the proverb, **'There is no pot, however ugly, that does not one day find a cover.'**"

There's an app for that / They have an app for that+

This is a 21st century cliché which arose from the smart phone boom. The word 'app,' short for application, became popular in 2010. It means that no matter what task one needs to accomplish online, someone has designed a software app, or program, which will 'fit or fill the bill' (See) They are designed for use on all smart phones, and mobile devices such as 'pads.' There are also Web apps for use on computers.

There's a new sheriff in town

This comedic idiom has been used by numerous celebrities from Charlie Sheen to Chazz. It means that no matter who was thought to be in charge, or have the most pull in the past, that has all changed. Someone has 'built a better mousetrap' (see first volume). The earliest known use of the saying is from *Heathers*, a 1988 black comedy film written by Daniel Walters. After one of the two Heathers, Heather Duke (Shannon Dougherty), kills J.D. (Christian Slater) who was out to get her, Veronica (Winona Ryder) confronts her, and after taking her hair tie, says:

> "Heather, my love, **there's a new sheriff in town**."

There's no time like the present

This is also proverbial, and quite old. It is a push to avoid procrastination, and was first recorded in 1562 in Gerald Leigh's *Accidence of Armoury*:

> "Mary, [to be sure] sir **no time better than even now**."

In 1790, John Trusler expounded on it in *Proverbs Exemplified*:

> "**No time like the present**, a thousand unforeseen
> circumstances may interrupt you at a future time."

They broke the mold when they made somebody or **something**

This is an idiom used to mean that the person or thing being discussed is very special and there is no other like him, her or it. This is often quoted from *Death of a Salesman*, Arthur Miller's excellent 1949 play, later a major motion picture. It was in use much earlier, however. The earliest known citation is from *The*

American Magazine, July, 1913, on page 49, in 'Salvation' by John Taintor Foote, a tale of a Kentucky race horse:

> "'Well, **they broke the mold** when they made that one!' I says."

See also: 'Break the mold'.

They saw you coming!

This means that the person being addressed was an easy target for a scam or swindle. He or she definitely got cheated. It came into use in the 1920s. The earliest known verifiable citation is from *Sham*, a short satire by American playwright Frank G. Tompkins, published in 1921, in 'Fifty Contemporary One-Act Plays,'

> "If you gave more than $3.98 for it, **they saw you coming,** Clara."

Think on one's feet

This means to react to circumstances decisively and effectively without the need for prior planning or strategizing. It derives from persons such as attorneys or athletes who of necessity are forced to make split-second decisions while standing up. Figuratively it may also apply to someone setting who is in the same situation. It came into use in the U.S. in the early 20th century. The first known example in print comes from the New York publication, *Judge,* July 22, 1918, in 'Editorial:'

> "The man can tell his employees where they get off. He can look his competitors in the eye and tell them what's what. But he can't face a dinner party and **think on his feet**, so he dies a thousand deaths for lack of a little training."

Two years later, in *The New Success*, Volume 4, 1920, has a clearly defined citation:

> "Even though he is not an orator, he should be able to **think on his feet**; to say a few intelligent words; to keep his mental balance, and not allow himself to be stampeded in such a foolish way."

Think someone hung the moon

This means to believe someone is amazing. The person is idolized, can accomplish anything and can do no wrong. It is fairly recent in origin. The earliest known use is from *Old Man Joseph and His Family*, a 1978 play by Romulus Lenney; Act One, Scene Six:

> "Send you out in life trying to do God knows what. That's what happens to Momma's boys, Jesus. They're just one little grain of sand, but they think they **hung the moon**. Truth is, nothing in their minds but Momma."

Three hots and a cot

This rhyming expression is 'cop slang' used to describe the only items which a prison inmate is entitled to have: three hot meals and a bunk on which to sleep. This has also been used as a way in which workers were paid, both in the military, and civilian jobs. The following is the earliest known actual citation in print, and appeared in an article, Delinquent Boys Learn at Camp by Joan Lee Faust in *The New York Times,* September 28, 1969:

> "The conservation tasks include trail cutting, thinning timber, planting tree seedlings,…For a day's work each youth is paid 50 cents plus earning his room and board, or '**three hots and a cot**,' as one youth described it."

Three-ring circus (See: **Become a three-ring circus**)

thrill of victory (The) and the agony of defeat

This is an opening line spoken on the ABC TV series, *Wide World of Sports* by Jim Mc Cay from 1961-1997.

> "Spanning the globe to bring you the constant variety of sports... **the thrill of victory... and the agony of defeat**... the human drama of athletic competition... This is 'ABC's Wide World of Sports!'"

It has come to symbolize the extreme emotions experienced by athletes after a major competition. The thrill of victory invigorates a player; the agony of defeat humbles him or her.

Through adversity to the stars[2]

This comes from the Latin *Per ardua ad astra* and is the motto of the British Royal Air Force, and other air forces of the Commonwealth, dating to 1912. It was that year, just after the Royal Flying Corps was formed, when the first commanding officer, Col. Frederick Sykes, asked his officers to develop a motto for their division. Two junior officers discussing it mentioned a Latin phrase from Virgil, *Sic itur ad Astra.* This was expanded to the current slogan. Later it also became the motto of the American space program, NASA, and other entities in the U.S. It is used proverbially to mean that there are often many struggles on the way to victory and success in life.

Through the mill

Going, being run, or put through the mill means to be badly treated or abused through hardships and exhausted. In some cases it may refer to being seasoned and knowledgeable, particularly because of this harshness. It is derived from grain which must be crushed in a grist mill to be made into flour or cornmeal. Figurative use dates to the late 19th century. The earliest verifiable citation comes from the weekly *Northwestern Miller*, June 6, 1888, and is found in 'Mill Insurance' by R. W. Arndt, page 11, here in quotes, indicating recent coining:

> "Does not his suit of over-alls and jacket of duck covered with flour dust indicate that he has been **'through the mill**,' and not over it?"

Throwback Thursday

This is a term used for a modern trend by users of social media sites such as Facebook, Twitter and Instagram when posting or reposting old photos. According to an article in *Sports Illustrated Magazine,* August 22, 2013, 'From Hardwood to Hashtag: How NBA Culture Gave Rise to **Throwback Thursday**' the term was coined on a blog named 'Nice Kicks' about sneakers in 2006.

Throw caution to the wind

This idiom means to do something without any regard to the result of your action, even if it is potentially disastrous. A precursor of the phrase was used by John Milton in his classic poetic satire, *Paradise Lost*, first published in 1667:

> "Taste so divine, that what of sweet before
> Hath touched my sense, flat seems to this, and harsh.
> On my experience, Adam, freely taste,
> And **fear of death deliver to the winds**."

Here, the implication was that the original man did not think of consequences for his actions. The next version in the evolution of the saying came in the late 19th century. On June 19, 1887 *The New York Times* published a story titled, "*Sharp Sleeps In A Jail: Sheriff Grant Had Begun To Get Nervous.*" It chronicles the adventures of millionaire Jacob Sharp, on trial, when an uproar occurred over the condition of the jail and services there. Court was dismissed for the weekend and it was uncertain what to do with the jury.

> "...brought face to face with those follies and vices of the world which they usually took pains to avoid, might impulsively **throw discretion to the winds** and be detected in the act of buying popcorn and lemonade from some of those snub-nosed Circes from the factories who go to Coney Island on Sunday prepared to 'mash' anything and everything that is mashable in all the width of the world."

The same term was used in by H. W. Norris in his Annual Address to the President in *The Proceedings of the Iowa Academy of Science for 1895*, Volume III, published in Des Moines the following year:

> "We are too much under the impression that everything — life, health and happiness, can be purchased with the almighty dollar. So we **throw discretion to the wind** and leave the results to the Lord and the doctors."

Just a few years later, on August 24, 1901, the *Baltimore American* newspaper used the current rendering in 'Another Race for Motors: Four Noted Crews and Motors to be Again Tested around the Bowl Track.'

> "There is great rivalry between the Nelson brothers as to the speeds of the motors, while the 'Blues' are a distinct camp full of all that professional jealousy that animates actors and motor riders. The outlook is that there will be more races of **throwing caution to the wind** after the crack of the pistol and of thrilling rides with death for the satisfaction of victory and the purses."

Throw someone to the lions

This refers to causing someone to be in an extremely dangerous or precarious position for which he or she is totally unprepared. It is said to have came from the practice of Ancient Romans who threw Christians to the lions in the Coliseum. This practice, however, is actually much older, and was ordered by Persian King Darius for Daniel (c 605 BCE-533 BCE), a Hebrew in authority, on a trumped-up charge by the princes of the kingdom, as described in the biblical book of *Daniel, Chapter 6, verse 16 (KJV):*

> "Then the king commanded, and they brought Daniel, and **cast him into the den of lions**. Now the king spake and said unto Daniel, Thy God whom thou servest continually, he will deliver thee."

A similar expression is 'Throw someone under the bus' (see original volume).

Throw the book at someone

This means to punish or criticize someone very severely. It comes from a judge finding as many laws as possible in an imaginary law book with which to charge a suspect. It came into use in the American court system in the late 1930s to early 1940s, and the first verifiable example in print is found in *New York Court of Appeals Records and Briefs,* in a written statement by Charles Schneider sworn to on 25 February, 1942 before Alvin A Rabinowitz, Attorney and Counselor at Law, here in quotes, recognizing a recent but known term:

> "Deponent readily appreciates that Judges, too, become emotional, and confronted by so calloused a violator, are impelled to **'throw the book' at** him, but the law must always be observed, most certainly so, by Judges."

Throw up a red flag

This refers to sending a warning signal which should be heeded in order to avert disaster. Red flags are used by work crews or on the backs of extended truck loads to alert other traffic of danger. Use of a literal red flag, however, as a warning signal dates back as far as the 1600s. An early example which gives a good definition is in *The English and Dutch Affairs Displayed to the Life, Both in Matters of Warr, State and Merchandize*, by Edward Thomas, 1664:

> *"Van Trump* the Dutch Admiral…refused to vail his Flag, a Ceremonial Honour, which the English appropriate to themselves, as being Lords of these Narrow Seas., instead thereof hanging out his **Red Flag**, the usual signal of Defiance,…"

This same connotation is evident through the 19th century in other texts. By the 1960s it was being used with 'throw up' as a warning of something very wrong. In the *Hearings of the Committee of Appropriations of the United States* Senate, 1961, we find on page 26 the following citation:

> "Anything that is found to be an unusual variation would **throw up a red flag**."

Thumbs up (or **down)**

This is an indication of either approval or rejection. This may be spoken or indicated with a symbol on online social media sites. It has been long believed that the actual gesture originated in the Ancient Roman Coliseum in gladiator fights, and that the loser's fate was decided by the gestures of the attendees. The

1601 translation of Pliny the Elder's first century CE *Natural Historie* by Philemon Holland reads:

> "To **bend or bow downe the thumbes** when wee give assent unto a thing, or doe favour any person."
>
> *History of Rome, for Young Persons* by Elizabeth Caroline Gray, published in 1847, page 191, clarified this and popularized the belief for future generations:
>
> "If they were pleased with him, they turned **down their thumbs**, and he was spared; but if they turned their **thumbs up**, his fate was sealed."

Within a few years the signs were used in Alice Fay's novel *Lily Bell: or The Lost Child*, 1857 (page 266) in the children's game, Simon Says, a practice which is echoed in later books of games:

> "The party ranged themselves against the wall, alternately a boy and girl, while Uncle Joseph, standing before them and raising his thumb, said: 'Simon says, **thumbs up**.' The company raised their thumbs. 'Simon says, thumbs down.' All lowered their thumbs downwards"

The actual Roman origin has recently been debated by some scholars who have questioned the translations by Holland of Pliny's Latin texts, stating that it should have been rendered 'press the thumbs' instead of 'bend the thumbs'.

Nevertheless, as is the usual, what was believed persisted. It wasn't until the late 20th century when thumbs up started to mean something good and positive. In *Chained Eagle: the Heroic Story of the First American Shot down over Vietnam* by Everett Alvarez, Jr., 1989 in Chapter 18, we read:

> "Many of those along the route gave the **thumbs-up** sign. It was a sweet and wonderful homecoming because it was so unforeseen. As we set foot in the hospital I took a deep breath."

It has been further popularized by movie being given thumbs up or down in reviews.

Tick all the boxes+

This earliest form (used in a literal sense from the mid-20th century in the U.K. for making checkmarks in boxes beside all of the items on a checklist), or the alternative American phrase 'check all the boxes' has come in very recent years to mean fulfill all the requirements or have everything needed to complete a process in an orderly manner.

Tickety-boo[2]

Now heard more in Canada than any other country, this means doing alright or going very well. It has been in use since the 1920s-1930s, and may have originated in Scotland, where it is in the title of a popular children's song titled, *Everything is Tickety-Boo.* It is in the 1958 MGM movie, *Merry Andrew*, sung by Danny Kaye. The most likely origin, however, is in the in the British military, and may have come from the Hindi term 'tickee babu' having basically the same meaning, due to the large British Military presence in India from 1848-1947. This citation from *The Motor,* Volume 80, 1942, on page 14, calls it a 'war-time expression:'

> "…about 6 p.m. it had been replaced, likewise the floorboards, and Bryon pronounced that everything, to use a war-time expression, was once again '**tickety-boo**.'"

Tight-lipped+

This is an idiomatic expression meaning unwilling to talk about something. It implies that one's lips are pressed tightly together because the person is either contemplating, angry or perplexed. *Merriam Webster* places origin at 1876 in the connotation of having ones lips pressed firmly together. By the early 20th century it was being used figuratively, as seen in a 1918 poem by Benjamin Robbins Collins Low titled *The Pursuit of Happiness*, stanza XLVII:

> "By wager of some feet in death's renown,
> On Shining fields of bravery;
> Unless it were some **tight-lipped** loyalty"

Time is money

This one is credited to Benjamin Franklin in *Advice to a Young Tradesman, Written by an Old One,* published July 17, 1748. It means that time is a very valuable asset and should be used wisely. But the thought goes all the way back to 1572, when Thomas Wilson published *A Discourse upon usury by way of Dialogue and Orations*:

> "**Time is precious**."

Time is of the essence

This is a very close expression to the one above, the thought being basically the same. Its beginning can also be traced to Thomas Wilson's remarkable 1572 tome. This precise term, however, is used in both British and American contract law. It means that since time is short, the task at hand is urgent and needs to be completed as quickly as possible. The earliest known use of it in print is in Reports of *Cases Decided in the High Court of Chancery by the Right Honorable John Leach*, London, 1824, page 197:

> "**Time is of the essence** of the Contract. It was not, till the Answer to the Supplemental Bill in 1819, that this objection was taken by the Defendant."

It is often used as an idiom when something needs to be done at once.

Time's a wastin'^

Often attributed to Billy de Beck's cartoon character, Snuffy Smith, originally part of the Barney Google cartoon strip started in 1919, this saying is somewhat older. It did come from the area in which the mythical Snuffy Smith supposedly lived. *In the Tennessee Mountains* by Charles Egbert Craddock, page 18, has the following realistic lines of area dialect, also found in other novels os the day:

> "'**Time's a-wastin,' — time's a-wastin'**!' When Evander was half-way up the steep slope, he turned and looked down at the embowered little house, that itself turned its face upward, looking as it were to the mountain's summit."

Tinnie[3]

Deriving from tin, literally, a tinnie or tinny is a commemorative medal made from either zinc or tin. In Australia and New Zealand and in some parts of the U.K. it is slang for a can of beer. But there are other meanings. In Australia, 'tinnie' also means a good friend or 'mate.' In New Zealand it can also be a small pack of cannabis wrapped in tin foil or a small, open aluminum boat. When used as an adjective, tinny can mean 'lucky.' If and when the term is used in the U.S., tinnie refers to a tin foil most often used as a smoking device for cannabis (marijuana). It can almost refer to anything made of a non-precious metal, like tin, zinc or aluminum;

The earliest citation available is from William Ferguson's *America by River and Rail,* 1856, page 325, is in quotes, and refers to a tin or aluminum well bucket:

"Madam lent us **a 'tinnie**,' and we went to the well ourselves. It was about sixteen feet deep, and the water was got at by means of a bucket attached to a long pole. So we drank, and 1 emptied my pockets of all the odd cents…"

Tip the scales

This is a metaphor for having profound influence affecting change which will make something more or less likely to happen. It is often used in cases of getting justice. The two earliest available citations are from 1943, one of which is in *The Journal of Electrical Workers and Operators*, September issue:

"This is a world of keen competition and often little things will **tip the scales** for or against you."

To be great is to be a non-conformist^

This is actually a *misquote* of Ralph Waldo Emerson, who said two things which are similar in scope, but not this. In his *Essays,* in Essay II on Self Reliance, first published in 1841, he actually said, 'Whoso would be a man, must be a **nonconformist,**' and '**To be great is to be** misunerdstood.' But the meaning is there.

To each his own

This very ancient proverb means that every person is entitled to his or her own individual likes and dislikes. It is a calque of Latin *suum cuique*, short for ***suum cuique*** *pulchrum est* meaning 'to each his own is beautiful.' It has a long history back to the Greek principle os justice as described by Socrates in Plato's *Republic* (380 BCE). The Latin phrase was made famous by Roman author and orator, Marcus Tullius Cicero (106 BCE – 43 BCE): Translated, he said, 'Justice renders to everyone his due…so that fortitude (courage) may be seen in hardship and danger, (...), justice in attributing **to each his own**.'

Before coming into English, is said to have been first a German proverb **Jedem das Seine,** 'to each what he deserves.' This was the motto of the Order of the Black Eagle in ancient Prussia under King Frederick.

Togs[3]

In Queensland, Austtralia and New Zealand, 'togs' refers to a bathing suit. This reflects the regional difference. In other areas of Australia swim suits are either referred to as swimmers, cossies, bathers or one type called speedos (see). The differences in terms for this and other items stems from the colonists who settled the country from different parts of the British Isles. Some regional expressions are also derived from local Indigeonous languages. *A Dictionary of Slang, Jargon and Cant Embracing English* by Albert Barrère, 1889 defines togs as simply 'clothes,' and gives a quote from Dickens popular novel, *Oliver Twist*:

> "**Togs** (common), clothes. Look at his **togs**! Superfine cloth, and the heavy swell cut! Oh, my eye, what a game! — Dichens: Oliver Twist. 'It mightn't spoil some sort of **togs**,' I replied, with a scornful glance at poor Sam's wretched rags."

To have a friend, be a friend

This popular proverbial saying is a close quote to Ralph Waldo Emerson in *Essays, Lectures and Orations,* 1848, in 'Friendship,' page 113:

> "The only reward of virtue is virtue; the only way **to have a friend** is to **be one**."

An even closer example is a quote attributed to American philosopher, writer and publisher Elbert Hubbard (1856-1915):

> "In order **to have friends you must first be one."**

The earliest citation available for the above saying, however, is in a book titled *Leadership* by George H. Knox, copyrighted in 1909, published in Des Moines, Iowa, 1911, where is is in quotes giving no attribution on page 132.

But the principle in its entirity goes all the way back to the biblical book of *Proverbs, 18:24 (KJV)*:

> "**A man that hath friends must shew himself friendly**: and there is a friend that sticketh closer than a brother."

Tom-catting around

This idiom refers to a man who is 'on the prowl,' searching for 'hook ups' with numerous women. The earliest known citation is from *Dialect Notes, Volume 5.* 1927, page 478:

> "**tom catting**, v. To seek illicit sexual adventure."

The earliest example of 'tom-catting around' in print, followed by many more from the 1940s forward, is from 1938, here in quotes, in *Southern Folklore Quarterly*, Volume 2-3, page 109:

> "Kelly Combs said he learned this song at camp meetings when he was young and '**tom-catting around**.'"

Tomorrow is another day

This saying was made famous by the memorable words from Vivian Leigh as Scarlet O'hara in the 1939 classic motion picture, *Gone With the Wind,* after their plantation, Tara, had been destroyed in the American Civil War at the end of her powerful dramatic dialogue:

> "After all... **tomorrow is another day!**"

As one might imagine, this was not the first time this statement had been expressed in literature. The earliest known recorded reference is from *Harper's Weekly*, May 23, 1857, in 'Foreign News,' here in quotes, indicating that it was already in use, though likely recent:

> "To each of the limited circle of duties he devotes in which his life is passed—eating, drinking, sleeping, strip-running, and swimming—he devotes a most unreasonable space of time; seemingly determined to divide his life into a few regular periods, and never losing sight of that, to him, great and glorious fact, that '**tomorrow is another day**.'"

Too clever by half[2]

In British colloquialism this is used to criticize someone for being too cocky and overconfident. It often also involves being devious and manipulating. It's a bit like saying the person thinks he or she is twice as smart as he or she really is. Other expressions involving 'by half' include 'too slow,' 'quick,' and 'fat by half'. The earliest known citation using 'by half,' which may give a hint to the reasoning of how it came into being in the first place, is in *England's Chronicle* by James Heath, 1689, page 70:

> "This was the King who built *Westminster* Hall ninety yards in length, and twenty-four yards two feet in breadth, yet when he came to see it, he complained it was **too little by half**, and therefore he would reserve it for a lodging Room…"

This was actually saying that the building should be twice the size it is. Then, in 1783, the title of a play by John Dent was ***Too Civil by Half***, *A Farce in Two*

Acts. It seems logical that being a farce, this could have begun the figurative use, made in jest, which continued to expand with time.

The earliest printed example available of 'too clever by half' is found in *Curiosities of Modern Times: A Yearbook of Adventure*, published by David Bogue in London in 1844:

> "With us, at such an age, children are helpless, timid, childish, and childlike; in Russia they are adroit, cunning, and **too clever by half**."

Too little, too late^

This is an idiom meaning that something offered was inadequate to solve the existing delima and not in time to be an effective solution. In spite of a well-intentioned online etymology source which attributed this saying to American Historian, Allan Nivens in an article the May, 1935 issue of Current History, this phrase, even more precisely, appeared in fourteen years earlier in *World Without End*, a 1921 novel by Grant M. Overton, on page 25:

> "'I have come to believe it is a mistake to see too much too early.'
> 'Or **too little too late**.' His discomfiture was evident, yet he appeared almost a social creature as he answered:
> 'You have allowed us to see too little of you.'
> 'And too late.'"

Too much of a good thing

This idiom means that excess of anything may cause harm. It goes back to William Shakespeare in *As You Like It*, 1599, Act IV, Scene i:

> "ROSALIND: Why then, can one desire **too much of a good thing**?
> Come, sister, you shall be the priest and marry us.
> Give me your hand, Orlando. What do you say, sister?"

Another way of saying it is, 'Taking a good thing too far.'

Too vanilla

In modern American slang, this means not exciting enough; very boring. The earliest known citation appeared in the light novel *Ever After* by Rachel Vail, first published in 1994, page 19:

> "I think if I weren't me, I wouldn't like me because I'm **too vanilla."**

Top dog

This is a sarcastic term for a person in charge of a company, office or operation, especially someone who uses nepotism or pushes his or her way to the top position. The earliest citation available is from *People Magazine*, August 29, 1994, in an article titled 'Man Bites Dog Food' about Edwin Rose, who tasted canine cuisine for a British corporation:

> "Rose's culinary habits may seem peculiar, but he's the **top dog** for Britain's 371-store Safeway supermarket chain (not affiliated with the U.S. stores)."

Top of the greasy pole[2]

This means reaching the top after encountering many difficulties on the way. It is derived from competetitive events invloving climing a greased pole. One such well known event in the U.K. is aat the Crab Fair in Egremont, Cumbria, a coastal market town on the Borough of Copeland. As a metaphor, it has been in use since the late 19th century. The earliest known citation is from 'The Parliments and Ministries of the Century,' in speaking of British Prime Minister Benjamin Disraeli, who may have coined it based on the text, first published in *McMillians Magazine*, then reprinted in *Littell's Living Age,* June 23, 1894:

> "To use his own expression, which is more forcible than elegant, he had climbed to the **top of the greasy pole**. It proved more slippery than probably even be imagined, and in a very few months he came down with a run, when Mr. Gladstone's resolution on the Irish Church placed him in a minority."

Three years later it was used in *The Book of Parliament*, page 76, in the actual quote from Disraeli:

> "'Yes,' said Disraeli, 'I have climbed to the **top of the greasy pole**,' as an old acquaintance, meeting him within a few days of his first Premiership, congratulated him on his triumph."

Touch and go

This means dangerous and uncertain as to outcome; precarious. The earliest use of this idiom on record is from a sermon English preacher, Hugh Latimer, who was martyred a few years later by being burned at the stake, recorded in *Seven*

Sermons before Edward VI, on Each Friday in Lent, 1549, published in 1869 in London, in 'The Fyrst Sermon,' on page 26:

> "As this texte dothe ryse I wyl **touche and go**, a lytel in euery parte, vntyl I come vnto to muche."

This connotation is slightly removed from current meaning; it indicated that he would only briefly make mention of the ideas he wanted to bring out before expanding upon them. Over the next 250 plus years, it began to change slightly. The earliest citation which seems to come close to our understanding is found in the British legal findings book, *Reports of Cases Determined at Nisi Prius, in the Courts,* 1816 by John Campbell in McDougle v. Royal Exchange Assurance:

> "To use a vulgar phrase, which has been applied to this subject, if it is '**touch and go'** with the ship, there is no stranding. It cannot be enough that the ship lay for a few moments on her beam ends."

Touch wood[2]

This is a British form of 'knock on wood' (see in first volume), and derives from the ancient pantheistic religions which believed that trees were inhabited by spirits or dieties, and that by touching or knocking on a tree it would ward off evil spirits. This phased into Christianity in the Middle Ages when 'summoners and pardoners' sold relics which were passed off as parts of the 'True Cross' of Jesus, which were carried in the pockets, and touched when the plague or other great disasters were mentioned for power and safety because of the belief that Christ had defeated the powers of darkness by dying on the cross.

In the 19th century a children's game was devised using this principle, as mentioned in *The Playground; or, the Boy's Book of Games,* 1858, by George Forrest, Chapter IV; page 42:

> "At last one of them suggested '**Touch wood**,' and this proposition was at once accepted. 'What is **Touch wood**?' said Tom. 'Much the same as 'Touch,' except that while you are touching wood, you are safe."

Touch wood, like 'knock on wood,' became a common expression to insure safety, mostly done now jokingly for fun.

Touchy feely

This refers to having a tendancy to show emotions openly. A person having this characteristic encourages empathetic interpersonal touching and hugging. It is American in origin and began to be used in the late 1960's to early 1970s. The earliest available citation comes from *Newsweek*, Volume 72, issue 10, page 61, 1968. Here in quotes, being very new:

> "The Congress was not all politics. It also offered '**touchy-feely**' sensitivity training— an enterprise in which six strangers sit in a circle in a dimly lighted room and try to understand each other and to create a group solidarity using words and touch."

Tough as nails+

This old metaphor may be used either as a compliment, meaning that the person is able to handle difficult situations, or an insult, to say that someone is cold and harsh. According to the online forum, *Writing Explained* it originated as early as the 1860s, preceded by 'hard as nails.' Research bears out popular usage in American newspapers and Broadway plays by the early 20th century.

Tough cookie^

This is used as a metaphor for someone who can endure physical and mental hardship and abuse and be resilient. Despite the stated time of origin on a much-respected online site as the 1920s, an earlier citation is in *Photoplay Magazine*, June, 1918, in and artiocle titled, 'And the Elephants Beckoned,' page 116:

> "By the rules of the plot, Miss Bessie made her exit from Coffee Dan's and a new waitress, a **tough cookie**, as it were, gum-chewing and sarcastic, took her place."

Train of thought^

This metaphoric idiom refers to the connection between the sequence of ideas in a pattern of thought in the brain, and how these lead to other ideas a person desires to bring out in conversation or writing. This is often expressed when one 'loses' this train of thought, thus having trouble connecting intended phrases. Note has often been made that Thomas Hobbs first used the phrase and defined it in *Leviathan*, 1651, and suggested by a major cliché dictionary that Hobbs may have coined it. In 1750, in the English Translation of *The Thoughts of Cicero* (Roman philosopher, 106 BCE – 43 BCE), printed in London for J. Newberry, we find this sitation on page 127, 'On Probability:'

> "By such a **train of thought** he will be led to say, this indeed is equitable, but that advantageous, by such a fatal mistake disjoining things in their own

> nature inseparable; which is the fource of all manner of treachery, injustice and wickedness."

By this we see that the idea of a train of thought existed long before it appeared in English.

Trash-talk (See: **Talk trash**)

Trial by fire

Figuratively, this refers to an ordeal in which the pressure involved tests a person's endurance, strength or resolve. Metaphoric use goes back to the *Bible*, in which the testing of a person is compared to the smelting of gold. The earliest is in the Old Testament: *Zechariah 13:9, KJV*:

> "And I will bring the third part **through the fire**, and will refine them as silver is refined, and will **try them as gold is tried..."**

Two more are found in the *New Testament: I Corinthians 3:13*, and *I Peter 1:7*, which reads in the *KJV*:

> "That the **trial** of your faith, being much more precious than of gold that perisheth, though it be **tried with fire**, might be found unto praise and honour and glory..."

Tricks of the trade

This is an old idiom used to mean special skills and knowledge which helps someone perform better and faster in a profession. The erarliest verifiable citation comes from *The Works of Maria Edgefield*, Volume VII, 'Patronage,' 1825, page 239, originally published in 1814, in Ireland:

> "Solicitor Babington, the solicitor employed against us in that suit, a man who knows, without practising them, all the **tricks of the trade**, and who is a thoroughly honest man, saw the trick that was played by Nameless, and took occasion afterwards to recommend me to several of his own clients."

Trojan horse

Literally, this is a tale from Ancient Greek Mythology. A large wooden horse was constructed by Epeius, a master Greek carpenter and pugilist. During the Trojan War (traditionally 1194 BCE to 1184 BCE) the Greeks presented it to the

Trojans, pretending it to be a goodwill offering to Athena, goddess of War (see: Beware Greeks bearing gifts). The horse was filled with soldiers, who, once inside the impregnable city of Troy, came out that night, opened the gate, and let in their army who conquered their unsuspedting foe.

Metaphorically speaking, a Trojan horse is anything that is used to mask the truth in order to trick or harm an ememy. The earliest known figurative use in print is in William Drummond's *The History of Scotland, from the year 1423 until the year 1542*, published in 1655, page 248:

> "...they directed me to ravage and plunder the more peaceable neighbours about; this **Trojan Horse** laboured to give me a command over Horses. All which imployments being contrary to my education..."

Trouble in Paradise

This means an unexpected problem in a situation thought to be positive, particularly applied in marriage. The allusion in this expression is of the biblical story of Adam and Eve in the Garden of Eden, often called the original 'Paradise,' and the decision by God to chase them out after their disobedience. (*Genesis 3:8-19*) Sermons and illustrations with this were prevalent as early as the 18th century, as seen in *The Best Treasure* by Bartholomew Ashford, 1781:

> "If you would have the World, it will cost you a great deal of sorrow, **trouble**, and pains, you must tug hard Adam being turn'd out of **Paradise** must work in the sweat of his brows for his bread."

The phrase itself was first printed in *The Aberdeen Evening Express,* Aberdeenshire, Scotland; Thursday November 5, 1885.

> "...Job says, understanding is dimmed with words, permitted to make perpetual **trouble in Paradise**."

Ten years later it was used in *Around the Tea-table* by Thomas DeWitt Talmage, where it speaks of problems caused by females, and alludes to the Adam and Eve saga. In 1932 it was the title of a dramatic motion picture starring Miriam Hopkins and Herbert Marshall as partners in crime and love.

True blue[3]

Universally referring to loyalty, this is just a bit different in Australia, where it now has to do with having having true Australian values. It comes from the British English, first attested in the 17th century, meaning faithful, staunch and unwavering in one's commitments. It was later that in England it came to mean being very politically Conservative; but it was an emtirely different political view in Australia. This sense was expressed first in writing near the end of the 19th century, as seen in the following citation from *Worker* (Sydney) September 18, 1897, where it meant being loyal to union values:

> "Reports from the sheds are cheering, both reps. and men being of the sort called '**true blue**.'"

Turf war

In the modern sense, this term stemmed from 1970s protection of urban areas, particularly among street gangs, regarded as specific group territories. It also applies to crime syndicates, motorcycle gangs and drug cartels, and goes to maintaining power and control. It has expanded to refer to battles over technology and innovations, and market control.

But the literal use goes back much further, and was cited in *Turf, Field and Farm*, January 3, 1902, page 5, in 'The Rule of the Western Jocky Club:'

> "The few remaining owners, trainers, horsess and jockeys that are in any consequence to the turf, that have not already been reinstated, are to apply for reinstatement at the coming January meeting of the Jockey Club in Chicago, and when they are taken in the end of the short and lively **turf War** in the West and South Will be over."

The use regarding conflicts among jockey clubs continued through the early 20th century. Although the Chicago race riot of 1919 stirred up what would later be called 'turf wars,' the term seems not to have been used about it and other such clashes until 1975, when the following appeared in a report titled *Violence by youth gangs and youth groups as a crime problem in major American cities,* published by the U.S. Department of Justice, Law Enforcement Administration, Office of Juvenile Justice and Delinquancy Pervention, on page 41:

> "On October 27, 1919, a Chicago newspaper ran a story on the killing of a member of the Elston youth gang by a 15-year-old member of the Belmonts—a Northwest Side gang in the course of a continuing '**turf war**' between the two gangs."

Turn back the clock

This idiom is used in reference to relishing the memories of naustalgic times and events of the past and wishing they could have remained that way. The earliest known citation is from *Watson's Magazine,* March, 1879, in 'Miscellaneous:'

"'As authors of some sorts of literary material complained of, we desire to enter a counter protest.' They say; then they write that their critics are 'curiously misguided,' and would, if successful, '**turn back the clock** in mational morals and national art.' Do not be astounded at this effrontery. 'National morals,' indeed! The creatures who are grinding out degenerates by millions are merely endeavoring to keep within the law by beginning and ending the products of their diseased imaginations by assertions that they would teach a moral lesson."

Turn (something) on its head

This means to treat something in a completely new and different way; to cause something to be the opposite from what it was before. It can also refer to causing a person to have a completely different view of something than in the past. The earliest reference in print available is from *Gogol: Plays and Selected Writings* by Nikolaĭ Vasil'evich Gogo (1809-1852), 1980, in the Introduction on page xix:

"In his task of destruction, however, he was highly dialectical, taking from the past what he could use but manipulating it in such a way as to **turn it on its head**."

Turn the world upside down

This hyperbolic metaphor refers to making monumental changes in the patterns of belief and worldview of a great number of people. The earliest citation is from the *Bible*, in *Acts 17: 6 (KJV)* where Jewish leaders in Thessalonica were forming a mob to go against Paul and Silas for preaching that Jesus was the Messiah and winning many converts to Christianity:

"And when they found them not, they drew Jason and certain brethren unto the rulers of the city, crying, These that have **turned the world upside down** are come hither also;"

In the 1640s a ballad was published in England titled, '*The World Turned Upside Down,*' protesting the policies of Parliament regarding celebrating Christmas as a 'solomn occasion,' outlawing traditional joyous British Christmas festivities.

Turn up the heat

This means to increase the amount of pressure or intensity of activity on something or someone. The earliest known metaphoric citation appeared in *Welding*, Volume 53, 1985, as a campaign name:

> "The campaign which was entitled '**Turn Up the Heat**' was divided into four categories in order to pitch similar distributors with similar market conditions and sizes against each other."

Twin flames+

This is another metaphor for 'soul mates,' or two persons destined to be together in a love relationship. The concept originated in Plato's mythical dialogue, *The Symposium*, in which he wrote: "So ancient is the desire of one another which is implanted in us, reuniting our original nature, seeking to make one of two, and to heal the state of man."

He further stated that humans originally had two faces, four arms, and four legs. Under the threat of being overpowered, he claimed. The gods split them in half, making us as we are today. From this concept emerged the teaching that we all have one twin soul somewhere in the world. Later it came to be called 'twin flames,' and is is believed that once they are enlightened to their true identity the will burn together as one. First common use of the term in books occurred in the 1960s in the peace and love movement.

Two left feet^

In colloquial English, having two left feet refers to moving in a very clumsy way; especially being awkward when dancing. A major online dictionary places first printed use at 1915. It was actually cited as early as 1902, in *Chimmie Fadden and Mr. Paul* by Edward W. Townsend, Chapter XIII, page 175:

> "He's a good boy, only he **has two left feet**, and I could learn Little Miss Fannie's doll to dance easier nor him."

U

Uncharted territory

This is an idiom for an activity or subject with which people have had no experience before and have no knowledge about. It is derived from places or waters which had not been explored in the distant past; therefore no maps were available to guide the explorers. The earliest known figurative citation is from *The International Congressional Council, London, 1891*, page 179:

> "'The social wreckage'—is not this, indeed, the very element which should cause us solicitude? The social movement is swift and relentless; the mighty industrial machine plunges forward through **uncharted territory**, making a track for itself..."

Uncle Sam

This is a common National Personification of the United States Government (U.S.). According to legend, it was coined in 1813, during the War of 1812, and was said to have been named such for Samuel Wilson (1766-1854), a Troy, New York meat packer, who supplied barrels of beef to the United States Army during the War, stamped with **U.S.** for United States. The story goes that the soldiers started referring to the meat as "Uncle Sam's." The local newspaper picked this up, and eventually Uncle Sam became the nickname for the Federal Government. During the late 1860s and 1870s, popular German-born political cartoonist Thomas Nast (1840-1902), who did a lot of features for *Harpers Weekly,* began developing an image of Uncle Sam which took on the white beard and Stars and Stripes suit. It was also Nast who developed the images of the donkey and elephant as the symbols for our political parties.

The most famous image of Uncle Sam, however, was drawn by artist James Montgomery Flagg (1877-1960) during World War I, in which a stern figure in a top hat staring forward, points a finger with the statement, "I Want You for the U.S. Army." It first appeared on the cover of *Leslie's Weekly* on July 6, 1916.

Uncle Tom Cobley and all[2]

In British English, this is a cute, whimsical way to say, 'and everyone,' and is often used to avoid naming an endless list of people. It is taken from the Devon folk song, *Wildcombe Fair,* published by Sabine Baring-Gould in the book *Songs and Ballads of the West* (1889–1891). The chorus ends with a long list of persons on the way to the fair:

> "Bill Brewer, Jan Stewer, Peter Gurney, Peter Davy, Dan'l Whiddon, Harry Hawke, Old **Uncle Tom Cobley and all**."

Under fire

Literally, (dating to the late 18th century) this means under attack; as an idiom it refers to being harshly criticized. The earliest known figurative use is from the mid-20th century. In *Subversive Influence in the Educational Process: Hearings Before the Subcommittee to Investigate the Administration of the Internal*

Security Actand Other Security Laws of the United States Senate, Eighty-Second Congress Second Session, September & October, 1952,

> "Senator GOLDMAN...The fact that I am **under fire** is no reason for abandoning a principle.
>
> "Senator WELKER. What do you mean by '**under fire**'? You have been a very cooperative witness here; you have gone all the way with us; you have been very free with your testimony..."

Under one's belt

This is a metaphor for something which has been safely and satisfactorily achieved. It comes from good food or drink which has been injested and satisfied one's hunger or thirst. The earliest printed reference in existence comes from Samuel Foote's *The Young Hypocrite*, 1762, here being applied to alchoholic beverage:

"COUNT

> "Pshaw! You talk like a young milksop, Mr. Mayor!
> "Why I'm never so sensible, as when I am soaking; with six bottles **under my belt** I am fit to govern the world."

Up a gum tree

Accorsing to etymologists in the U.K., this idiom has various meanings including 'in great difficulties,' which is most common, contented, and done very fast. Earliest citations are from the 19th century, and it is usually thought to have originated in Australia, where it is most used. A gum tree is a common name for the Eucalyptus. The earliest citation, however, in print is of an o'possum up a gum tree, and are from America, where the black gum grows. The first is from 1825 in *The Portfolio* by Oliver Oldschool printed by H. Maxwell, published in Philidelphia, Pennsylvania, where the saying is listed on page 148:

> "168. **O'possum up a gum tree"**

Just four years later, famed British author William Makepiece Thackery used it in *The Oxford Thackery, Volume IV,* page 442:

> "'Possom **up a gum-tree**, eh? Fill him up. Dere he go! (imitating the Mandingo manner of speaking English)."

This reference, strangely, was of a Brit speaking to a West African, who was mocking his accent. Another reference, soon thereafter, also pointed to blacks. In *The Universal Songster; Or, Museum of Myrth,* published in London in 1832, and may give us the true origin:

> "OPOSSUM **UP A GUM-TREE**.
> *A real Negro Melody*.
>
> "OPOSSUM **up a gum-tree**,
> His tail his body follow;
> Lacoon quickly him see,
> Looking out o' hollow…"

By 1838 it was used without the o'possom reference in *The Literary and Pictorial Repository*, by George Burger, where the saying is viewed as American;

> "America — the ample sky seemed literally dyed with streaks of red and purple, and light fleecy clouds of a golden hue ... of interrogations was from time to time showered upon me with a volubility only possessed by your genuine American, and embracing almost every subject that could be mentioned; each asseveration that he made concluding with an oath of 'Slike-slick and poke me **up a gum-tree**;'"

The next year *New Monthly Magazine* printed an article, 'Some Passages in the Life of Major Gahagan' by Thackery in which he indicated America as the place of origin:

> "I had her in my power - **up a tree**, as the Americans say."

Up for grabs

This term is applied to anything which is available and obtainable by anyone wishing to compete for it, particularly jobs or funds. It is believed to have been derived from someone throwing paper currency up in the air. The earliest known citation comes from the publication *Nature,* a journal by Sir Norman Lockyer, published in London in Volume 342, page 327, 1869:

> "That, at least, seems to be one of the portents of this month's elections in the United States, when New York elected its first black mayor, when governorships were **up for grabs** in states such as New Jersey and Virginia and when several ..."

Uphill climb / battle

This metaphor means some task or goal which will take a great deal of effort and determination but which is obtainable. It comes from the obvious; manually ascending a steep slope. The earliest figurative citation available, though obviously a known phrase at the time, is from the novel *Lizzie Loren of Greyrigg* by Eliza Lynn Linton, 1866, page 16:

> "The effort was what we have all felt when we have left friends who whispered to us tenderly how much better we are than others, for those who tell us unflinchingly how much worse than what we ought to be—sometimes a little anger, and sometimes a great deal of pain, a sudden writhing of wounded vanity, and a sudden flaming up of wrathful pride, but improvement all the same, and a few steps more accomplished of that toilsome **uphill climb**."

Up in the air

This idiom is used of anything with a feel of uncertainty and with unknown results. It comes from an object in the sky which is unknown or uncertain how it got there and what is going to happen to it. Figurative use began early in the 20th century. The earliest known citation is from *The American Home Missionary*, March, 1916, in an article by C. F. Swander, here in quotes, indicating a fairly new use of the expression:

> "In reference to your reason for discontinuing the appropriation to our city work, that this work **is 'up in the air**,' I would say that you are taking a snap judgment that is hardly warranted."

Upping the ante

In poker, the ante is the amount of money required to get in or stay in a game. Literally speaking, upping the ante is increasing the amount of the 'pot' which will be 'up for grabs' (see), but more immediately, it increases the risk of staying in. Figuratively, upping the ante of anything means rasising the stakes, or taking more risk in order that the potential gain might be greater. Figurative use came as early as 1964, when it was used in *Investigation of the Assassination of President John F. Kennedy...*, Volume 14, 1964, page 351: .

> **"MR. RICH**. We were to be notified as to the time and place of the next meeting and as to the decision on **upping the ante**, so to speak."

Up to one's neck in (anything)

This means that a person is very involved in something and has too much of it. It comes from someone who can't swim being so immersed in deep water that drowning in it is the next possibility. It came into figurative use in the early 20th century. One early example is from *Punch, or The London Charivari*, March 1, 1905, in 'At a Moment's Notice,' Chapter II:

> "I was simply **up to my neck in** money worries of all kinds."

Use it or lose it

This is a saying used to mean that the right to something will expire if not used by a specific date, or figuratively that if a person's talent or privilege is not practiced or kept active, his or her ability to perform will grossly decline. The saying came into use in the mid-to-late 19th century. The earliest known example of the phrase in print is from *Nothing New Tales* by Dinah Maria Craik, 1857, page 187:

> "…the worthy old fellow, once a creditor of my father's, had offered me as a loan, the amount of his long paid debt.
> "'**Use it, or lose it**, or give it me back any time these ten years."

This citation, however, did not have the current connotation. The first printed reference to it as an axiom is from December 15, 1883, in *United States Medical Investigator*, in 'Clinical Medicine' by W.A. Knight, M.D., where it is in quotes:

> "We are all familiar with the physiological axiom, '**Use it, or lose it**,' and there is good reason to believe that after a lapse of time, tissues which have not fulfilled their functions, cease to have the ability to do so."

Using a sledgehammer to crack a nut[2,3]

This British and Australian metaphoric idiom means using greatly excessive force to solve a minor problem. Originally only called 'sledges,' these are very large hammers which were designed and utilized as early as the 15th century in England for major tasks such as breaking boulders. Prior to the use of 'crack a nut' in this metaphor, there was 'kill a fly;' other variations came. The earliest known uses were actually in America, two of which were in 1854. The first was in the *Boston Medical and Surgical Journal*, February 1, that year, under '***The Quick Festival***,' about an address given before the Medical Socioety of the University of Nashville, Tennessee, now defunct, which spawned Vanderbilt

University Medical School, Peabody College, Montgomery Bell Academy and the University School of Nashville:

> "The Mustang Liniment, the Pain Killer, and a variety of other nostrums, are harpooned outright; but it strikes us that it is unnecessary to swing a **sledge-hammer to kill a fly**."

The earliest citation with 'crack a nut' known was in *The Autobiography of Thomas Anthony Methuen,* published in London in 1870, page 164:

> "It was taking a **sledge-hammer to crack a nut**, but it seems to have produced a profound impression on my father's sensitive and scrupulous mind."

Ute[3]

In Australia and New Zealand, the term 'ute' is short for utility vehicle, which in the literal interpretation, is a passenger vehicle with a cargo section in the rear which is a continuation of the passenger area, much like the old Ford Ranchero and Chevrolet El Camino in America. In fact, General Motors has a model for sale in Australia called the Holden Ute. However, it may also be used for the vehicle referred to as a pickup truck in the rest of the world.

V

Variety is the spice of life

This proverb means that trying many different experiences helps to make life interesting and is from English poet William Cowper's narrative, *The Task*, 1785:

> "**Variety's the very spice of life**, That gives it all its flavour."

The thought was expressed over 100 years earlier in *The Rover,* a play by dramatist Alphra Behm, first performed March 24, 1677, at Dorsett Garden Theater in London:

> "**Variety is the** soul of pleasure."

Velvet glove[2]

This metaphoric term illudes to the subtle but effective use of gentle persuasion to obtain a desired result. The glove is a depiction of the imaginary hand which becons someone into a state of ease, and velvet is figurative of subtlety. The initial citation involved the obviously variant 'iron hand' in the glove in *The Appendix to the Seventh-Eighth Volume of The Monthly Review Enlarged*, 1815 by Ralph Griffiths, in quoting the Russian czar, Paul I, who reigned from 1796 to 1801:

> "Like other men of coarse minds, he had no idea of governing but by force; and he was accustomed to say that the 'Russians could be ept at their duty only by an iron hand covered by a **velvet glove**.'"

Thomas Carlyle's *Latter Day Pamphlets*, 1850, also has the iron hand metaphor and states that it was used by Napoleon:

> "'Soft of speech and manner, yet with an inflexible vigour of command...'iron hand in a **velvet glove**,' as Napoleon defined it."

Virtual ghost town

The term 'ghost town' has been around since the 19th century when abandoned mining towns in the American West were called by that name. But 'virtual ghost town' is much newer.

This is an oft-used phrase in the Internet. On September 12, 2005, Trip Advisor carried a review of Casa Velos, a resort in Puerto Vallarta, Mexico, calling it 'a virtual ghost town.'

On May 16, 2012, Rob Waugh did an article on DailyMail.com with the headline, "The 'virtual ghost town:' One-third of users of Google Plus social network post once - and then NEVER post again."

Kristen Dalgren, on *NBC Nightly News*, Friday, January 23, 2016, described LaGuardia being shut down by the 'blizzard of a generation,' using this term.

Billboard Magazine, in the August 1, 1942 issus, may have been the first to call an abandoned place a 'virtual ghost town,' in 'Clubs Feel Effects of War; Late Shows Empty; More Bar Trade; Unescorted Fems Welcomed,' on page 11:

> "Taverns near the waterfront and the few night spots In that sector which catered to seamen and which up to the Pearl Harbor attack enjoyed a

lucrative patronage, are now **virtual 'ghost town'** spots, as seamen patronage is no more."

W

Waffling on the issues

This is most often used of politions when they are nebulous about the important concerns of constituents, especially during an election year, going on an on with meaningless rhetoric. The word 'waffle' came from the Middle Low German *wāfel* and was brought into English in 1377 as wafer. *Waff*, meaning to bark like a dog is antiquated and virtually obsolete, but is now used as *woof*. In *An Etymological Dictionary of the Scottish Language* by minister and lexicographer John Jamieson, published in 1808, *waff* in Scottish meant someone who was worthless. Waffle, in this sense, means to talk aimlessly and trivially, and is actually derived from *waff*. It is easy to see how this might relate to barking like a dog and being worthless. In America the term came into ues in politics in 1972 (an election year), and the earliest known citation is from *New York Magazine* that year, Volume 5, page 138:

> "Can a network that fails to grasp the women's issue understand **problems** like McGovern's strategy on South Carolina? .... Instead people are beginning to say they are forcing **issues**: 'We/she/he/they **waffles**, is **waffling, waffled on the issues**, ...'"

Walk in someone's shadow

This metaphor is used to describe the sometimes uncomfortable position that a child or younger sibling of a very famous person, particularly one following in the career choice of his or her parent, brother or sister occupies. Though it has been stated that each person is an individual and not to be likened to any other person, the fact remains that the public many times views the younger family member of a popular public figure through the same window as the famous predecessor. The earliest reference to a form of this, and possibly the inspiration for the expression, comes from the *Bible*, and is speaking of man's relationship to God. *Hosea 14:7, KJV* says:

> "They that **dwell under his shadow** shall return; they shall revive as the corn, and grow as the vine: the scent thereof shall be as the wine of Lebanon."

The earliest reference available to walking in someone's shadow is in Dorothy Charquez's *The Tramp and His Woman*, 1937, page 18:

> "Strange, when she thought of it, how everything in the house moved round him, how her mother always seemed to **walk in his shadow**, and the others, Tom and Elsie, would always do as he wished, out of habit or because they really thought it was best."

(See also: '**In the shadow of**')

walk on the wild side, A+

This is an idiomatic expression meaning to be involved in adventuresome, risky, or morally questionable behavior. It is actually not very old. The earliest use of this exact phrase was as the title of a 1956 Depression-era, tragic comedy novel by American author Nelson Algren, which was adapted to a major motion picture in 1962, with such stars as Lawrence Harvey, Jane Fonda and Barbara Stanwyck. The book was inspired by a country song by Arlie Carter and William Warren titled *The Wild Side of Life* first recorded by Johnny Heap in 1951, which hit big for Hank Thompson the following year.

Walk someone through something

This idiom refers to leading another person slowly and patiently, 'step by step,' through a complex problem or thought process. It came into figurative usage in the second half of the 20th century. A good early example is in *Don't Take My Grief Away* by Doug Manning, 1984, page 17:

> "I want to **walk you through** grief."

Walk the walk and talk the talk

This cliché statement is often made by a person who has doubts as to the authenticity of another person's sincerity concerning a capability or stringent belief. It means living up to one's public persona, and was first attested in June, 1921, in the *Mansfield* (Ohio) *News*:

> "Although he has no guilded metals upon his bosom, Howard Herring of the North American Watch Company **walks the walk and talks the talk** of a hero today."

A similar saying is 'Actions speak louder than words.' (See original volume)

Wall to wall

Coming from the literal definition of covering a floor in its entirety, or reaching from one wall to the other, this is a colloquial saying meaning either occupying a space or period of time completely, or the market being saturated with something. It was used poetically in a somewhat firurative way as early as 1762 by English poet Edward Bysshe, in his epic *War,* in Volume II of *The Art of English Poetry*:

> "Undaunted, they no Dangershun;
> From **Wall to Wall** the Shouts and Clamours run."

A more clearly figurative usage comes by the last half of the 20th century. A good example is a Christian self-help book entitled *Happiness Wall to Wall* by Gelrge E. Vandeman, 1968.

War chest+

This is a figurative phrase describing a reserve fund, collection of tools, etc. used for fighting a war or for use in any challenging or dangerous situation. It originally, in medieval times, referred to a literal chest located in the homes or barracks of soldiers in which they stored arms and armor.

Today, the term may also be used today to describe a fund received from donors in advance of a political campaign by an incumbent up for reelection.

In business it can mean a stash of money set aside to set aside to deal with unexpected changes in thte business environment.

Wasp waist

Figuratively, this refers to a woman's very slender waistline. It comes from the fact that a wasp, with its segmented body, has the thinnest waist of any insect. The term was popularized by a style of corset and girdle designed in the 19th century to slenderize a feminine waist, thus exaggerating the hips and bust. The earliest known citation referring to the wasp shape of a woman's figure is found in *The Tattler; or, Lucubrations of Isaac Bickerstaff*, 1764, page 97:

> "Our tight-laced grandmothers were nothing to the **wasp**-shaped dames of the court of Catherine de Medicis."

In 1809, 'Helena, the Grecian Beauty' was one of the poems in *The Cypriad in Two Cantos with Other Poems and Translations* by Henry C. Knight published in Boston. The following lines expressed the male view of a wasp waist:

> "Her form, it surely was divine,
> Compress'd like a **wasp** in the **waist**;
> A churn at the bottom so fine,
> And other parts all in the taste."

Watchdog

From the literal canine which is used to guard property comes this metaphoric term meaning a person or organization which serves a guardian against waste, loss or illegal practices. It came into general use early in the 20th century. The earliest available citation is from *The American Monthly Review of Reviews*, August, 1902, in an article titled, 'Spooner of Wisconsin, A Sketch of the Present Leader of the Senate:'

> "As a lawyer and maker of laws, as a **watchdog** against the furtive slipping in of blunders, as a suggester of stronger and bcttcr methods, as a deviser of practical schemes which will meet existing conditions in the Senate and the country, he is without a peer in public life."

Watching the world go by

This phrase means sitting or standing in one location and enjoy seeing others as they pass by. Dean Martin had a hit song by this title in 1956 which began:

> "**Watching the world go by** under a sunny sky
> Strolling 'round the park on a Sunday afternoon
> Oh, how the moments fly watching the world go by
> When you're with your love life is a beautiful tune…"

But the saying was around about 100 years earlier. The first known citation is from *Rhymes with a Reason* by Alan Brodrick, 1857, on page 9, in 'The Bridge of Boats (Stamboul, 1855):'

> "I had been standing on the bridge for hours
> **Watching the world go by**,
> Until the little steamer, piled up high
> With city Turk and Greek, had left the side,

And borne her freight away upon the tide,
And landed them amid their 'orange bowers'"

Watch that first step, it's a doozy!+

This popular saying is usually credited as a quote from the 1993 comedy film, Groundhog Day starring Bill Murray. But it has been around quite a bit longer. It was first used by Warner Brothers in *Bugs Bunny* cartoons in the 1950s. Then it was in an episode of *Top Cat* titled All that Jazz in late 1961. The word doozy also spelled doozie, was used as a short form of Dousenberg, a car made by Auburn Motor Company in the late 1920s and 1930s. But the word doozy was in use long before that, even. The Random House Dictionary of American Slang suggests that it first appeared about 1903. It may have even came earlier, as some experts believe it was first taken from famed Italian actress Elnora Duse, who appeared in New York in 1893. 'Dusey' was originally applied to something excellent in its field.

Watch this space[2]

This British expression is used to express the opinion that there will soon be an exciting change in the situation. It became known in the late 19th century, and the earliest known citation is from *The Lansing College Magazine*, April, 1878, in Advertisements under the heading, 'Don't Read This:'

> "'Patent Blue' is bewildering, and exerts over the quiet contemplative mind, in connection with the royal nursery, a strange fascination. Or consider the imperative injunction to '**Watch this space**.' What may not hang on the strict performance?"

Weakest link (See: **Chain is only as strong as its weakest link, A**, original volume)

Wear out one's welcome+

This old metaphor means that one has stayed in a place so long, or visited so often, that he or she is no longer wanted. The principle comes from the *Bible, Proverbs 25:17*:

> "Withdraw thy foot from thy neighbor's house; lest he be weary of thee, and so hate thee." (*KJV*, 1611)

The *NLT* (1996) brings it into modern wording:

> "Don't visit your neighbors too often, or you will **wear out your welcome**."

This exact phrase was in use in English by at least 1889 when Lewis Carroll used it in *Sylvie and Bruno*, chapter 16, where it appears in quotes:

> "No, he feared to '**wear out his welcome**,' he said: they had 'seen enough of him for one while.'"

Wear the pants (in the family)

This idiomatic expression means be the person with controlling authority of a marriage or family. It is based on the tradition that a man is the head of the family. Originally it was 'wear the breeches.' It has been in use for hundreds of years, and the earliest verifiable example is from *The Craftsman*, Volume XII by Caleb D'Anvers of Grey's Inn, 1737, page 294:

> "It may be farther urged in her Defence that **She wears Breeches**, not in a figurative Sense, like several notable Dames about Town, but according to the strict and literal Meaning of those Words."

Here it mentions 'figurative' use of the term, indicating that it was used that way in the 1730s. In *The London Magazine*, Volume 43, 1774, in a poem on page 216 we see a clear example:

> "Now all the good he sets of this read wife,
> **She wears the breeches**, he the horns for life."

Web of deceit or **lies**

This refers to a vast weaving together of untruth which engulfs a person as a spider entangles its prey in its web. The earliest known reference in print of 'web of deceit' is from Sir Walter Scott, in one of the *Waverly Novels,* in the *Tales of My Landlord* series, *Count Robert of Paris*, published in 1831 in Baudry's Foreign Library in Paris, Chapter XIV, page 187:

> "Beginning by being the buffoon of the court, he has wormed himself into all its secrets, made himself master of all its intrigues, conspired with my own

> son-in-law against me, debauched my guards, — indeed so woven his **web of deceit**, that my life is safe no longer…"

Earlier, Lord Byron had used 'web of wiles' in his poem, *A Sketch from Private Life* in 1821. The 'lies' version came slightly later, but before Scott's web of deceit. In 1825, in *The Pocket Magazine* of which Scott was a major contributor, in a letter to the Editor signed by Tristissima Tims, Liverpool, Sept. 8, 1825, we find:

> "Mr. B. with that facility of falsehood which veils his real character beneath a **web of lies**, as the rotten fertility of a dunghill overspreads its disgusting surface with a tissue of verdant but baleful weeds, has endeavoured, under pretence of ..."

We have two ears and one mouth, so we should listen more than we say.

This proverb is currently attributed to both Zeno of Citium, a Greek Stoic Philosopher born in 334 BCE, and Epictetus, another Greek Stoic Philosopher (55-135 CE). The earliest available text, *Bibliotheca Classica, Or A Dictionary of All the Principal Names and Terms* by John Lemprière, 1851, states that it is from Zeno, on page 665:

> "Zeno in his maxims used to **say**, that with virtue men could live happy under the most pressing calamities. He said that nature had given us **two ears**, **and** only **one mouth**, to tell us that **we ought to listen more than speak**."

It is likely that Epicteus was a student of Zeno and therefore carried the saying onward.

Weigh in

In a literal sense this refers to a person stepping on the scales to record weight, particularly in weight loss programs or fighters going into the ring; to animals being weighed for market, and for game which is bagged or caught. Figuratively, it means to express one's opinion on some particular matter, especially in a discussion or argument. This use began in the mid-20th century, and the earliest available citation is from *The Aeronautical Journal*, Volume 57, 1953, page 462, here in quotes indicating a fairly new but known expression:

> "The lecturer had not spotlighted that particular aspect but he felt that improvement in fatigue properties would also **'weigh in'** on the side of integral construction."

Well begun is half done

This ancient proverb, meaning that a lot of any project's success is dependent upon a good beginning, goes back to Ancient Greek philosophy. Variations of it were used in the works of Hesiod (c 750-650 BCE)[*Works and Days 40*] quoted by Lucian (125-180 CE) [*Hermotimus*]; Plutarch (45-120 CE) [*Moralia 16A*] citing Sophacles (c 496-406 BCE) in *frag 747 Nauck;* Plato (c 428-348 BCE), [*Laws Book 6*], Aristotle (384-322 BCE) [*Politics Book 5*], Horace (65-8 BCE) [*Epistles*]; the Roman poet Ausonius (c 310 –395 CE) *[Epigrammata 15 (81*)]; and Suidas (10th century CE) [*A 1491*].

Since Hesiod came first, it is possible that he originated the saying; however, he, like other ancient philosophers, may have carried it down from someone before him.

Well, butter my butt and call me a biscuit!

This is a rural American expression of surprise that just came to light early in the 21st century. It indicates that something that has just been said was not expected, or something that was not thought probable. There are several other such sayings, such as 'paint me green and call me a cucumber' and 'slap me with bread and call me a sandwich.' It likely was made popular on social media. The earliest citation available is in the book, *Off the Internet for Everyone: Stories, Jokes and Inspiration from the World Wide Web for You*, 2002, by Tammy Wright, on page 92.

Well-healed

This is most commonly used to describe someone for whom money is no problem. Before the late 19th century, the term only referred to a wound which had become well. The earliest known reference in which it refers to financial status is in *Bound in Shadows, A Novel,* by American author Eva Wilder Brodhead, 1897, on page 153:

> "I always figured that there walnut wood of ours would come into the market sooner or later, and I never worried much. But t' tell you the dead truth, I ain't so **well-healed** right now as I'd find accomidating. I got to figure round a heap."

This could be the beginning of this saying, and may have meant that the person could use a new pair of shoes ('well heeled' was used earlier re shoes). But obviously, the metaphor caught on.

Well-oiled machine

This idiom describes anything that operates effectively as a whole by coordinated efforts of its parts or facets. The earliest known figurative citation is from *Phantasmagoria: Or, Sketches of Life and Literature* by Mary Jane Jewsbury, published in Edinburg, 1825, p 230:

> "In her voice there is nothing sharp or querulous, it has a body of sound, like that which proceeds from **a well oiled machine** in constant use; at the same time, you detect the true gossip-tone in every sentence she utters."

Well shut my mouth!

Like the previous entry, 'Well butter my butt and call me a biscuit!' this is an exclamation of surprise, used primarily in the Southern U.S. The earliest known usage in print is from *Freedom and Union*, Clarence Kirshman Streit (1896-1986), 1953, Volume 8, page 61:

"'Well Shut My Mouth!'

> "The junior Senator from Wisconsin (when over-ruled by the Chairman of the Watkins Committee during the recent censure hearings): 'This is the most unheard of thing I have ever heard of!'"

We must, indeed, all hang together, or, most assuredly, we shall all hang separately

Meaning that in order to gain true freedom and independence, the founders of the American Colonies must unite in their rebellion against England; Benjamin Franklin made this statement at the signing of the Declaration of Independence on July 4th, 1776.

Wham bam, thank you ma'am!

Initially used to describe a very quick sexual encounter, this may now refer to any transaction between two or more parties conducted with no emotion and usually disregard for one or more party involved. The saying originated in a 1948 World War II play titled, *Mr. Roberts*, based on a 1946 Thomas Heggen novel, written by and Heggen and Joshua Logan, in which a sailor named Gerhart said:

> "Well there goes the liberty. That was sure a **wham-bam-thank-you ma'am!**"

What are you trying to prove?+

This cliché expression is used to ask someone why he or she is behaving in a way that seems unreasonable. Though it reached heights of popularity in the mid-20th century, it had been in use much longer. French protestant author Jean-Paul Rabaut Saint-Etienne utilized it in *The Old Cevenol* (1743-1793), first translated into English in 1893. This is from the American version, 1911:

> "CEVENOL. **What are you trying to prove?**"

What can I do you for?

This is a rhetorical expression with intended inversion aimed at jovially asking how the speaker can help someone. It came into the American slang vernacular near the close of the 20th century. The earliest available examples are from 1999. One of these is *The Woman in the Yard* by Stephen E. Miller, 1999, page 68:

> "'**What can I do you for** today, Kewpie?' the man behind the counter called out."

What doesn't kill you makes you stronger

This proverbial axiom comes from Frederich Neitzsche's book, *Twilight of the Idols, or, How to Philosophize with a Hammer,* originally written in German in1888, translated by R. J. Hollingdale, published in 1889. The actual quote is:

> "**That which does not kill us, makes us stronger**."

On January 17, 2012, Kelly Clarkson released a CD single titled *Stronger* on RCA Records, written by Jorgen Elofsson and David Gamson embracing the proverb which became one of the best selling singles of all time.

What do you do for a crust?[3]

This Aussie expression is equal to 'How do you earn a living?' Crust, of course, is the outside, visable layer of bread, used commonly in English to mean money, which equates to 'our daily bread' in The Lord's Prayer. The earliest available citation is for 'earn a crust' in *Once a Week: an Illustrated Miscellany* published in London, December 1, 1865, in 'The Golden Wedding in the Workhouse:'

> "I slept in the hayloft and did odd jobs just to **earn a crust** for the two boys and myself."

What's his (or **her**) **face**

Like 'What can I do you for' above, this is another jovial play on words, actually meaning 'What's his name,' and sometimes having been applied when the person's name is really not forgotten, but talking about him or her is likely painful. This one, however, is dated, hardly being used any more in Southern America. It is of note that it is not really a question. It became polular in the late 1970s, and the earliest known use in print is as the title of a poem in the book, *Resident Alien: Poems* by Canadian-American poet and editor, Daryl Hine, 1975, on page 52.

What the Sam Hill?!+

There are numerous conflicting stories about how and when this expression was coined. It is believed by some that Sam may have come from *salmon*, meaning an oath. Another suggestion is that Sam came from Samuel, a name for the devil in the opera, *Der Freischutz*, by Carl Maria Von Webber; but since first use was by uncultured frontiersmen; this seems unlikely. Various people named Samuel Hill became associated with the phrase through the 19th and early 20th centuries.

The plain truth, however, is that Sam Hill is a euphemism or 'minced oath'. It most likely was first used in the Pacific Northwest for 'damn(ed) hell', by American frontiersmen who wanted to 'clean up their language' when ladies were around, coming into common use in the early 1800s, according to an editor, Elmer Roessner, who reported this in The Seattle Times in 1839.

What you see is what you get^

Today, this is most commonly used concerning computer print outs. It has the popuolar acronym, WYSIWYG, and means that what is displayed on the computer screen is exactly what will be printed out. A product of Xerox PARC, the explanation of this acronym was explained in *Byte Magazine* in the April, 1982 issue. But that was not the original coining of the acronym, though then it did not refer to computers at all. On January 23, 1972, the Texas newspaper, the

Victoria Advocate carried a story about teams of local students who competed for a new business idea, in which they were to use an acronym in the business name. Here are the names the teams chose:

> "SPOT - Selling Products of Tomorrow
> LIFE - Lets Insure Future Existence
> **WYSIWYG - What You See Is What You Get**"

It is possible that this carried over into the later use of the acronym as a computer term. But the expression did not start there, neither was it coined by Flip Wilson in his Geraldine character on *Rowen and Martin's Laugh In* (1968-1973), and later his own variety show, which premiered September 17, 1970, as widely reported and believed, though he did popularize it. In November, 1949, *The Charleston Gazette* (South Carolina), ran ad ad for a Filmo Sportsware camera which used something very close:

> "You just sight, press a button and **what you see, you get**!"

The exact phrase came in May, 1966, in an ad for a house that was for sale in *The Oakland Tribune* in California:

> "So with the exception of landscaping and decorator furnishings, **what you see is what you get.**"

This saying has since also been used as a catchphrase for anything or anyone which may be taken at face value. Thanks to *The Phrase Finder* for most of this info.

Wheels within wheels[2]

This is a British metopher for hidden facts which make a situation more complicated or complex. It is derived from a prophetical biblical text in *Ezekiel 1:16*:

> "As for the appearance of the wheels and their construction: their appearance was like the gleaming of a chrysolite; and the four had the same likeness, their construction being as it were a **wheel within a wheel."** (*ESV*)

Irish blues rocker, Rory Galligher released a studio album with a mixed bag (see) of a wide range of acoustic styles including some traditional Irish tunes on the Capo label in 2003 titled, *Wheels Within Wheels.*

When God closes a door He opens a window

Having become classified as 'a Christian cliché,' many may expect this to have originated with some popular minister or Christian philosopher. *Au contraire.* It comes from the 1965 Rogers and Hammerstein classic motion picture, *The Sound of Music,* and was spoken by Mother Superior to Maria, who has made a decision to leave the abbey.

It is a close rephrasing of a statement attributed to Alexander Bell which had no reference to God 'When one door closes, another door opens' (see original volume for full quote).

When life passes out lemons make lemonade

This proverbial saying encourages people who are facing adversity to be positive, take the misfortunes of life and find ways to improve oneself through these experiences. The thought was coined by Elbert Hubbard, a Christian anarchist writer, in the 1915 obituary of Marshall P. Wilder, a dwarf actor, headed with the praise: King of Jestors, according to *Select Writings of Elbert Hubbard*, 1922, page 237:

> "He was a walking refutation of that dogmatic statement, *Mens sana in corpore sano*. His was a sound mind in an unsound body. He proved the eternal paradox of things. He cashed in on his disabilities. **He picked up the lemons that Fate had sent him and started a lemonade-stand."**

The September, 1916 issue of the *Auburn Seminary Record* was next to use the maxim:

"[Hugh K. Walker] described a pessimist as one who fletcherizes his bitter pill, the optimist as the man who **made lemonade of the lemon handed him."**

It then picked up by other writers, and was later popularized by Dale Carnegie in *How to Stop Worrying and Start Living*, 1948, page 138, where he credited Joseph Rosenwald for passing it along to him,

> **"If You Have a Lemon, Make a Lemonade."**

Whisper sweet nothings

'Sweet nothings' refers to flattering or wooing words and before the term began with 'whisper' or possibly ended with 'in (someone's) ear,' the first mention of 'nothings' was in poetry. In August, 1796, *The European Magazine and London*

Review, had a poem titled 'Ode to Love,' containing the following lines, clearly carrying the same connotation:

> "Thou, whose veriest **nothings** teaze,
> And as very **nothings** please;"

The earliest use of 'sweet nothings' in print known are found in the London publication, *The Lady's Monthly Museum,* February, 1811, in a letter to the Editor:

> "As for the lady, her eyes sparkled, and her tongue talked such **sweet nothings**, that I can scarcely wonder Ned forgot his supper.—Suffice it, Mr. Editor, that Ned danced with her the rest of the night, and, at the conclusion, I hardly need say that he had the pleasure to see her home."

White wedding[2]

This term is applied to the traditional wedding format which originated in England after Queen Victoria wore a dazzling white satin dress in her wedding to Prince Albert on February 10, 1840. Her dress came at a cost of £1000, a virtual fortune at the time. Later it was described in *The Permanent Record of Queen Victoria's Visit to Derby* this way:

> "Lady readers will be especially interested to know that her Majesty's **wedding** dress was of **white** satin, with a very deep trimming of Honiton lace. The body and sleeves were richly trimmed with the same material. The train, also was of white satin, lined with the same material, and was trimmed with orange blossoms."

During the Victorian age some women were intent on imitating this exquisite garment, and were able to do so at much less cost according to fasion reports in London publications. Later the term 'white wedding' came to encapsulate the Christian traditional Western wedding format.

Who'd a thunk it?^

This is a humorous, jovial way to say, 'I would have never thought of that.' It is often credited to vaudeville ventriloquist Edgar Bergan, who popularized it via the mouth of his buck-toothed dummy, Mortimer Sneed, in the 1930s and 1940s. It was around much earlier, however. The earliest known citation is from *The Knickerbocker; or, New York Monthly Magazine*, December, 1855, in 'Gossip with Readers and Correspondents:'

> "**Who'd** ha' **thunk it?** — 'spected to be married in less 'n tew months!"

Numerous other publications used it in the late 19th century, either as who'd have thunk it' or 'who'd a thunk it.'

Whodunnit^

This is a colloquial term which has been applied to detective stories which retain an aura of mystery, keeping the reader, listener or viewer guessing throughout the plot as to who committed the crime, usually a murder or string of murders. The term was coined early in the 1930s. In spite of Journalist Wolfe Kaufman's claim that he came up with the word around 1935 while working for *Variety Magazine*, the editor of *Variety*, Able Green, attributed it to Sime Silverson who preceeded Kaufman, and the first use in that magazine was in the edition of August 28, 1934, referring to the motion picture adaptation of *Recipe for Murder*, later titled 'Blind Justice,' printed in the headline:

> "U's **Whodunit**: Universal is shooting 'Recipe for Murder'"

But there is an even earlier claim, one which checks out. On April 11, 1943, *Publisher's Weekly* attributed the expression to outspoken book critic, Donald Gordon, in *America's News of Books*, July, 1930. The coining was in regard a murder mystery:

> "*Half-Mast Murder* by Milward Kennedy—A satisfactory **whodunit**"

Whole new ball game

This idiomatic expression has reference to an entirely different situation from that which had prevailed, one which is difficult to predict. It is derived from baseball, and used initially to mean that because of a totally unexpected turn of events in an inning, the outcome may be sharply reversed. It came into figurative use in the 1970s, and the earliest known citation of a close form is in *Congressional Record, Senate*, Washington, DC, July 15, 1974, referring to technology:

> "There have been important changes, especially in the technology of radio and television. There is **an entirely new ball game** now."

The following year, after the resignation of President Richard M. Nixon and the inauguration of Gerald Ford, in *Hearings before the Select Committee on Intelligence, U.S. House of Representatives 94th Congress, First Session,* on Friday, August 1st, a statement was made by Connecticut Democtatic Representative Robert N. Giaimo, to James T. Lynn, Secretary of HUD under Nixon, who was now Director of OMB:

"This is **a whole new ball game** insofar as both of us are concerned."

whole nother, A+

Formed by insertion of whole into another by 'tmesis,' this is a term which has come to be accepted as an alternative form of 'another whole.' It is not new, as some may believe, as earliest known use in print was actually in 1890 in Mary Louisa Molesworth's short story, 'The Mysterious Guide' in the collection, *The Story of a Spring Morning and Other Tales*, on page 315:

"I don't know what we shall do if we have to be **a whole 'nother** day in the house and in the dark."

Who's your daddy?

This American colloquial expression may be used to bragadociously claim dominance over its target. The earliest known use of the phrase in print is actually long ago—in April, 1851, in "Uncle Sam and His 'B'hoys,'" Chapter II, published in *The U.S. Democratic Review:*

"Didn't I give you every foot of land you own, you rebellious rascals? Answer me that—**who's your daddy?**—hey!"

Modern use of a close form is in the comedy movie, *The Adventure of Sherlock Holmes' Smarter Brother*, 1975, starring Gene Wilder as Holmes, who harshly questions Jenny Hill, played by Madeline Kahn, who claims to be the daughter of the British Minister of External Affairs. While massaging her exposed breasts, he repetedly asks her, "**Who's your father?**"

The Zombies' 1968 song, *Time of the Seasons*, asks, "What's your name, **who's your daddy?**" but this still hardly qualifies as having the meaning of the idiom.

Through the 1970s and 1980s it was used in numerous books and publications, though the meaning didn't seem to evolve until the late '80s and early '90s. The 1991 comedy routine of Saturday Night Live's Dennis Miller really popularized the expression. It was used on numerous TV shows; then actress Fiona Hughes did a primetime 90 mintute special based around a young woman, T. J. Myers, being reunited with her biological father titled *Who's Your Daddy*, which was aired on Fox on January 3, 2005. A series was developed with six planned episodes. Low ratings and sharp controversy caused quick cancellation, and the remaining episodes only aired on Fox Reality.

Widowmaker

This term is applied to anything with the potential to kill men. It comes from Shakespeare's *King John*, 1595, Act V, Scene ii:

> "Oh, it grieves my soul, that I must draw this metal from my side, to be a **widowmaker."**

Wilco (Roger, wilco, over and out)+

According to the *ACP 125 (F) Communications Instructions Radiotelephone Procedures,* September, 2001, this is a military 'proword' (procedure word) meaning that a radio transmission has been received and will be complied with. It was first recorded in the U.S. military between 1935 and 1940, and is short for will comply. Roger indicates understanding,

Wild card

This term, meaning something that is unpredictable, came from a card game, particularly poker, where a certain card is 'wild' and may be used as any other card. It came into figurative use early in the 20th century. The first verifiable citation available is from *Visions and Beliefs in the West of Ireland* by famed Irish poet and writer William Butler Yeats, 1920, page 191:

> "There was one time a tailor, and he was a **wild card**, always going to sprees."

Wild hair (See: **Have a wild hair**)+

Windbag (See: **Bag of wind**)

Windfall

This means an unexpected acquisition. It derived from fruit bown down from a tree by the wind, which was considered free for all. The earliest verifiable printed example of figurative usage is in *Epistolæ Ho-Elianæ: Familiar Letters, Domestic and Forren. Divided into Four Books* by James Howell, Sixth Edition, printed in London in 1688, page 446:

"Sir, I Am one among many who much rcjoyce ar the fortunate **windfall** that happen'd lately, which hath so fairly rais'd and recruted your Fortunes."

wink's as good as a nod (to a blind horse/mule, etc), A

This proverbial saying originated in England by the 18th century. It means that for someone who is ready and able to understand something, any subtle signal will be sufficient. It usually is said of something thought off color or possibly illegal. The earliest citations are slightly different and use horse. The first one is from the play *Scottish Volunteers* a farce performed first in 1745:

"LOVES: Where are you going; —what will you say when you're there?

"THOM: I'm not there yet.—

"LOVES: Do you mind what I say to you.

"THOM: Let me alone for that, **a nod's as good as a wink to a dead horse**.

"LOVES: A **blind horse** you mean, you beast!"

In *The Egotist: or, Sacred Scroll*, 1798, it is attributed to Milton:

"I do not say they had better not – but I say nothing! – 'a **nod is as good as a wink to a blind horse**' as Milton beautifully expresses it."

As time went on, 'a nod is as good as a wink' was most often reversed, and other things were used for horse (mule, man). Eventually it was mostly used without the ending all together.

Win, lose or draw

As an idiom, this means that a contest should be held and the results should be accepted by all involved. It comes from sports and games where a draw means a tie. The earliest available citation expressing the three cases is in *Transactions of the Asiatic Society of Japan from 30th October 1872 to 9th October 1873* published in Yokahama, Japan in 1874. On page 151, in a section titled, 'The Games and Sports of Japanese Children' by Professor W.E. Griffis, is a description of the game called *Ishiken*, today known in America as rock, sizzors, paper, in which a stone, a pair of sizzors and a piece of wrapping cloth are represented, the stone is the clenched fist, the parted fore and middle fingers are the sizzors and at that time the cloth was the curved forefinger and thumb. The senerio was the same as today. The book states that:

> "The two players sit opposite each other at play, throwing out their hands so as to represent either of the three things, and **win, lose, or draw**, as the case may be."

Then, nine years later, *The Chess Player's Chronicle*, Tuesday August 30, 1881, in the article, 'Telegraph Match in South Australia,' had the following statement:

> "If the Ports **win** one and **lose or draw** the other, they will win the match, provided that Mr. Henderson's game remains theirs."

From 1987 to 1990, an American TV game show named ***Win, Lose or Draw*** aired on NBC narrated by Bob Hilton and by Gene Wood in syndication. Later versions appeared on Disney. In 1987, a board game version was released.

Win the day

This idiom refers to being victorious in battle, sports competition or argument. It infers that it is better to concentrate on winning the day rather than looking too far forward. Like so many other old expressions, this one is from Shakespeare. It is found in *King John*, Act V, Scene vi, 1595, where it appears twice in a discourse of Melun. The first is:

> "I say again, if Lewis do **win the day**, He is forsworn, if e'er those eyes of yours Behold another day break in the east:"

Wipe the slate clean

This old idiom means to expunge one's record of all wrong doing, or to consider a person blameless though he or she has had past infractions. In the old days, storekeepers kept their customers' credit records on a small chalk slate. When the bill was paid he would 'wipe the slate clean' and begin anew. The earliest citation known is in *The Parlimentary Debates of Great Britain, from the 24th Day of June to the 29th Day of July, 1864,* page 1503:

> "Friend the Member for Taunton said they had better **wipe the slate clean**, and start afresh. He (Mr. Adderley) said the better plan would be to wipe the slate and not start afresh."

Wise as an owl

This simile is based purely on myth, since owls are not really wise, and have a smaller brain than most other birds. It comes from Greek mythology, and likely was inspired by the serious look and bright, wide-awake eyes of the species. An owl cannot even move its eyes, but obtains its peripheral vision form turning its head from side to side. In *Fables* by John Gay, 1728, on page 124 we read these poetical lines in Fable XXII, 'The Two Owls and the Sparrow:'

> "I grant you were at Athens grac'd,
> And on Minerva's helm were placed,
> But ev'ry bird that wings the sky,
> Except an **owl**, can tell you why.
> From hence they taught their schools to know
> How false we judge by outward show,
> That we should never looks esteem,
> Since fools as **wise** as you might seem."

An old nursery rhyme, first published in *Punch* on April 10, 1875 is titled, 'A **Wise Old Owl**:'

> "There was an **owl** liv'd in an oak
> The more he heard, the less he spoke
> The less he spoke, the more he heard.
> O, if men were all like that **wise** bird"

A version of this rhyme is found in *The Best of Mother Goose and Other Nursery Rhymes, Illusrtated*, on page 83, published by St. Clair Publications, 2013.

With all due respect^

This cliché infers that the person being addressed is admired and that the one speaking or writing is acknowledging a certain appreciation. However, it is usually followed by an exception in belief or view on a given point of mutual interest. An online reference forum places origin at circa 1800; however, it was in use long before that date—almost 150 years earlier—in *The Tears, Sighs, Complaints, and Prayers of the Church of England* by John Gauden, 1659, page 466:

> "…when they knew who were their *Bishops, Pastors*, and Spirituall Fathers, owning them **with all due respect** and love as in Christs stead, submitting to them for conscience sake, as to the Lord, and receiving from them good

instructions, just reproofes, holy comforts, and heavenly Mysteries, not as from man, but God..."

A clearer expression of current meaning comes only a few years later in *Thirtheism Charges upon Doctor Sherlock's New Notion of the Trinity* by Robert South, 1695, page 249:

"That it is *Natur œ Rationabilis Individua Substantia*, Though he has been told before, That this Definition (**with all due respect** to Boetins be it spoke) was long since rejected by most Divines, Schoolmen and others as defective;"

With a vengeance

This cliché is used to emphisize the tremendous force or extreme energy with which something occurs, or the great degree of truth which something conveys. The word 'vengeance' came into Middle English from the Anglo-French *vengeaunce* circa 1300 CE. This term had come into use in English by 1681 when it appeared in two separate publications. One of these was *The Best Treasure; or, The Way to be Truly Rich* by Bartholomew Ashwood, pp 377, 378:

"The things of the world bar up the way to Heaven, and open the way to Hell, and hasten the soul **with a vengeance** to distruction; They are like the Devils sleep-drench, that casts Souls into a deep trance, and 'till they come to the end of their lives they never awake, and then they awake **with a vengeance..."**

Wither on the vine (or **branch)**

This metaphoric expression means to fail to be implemented or dealt with because of neglect or inaction. When this is done, a person or thing is destroyed gradually, like fruit which is not cared for or harvested in a timely manner. The principle is taken from at least three verses in the *Bible. Isaiah 34:4, KJV* reads:

"And all the host of heaven will wear away, And the sky will be rolled up like a scroll; All their hosts will also **wither** away As a leaf **withers from the vine**, as a falling *fig* from the fig tree."

Hebakkuk 3:17, CEB also mentions olives and figs withering on the vine:

"Though the fig tree doesn't bloom, and there's no produce on **the vine**; though the olive crop **withers**, and the fields don't provide food; though the sheep are cut off from the pen, and there are no cattle in the stalls;"

Then in *John 15, 5-6 (BSB)*, Jesus calls himself the vine, and says that those who do not remain in him will wither:

> "I am **the vine** and you are the branches. The one who remains in Me, and I in him, will bear much fruit. For apart from Me you can do nothing. If anyone does not remain in Me, he is like a branch that is thrown away **and withers**. Such branches are gathered up, thrown into the fire, and burned."

With guns blazing

Conjuring up the familiar stereotype of the Western style shootouts portrayed in motion pictures, this idiom refers to doing something with great force and energy. The earliest citation, however, was long was before Hollywood embraced this image: in 1876. *Cassell's Illustrated History of India, Volume II*, by James Grant, published simultaneously in London, Paris and New York, in 'The Tarai of Nepaul,' the description of a hunt in the jungle by dignatories has the following on page 502:

> "At times, a deer or hog will be knocked over at the first or second shot; but some animals will run the whole gauntlet, **with guns blazing** from every howdah, and may get off without a wound."

Women of a certain age

Owing to the fact that women are traditionally tight-lipped about their actual age, this term is used to keep from saying 'middle aged or older,' and is usually referring to unmarried, sassy women who want to remain unwed, most normally between 50 and 60. The expression, 'a certain age' has been in use in English since at least the late 17th century. Early in the 18th century, it was evident that the idiom was ambiguous, as seen in *Monsuir Bossu's Treatise of the Epick Poem*, published in London in 1716, page 209:

> "In one corner a lady sat on a rocking-chair, moving to and fro like the pendulum of a clock: she seemed to have attained that time of life called '**a certain age**,' a term so very indefinite, it has puzzled physiologists to fix the precise period.."

Wooden spoon[2]

In Birtish colloquial English, this is an imaginary prize to be awarded to the individual coming in last in a competition, particularly used nowadays in the annual Rugby Union Six Nations Championship. It was originally an actual prize used in Cambridge University mathematical tripos exams awarded by the students as a 'booby prize' for the student finishing last. The custom dated back to at least the early 19th century and continued for about 100 years until 1909, after which the results of the competition were called out in alphabetical order, rather that by the highest to lowest scores. Spoons used during this century-long farce continued to grow in size until they reached 1.5 meters in length, and were dangled from the upstairs balcony of the Senate house when the 'winner' came forward to receive his degree.

In *A Collection of College Words and Customs* by Benjamin Homer Hall, 1856, published at Cambridge, on page 496, there is a comical story regarding an earlier 'wooden spoon' prize:

> "Many men prefer the **Wooden Spoon** to any other college honor or prize, because it comes directly from their classmates..." "The '**Wooden Spoon**,' tradition says, was in ancient times presented to the biggest glutton in the class, by his appreciating classmates. It is now **given** to the one whose name comes last on the list of appointees for the Junior Exhibition, though this rule is not strictly followed."

It seems likely that a wooden spoon was chosen because of the negative connotation which it carried. In *The Gentleman's Magazine; or, Monthly Intelligencer, Volume 3*, page 306, 1776, we find 'wooden-spoon' used as an adjective with a less-than-pleasant meaning:

> "...himself made a Secretary of State, or a **wooden-Spoon** of a Lawyer angry that, as he sunk in Fees, he did not rise in Preferment..."

Woop woop[3]

In Aussie slang, this is a term for an imaginary remote town or district symbolizing isolation and backward ways, similar to 'the boondocks' in America. It has been in use the late 19th century and was originally a mimic of Aboriginal placenames such as *Oodnagalahbi*, *Bullamakanka*, and *Bandy-wallop*. *The Victorian Railways Magazine*, published in Melbourne, in 1926 (Volume 3-4, page 102) has an example of a place being called by this name in quotes:

> "How the Staff of our annual cricket match... (who one day instructs us to proceed to '**Woop Woop'** and then compassionately tells us a week or two later to proceed to 'Suberbanville') that, together with two other R.S.M.'s, I was being sent to the Powers District."

Word cloud

This modern term is used to describe a visual representation containing individual words in a particular text or on some certain subject, in which the size of each word is determined by that word's importance to the overall topic. *Information Assurance and Security Education and Training* edited by Ronald C. Dodge and Lynn Futcher, 2013, tells us how the web app was created:

> "TagCrowd is a web application for visualizing word frequencies in any text by creating what is commonly known as a **word cloud**, text cloud or tag cloud. It was created in July 2006 by Daniel Steinbock, while a PhD student at Stanford University."

Microsoft Publisher 2013 contains a program which allowed the user to develop such a visual offline and print it or prepare it for being displayed on a screen in business meetings or classes.

Work one's fingers to the bone

With several variations, this idiom means to work excessively or to the point of exhaustion. It was in use by the late 18th century. The earliest available citation is from *The Spirit of the Public Journals for 1798*, Volume II, New Edition, poetry and prose taken from newspapers, published in London in 1805, in 'A Consolatory Address to his Gunboats' by 'Citizen Muskein,' page 284:

> "Though lovely Stael, and lovelier Stone,
> Have **work'd their fingers to the bone**,
> And cut their petticoats to rags
> To make you bright three-colour'd flags"

Works like a charm

This indicates that something was very effective, and likely surprisingly so. In the olden days a 'charm' was a magic spell, so this meant that something worked in a magic way. The earliest citation known is from *An Account of Some Remarkable Passages in the Life of a Private Gentleman* by Daniel Defoe, 1711, pp 319-320:

> "The devil, I know, abuses many, urging the Impenitent to come out of false Ends and base Designs; to stop the Clamours of Confidence, to gain repute or qualifications, and some are so stupid, as to think it **works like a Charm**, and content themselves with meer Formalities."

world is your oyster, The

This means that you can achieve anything you desire in life because you are in a position to take the opportunities that come your way. It comes from Shakespeare's *The Merry Wives of Windsor*, Act II, Scene ii, penned by1597:

> "Pistol: Why then **the world's mine oyster**/Which I with sword will open**."**

Worry wart+

This Americanism is used to a greater degree in the South today, and means someone who worries a lot. It was coined by J.R. Williamson a highly popular comic strip titled *Out Our Way* which ran from 1922 to 1977. The strip featured a small town family in which one of the boys, about eight years old, was nicknamed Worry Wart by his older brother. In the April 3, 1929 issue of *Canton Daily News*. Canton, Ohio, the boy is by an open window, blackened with soot from nearby factory chimneys. His brother says dryly:

> "So somebody told you it was good fer you t'sleep with a winder open, hah? Well answer me this, **Worry Wart**, without no sarcasticism — does this somebody live in a shop neighborhood?"

Worse for wear

This may refer to a person or thing which is tired or in poor shape because of excessive work or use; basically the equal to 'worn out.' It is also used as 'worse for the wear,' and was first recorded by John Heygood in his 1546 tome, *A Dialogue Conteinyng the Nomber in Effect of all the Prouerbes in the Englishe Tongue.*

> "Al thyng is the **wors for the wearyng.**"

Would argue with a fencepost+

This is an old Southern American metaphoric expression used to illustrate that someone is excessively stubborn and won't listen to reason. According to expert etymologist, Elyse Bruce, in an Internet blog on idiomization, though not known to be used as an idiom until later, the expression seems to have evolved directly from the strict fence laws of the Virginia colony enacted in 1631. At that time, once a fence was erected, and there was a fence agreement between neighbors, nothing could be done to bring the fence down. It was to stay in place and be maintained by both landowners who shared the fence between them. No one could 'argue with the fence posts.' It was a popular saying throughout the South since at least the early 20th century, and likely much earlier.

Woulda, coulda, shoulda (See: **Coulda, shoulda, woulda**)+

Would kill for

This hyperbolic saying means that the person has a near unquenchable desire for something. The earliest known citation of the phrase is from *Niles Weekly Register*, Volume 37, 1829, page 85:

> "We hope that even in that country, a 'missionary of the college of the Holy Cross,' attending a band of armed mercenaries will be treated with very liltle respect, if falling iuto the hands of those whom he **would kill for** the good of their souls!"

Other citations in the late 18th and early 19th century were also difficult to determine whether they were literal or figurative, such as this one from James Oliver Cromwell's *A Fight for Life*, Chapter IX, which appeared in *Munsey's Magazine* in January, 1910:

> "Don't you understand, man? I love her! I didn't mean what I said. I **would kill for** her, too, Jean."

For decades the phrase went missing from publications. Clearly figurative use came in the 1990s, when the saying gained tremendous popularity. A great example comes from *Talk of Drama: Views of the Television Dramatist Now and Then* by Sean Day Lewis, 1998, in Chapter 4: From the Heart and Soul, Jimmy McGovern, page 59:

> "Producers **would kill for** a good, young, passionate honest writer."

Wouldn't say boo to a goose

This is an old country proverb started in England. Most country folk had or knew someone who raised geese. It has been said that saying boo to a goose is a symbol of intimidating them. The saying indicates that someone who wouldn't even dare intimidate a goose is a wimp. However, stirring up a goose can cause an attack by the threatened foul. Geese are well known for grabbing a person's flesh and causing quite a bit of pain.

But there is more to this saying that meets the eye (see: More than meets the eye). From the 1500s, figuratively, a goose has meant a simpleton. Saying 'boo' to a 'goose' was thought to be the least brave act a person could do; so, yes, the meaning is basically the same. The person incapable of this is extremely timid and 'afraid of his or her own shadow.' (See: Afraid of one's own shadow)

The earliest known reference in print is from *The Humours of an Election, a Farce,* as Performed at the Theater Royal in Covent Garden by F. Pilon, Scene I, 1780:

> "*Letit*...But surely, you can never think my booby cousin will cut any figure in the House of Commons.
> *Parma.* Why not, why not, you satyrical baggage?
> *Lelit.* He can't **say boo! to a goose**."

Would you Adam and Eve it?[2]

This odd expression is Cockney rhyming slang for 'would you believe it.' This type of sayings came about in the late-19th century in the East End of London. A mate became a 'china plate.' Why this was invented, no one is certain; but, like 'Pig Latin,' some think it was intended as a sort of code, so folks could communicate questions without everyone knowing what they were saying. It didn't make its way into print for many years, as expressed in the Chinese English publication, *Annual Report on the Researches*, 1978, page 75:

> "Although the tradition does not seem to go back further than the 19th century, it is a privilege that can only be passed on ... Adam and Eve. Believe (late 19th or early 20th c.); **Would you Adam and Eve it**? (to express disbelief), airs and graces."

The idea has carried over into other English speaking sountries. Two examples are 'bread' for money, and 'raspberry' for passing gas.

Wow factor

This modern expression refers to a specific set of qualities belonging to a person, place or thing which strike someone as being extremely impressive; worthy of admiration. The earliest verifiable citation is actually from an Australian author, Jon Casimir, in *Postcards from the Net: An Australian's Guide to the Wired World,* 1996, page 8:

> "The producers always seem to go for the romantic, memorable image, for the tug at the heartstrings or the **wow! factor**."

Wrap one's head around something

This is a modern figurative phrase meaning to come to a good understanding of something difficult to comprehend. It came into common use early in the 21st century. A very early example is from *Mistakes Worth Making: How to Turn Sports into Atheltic Excellence,* by Sandra Halden-Brown, page 275:

> "Take your time, now... relax... focus. **Wrap your head around** this one because nothing is more fundamental to your success than getting the right answer to this question."

Wrecking ball+

In the literal sense, this is a large iron or steel ball dropped by a derrick to demolish buildings. In this meaning it was first attested in 1947, according to *Merriam Webster.* In August, 2013, Miley Cyrus recorded a song on RCA Records titled *Wrecking Ball*, written by Mozella, Stephen R. Moccio and others, which quickly became a Billboard top 100 hit, then her first number one single in the U.S. The pop ballad discusses the deterioration of a relationship. The video shows Cyrus scantily clothed swinging on top of a wrecking ball. The term 'wrecking ball' became used metaphorically do describe someone who came crashing into someone's life, tearing the other down.

Wrong end of the stick^

Unlike 'getting the short end of the stick' (see in first volume), which refers to receiving the raw end of a deal, having the 'wrong end of the stick' means misunderstanding something. It has been reported that 'stick,' in this sense, meant the hand-held device a typesetter used for putting together text with individual letters. Again, this is folk etymology, and incorrect. To get the wrong end of this stick would have been nearly impossible, and the typesetter would have had to know nothing about setting type.

Walter Skeat, a British pioneer philologist, suggested in 1895 that the source was a master beating his servant:

> "The right end of the stick was that held in the master's hand, whilst the other was the wrong end, or (as our American cousins

> would say) the 'business end.' The servant would naturally 'get hold of the wrong end of the stick,' but it would not much avail him, it would soon be wrested from him, and the result would be more stick."

The earliest known citation is from *The Dr---yt---n Review: Or, Characteristic Sketches* by Yorick, Part the First, published in London in 1793, page 67:

> "He's certainly Curs'd, This Yorick is surely in League with Old Nick,
> We Saints have sure got the **Wrong End of the Stick**,
> Part the Second is coming, 'twill contain nothing Good,
> So don't let us Halloo till we're out of the Wood."

This would not contradict Skeat's deduction on the matter, which seemed to be supported by another citation, July 29, 1820, in London's *Morning Post*:

> "This florid opinion, directly contrary to matter of fact, is the **wrong end of the stick** — the *argumentum baculinum*, which you unfortunately got hold of."

The Latin phrase *argumentum baculinum*literally means 'the argument of the cudgel,' appealing to force.

WWJD

This is a Christian inspired acronym which came into popular use in the 1990s and stands for 'What Would Jesus Do?' But the slogan had been used for centuries by ministers, including Charles Spurgeon, and achieved great popularaty 100 years earlier. It was used in 1886 in a series of sermons by minister and social activist Charles Sheldon in Topeka, Kansas. Because of the status of the theme, he got them published in the *Congregationalist Magazine*, and they were soon the subject of a novel first published in 1896, eventually translated into 21 languages, *In His Steps: What Would Jesus Do?* Sheldon was a Socialist, wanted nothing to do with capitalism, supported gender and racial equality and was a vegetarian with strict views on humane treatment of animals.

X

XOXO

This popular symbol, often used, first at the end of letters and notes, today in texts and emails, means 'Hugs and kisses,' and may be used to show affection even when not actually involving a romantic interest. It is uncertain exactly how these letters in combination came to be used in this manner. Signing letters with an X goes back to the Middle Ages, and was practiced for hundreds of years by persons who could not read and write as a mark of one's name. This began as a symbol of the Cross of Christ, and designated that what preceded it was true, 'in Christ's name.' The X in the shortened form of Christmas was actually the Greek letter 'Chi,' not the English 'X.' Greek for Christ was χριστος.

It is believed by scholars that the X may have begun to be used as a kiss when Christains would kiss the X in the same manner that the Bible would be kissed, thus, 'sealing something with a kiss.'

According to the OED, the first use of X's to mean 'kisses' was in a letter by a priest named Gilbert White in 1763:

> "Madame, … In the whole it is best that I have been the loser [of a friendly bet], as it would not be safe in all appearances to receive even so much as a pin from your Hands.
>
> "I am with many a xxxxxxx and many a Pater noster (Our Father) and Ave Maria (Hail Mary), Gil. White."

In *Laetus Sorte Mia* by J. W. Ewing, Chapter VIII, serialized in *Aunt Judy's Magazine*, in 1882, the following reference (Issue XI, p. 669) indicates that the practice of using 'crosses' as they were, as kisses was known:

> "P.S.—Uncle Henry says his father was very old-fashioned, and he always liked to put, 'Your dutiful son,' so I put it to you.
>
> "'All these crosses mean kisses, Jemima told me.'"

According to the 'Today I Found Out' website, the most prominent theory for the O coming into use is much like the X; from illiterate Jewish immigrants to America refusing to sign with an X, due to the Christian perception, who chose to sign with an O. Another theory is that it came from tic-tac-toe, and that the two became used together because of the need for a symbol for higs to go with the X. Other theories exist. Some say the X is actually the hug and O the kiss now.

Whatever the origin, by the early 20th century, the two were being used together just as they are today. In *Reports of Cases Determined by the Supreme Court of the State of Missouri*, Volume 191, October term, 1905, in the Case of State v. Kelley we read:

> "Prosecutrix also testified that defendant told her that when he wrote X and O he meant **hugs and kisses**."

XYZ

This is an acronym for 'Examine Your Zipper,' mostly used by a friend when a man or adolescent has forgotten to zip up his pants following a restroom visit. It was started in the early 1970s, likely in colleges. The earliest citation known is from *Journal of Open Education,* published by Los Angeles, California area Newton College in 1971, Volume 3-4, on page 68:

> "A knowledge of Greek names might be helpful in this case. Example: Sell Everything Xenophon, Xerxes Yelled, 'Zorba.' Students have been known to give **Examine Your Zipper** for the latter."

By the mid-1980s it was picking up use all around America, as seen in *Social Behavior in Autism* edited by Eric Schopler and Gary B. Mesibov, from the University of North Carolina School of Medicine at Chapel Hill, North Carolina, 1986:

> "'I don't say that because it would be rude. Impolite.' Well, it's not exactly that, I say, it's because you don't talk about that part of your body in public places. And Jessy, enlightened, relates it to another such subject: 'Like XYZ; that means **Examine Your Zipper**.'"

Y

Ya think?

This modern expression is used often to answer someone who has just made a statement which is an obvious truism. It means about the same as 'well, duh?' or 'You know that's the truth!' which would have been more commonly said in the late 20th to early 21st century. 'Ya think' has been used in statements and questions often since the 1970's, and excessively so since the 1990s, but in the way it is now, not so much. It got close in *Fisherman Down*, 2005 by E. Bruce Bushong, page 80:

"'...with your vocabulary and your experiences, you can't miss.'

"'**Ya' think**?'

"'Yeah, I think.'"

By 2007 the present usage was beginning to catch on. An example is in a book titled, *The Message: A Conversation with Christ and the Events That Preceded It* by Peter Mercuro, Second Session:

"Peter: There's times when I feel that there's someone around me.
"Karen: And you know he's even saying, you know, 'you could lighten up bud'.
"Karen: Life.
"Peter: Gee, **ya think**? (laughing)
"Karen: Yeah."

You ain't seen nothin' yet!^

This, we have been told, was taken from one of the most powerful statements ever made in entertainment, and has since been a cliché to announce something unexpectedly grand. On October 6, 1927, at the Warner Theater on Broadway, Al Jolson changed history when he called to the orchestra in the premier of *The Jazz Singer*, the first talkie film ever:

"Wait a minute, wait a minute, I tell yer, **you ain't heard nothin' yet**."

From that moment on, silent films were a thing of the past. Very close to this cliché. That, however, was not the origin of a form of this saying. Certainly Jolson helped to popularize it. But the actual cliché had been around for almost 40 years before that. In *The Island Treasure; or, Harry Darrel's Fortunes* by Frank H. Converse, 1888, on page 193 we read:

"Doris shivered and clung a little closer to her father's arm.
'It is like a dungeon,' she said in a low tone.
'More like a wine-cellar,' suggested Lord Masters. But Dan's trump card was yet to be played.
'**You ain't seen nothin' yet**,' he remarked, with the same mysterious air.'"

This has been used as the title for several songs and an album.

You and what army?

This rhetorical question, popular in the mid-20th century, simply means, 'You can't do that on your own!' Actual origin is unclear, but the earliest verifiable citation comes from *The Sin of Patrick Muldune,* a John McLiam play originally copyrighted in 1952 and published later in 1957, Act I, Scene i:

> "CORNELIUS. Buy the best and you buy satisfaction. Never mind, I'll change into my uniform. Someone ought to give you a good skelpin'. (Cornelius exits upstairs with ice cream.)
>
> "GERTRUDE. (Sits R. of table.) **You and what army**?"

You can fool all the people some of the time, and some of the people all the time, but you can't fool all the people all the time^

This proverbial statement has repeatedly been ascribted to Abraham Lincoln, however, there is no definitive proof that he actually said it, and it is certain that the thought did not originate with him. According to the excellent online site, *Quote Investigator*, the earliest reference in print in English is from the *Syracuse Daily Standard*, Syracuse, New York, September 9, 1885, 20 years after Lincoln's death, in a story about a convention of Prohibitionists during which a judge, William J. Groo, reportedly used a version of this saying, without attributing its origin, in a speech complaining about polititions:

> **"You can fool all the people part of the time, or you can fool some people all the time, but you cannot fool all people all the time**."

Then on March 8, 1886, *The Albany* (New York) *Times* published an interview with Prohibitionist state chairman Fred Wheeler who, in a statement also criticizing polititions, gave the earliest known accreditation of the saying to Lincoln:

> "They should remember Abraham Lincoln's famous saying: '**You can fool part of the people some of the time, you can fool some of the people all of the time, but you cannot fool all the people all of the time,**' and take their stand boldly and fearlessly on this question and abide the result at the ballot box.".

This opened the proverbial floodgate for others to credit the 16th President for this astute adage. Numerous other citations followed that year and thereafter.

But the proverb predates this in French by two centuries. The earliest known is in *Traité de la Vérité de la Religion Chrétienne,* a popular 1684 Protestant work of apologetics by Frenchman Jacques Abbadie, in Chapter 2:

> "*...ont pû tromper quelques hommes, ou les tromper tous dans certains lieux & en certains tems, mais non pas tous les hommes, dans tous les lieux & dans tous les siécles*."

This translates to:

> "**One can fool some men, or fool all men in some places and times, but one cannot fool all men in all places and ages**."

You can't make bricks without straw

This proverb refers to the inability to complete a task without the necessary materials. It derives from the biblical story of the Israelites in Egypt not being supplied the straw needed to make bricks by the irate Pharaoh who was bitter over the attempts of Moses to secure their freedom from slavery. *Exodus* 5:7:

> "Ye shall **no more** give the people **straw to make brick**, as heretofore: let them go and gather straw for themselves," (*KJV*)

This was actually a misinterpretation by some that they were to make bricks without straw; however, in actuality they were required to find their own straw, and then make the same number of bricks as if it had been provided. The earliest known figurative reference in print in English to making bricks without straw is found in *A Discourse*, by Daniel Whitby, DD, 1710, page 167:

> "There is no Straw given to us, and thou fayest to us, make Bricks; no fpecial Grace, no Divine Energy afforded us, and thou fayeft to us, do that, which can no more be done without it than Men can **make Bricks without Straw**, and thy Servants are beaten..."

Numerous citations appeared in books in the subsequent years after that, but the earliest known usage of 'cannot make bricks without straw' (purely metaphoric) context is from *Brownson's Quarterly Review*, July, 1845:

> "We have abated nothing of our young zeal for reform nor are we conscious of having lost the ability of the disposition to make as painful sacrifices for the amelioration of our brethren even in this life as our contemporaries are prepared to make; but we **cannot make brick without straw** and we have learned too much from our past experience to be willing to erect a mill where we can have neither wind or water, nor even steam, to drive its machinery."

You can't put the toothpaste back in the tube

This American proverb means that once a person has committed to something it is impossible to turn back. This is a quote from H.R. 'Bob' Haldeman (1926-1993), one time White House Chief of Staff to Richard Nixon. Haldeman, who was well known for his noteworthy sayings, was convicted of conspiracy and obstruction of justice in the Watergate Scandal and imprisoned for 18 months.

You could have knocked me over with a feather+

This old hyperbolic axiom means that something that happened was so unexpected that it took someone by utter surprise. It goes back to the 18th century. The earliest known reference in print to a form of it is found in the epistolary novel, *Pamela; or, Virtue Unrewarded,* about unwanted advances made on a 15-year-old maidservant, by English writer and printer, Samuel Richardson, 1740, Letter VII, page 15:

> "I was so confounded at these words, **you might have beat me down with a feather**."

Then a bit of a change came, using 'knocked' rather than beat, in English author William Corbett's *Porcupine*, September 1796, page 131:

> "As the old women say, **you might have knocked me down with a feather**."

The statement was repeated in Corbett's *Rural Rides* in 1821.

You don't (or **never) get a second chance to make a first impression**

Like many other bits of proverbial wisdom this one has been attributed to both Will Rogers and Oscar Wilde. It is possible that both could have picked it up and popularized it. The earliest citation of the ideal is found in *The Rambler* by Samuel Johnson (1709-1784), first published in 1750, page 286:

> "Few have strength of reason to overrule the perceptions of sense, and yet fewer have curiosity or benevolence to struggle long against the **first impression**: he who therefore fails to please in his salutation and address is at once rejected, and **never obtains an opportunity of showing his latest excellences or essential qualities**."

You don't have to be crazy to work here, but it helps

This comical cliché means that working at a particular place of employment is so challenging that it tends to make a person feel like the employer is driving him or her 'crazy.' It is spoken or posted in jest, and certainly is not to be taken literally. This implies that being insane would help a person cope with the job. It dates back to the 1940s, and may have been coined to apply to working for the U.S. Government. The earliest citation available is from *Newsweek Magazine*, Volume 20, page 113, 1942:

> "A sign decorating one of the offices occupied by the National Inventors' Council, repository of many a crackpot idea, reads: **'You don't have to be crazy to work here, but it helps'…"**

A 1943 publication states that the same sign hung in 'some agencies in Washington,' and other references from the 1940s also state that it was either on a sign or a post card.

You do the math

Although this expression was coined in the 1990s at American college campuses (very likely in the Boston area at either Harvard or M.I.T. in Cambridge, Massachusetts), it is gaining rapid popularity in the U.K., where it often ends up as 'maths.'

It means, 'It's not that difficult, you figure it out.' An early printed example came from the *Harvard Conference on the Internet and Society*, 1997, page 162:

> "So **you do the math**."

The saying was spread quickly by loquacious TV talk show hosts and comedians, thus becoming entwined into our pop culture.

You get what you pay for

Sometimes now shortened to the acronym YGWYPF, this proverbial phrase simply means, 'What did you expect at that price?' It is fueled by marketers of better quality goods who encourage consumers to step up by purchasing better quality merchandise which tends, on the whole, to last longer and be of greater value in the long run. The earliest known example in print of the phrase is from *Elmo's Model Speaker for Platform; School and Home*, 1888, containing a selection of programs for various events, on page 358 in 'Peck's Bad Boy; He Becomes a Druggist' by George W. Peck:

> "If you have a prescription you want filled you can come down to the store and I will put it up for you myself, and then you will be sure **you get what you pay for**."

A better example of the modern meaning comes in January, 1905, in an ad on page 35 of *Successful Poultry Journal*:

> "You should buy your stock of me because **you get what you pay for** and you don't pay three prices for stock that is not as good as mine. I have Al stock and prices that are eye-openers.— KINEY MILLER, LANCASTER, MO."

You got that right!

For almost 100 years, this has been a way of expressing one's agreement with some surprising statement that has just been made. The earliest known citation is from *The Saturday Evening Post*, April 11, 1920, in 'Gloma, the Beautiful Ticket Agent, or The Strike for Love' by George Kibbe Turner:

> "When he argued he always yelled, '**You got that right**, I guess,' said Clancey, letting up a minute."

You'll never work in this town again!+

This cliché is thought to have originated in Hollywood in regard to actors and actresses who had offended producers. However, a 1991autobiographial book by Julia Phillips about her work as a producer in the New Hollywood in the 1970s and 1980s titled *You'll Never Eat Lunch in This Town Again* told the following story:

> "In 1882, the committee for Preston Guild awaited the arrival of Prince Leopold, Duke of Albany. An enigmatic letter arrived from Windsor Castle saying, 'Were it not for a slight indisposition, I would have enjoyed attending the Preston Guild.'
>
> "'Does that mean he's not coming?' asked one.
>
> "'Aye,' replied another.
>
> "'Reet. **He'll never work in Preston again**!' '

> "The cotton lords certainly had the power to prevent unpopular workers from working in a town."

From this it appears that the idea was introduced much earlier. Earliest use in films seems to have been in the 1954 Italian melodrama, *La Shchiava del Pecato,* directed by Raffaello Matavazzo, which had in the English captioning:

> "But don't think that's all, **you'll never work in this town again**."

Your chariot awaits+

This is a common phrase used humorously to say that a vehicle, supposedly one of high quality (whether in reality or not), is ready to take the person to his or her desired destination. It has been used in numerous novels, beginning with *The Voyage of the 'Petula'* by Frank Evans, page 89, 1957:

> "Roland, who was holding the dinghy painter, agreed with him. 'It's right, Frank,' he said. 'You know he can never resist a boating trip. O.K., Dick, **your chariot awaits**.'"

But it was used as early as Sunday, February 18, 1866, by noted English minister, Charles Spurgeon, in a sermon titled *The Almighty Warrior* delivered at the Metropolitan Tabernacle in Newington, UK, and refers to "a fine old Welsh hymn," obviously even older:

> "There is a fine old Welsh hymn which I wish I could turn into English without spoiling it—it runs somewhat to this effect, 'O Jesus, come forth! Leave the ivory palaces! **Your chariot waits for You**. Come forth, come forth! Hell trembles before You, all Heaven adores You, earth owns Your sway, men's hearts cannot resist You. Come forth, come forth! Bars of brass You break, gates of iron give way before You, come forth, come forth, O Jesus for **your chariot awaits You** now!'"

You're (or **he,** or **she is) a hoot!**

This is said of someone who has done something odd or out of the ordinary, whether it is considered to be weird or hilariously funny. Surprisingly, this was first cited in *Best Short Plays in World Theater*, 1958-1968, in '*The Disposal*,' a One Act play first produced in 1968, later titled, 'The Pad,' in 1972, by Academy Award winning playwright William Inge:

"**ARCHIE**. You're too much. Honestly, **you're a hoot**."

Your guess is as good as mine

This familiar cliché is a casual answer to what is seen as an ambiguous query and means that the person using it has no way of knowing what has happened, or will happen, in a certain given situation, or just doesn't know the answer to the question being asked. It may mean that the person using it is a bit exasperated with the other person for even asking such a rhetorical question, while the other person may feel that he or she is being shrugged off. The earliest citation known is from 1902 in *Miscellanies* by Henry Strong, page 273:

> "You ask who will be the probable presidential candidates. **Your guess is as good as mine.**"

Your money's no good here

Originally this catchphrase was used negatively to tell someone that they were unwanted. Through the years it evolved into a positive. It means, 'Whatever you want in this place, I'll pay for,' and is usually spoken by the owner or manager of a business intending to treat a particular guest in a special way. The earliest example available of the current use is in *The Strength of Gideon: And Other Stories* by Paul Laurence Dunbar, 1900, page 293, in 'The Finding of Zach:'

> "Oh, I'll res' myself but I ain' gwine sponge on you dat way. I got some money," and the old man dug down into his long pocket. But his host laid a hand on his arm.
>
> "**Your money's no good** up **here**."
>
> "Wh—wh—why, I thought dis money passed any whah in de Nunited States!" exclaimed the bewildered old man.
>
> "That's all right, but you can't spend it until we run out."

You're not the boss of me!+

This is a common exclamatory phrase used to express disdain over another person's unwarranted demands. It is often used by children resisting bossing by older siblings. Though it has reached new heights of use in recent decades, it is actually over 100 years old, according to Ben Zimmer, 'On Language' columnist for *The New York Times*, in a NPR interview on March 19, 2010. Of course, he was right. The earliest known citation in print is from *The Church*, New Series, Volume III, 1883, in the Chapter One of 'As by Fire' on page 70:

> "His sister was going to put her arms around him, but he whirled, and facing her with a very angry face, snapped—
>
> "'Let me alone; **you are not the boss of me** now, I tell you, and I'm going to do as I please."

Other examples followed in the next few years. The exact modern verbiage appears in A.C. Stevenson's *Unspotted from the World* in 1899, on page 48:

> "'Blacksmithing is honorable enough, but ignorance and selfishness are not. You ought to be made to stop going with him, that's all.'
>
> "'Well I guess **you're not the boss of me**."

Your shout[3] +

In Australian slang, this means it is the other person's turn to buy, usually used in reference to a round of drinks. It was in use by 1888, when it appeared in *Camiola, A Girl of Fortune* by Justin McCarthy, page 59, here in quotes:

> "It's partly '**your shout**,' you know, as they say in Australia.
> "Partly my shout?" Mrs. Pollen asked; "as they say in Australia? And what might that mean? I have never been in Australia."
> "Well, **your shout**; that means your treat."

Yours, mine and ours+

A very well-known movie by this title was released in 1968 starring Lucille Ball, Henry Fonda and Van Johnson; but that was by no means the origin of the cliché. The earliest known printed reference is found in *Public Opinion*, June 27, 1891, in an article titled, 'Sociology; Various Timely Topics: Marriage and Divorce,' taken from the *New York Herald*:

> "Homes are thus broken up; children get so mixed that they are divided into groups, denominated **'yours,' 'mine' and 'ours**,' and Heaven knows what misery is entailed."

Youth is a wonderful thing. What a shame it's wasted on children^

Although this bit of quirky proverbial thought has been attributed to Oscar Wilde, the earliest known citation actually says it came from George Bernard Shaw. *Cook Coos*, a syndicated column by Ted Cook, in February, 1931, had the following:

> "Someone asked Bernard Shaw what, in his opinion, is the most beautiful thing in this world.
>
> "'**Youth,**' he replied, '**is the most beautiful thing in this world—and what a pity that it has to be wasted on children!**'"

Z

Zero in on something+

There are various theories as to the origin of this term; however, the most accurate is from aiming a rifle at target and setting the sights on the center of the rifle's crosshairs, where there is a small circle. *Barnhart's Concise Dictionary of Etymology*, 1995, states that 'zero in' was first used for setting an instrument to the zero point to take aim at a target in 1913. *Etymology Online* dates this at 1909. Both sources further state that 'zero in on' was first attested in 1944. As a metaphor it means to give all of one's attention to a particular person or subject.

Zig-a-zig-ah

This catchphrase, meaning to enjoy oneself, was coined and made popular in 1996 by British girl group, Spice Girls, in their hip-hop rap runaway hit dance song, *Wannabe*.

Bibliography

Books

A Banker in Bankersville, Maurice Thompson, p 17; Street and Smith, New York, NY, U.S.A., 1900

A Boy's Book of Rhyme, Clinton Scollard, "Fraidie-cat", p 17; Copeland and Day, Boston, MA, U.S.A., 1896

A Bride-bush, Or, A Direction for Married Persons, by William Whately, page 166, Felix Kyngston, London, England, 1619

A Brief Relation of a Journey, Lately Preformed by Mafter H.P. Gentleman printed by I.L. for Andrew Crooke, London, England, 1637

A Bunch of Roses and Other Parlor Plays by MEM Davis, Small Maynard and Company Boston, 1903 previously published by Curtis Publishing Co., 1899.

A Catalogue of Manuscripts and Rare Books; Myers and Co., London, U.K., c 1900

Accidence of Armoury; Gerald Leigh, London, England, 1562

Accident and Injury, Their Relations to Disease of the Nervous System, by Pierce Bailey, AM, MD, D. Appleton and Co., NY, 1898

Accidents with Step; Kingsley Hendrick and Ludwig Benner, page 19; Marcel and Dekker, New York, NY, U.S.A., 1986

Across the Continent: A Summer's Journey to the Rocky Mountains, the Mormons and the Pacific States; Samuel Bowles, p 368; Hurd & Haughton, New York, NY, U.S.A., 1866

A Charge of Error, Heresy, Incharity, Falshood; Henry Pickworth, p 310: printed for S. Noble, London, England, 1718

A Choice Collection of Original Essays on Various and Entertaining Subjects; London, England, 1748

A Classic Dictionary of the Vulgar Tongue, Francis Grose, printed for S. Hooper, London, U.K., 1785; Second Edition, 1788

A Collection of College Words and Customs by Benjamin Homer Hall, p 496; John Bartlett, Cambridge University, Cambridge, U.K., 1856

A Collection of English Proverbs, Second Edition; John Ray, p 254; John Hayes, Cambridge, England, 1678

A Collection of Farces and Other Afterpieces; David Garrick's 2 act comedy, 'The Irish Widow,' Act I, Scene iii, p 56; Longman, Rees, Hurst, Orme and Brown, London, U.K., 1815

A Collection of Letters on the Most Interesting and Important Subjects and on Several Occasions by William Law, Letter XVI, p 159; W. Hardcastle, London, U.K., 1815

A Collection of Miscellanies – The Ninth Edition; John Norris, MA, London, England, 1730

A Collection of State Tracts, Publifh'd on the Occasion of the Late Revolution in 1688 and During the Reign of King William III, Volume I, p 367; London, England, 1705

A Collection of Voyages: In Four Volumes: Volume 1: A New Voyage Round the World, James and John Knapton, London, England, 1729

A Commentary Upon The Fourth Book of Moses, Called Numbers by Simon Patrick, Lord Bishop of Ely, p 193; Ri. Criswell, London, England, 1699

A Compleat Collection of English Proverbs; John Ray, Third Edition, p 97, p 210; J. Hughs, London, England,

A Complete Collection of State Trials and Proceedings for High Treason from the Reign of Richard II Vol. 1, London, England, 1730

A Compleat Dictionary Dutch and English; Egbert Buys, p 790; Kornelis de Veer, Amsterdam, Holland, 1766

A Compleat History of the Lives and Reigns of Mary Queen of Scotland and of her Son and Successor, James the Sixth, King of Scotland; And (After Queen Elizabeth) King of Great Britain, France and Ireland, The First (of evre Blessed Memory) by William Sanderson, page 123; printed for Humphrey Moseley, Richard Tomlins and George Sawbridge, London, England, 1656

A Copious Dictionary in Three Parts, Francis Gouldman; printed for John Field, London, England, 1664

Acts of the General Assembly of the Province of New Jersey, by Samuel Allison, pp 264, 265; Printed for Isaac Collins Burlington, NJ, U.S.A., 1776

Address before the Masonic Veterans of Pennsylvania, I. Layton Register; Philadelphia, PA, U.S.A., February 27, 1885

A dialogue containing the number in effect of all the proverbs in the English Tongue; John Haywood, London, England, 1546

A Dictionary of Slang and Unconventional English, Eighth Edition, Eric Partridge; McMillan, New York, NY, U.S.A., 1984

A Dictionary of Slang, Jargon and Cant Embracing English; p 347; Albert Barrère, 1889 George Bell & Sons, London, U.K., 1889, 1897

A Dictionary of the French and English Tongues Composed by Randle Cotgrave; printed for Adam Islip, London, England, 1611

A Discourse, by Daniel Whitby, DD, page 167, printed for John Wyatt, London, England, 1710

A Discourse upon usury by way of Dialogue and Orations; Thomas Wilson, London, England, 1572

A Defense of Natural and Unrevealed Religion; Robert Boyle S. Powell, p 194; Dublin, Ireland, 1737

A Description of Millennium Hall and the Country Adjacent, the Fourth Edition by Barbara Montagu, pseudonym 'A Gentleman on His Travels;' T. Carnan & F. Newbery, London, U.K., 1768

A Description of New England, John Smith, Humfrey Lewnes, London, England, 1616

Advice to a Young Tradesman, Written by an Old One; Benjamin Franklin; Philadelphia, PA, U.S.A., July 17, 1748

Aesop's Fables; Greece, 620-560 BCE

Aeneid, Book 6, line 727, *Aeneid, Book II,* Virgil, Rome, 19 BCE.

Aesop's Fables attributed to Aesop (c. 620-564 BCE) printed by German printer Heinrick Steinhowel, 1480; English version; William Claxton, London, England, 1484

Aesop's Fables, 'A Daw with a String at's Foot,' Roger L. Estrange's translation; London, England, 1692:

A Free Discourse Concerning Truth and Error, Especially in Matters of Religion, John Edwards, DD, 36; London, England, 1701

***A French and English Dictionary* compiled by M. Randle Cotgrave**; Anthony Dole, London, England, 1611, 1673

After Everest: The Experiences of a Mountaineer and Medical Missionary, Theodore Howard Somervell; Hodder & Stoughton, London, U.K., 1936

After the Fact: The Art of Historical Detection, First Edition; James West Davidson and Mark Hamilton Lytle; Alfred A. Kompf, New York, NY, U.S.A., 1982

A General History of the Netherlands, Ed Grimeston, Jean François Le Petit, page 1244, A Islip, G. Eld, London, England, 1609

A Gift; A Christmas and New Year's Present for 1812, Eliza Leslie, p 104; Carey and Hart, Philadelphia, PA, U.S.A., 1841

A Glossary of Words and Phrases; John Russell Bartlett; Little, Brown and Co., Boston, MA, U.S.A., 1860

A Glossary of Words and Phrases Pertaining to the Dialect of the Cumberland; William Dickinson, New York, NY, U.S.A., 1899

A Glossary, The Lancaster Dialect, Part II, F – Z, English Dialect Society, London, U.K., 1882

Agricultural Innovation: The Process of Ecological Change in Indonesia, Clifford Geertz, p 62; University of California Press, Berkley and Los Angeles, CA, U.S.A., 1968

A Handbook of Travel-talk: A Collection of Dialogues and Vocabularies Intended to Serve as an Interpretor to Travelers in Germany, France or Italy; John Murray, page iv: London, U.K., 1847

A History of Green Ridge Forest, Champ Zumbrun; The History Press, Charleston, SC, U.S.A., 2010

A History of Music, Volume One, John Frederick Rowbotham, page 72; Trubner and Co., London, U.K., 1885

A History of the English People Volume VIII, 1660-1683 by John Richard Green, p 162; Funk & Wagnalls, New York, NY, U.S.A. and London, U.K., 1880

A History of Origins, Sampson Low, London, U.K., 1824

A History of the Life of James Duk.e of Ormonde, Volume I, Thomas Carte, p 461; J. Battenbam, London, England, 1736

Air War in the South Atlantic, by Jeffery L. Ethell and Alfred Price, Sidgwick & Jackson, London, U.K., 1983

A Jacobean Company and its Playhouse, The Queen's Servants at the Red Bull Theater (c. 1605-1619) by Eva Griffith, p 172; Cambridge University Press, New York, NY, U.S.A., 2013

A Journal or Historical Account in the Life and Ministry of George Fox, Volume I, p 407; Thomas Northcutt, London, England, 1694

A Large Dictionary in Three Parts, Thomas Holyoake; W. Rawlins, London, England, 1677

A Latin-English and English-Latin Dictionary for the use of Schools; Charles Anthon, London, U.K., 1853

A Letter to G______W______. Esq. Concerning the Present Condition of the College of Dublin; Dublin, Ireland, 1734

A Life on the Edge: Memoirs of Everest and Beyond, Jim Whitaker; Mountaineers Books, Seatle, WA, U.S.A., 1999

A Etymological Dictionary of the Scottish Language, Supplement, Vol. 2, John Jamieson, p 426; University Press, Edinburgh, UK, 1825

All Sides of the Fiscal Controversy, in Mr. Chamberlin at Tynemouth. 21st October, 1903Edited by T. L. Gilmore; Lawrence and Bullen, Ltd., London, U.K., 1903

A Man Without Principle? Retsel Terreve (Lester Everett Broyles), p 84; Lowenthal Wolfe Co., Baltimore, MD, U.S.A., 1906

A Mauriac Reeder; François Mauriac, p 178; Farrar, Strausand Giroux, New York, NY, U.S.A., 1968

A Memoir of the Rev. Richard Sluyter, Late Pastor of the Ref. Prot. Dutch Church of Claverace New York; R. Ormaston Currie, page 79; John Moffet, New York, NY, U.S.A., 1846

America by River and Rail; William Ferguson, p 325; James Nisbet and Co, London, U.K., 1856

Americanisms, Old and New; John Stephen Farmer, p 127; Thomas Poulter and Sons, London, U.K., 1889

Americanisms, the English of the New World; Maximilian Schele de Vere, p 472; Charles Scribner and Co., New York, NY, U.S.A., 1872

America, Inc. Who Owns and Operated the United States; Morton Mintz and Jerry Cohen, Chapter 6; Dell Publishing Co., Inc., New York, NY, U.S.A., 1971

America Taken Hostage; Hayden Lee Hinton, p 142; Arbor House, Bloomington, IN, U.S.A., 2010

Among the Fans; Patrick Collins, p 148; Wisden Sports Writing, Brisbane, Queensland, Australia, 2011

An Account of Some Remarkable Passages in the Life of a Private Gentleman; with Recollections Thereof; Daniel Defoe, pp 319-320; J. Downing, London, England, 1711

An Accurate Description of Newgate: With the Rights, Privileges, Allowances, fees,

Dues and Customs Thereof; Betty Langley; printed for T. Warner, London, England, 1724

An Act for Dividing and Inclosing the Open Fields and Commonable Places; Parliament, London, U.K., 1767

An Address Delivered before the Insurance Society of New York, William H. Stevens; New York, NY, U.S.A., October 8, 1919

An Address from John Zephaniah Holwell, Esq.: to Luke Stanton, Esq., p 26; T. Becket and P.A. de Hondt, London, England, 1767

An American Tragedy, Theodore Drieser, Horace Liveright, New York, NY, U.S.A., December 17, 1925

An Antient and Present State of the Country and City of Cork: Book II, Chapter VI, Charles Smith; printed for A. Reilly, Dublin, Ireland,

An Apology for the Life of Mr. Colley Cibber, Comedian; (written by himself), p 117; George Faulkner, Dublin, Ireland, 1746

A Narrative of the Adventures and Sufferings of J.R. Jewitt, Only Survivor of the Ship Boston by John Rogers Jewitt, P 78; Loomis and Richards, Middleton, U.K., 1820

An Art Student in Munich; Anna Mary Watts, Volume II, p 178; Longman, Brown, Green and Longmans, London, U.K., 1853

Ancient History from the Monuments. Assyria from the Earliest Times to the Fall of Nineveh; Society for Promoting Christian Knowledge, London; Clarendon Press, Oxford, U.K., 1875

And the Sun Stood Still; Guy Parish, p 101; Xulon Press, Fairfax, VA, U.S.A., 2002

An Easy and Compendious Introdvction for Reading All Sorts of Histories; Mathias Prideaux, A.&L. Litchfield, Oxford, England, 1664

An Elegant and Learned Discourse of the Light of Nature; Nathanial Culverwel and William Dillingham, page 87; Oxford, England, 1669

An Essay to the Genius of Shakespeare &c; Henry Mercer Graves,' p 112, 'A Letter on Taste, Judgment and Rhetorical Expression;' London, U.K., 1826

An Elementary Course in Civil Engineering for the Use of Cadets in the United States Military Academy; Dennis H. Mahan, Second Edition, p 319; Wiley and Halstead, New York, NY, U.S.A., 1857

An Enquiry into the Power of Dispensing with Penal Statutes; **Sir Robert Atkyns**; printed for Timothy Goodwin, London, England, 1689

An Etymological Dictionary of the Scottish Language; John Jamieson Edinburg, Scotland, U.K., 1808

An Etymological Dictionary of the Scottish Language, Supplement, Volume 2; Edinburgh, Scotland, U.K., 1825

A New Dictionary of Spanish and English and English and Spanish; John Stevens, London, England, 1726

An Essay toward the Amendment of the last English-Translation of the Bible; Robert Gel, p 365; R. Norton and Andrew Crook, London, England, 1659

An Exact Abridgement of All the Statutes of King William and Queen Mary and of King William III in Force and Use; London, U.K., 1741

An Exposition Vpon the Prophet Ionah Contained in Certain Sermons, Preached in S. Maries Church in Oxford, George Abbot, Professor of Divinitie; Richard Field, London, England, 1613

An Humble Supplication to Her Maistie; pp 22, 23; London, England, 1595

An Introduction to the Philosophy Law; Roscoe Pound, p 58; Yale University Press, New Haven, CT, U.S.A., 1922, 1954

An Irish Beauty of the Regency; Knox Blake, p 177; John Lane, London and New York, NY, U.S.A., 1911

A Large Dictionary: In Three Parts, English and Latin; Thomas Holyoke, DD; W. Rawlins, London, England, 1677

An Essay on the Archeology of Our Popular Phrases, Vol. I; John Bellenden Ker, p112; Longman, Rees, Orme, Brown, Green, & Co., London, U.K., 1837

A New Dictionary of the Spanish and English Languages, (Dictionario Nueva de las dos Lenguas, Español e Englesa); Thomas Connelly; London, England, 1798

An Open Letter to the Christian Nobility of the German Nation Concerning the Reform of the Christian Estate; Martin Luther and Charles Michael Jacobs, pp 57, 58; London, England, 1520

An Other Boke Against Rastel; John Firth, London, England, 1533

Annual Labor Bulletin, Proceedings of the Eleventh Conference; quote from David Clark, Editor of the Southern Textile Bulletin, p 74; National Child Labor Committee, New York, NY, U.S.A., May, 1915

Annual Report on the Researches; p 75; China, 1978

Another Collection of Philosophical Conferences of the French Virtuosi, upon Questions of all Sorts for the Improving of Natural Knowledg. Render'd into English by G. Havers, Gent and J. Davies of Kidwelly, Gent; Printed for Thomas Dring and John Starkey, London, England, November 20, 1663

Apoligia Pro Vita Sua, Dr. John Henry Newman, DD, p 21; Longman, Green, Longman, Roberts and Green, London, U.K., 1864

Apophthegmata; Plutarch, Greece, 45 - 120 AD

Apophthgmes, that is to saie prompte saiynges First gathered by Erasmus, Udall, English Translation, London, England., 1542

A Quarter Race in Kentucky: And Other Sketches; William Trotter Porter, p 86; T. B. Peterson and Prothers, Philadelphia, PA, U.S.A., 1846, 1854

Archibald Cary Coolidge: Life and Letters; Harold Jefferson Coolidge, p 308; Haughton, Mifflin and Co., Boston, MA, U.S.A., 1932

A Rejoindre to M. Jewels Replie against the Sacrifice of the Masse; Preface to the Catholic Reader; Rome, 1567

A Review of the Affairs of France, with Observations on Transactions at Home; 'Advice from the Scandal Club;' London, England, Saturday, March 12, 1705

A Review of the 'Great' Speech of Senator John P. Jones on the Banking and Currency Bill, delivered in the United States Senate, April 1st. 1874, Henry S. Fitch; E. Bosqui & Co., San Francisco, CA, U.S.A., 1875

A Reviving Cordial for a Sin-sick Despairing Soul in the Time of Temptation; Rev. James Barry; London, England, 1699

A Rich Cabinet with a Variety of Inventions, collected by "J.W.;" London, England, 1668

Are We Having Fun Yet? Bill Griffith, Fantagraphics Books, Seatle, WA, U.S.A., 1985

A Rod for Turnbridge Beaus, Bundl'd up at the Request of Turnbridge Ladies; a Burlesque poem, p 19; London, England, 1701

Around the Tea-table; Thomas DeWitt Talmage; Christain Herald, New York, NY, U.S.A., 1895

Artie; George Ade, p 92; 1896; Herbert S. Stone & Co., Chicago, IL, U.S.A., 1898

A Searching Heart; Jeanette Oak, p 165; Bethany House, Bloomington, MN, U.S.A., 1998

A Select Collection of Novels, Volume the Second; 'The History of the Captive,' p 365; John Watts; London, England, 1720

A Shakespeare Dictionary: Part One, Julius Caesar; comments on Scene II act I, Arthur E. Baker, Borough Librarian in Taunton, England, p 26, London, U.K., 1623

A shorte dictionarie most profitable for yong beginners the second tyme corrected, and augmented, with diverse phrasys, & other thinges necessarie thereunto added; John Withals; Thomas Purfoot, London, England, 1574

A Souvenir of the Anchor Line Agents Excursion on the Steamer California; To Thomas Henderson of Glasgow; New York, NY, 1872

A Supplementary English Glossary; Thomas Davies; London, U.K., 1881

A Suruey of the Popes Supremacie; Francis Bunny Valentine Simmes, London, England, 1595

A Survey of the Summe of Church-discipline: Wherein the way of the Churches is Waranted out of the Word; Thomas Hooker, p 12; A.M. for John Bellemy, London, England, 1648

A Tale of Two Cities; Charles Dickens (1859), p 306; Doubleday and McClure, New York, NY, U.S.A., 1900

A Tariff Talk among Working Men; I. E. Smith; J.T. Miller, New York, NY, U.S.A., 1887

A Ternary of Paradoxes; Jean Baptist Van Helmont, trans. Walter Charleton; James Fleshner, London, 1650

Atlas Japannensis, Being Remarkable Addresses by Way of Embassy from the East India Company of the United Provinces to the Emperor of Japan certified in several Writings and Journals; by Arnoldis Montanis English'd and Adom'd by John Ogilby; London, England, 1670

A Third Story; Carole Taylor Lace Publications, p 11; Denver, CO, U.S.A., 1986

A Treasury or Storehouse of Similes: Both Pleasant, Delightful, and Profitable for all estates of men in general; Robert Cawdry; Thomas Creede, London, England, 1609

A Treatise of the Passions and Facvlties of the Soul of Man; Edward Reynolds; Robert Bostick, London, England, 1647

A Treatise on Miracles; Abraham Lemoine, Chaplin to His Grace the Duke of Portland; J. Nourse, London, England, 1747

At the Village Post Office; Seymore Seldon Tibbles; Eldridge Entertainment House, Franklin, Ohio, U.S.A., 1906

Aussie Slang Dictionary; John Blackman; Pan Macmillan Australia Pty Ltd; Sydney, Australia, 2012

Australian Poems; How Sweet it Is, Emma Styles, p 27; Thomas, Adelaide, Australia, 1883

Australians and the Gold Rush: California and Down Under (1849-1854); Jay Monaghan, p 29; University of California Press, Berkley and Los Angeles, CA, U.S.A., 1966

Authentic Memoir of His Late Royal Highness, Frederick, Duke of York; Robert Huish, p 53; John Williams, London, U.K., 1828

Autism's False Prophets: Bad Science, Risky Medicine and the Search for a Cure; Paul Offit, M.D.: Columbia University Press, New York, NY, U.S.A., 2010

A Vindication of the Ordinations of the Church of England; Gilbert Beunet, p 70; E.H. & T.H., London, England, 1877

A Vindication of the Rights of Woman; Chapter 5; Mary Wollstonecraft; Simone de Beaulivior, Paris, France, London, U.K., 1792

A Vocabulary of Criminal Slang, Louis E. Jackson, p 46; C.E. Hellyer, City Detective Dept., Portland, OR, U.S.A., 1914

A Vocabulary Persian Arabic and English; William Kirkpatrick, p 85; London, U.K., 1785

A Walk on the Wild Side, Nelson Algren, Farrar, Straus and Cudahy, New York, NY, U.S.A., 1956

A Year in Spain by a Young American; Alexander Mackenzie, p 379; John Murray, London, U.K 1831

Babylonian Talmud, Rabbis; Galilee, c. 500 C.E.

Barnhart Concise Dictionary of Etymology, Robert K. Barnhart; HarperCollins Publishers, New York, 1995

Base-ball Ballads, Grantland Rice, Rooter's Row, p 102, The Tennessean Co., Nashville, TN, U.S.A., 1910

Bell's Edition: The Poets of Great Britain complete from Chaucer to Churchill; John Bell, London, U.K., 1777

Bentley's Miscellany, American Edition; Volume III; Handy Andy, Samuel Lover; Jemiman M. Lewer, New York, NY, U.S.A., 1839

Between Parent and Teenager, Dr. Haaim Gennot; McMillian, New York, NY, U.S.A., 1969

Bible *in Chronological order:*

Lindisfarne Gospels, 10th Century

Genesis 1:27; 3:8-19

Exodus 5:7, KJV, **1611,** ***21:34; KJV; 32:4, KJV***

Leviticus 13:8, 10, KJV

II Kings 2:12-13; 10:18-31

Job 41:24, KJV

Psalm 23: 4 KJV; 58, 3- 4, KJV; 91:11, NIV; 115:3

Proverbs 9:9, KJV; 10:4, NIV; 16:18-19; 18:24, KJV; 25:17, KJV; 29:23 (1611), ***NLT*** (1996)

I Samuel 20:27, KJV, WYC

Isaiah 34:4, KJV

Jeremiah 31:29, KJV

Ezekiel 1:16, ESV; 3:18 NASB; 19:2, KJV, 1611

Daniel 2: 31-33, KJV; 6:16, KJV

Hosea 14:7, KJV

HebakkU.K. 3:17, CEB

Zechariah 13:9, KJV:

Matthew 5:41, NASB; 6:2, New World Translation, 7:24, NIV; 16:3, TYN, **1526;** ***15:8; 18:10 NIV; 24:33, KJV***

Luke 1:28, 42

John 9:6; 11:44, KJV; 15, 5-6, BSB

Acts 17: 6, KJV

I Peter 1:7, KJV

Revelation 21: 8 KJV

Bibliotheca Classica, Or A Dictionary of All the Principal Names and Terms; John Lemprière, p 665; Fifteenth American Edition; W.E. Dean, New York, NY, U.S.A., 1851

Bibliotheca scholastica instructissima, or, A treasury of ancient adagies and sententious proverbs selected out of the English, Greeke, Latine, French, Italian, and Spanish; Thomas Draxe, London, England, 1616

Bill Drafting, James McKirdy, p 12; C. K. Aughinbaugh, Harrisburg, PA, U.S.A., 1912

Bill for Provision of Gradual Resumption of Payments in Cash by Bank Ireland, Dublin, Ireland, 1821

Billy Bounce, William Wallace Denslow, M.A. Donohue, Chicago, IL, U.S.A., 1906

Biography of Edmond Pendleton Gaines by 'A Friend'; Library of Congress, Washington, DC, U.S.A., 1844

Bird Display: An Introduction to the Study of Bird Psychology; Edward Allworthy Armstrong, p 142; Cambridge University Press, London, U.K., 1942

Bishop Burnet's History of His Own Time; From the Restoration of King Charles II to the Conclusion of the Treaty of Peace at Uthecht in the Reign of Queen Anne; Gilbert Burnet, p 254; London, U.K., 1809

Blackbeard: A Page from the Colonial History of Philadelphia; Chapter XIX, p. 225; Matilda Douglas; Harper and Brothers, New York, NY, U.S.A., 1835

Bleak House; Charles Dickens; Bradberry and Evans, New York, NY, U.S.A., 1853

Blue-Beard; George Coleman, the Younger, p 18; T. Woodfall, London, U.K., 1798

Blue Movie; Terry Southern, p 13; Grove Press, New York, NY, U.S.A., 1970

Bolshevik Propaganda: Hearings Before a Subcommittee of the Committee on the Judiciary United States Senate, *Sixty-Fifth Congress;* p 929; Washington , DC, 1919

Border Tales around the Campfire, in the Rocky Mountains; Chaplain Tuttle, p 132; E.P. Dutton, New York, NY, U.S.A., 1878

Bound in Shadows, A Novel; Eva Wilder Brodhead, p 153; Harper & Bros. New York, NY, U.S.A., 1897

Brewer's Dictionary of Phrase and Fable; Ebenezer Cobham Brewer; Henry Altemus, Philadelphia, PA, U.S.A., 1898

British Corruption to the Europe of the Twenty-first Century; Basil S. Markesinis, p 78; Hart Publishing, Oxford, U.K., 2002

British History Chronologically Arranged; John Wade, p 739; Effingham Wilson, Royal Exchange, London, U.K., 1839

Buffet for Unwelcome Guests; Christianna Brand; Southern Illinois University Press, Edwardsville, IL, U.S.A., 1983

Bulletin of the University of Texas, A Word-List from East Alabama, p 314, Austin, TX, U.S.A., May 1, 1909

Bully for Brontosaurus: Reflections in Natural History; Stephen Jay Gould, (1991), pp 240, 241; W.W. Norton & Co., London, U.K., 1992

Calendar of State Papers, Foreign Series, of the Reign of Elizabeth; Public Records, Great Britain; Longman, Green, Longman, Roberts, & Green, 1589

Camiola, A Girl of Fortune; Justin McCarthy, p 59; Chatto & Windus, Piccadilly, London, U.K., 1888

Canterberry Tales; ***The Man of Law's Tale;*** Geoffrey Chaucer; London. England, c 1387

Caroline Mordaunt; or, the Governess; Mrs. Sherwood (Mary Martha), p 17; Darton & Clark, London, U.K., 1853

Case Histories in Abnormal Psychiatry; p 12, Case 8, 'Paraplegia;' Stanford University Press, Stanford, CA, U.S.A., 1940

Cases and Materials in Company Law; p 170; Cambridge University Press, London, U.K., 1971

Cases Decided in the High Court of Chancery, by the Right Honorable John Leach; p 197; London, U.K., 1824

Cases Determined by the St. Louis and Kansas City Court of Appeals for the state of Missouri; Volume LXII, p 196; 1895

Cash is King; William A. Reed; Drane, London, U.K., 1901

Cassell's Dictionary of Slang, Jonathan Green, p 927; Wellington House, London, U.K., 1998

Cassell's Illustrated History of India, Volume II; James Grant, p 502; Cassell, Petter & Galpin, London, U.K.; Paris, France, New York, NY, U.S.A., 1876

Catalog of Copyright Entries, Part 3 - Musical Compositions, New York, NY, U.S.A., 1937

Catalogue of Copyright Entries*, Musical Compositions;* part 3; Washington, DC, U.S.A., 1939

Catalogue of Copyright Entries for Musical Compositions, Washington, DC, U.S.A., 1942

Catalogue of Copyright Entries, Washington, DC, U.S.A., July through December, 1976

Catalogue of the U.S. Library of Congress; Washington, DC, U.S.A., Last Half, 1944

Cato's Letters; John Trenchard and John Gordon; London, U.K., 1724

Chained Eagle*: The Heroic Story of the First American Shot Down over Vietnam*; Everett Alvarez, Jr., Ch. 18; Donald I. Fine, New York, NY, U.S.A., 1989

Chained Lighting: A Book of Fun; Ike Philkins, p 79; J. S. Ogilvie and Co., New York, NY, U.S.A., 1883

Charades; 'Janette Turner Hospital,' p 179; University of Queensland Press, Queensland, Australia, 1988

Children of the Ghetto: A Study of a Peculiar People; Israel Zangwill; London, U.K., 1892

Chimmie Fadden and Mr. Paul; Edward W. Townsend, ch. XIII, p 175; The Century Co., New York, NY, U.S.A., 1902

Chinese Characteristics; Arthur H. Smith, Fourth Edition, p 18; Fleming H. Royal, New York, U.S.A., 1894

Chronicle of Troy; John Lydgate; London, England, 1430

Civill Considerations Vpon Many and Svndrie Histories, as Well Ancient and Modern; Lord Leme of Florence, French by Remigio Nannini, Gabriel Chappuys, English by W.T. p190; Matthew Lownes, London, England, 1601

Clear and Present Danger; Tom Clancy, p 210, p 111; Jack Ryan Enterprises, Berkley Books, New York, NY. U.S.A., 1989

Clarissa; or, the History of a Young Lady, Samuel Richardson, London, U.K., 1748

Cobbers: Journey Essex to Australia; Thomas Wood; Oxford University Press, London, U.K., 1934

Collection of English Proverbs, John Ray; London, England, 1670

Colonial Times; Hobart Town; Tasmania, Australia, Friday July 28, 1826

Coming Attractions, Katie Weldon #3, Robin Jones Weldon, Thorndike Press, Waterville, ME, U.S.A., June 2009

Comin' Thro' the Rye; Helen B. Mathers, p 14; Richard Brantley & Son, London, U.K., 1875, 1876

Commandments on the Laws of England; William Blackstone; London, U.K., 1769

Concluding; Henry Green, p 182; Viking Press, New York, NY, U.S.A., 1950

Confessio Amantis; Middle English text, John Gower; London, England, 1390

Confession of Child of the Century; Alfred de Musset; Current Literature Publishing Co., New York, NY, U.S.A., 1910

Congressional Record, Senate; Washington, DC, U.S.A., July 15, 1974

Consequences of Failure; William R. Carson, p 156; W.W. Norton & Co., New York, NY, U.S.A., 1974

Catalogue of Copyright Entries Third Series, Vol 28; Pt 5, No 1, Sec 2; Music, Washington, DC, U.S.A., January – June, 1974

Complete Collection of Scottish Proverbs; James Kelley, p 270; Wm and John Innys; Oxford University Press, Oxford, U.K., 1721

Congressional Record: Proceedings and Debates of the 92nd Congress, Second Session; Washington, DC, 1974

Corbett's Two Penny Trash or Politics for thee Poor; John Corbett, p 257; Corbett, London, U.K., 1831

Cornish Saints and Sinners; J. Henry Harris, Ch. 2; Bodley Head, London, U.K., 1906

Court of Appeals, State of New York Notice of Motions, Affidavit, Exhibits A, B & C; Gaspere Puccio versus Metropolitan Jockey Club, p 32; Albany, NY, U.S.A., 1942

Cricket at the Seashore; Elizabeth Westin Timlow, p 315; Press of the Commercial Bookbinding Company, Cleveland, Ohio, U.S.A., 1896

Criminal Slang: the Vernacular of the Underworld Lingo; Captain Vincent J. Monteleone, p 181; Christopher Publishing House, Boston, MA, U.S.A., 1949

Criminal Slang: The Vernacular of the Underground Lingo; Vincent Joseph Monteleone, p 123; The Law Book, Ltd., Clark, NJ, U.S.A., 2003

Criminal Trials and Other Proceedings before the High Court of Justiciary in Scotland during the Reigns of King James the Fourth and Fifth, Part IX; 1537; printed Edinburgh, Scotland, U.K., 1831

Cruel Sea; Nicholas Monsarrat; Cassell & Company Ltd., London, England, 1951

Curiosities of Modern Times: A Yearbook of Adventure; published by David Bogue; London, U.K., 1844

Dangers of Working Girls or, Dealers in White Women; Grace Miller White; J.S. Ogilvie New York, NY, U.S.A., 1904

David Balfour, Chapter XVII; Robert Louis Stevenson; London, U.K., 1892

Dear Judy, Did You Ever Like a Boy (who Didn't Like You?); Judy Baer, pp 9 and 40; Bethany House, Bloomington, IN, U.S.A., 1993

De Augmentis Scientarium, Frances Bacon, London, England, 1623; English Translation, Works of Frances Bacon, p 41; Hurd & Haughton, New York, NY, U.S.A., 1862

Decisions of the Court Sessions; 1781-1822, sess. June 9, 1803; David Hume, Edinburgh, Scotland, 1839

Democracy Made Safe, Paul H. Drake, p 55; L. Phillips, Boston. MA, U.S.A., 1918

Depositio cornuti typographici: that is, A Comical or Mirthful Play; John Rist, John George Dullman, Frankfurt-On-the-Main, Germany, 1677

***Dialect* Notes *I*;** 232; London, U.K., 1892

Diary of Samuel Pepys; 1660, p 2191; 1893 Unabridged Version edited by H.B.W. Brampton; Reprinted by Hayes Barton Press, Raleigh, NC, U.S.A., 2007

Dick's Reflections and Readings Number Twelve; Dick Fitzgerald; 'The Language of the Rail' by Bill Nye, p 117; New York, NY, U.S.A., 1881

Dictionarium latinogermanicon; Peter Dasypodius; Strasbourg, France, 1536

Dictionary of Americanisms; John Russell Barett, p 302; Bartlett and Welfors, New York, NY, U.S.A., 1848

Dictionary of Americanisms; John Russell Bartlett, p 332; Little, Brown & Co., Boston, MA, U.S.A., 1859

Dictionary of American Regional English, Belknap Press of Harvard Press, Cambridge, MA, U.S.A., 1965

Dictionary of Idiomatic English Phrases; James Main Dixon; Thomas Nelson snd Sons, London, Edinburgh and New York, U.S.A., 1891

Dictionary of Phrase and Fable, New and Enlarged Edition, E. Cobham Brewster, Unk. Pub., London, U.K., 1894

Dictionary of Regional English, University of Wisconsin-Madison; Belknap Press, Harvard University, Cambridge, MA, U.S.A., 1985

Dictionary of the Vulgar Tongue; Francis Grose, London, U.K., 1811

Director; Leslie Coulthard, p 228; Unknown Locale, August, 1966

Divi Britannici: Being a Remark Upon the Lives of All the Kings of this Isle from the Year of the World, 3855 unto the Year of Grace 1660; Sir Winston Churchill, p 148; London, England, 1675

DNA Doesn't Lie: Is the Real Criminal Behind Bars, Anna Prokos, Scolastic, New York, NY, U.S.A., 2011

DNA Doesn't Lie, Trudy N. Wassenaar, Create Space, U.S.A., 2015

Dodsley's Annual Register for the Year of 1765, p 200; 'An Essay on the Ancient English Minstrels, from the Same;' London, England, 1766

Dog in the Manger; fable as told by Straton of Sardis; Greece, 3rd century CE

Don't Take My Grief Away: Ehat to Do When You Lose a Loved One; p 17: Doug Manning; Harper One, New York, NY, U.S.A., 1984

Down in the Zero; Andrew Vachss Knopf, New York, NY, U.S.A., 1994

Drawing Blood; Poppy Z. Brite, pe 261; Dell Books, New York, NY, U.S.A., 1993

Dream On: Living on the Edge with Steven Tyler and Aerosmith, Cyrinda Foxe-Tyler, 1996, Newstar, New York, NY, U.S.A., Jan. 1, 1997

Du Bartas: His Divine Weekes and Workes; 'The Third Book of Judith,' Lib 4 by Guillaume de Saluste Du Bartas, translated by Josuah Sylvester, p 365; London, England, 1641

Effective Men's Ministry: The Indispensible Toolkit for Your Church; Phil Downer, editor, p 12; Zondervan, Grand Rapids, MI, U.S.A., 2001

Eleven Sermons Preached Upon Special Occasions; *Sermon on Union and Peace, preach'd to several Congregations,* John Piggott, April 17, 1704, p 290, John Darby, London, England, 1714

Elizabeth Evanshaw; William Pitt Scargill, p 115; Hunt and Clark, London, U.K., 1827

Elmo's Model Speaker for Platform; School and Home; 'Peck's Bad Boy; He Becomes a Druggist' by George W. Peck, p 358; Bedford, Clarke and Co., Chicago, IL, U.S.A., 1888

Elocution Do's and Don'ts, Frederick A. Stokes Co., Rochester, NY, U.S.A., January 1, 1926

Emerson, Yearbook, Emerson College, Los Angeles, CA, U.S.A., 1961

Encyclopedia Britannica, A Dictionary of Arts, Sciences, Literature and General Information, Eleventh Edition, Volume VII; New York, NY, U.S.A., 1910

***England's Chronicle*; James Heath**, p 70; Benjamin Crayle, London, England, 1689

Epistolæ Ho-Elianæ: Familiar Letters, Domestic and Forren. Divided into Four Books; James Howell, Sixth Edition, p 446; Thonas Gay, London, England, 1688

Eshter Damon; Mrs Fremont Older, p 227; Charles Scribner's Sons, New York, NY, U.S.A., 1911

Essays: First Series; Ralph Waldo Emerson; T.Y. Cowell & Co., London, U.K., 1841

Essays in Criticism; Matthew Arnold, p xiv; London, U.K., 1867

Essays, Lectures and Orations; Ralph Waldo Emerson, 'Friendship,' p 113; William S. Orr, London, U.K., 1848

Essays Moral and Humorous; Joseph Addison; published for William and Robert Chambers, Edinburgh, Scotland, U.K., 1839

Eternal Fragments; Francis Castro, p 29; Lulu Press, Raleigh, NC, U.S.A, 2010

Etymological Dictionary of the Scottish Language; John Jamieson, p 683; University Press, Edinburgh, Scotland, U.K., 1825

Ever After; Rachel Vail, first published in 1994, p 19; Harper Collins Publishers, New York, NY, U.S.A., 2005

Evidence; Thomas Starkie; London, U.K., 1824

Evils & Abuses in Naval & Merchant Service, William McNally; London, U.K., 1839

Fables of Aesop and Other Mythologists with Morals and Reflections; reflection to one of Aesops Fables, 'The Dog and His Master' written between 620 and 560 BCE; Sir Roger L. Estrange, London, England

Fables; John Gay, Fable XXII, 'The Two Owls and the Sparrow,' p 124; J. Tonson & J. Watts, London, U.K., 1728

Farmer Hiram on the World's War; Lindley Grant Long, p 171; Christian Publishing Assoc., Dayton OH, U.S.A., 1920

Father Hubburds Tales or the Ant and the Nighting; Thomas Middleton; London, England, 1604

Fisherman Down; E. Bruce Bushong, p 80; iUniverse, Lincoln, NE, U.S.A., 2005

500 of the Most Witty, Acerbic, and Erudite Things Ever Said about Money; Stephen Eckett; Harriman House, Petersfield, U.K., 2005

Five Hundreth Pointes of Good Husbandrie; Thomas Tusser; London, England, 1573

Felo de se; or, Bishops Condemned out of their own Mouthes; Rome, Italy, 1668

Feminism and Philosophy; edited by Mary Vetterling-Braggin, Frederick Elliston and Jane English, p 355; Littlefield and Adams, Savage, MD, U.S.A., 1977

Fire Underwriter's Association of the Pacific 1903, Proceedings of the 27th Annual Meeting; p 198; San Francisco, California, U.S.A., February 17-18, 1903

First Person Singular; Florence Ryerson and Colin Clements; Samuel French, New York, NY, U.S.A., 1937, 1965

Free Thoughts on Quacks and Their Medicines; Francis Spilsbury, p 76; J. Wilkie, London, U.K., 1776

Flexible Ferdinand; Julie M. Lippmann, p 32; Grosset and Dunlap, New York, NY, U.S.A., 1919

Four Boys in Mississippi; Frank Eugene Kellogg, p 38; Saalfield Pub. Co., Akron, OH, U.S.A., 1909

Four Letters and Certain Sonnets Especially Touching Robert Greene and Divers Excellent Persons; Gabrielle Harvey: Imprinted for John Wolfe, London, England, 1592

From the First Shot: A Picture History of the Great War; Hannah White, 'Paris with a Difference' by Harold Howland; Independent Corporation, New York, NY, 1918

Frontiers of American Culture; Ray B. Browne, p 192; Purdue University Studies, Lafayette, IN, U.S.A., 1968

Funny Dogs with Funny Tales; 'The Good Natured Dog,' James Hannay, p 80; Addey & Co., London, U.K., 1852

Gales and Seaton's Register of Debates in Congress; First Session of the 20th Congress, p 255; Washington, DC, U.S.A., February 7, 1828

Gaping Gulf, with Letters and Other Relevant Documents; John Stubbs, 1579; reprinted by University Press of Virginia, Charlottesville, VA, U.S.A., 1968

Genesis through Revelation; J. Vernon McGee, ch. 5; Thomas Nelson, Nashville, TN, U.S.A., 1984

Genevra: Or, The History of the Portrait; Geneviere Genevra Fairfield, p 143; T.B. Peterson, Philadelphia, PA, U.S.A., 1851

Georgetown's North Island: A History; Robert McAllister, p 33; History Press, Charleston, SC, U.S.A., 2015

Gilt Kid; James Curtis; Jonathan Cape, London, U.K., 1936

Glenlonely; or, The Daemon Friend; Volume 3; William Henry De Merle, p 171; Longman, Orme, Brown, Green, and Longmans, London, U.K., 1839

Gnomologia: Adagies and Proverbs; Wise Sentences and Witty Sayings, Ancient and Modern, Foreign and British; collected by Thomas Fuller, MD, p 99; B. Barker, London, England, 1732

Go, Get 'em!: The True Adventures of an American Aviator of the Lafayette; William A, Wellman; The Page Co., Boston, MA, U.S.A., 1918

Gogol: Plays and Selected Writings; Nikolaĭ Vasil'evich Gogo, Introduction, p xix; University of Chicago Press, Chicago, IL, U.S.A., 1980

Gone With the Wind, Margaret Mitchell, Macmillan, New York, NY, U.S.A., 1936

Good News for Evil Tiles for Fainting Believers or, the Sum of a Lecture upon Jeremiah 45 Chapter together with another Lecture on the 28 Chapter of Matthew throughout; Mr. Michael Bruce, Minister of the Gospel, written in 1671; pub. London, England, 1708

Going Rogue; Sarah Palin, p 168; Harper Collins, New York, NY, U.S.A., 2009

Gospel of Thomas; Gnostic gospel; 1st century, discovered in Nag Hammadi, Egypt in 1945

Granada Manchester's Plays; 'Independent Means' by Stanley Haughton, Act II, p 118; Published on Behalf of Granada TV Network, Manchester University Press, Manchester, U.K., 1962

Greene Brothers Clinical Course in Dental Prosthesis in Three Lectures, Jacob W. Greene, p 75; Chilliothe, Detroit Dental Mfg. Detroit, MI, U.S.A., 1910

Greenwich Hospital, A Series of Naval Sketches Descriptive of Life of a Man-of-War's Man; 'An Old Sailor,' p 181; James Robins and Ivy Lane, London, U.K., 1826

Gregory's Chronicle of London; London, England, c 1470

Guerilla Marketing Attack; Jay Carrad Levinson Houghton; Miffin Co, Boston, MA, U.S.A., 1989

Happiness Wall to Wall; George Vandeman; Pacific Press, Oakland, CA, U.S.A., 1968

Harry Pell's Ebony Songster; 'Hunky-Dory, Air – Limerick Races,' p 7; Dick and Fitzgerald Publishers, New York, NY, U.S.A., 1866

Harvard Conference on the Internet and Society; p 162; Harvard, Boston, MA, U.S.A., 1997

Hearings before the Select Committee on Intelligence, U.S. House of Representatives 94th Congress, First Sessio; Washington, DC, U.S.A., Friday, August 1, 1975

Hearings of the Committee of Appropriations of the United States Senate; p 26; Washington, DC, U.S.A., 1961

Here's Luck; **Lennie Lower**, Australia, 1930, Prion Humer Classics, London, U.K., 2001

Hesperides, Robert Herrick, 'No Pains, No Gains;' London, England, revised ed., 1650

Hey, It's O.K.!; Jane E. SKILLICORN, 2013, p 37; Xlibris Books, Gordon, Australia

Hezekiah's Wives, Leslie Hamilton French, Preface, p vi, Haughton, Mifflin, Cambridge, Boston, MA, New York, NY, U.S.A., 1902

Historia Ecclesiastica Gentis Anglorum; St. Bede (Bēda Venerābilis); London, England, 8th century CE

Historical Collections, *Volume III*; John Rushworth, London, England, 1706

Historical Connections of Ohio: An Encyclopedia of the State, Volume II; p 174; Henry Howe, LL.D.; Henry Howe and Son, Columbus, OH, U.S.A., 1891

Historical Sketches of the Ten Miles Square Forming the District of Columbia; Jonathan Elliott, p 116; J. Elliott, Washington, DC, U.S.A., 1830

History of Edinburgh from its Foundation to the Present; William Maitland; Edinburgh, Scotland, 1753

History of England, David Hume; London, England, 1529

History of England; Thomas Macaulay; London, U.K., 1848

History of Ireland, Ancient and Modern; Martin Haverty, Esq.; James Duffy, Dublin, Ireland, 1860

History of Ireland from the Earliest Times to the Present Day; Edward Alfred D'Alton, Half Volume 3, 1547-1659; Gresham Publishing, London, U.K., 1920

History of Rome, for Young Persons, Vol. II; Elizabeth Caroline Gray; J. Hatchard and Son, London, U.K., 1847

History of the New Netherlands, Province of New York and State of New York; William Dunlap, p 154; Carter and Thorpe, New York, NY, U.S.A., 1839

History of the World, the Second Book of the First Part; p 552 Sir Walter Raleigh; London, England, 1614

Hitch 22, A Memoir, Christopher Hitchens; Atlantic Books, London, U.K., 2010

Home Study for Machinists Steam Engineers, Etc., Volume I; July 1897 to July, 1898, p 169; Colliery Engineer Co., Scranton, PA, U.S.A., 1898

Honey Moon; Susan Elizabeth Phillips, p 182; Pocket Books, New York, NY, U.S.A., 1993

Hoops Nation: A Guide to America's Best Pick-Up Basketball; Chris Ballard; Henry Holt, New York, NY, U.S.A., 1998

Horace, his Arte of Poetrie, Pistles and Satyrs Englished; Quintus Horatius Flaccus (65 BCE –8 BCE), Rome; Thomas Drqant's English translation; London, England, 1566

Hottie; Jonathan Bernstein, p 126; Penguin Books, New York, NY, U.S.A., 2009

Houser: Pride of America; Robert Dunn, p 213, ch. 51; Infinity Publishing, W. Conshohocken, PA, U.S.A., 2006

How the Good Guys Finally Won: Notes from Impeachment Summer; Jimmy Breslin; Viking Adult, New York, NY, U.S.A., 1975

How to Become an Athlete, James Edward Sullivan. P 23; American Sports Publishing Co., New York, NY, U.S.A., 1916

How to Gain Health and Long Life; P.M. Haney, p 76; The Hazel Pure Food Co., Chicago, IL, USA, 1899

How to Stop Worrying and Start Living; p 138; Simon & Schuster, New York, NY, U.S.A., 1948

How to Win Friends and influence People; Dale Carnegie; Simon & Schuster, New York, NY, U.S.A., 1936

Humanitarian Operations in Northern Iraq, 1991; Ronald J. Brown, The Mission of MSSG-24, p 44; U.S, Marine Corp History and Museums Division, Washington, DC, U.S.A., 1995

Hyman's Love Praeludia: Or; Love's Masterpiece; French by Gaultier de Coste La Calprenède, English rendition by 'J.D.;' Humphrey Moseley; London, England, 1659

I Can Jump Puddles; Alan Marshall, p 186; F. W. Cheshire, Melbourne, Victoria, AU, 1955

If You're Not Living on the Edge, You're Tasking up Too Much Space; Willis and Assoc., LLC, Singer Island, FL, U.S.A., 1999

Illiad; Homer; XXXII, 503, Greece, c. 1200 BCE

In a Little Town, Rupert Hughes, p 51; Harper and Bros., New York, NY, U.S.A., 1917

Incomparable Bellairs; Agnes and Egerton Castle; Thomas Nelson & Sons, London, U.K., 1907

Information Assurance and Security Education and Training; edited by Ronald C. Dodge and Lynn Futcher; Springer, Heidelberg, Dordrecht, London, U.K., New York, NY, U.S.A., 2013

In His Steps: What Would Jesus Do? Chicago-Advance, Charles M. Sheldon; Chicago, IL, U.S.A.1896

In It, to Win It: A Personal Memoir; David Kenney; Sunny Slope Press, Carbondale, IL, U.S.A., 1998

Inside My Skin; Susan Lucas, p 384; National Library of Australia, Parkes, AU, 2011

Inside the Ropes; Charles Emmitt Van Loan, p 274; Small, Maynard and Co., Boston, MA, U.S.A., 1913

Instructions for Officers and Non-commissioned Officers of Cavalry by Lieut. Colonel Von Arentschildt, First Hussars German Legion; p 56; J.W. Randolph, Richmond, VA, U.S.A., 1861

In the Shadows: Thirty Detective Stories Showing Why Crime Doesn't Pay, A Series of Famous Cases; Nick Harris, The Times Mirror Press, Los Angeles, CA, U.S.A., 1923

In the Tennessee Mountains; Charles Egbert Craddock; Haughton, Mufflin & Co., Boston, MA, USA, 1884

Investigation into the Alleged Official Misconduct of the Late Superintendent of the Philadelphia, Wilmington and Baltimore Railroad Co. Volume I; photographed and reprinted by Arthur Cannon, p 542; Philadelphia, PA, U.S.A., 1854

Investigation of the Assassination of President John F. Kennedy; Volume 14; p 351; Washington, DC, U.S.A., 1964

Investigation of Un-American Propaganda Activities in the United States Congress; page 272; Washington, DC, U.S.A., 1947

It Cannot Rain but it Pours; or In London Strow'd with Rarities, John Arbuthnot, London, England, 1726

I Think We Should Go into the Jungle; Barbara Anderson, p 38; Victoria University Press, Melbourne, Victoria, Australia, 1989

It Takes a Village and Other Lessons Children Teach us; Hillary Rodham Clinton with Barbara Feinman; Simon & Schuster, New York, NY, U.S.A., 1996

It Takes a Village; Jane Cowan-Fletcher; Scholastic, New York, NY, U.S.A., 1994

Ivanhoe; Sir Walter Scott, page 367; Samuel H, Parker, Boston, MA, U.S.A., 1820

Jackspeak the Pusser's Rum, Guide to Royal Navy Slanguage; Rick Jolly and Tugg Wilson, p 210; Maritime Books, London, U.K., 1989, & p 199 in rev. 2012, 2014

J.A. Hamilton's Historical, Descriptive and Practical Catecism of the Organ; pp 59,60; R. Cocks and Co., London, U.K., 1845

James G. Blaine, A Sketch of His Life, with a Brief Record of the Life of John A. Logan; Charles Wolcott Balestier, p 73; R. Worthington, New York, NY, U.S.A., 1884

Jane Brody's Good Food Book: Living the High-Carbohydrate Way; Jane E. Brody, p 240; W.R. Norton, New York, NY, USA & London, U.K., 1985 [1st Ed. 1980]

John Bull and His Senses, Being the Third Part of Law is a Bottomless Pit; John Arbuthnot, p 14; John Murphew, London, England, 1712

Journal of a Young Lady in Virginia 1782; Lucinda Lee Orr, Murphy & Co., Baltimore, MD, U.S.A., 1871

Journal of the Proceedings of the Missouri State Convention; p 188; Jefferson City, MO, U.S.A., 1862

Journal of the Senate of the General Assembly of the State of Iowa; Des Moines, IA, 1929

Just Say the Word; Writing for the Ear; G. Robert Jacks' p 175; William B. Eerdmans Publishing, Grand Rapids, MI, U.S.A., 1996

Kaffirland; Or, Scenes and Adventures in the Kaffir War of 1851-2; William Ross King, Second Edition; p 230; Saunders and Otley, London, U.K., 1855

Keeper of the Bees; Jean Stratton-Porter, p 266; Jean Stratton Porter, Inc, Indianapolis, IN, U.S.A., 1930

Kellys and O' Kellys; Anthony Trollope; Thomas Cautley Newby, London, U.K., 1848

Kenya National Assembly National Debates, Hansard Official Report; p 64715; Kenya, West Africa, November, 1994

Knights and Their Days; Dr. Doran; Richard Bentley, London, U.K., 1854

Lancelot Biggs, Spaceman; Nelson Bond; Wayside Press, Berkley Heights, NJ, U.S.A., 1950

Latter Day Pamphlets; Thomas Carlyle; London, U.K., 1850

Laurel and Hardy: A Bio-Biography; Wes D. Gehring, p 107; Greenwood Press, New York, NY, U.S.A., 1990

Leadership; George H. Knox, copyright 1909, p 132; Personal Help Publishing, Des Moines, IA, U.S.A., 1911

Leadership: Lessons from the Coyote, Volume One; Johnny R. Purvis and John W. Smith, Jr., pe 21; Author House, Bloomington, IN, U.S.A., 2008

Leaves from a Squatter's Note Book; Thomas Major, Sands and Co., p 132; London, U.K., 1900

Leaves of a Stunted Shrub: Genealogy of the Scrogen-Scroggin-Scroggins Family, Volume 5; compiled by William G. Scroggins, p 15: Nativa, LLC, Cockeysville, MD, U.S.A., 2009

Legions of Space; Keith Laumer; Baen Publishing Enterprizes, New York, NY, U.S.A., 2004

Leni Leoti Or, Adventures in the Far West; Emerson Bennett; J.A. and U.P. James, Philidelphia, PA, U.S.A., 1849, 1853

Letters and Dispatches; Earl of Stratford; London, England, 1636

Letters from a Gentleman in the North of Scotland, Edward Burt, Edinburgh, Scotland, circa 1730:

Letters of Madame Guyon* (1645-1717), *Being Selections of her Religious Thoughts and Experiences, Letter XV; trans. Mrs. P.L. Upham; pub. Bible House, New York, NY, U.S.A., 1870

Letters from Victorian Pioneers; Thomas Francis McBride; Robert S. Bain, Melbourne, Victoria, Australia, 1853

Letters Written by His Excellency Hugh Boulter, D.*D.* to several ministers of the State of England, 1672-1742; G. Faulkner and J. Williams, Dublin, Ireland, 1770

Leviathan; Thomas Hobbs; London, England, 1651

Life of the Party; Irvin Shrewsberry Cobb; Haughton Mifflin, New York, NY, U.S.A., 1919

Life of Henry W. Grady; Joel Chandler Harris, p 258; Cassell Publishing Co., New York, NY, U.S.A., 1800

Life of Tom Horn, Government Scout and Interpretor, Written by Himself; p 82; University of Oklahoma Press, Norman, OK, U.S.A., 1964

Life's Work As It Is; or, The Emigrant's Home in AusStralia; 'A Colonist;' Sampson, Low, Son and Marston, London, U.K., 1867

Like One of the Family, Alice Childress, Independent Publishers, Brooklyn, NY, U.S.A., 1956

Lily Bell: or The Lost Child; Alice Fay; James French and Co., Boston, MA, U.S.A., 1857

Lionel Lincoln; James Fenimore Cooper, p 111; John Miller, London, U.K., 1825

Little Dorrit, Charles Dickens, Bradbury and Evans, London, U.K., 1857

Lizzie Loren of Greyrigg; Eliza Lynn Linton, p 16; Tinsley Bros., London, U.K., 1866

Loch Creran, Notes from the West Highlands; William Anderson Smith, p 279; Alexander, Gardner, Paisley, London, U.K., 1887

Looking Forward to It; Stephen Elliott; Picador, St. Martin's Press, New York, NY, U.S.A., 2004

Love Story, Erich Segal, Harper & Rowe, New York, NY, U.S.A., 1970

Macon Moore, the Southern Detective; Jonathan R. Taylor, p 113; Street and Smith; J.S. Oglivie and Co., New York, NY, U.S.A., 1881

Maid of the Mist; John Oxenham (psu); London, U.K., 1914

Manning's Chronicle of English; London, England, 1338

Margaret: A Tale of the Real and Ideal Blight and Bloom; Jordan and Wiley, Boston, MA. U.S.A., 1845

Margaret Ogilvy; J. M. Barrie, p 156; pub. U.K., 1896; Charles Scribner & Sons, New York, NY, U.S.A., 1912

Marine Corps Stock Fund 1953-1967, p 214, U.S. Marine Corp, Washington, DC, U.S.A., January 1, 1968

Marked for Life; A. Frank Pinketton, p 75; Laird and Lee, Chicago. IL, U.S.A., April, 1887

Master Humphreys Clock aka ***The Old Curiosity Shop;*** Charles Dickens; page 142; London, U.K., 1840-1841

Mechanick Exercises, or. The Doctrine of Handy-works, Joseph Moxon, London, England, 1683

Meditationes Sacrae; Francis Bacon; London, England, 1597

Melodies and Mountaineers, Isabel McMeekin, Johnnie (B.A.A.), p 41; The Stratford Co., Boston, MA, U.S.A., 1921

Memoirs, Correspondence and Private Papers of Thomas Jefferson, Vol. 1; page 75; Henry Colburn and Richard Bentley, London, U.K., 1829

Memoirs, Historical and Military; Antoine de Pas marquis de Feuquières, trans. from French, p 453: T, Woodward, London, 1735

Memoirs of Ancient Chivalry from the Romance Writers and Historians of Those Ages; translated from the French by Monsieur de Sainte-Palaye, pp 213-214; London, England, 1784

Methods of Housing Analysis; James W. Hughes, p 119; Transition Publishers, New Brunswick, NJ, U.S.A., 1977

Memoirs of the Dead and Tomb's Remembrancer, Prayer for George Waashington; Baltimore, MD, U.S.A., 1806

Milestones in Midwifery; Walter Radcliffe; W. Heinemann, London, U.K., 1947; Bristol Wright, New York, NY, U.S.A., 1967

Michiganensian; 'Freshman This and Freshman That,' p XT-28; University of Michigan, Ann Arbor, MI, U.S.A., 1908

Millionaire Republican; Wayne Alyn Root, 'Secret #18;' Penguin Group, New York, NY, U.S.A., 2006

Million Dollar Advice from America's Top Marketing Consultant; Regis McKenna, p 27; Business & Economics Textbook, Addison-Wesley Pub. Co., Boston MA, U.S.A., 1985

Mining in the Pacific States of North America; John S. Hittell, p 116; H.H. Bancroft and Co., San Francisco, CA, U.S.A., 1861

Minor Characters: A Young Woman's Coming-of-Age in the Beat Orbit of Jack Kerouvac; Joyce Johnson, p xxii; Haighton Mufflin, New York, NY, U.U.A., 1983

Miriam Copley; John Cody Jeaftreson, p 154; Hurst and Blackett, London, U.K., 1859

Miscellanies; Henry Strong, p 273; R.R. Donnelley & Sons, Chicago, IL, U.S.A., 1902

Mistakes Worth Making: How to Turn Sports into Atheltic Excellence; Sandra Halden-Brown, p 275; Humnan Kinetics, Champaign, IL, U.S.A., 2003

Moby Dick; Herman Melville, p 91; The St. Botolph Society, Boston, MA, U.S.A., 1892

Modern Chivalry, Vol. I; page 98; Cary and Hart, Philadelphia, PA, U.S.A., 1846

Monsoon; Di Morrissey; Pan Macmillan Australia Pty. Ltd., Sydney, Australia, 2007

Monsuir Bossu's Treatise of the Epick Poem; Rene Bossu; J Krapton & H. Clements, London, England, 1716

More Money than God: Hedge Funds and the Making of the New Elite; Sebastian Mallaby; Penguin Press, New York, NY, U.S.A., 2010

More Money than God: Living a Rich Life without Losing Your Soul; Steven Z. Leder; Bonus Books, Chicago, IL, U.S.A., 2003

Moving the Needle: Get Clear, Get Free, and Get Going in Your Career; Joe Sweeney and Mike Yorkey; John Wiley & Sons, Hoboken, NJ, U.S.A., 2014

Mr. Rutherford's Letters, Now Divided into Three Parts; E. & J. Robertsons, Edinburg, Scotland, U.K., 1761

Mrs. Dymond; Anne Isabella Thackeray Ritchie; Leipzizig, Bernhard, Tauchnitz, Paris, France, 1885

Murphy's Law Book Two; Arthur Bloch; Price/Stern/Sloan Publishers, Inc., Los Angeles, CA, U.S.A., 1980

Nahj Al-Balagha; Col. by Sahrif Razi, Inam Ali (599-661 AD); Persia, 10th century CE

Narrative of a Journey into Khorasan; James B. Frasier, p181; Longman, Hurst, Rees, Orme, Brown and Green, London, U.K., 1825

Narrative Structure in the Novels of Sir Walter Scott; Michael H. Cusac, p 65; Mouton and Co., The Hague, Netherlands, 1969

Natural Historie; Pliny the Elder; first century bef. 70CE; English trans. Philemon Holland; London, England, 1469, 1601

Never Come Morning; Nelson Algren, p 14; Harper & Bros, New York, NY, U.S.A., 1942

New Annual Register or General Repository of History, Politics and Literature for the Year 1804, Part I, p 297; John Stockdale, London, U.K., 1805

New Dictionary, Spanish and English; Pedro Penida; London, England, 1740

New Double Grammar: English-French, French-English; p 109; Eugene Henri Frix, Paris, 1696

New-England's Memorial; Nathanial Morton; William Bradford and Thomas Prince, editors; printed for John Usher, Cambridge, MA, U.S.A., 1669

New Letters, Thomas Carlyle; London, U.K., 1836

New Theories and the Old Faith; James Allison Picton, p112, Williams and Norgate, London, U.K., 1870

New York Court of Appeals, Records and Briefs; p 59, 1935; p 44, New York, NY, U.S.A., 1942; statement by Charles Schneider sworn to on February 35, 1942 before Alvin A Rabinowitz, Attorney and Counselor at Law; p 900, Albany, NY, U.S.A., 1943

Nicholas Nickelby; Chapter LIV; Charles Dickens; London, U.K., 1854

Niles Weekly Register; 'Tennessee Militiamen;' Niles and Sons, Baltimore, MD, U.S.A., March 3, 1828, Volume 37, Hezekiah and William Niles, p 85; Baltimore, MD, U.S.A., 1829

Ninth Session, 1877, The Acts and Resolutions Adopted by the Legislature of Florida; Tallahassee, FL, U.S.A., February 17, 1877

No Other Way to Tell It; Derek Paget; New York, NY, U.S.A., 1996

Nothing New Tales; Dinah Maria Craik, p 187; Hurst & Blackett, London, U.K., 1857

NTC's Thematic Dictionary of American Slang; Richard Spears, p 40; McGraw Hill, New York, NY, U.S.A., 1998

Objects Interesting to the English Nation; Elias Habesci, p 186; London, U.K., 1793

Observations on the Principal Medical Institutions and Practice of France Italy and Germany; Haswell; Barington and Haswell, Philadelphia, PA, U.S.A., 1837

Occasional Fac-similie Reprints of Rare English Tracts; Edmond William Ashbee, 'Taylor's Westerne Voyage to the Mount,' p 4; London, England, 1649

OED, Oxford English Dictionary, Oxford University Press, Oxford, U.K., 1989

OED, 3rd Ed.; ref. on raking over the coals, p 69; Oxford University Press, Oxford, U.K., 2010

Of All Things! Robert Benchley, H. Holt and Co., New York, N.Y., U.S.A., 1921

Off the Internet for Everyone: Stories, Jokes and Inspiration from the World Wide Web for You; Wright Corp., Aylett, VA, U.S.A., 2002

O. Henry, the Story of William Sidney Porter, Jeanette Covert Nolan; Mesner, New York, NY, U.S.A., 1943

Ohio State Bar Association Reports, Volume 4, Proceedings of the Annual Meeting of the Association held at the City of Dayton, Ohio, December 29 and 30, 1885; p 26; Columbus, OH, U.S.A., 1886

Old Bachelors, Their Varieties Characters and Condition; pp 103-104; James McCrone, London, U.K., 1835

Older England; a Course of Seven Lectures; J. Frederick Hodgetts; Whiting and Co., London, U.K., 1887

On Board the "Rocket;" Robert Chamblett Adams, p 128; D. Lothrop Co.; Boston, MA, U.S.A., 1879

One Thousand Jokes from Vaudville; Jack Hazard joke; L. & M. Ottenheimer, Baltimore, MD, U.S.A., 1908

On Human Science and Its Works and On Divine Revelation and Its Works and Sciences; James John Garth Williamson; J,P. Lippincott, Philadelphia, PA, U.S.A., 1876

On the Death of Rev. Mr. George Whitefield; sermon, Charles Wesley, Chapel in Tottenham-Court Road and at the Tabernacle, near Moorfields, Emgland, November 18, 1770; p 2, pub. By Thomas Jackson, London, U.K., 1872

On with Torchy; Sewell Ford, p 351; Grosset and Dunlap, New York, NY, U.S.A., 1914

Out of the Nest; A Flight of Verses; Mary McNeil Fenollosa, 'Behind Bars,' p 77; Little, Brown & Co., Boston, MA, U.S.A., 1899

Out of the Night: Memoir of Richard Julius Herman Krebs alias Jan Valtin; Jan Valtin; Alliance Book Corp., New York, NY, USA, 1941

Outsiders; Robert William Chambers; Frederick A. Stokes Co., New York, NY, U.S.A., 1899

Oxford English Dictionary; Editors: William Craigie, James Murray, John Simpson; definition of cook; London, U.K.. 1884

Oxford English Dictionary, Oxford Press, Oxford, U.K., 1933, 1967

Pamela, or, Virtue Unrewarded, Samuel Richardson, Letter VII, p 15; London, England, 1740

Paradise Marred; Robert Hardin; iUniverse, Lincoln, NE, U.S.A., 2007

Parenting with Love and Logic: Teaching Children Responsibility; Foster W. Cline and Jim Fay, p 25; Pinion Press, Colorado Springs, CO, U.S.A., 1990

Parliamentary and Political Tracts, etc.; Sir Robert Atkyns, Knight of the Bath, p 262; printed for R. Gosling, London, England, 1734

Parliamentary Debates; New South Wales Parliament, AUStralia, p 728, 1862; page 1113, 1899 *Parliamentary Debates, HoUSe of Representatives*, p 3350; Canberra, ACT, Australia, 1983

Parliamentary Papers, HoUSe of Commons and Command, Volume 220; Reports of Commissioners, Army, Military Punishment, Session, 4 February to 20 August, 1836, p 218; London, U.K., 1836

Parlimentary Papers Volume 3, Queensland Parliament; page 648; Queensland, Austrralia, 18 November, 1928

Partners in Providence; Charles D. Stewart; The Century Co., New York, NY, U.S.A., 1907

Patricia of the Hills; Charles Kennett Burrow, p 30; G.P. Putnam & Sons, New York, NY, U.S.A.; London, U.K., 1909

Paul's Case: The Kingston Letters; Lynn Crosbie, p 127; Insomniac Press, Toranto, ON, Canada, 1997

Pearls of Thought; Maturin Murray Ballou, p 56; Haughton, Mufflin and Co., Boston, MA, U.S.A., 1881

Peasant Life: Sketches of the Villagers and Field Laborers in Glenaldie; Malcolm McLennan. P 230; Strahan and Co., London, U.K., 1872

People You Know; George Ade; University of Michigan Library, Ann Arbor, MI, U.S.A., 1902

Performance Appraisals Made Easy; Lisbeth S. Margulus and Jaquelyn Ann Melin; Corwin Press, Thousand Oaks, CA, U.S.A., 2005

Perimedes the Blacke-smith; John Payne Collier, p 40; printed for John Wolf, London, U.K., 1588

Peter Simple, Volume III; Frederick Marryat pp 227-228; Saunders and Otley, London, U.K., 1834

Phantasmagoria: Or, Sketches of Life and Literature; Mary Jane Jewsbury; p 230; Hurst, Robinson and Company, and Archibald Constable and Company, Edinburg, Scotland, U.K., 1825

Philosophy of Sir William Hamilton; Bart, London, U.K., 1853

Phyllis; Howard Fast, p 204; Andre Deutsch; London, U.K., 1962

Picket; Renfrey Clark, p 11; Pathfinder Press, Chippendale, New South Wales, Australia, 1984

Pierce Egan's Book of Sports and Mirror of Life; Pierce Egan, p 158; William Tegg, London, U.K., 1832

Pilgrim's Progress, John Bunyan, London, England, 1678

Pioneers of Beverly: Series of Sketches; John A. Cornell, p 354; The Dundas True Banner Printing and Publishing House, Dundas, Ontario, Canada, 1889

Pirkei Avot (Ethics of the Fathers) 5:21; Palestine, c 120 CE

Plautus's Comedies, Amphitryon, Epidicus, and Rudens; made English, by Titus Maccious Plautus, p 6; London, England, 1694

Poems by Allan Ramsey, Volume II; "Epigram on Mr. Drummond;" p 244; first published in Edinburgh, Scotland, May, 1728

Poetical Version of Certain Psalms of David, Psalm L, v 23; p 64; J. Sprange, London, U.K., 1801

Pole Baker; Will N. Harben, p 23; Harper & Brothers; New York, NY, U.S.A.; London, U.K., 1905

Political Essays with Sketches of Public Figures; William Hazlitt; William Hone, London, U.K., 1819

Political Science Fiction; edited by Donald M. Hassler and Clyde Wilcox, 'Governing the Alien Nation,' p 168; University of South Carolina Press, Columbia, SC, U.S.A., 1997

Porcupine, William Corbett, p 141, Barbour, Oxford, England, 1796, 1801

Postcards from the Net: An Australian's Guide to the Wired World; Jon Casimir; Allen & Unwin Pty, Ltd. St. Leonards, NSW, Australia, 1996

Private Sea Journals; Admiral Sir Thomas Pasley, Bart, written, 1778-1782; published by J. M. Dent and Sons, London, U.K., 1931

Proceedings for Phychical Research; A.W. Verrall p 403; Appendix dated August 21, 1904; Robert Mclehose and Co, Glasgow, Scotland, U.K., 1906

Proceedings of the Alabama State Bar Association, Held at Southern Club, Birmingham Alabama, April 28, 29, 1922; p 42; Paragon Press, Montgomery, AL, U.S.A., 1922

Proceedings of the American Street and Interurban Railway Association; 'Publicity Symposium Paper;' G.H. Gall, p 227; New York, NY, U.S.A., 1908

Proceedings of the Illinois Bar Association, Forty-fifth Annial Meeting at Dixon, June 9, 10, 11, 1921, p 61; Interstate Printing, Danville, IL, U.S.A., 1921

Proceedings of the Parliament of South Australia: Volume 2; 1872, p 67; W.C. Cox, Govt. Printer, Adelaide, AU, 1873

Proverbs Exemplified; John Tresler; London, U.K., 1790

Proverbs in Scots, James Carmichael; Edinburgh, Scotland, 1628

Psychology from the Standpoint of a Behaviorist; John B. Watson; P.P. Lippincott, Philadelphia, PA, U.S.A. and London, U.K., 1919

Public Papers of the Presidents of the United States, "A Conversation with the President" Interview with Howard K. Smith of the American Broadcasting Network; New York, NY, U.S.A., March 22, 1971

Pudd'nhead Wilson; Mark Twain, first serialized in *The Century Magazine;* New York, NY, U.S.A., 1894

Qanoon-e-Islam or the Customs of the Moosulmans of India; Jaffur Shurref, p 97: Parbury, Allen and Co., London, U.K., 1832

Queen Anna's New Words; John Florio; London, England, 1611

Railroad Men; Railroad Branch of the YMCA, New York, NY, U.S.A., May, 1907

Random House Historical Dictionary of American Slang, Volume 1, A-G by J.E. Lighter, Random House, New York, 1994

Ransom Unpaid; Fred Hunter, p 163; St. Martin's Press, New York, NY, U.S.A., 1999

Reading Myself and Others; Philip Roth, p 61; Farrar, Straus and Giroux, New York, NY, U.S.A., 1971

Reading the Bromance Homosocial Relationships in Film and Television; DeAngelis M. (editor); ISBN 9780814338988, p 328; Wayne State University Press, Detroit, MI, U.S.A., 2014

Recollections of Rifleman Bow; Allen Bolby, 1969, page 122; Leo Cooper, Ltd., London, U.K.; Melbourne, Austraalia; Aukland, NZ, 1969

Relations and observations historical and political upon the Parliament begun Ano Dom. 1640; page 17; London, England, 1648

Relique Wottenianie: Or a Collection of Lives; Sir Henry Wotton; London, England, 1672

Remaines Concerning Britaine; William Camden and John Philipot, p278; 'Wife Speeches;' London, England, 1636

Remaines of a greater worke concerning Britaine; William Camden, 1605; London, England, 1614

Remarks addressed to an illiterate book fancier, Timon the Misanthrope; 'Dog in the Manger,' Lucian of Samosata; Greece, 2nd century CE

Report of the Commissioner of Agriculture; page 204; U.S. Government Printing Office, Washington, DC, U.S.A., 1863

Reports from Commissioners in the British Parliament and House of Commons; p 77; London, U.K., 1866

Reports of All the Cases Decided by All the Superior Courts; p 488; London, U.K., 1864

Reports of Cases Argued and Determined in the English Courts of Common Law, Volume XIV; Edited by Thomas Sergeant and John Lowber, p 181, in Trane Versus Bennett, T.T., 1827; P.H. Nicklin, P. Johnson, Philadelphia, PA, U.S.A., 1830

Reports of Cases Determined at Nisi Prius, in the Courts; John Campbell; McDougle v. Royal Exchange Assurance, Tuesday, December 19, 1815; Joseph Butterworth, London, U.K., 1816

Reports of Cases Determined by the Supreme Court of the State of Missouri, Volume 191; October term, 1905; Case of State v. Kelley; Perry S. Rader, p 3; E.W. Stephens, Columbia, MO, U.S.A., 1906

Republic; Plato, Greece, 380 BCE

Resident Alien: Poems Anthenum; Daryl Hine, 'What's His Face,' p 52; New York, NY, U.S.A., 1975

Rhymes with a Reason; Alan Brodrick,'The Bridge of Boats (Stamboul, 1855),' p 9; Piper, Stephenson & Spence, London, U.K., 1857

Rhymes with a Red Cross Man; Robert William Service, 'Wounded,' p 158; Barse & Hopkins, New York, NY, U.S.A., 1916

Rights of Man; Thomas Paine, p 45; printed for the Whigs of the Capitol; Dublin, Ireland, 1791

Ritual and Cult at Ugarit, (written late twelfth-early eleventh centuries BCE); Trans. and pub. Dennis Pardee, Chicago Center for Jewish Studies, Chicago, IL, U.S.A., 2002

Rofallnde Eupheus golden legacie: Memoir of Thomas Lodge; Edmond W. Gosse, p 11; Thomas Orwin, London, England, 1590

Rory O'More: A National Romance; 'Samuel Lover,' Vol. 1, p 81; Richard Bentley. London, U.K., 1837

Roughing it in the Bush, Or, Life in Canada, Susanna Bush, George P. Putnam, New York, NY, U.S.A., 1852

Rowland Bradshaw: His Struggles and Adventures on the Way to Fame; p 104: Sherwood, Gilbert and Piper, London, U.K., 1848

Rules for Spelling and Writing English, Second Edition; William Baker, p 79; Joseph Penn, Bristol, England, 1724

Salve Deus Rex Judaeorum; Amelia Lanyer; London, England, 1611

Samantha at Saratoga; Marietta Holley, Hubbard Bros., Philadelphia, PA, U.S.A., 1887

Saratoga: An Indian Tale of Frontier Life; Daniel Shepherd, p 179; T.B. Patterson and Bros., Philadelphia, PA, U.S.A., 1877

Saved by a Smile; James Siree, p 39; Vizetelly and Co., London, U.K., 1886

Scots Poems; William Taylor of Currie; Edinburgh, Scotland, U.K., 1787

Scottish Proverbs, James Kelly, Edinburgh, Scotland, 1771

Scripture Songs for Zion's Travelers; Song VI; John WIllison, p 242; Geo. & Robt. King, Aberdeen, Scotland, U.K., 1767, 1793

Select British Classics, Volume 29; p 101; Samuel Bradford, Philadelphia, PA, U.S.A., 1803

Select Circuit Library, Part 1; Adam Waldie, p 178, London, U.K., 1834

Select Writings of Elbert Hubbard; Elbert Hubbard, p 237; William H. Wise & Co., New York, NY, U.S.A., 1922

Seneca's Morals Abstracted in Three Parts; Roger L'Estrange, pp 104-105; Homer Broome, London, U.K., 1679

Sermons on Various Subjects, Volume III; Thomas Francklin, 'On Vigilance,' p 233: printed for T, Cadell, London, U.K., 1787

***Session Cases: Cases Decided in the Court of Session*, &c, Volume** 3; House of Lords, London, U.K., 1864-1865

Seven Day Magic; Edward Eager, p 172, 1962; Children's Classics, Harcourt, Inc., San Diego, CA, U.S.A., 1990

Seven Sermons before Edward VI, on Each Friday in Lent, 1549; p 26; 'The Fyrst Sermon;' London, U.K., 1869

Shakespeare and His Friends; Robert Folkestone Williams: Stringer and Townsend, New York, NY, U.S.A., 1847

Shaw's Annotated Report, of the Irish State Trials; p 75, Henry Shaw, Dublin, Ireland, 1844

Sheridan's Troopers and Borders; De Benneville Randolph Keim, Davin McKay, p 157; George Routledge and Sons, London, U.K., 1885

Shirley, A Tale, Volume I; Currer Bell (Charlotte Bronte) p 138; Smith, Elder and Co., London, U.K., 1849

Signs of the Times; Thomas Carlyle; Edinburg, Scotland, U.K., 1829

Sinister Street; Compton Mackenzie, Volume II, chapter 3; Martin Secker, London, U.K., 1914

Sir Richard Calmady; Lucas Malet; London, U.K., 1901

Sir Thomas More, First English Collectivist; James Leatham,p 53; Abraham Vele, London, England, 1551

Sketches in Lyric Prose and Verse; 'Your Day Dreams,' Natalie Whited Price, p 48; Ralph Fletcher Seymour, Chicago, IL, U.S.A., 1920

Skyscraper; Faith Baldwin, p 265; Dell Publishing, New York, NY, U.S.A., 1931

Small Bachelor; P.G. Wodenhouse, London, U.K.; George H. Doran, New York, NY, U.S.A., 1927

Snagged and Sunk, or, The Adventures of a Canvas Canoe; Harry Castlemon, p 354: Henry T. Coats and Co., Philadelphia, PA, U.S.A., 1888

Social Behavior in Autism; Edited by Eric Schopler and Gary B. Mesibov; University of North Carolina School of Medicine at Chapel Hill, North Carolina, U.S.A., 1986

Social Darwinism in American Thought; Richard Hofstadter; University of Pennsylvania Press, Philadelphia, PA, U.S.A., 1944

Social Theory and Social Structure; Robert King Merton, p 249; enlarged edition, The Free Press; New York, NY, U.S.A., 1968

Solomonis Panaretos: Commentary upon the books of Proverbs, Ecclesiastes and the Song of Solomon; John Trapp; London, England, 1650

Some Account of the Life, Writings and Speaches of William Pinkney; Henry Wheaton, p 593; Richardson and Lord, Boston, MA, U.S.A., 1826

Some Old Love Stories; Thomas Power O' Connor, pp 247-248; Chapman and Hall, London, U.K., 1895,

Songs and Sonnets written by the ryght honorable Lord Henry Haward late Earle of Surrey; section, 'Nicholas Grimald's Poem's,' p 152, 'A funerall song, upon the deseas of Annes his mother;' Apud, Richardson, Totte, London, England, 1557

Songs of London: A Melody Grave and Gay; Herbert Furst, 'A Dance of the Muses in Princes Road, Notting Hill,' p 24; Gowans, London, U.K., 1908

Speaking to Persuade; LeRoy Brown, p 74; Frederick Fell, New York, NY, U/S.A., 1960

Steelwork; Gilbert Sorentino, p 5; Dalky Archive Press, Elmwood Park, IL, U.S.A., 1992

***Store Manager**: The Professional Experience;* Larry Frazio; Focal Press, Burlington, MA, U.S.A., 2000, 2013

Stories of Irish Pleasantry; Mrs. S. C. Hall, '*The Landlord Abroad*'; William and Robert Chambers, Edinburgh, Scotland, U.K., 1840

Stories of the Sea; Frederick Marryat, Harper, New York, NY, U.S.A., 1835

***Standing By: The Making of an American Military Family in a Time of** War;* Alison Buckholtz; Penguin, New York, NY, U.S.A., 2009

Star Dust; Fannie Hurst, p 198; Harper & Bros, New York, NY, U.S.A., 1921

Star Trek II Distress Call; William Rotsler, p125; Wanderer Books, New York, NY, U.S.A., 1982

Strange Histories Consisting of Ballads and Other Poems Principally; Thomas Deloney; London, England, 1607

Strategic Project Management; **Michael J. Termini**, p 47; Society of Manufacturing Engineers, Dearborn, MI, U.S.A., 1999

Studies in English, Written and Spoken; Cornelis Stoffel; W.J. Phieme and Co., Zutphen, Netherlands, Luzac and Co., London, U.K., 1894

Subversive Influence in the Educational Process: Hearings Before the Subcommittee to Investigate the Administration of the Internal Security Actand Other Security Laws of the United States Senate, Eighty-Second Congress Second Session, September & October, 1952; Washington, DC, U.S.A., 1952

Sudden Death; Rita Mae Brown; Banham Books, New York, NY, U.S.A., 1983

Summer Pictures - From Copenhagen to Venice; Henry Martyn Field, p. 21; Sheldon and Co., New York, NY, U.S.A., 1859

Summer's Tales, Volume III; John Iggulden, p 123; Macmillan and Co., Ltd, London, U.K., 1966

***Supplements to the Connecticut Couramt for the year 1855**;* Thomas M. Day, Hartford Connecticut, U.S.A., 1855

Supreme Court Appellate Division – Fourth Department; p 185; The Reporter Co., Walton, NY, U.S.A., 1934

***Sweet Thursday**,* John Steinbeck, p 69; Viking Press, New York, NY, U.S.A., 1954

Sylva, Discourse of Forest-Trees and Propagation of Timber in His Majesties Dominions; John Evelyn, fellow of the Royal Society; London, England, 1670

Sylvie and Bruno; ch.16, Lewis Carroll; Macmillan, New York, NY, 1889

Symbola divina et humana Pontificum, Imperatorum, Regum; Rome, Italy, 1601

Tak Your Auld Cloak about Ye; To which are Added, Tom Bowling. Thou art gan awa, Auld Saunders M'Craghan. Lady Onlie; W, Macnie, Sterling, U.K., 1825

Tales of Fashionable Life: Manoeuvring, Almeria and Vivian, Maria Edgeworth, J. Johnson, London, U.K., 1800, 1809

Talk of Drama: Views of the Television Dramatist Now and Then; Sean Day Lewis, Ch. 4: From the Heart and Soul, Jimmy McGovern, p 59; University of Luton Press, Bedfordshire, U.K., 1998

Tail of the Storm: Flying Missions in the Gulf War; Alan Cockrell; University of Alabama Press, Tuscaloosa, AL, U.S.A., 1995

Tarzan the Untamed; Edgar Rice Burrows, p 273; Gossett and Dunlap, New York, NY, U.S.A., 1920

Tea and Tea Drinking; Arthur Reed, pp 11-12; Samson, Low, Marston, Searle & Rivington, London, U.K., 1884

Teen Talk: Sixteen Character Sketches for Teen-Aged Boys and Girls; Joyce R. Ingalls; Baker's Plays, Quincy, MA, U.S.A., 1953

Test Case: Italy, Ethiopia, and the League of Nations; George W. Baer, p 276; Hoover Institution Press, Sanford, CA, U.S.A., 1976

Texas and Southwestern Lore; J. Frank Dobie, Texas Fokelore Society, Austin, TX, U.S.A., 1927

That's Life; William Herrick, p 57; New Directions Publishing Co., New York, NY, U.S.A., 1985

The Academic Man; Logan Wilson, p 197; Oxford University Press, Oxford, U.K., 1942

The Acharnians, Knights, Wasps and Birds or Aristophanes; Translated into English Prose; written 4th century BCE by Aristophanes; trans. 1824 by Henry Carey; pub. Harry Slatter, Oxford, U.K., 1830

The Adventures of a Carpet Bag; Ernest Thomson, Piper, Brothers and Co., London, U.K., 1853

The Adventures of Huckleberry Finn; Mark Twain, Chap. VI, Harper & Bros., New York, NY, U.S.A., 1896

The Advantures of Tom Sawyer; Mark Twain, American Publishing Co., Hartford, CT, U.S.A., 1876

The Anatomy of Melancholy; Robert Burton, London, England, 1621

The Amarnth or Token of Remembrance; Edited by Emily Percival; Phillips, Samson and Co., Boston, MA, U.S.A., 1854

The American Heritage Dictionary, Second Edition; Christine Amur, Haughton, Mufflin, Harcourt, Boston, MA/ New York, NY, U.S.A., 2013

The American Language; Henry Louis Mencken, first published in 1919-1921; 1936 edition; Alfred A Knopp, New York, NY, U.S.A.

The American Library Annual 1914-1915; p 106; R.R. Bowker Co., New York, NY, U.S.A., 1915

The Angel of the Chimes; Fortuné Du Boisgobey, English version; London, U.K., 1896

The Annals and Magazine of Natural History; 'Notes on the Mexican Coccidae' by T.D.A. Cockarell p 47; Taylor and Freancis, London, U.K., July, 1893

The Annotated Classic Fairy Tales; Maria Tartar, p 44; BCA, London, U.K., 2002

The Annual Miscellany for the Year of 1694; Art of Poetry, Cant. III, Boileau; John Dryden, London, England, 1708

The Arethusa: A Naval Story, Volume 1; Frederick Chamier; E.L. Carey and A. Hart, Philadelphia, PA, U.S.A., 1837

The Art of English Poetry, Vol II; Edward Bysshe, War; London, U.K., 1762

The Art of English Possie; George Puttenham; London, England, 1589

The Athenian Oracle, 3rd Edition, Volume 2, John Dunton, p 19; London, England, 1728

The Autobiography of Thomas Anthony Methuen; p 164; Hachards, London, U.K., 1870

The Balloon; Sir Henry Phelps Brown, p 184; Macmillan, London, U.K., 1853

The Bee Hive of the Romishe Church; 'translated out of the Dutch to the Englishe by George Gilpin the Elder;' London, England, 1579

The Best Plays, 1938-39; Burns Mantle, 'Kiss the Boys Goodbye,' Act III; Dodd, Mead & Co., New York, NY, U.S.A., 1938

The Best of Mother Goose and Other Nursery Rhymes, Illusrtated; Stanley J. St. Clair, p 20, p 86: p 83; St. Clair Publications, 2013

The Best Treasure*; or, *The Way to be Truly Rich; Bartholomew Ashford; William Marshall, London, U.K., 1781

The Boke of Nature, or, School of Good Manners for Men, Servants and Children; Hugh, Rhodes, p xiii; London, England, 1577

The Book of British Poets; C. H. Monike, 'From the Chase'; William Somerville, p 306; George Wigand, Leipzig, Germany, 1858

The Book of Parliament; Michael Macdonagh, p 76; Ibister & Co., London, U.K., 1897

***The Book of Popular Songs**,* G.G. Evans, Philadelphia, PA, U.S.A., 1861

The Broken Wheel; Florence Land May, p 355; C.M. Clark Publishing Co., Boston, MA, U.S.A., 1910

***The Building of the Tower of Salvation: Being a Preparation Sermon**,* James Simson d. c 1694, Edinburgh, Scotland, 3rd Edition 1723

***The Cane Mutiny**;* Herman Wouk, p 123; Doubleday, New York, NY, U.S.A., 1951, 1954

The Casquet of Literature, Volume III; edited by Charles Gibbon, *Chanet* by J.W. De Forest; p 107; Blackie & Son, London, U.K., 1873

The Catcher in the Rye; J.D. Salinger; Little, Brown & Co., New York, NY, U.S.A., 1951

The Century Dictionary and Cyclopedia, Volume III; p 2104; The Century Co., New York, NY, U.S.A., 1911

The Century Dictionary of the English Language, Volume IV; prepared under the supervision of William Dwight Whitnet, Ph.D., LL.D., p 3588; The Century Co., New York, NY, U.S.A., 1890

The Chameleon Manager; Brian Clegg, p 28; Rutledge, London, U.K., 1998

***The Chaplin of the Fleet**: A Novel,* Volume 1; Sir Walter Besnant and James Rice, p 92; Chatto and Windus, London, U.K., 1881

***The Building of the Tower of Salvation: Being a Preparation Sermon**,* James Simson d. c 1694, Edinburgh, Scotland, 3rd Edition 1723

***The Classic Dictionary of the Vulgar Tongue**;* Francis Grose; London, U.K., 1785

The Chess Player's Chronicle and Journal of Indoor and Outdoor Amusements; Howard Staunton, London, U.K., August 30, 1881

The Christian in Combat Armour; William Gurnall, 5th Edition, page 26; Printed for Ralph Smith, London, England, 1669

The Citizen and the State; Nathan Matthews, p 4; Massachusetts General Court, Committee on Education; G.H. Ellis, Boston, MA, U.S.A., 1889

The Civil Engineer and Architect's Journal; July, 1845; 'Candidus's Note-book;' R. Groombridge & Sons, London, U.K., July, 1845

The Clue of the Broken Blade; Franklin W. Dixon (psu.), Grossett and Dunlap, New York, NY, U.S.A., 1942

The Code of Federal Regulations of the United States of America; Federal Register, National Archives, Washington, DC, U.S.A., January 1, 1984

The Comic Annual; Thomas Hood, The Rope Dancer, p 2; Charles Tilt, London, U.K., 1834

The Comics; Coulton Waugh, p 259, p 329; University of Mississippi Press, Jackson MS, U.S.A., 1947

The Common Purse: Income Sharing in New Zealand Families; Robin Fleming and Susan Kell Easting, p 106; Auckland University Press, Auckland, NZ, 1997

The Compleat Body of the Art Military; Second Edition; Richard Elton Leivtenant Collonel, 1659, page xxxi; R. & W. Leyburn, London, England, 1659

The Complete Works of Sir Walter Scott, Vol. VII; p 139; Connor & Combs, New York, NY, U.S.A., 1833

The Conscience of Coralie; F. Frankfort Moore, p 410; Herbert & Stone, Chicago, Il, New York, NY, U.S.A., 1900

The Confessions of James Baptiste Couteau; Robert Jephson; London, U.K., 1794

The Contested Castle: Gothic Novels and the Subversion of Domestic Ideology; Acknowledgements, p vii; Board of Trustees, University of Illinois, Urbana, IL, U.S.A., 1989

The Converted Catholic; James A. O'Connor, Dr. Pentecost's Address; New York, NY, U.S.A., January, 1909

The Correspondence of Sir Philip Sidney and Hubert Languet; Published, London, U.K., 1577

The Cost of a Secret, Vol. III; Isa Blagden, Volume 3, p 33; Chapman and Hall, London, 1863

The Countesse of Pembrokes Arcadiam, Sir Phillip Sidney, London England, 1580

The Coursing Calendar for the Autumn Season 1868, Containing Results of All the Public Courses Run in Great Britain and Ireland; Ed. 'Stonehenge,' p 243; London, U.K., 1869

The Court of the Air; Stephen Hunt; Harper Voyager, London, U.K., 2007

The Craftsman: Being a Critique on the Times, Volume 6; Caleb Danvers at Britain's famous Grey's Innp 235; R. Francklin, London, 1761; Volume XII; Caleb D'Anvers of Grey's Inn, p 297; R. Francklin, London, England, 1737

The Critical Review; Or Annals of Literature, Extended and Improved; by 'A Society of Gentlemen;' Volume II; in 'William's Letters from France,' p 66; Hamilton, London, U.K., 1792

The Cypriad in Two Cantos with Other Poems and Translations; Henry C. Knight; Helena the Grecian Beauty, J, Belcher, Boston, MA, U.S.A., 1809

The Day's Work, Part I, 'The Devil and the Deep Sea;' Rudyard Kipling, pp 186-187; Charles Scribner and Sons, New York, NY, U.S.A., 1909

The Devil Made Me Do It, Georgina Spelvin, Georgina's World, Inc, 2008

The Diaries of Paul Klee (1898-1918), Diary 11; p 102; University of California Press, Berkley and LA, CA, U.S.A., 1964

The Diary of Lady Lucy Cavendish; entry for February 7, 1857, Lucy Cavendish; Frederick A. Stokes Co., New York, NY, U.S.A., 1927

The Dictionary of New Zealand English; Oxford University Press, Oxford, U.K., 1998

The Dr---yt---n Review: Or, Characteristic Sketches; Yorick, Part the First; p 67; William Howell, London, U.K., 1793

The Duty of Executors and Administrators; John Facuhereaud Grimke; T. & J. Swords, New York, NY, U.S.A., 1797

The Dyestuffs of the Berlin Aniline Works; p 12; Berlin, Germany, 1904

The Educational Technology Reviews Series, Using Programed Instruction; p 128; Educational Technoloogy Publications, Englewood Cliffs, NJ, U.S.A, January, 1973

The Egotist: or, Sacred Scroll; annon; Murray and Highley, London, U.K., 1798

The Egyptian Sketchbook*;* Charles G. Leland; Hurd and Haughton, Cambridge, NY, U.S.A., 1874

The Electrical Researches of Henry Cavendish*;* p 309; University Press, Cambridge, U.K., 1879

The Electrical Worker*;* letter from Portland Oregon member W.H. Emrick to the Editor, Springfield, IL, U.S.A., April, 1914

The Encyclopedia Britannica, Volume 1; p 95, Werner and Co., Chicago, IL, U.S.A., 1896

The Endless Moment*;* Wayne C. Allen, p 26; Phoenix Center Press, Waterloo, Ont., Canada, 2005

The English and Dutch Affairs Displayed to the Life, Both in Matters of Warr, State and Merchandize*;* Edward Thomas; Thomas Mabb, London, England, 1664

The English Dialect Dictionary*;* New York, NY, U.S.A., 1902

The English Language in Elements and Forms*;* William Chauncer Fowler; Harper and Brothers, New York, NY, U.S.A., 1861

The Essayes of Montaigne, Vol. 5; Translated by John Floro, p 86: Gibbings & Co., London, England, 1603

The Essays or Counsels, Civil and Moral*;* Francis Bacon; M. Clark, London, England, 1680

The Eye of the Sibyl*;* Philip K. Dick, p 289; Citidel Press, New York, NY, U.S.A., 1992

The Failures of Ethics*: Confronting the Holocaust, Genocide, and Other Mass Atrocities;* John K. Roth; Oxford University Press, Oxford, U.K., 2015

The Falcon, Minnechaug Regional High School yearbook ,Wilbraham, Massachusetts, 1985

The False Prophets of Ecological Apocalypse*;* Ronald Bailey; St. Martin's Press, London, U.K., 1993

The Famous Chronicle of King Edward the First*;* George Peale; London, England, 1593

The Famous Romance of Tarsis and Zell; Roland Le Vayer de Boutigny, translated into English by Charles Williams, Book III, p 247; printed for Nathanial Ponder; London, England, 1685

The Fog*;* William Dudley Pelley; Little, Brown & Co., Boston, MA, U.S.A., 1921

The Forayers: or, The Raid of the Dog-days; William Gilmore Simms, Redfield, New York, NY, U.S.A., 1855

The Foreign Quarterly Review; 'Minch's Studies and Recollections,' p 315; Black and Armstrong, London, U.K., January, 1838

The Forged Note: or Julian and Marianne, A Moral Tale, Founded on Recent Facts; Hannah Maria Jones, J. Jaques and W. Wright; London, U.K., 1824

The Fortunate Country Maid; written in French author credited as L_____ V_____, translated by Charles de Fieux Mouhy; Volume One, p 290; London, England, Hitch & L. Hawes, London, England, 1758

The Foundation of Education for Librarianship; Jesse Hauk Shera, p 433; Becker and Hayes, New York, NY, U.S.A., 1972

The Fourteenth Ohio National Guard; Sergt. Maj. Chas. E. Creager; Landon Printing, Columbus, OH, U.S.A., 1899

The Frauds and Villanies of the Common Practice of Physicke; Rob Pitt, 1705, Preface; John Matthews, London, England, 1705

The Gamblers; or a Treacherous Friend, A Moral Tale, Founded on Recent Facts; author unknown; E. Livermore, London, U.K., 1824

The G.A.P.P., Great American Pity Party and Social Musings; Lee Cain, p 19; iUniverse, Lincoln, NE, U.S.A., 2006

The Gawain Poet, a Critical Study; poem, 'Patience;' A.C. Spearing; Cambridge University Press, Cambridge, U.K., 1970

The Gem of Song, Part First, Containing a Large Collection of Sentimental and National Songs**;** Dream On,' An Amateur' p 75; E. Howe, Boston, MA, U.S.A.,1846

The General Historie of the Turkes from the First Beginning of that Nation to the Rising of the Ottoman Families; Richard Knolls; printed by Adam Islip, Oxford, England, 1610

The General Historie of the Turkes; Richard Knolles; Adam Islip, London, England, 1603

The General Historie of Virginia, New England and the Summer Isles, John Smith, I.D.&H for Michael Sparkes, London, England, 1624

The Golden Spy: Or, a Political Journal of the British Nights Entertainments of War and Peace and Love and Politics; p 149; J. Woodward, London, U.K., 1709

The Grand Debate between the Most Reverend, the Bishops and the Presbyterian Divines, appointed by His Sacred Majesty as Commissioners for the Review and Alterations of the Book of the Common Prayer; p 74; London, England, 1661

The Grand Essay: Or, A Vindication or Reason and Religion against Impostures of Philosophy; W.C. M.D. C.M. L.C.; printed for P.G.; London, England, 1704

The Great All-Star Animal League Ball Game; Vincent Starrett; Dodd, Mead, New York, NY, U.S.A., 1950

The Great Duty of Labour and Work, and the Necessity There is at Present for a General Work-house for the Poor of this Place; John Mickleburgh, p 22; Cambridge, England, 1751

The Great Gospel; Simon Peter Long; Sermons, American Lutheran Church; Lutheran Book Concern, Columbus, OH, U.S.A., 1904

The Great Secret; Osho, ch.10, p 181; India, orig. 1975

The Green Mountain Boys: A Historical Tale of the Early Settlement of Vermont; Daniel Pierce Thompson, p 232; E.P. Walton and Sons, Montpelier, VT, U.S.A., 1839

The Guardian Angel; Oliver Wendell Holmes; Boston, MA, U.S.A., 1867

The Gvnner Shewing the Whole Practise of Artillery; Robert Norton; Humphrey Robinson, London, England, 1638

The Happinesse of Practice: A Sermon on John xiii 17; Samuel Ward, p 19; printed for John Marrot and John Grifmond, London, England, 1622

The Harmonies of Creation; Or, The Music of the Morning Stars; John C. Newman, 'An Address to the Ladies and Gentlemen of Baltimore' p xiv; J.W. Woods, Baltimore, MD, U.S.A., 1836

The Historie and Chronicles of Scotland 1436–1565, Robert Lindsay of Pitscottie, Edinburgh, Scotland, first published 1728

The Historie of Ane Nobil and Walieand Sqviel, William Meldrum; Sir David Lyndesay of the Mont, p 531; Henrie Chartteris, London, England, 1594

The History of John Bull (1667-1735), 1712, p 48, Cassel, London, U.K., 1889

The History of Ophelia, Volume II; p 11; R. Baldwin, London, England, 1760

The History of Scotland, from the year 1423 until the year 1542; p 248; London, England, 1655

The History of Sir William Harrington, Volume I, Second Edition; Thomas Hull, p 226; John Bell, London, U.K., 1772

The History of the Government of France: Under the Administration of the Great Armand Du Plesis, Cardinal and DU.K.e of Richlieu and Chief Minister of State of that Kingdome; Tran. J.D., Esq.; J. Maycock, London, England, 1657

The History of the Kiss; Marcel Danesi; Palgrave McMillan, New York, NY, U.S.A., 2013

The History of the Principality of Wales: In Three Parts; Robert Burton, Second Edition; printed for A. Bettesworth, London, England, 1730

The History of the Most Ingenious Knight, Don Quixote de la Mancha; Miguel de Cervantes Saavedra, translated by Capt. John Stevens, Volume II, p 190; R. Chriswell, London, England, 1706

The History of the Renowned Don Quixote de La Mancha; Miguel de Cervantes Saavedra English translation by 'Several Hands,' Volume II; London, England, 1719

The History of the Trial of Warren Hastings, Esq., Late Governor General of Bengal; London, England, 1796

The Hoosier Volunteer; Kate and Virgil D. Boyles, p 49; A.L. Burt, New York, NY, U.S.A., 1914

The Housekeeper's Instructor, or Universal Family Cook; W.A. Henderson, p 461; J. Stratford, London, U.K., 1895

The Huguenot: A Tale of the French Protestants; (Volumes I, II and III), originally published from 1832-1837, *The Maid of Thilouse* by Honoré de Balzac; English translation by George Payne Rainsford James; London, U.K., 1874

The Human Touch, Carleton Everett Knox; 'Whistle an Old Time Tune', p 29; The Knox Art Co., Kansas City, MO, U.S.A., 1922

The Ideal of a Gentleman; Abram Smith Palmer, DD, p 353; George Rutledge & Sons, London, England, 1586

The Ignorance Explosion: Understanding Industrial Civilization; Julius Lukasiewicz, p 136; Carleton University Press, Ottawa, Canada, 1944

The International Congressional Council, London, 1891; p 179; James Clark & Co., London, U.K., 1891

The Island Treasure; or, Harry Darrel's Fortunes; Frank H. Converse, p 193; A.L. Bert, New York, NY, U.S.A., 1888

The Isaac Question; David S. Brody, chap 4, p 95; Eyes That See Publishing, Westford, CT, U.S.A., 2015

The Jew and the Foundling; Thomas Peckett Prest, p 139; E. Lloyds, London, U.K., 1847

The Job: An American Novel; Sinclair Lewis, p 257; University of Nebraska Press, Lincoln, NE, U.S.A., 1917

The Journal of Education, Volume 37; page 288; London, U.K., 1915

The Keepsake; Frederick A. Heath, Edited by the Late Countess of Blessington, p 2; David Bogue, London, U.K., 1850

The Land Log-book: a Compilation of Anecdotes and Occurrences Extracted from the Journal of the Author; Sarah Hoding, p 15; Simpkin, Marshall & Co., London, U.K., 1836

The Land That Time Forgot; Chap. 4, Edgar Rice Burroughs; McClurg, London, U.K., 1908

The Last American Frontier, Frederick L. Paxson, Simon Publications, New York, NY, 2001

The Last Battell of the Soul in Death; Zacharie Boyd, minister of the Barony Church in Glasgow, Scotland; Edinburgh, Scotland, 1629

The Last Hurrah; Edwin O'Connor, Brown, Little, New York, NY, U.S.A., 1956

The Last Magician; Jeanette Turner Hospital, p 184; University of Queensland Press, St. Lucia, Queensland, AusStralia, 2003

The Last Night of Pompeii; Sumner Lincoln Fairfield; Elliott and Palmer, New York, NY, U.S.A., 1832

The Last Poems of Alice and Phoebe Cary; 'Cottage and Hall,' Cary and Cary; Ed. Mary Clemmer Ames; Hurd and Haughton, New York, NY, U.S.A., 1873

The Letters of Hon. Horace Walpole, to George Montagu, Esq. from the year 1736 to the year 1770; pub. in *The British Critic;* printed for F.C. & J. Rivington; London, U.K., June, 1818

The Library of Romance, Leitch Richie; *The Ghost Hunter and His Family*; The O'Hara Family, p 133; Carey, Lee and Blanchard, Philadelphia, PA, U.S.A., 1833

The Life and Adventures of Dr. Dodimus Duckworth; Asa Greene, p 196; Peter Hill, New York, NY, U.S.A., 1833

The Life and Adventures of Obadiah Benjamin Franklin Bloomfield...Written by Himself; p 138; Philadelphia, PA, U.S.A., 1818

The Life and Adventures of Martin Chuzzlewit; Charles Dickens; Bradbury and Evans, London, U.K., 1844

The Life and Adventures of Valentine Vox, the Ventriloquist; Henry Cockton, p 289, p 508; Willoughby & Co., London, U.K., 1840

The Life and Opinions of Tristam Shandy, Gentleman, Volume I; Laurance Sterne, p 33; J. L. LeGrand, Basil, 1792

The Life and Works of John Arbuthnot, MD, Fellow of the Royal Court of Physicians, George Atherton Aitken, p 107/108; Clarendon Press, Oxford, U.K., 1892

The Life and Writings of Major Jack Downing of Downingville; Seba Smith, p 228; Lillie, Wait, Colman and Holdon, Boston, MA, U.S.A., 1834

The Life of Frederich Schiller; Thomas Carlyle, p 229; Chapman and Hall, Ltd., London, U.K., 1825

The Life of James II, the Late King of England; David Jones, p 347; J. Kanapton, London, England, 1705

The Life of Mr. James Quin, Comedian, with the History of the Stage; J. Bladon, London, England, 1766

The Life of Samuel Johnson, LLD; James Boswell, p 390; Henry Baldwin, London, U.K., 1791

The Life of the Reverend Jonathan Swift; Thomas Sheridan, Second Edition, J.F. & C. Rivington, London, U.K., 1787

The Life of Thomas Dermody Interspersed with Pieces of Original *Poetry*; James Grant Raymond, p 131; William Miller, London, U.K., 1806

The Literary Panorama, Volume XIV; Address, p 1004; London, U.K., 1813

The Logic of Decisions and Actions; Nicholas Rescher, p 67; University of Pittsburg Press, Pittsburg, PA, U.S.A., 1967

The Long Trick; 'Bartimeus,' Chapter IV, War Babies, p 79; George H. Doran and Co., New York, NY, U.S.A., 1917

The Love Match; Henry Cockton; Burgess, Stringer and Co., New York, NY, U.S.A., 1845

The Lusiad; or, the Discovery of India: an Epic Poem; Luís de Camões, translated into English by William Julius Mickle, Dissertation, p ccxv; London, Jackson and Lister, London, U.K., 1778

The Magic Journey, A Novel; John Nichols, p 241, p 248; Holt, Rinehart and Winston, New York, NY, U.S.A., 1978,

The Magnetic North; Elizabeth Robins, p 42; Frederick A. Stokes Co., New York, NY, U.S.A., 1904

The Making of a Scientist; Anne Roe, Dodd Mead, New York, NY, U.S.A., 1953

The Manners of the Age in Thirteen Moral Satirs, Sat VII; Thomas Newcomb; Jer. Batley, London, England, 1733

The Men in the Jungle; Norman Spinrad; Leisure Books, Cape Town, South Africa, 1967

The Message: A Conversation with Christ and the Events That Preceded It; Peter Mercuro, Second Session; Dog Ear Publishing, Indianapolis, IN, USA, 2007

The Metal; John Dryden; London, England, 1682

The Michigan Technic; Engineering Management Decisions; Bryan Whipple; Ann Harbor, MI, U.S.A., May, 1958

The Minnesota Community: Country and Town in Transition; Lowry Nelson, p 54; University of Minnesota Press, Minneapolis, MN, U.S.A., 1960

The Militarizarion of South African Politics; Kenneth W Grundy, p 85; I. B. Tauris and Co., Ltd, London, U.K., 1986

The Mirror of Literature, Amusement and Instruction; 'The Sketch-Book' p 45; Columbia College, New York, NY, U.S.A., July 19. 1828; 'Memoirs of Vidoco, The French Thief Taker,' John Limbird; London, U.K., December 20, 1828

The Monthly Review Enlarged, Seventh-Eighth Volume Appendix; Ralph Griffiths; Beckett and Porter, London, U.K., 1815

The Mythologizing of Mark Twain; Sara Davis, p 65; University of Alabama Press, TUScaloosa, AL, U.S.A., 1984

The Money Question; William A. Berkey, p 413; W.W. Hart Steam Book, Grand Rapids, MI, U.S.A., 1876

The Morte Arthure; Ed. E.J. Brock, London, England, 1440

The Moving Picture Boys on the Warfront; 'Victor Appleton,' p 84; Grosset and Dunlap, New York, NY, U.S.A., 1918

The Muses Mirror: Being a Collection of Poems, Vol II; 'The Noble Game of Cricket,' p 180; Royal Exchange, London, U.K., 1783

The Mysteries of London; George W. M. Reynolds, 1845, Volume I, Chapter LXVII, p 210; George Vickers, London, U.K., 1845

The Mystery of Sacrifice, A Meditation on the Liturgy, Evelyn Underrhill; Chapter One; Longmans, Green & Co., Richmond, VA, U.S.A., 1938

The Mythology and Fables of the Ancients; the Abbe Banier, London, England, 1739

The New Covenant, or, the Saints' Portion, 5th Edition; corrected, John Preston, p 476; I.D. for Nicholas Bourne, London, England, 1630 (Original, 1629)

The New Idea of Astronomy, p 40, D. Woodwell Hunt, Bacceton Scofield and Co., San Francisco, CA, U.S.A, 1878

The New Song Era; 'Dream On, A Serenade,' Frederic W. Root, p 74, J. Church, Cincinnati, OH, U.S.A., 1877

The New World of English Words, Or, A General Dictionary; E.P.; Nath. Brook, London, England, 1663

The New York Court of Appeals, Records and Briefs; pp 17-18; Albany, NY, U.S.A., 1943

The New York Supplement, Volume 46; Dunn et el v. Wehle, Supreme Court, Appellate Term, July 29, 1897; W.C. Little and Co., Albany, NY, U.S.A., 1897

The Nine Tailors; Dorothy Lee Sayors, 1934, p 194; Harvest Books, Orlando, FL, U.S.A., 1962

The Official Report of the Annual Meeting of the Church *Congress;* 'Middle Class Education and the Bristol Diocesan Trade School,' Rev. Preb. Brereton; Bristol, U.K., October 13, 1864

The Old Cevenol, Jean-Paul Rabaut Saint-Etienne, France, 18th century, English translation; Standard Pub., Cincinnati, OH, U.S.A., 1911

The Orphan, or, Memoirs of Matilda; Eugene Sue; trans. by the Honorable D.G. Osborne, Volume I, p 303; T.C. Newby, London, U.K., 1846

The Overthrow of the Protestants Pulpit-Babels; John Floyd, pp 322, 323; London, U.K., 1612, (Scolar Press facsimile)

The Oxford Entertaining Miscellany, Volume 1; F. Trash, Oxford, London, U.K., 1894

The Oxford Thackery, Volume IV; p 442; Oxford University Press, Oxford, U.K., 1829

The Parlimentary Debates of Great Britain, from the 24th Day of June to the 29th Day of July, 1864; p 1503; Cornelius Buck, London, U.K., 1864

The Parliamentary Register; Or, History of the Proceedings and Debates of the House of Commons; p 207; London, U.K., 1791

The Parriana or Notices of the Rev. Samuel Parr, LLD; and in part written by E.S. Barker, Esq., Vol. II; John Bohn, London, U.K., 1829

The Parson's Tale, Geoffrey Chaucer, London, England, c 1390

The Parterre of Poetry and Historical Romance: With Essays, Sketches and Anecdotes; Effingham Wilson, Junior, Volume Five, p 218, Manning and Smithson, London, U.K., 1836

The Passage; Vance Palmer, Australia, 1930; Halstead Press, Sydney, Australia, 2001

The Permanent Record of Queen Victoria's State Visit to Derby; Derby, Ireland, 1891

The Prerogative of Popular Government; James Harrington, p xiii; London, England, 1658

The Petition Apolojeticall of Lay Papists, Calling Themselves the Lay Papists, calling themselves the Lay Catholics of England; William Cotton and William Welby, London, England, 1606

The Pilgrim's Progress; John Bunyon; printed for A.W. & J. Clarke; London, England, 1743

The Pinecone, yearbook, Dorothy Ogletree entry, p 34; Georgia State Women's College, Valdosta State University, Valdosta, GA, U.S.A., 1935

The Pioneers, or the Sources of the Susquehanna; a Descriptive Tale; James Fenimore Cooper, p 156; John Murray, London, U.K., 1823

The Playground; or, the Boy's Book of Games; George Forrest, Chap. IV; p 42; G. Rutledge and Co., London, U.K., New York, NY, U.S.A., 1858

The Plays of William Shakespeare; 'The Historical Account from the English Stage, Vol. II; Malone, London, U.K., 1793

The Poems of John Dryden; ed. John Sargeaunt, *Absalom and Achitophel,* p 51; Henry Frowde; Oxford University Press, London, U.K., 1905

The Poetic Melange, Volume II; George A. Douglas; Edinburgh, Scotland, U.K., 1828

The Polar Star or Entertainment and Popular Science, Vol. II; 'Prosers of all Kinds,' p 148; H. Flower, London, U.K., 1830

The Political and Miscellaneous Works of Thomas Paine, Volume II; 'Speech on the Constitution,' read July 7. 1775; R. Carlisle, London, U.K., 1819

The Poor White: or, The Rebel Conscript; Emily C. Pearson; Graves and Young, Boston, MA, U.S.A., 1864

The Post Captain; or, the Wooden Walls Well Manned; Comprehending a View of Naval Society and Manners; John Davis, London, U.K., 1804

The Posthumous Papers of the Pickwick Club; Charles Dickens (1837), p 62; Galignani & Co., Paris, France, 1838

The Present State of Europe Volume IV; for the month of January, 1693, Henry Rhodes; London England, 1693

The Principles of Natural and Revealed Religion Occasionally Opened and Explained in a Course of Sermons Preached before the Honorable Society of Lincolns Inn, in Two Volumes, Volume the First; Reverend Mr. Warburtin; J. & P. Knapton, London, England, 1753

The Principles of Population and Production as They are Affected by the Progress of Society; John Weyland; Baldwin, Craddock and Joy, London, U.K., 1816

The Proceedings of the Annual Conclave of the Great Commandery Knights Templar of the State of Mississippi; Held at Natchez, Thursday and Friday, May 10th and 11th; p 74; Jackson, MS, U.S.A., 1877

The Palace Miscellany; 'The Progress of Matrimony,' Canto II; p 35; J. Dormer, London, England, 1733

The Proceedings of the Iowa Academy of Science for 1895, Volume III; Annual Address to the President, H. W. Norris; Des Moines, IA, U.S.A., 1896

The Promptorum Parvulorum Sive Clericorum; p 153; London, England, 1440

The Proverbs, Epigrams and Miscellanies of John Heywood; Early English Drama Society, London, England, 1562

The Proverbs of John Heywood: Being the 'Proverbes' of that Author Printed 1546; London, England, 1546

The Rambler; Samuel Johnson, first published in 1750, p 286; John & Co., London, U.K., 1825

The Red Dawn; Stewart Edward White, p 141; Doubleday, Page & Co., Garden City, New York, 1920

The Red Stockings of Cincinnati: Base Ball's First All-Professional Team; Stephen D. Guschov, p 115; McFarland & Co., Jefferson, NC, U.S.A., 1998

The Reign of Henry II; 'The Battaile of Crescey;' Charles Aleyn, p 43; London, England, 1633

The Religion Virus; Craig A. James, p 73; Create Space, Charleston, SC, U.S.A., 2010

The Rights, powers, and Priviledges, of an English Convocation; Francis Atterbury, Preface, p xxxvi; Thos. Bennett, London, England, 1701

The Road of the Rough; Maurice M. Minton, 1893, p 74; The Illustrated American Publishing Co., New York, NY, U.S.A., 1893

The Royal Rake: and the Adventures of Albert Chesterton; William Leman Rede, p 149; Chapman and Elcoate, London, U.K., 1842

The Rule and Exercise of Holy Dying…Together with Prayers and Acts of Virtue; Jeremy Taylor, DD, p 128; Longman, Hurst, Rees, Orme and Brown, London, U.K., 1812

Thesaurus; Thomas Cooper; London, U.K., 1565

The Science of Getting Rich; Wallace D. Wattles, p 29; Elizabeth Townes Co., New York, NY, U.S.A., 1910

The Scotch Rogue, or Life and Actions of Donald MacDonald; Donald Macdonald, p 66; Robert Gifford, London, England, 1706

'***The Secret Service Old and Young King Brady Detectives'*** story, *The Bradys and the 'Chink' Smugglers; Or The Hurry Call to Canada;* Frank Tomacy, p 18; New York, NY, U.S.A., April 5, 1907

The Slang Dictionary, Etymological, Historical and Anecdotal, a New Edition; Chatto & Windus, Piccadilly, London, U.K., 1873

The Soccer Tribe; Desmond Morris; Cape, London, U.K., 1981

The Sound Believer, A Treatise of Evangelicall Conversion; Thomas Shepphard; printed for R. Dowlman, London, England, 1645

The Southwest Reporter; Casanova v State; April 14—May 5, 1920

The Spirit of the Public Journals for 1797, Volume I, 3rd Edition; letter to the editor of the Morning Chronicle; printed for James Ridgeway, London, U.K., 1802

The Spirit of the Public Journals for 1798, Volume II, New Edition; 'A Consolitory Address to his Gunboats;' Sitizen Muskein, p 284; London, U.K., 1805

The Sportsman's Directory or Park and Groundkeeper's Companion, 3rd Edition; John Mayer; Baldwin Cradock and Joy, London, U.K., 1819

The State: Elements of Historical and Practical Politic; Woodrow Wilson, p 235; DC Heath and Co., Boston, MA, U.S.A., 1898, 1911

***The Steele Glas;* George Gascoigne**; London, England, 1567

The Story of a Spring Morning and Other Tales, Mary Louisa Molesworth, The Mysterious Guide, p 315; Longman, Green and Co., London, U.K., 1890

The Strength of Gideon: And Other Stories; Paul Laurence Dunbar; Dodd, Mead & Co., New York, NY, U.S.A., 1900

The Stricket Minister: And Some Common Men; Samuel Rutherford Crockett, p 62; MacMillan and Co., New York, NY, U.S.A., 1894

The String of Beads for the Romanisers; Peter Plapet (pseudonym), p 33; J. Hatchard and Son, London, U.K., 1844

The Submissions of Dependence, A Novel, Interspersed with Poetry; p 89; Hookham and Carpenter, London, U.K., 1797

The Sunset Trail; Alfred Henry Lewis, p 349; A.L. Burt and Co., New York, NY, U.S.A., 1905

The Supremity of Mind: A Lecture; Reverend Samuel W. Fisher, p 20; Monsell and Tanner, Albany, NY, U.S.A., 1845

The Tattler; or, Lucubrations of Isaac Bickerstaff; Isaac Bidkerstaff, p 97; R. Tonson & Others, London, England, 1764

The Tattler; Isaac Bickerstaff, Memoirs of Sir Richard Steele, p 74; J. Parsons, London, U.K., 1994

The Tears, Sighs, Complaints, and Prayers of the Church of England; John Gauden, p 466; Church of England, London, England, 1659

The Tenth Man; Edward Francis Murphy, p 21; Dolphin Press, Philadelphia, PA, U.S.A., 1937

The Thesaurus of English Words and Phrases; Peter Mark Roget; Sheldon and Co., New York, NY, U.S.A., 1878

The Third American Edition of Nicholson's British Encyclopedia; or Dictionary of the Arts and Sciences; Physiology; W. Brown; Philidelphia, PA, U.S.A., 1821

The Thoughts of Cicero (Roman philosopher, 106 BCE – 43 BCE); London 'On Probability,' English trans., J. Newberry, p 127; London, England, 1750

The Tramp and His Woman; Dorothy Charquez, p 18; Macmillan Co., New York NY, U.S.A., 1937

The Travels of Antenor in Greece and Asia; Étienne-François de Lantie, English translation, E. F. Lantier, p 46; London, U.K., 1799

The True and the False: The Domain of the Pragmatic; Charles Travis, p 5; John Benjamins Publishing Co., Amsterdam, Holland, 1981

The Tryal of Nathaniel Reading, Esq. for Attempting to Stifle the King's Evidence as to the Horrid Plot; Robert Powlet; London, England, 1679

The Trimming of Thomas Nash, Gentleman; Ricardo de Medico Simpkin, p iv, p 17; Philip Scarlet, London, England, 1597

The True Anti-Pamela, Second Edition; James Parry, p 115; London, England, 1742

The Tyde tarryeth No Man; John Payne Collier; Hugh Jackson, London, England, 1576

The Tryal of Thomas, Earl of Stafford, Lord Lieutenant of Ireland, upon Impeachment of High Treason; p 229; printed for John Wright, London, England, 1680

The Universal Songster; Or, Museum of Myrth; Routledge, London, U.K., 1832

The Urgent Task of Homiletics; a seminary textbook; Jay Edward Adams; Zondervan, Grand Rapids, MI, U.S.A., 1982

The U.S. at 200; Compiled by Sharifah Abdulah, p 201; Singapore University Press, Kent Ridge, Singapore, 1978

The Vocabulary of East Anglia; Robert Forby; London, U.K., 1830

The Waverly Novels; The Heart of Mid-Lothian; Sir Walter Scott, p 173; Waddell and Co., Edinburgh, Scotland, 1830 *Waverly Novels*; *Tales of My Landlord*; *Count Robert of Paris*, Sir Walter Scott; Chap. XIV, p 187; Baudry's Foreign Library, Paris, France, 1831

The Way to Christ Discovered; Jacob Boehme, p 222; Joseph Harrop, Manchester, England, 1752

The Way to Wealth; Benjamin Franklin; Philadelphia, PA, U.S.A., 1758; reprint: Applewood Books, Carlisle, MA. U.S.A., 1986

The West Australian Settler's Guide and Farmer's Handbook; L. Lindsay-Cowen; E.S. Wigg & Son, Perth, Australia, 1897

The Wharton's Sketch Book; Jim and Phil Wharton, 'Coaches' Notes, p 139; The Rivers Press, New York, NY, U.S.A., 1996

The White Rose of York; Edited by George Hogarth, pp 30, 31; printed for John Murray, London, U.K., 1834

The Whole World is Watching, Mass Media in the Making; Todd Gitlin, p 224; University of California Press, Berkley and Los Angeles, CA, U.S.A., 1980

The Wit and Wisdom of Mark Twain; edited by Alex Ayers; Harper and Row, New York, NY, U.S.A., 1987

The Wits Paraphrased: Or, Paragrafe upon Paragrafe in a Berlesque on the Several late Translations of Ovids Epistles; Printed for Will. Cademan, London, England, 1680

The Woman in the Yard; Stephen E. Miller, p 68; First Edition, St. Martin's Press, Pan Books, Ltd., New York, NY, U.S.A., April, 1999

The Workes of that Late Learned Minister of God's Holy Word, William Pemble; p 69; Printed by Henry Hall for John Adams, Oxford, U.K., 1659

The Works: Containing His Plays and Poems; George Etherege, 'Love in a Tub,' Act III, Scene vii; London, U.K., 1794

The Works of Charles Dickens; Chapter LIV, Vol. 4; p 350; Getz and Buck, Philidelphia, PA, U.S.A., 1854

The Works of Dr. Jonathan Swift, Volume V, p 165, C. Bathurst, London, England, 1766

The Works of Francis Rabelias; Navarre Society, London, England, 1653

The Works of George Whitefield, Volume II; p 362, Letter to Mr. B_____, dated June 29, 1750; Edward and Charles Dilly, London, U.K., 1771

The Works of John Ruskin, Vol. 5, Fors Cavigera; John Ruskin, p 187; George Allen, Kent, England, U.K., 1875

The Works of Maria Edgefield, Volume VII; 'Patronage,' p 239; Samuel H. Parker, Boston, MA, U.S.A., 1825

The Works of Mr. Francis Rabelais, doctor in physick, Volume II; Francis Rabelias, pp 298, 299; Navere Society, Ltd., London, England, 1653

The Works of John Dryden, Volume XVII; Letter II; London, U.K., 1808:

The Works of John Knox; 'A Godly Letter to the Faithful in London,' 1548, p 170; published in Edinburgh, Scotland, U.K., 1853

The Works of Molière, Volume X; p 134; 'Psyche,' 1671, Act V, Scene iii, J.B.P Molière; first printed Paris, France, c 1739

The Works of Mons. de la Bruyere; Jean de la Bruyere, a Translation from the last Paris Edition by N. Rowe, Esq.; Printed for D. Brown, London, England, 1752

The Works of Mr. Frank Beaumont and Mr. John Fletcher, Volume the Eighth; "Women Pleased," Act I, Scene iii, A 'Tragi-Comedy; printed for J. & R. Tonson and S. Draper, London, England, 1750

The Works of the Most Reverend John Tillotson, Late Lord Archbishop of Canterbury; p 1417; London, U.K., 1757

The Works of Thomas More, Knyght, Sometyme Lorde; London, England, 1557

The Works of Thomas Moore; poem, 'Tom Cribs Memorial to Congress'; p 515; Ernst Fletcher, Leipsic, Germany, 1826

The Works of William Bridge; William Bridge, p 34; Peter Cole, London, England, 1654

The World of London, John F. Murray, William Blackwood & Sons, London, U.K., 1843

The Writings and Prose of Rudyard Kipling, The Man Who Would Be King; 1888, 1895, McMillian and Co., p 197; Charles Scribner's Sons, New York, NY, U.S.A., 1911

The Year 2000 Problem Solver: A Five Step Disaster Prevention Plan; p 11; McGraw Hill, New York, NY, U.S.A., 1997

The Young Hypocrite; Samuel Foote; London, U.K., 1762

Thirtheism Charges upon Doctor Sherlock's New Notion of the Trinity; Robert South, p 249; John Whitlock, London, England, 1695

Three Elephant Power and Other Stories; A. B. 'Banjo' Paterson, first published in 1917, p 38; Hayes Barton Press, Raleigh, NC, U.S.A., 2007

Three Lives for Mississippi; William Bradford Huie, p 81; WWC Books, 1965; University Press of Mississippi, Jackson, MS, U.S.A., 2000

Trumbull Park, Frank London Brown; Regnery, Chicago, IL, U.S.A., 1959

Time Must Have a Stop; Aldous Huxley, Dalkey Press, p 115; Chicago, IL, U.S.A., 1944

To Diapheronta, or Divine Characters, in Two Parts; Samuel Crook and Christopher Barker, chap. XI, Part 1, p 105; printed for Adimiram Byfield, London, England, 1658

To Keera with Love: Abortion, Adoption or Keeping the Baby: the Story of One Teen's Choices; Kayla M. Becker with Connie K Heckert: Sheed and Ward, Kansas City, MO, U.S.A., 1987

Totemwell; George Payson, p 166; Riker, Thorne and Co., New York, NY, U.S.A., 1854

Traité de la Vérité de la Religion Chrétienne; Jacques Abbadie, Ch. 2; Chez Reinier Leers; Rotterdam, Holland, 1684

Transactions of the Asiatic Society of Japan from 30th October 1872 to 9th October 1873; 'The Games and Sports of Japanese Children'; Professor W.E. Griffis, p 151; Yokahama, Japan in 1874

Transactions of the Section on Laryngology, Otology and Rhinology; American Medical Assn., Chicago, IL, U.S.A., 1822

Transitions of the Department of Agriculture of the State of Illinois; Springfield, IL, U.S.A., 1880

Travels in America performed in the year 1806 for the purpose of Exploring the Rivers Allegheny, Monongahela, Ohio and Mississippi; Thomas Ashe p 225; Richard Phillips, London, U.K., 1808

Travels in Russia, &c, &c; William Rae Wilson, Esq. F.S.A., p 316; Longman, Rees, Orme, Brown and Green, London, U.K., 1828

Travels of Four Years and a Half in the United States of America; p 427; John Davis E. Edwards, London, U.K., 1803

Travels Through the South of France and in the Interior Provinces of Provence and Languedoc; Ninian Pinkney; p 22; T. Purday and Son, London, U.K., 1809

Treasure Island; Robert Lewis Stevenson, Ch. 19; Cassell and Co., London, U.K., 1883

Trials of the Persons Concerned in the Late Riots, Before Chief Justice of Great Britain; p 10; P. Rose, London, England, 1832

Trina Wants to be a Duck; 'C Card', p 18; Trafford Publishing, Victoria, BC, Canada, 2007

Truth's Triumph: Or, A Witness to the Two Witnesses from that Unfolded; Thomas Tomkinson, written in 1676, Ch. VII, p 315; W. Smith, London, England, 1690

Twenty Years in Wall Street; Henry Clews; Irving Publishing Co., New York, NY, U.S.A., 1888

***Twilight of the Idols**, or, How to Philosophize with a Hammer;* 1888, Germany; trans. R. J. Hollingdale, London, U.K., 1889

Two Proposals Humbly Offer'd to the Honorable Houfe of Commons, Now Assembled in Parliament, London, England, 1696

Uneasy Rider; Mark Bryan, p 313; Alfred A. Kompf, New York, NY, U.S.A., 1977

United States Army in Vietnam 1965-1973; Jeffery J. Clark; Center of Military History, Washington, DC, U.S.A., 1988

Unspotted from the World, A.C. Stevenson, p 48; F. Tennyson Neely, New York, NY, U.S.A., 1899

Up: A Little Book of Talks on how to Wake Up, Get Up, Think Up, Climb Up; George Mathew Adams, p 108; The Reiley and Lee Co., Chicago, IL, U.S.A., 1920

U.S. Intelligence Agencies and Activities, Committee Procedings; U.S. House of Representatives, 94th Congress (September, October and November); Washington, DC, U.S.A., 1976

U. S. Policy in Central America: The Endless Debate; Dario Moreno, p 78; Florida International University Press, Miami, FL, U.S.A., 1990

Van Cleve; Mary S. Watts, p 212; Macmillan & Co., New York, NY, U.S.A., 1913

Very Hard Cash: A Novel; Charles Reed, p 42; Chatto and Windus, Picadilly, London, U.K., 1864

Victoria Parliamentary Debates Session 1872; Vol. XV; Melbourne, Australia, 1872

Village Verse Srories and Other Poems; Crawford C. Slack, p 43. Athens, ON, Canada, 1890

Vindiciœ veritatis: a narrative vindicating the truth; John Humphreys, p 12; London, England, 1680

Violence by youth gangs and youth groups as a crime problem in major American cities; p 41; U.S. Department of Justice, Law Enforcement Administration, Office of Juvenile Justice and Delinquancy Pervention, Washington, DC, U.S.A., 1975

Vulgaria; Robert Whittington; London, England, 1520

Warfare, Recreation and Morale, United States Army, Washington, DC, U.S.A., March, 1985

Warren-Adams Letters; (letters between U.S. President John Adams, Samuel Adams and James Warren); U.S.A., 1743-1777

Washington's War on Nicaragua; Holly Sklar, p 333; South End Press, Cambridge, MA, U.S.A., 1988

Wayward the Wake, "Last of the English;" Charles Kingsley, p 97; McMillan & Co., London, U.K., 1831

Westminster Abby; Emma Robinson, Volume I; p 282; John Mortimore, London, U.K., 1854

We Too Are the People; Louise Van Voorhis Armstrong, pp 441, 442; Little, Brown & Co., Boston, MA, U.S.A., June, 1938

What Economists Think of the Kelley Resale Price; Bill Carol W. Doton, Mass Tech; *New York Court of Appeals Records and Briefs*, p 24; Albany, NY, U.S.A., 1935

What's for Dinner*;* James Schuyler and James McCourt; NYRB, New York, NY, U.S.A., 1978

What the Best CEOs Know*;* Jeffery E, Krames, p 6; McGraw Hill, New York, NY, U.S.A., 2003

While the Billy Boils*;* Henry Lawson; Angus and Robertson, Sidney, Australia, 1896

Whimwhams; 'Four of us;' G.S. Goodrich, Boston, MA, U.S.A.; A.K. Newman and Co. London, U.K., 1828

Who Gave Pinta to the Santa Maria; Robert S. Desowitz; W.W. Norton, New York, NY, U.S.A., 1980

Who Governs Scotland*;* Alex Wright, p 168; Rutledge, London, U.K., 2005

Who Said that First*,* Max Cryer, Gobbledygook, p 82; Summersdale Publishers, Ltd., West Sussex, U.K., 2010, 2011

Whose Revolution?: A Study in the Future Course of Liberalism in the United States*;* Roger N. Baldwin and Alfred M. Bingham, p 81; Howell Soskin, New York, NY, U.S.A., 1941

Why Time Begins on Opening Day*;* Thomas Boswell, p 168; Doubleday, New York, NY, U.S.A., 1984

Wilhelm Meister's Apprenticeship and Travels, Volume II, Book VII; Johann Wolfgang von Goethe, first published 1795-1796, as trans. by Thomas Carlyle, p 120; Chapman and Hall, London, U.K.

Wines and Vines of California; Frona Eunice Wait, p 214; The Bancroft Co., San Francisco, CA, U.S.A., 1889

Wit and Mirth or Pills to Purge Melancholy; 'A Prologue Spoken like A Scotch Highlander' p 348; W. Pearson, London, England, 1719

With Harp and Crown; Walter Besant and John Rice, p 106; Chatto and Windus, London, U.K., 1800

Wobegon Boy*;* Garrison Keillor; Penguin Books Ltd., London, U.K., 1996

Works of British Poets: With Prefaces, Volume Eight*;* compiled by Robert Anderson, MD, p 56; printed for John & Arthur Arch, London, U.K., 1795,

Works of Fisher Ames*;* in Letters, p 515; T. B. Watt, Boston, MA, U.S.A., 1809

World Without End; Grant M. Overton, p 25; Doubleday, Page & Co., Garden City, NY, U.S.A., 1921

Writings; George Washington, G. P. Putnam's Sons, New York, NY, U.S.A., 1793-1799

Writings of Benjamin Franklin; letter to Benjamin Vaughn dated March 14, 1785; edited by Albert H. Smyth, Volume 9, p 293; McMIllian, New York, NY, USA, 1906

You and Me Both, "Including You and Me," Strickland W. Gillian, P 22, Forbes and Co., Chicago. IL, U.S.A., 1916

You'll Never Eat Lunch in This Town Again, Julia Phillips, Random House, New York, NY, U.S.A., 1991

Zadig: The Book of Fate, An Oriental History; Voltaire, English Translation, p 53; John Brindley, London, England, 1749

Zingis, A Tragedy in Five Acts; Alexander Dow, London, England, 1769

Zollenstein; W.M.B. Ferguson, p 7; D. Appleton & Co., New York, NY, U.S.A., 1908

Miscellaneous

Allen Kay; Manhattan ad exec slogan for New York MTA, NY, U.S.A., 2001

Appalachian Stories Quotes and Antecdotes online blog, Dave Tabler

Barry Popik of the American Dialect Society: quote from comedian Martin Lawrence, when talking to *Entertainment Weekly* in 1994 about his Fox sitcom

Contingent Fees, an Address to the Graduating Class of 1905, Being One of the Lectures of the Hubbard Course of Legal Ethics by Irving G. Vann, LLD, Associate Judge of the Court of Appeals, Albany, NY, U.S.A., 1905

Cook Coos, syndicated column, Ted Cook, February, 1931

ESPN article, ***The History and the Mystery of the High Five;*** online July 39, 2011

"Holt, Alfred." Review of the Progress of Steam Shipping during the last Quarter of a Century," Minutes of Proceedings of the Institution of Civil Engineers, Vol. LI, Session 1877–78—Part I, at 2, 8 (November 13, 1877 session, published 1878)
If You're Not Living on the Edge, You're Tasking up Too Much Space, YouTube Film Courage film by Tiffany Shlain, 2015

Instagram posting: attribution of saying to 07-09-93, subscriber genernow

Letter by Fr. Gilbert White, 1763

Meanings and Origins of Australian Words; Australian National Dictionary Center online

Motto, British Royal Air Force, *Per ardua ad astra*

Nike slogan, campaign, 1988-

Otago; Its Goldfields & Resources, Vol. 6, no. 10; Hocken Pamphlet Collection; Melbourne, Australis, W. H. Williams, 1862

Poster: WW II: If you must talk, tell it to the marines

Quote, 'Aero Windmaker' pseudonym, modern Chinese language expert

Quote attributed to Elbert Hubbard (1856-1915)

Quote, Coach Jimmy Johnson, Dallas Cowboys locker room, Candlestick Park after 30-20 NFC Championship Victory over San Francisco 49ers, January 17, 1993

Quote: Edgar Bergan, dummy, Mortimer Sneed, 1030s-1840s

Quote: George Bernard Shaw

Quote: Henry 'Ole Pete' Peterson, 1974

Quote: H. R. Haldeman, Nixon Chief of Staff

Quote Investigator website: http://quoteinvestigator.com/2013/12/11/cannot-fool/

Quote: Irish Central, irishcentral.com

Quote; Jesse Ventura, American wrestler, political commentator

Quote: Julia Turner, Slate online magazine

Quote: Marcus Tullius Cicero; Rome, 106 BCE – 43 BCE

Quote: Mark Shields, American political columnist and commentator

Quote: Professor John McWhorter

Quote: Randy Jackson, American Idol, NBC TV

Quote: Rob Waugh, DailyMail.com, May 16, 2012

Quotes from various Ancient Greek and Roman Philosophers: Hesiod, Lucian, Plutarch, Sophacles, Plato, Aristotle, Horase, Ausonius, and Suidas: numerous works: (see: Well begun is half done)

Quote: Socrates (496-406 BCE)

Quotes: Thomas Jefferson, letter to George Ticknor November 25, 1817; letter to Joseph C. Cabell, January 22, 1820

Quote: Volleyball great, Gabrielle Reece

Quote, Walter Skeat, London, U.K., 1895

Sammy Hagar, Are We Having Fun Yet website

Sceptictank.org, Greenpease U.S.A. quote

Speech, Winston Churchill; Fulton, MO, U.S.A., March 5. 1946

Suppose; 1902, discovered by Joanne Despres of Merriam-Webster

The Inquisitive Man; fable by Ivan Andreevich Krylov, Russia, 1814

The Official Report of the Annual Meeting of the Church Congress; 'Middle Class Education and the Bristol Diocesan Trade School,' Rev. Preb. Brereton, October 13, 1864

The Online Slang Dictionary; onlineslangdictionary.com/meaning-definition-of/grape-smugglers, April 10, 1998

The Presidential Incentive for Making .08 BAC the National Legal Limit Recommendations from the Secretary of Transportation, Washington, DC, U.S.A., 1998

The Windmill; (short story) M.T. Shanley, in *The National Times*, Brisbane, Australia 25 January 1985

Thorleif Schjelderup-Ebbe; PHD dissertation; 1921

TOCWC – A Civil War Blog, Fred Ray, 'Origin of Sharpshooter,' Sept. 23, 2006

todayifoundout.com: 'How XOXO Came to Mean Hugs and Kisses'

U.S. Department of Agriculture Technical Bulletin 206, p 106; Washington, DC, U.S.A., November, 1930

Usernet posting by 'David Jakovak,' February, 1995

Usernet posting by "Ernst Berg" December, 1994

University of Ohio football website: http://beatmichigan.osu.edu/history

U.S. Dept. of Homeland Security Campaign, Washington, DC, U.S.A., 2010

Vegemite jingle, 1950s

Wndu.com/news, "Dealing with 'Porch Pirates';" December 9, 2013

Writings of William of Ockham (c 1285-1348 CE)

Zippy the Pinhead cartoon, Bill Griffith, 1979

Movies and TV Shows

All the President's Men; Docudrama; Robert Redford, Dustin Hoffman, dir. Alan J. Pakula, Warner Bros., Hollywood, CA, U.S.A., 1976

Alright Already; sitcom, Carol Leifer, Amy Yasbech, The WB, Hollywood, CA, U.S.A., 9-7-1997—5- 4-1998

Arsenio Hall Show, CBS TV, Hollywood, CA, U.S.A., 1989-1994

A Walk on the Wild Side, Movie, Lawrence Harvey, Jane Fonda, Anne Baxter, Barbara Stanwyck, Columbia Pictures, Hollywood, CA, U.S.A., 1962

Bikie Wars: Brothers in Arms; Australian TV series, 2012-

Blade Runner, Harrison Ford, Rutger Hauer, pro. Michael Deeley, dir. Ridley Scott; Ladd Co., Warner Bros.' Hollywood, CA, U.S.A., 1982

Contact; starring Jodie Foster, dir. Robert Zemeckis, Warner Bros., Hollywood, CA, U.S.A., 1997

Damaged Goods; American silent short film; dir. Tom Rickets; Richard Bennett; starring Richard Bennett; Mutual Film Corp., Hollywood, CA, U.S.A., 1914

Damaged Goods; British silent version; Wolf and Freeman Films, London, U.K., 1919

Damaged Goods; American sound film; dir. Phil Gladstone; Grand National Pictures, Hollywood, CA, U.S.A., 1937

Dennis Myers Comedy Routine; SNL, NBCTV, Hollywood, CA, U.S.A. 1991

Empty Nest; starring Richard Mulligan and Dinah Manoff, NBC TV sitcom, Hollywood, CA, U.S.A., 1988-1995

Futurama, cre. Matt Groening, voice Billy West; 20th Century Fox TV, Hollywood, CA, U.S.A., 1999-2003

Gone With the Wind; Vivian Leigh quote as Scarlet O' Hara, MGM, Hollywood, CA, U.S.A., 1939

Grey Nomads; Marciniak and Steve Westh, Doc., Australian public TV, ABC, 1997-

Heathers; Daniel Walters; starring Shannon Dougherty, Winona Ryder, Christian Slater; New World Pictures, Hollyood, CA, U.S.A., 1988

How Sweet it Is! Movie, James Garner, Debbie Reynolds, National General Pictures, Hollywood, CA, U.S.A., 1968

It's a Wonderful Life; starring James Stewart, Donna Reed, Henry Travers; dir., Frank Capra, RKO Radio Pictures, Hollywood, CA, U.S.A., 1946

La Shchiava del Pecato, Silvana Pampanini, Franco Fabrizi; dir. Raffaello Matazzo; Titanus Studios, Rome, Italy, May 8, 1954

Listen Darling; Judy Garland, MGM, Hollywood, CA, U.S.A., 1938

Living with Ed; Ed Bagley, Jr., Home and Garden TV, Planet Green, Silver Spring, MD, U.S.A., January 1, 2007 – May 14, 2010

Love Story; Ali McGraw, Ryan O'Neal, Paramount Pictures, Hollywood, CA, U.S.A., 1970

Merry Andrew; Dir. Michael Kidd, starring Danny Kaye, Pier Angeli, MGM, Hollywood, CA, U.S.A., 1958

Mommie Dearest; Faye Dunaway, Diana Scarwid; MGM, Hollywood, CA, 1981

NBC Nightly News; New York, NY, U.S.A., Friday January 23rd, 2016

NBC's Today Show, New York, NY, U.S.A., Wednesday, January 27, 2016

Never Take Candy (Sweets) from a Stranger; dir. Cyril Frankel, filmed U.K.; Hammer Films, London, U.K., 1960

Pinocchio; Walt Disney, Hollywood, CA, U.S.A., 1940

Rowen and Martin's Laugh In; Dick Rowan, Dan Martin; Flip Wilson Geraldine character, NBC TV, Hollywood, CA, USA, 1968-1973

Seinfeld; 'The Boyfriend' (Season 3, Episode 15); Jerry Seinfeld; NBC TV, Hollywood, CA, U.S.A., 1992

Snow White and the Seven Dwarfs; Walt Disney, Hollywood, CA, U.S.A., 1937

Some Like it Hot, Tony Curtis, Jack Lemon, Marilyn Monroe, Ashton Prod., Hollywood, CA, U.S.A., 1959

Star Wars Episode IV, A New Hope; quote; George Lucas, 29th Century Fox, Hollywood, CA, U.S.A., May 26, 1977

Sweet Smell of Success; Dir. Alexander Mackendrick; Burt Lancaster, Tony Curtis, Susan Harrison and Martin Milner; Norma Productions; Hollywood, CA, U.S.A., 1957

Tell It to the Marines; Lon Chaney, Eleanor Broadman, MGM, Hollywood, CA, U.S.A., 1926

The Adventure of Sherlock Holmes' Smarter Brother; Gene Wilder, Madeline Kahn, 20th Century Fox, London, U.K., Hollywood CA, U.S.A., 1975

The Flip Wilson Show; Geraldine character, NBC TV, Hollywood, CA, U.S.A., 1970-1974

The Jackie Gleason Show, Jackie Gleason, CBS TV, Hollywood, CA, 1952-1957

The Jazz Singer; Al Jolson, premier, Warner Theater, Broadway, New York, NY, U.S.A., October 6, 1937

The Shadow; Walter B. Gibson, New York, NY, U.S.A., 1930- serialized radio crime drama, 1937-1954.

The Sound of Music; starring Julie Andrews, Christopher Plummer, Rogers and Hammerstein, 20th Century Fox, Hollywood, CA, U.S.A., 1965

The Wizard of Oz; Judy Garland, MGM, Hollywood, CA, U.S.A., 1939

The World and His Wife, silent film; Cosmopolitan Productions, distributed by Paramount Pictures, Hollywood, CA, U.S.A., 1920

Trouble in Paradise; Dir. Ernst Lubitsch, starring Kay Frances, Miriam Hopkins and Herbert Marshall, Paramount Pictures, Hollywood, CA, U.S.A., 1932

Up the Track; Douglas Lockwood, Rigby Ltd., Adelaide, South Australia, 1964

What Not to Wear; Stacy London, TLC TV show; Hollywood, CA, U.S.A. (2003-2013).

Who's Your Daddy, Fiona Hughes, T. J. Myers, Fox TV, Hollywood, CA, U.S.A., 2005

Wide World of Sports; Jim Mc Cay; ABC TV network, New York, NY, U.S.A., 1961-1997

Win, Lose or Draw; Game show, NBC, syndication, Hollywood, CA, U.S.A., 1987-1990

Yours, Mine and Ours; Dir Melvin Shavelson, starring Lucille Ball, Henry Fonda, Van Johnson, United Artists, Hollywood, CA, U.S.A., 1968

Music, Songs and Albums

All That Jazz; music by John Kander and lyrics by Fred Eb, play *Chicago*, New York, NY, U.S.A., 1975

Alright Already; Emil Stern, copyright app. Library of Congress, Washington, DC, U.S.A., January – June, 1957

Alright Already; Larry Stewart; Byron Hill, J.B. Rudd; RCA Records, Nashville, TN, U.S.A., 1993

At a Darktown Cakewalk; Charles Hale; Belmont Music Co.; Philadelphia, PA, U.S.A., 1899

Babes in Toyland; Victor Herbert, Wonderland Records, New York, NY, U.S.A., 1978

Bless Your Pea Pickin' Heart; Tennessee Ernie Ford Pickwick Label, Nashville, TN, U.S.A., 1966

Brothers in Arms, Mark Knopfler, 1982; released by Dire Straits, Virgin Records, London, U.K., 1985

Clean up Your Own Backyard; by Mac Davis and Billy Strange; Elvis Presley, RCA, New York, NY, U.S.A., 1969

Crash and Burn; writers Jesse Frasure and Chris Stapleton; Thomas Rhett; The Valory MUSic Co., Nashville, TN, U.S.A., 2015

Diggin' Up Bones; Randy Travis, written by Nat Stuckey, Paul Overstreet and Al Gore; Sony, ATV MUSic Publishing, Nashville, TN, U.S.A., 1986

Don't Give up Your Day Job (LP); Country Gazette; United Artists, Nashville, TN, U.S.A., 1973

Don't Go Away Mad (Just Go Away); Mötley Crüe. Nikki Sixx. Mick Mars; released Elektra Entertainment, New York, NY, U.S.A., May 28, 1990

Down and Dirty; (later *Hoe Down and Dirty*) Al Cohen c. Planetary Music Publishing Corporation, New York, NY, U.S.A., 1957

Down Memory Lane; copyright app., Library of Congress Washington DC, U.S.A., 1931

Down Memory Lane; Universal Pictures; dir. Monte Bruce; Library of Congress, Washington, DC, U.S.A., December 9, 1932

Down Memory Lane with You; words Nelle Stratton; music E.S.S. Huntington Library of Congress, Washington DC, U.S.A., c. August 5, 1921

Down Memory Lane; Vaughn Morrison, album, RCA Records; New York, NY, U.S.A., 1940s

Dream On, Steven Tyler, Aerosmith, Columbia Records, New York, NY, U.S.A., 1972

Everything is Tickety-Boo; Scotland, sung by Danny Kaye, Hollywoo,. CA., U.S.A.,1958

Five O'clock Shadow; Elliott Lawrence, Columbia Records, New York, NY, U.S.A., 1946

Flattery Will Get You Everywhere; Lyn Anderson, Columbia Records, Nashville, TN, U.S.A., 1968

Flattery Will Get You Nowhere; Gordon MacRae, Royale Records, London, U.K., 1946

Full Musical Score of 'The Oolah;' as Played by Francis Wilson and Company at the Broadway Theater by Charles Lecocq and Sydney Rosenfeld in 'The March and Entrance of the Prince,' p 45, New York, NY, U.S.A., 1889

How Sweet it Is (To be Loved by You), by Holland-Dozier-Holland, Marvin Gay, Tamia Records, Motown, Detroit, MI, U.S.A., 1964

Hunkey Dorey, "Air—Limerick Races," Christy Minstrels, Philadelphia, PA, U.S.A., 1862

I Ain't Broke but I'm Badly Bent; written by H. Payne (or Fred Carter), recorded by Del Reeves; Columbia Records Nashville, TN, U.S.A., January, 1968

If You Can Live With It (I Can Live Without It); Bill Anderson, RCA, Nashville, TN, U.S.A., 1973

If You See Something, Say Something; Taking Black Sunday, Warner Bros. Records, New York, NY, U.S.A., 2014

I Go Ape; Neil Sedaka, RCA Records, New York, NY, U.S.A., 1959

It's Five O'clock Somewhere; Jim 'Moose' Brown and Don Rollins; rec. Alan Jackson and Jimmy Buffett, Arista, Nashville, TN, U.S.A., May, 2002

It's Lonely at the Top; Randy Newman, Reprise, Los Angeles, CA, U.S.A., 1972

It's My Party, Leslie Gore, (Walter Gold, writer) Mercury Records, New York, NY, U.S.A., 1963

I Wanna Be Like You; Robert and Richard Sherman, Jungle Book, Walt Disney Films, Hollywood, CA, U.S.A., 1967

Kindly Keep it Country; The Older the Violin the Sweeter the MUSic, Hank Thompson, written by Curley Putman, Dot Records, Nashville, TN, U.S.A., 1973

My Main Man; Sonny Stitt and Bennie Green, Ter Mar Studio, Chicago, IL Argo label, New York, NY, U.S.A., 1964

No More Mr. Nice Guy, Billion Dollar Baby; album, Alice Cooper, [A. Cooper and Michael Bruce] Warner Bros., New York, NY, U.S.A., April, 1973

One Size Fits All; Frank Zappa, Zappa Records, Los Angeles, CA, U.S.A., June 25, 1975

Pity Party; Barbara Mandrell, Moods Album, ABC Records, Nashville, TN, U.S.A., 1978

Pity Party; Melanie Martinez, Atlantic Records, New York, NY, U.S.A., 2015

Poetry In Motion; Johnny Tillotson, written by Paul Kaufman and Mike Anthony; Cadence label, Nashville, TN, U.S.A., 1961

Settle Down Zelda; Timothy M. Bracy, The Mendoza Line, album, Full of Light and Fire, Misra Records, Pittsburg, PA, U.S.A., 2005

Shave and a Haircut; Rosalind Rosenthal and Herbert Halpert, Music Division Recording Lab. 3646 B4 New York, NY, U.S.A., 1939

Shave and a Haircut—Shampoo; Dan Shapiro, Lester Lee and Milton Berle; Larry Spier, New York, NY, U.S.A., 1939

Singing the Blues; Aliene Stanley (Victor Records), copyright book, Washington, DC, U.S.A., 1921

Singing the Blues; Melvin Endsley, Marty Robbins, Columbia Records, Nashville, TN, U.S.A., 1956

Stronger; Kelly Clarkson; by Jorgen Elofsson and David Gamson; RCA Records, New York, NY, U.S.A., January 17. 2012

The Devil Made Me So It, debut album, Paris, Tommy Boy Records, New York, NY, U.S.A., 1990

The Task; William Cawper, London, U.K., 1785

The Wild Side of Life, Arlie Carter and William Warren; Johnny Heap, Hank Thompson, Capitol Records, Los Angeles, CA, 1951, 1952

The World Turned Upside Down; English ballad, 1640s

Time of the Seasons; song; The Zombies, Abby Road, CBS, London, U.K., 1968

Waiting for Columbus; Little Feat, Warner Brothers, Burbank, CA, U.S.A., 1978

Wannabe; Spice Girls, Virgin Records, London U.K., 1996

Watching the World Go By; Dean Martin; Capitol Records, New York, NY, U.S.A., 1956

What a Crying Shame! The Mavericks, studio album, MCA Records, Nashville, TN, U.S.A., February 1, 1994

Wheels Within Wheels; studio album, Rory Galligher; Capo label, Brooklyn, NY, U.S.A., 2003

Wildcombe Fair; Songs and Ballads of the West; Sabine Baring-Gould, London, U.K., 1889–1891.

Wrecking Ball, Mozella, Stephen Moccio and others, Miley Cyrus, RCA Records (Sony) Nashville, TN, U.S.A., August, 2013

Yo! Bum Rush the Show; debut album; Public Enemy, Def Jam Records, Columbia, New York, NY, U.S.A., 1987

You Really Did a Number on Me; song by Keith Colley, copyright 1971

Newspapers, Magazines and Journals

Ainsworth Magazine: A Miscellany of Romance; William Harrison Ainsworth, Volume 7; Hints of Servants, John Mortimer, London, U.K., 1845

Alexandra & Yea Standard; Alexandra, Victoria, Australia, January 10, 1896

All the Year Round; 'Picture Words,' p 14; London, U.K. September 13, 1862; 'How the Bank Was Wound Up,' Charles Dickens;' London, U.K., April 15, 1865

American Blacksmith and Motor Shop; 'Sam Thomas Plans for Christmas BUSiness,' p 52; Buffalo, NY, U.S.A., September, 1923

American Druggist and Pharmaceutical Record; Business Building section, p 12; New York, NY, U.S.A., July 12, 1909

American Insurance Digest and Insurance Monitor; 'Pluck, Determination and Hard Work Brought Judge Dugan Success,' p 11; Wadsworth Publishing, Chicago, IL, U.S.A., June 10, 1922

American Poultry Journal; Thanksgiving Turkey, Mrs. M.E.C. Bates; Chicago, IL, USA, November, 1889

American Legion Magazine; 'The Fight Against Filth;' New York, NY, U.S.A., May, 1961

American Motorcyclist Magazine; A Common Road, Celebrating Women and Motorcycling, Kelly Friend quote; Westerville, OH, U.S.A., November, 1997

American Opinion; Volume 18, p 86; John Birch Society, Robert Welch, Appleton, WI, U.S.A., 1975

American Speech, Journal, American Dialect Society, Duke University Press, Durham, NC, 1955

America's News of Books; New York, NY, U.S.A., July, 1930

Anamosa Prison Press; Anamosa, IA, U.S.A.; Saturday, October 24, 1903

Atkinkin's Casket; Gems of Literature, Wit and Sentiment; 'Autobiography of a Jack-knife,' Philadelphia, PA, U.S.A., March, 1831

Atlantic Monthly; Vol. 162, (July-December); Washington, DC, U.S.A., 1938

Auburn Seminary Record; New York, NY, U.S.A., September, 1916

Aunt Judy's Magazine; Laetus Sorte Mia; J. W. Ewing, Ch. VIII; David Bogue, London, U.K., 1882

Austin Chronicle; 'Janice Joplin, Texas and the Big Beat;' Margaret Mosser; Austin, TX, U.S.A., December 31, 1969

AUUGN Magazine; 'An Update on UNIX-Related Standards Activities,' p 75; Kensington, NSW, Australia, April, 1994

Baily's Magazine of Sports and Pastimes; 'Our Jockeys;' Baily Bros., July, 1860; 'Our Van,' November, 1874; 'Our Van; Vinton & Co., London, U.K., December, 1901

Baltimore American; 'Another Race for Motors: Four Noted Crews and Motors to be Again Tested around the Bowl Track;' Baltimore, MD, U.S.A., August 24, 1901

Belgravia, A London Magazine; 'His Second Inheritance,' Ch. VIII; London, U.K., September, 1875

Bentley's Miscellany, Volume 4; 'Some Passages in the Literary Life of Olinthus Jenkinson,' p 74; Jemima M. Mason, New York, NY, U.S.A., July, 1839

Billboard Magazine; Editor's Desk, p 43; January 17, 1942; article p 11, August 1, 1942; 'Now Play on Broadway' Reviewed by Eugene Burr p 10: September 12, 1942; 'The Crossroads,' Nat Green, Chicago, p 43; February 20, 1943; 'Pubs Edging into Disk and Bank Fields,' p 67: April 15, 1944; 'Bless Your Little Heart,' April 6, 1946; New

York, NY, USA; December 7, 1946; Best Direct to Location Sales of Venders at NAMA Cigarette Operator Clinic;' Is Horowitz, p 2; December 10, 1949; ad, p 61, December 22, 1951; 'Ted Lewis,' p 56, January 3, 1942; **'**Coin Ride Trade Counts Every Dime' by Ken Knauaf, p 1, AugusSt 10, 1959; "WB's Conkling Sets 'PIUS 2' Singles Plan" by Lee Zhito, p 1, August 28, 1961; June 14, 1952; February 27, 1965, page 24; AugUSt 20, 1966; Ella Fitzgerald ad; February 1, 1964; Article; Elliott Tiegel, p 20, November, 1967; November 30, 1968; 'Snuff's Philosophy,' p 40; December 15, 1973; Vox Jox, Claude Hall p 38, November 23, 1974; ad, p 51, December 12, 1976; 'BOOK REVIEW: Radcliff Joe Probes '70s Disco Evolution,' October 18, 1980; 'Rock 'n' Rolling,' p 16, quote from Marianne Faithful, October 17, 1981; 'First Time,' Brent Maher p 43; Chicago, IL, U.S.A., May 30, 1998

Bird Lore Magazine; 'Notes from Field and Study,' Audubon Society, McMillan Co., Englewood, NJ, U.S.A., March-April, 1914

Black and White: A Monthly Magazine of Facts for Insurance Policy Investors; Kellogg & Son, Chicago, IL, U.S.A., 1895

Black Belt Magazine; caption; Burbank, CA, U.S.A., May, 1980

Black Belt Magazine; p 9, Rainbow Productions, North Hollywood, CA, U.S.A., March, 1997

Blackwood's Magazine; 'Hounds and HousSes at Rome;' London, U.K., October, 1847

Blackwood's Edinburg Magazine; Mine is Thine, Part II, Edinburg, Scotland, U.K., August, 1877

Boston Medical and Surgical Journal; '***The Quick Festival***, Boston, MA, U.S.A., February 1, 1854

Boy's Life; "'Meramec Dan' McDonald" p 14; November 1912; 'The Pilot of the Cloud Patrol,' Irving Crump,' p 48; May, 1929; 'Dynamite for Senor McGonigle' Selden M. Loring, p 47; April, 1934; 'Florsheim Shoes ad, p 11; June 16, 1941; 'Don't Look at the Log Books,' J. Marquis Irwin, p 9; September, 1943; High Jinx, p 34; October, 1943; 'Tropical Snow Climb;' James W. English, p 47; November, 1948; A Bad Town for Pull Hitters, p 15; June, 1964; Peace Corp Ad, p 8; 'For the Freedom of the Seas,' Ralph Henry Barber, Chapter VI, p 14; January 5, 1968; 'High Adventure Ahead,' William B. Mc Morris, pp 6-8; Boy Scouts of America, New York, NY, U.S.A., February, 1972

Broadcasting Telecasting, Broadcasting Productions, New York, NY, U.S.A., Oct-Dec 1957

Brownson's Quarterly Review; published by William H. Greene, Boston, MA, U.S.A., July, 1845; January, 1846

Bulletin of the Atomic Scientists; 'A Slippery Slope,' Edward Shills, June, 1954 'Can We Halt the Race for Atomic Arms?;' Clinton Anderson, p 226; University of Chicago Press, Chicago, Ill, U.S.A., June, 1956

***Bulletin**;* Sydney, New South Wales, Australia, March 3, 1962; April 14, 1981

***Byte Magazin**;,* UBM, Petersborough, NH, U.S.A., April, 1982

***Chambers' Edinburgh Journal**;* 'Cromwell in Scotland;' Saturday, February 28, 1846; 'The Suez Canal,' p 2; W. & R. Chambers, London & Edinburgh, U.K., April 2, 1870

***Chicago Commerce**;* reprint of article from Chicago Herald, p 7: 'Sit Tight! Don't Rock the Boat!' Chicago, IL, U.S.A., August 7, 1914

***Chicago Dairy Produce**;* 'Timely Hints for the Buttermaker,' p 46: Chicago, IL, U.S.A., May 26, 1914

Chips Ahoy; magazine, U.S. Navy, Washington, DC, U.S.A., July, 1996

***Christian Science Monitor**;* article by John K. Cooley, quoting U.S. General Volney Warner; Boston, MA, U.S.A., April 11, 1980

***Church Building Quarterly from the Church Building Society, American Congregational Union**;* p 94; New York, NY, U.S.A., January, 1901

***Church Register**;* Rev. C. Weller, 'The Young Midshipman;' Philadelphia, PA, U.S.A., November 17, 1827:

***Coburn's New Monthly Magazine**;* 'The Flying Island,' p 44; London, U.K., January, 1835

***Collier's Weekly**;* 1847 Rogers Brothers ad, p 21, New York, NY, U.S.A., April 20, 1907

***Collier's**;* 'The Soldier who went AWOL: U.S. to Korea;' New York, NY, U.S.A., June 20, 1953

***Commercial Telegraph's Journal**;* St. John, New Brunswick, Canada, August, 1920

Computerworld; 'The Hotel Welcome Mat is Out;' Helen Pike; San Francisco, CA, U.S.A., July 30, 1990

***Cosmopolitan**;* 'Propriety Pratt, Hypnotist;' Alfred Henry Lewis, p 18; New York, NY, U.S.A., June, 1910

***Country Life Magazine**;* 'You'll Like It,' Frances Buzzell; Doubleday, Page and Co., Garden City, NY, U.S.A., January, 1919

***Cruise Travel**;* Interview at Sea: Lady Maitre D*;'* Beverly Shaver p 55; May, 1993

***Current Literature**;* 'The Sketch Book: Character in Outline,' Stephen Gwyan; reprinted from Cornhill Magazine; New York, NY, U.S.A., November, 1897

Cycle and Automobile Trade Journal; in 'How Pete Put One Over;' Philadelphia, PA, USA, April 1, 1920

Cycle World Magazine; page 57; CBS Publications, Los Angeles, CA, U.S.A., January-May, 1984

Daily News; London, U.K., June 19, 1897

Demorest's Monthly Magazine; 'A Painful Lift' by 'Madge,' p 63; New York, NY, U.S.A., February, 1879

Dialect Notes, Volume *5;* p 478; American Dialect Society, New York, NY, U.S.A., 1927

Dickenson's Theological Quarterly; Richard D. Dickenson; London, U.K., July, 1877

Dublin University Magazine; 'A Leaf from the Fortunes of Mordaunt Mervale;' William Curry, May, 1841; 'Gasper the Pirate: A Tale of the Indian Seas,' chapter VIII, February, 1842 'A Flying Shot at the United States;' Dublin, Ireland, October, 1852

Ebony Magazine; 'The Soul of Ray Charles,' p 106; September, 1960; letter to the editor from James Lopez, p 11; Chicago, IL, U.S.A., October, 1965

Edinburgh Review; Professor Jowell's Translation of Plato, Edinburgh Scotland, U.K., October, 1871

Electric Railway Journa; Daily Edition, 'Conventionalities' p 2; McGraw Publishing Co.; Chicago, IL, U.S.A., Tuesday, October 9, 1912

Engineering News; editorial, 'Rail Troubles Not Ended;' Hill Publishing, New York, NY, U.S.A., August 24, 1916

Everybody's Magazine; 'The Rider of Golden Bar,' William Patterson White; Ridgeway Co., New York, NY, U.S.A., September, 1921

Fibre and Fabric; 'The Woolen Factory,' Observations of 'Peter;' Saturday, December 31, 1898

Field and Stream; 'Cottontail Hunting, Eastern Style' p 91; October, 1971; 'Hotspot for Brookies,' Ed Zern, p 96; New York, NY, U.S.A., February, 1980,

Flying Magazine; 'Love Birds,' Hamilton Thornquist, p 35; February, 1939; 'I Learned about Flying from That!,' Edna Ungerer, p 50; December, 1950; 'The Gremlin Corner,' Weyman C. Carver, p 58; November, 1954; 'Aviation Down Under;' Gregory R. Copley, p 93, AugusSt, 1966; Westerlies, Geo. Clarson, p 80; Zif Davis Publishing, Chicago. IL, U.S.A., July, 1977

Forest and Stream, p 99, Forest and Stream Pub. Co., New York, NY, U.S.A., August 21, 1890

Forest and Stream*;* Game Bag and Gun: Where to Go; New York, NY, U.S.A., December 19, 1896

Frasers Magazine*;* 'Miru and the Man Spirit,' William Ellis; 1831; 'The Last Duel I Had a Hand In;' C. O'Donoghue; London, U.K., August, 1833

Gaillard's Medical Journal*;* New York; August, 1881

Freedom and Union*;* Clarence Kirshman Streit (1896-1986), Vol. 8, p 61; Washington, DC, U.S.A., 1953

Geological Society of America Bulletin*;* article on Buttes: Rochester, NY, U.S.A., March 30, 1985

Golf Illustrated*;* p 7; London, U.K., June 16, 1899

Good Health Magazine, Western Health Reform Institute, Battle Creek, MI, U.S.A., May 1, 1883

Good Housekeeping*;* 'Kiss of the Wife that's True,' Holyoke, MA; New York, NY, U.S.A., September 18, 1886

Graham's American Monthly Magazine of Literature*;* 'The Young Widow;' Philadelphia. PA, U.S.A., March, 1842

Grammophone*;* Mark Allen Group, London, U.K., November, 1940

Green Book Album Magazine*;* 'Broadway Gossip;' Donald Morris Jones, New York, NY, U.S.A., September, 1911

Herald Sun*;* Melbourne, Victoria, Australia, November 23, 2002

Hardwood Record*;* 'Cupid and Inspection,' p 29; Detroit, MI, U.S.A., March 25, 1909

Harpers New Monthly Magazine*;* 'The Quiet Home;' Harper & Bros.; New York, NY, U.S.A., August, 1858

Harper's Weekly*;* May 23, 1857, 'Foreign News;' Harper & Bros.; New York, NY, U.S.A., September 19, 1857

Harvard Business Review reprint series, Issue 81512; article "Big Hat, No Cattle: Managing Human Resources" Harvard University, Cambridge, MA, U.S.A., 1981

Hearst's International*;* article, Damon Runyon; Hurst's International Magazine Co., New York, NY, USA, October, 1929

Indiana Quarterly Magazine of History, Fourth Quarter*;* 'Folk Speech in Indiana,' Paul L. Hawthorne and O.G.S.; Indiana University, Bloomington, IN, U.S.A., 1905

InfoWorld; Vol. 6, Issue 23; June 9, 1986; AT&T article, p 32, Menlo Park, CA, U.S.A., October 21, 1996

Illustrated World; 'Smashing Machine Gun Nests;' E.T. Bronsdon; New York, NY, U.S.A., October, 1918

Irish Times; article, Donald Clarke, 'Taking a Bare Knuckle Ride;' Dublin, Ireland, Wednesday, August 3, 2011

Jacksonville Journal; photo by Rocco Morabito, Jacksonville, IL, U.S.A., 1967

Jet; 'Sugar Ray's Money,' p 53; February, 1955; Gerri Major's 'Society World,' p 42; Johnson Publishing, Chicago, IL, U.S.A., August 25, 1955

Journal of Open Education, Vol. 3-4; p 68; Newton College, Los Angeles, CA, U.S.A., 1971

Judge; 'Editorial;' New York, NY, U.S.A., July 22, 1918

Judy, or; The London Serio-Comic Journal; 'Poor Will Bunion,' p 29; London, U.K., July 20, 1887

Kansas State Collegian, p 13; Kansas State University, Manhattan, KS, U.S.A., April 30, 1972

Kiplinger's Personal Finance Magazine; 'Whoa, Take it Easy! You'll Do Better, Live Longer,' p 9; August, 1955; p 12; June, 1974; 'Spell Profits,' Ken Sheets, p 129; Washington, DC, U.S.A., March, 1995

Knickerbacker; or, New York Monthly Magazine; 'A Question in Single Rule of Three;' August, 1847 *Knickerbocker; or, New York Monthly Magazine*, 'Gossop with Readers and Correspondents;' New York, NY, U.S.A., December, 1855

Ladies Home Journal; LePage's glue ad; New York, NY, U.S.A., March, 1921

Leslie's Weekly; Uncle Sam image, James M. Flagg; New York, NY, U.S.A., July 6, 1916

Lewiston Evening Journal, Lewiston, Maine, U.S.A., April 16, 1894

Life Magazine; 'The Matter with Montaigne,' June 17, 1909; Buick advertisement, p51; March, 1937 Heinz Ketchup ad p 8; p 35; caption under a picture from 1930 WW I Errol Flynn war movie, *The Dawn Patrol,* December 26, 1938; Speaking of Pictures; January 9, 1939; ketchup ad, p 8; August 28, 1939; 'The Midwest,' p 32; November 8, 1940; article headed "Never mind 'who done it'—pitch in and help get it done!" p 120; December 6, 1943; 'New York City's Able Mayor' p84; October 27, 1941; 'Argentine Crisis Spotlights Rivalry of America and Rudsia;' John K. Jessup, May 14, 1945; 'Shall We Have a Depression,' p 69; Time, Inc., Chicago. IL, USA, May, 1946 in 'The Tragedy of Liberalism;' Joseph and Stewart Alsop, p 65; October 7, 1946; caption, photo, 'Death of a Salesman' p 118; February 21, 1949;'Gang War,' p 137; April 14, 1958; 'The Scary Sappy Life of the Nation's Ski Maniacs' by Sports Editor Marshall Smith; February 2, 1959; caption under photo, p 95; November 10, 1961; Perry Como ad, p 14; January, 1962; 'Great Dinners,' p 47; January 31, 1964; 'You Can Stop Snapping at My Heels Now,' p 36; May, 1969; 'The New Arithmetic of Vietnam,' p 24; Time-Life, Chicago, IL, U.S.A., July 11, 1969

Lippincott's Monthly Magazine; Book-Talk, June, 1887; January, 1888; article 'The New Womanhood;' July, 1895; 'Queen Mary of Memory Lane,' Carolyn Wood Morrison; J.P. Lippincott Co., Philadelphia, PA, U.S.A., December, 1906

Literary Garland and Canadian Magazine; p 46; 'Notices of New Works,' Valentine Slyboots; Lovell and Gibson, Montreal, Canada, March, 1846

Littell's Living Age; 'Three Friends,' July 18, 1846; 'The Rooster Pecked Wife,' Eliza L. Sproat, Scene First; February, 1853; 'The Parliments and Ministries of the Century;' Waite, Pierce & Co., Boston, MA, U.S.A., June 23, 1894

Logansport Pharos-Reporter; Logansport, Indiana, May, 1917

London Gazette; London, U.K., March 16, 1716

London Saturday Journal; London, U.K., November, 1839

Los Angeles Times; article by Kevin Thomas re: *The Great Outdoors,* starring John Candy and Dan Aykroyd; Los Angeles, CA, U.S.A., June 17, 1988

Maryland Historical Magazine, pp 243-244; Baltimore, MD, U.S.A., Fall 1975

McClure's Magazine; 'The Property Man;' Booth Tarkington; New York, NY, U.S.A., August, 1905

Melbourne Punch; 'The Old Hen's Lament' p 57; August 22, 1867; Melbourne, Victoria, Australia, September 22, 1887

Metropolitan Magazine; 'Snarlleyyow, or the Dog Fiend,' Capt. Marryat, Chapter XII; Theodore Foster, New York, NY, U.S.A., May, 1836

Michigan Business Review; 'Achieving Administrative Confidence—The Supervisor;' Robert Hilkert, p 6; University of Michigan, Ann Arbor, MI, U.S.A., May, 1959

Michigan Farmer; 'Young and Old England,' p 3; Detroit, MI, U.S.A., January 1, 1852

Michigan Technic; Northrup Aircraft ad, p 37; U.M., Ann Arbor, MI, U.S.A., January, 1958

Monthly Weather Review; 'The Term Indian Summer,' Albert Matthews; Washington Weather Bureau, Washington, DC, U.S.A., February, 1902

Morning Post; London, U.K., July 29, 1820

Motion Picture; 'The Talkies,' p 56; Macfadden-Bartel, New York, NY, U.S.A., February, 1936

Motorboating; magazine, article p 111; New York, NY, U.S.A., July, 1935

Mother Jones Magazine; February, 1984

Munsey's Magazine; 'The Stage,' April, 1905; 'A Fight for Life,' James Oliver Cormwell, January, 1910; 'Paddling Sam,' J.E. Rath, Volume 85, p 59; Frank A. Muncey Co., New York, NY, U.S.A., January, 1912

Museum of Foreign Literature, Science and Art; 'Master Humphrey's Clock,' Charles Dickens, Chapter I; Littell and Co. Philadelphia, PA, U.S.A., April, 1840

Nature; Sir Norman Lockyer, V 342, p 327; London, U.K., 1869

New England Farmer; p 2; Boston, MA, U.S.A., Wednesday September 25, 1844

New England Magazine; Boston, MA, U.S.A., April, 1834

New Monthly Magazine; 'Scenery and a Scene' p 9; London, U.K., June, 1935

New Monthly Magazine; Some Passages in the Life of Major Gahagan' William Makepiece Thackery; New York, NY, 1829

New Outlook; article by A.S. Pearce 'Success' p 83; Los Angeles CA, U.S.A., December, 1953

New Scientist, review of *Mankind in the Making: The Story of Human Evolution;* (1959) William Howells, written by W. Holmes, London, U.K., November 23, 1961

Newsweek Magazine, Vol. 20; p 113; 1942; Newsweek LLC, New York, NY, U.S.A., Volume 72, issue 10, p 61, 1968

New York Literary Journal; 'Men of Pleasure,' p 1; New York, NY, U.S.A., Saturday, March 11, 1826

New York Magazine, Volume 5; p 138; 1972; article "The Raise of the Year from a 'Board of Robots'" Dan Dorfman; 'The Learning Annex,' p 58, December 28, 1981; McEnroe, a Player for All Courses,' p 82; July 4, 1977, New York, NY, U.S.A., April 25, 1983

New York Times, ad, Halpert, Oberst and Co., June 19, 1977

Niles Weekly Register; Baltimore, MD, U.S.A., May 7, 1831

Northern Vendicator; Estherville, Iowa, U.S.A., 1868

Northwestern Miller; 'Mill Insurance,' R. W. Arndt, p 11; C. M. Palmer, Minneapolis, MN, U.S.A., June 8, 1888

Nottingham Evening Post; Lincolnshire, U.K., February, 1882

Once a Month: An Illustrated Australian Magazine; 'Scalping Extraordinary,' James Rae Dixon; Melbourne, Victoria, Australia, March 1, 1886

Once a Week, an Illustrated Miscellany; 'A Winter in a Tipperary Household Fourteen Years Ago,' Eneas Sweetland Dallas, chapter II, March 22, 1862; 'The Golden Wedding in the Workhouse;' December 1, 1865; Enheas Sweetland Dallas, 'The Casual Observer;' London, U.K., November 20, 1875

Opportunities of To-day; article, p 31; 'Fifty Million Steers in the U.S. Should Rejoice for Coming Changes,' Chicago, IL, U.S.A., February, 1908

Orange Coast Magazine; 'Yabber,' p 133; Irvine, CA, U.S.A., September, 1984

Oregon Teachers Monthly; 'Ashland Normal News' by editor Armilda Daughty; Salem OR, U.S.A., January, 1906

Our Paper; 'They Risk Their Lives Taking Pictures in the Air,' p 2; Massachusetts Reformatory, Concord Junction, MA, U.S.A., November 6, 1920

Our Young Folks Illustrated Magazine for Boys and Girls; 'A Deer Hunt in the Adirondacks;' Tickner and Fields, Boston, MA, U.S.A., September, 1867

Our Young People; 'Advice of Evangelist to Girls,' p 22; Milwaukee, Wisconson, October, 1912

Overland Monthly; 'A Piney-Woods Character;' A. Roman and Co., San Francisco, CA, U.S.A., May, 1870

Ozwords; Oxford University Press, ANU, Australia, October, 2009

Pacific Coast Law Journal; San Francisco, CA, U.S.A., March 24, 1883

Paint, Oil and Drug Review; 'For Oleomargerine Relief,' p 10; Wednesday, Chicago, IL, U.S.A., December 14, 1904

P.C. Magazine; 'File Management for Windows 95,' p 18; Davis Publishing Co., New York, NY, U.S.A., June 15. 1996

Pearson's Magazine; 'Getting the Break,' Billy Evans; New York, NY, U.S.A., June, 1914

People Magazine; 'Man Bites Dog Food,' New York, NY, U.S.A., August 29, 1994

Phi Delta Kappan; 'Mad Avenue Aids the School Crisis' p 173; Bloomington, IN, U.S.A., January, 1959

Phi Gamma Delta; Fijis on the Basketball Courts, Philip Lyon; East Palestine Ohio, U.S.A., April, 1822

Photoplay Magazine; 'And the Elephants Beckoned,' p 116; Chicago, IL, U.S.A., June, 1918; 'Orange Blossom' ad; McFadden Publications, New York, NY, U.S.A., June, 1927

Phrenological Journal and Science and Health; 'Thoughts and Things;' Fowler and Wells, New York, NY, U.S.A., March, 1890

Pix; Associated Newspapers Limited, Sydney, Australia, September, 1947

Popular Mechanics; 'Television…The New War Baby,' p 69; October, 1943; 'The Army Adopts a New Rifle' p 150; Chicago, IL, U.S.A., January, 1958

Popular Science Magazine, Strongfort Ad, p 102; January, 1921; 'How to Time a Rough Riding Car;' September, 1929; 'New Prisons are Proof Against Riot and Outbreak,' p 16; August, 1932; 'How Auto Makers Spy on Each Other,' James Jones, p 136; p 113;, January, 1949; 'Nuts Bolts and People,' Perry Githens, p 103; Bonnier Corp. Harlan, IA, U.S.A., March, 1949

Poultry Success; p 34; CE Hosterman, Springfield, OH, U.S.A., November, 1909

Power; 'Engineering or Engineman,' E. L. Jessup; McGraw Hill, Inc., New York, NY, U.S.A., October 25, 1921

Prairie Farmer; "Letters to the Editor: Household Affairs, Soap Making,' Chicago, IL, U.S.A., September, 1816

Primary Education; Boston, New York, Chicago, San Francisco, U.S.A., November, 1920

Primitive Monitor and Church Advocate; R.W. Thompson; Greenfield, IN, U.S.A., May, 1892

Princeton Alumni Weekly; Refutation, Mr. Casement; April 1, 1931; Francis H. Glafebrook, Jr., Princeton Theological Seminary, January 19, 1940; November 24, 1975, 'Class Notes' 74, p 35; 'Class Notes'72 by Larry Kurtz, p 48; Princeton University, Princeton, NJ, U.S.A., July 13, 1983

Professional Engineer; p 27; National Society of Professional Engineers, Alexandria, VA, U.S.A., December, 1927

Public Opinion, 'Sociology; Various Timely Topics: Marriage and Divorce,' from *New York Herald*; New York, NY, U.S.A., June 27, 1891

Public Safety; 'It did Happen Here,' Paul Jones, p 18; December, 1938; 'An Award Dinner Packs 'Em In,' p 44; National Safety Council, Chicago, IL, U.S.A., May, 1938

Publisher's Weekly; New York, NY, U.S.A., April 11, 1943

Puck; poem 'Puckerings;' Keppler and Swartzmann, New York, NY, U.S.A., May 28, 1884

Puck's Library; 'Base-ball Mechanism-Two Prophecies.' p 20; Keppler & Swartzmann, New York, NY, U.S.A., July, 1887

Punch, or The London Charivari; A Wise Old Owl, April 10, 1875; 'At a Moment's Notice,' Chapter I; London, U.K., March 1, 1905

Quarterly Review; 'View of Grecian Philosophy-The Clouds &c,' London, U.K., April, 1819

Queenslander; Brisbane, Queensland, Australia, August 15, 1837

Queensland Times; Ipswich, Queensland, Australia, June 12, 1900

Reformatory Pressus; 'The Silent School Hours,' Sonny Jim; Anamosa, IA, U.S.A., Saturday October 10, 1909

Religious Intelligencer; New Haven, CT, U.S.A., February 26, 1826

Roberts' Semi Monthly Magazine; 'The Poacher,' a novel, 'Captain Marryat,' Chapter XIV; Boston, MA, U.S.A., April 1, 1841

Rollins Magazine; 'Unburied Treasures,' Richard Maxwell Winans, p 10; E. H. Rollins and Sons Investment Bonds, Boston, MA & New York, NY, U.S.A., July, 1911

St. Louis Daily Pennant; St. Louis, MO, U.S.A., May, 1840

San Francisco Daily Times; 'Social Profile,' by Tantalus; 'Zoloags and Fraser,' p 12; San Francisco, CA, U.S.A., February 23, 1918

Salt Lake Tribune; 'Mr. Dooley on Change of Politics,' p 15, column 3; Salt Lake City, UT, U.S.A., October 13, 1895

School Education; 'A Workman's Hints on Teaching Work;' Sanford Niles, Minneapolis. MN, U.S.A., July, 1887

Scientific Monthly; Ernest Henry Starling, Volume 11, p 295; Henry Holt and Co., New York, NY, U.S.A., July, 1920

Secret Service, Old and Young King Brady Detectives; 'The Opium King,' ch. 5, p 9; New York, NY, U.S.A., June 30, 1899

Sydney Morning Herald; Sidney, New South Wales, Australia, November 2, 1992

Skiing Magazine; New York, NY, U.S.A., November, 1966; March, 1992

Southern Cultivator and Dixie Farmer; The Franklin Publishing House, Atlanta, GA, U.S.A., April, 1893

Southern Folklore Quarterly, Volume 2-3; p 109; Southern Folklore Society, University of Florida, Gainesville, FL, U.S.A., 1938

Sporting Magazine; 'A Fashionable Sportsman and His Friend' included in the feature 'Feast of Wit or Sportsman's Hall,' January, 1803; 'Second Letter from Ant. Arab on Our Breed of Horses and Other Subjects,' p 82; J. Pittman, London, U.K., December, 1826; Nimrod's Yorkshire Tour, p 12; M.A. Pittman, London, U.K., May, 1838

Sports Illustrated Magazine; 'From Hardwood to Hashtag: How NBA Culture Gave Rise to Throwback Thursday', New York, NY, U.S.A., August 22, 2013

Standard Player Monthly; New York, NY, U.S.A., February, 1919,

Successful Poultry Journal; ad, p 35; Chicago, IL, U.S.A., January, 1905

Sunday Mercury; p 2, col 5; New York, NY, U.S.A., March 18, 1876

Sunshine Advocate; Sunshine, Victoria, Australia, 22 March 1951

***Sunset: The Pacific** Monthly*; 'The Vision of the Ram and He- Goat,' Peter B. Kyne, p 66; San Francisco, CA, U.S.A., May, 1916

Susquehanna, p 4; 'Orange and Maroon End Road Jinx,' Susquehanna University, Selinsgrove, PA, U.S.A., September 6, 1956

Sydney Morning Herald; Section: News and Features "COLUMN 8," Quote, p 1; Sydney, Australia. (NewsBank Access World News), September 13, 1997

Syracuse Daily Standard; Quote from Judge William J. Groo; Syracuse, NY, U.S.A., September 9, 1885

Tait's Edinburgh Magazine; 'Sam Pogson's Jealousy;' Edinburgh, Scotland, U.K., March, 1836

Tao Te Ching, Lao Tzu; China, 6th century BCE, pub. 4th century BCE, English, 1868

Telegraph Age; 'To Everybody Everywhere;' John F. Skirrow; Western Union Telegraph Co., New York, NY, U.S.A., December 16, 1919

Temple Bar; 'Edged Tools: A Romance of Two Summers;' Ethyl M. Arnold, chapter 2; London, U.K., August, 1887

Texas Monthly; p 244; Austin, TX, U.S.A., October 1983

Textile Worker; 'Straightening Out the Fade Away;' National Union of Textile Workers, New York, NY, U.S.A., September, 1919

The Aberdeen Evening Express; Aberdeenshire, Scotland, U.K., Thursday 5 November 1885

The Aeronautical Journal; Volume 57, p 462; Royal Aeronautical Society, Cambridge University Press, London, U.K., 1953

The African Repository and Colonial Journal, Volume 23; p 41; C. Alexander, Printer, Washington, DC, U.S.A., February, 1847

The Albany Law Journal; 'Evidence of the Accused;' Albany, NY, U.S.A., December 17, 1898

The Albany Times; Quote from Fred Wheeler; Albany, NY, U.S.A., March 8, 1886

The Alpine Journal; 'The Ascent of Tetnuld Tau;' Clinton Dent; Longmans, Green, and Co., London, U.K., May, 1887

The Amateur's Magazine; 'The Mammoth Grub, Part II;' Piper, Stephenson & Spence, London, U.K., November, 1859

The American Bee Journa; 'A General Law is Needed,' G.W. Demekee; Chicago, Il, U.S.A., February 16, 1881

The American Hereford Journal; 'The Sothams Have Mastered the Business of Handling Public Sales;' Kansas City, MO, U.S.A., December 15, 1916

The American Home Missionary; 'Up in the Air,' C. F, Swander; Cincinnati, OH, U.S.A., March, 1916

The American Journal of Dental Science; edited by FJS Georges, MD. DDS and Richard Grady, MD, DDS, Vol. XXXII, p 430; Snowden & Cowman, Baltimore, MD, U.S.A.; Trubner & Co, London. U.K., 1899

The American Magazine, Article, B.C. Forbes; May 16, 1920

The American Monthly Review of Reviews; 'Spooner of Wisconsin: A Sketch of the Present Leader of the Senate;' New York, NY, U.S.A., August, 1902

The Apache Pow Wow, 'Question Box,' p 3;Tyler Junior College Tyler, TX, U.S.A., December 12, 1946

The Athenaeum: Journal of Literature, Science, the Fine Arts; 'Reviews,' July 20, 1844; March 25, 1854; Longman, Green, Longman, Roberts and Green, London, U.K., October 29, 1864, August, 1919

The Atlanta Constitution; article; Atlanta, GA. U.S.A., April 14, 1896

The Atlantic Monthly; 'The North Shore Watch;' London, U.K., April, 1800

The Australian Journal: A Weekly Record of Literature, August Travers; 'Europa,' Chapter VII; November, 1876

The Automobile; 'Rapid Growth of Automobiling in the South;' New York, NY and Chicago, IL, U.S.A., April 9, 1908

***The Auto**: The Motorist's Pictorial;* published by Stanley Spooner in an article titled 'Effects of Road Surface on Cars,' London, U.K., October 17, 1908

The Auto Trade Journal; Crew Levick headlamp ad, Philadelphia, PA, U.S.A., January 1, 1917

The Bee, (Newspaper) 'Back to Principles' col 2, p 3; Earlington, Kentucky, U.S.A., May 26, 1916

The Bisbee Daily Review, Section Two, "I'll Leave Congress with Friends of Both Sides," Says "Uncle Joe" Cannon, Harry Hunt; Bisbee, Arizona, Sunday, February 26, 1922

The Bookman, a Journal of Literature and Life, Volume 9; story, 'Janice Meredith' by Paul Leicester Ford, p 325; New York, NY, U.S.A., 1899

The Boston Examiner; Boston, MA, U.S.A., August 6, 1803

The Boston Times; "Thoughts;" Boston, MA, U.S.A., January 16, 1808

The Bulletin; Sydney, Australia, 1884; June 3, 1972

The Century Illustrated Magazine; 'The Mountaineers about Monteagle,' September, 1888; 'Mrs. Northmere's Treasure,' Gertrude Hall, August, 1910; 'A Vagabond in the Sun,' Harry A. Franck; The Century Co., New York, NY, U.S.A., June, 1922

The Chicago Commerce; 'Home and Front as One,' p 20; Chicago, IL, USA, July 19, 1918

The Chicago Tribune; 'In the Wake of the News;' David Condon, p A3; April 22, 1973

The Christian Review; 'Evil Made Subservience to Good;' Sheldon & Co., New York, NY, U.S.A., July, 1860

The Chronicle; University of Michigan, Ann Arbor, MI, U.S.A., June 30, 1881

The Congressional Globe; Rep. Robert Toomes, speech; John C. Rives, Washington, DC, U.S.A., February 27, 1850

The Clever Magazine; The Epic of Lone Wolf,' Melville Irvin Arni, p 102; The Standard Publishing Co., Kansas City, MO, U.S.A., November, 1903

The Colorado School of Mines Magazine; 'Tune, Everybody's Doin' It;' Golden, Colorado, December, 1912

The Commoner; William Jennings Bryan, p 4; Lincoln, Nebraska, U.S.A., July 25, 1904

The Cornhill Magazine; Smith, article, 'Big Birds,' Elder and Co., London, U.K., November, 1890

The Coshocton Tribune; 'New York Day-By-Day,' Oscar Odd 'O.O.' McIntyre; Coshocton, OH, U.S.A., October 1921

The Country Gentleman Magazine; 'Farm Mill,' S. Edwards Todd; Simon Marshall & Co., Lundon, U.K., March 1821

The Daily Gleaner; Kingston, Jamaica, December 20, 1966

The Dartmouth; 'Exchanges;' Dublin University, Hanover, MA, U.S.A., July, 1870

The Day of Rest, An Illustrated Journal of Sunday Reading; column titled, 'The Bright Side;' Church of England, London, U.K., August 23, 1873,

The Denver Post; 'Nubbins;' Burns Jenkins; Denver, CO, U.S.A., February 24, 1921

The Dollar Magazine; 'The Commencement Vision,' Mrs. E. Rockwell; New York, NY, U.S.A., November, 1842

The Electric Magazine; 'The Abbé's Repentance;' London, U.K., November, 1891

The End is Nigh; British Fanzine, Michael Molcher, Comic Expo, London, U.K., 2005

The Engineers' Review; 'Lubricators—Valves in Water Columns,' p 26; Cleveland, OH, U.S.A., January, 1907

The English Review, Or, An Abstract of English and Foreign Literature; Murray, London, U.K., September, 1788

The Epoch; p 3; New York, NY, U.S.A., June 21, 1889

The European Magazine and London Review; 'Ode to Love;' Philosophical Society of Britain, J. Feilding, London, U.K., August, 1796

The Evangelical Repository and United Presbyterian Review; article, 'Church Union;' Rev. D.F. Bonner; Philadelphia, PA, U.S.A., February, 1868

The Evening Bulletin, 'Buckner on Finance' in col 1, p 3, Maysville, KY, U.S.A., May 19, 1887

The Evening Post; article; Frederick, MD, U.S.A., September 6, 1911

The Examiner; Jonathan Swift; London, England, November 2-9, 1710

The Fortnightly Review; article, 'Wilkie Collins;' Chapman and Hall, London, U.K., November 1, 1889

The Forum; 'At the Height,' Russell Herts; Mitchel Kennerly, London, U.K., May, 1911

The French Revolution: a History; Volume II, Thomas Carlyle, p 459; Charles C. Little and James Brown, Boston, MA, U.S.A., 1842

The Galaxy; 'Two Women,' Chap. 1; Sheldon & Co., New York, NY, U.S.A., June, 1870

The Galveston Daily News, Galveston, TX, U.S.A., 1866

The General Magazine and Historical Chronicle; General Alumni Society, University of Pennsylvania; Sowers Printing, Lebanon, PA, U.S.A., January, 1939

The Gentlemen's Magazine and Historical Chronicle; 'Death's Promotions &c in April, 1734;' London, England, April, 1734

The Gentleman's Magazine; Life of Books Published with Remarks; London, U.K., April, 1756

The Gentleman's Magazine, General reference, London, U.K., 1756

The Gentlemen's or London Magazine, Proc. House of Commons Monday December 1, 1784, London, U.K., April 1785; article, August, 1785; Letter to the editor, printed for D. Henry by John Nichols, London, U.K., July, 1791

The Gentleman's Magazine; or, Monthly Intelligencer, Volume 3; p306; London, U.K., 1776

The Gettysburg Times (Pennsylvania) Question and Answer Column, 'Ask the Chief' by George T. Keeney; Gettysburg, PA, U.S.A., January 1997

The Glasgow Herald; Glasgow, Scotland, U.K., May 15, 1929

The Grip; article, 'Give US Fair Play;' Toronto, ON, CA, 3 March 1882

The Guardian; article by Michael Parkin, "Barnsley Bashers Face the Chop;" London, U.K., 17 July 1978

The Guardian; article, Michael Parkin, 'Barnsley Goes Down and the Fans Love it;' London, U.K., February 23, 1980

The Hartford Courant; Letter to the Editor; Hartford, CT, U.S.A., August 29, 1839

The Harlequin; p 12; New Orleans, LA, U.S.A., Wednesday, June 18, 1899

The History of the Works of the Learned; London, U.K., September, 1704

The Independent; 'Old Abram's Lament;' New York, NY, USA, March 17, 1884

The Inland Printer, Draper Hall ad; Chicago, IL, U.S.A., January, 1910

The Instructor, Get into the Act, Hazel West Lewis, p 103, Deseret Sunday School Union, Salt Lake City Utah, April, 1963

The International, edited by George Sylvester Verreck, Moods Pub., New York, NY, U.S.A., January 1917

The Investigator, 'Mr. Rathbun's Report,' p 27; London, U.K., January, 1846

The Journal of Business Forecasting Methods & Systems; p 5; Graceway Publishing Co., New York, NY, U.S.A., 1985

The Journal of Electrical Workers and Operators; Washington, DC, U.S.A., September, 1943

The Journal of Industrial Engineering Chemistry; p 390; American Chemical Society, Eschenbach Printing, Easton, PA, U.S.A., 1921

The Kentucky Kernel, Out Of This World, Tommy Rusk, p 2; The University of Kentucky, Louisville, KY, U.S.A., April 5, 1940

The Ladies' Repository; 'Gentle Hortense; Or, The Maiden's Leap,' Emma E.H. Specht; Methodist Episcopal Church, Hitchcock and Walden, Cincinnati, OH, U.S.A., November, 1873

The Lady's Monthly Museum; Letter to the Editor; Vernor, Hood and Sharpe, London, U.K., February, 1811

The Latter Day Saints' Millennial Star; The Mormons, Historical Address; Liverpool, U.K., March 26, 1850

The L.A.W. Bulletin and Good Roads; ad; Record Petal Manufacturing Company, Boston, MA, U.S.A., February 5, 1897

The Law Times Reports; Weltzar V Zachariah; Horace Cox, London, U.K., June 1, 1867,

The Lawyers and Magistrates Magazine; 'Trial of Rnewick Williams;' W. Jones, Dublin, Ireland, July, 1790

The Literary and Pictorial Repository; George Burger; London, U.K., 1838

The Literary Digest; 'Sociological, Dr. Rainsford on the Drink Question' Rev. John Tunis; Funk and Wagnalls, New York NY, U.S.A., July 30, 1892

The Literary Gazette, Vol. 2; p 570; 'The Hermit in London or Sketches of English Manners No. IX: A Day in the Country,' author uncertain; London, U.K., 1818

The Literary World; 'Drafts at Sight in the Southwest;' July 20, 1850; 'Literature;' F.A. and G. L. Duyckinck, New York, NY, U.S.A., March 20, 1852

The Locomotive Fireman's Monthly Magazine; Editorial Correspondence; Brotherhood of Firemen, Boston, MA, U.S.A., April, 1880

The London Magazine and Monthly Chronologer; Dublin, Ireland, September, 1742

The London Magazine; Charvari; Marshall and Co., London, U.K., April, 1840

The London Magazine or Gentleman's Intelligencer; Vol. 43, poem, p 216; London, U.K., 1774

The London Medical and Physical Journal, July to December, 1822; London, U.K., 1822

The Maryville Tribune; Maryville, Ohio, U.S.A., July, 21, 1858

The McGill Daily; poem ***Fell, Fell, Fell*** p 4, col 3; Montreal, Canada, Wednesday, February 5, 1947

The Medical Pickwick, a Monthly Magazine of Wit and Humor; Julian W. Brandis, Editor, p 1; New York, NY, U.S.A., 1918

The Medical Times and Gazette; Lectures on Insanity by Edgar Shepherd, M.D.; London, U.K., December 7, 1872

The Metal Worker, Plummer and Steam Fitter; 'News of the Trade Associates;' New York, NY, U.S.A., September 26, 1919

The Michigan Alumnus; 'Confessions of a Pseudo-Quadrangler,' Arthur G. Brown; Ann Arbor, MI, U.S.A., May 13, 1932

The Midwestern; 'Bryan in Iowa,' p 2; Des Moines, IA, U.S.A., April, 1907

The Milwaukee Daily Sentinel, article, Cushing Land Dispute, August, 1853

The Missionary Magazine; London, U.K., February, 1801

The Mixer and Server; p 75; letter from Nashville, Tennessee Local 517 President, T. L. Bradshaw; March 15,1904; 'Why Not Dissolve Congress,' p 40; Cincinnati, Ohio, U.S.A., January 15, 1919

The Monthly Law Reporter; Tuttle, Denette and Chisholm, Printers, Boston, MA, U.S.A., November, 1838

The Monthly Magazine; published by Sir Richard Phillips, letter to the editor, Dr. John Aiken, London, U.K., February, 1798:

The Monthly Mirror; 'Rules for Punning;' J. Wright, London, U.K., September, 1807

The Monthly Traveller; 'The Lottery Ticket,' p 2; Boston, MA, U.S.A., April, 1931

The Motor, Volume 80; p 14; Temple Press, Ltd., London, U.K., 1942

The Mount Sterling Advocate, 'Merchants Try This,' p 6, col 1; Mount Sterling, KY, U.S.A., September 26, 1918

The National Temperance Mirror; 'Darkness and the Dawn of Another Day,' E. Harcourt Burrage; London, U.K., December, 1885

The Nation; 'Genius and Insanity,' Dr. Paul Radestock; The Evening Post Publishing, New York, NY, U.S.A., October 9, 1884

The New Monthly Magazine and Literary Journal; John Bull; Colburn and Bentley, Vol. 25, 1829 Part the Third, 'The Devorcee Devote,' p 25; Henry Colburn, London, U.K., 1833

The New Success; Vol. 4; Lowery- Madden, New York, NY, U.S.A., 1920

The New York Currier; New York, NY, U.S.A., June, 1829

The New Yorker Magazine, Volume 67, issue 11, p 43: New York, NY, U.S.A., 1991

The New York Times; *"*Sharp Sleeps In A Jail: Sheriff Grant Had Begun To Get Nervous,*"* June 19, 1887; Article, p 8, September 1, 1888; article, January 10, 1913; 'The Argot of Vaudeville Part I,' p. X7; Dec. 16, 1917; classified ad, February 16, 1953; June 20, 1959; Obituary of Ludwig van der Rohe, August, 1969; 'Fair Shake of the Sauce Bottle, Mate,' New York, NY, U.S.A., June 17, 2009

The North American Review; Editor William Tudor; Boston, MA, U.S.A., 1821

The Northern Miner newspaper, Toronto, Ontario, Canada, 1931

The Northern Monthly; May, 1864; Bailey & Noyes, p 182; Portland, OR, U.S.A., May, 1864

The Oakland Tribune; Oakland, CA, U.S.A., July, 1903; May, 1966

The Ohio Repository, Canton, OH, U.S.A., May, 1837

The Opal, A Monthly Periodical of the Lunatic Asylum, Utica, New York, 1852

The Oriental Herald; poem, 'The First Kiss of Love' by J.A. St. John, Esq.; London, U.K., November, 1828

The Ottawa Jewish Bulletin and Review, "Teams Invited to Join J.C.Y.", p 3; Ottawa Jewish Society, Ottawa, Ontario, Canada, January, 1975

The Outlook, A Family Paper; 'Bimetallism in City and County;' April 13, 1895; 'After a Year at War;' p 8; New York, NY, U.S.A., April 17, 1918

The Overland Monthly; 'South-western Slang,' p 131; August, 1869; 'A Set of Born Fools,' p 62; A. Roman Co., San Francisco, CA, U.S.A., July, 1890

The Pall Mall Magazine; The Luck of the Devil, Chapter III; London, U.K., May- Oct, 1893

The Pedagogical Seminary; June, 1903, 'Showing off and Bashfulness as Phases of Self ConcioUSness;' G. Stanley Hall and Theodate L. Smith, p 187; Lewis Wilson Worchester, MA, U.S.A., June, 1903

The Pursuit of Happiness and Other Poems, The Pursuit of Happiness, stanza XLVII; John Lane Co., J.J. Little and Ives, New York, NY, 1918, 1919

The Petroleum Gazette; 'An Easy Finishing Job,' p 9; Titusville, PA, U.S.A., January, 1910

The Phonetic Journal; Saturday, Intelligence; F. Pitman, London, U.K., July 11, 1885

The Phrenological Journal; Samuel R. Wells, Editor and publisher; New York, NY, U.S.A., March, 1870

The Pocket Magazine; letter to the Editor signed by Tristissima Tims, Liverpool, Sept. 8th, 1825, Vol. III, Knight and Lacey, London, U.K., 1825

The Portfolio; Oliver Oldschool; H. Maxwell, Philidelphia, PA, U.S.A., 1825

The Portland Gazette; Portland, MN, U.S.A., September 5, 1820

The Poster; 'The Growing USe of Poster Reds in Magazine Advertising,' Herbert Graham p 34; New York, NY, U.S.A., April 1, 1922

The Poultry Item; Sellersville, PA; February, 1921

The Principles of Human Psychology, James McKeen Catell, p 1156; London, U.K., July to December, 1918

The Public; Louis F. Post, editor, Chicago, IL, U.S.A., Saturday, June 30, 1903

The Railroad Telegrapher; Report from Illinois, M.E. Schooler; L.W. Quick, St. Louis, MO, U.S.A., December, 1904

The Rattle of the Theta Chi; 'An Audit of Fraternity Experience;' Dr. Henry M. Wriston; Norwich University, New York, NY, U.S.A., May-June 1936

The Rotarian Magazine; Rotary International, August 1913; p 29; March, 1929; 'There's Always a New Crowd,' George T Eager, p 20; August, 1937; August, 1951; Evanston, IL, U.S.A., April, 1986

The Rural Carolinian; 'Blue and Grey: The Story of the Late Civil War;' D.H. Jacques, Editor; Charleston, SC, U.S.A., April, 1873

The Saturday Evening Post; ad for Stewart's Duplex Safety Pins made by Consolidated Safety Pin Co., p 29; January19, 1901; 'A Meteorological Misadventure' by Kenneth Harris, p 7; April 22, 1905; August 8, 1914 in a Velvet Tobacco ad p 41; article, Gerald Stanley LeeMay, 1918; 'Gloma, the Beautiful Ticket Agent, or The Strike for Love' by George Kibbe Turner; Philadelphia, PA, USA, April 11, 1920

The Saturday Review of Politics, Literature, Science and Art; Austria and Naples versus England, p 1; September 6, 1856; August 31, 1872; John W. Parker and Son, London, U.K., October, 1896

The Scots Magazine; 'The Speech of Q. Marcius Philippus, in the Character of the Marquis of Tweeddale:' November, 1745; 'Parliament: Commons on the Address,' p 28; A. Murray, J. Cochran, January, 1779; 'Parliament: Commons on the Greenland Fishery;' Edenburgh, Scotland, U.K., July, 1786

The Sketch, a Journal of Art and Actuality; 'Small Talk of the Week;' London, U.K., December 6, 1899

The Southern Literary Messenger; 'The Duke of Wellington,' Asher Clarkson, December, 1853; Laurence Neville's *Lilias*, Chapter XXIII, Richmond, Virginia, U.S.A., February 1857

The Southern Pharmacutical Journal; 'Principle Success Qualities, Article III;' Dallas, TX, U.S.A., May, 1914

The Southwest Reporter; Vol. 75, case of *State v Kennedy*, West Publishing, St. Paul, MN, U.S.A., July 8 - October 7, 1903

The Speaker; 'Among the Mendips,' Theodore Compton; London, U.K., September 10, 1892

The Spectator, p 1; London, England, Friday, April 13, 1729

The Stanford Interior Journal; Ad, p 6; Stanford, KY, U.S.A., August 13, 1915

The Sunday Mail; article, Terry McCrann, 'Bare Knuckle Ride as Markets Tumble Worldwide,' *Queensland Australia,* posted on pressreader.com, August 23, 2015

The Sunday School Journal; Methodist Publishing House, Nashville, TN, U.S.A., April 12, 1890

The Tattler; Sir Richard Steele, London, England, 1709

The Taylorian; Vail and Co., 'Pleasant Hours;' Steam Printing Works, London, U.K., March, 1885

The Telegraph; New York, NY, U.S.A., Saturday June 20, 1825

The Telegraph; article by Richard Allenune, 'Coin tossing through the ages;' London, U.K., December 31, 2009

The Texas Medical Journal; 'Medical Politics in Epigram and Otherwise,' G. Frank Lydston, MD, Chicago; Austin, TX, U.S.A., January, 1909

The Text; Lowell Textile Institute, in 'Military Discipline in Girls Sanctuary,' p 1; Lowell, MA, U.S.A., January16, 1951

The Times News; Tuesday, 'New Tax Cut Bill Bobs up in Committee,' p 1; Twin Falls, ID, U.S.A., June 24, 1947

The Times News, The Golden Door; Twin Falls, ID, U.S.A., Monday April 2, 1962

The Toledo Blade, 'The Voice of Broadway; A fable from the Forties,' Dorothy Kilgallen; Toledo, IH, U.S.A., March, 1944

The Trenton Evening Times; Trenton, NJ, U.S.A., July 28, 1908

The Trenton Times; 'Letters to Editor,' p 3, col. 2; Trenton, NJ, U.S.A., November 8, 1888

The Typographical Journal; W. J. Hayes, p 49; Indianapolis, IN, U.S.A., July, 1913

The Union Postal Clerk; 'Famous Sayings of Clerks of the Mailing Division,' Washington, DC, U.S.A., January, 1921

The Union Signal; American National Women's Temperance Union Evanston, IL, U.S.A., May 8, 1919

The United States Catholic Magazine; 'Peré Jean, Or, The Jesuit Missionary, A Catholic Story Founded on Facts,' Chapter IX; J. Murphy, Baltimore, August, 1846

The U.S. Democratic Review; Thomas Printiss Kettell, "Uncle Sam and His 'B'hoys,'" Chapter II; Ketell & Moore, New York, NY, U.S.A., August, 1851

The Varsity, Big Ben Tolls Knell as Western Face Hell, p 11, col. 2; University of Toronto, Ontario, Canada, Friday October 9, 1959

The Veterinarian; Bazing; London, U.K., July, 1830

The Victorian Railways Magazine; Volume 3-4, p 102; Melbourne, Victoria, Australia, 1926

The Wall Street Journal, What do you like about your kid? p 3; New York, NY, U.S.A., June 1, 1987

The Wall Street Journal; article, Ben Zimmer; New York, NY, U.S.A., August 22, 2014

The West Coast, an Illustrated Monthly; News Notes and Comments; Los Angeles, CA, U.S.A., August, 1913

The Western Literary Messenger; 'Deacon Whitfield's Folks' from *National Era,* p 7; Buffalo, NY, U.S.A., September 1, 1891

Third Way; 'The theological book seller,' p 20; London, U.K., June, 1979

TJC Pow Wow, 'Band, 'Belles Plan White Christmas for Sunset Home,' p 1;Tyler Junior College, Tyler, TX, U.S.A., December 13, 1961

To-day; A Lost Lady of Old Years, Chapter 2, John Buchan, p 8; Howard House, London, U.K., November 5, 1898

Traffic Safety; 'One of us is Nuts,' Paul Jones; Chicago, IL, U.S.A., June, 1938

Trenton Evening Times; quote from *Washington Herald,* p 6, col. 3; Trenton, NJ, U.S.A., February 5, 1908

Turf, Field and Farm; 'Racing Notes;' November 12, 1897; 'The Rule of the Western Jocky Club, p 5; New York, NY, U.S.A., January 3, 1902

United States Interstate Commerce Commission Valuation Do*cket;* Washington, DC, U.S.A., January 7-9, 1920

United States Medical Investigator; 'Clinical Medicine;' W.A. Knight, M.D.; Duncan Bros., Chicago, IL, U.S.A., December 15, 1883

USA Today; report on off-the-grid living; Gannett Papers, New York, NY, U.S.A., April, 2006

Variety Magazine; New York, NY, U.S.A., August 28, 1934

Victoria Advocate; article, Victoria, TX, U.S.A., January 23, 1972

Washington Post; 14/ 4: December 10, 1923; 'TOYS, NOT JUST FOR KIDS,' Hank Burchard; Washington, DC, U.S.A., November 19, 1982

Water Ski Magazine; 'Oz Speak, How They Say it in Australia,' p 70; Winter Park, Florida, U.S.A., March, 1987

Watson's Magazine; 'Miscellaneous;' Thomson, GA, U.S.A., March, 1879

Welding; Louis Cassier Co., Vol. 53; London, U.K., 1985

Wesleyan-Methodist Magazine; obituary of Henry Farr; August, 1882; 'Gobo, and the War in Egypt: A Letter from the Reverend John Leverack;' London, U.K., November, 1882

Weekly World News; quote from *Chicago Tribune* re: Bo Derek; p 13; New York, NY, U.S.A., March 4, 1994

Winchester Journal, Winchester, IN, U.S.A., Oct. 25, 1876

Wisconsin State Journal; sec. 1, p 12, col. 2; 'It Happened One Night,' Earl Wilson; Madison, WI, U.S.A., July 13, 1960

With the Maine to South America, Journal, p 1; Eugeanie Hibbard, Supervising Sister of the American Hospital Ship Maine, Ovid Technologies, U.S.A., 1900

World Outlook; "The Town that Got Acquainted with Itself;" Margaret Widdemer, p 45; New York, NY, U.S.A., March, 1920

Worlds of IF, *Malice in Wonderland*, Evan Miller, ch. 2, p 14; Kingston, NY, U.S.A., January, 1954

Xi Psi Phi Quarterly, Vol. 40; p 1; Ovid Bell Press, Alton, IL, U.S.A., October, 1941

Plays and Poems

A Christmas Carol; Charles Dickens; London, U.K., 1858

A Faire Em; Act V, Scene I; William Shakespeare? England, 1592

Agamemnon; play by Aeschylus, Greece, 458 BCE

A Limb O' the Law, A Comedy in Two Acts, Act I, p 7; Martha Russell Orne, W. H. Baker, Boston, MA, U.S.A., 1892

All's Well That Ends Well; Act III, Scene ii.9, Act IV, Scene I; William Shakespeare, London, England, 1604-1605

A Midsummer Night's Dream; Act II, Scene ii.59; General Reference; William Shakespeare; London, England, first perf. 1595-1596, printed, 1600

Andrea del Sarto; Robert Browning; London, U.K., 1855

An Essay on Man, Alexander Pope, London, England, 1734

A Scout's Honor; Clifton Lisle; Penn Pub. Co., Philadelphia, PA, U.S.A., 1917

A Sketch from Private Life; Lord Byron; London, U.K., 1821

As You Like It; Act IV, Scene i; William Shakespeare; London, England, 1599, first pref. 1603

Aureng-zebe, John Dryden, London, England, 1876

A Virgin Widow: A Comedy in Five Acts, in Prose and Verse; Fra. Quarles, Second Edition; Printed for R. Royston, London, England, 1656

Borough Reform and City Deformity; Anonymous; Act I, Scene I; Edinburgh, Scotland, 1818

Canterberry Guests; Act V, Scene i; Edward Ravenscroft; Theater Royale, London, England, 1695

Cat Among the Pigeons; Georges Feydeau, trans. John Mortimer, Act I, p35; Samuel French, New York, NY, U.S.A., London, U.K. and Toronto, ON, CA, 1970

Cato; Joseph Addison; London, England, 1712

Cat's Cradle; a play by Leslie Sands, Act I, Scene i; Commercial Coulors Press, London, U.K., 1983

Catullus 101, Gaius Valerius Catullus, Rome, c. 57 BCE

Caught in the Act, Chrisnell Newton, Ames Publishing Company in Clyde, Ohio, 1888

Coriolanus; William Shakespeare; London, England, 1607

Coupon Bonds: A Play in Four Acts; John Townsend Towbridge; George M. Baker & Co., Boston, MA, U.S.A., 1876

Cymbeline; Act III. Scene iii, Exit; William Shakespeare; London, England, circa 1611, pub. 1623

Dancing Dolls, A Fantastic Comedy in One Act, Kenneth Sawyer Goodman, The Stage Guild, Chicago, IL, U.S.A., 1915

Death of a Salesman; Arthur Miller; Broadway, New York, NY, U.S.A., 1949

Detective Story; Sidney Kingsley, Act I; Dramatists Play Service, Inc., New York, NY, U.S.A., 1949

Don Juan; poem by George Gordon Byron, 6th Baron, Lord Byron; London, U.K., 1823

Douglas, A Tragedy, by John Home, Reduced to Scottish Rhyme, Chiefly the Broad Buchan Dialect; George Smith, p 57; printed for D. Chambers and Co., Aberdeen, Scotland, U.K., 1824

Every Night the Sun Goes Down; Philip Hayes Dean; Dramatist Play Service, Inc,. New York. NY, U.S.A., 1976

Faerie Queen, Volume II; Edmund Spencer, after Canto XII, notes on p 428; London, England, 1758

Gut Girls; Sarah Daniels, Act II, Scene iv; Samuel French, New York, NY, U.S.A., London, U.K., Toronto, ON, CA, 1989

Hamlet; Act I, Scent ii; William Shakespeare; London, England, 1599-1602

Helenore, Or, The Fortunate Shepherdess; Alexander Ross; Edinburgh, Scotland, 1778

Henry V; Act IV, Scene iv; William Shakespeare, London, England, 1600

Henry VI; Part II, Act I, Scene i; William Shakespeare; London, England, 1591

He Would Be a Soldier, a Comedy in Five Acts; Act III. Scene ii; Frederick Pilon; London, U.K., 1787

Hudibra; Part III, Canto iii, lines 547-550; Samuel Butler; London, England, c 1663-1878

Hush Money, play, George Dance; London, U.K., 1825

Inez, A Drama in Three Acts, Act II, Scene iv, Irene Ackerman; G.H. Bauer, New York, NY, U.S.A., 1882

Julias Ceasar; Act IV, Scene iii; William Shakespeare; London, England, 1599

King John; Act IV, Scene ii; Act V, Scene iv; Act V, scene ii, Act V, Scene vi; William Shakespeare; London, England, 1595 - 1596

King Lear; Act II; William Shakespeare; London, England, 1605 - 1606

Macbeth, Act I, Scene vii; Act II Scene ii, 721; William Shakespeare, London, U.K., 1606

Lady Windermere's Fan; Act I, Scene i; Oscar Wilde; Samuel French, New York, NY, U.S.A., 1893

La Logique des Vraisemblences; Johann Henri; Samuel Formey, London, England, 1748

Law Trickes; Act IV, p 66; John Day; London, England, 1603

Les Avaries; Eugene Briux, 1901; translated by Upton Sinclair, 1913

Love a la Mode; Act II, Scene i; Charles Macklin; John Cawthorn, London, U.K., 1806

Love Birds (2 Act Musical Comedy); Sigmund Romberg; Apollo Theater, New York, NY, U.S.A., 1921

Love Triumphant or Nature Will Prevail; Act V, Scene i; published in 'Don Sebastian, King of Portugal, Or, The Two Socias,' John Dryden; London, England, 1725

Lullaby: A Comedy; Act II, Scene ii; p 58; Dramatists Play Service, Inc., New York, NY, U.S.A., 1953

Memories; John Greenleaf Whitaker; Hartford, CT, U.S.A., 1834

Miss in her Teens, A Farce in Two Acts; Fourth Edition, Act I, Scene i; S. Powell, Dublin, Ireland, 1747

Much Adoe About Nothing; Act I, Scene i, William Shakespeare; London, England, 1598-'99, first perf. 1612

Noteriety: A Comedy; Frederick Reynolds; W. Woodfall, London, U.K., 1793

Old Man Joseph and His Family, Romulus Lenney; Act I, Scene vi; Dramatists' Play Service, New York, NY, U.S.A., 1978

Paradise Lost; John Milton; London, England, 1667

Piers Plowman, William Langland, London, England, 1730-1790

Pindarick Poem on the Happy Coronation of His Most Sacred Majesty, James II and His Illustrious Consort, Queen Mary; Mrs. Behn; printed for J. Playfors and Henry Playford, London, England, 1685

Polite Conversation,(play) Jonathan Swift, Samuel Reynardson, B. Notte, Middle Temple-Gate, England, 1738

Psyche, Act V, Scene iii, J.B.P Molière; Paris, France, 1671

Robert Bruce's March to Bannockburn; Robert Burns; Edinburgh, Scotland, 1793

Romeo and Juliette; Act II, Scene ii; William Shakespeare; London, England, 1597

Scottish Volunteers; Play, London, England, 1745

Sham; a short satire; Frank G. Tompkins; Fifty Contemporary One-Act Plays; Stewart & Kidd Co., Cincinnati, OH, U.S.A., 1921

Simply Heavenly; Play; Music by Langston Hall; Pres. Stella Hall,;New York, May 21, 1957

Sir Anthony Love; or The Rambling Lady; Act I; Thomas Southerne; Joseph Fox, London, England, 1691

Sixteen String Jack, Act I, Scene ii, Leman Rede G.H. Davidson, London, U.K, c.1835

So Long! Walt Whitman, Leaves of Grass, Thayer and Eldridge, Boston, MA, U.S.A., 1860

Stay, Carl Stay, the first play in *Stay Carl Stay; Best Half Foot Forward; Pillow Talk: Three One-act Plays;* Peter Tolan, p 35; Dramitists Play Service, Inc., New York, NY, U.S.A., 1991

Stoop to Conquer; Oliver Goldsmith; London, U.K., 1771

The Act of Preaching; by a French author, made English by F. B. Esquire, Cant. III, p 44, London, England, 1685

The American Magazine; 'Salvation;' John Taintor Foote, p 49; Phillips Publishing, New York, NY, USA, July, 1913

The Atheist: Or the Second Part of the Soldier's Fortune; Thomas Otway, Act II; printed for R. Bentley and J. Tonson, London, England, 1684

The Automobile; 'Guttenberg Meet Attracts Thousands;' The Class Journal Company, New York, NY, U.S.A., Thursday, June 22, 1911

The British Apollo; Or Curious Amusements for the Ingenious; London, Preformed December 31, 1708

The Broken Sword; Act I, Scene ii; William Dimond; Royal Covenant Garden Theater, London, U.K., 1816

The Busy Body; a Comedy, Act V, Scene vii; Susannah Centlivere; John Bell, London, U.K., 1791

The Charge of the Light Brigade; Alfred, Lord Tennyson; London, U.K., 1864

The Comedy of Errors; William Shakespeare; London, England, 1594-1595

The Diaboliad*: a poem. Dedicated to the worst man in His Majesty's **dominions;*** William Combe, p 24; G. Kearsley, London, England, 1677

The Disagreeable Surprise; Act I, Scene iii; John Cumberland; Cumberland's British Theater: With Remarks, Biographical and Critical, London, U.K., 1828

The Disposal; One Act play, William Inge; Philadelphia, PA, U.S.A., 1968

The Excellent Comedie of Two the Moste Faithfullest Freendes, Damon and Pithias; Ralph Edwards; London, England, c 1566

The Exercise; Lewis John Carlino p 46; Dramatist's Play Service, Inc., New York, NY, U.S.A., 1963, 1968

The False Count; a Comedy, Aphra Behn (Iii1); London, England, 1681

The Fatal Secret; A Tragedy, Mr. Theobald, Act IV, Scene i; p 37: London, England, 1737

The Follies of Fashion, A Comedy in Five Acts; Richard Butler, Earl of Glengail Act III, Scene i; London, U.K., 1830

The Gentle Shepherd, A Scotts Pastoral Comedy**,** Alan Ramsay, Edinburgh, Scotland, 1725

The Haunted Tower, a Comic Opera in Three Acts; Act III, Scene ii; James Cobb; printed for P. Burne; and J. Jones, **London, U.K., 1790**

The Honest Thieves, A Farce in Two Acts; Act II Scene iv; T. Knight; Theater-Royale, London, May 9, 1797

The Humours of an Election, a Farce; as Performed at the Theater Royal in Covent Garden, Scene One; F. Pilon Printed for G. Kearsly, London, England, 1780

The Iliad; XXXII, 503; Homer, Greece, c 1200 BCE; English translation, Alexander Pope; London, England, 1715

The Illustrated Magazine; 'A Peep at the Black Country;' Mrs. Carolyn A. White; London, U.K., 1865

The Inpossible Years, A Comedy in Two Acts; Act I, Scene ii; Bob Fisher; Arthur Marx, Samuel French, New York, NY, U.S.A., 1964

The Jew of Malta; Act II, Scene i; Christopher Marlow; London, England, 1633

The Lady's Magazine; 'The Trial of Mrs. Jane Butterfield,' p 3; London, U.K., August, 1775

The Lansing College Magazine; Advertisements, 'Don't Read This; Lansing College, Shoreham, Sussex, U.K., April, 1878

The Life and Death of Richard III; Act IV, Scene iii; written circa 1592; The Works of William Shakespeare; London, England, 1714

The Maiden Queen; Act II, Scene iii; John Dryden; London, England, 1667

The Merchant of Venice; Act I, scene ii; William Shakespeare; London, England, 1586

The Merry Wives of Windsor; William Shakespeare, Act II, Scene ii; London, England, circa 1597

The Miseries of Enforst Marriage; Played by His Majesties Servants by George Wilkins, Act V; I. N. for Richard Tharale, London, England, 1637

The Newtonton; 'Cricket, Tigenmouth v Newton College;' Newton Abbot; London, U.K., 1877

The Old Law; Thomas Middleton and Philip Massinger, Act V, Scene i; 1599, pub, London, U.K., 1618

The Open Gate: An Original Domestic Drama in One Act, Charles Haddon Chambers, Samuel French, New York, NY, U.S.A., 1887

The Padlock, A Comic Opera; 1766, Charles Dibdin; Act I Scene vi; Royal Theater, London, U.K., 1768

The Passing Regiment, A Comedy of the Day in Five Acts, Augustin Daly, New York, NY, U.S.A., 1884

The Pastime and Recreation of the Queen of Fairies in Fairyland, the Centre of the Earth; p 209; *Poems by Eminent Ladies Volume II;* London, U.K., 1755

The Plain-Dealer: A Comedy, as it is Acted at the Theater Royal a play by "Mr. (William) Wycherley," Act V; Scene I; p 77; London, England, 1677

The Pot of Gold; Act II, circa 210 BCE; Rome; English trans., Paul Nixon; William Heinsman, London, U.K., 1912

The Refusal, Or, The Ladies Philosophy; Act V; London, England, 1721

The Rent Day; Act I, Scene iv, Douglas William Jerrold; John Miller, London, U.K., 1834

The Road Not Taken; Robert Frost, in Mountain Interval; Henry Holt and Co., New York, NY, U.S.A., 1916

The Rover; Alphra Behm; Dorsett Garden Theater, London, U.K., March 24, 1677

The Royal Family: A Comedy in Three Acts; George S. Kaufman and Edna Ferber, Act I; Samuel Finch, New York, Hollywood, London and Toranto, ON, CA, 1929-1977

The Sin of Patrick Muldune; John McLiam; Dramitists Play Service, New York, NY, U.S.A., 1952, 1957

The Spanish Tragedy; Thomas Kyd; London, England, 1592

The Taming of the Shrew; Act V, Scene xii; William Shakespeare, London, England, 1590

The Tempest; Act V, Scene I; William Shakespeare; London, England, 1610

The Trve Tragedie of Richard III; (c. 1590) entered into the Stationer's Register; London, England, June 19, 1594

The Veteran of 1812, Act I, Scene i; T. Trask Woodward; DeWitt, New York, NY, 1883

The Wee Raggit Laddie; James Ballantyne, Edenborough, Scotland, 1883

The World and His Wife, Broadway Play, Charles Frederic Nirdlinger, New York, NY, U.S.A., 1908

Too Civil by Half, *A Farce in Two Acts*; John Dent; London, U.K., 1783

Tooth and Claw; Act I, Scene ii;, Greg McGee; Victoria University Press, Footscray, Victoria, Australia, 1984

Trinculo's Trip to the Jubilee, Edward Thompson; printed for A. Moran, London, U.K., 1769

Troilus and Criseyde; Geoffrey Chaucer; London, England, circa 1374

Turn Out! A musical farce, Matthew P. King, Washington and Roland, London, U.K., 1812

Two Gentlemen of Verona; Act IV Scene iv; William Shakespeare, 1589 -1592

Venus and Adonis; William Shakespeare; Richard Field, London, England, 1593

Websites: Specific URLs

http://cloanto.com/users/mcb/19950127giflzw.html

http://languagecaster.com/weekly-football-phrase-cliche-bad-day-office/

http://history.nasa.gov/SP-350/ch-13-1.html (Apollo Expeditions to the Moon, Chap. 13.1, James A. Lovell)

http://phrases.com/easy-as-rolling-off-a-log

http://quod.lib.umich.edu/cgi/k/kjv/kjv-idx?

https://archive.org/details/TheArtOfTranslationScholz/page/n11?q=%22greetings+and+salutations%22

https://archive.org/details/googlebooks

https://dare.wisc.edu/words/quarterly-updates/quarterly-update-1/beat-a-hen-a-pecking

https://d.lib.rochester.edu/teams/text/lupack-lancelot-of -the-laik-and-sir-tristrem-la

https://english.stackexchange.com/questions/226340/idiom-to-be-off-the-wall
https://english.stockexchange.com/questions/390539.when-has-a-hot-minute-meant-a-long-time, https://english.stackexchange.com/questions/290389/what-is-the -history-of-the-expression-many-moons-ago,
https://english.stackexchange.com/questions/43986/whats-the-evolution-of -the -phrase-milk-it-for-all-its-worth; https://englsih.stackexchange.com/questions/152446/much-obliged-old-fashioned-polite-pedantic

https://english.stackexchange.com/questions/188364/what-is-the-meaning-of-the-expression-handsome-devil
https://ell.stackexchange.com/questions/5498/does-to-put-something-in-mothballs-mean-the -same-as-to-mothball-something

https://en.wikipedia.org/wiki/.com

https://google.com/amp/s/amp.reddit.com/r/30Rock

https://idiomation.wordpress.com/tag/enough-to-feed-coxs-army/
https://idiomation.wordpress.com/2015/10/13/argue-with-a-fence-post/

https://merriam-webster.com/words-at-play/so-long-origin

https://newsmaven.io/indiancountrytoday/archive/theodore-roosevelt-the-only-good-indians-are-the-dead-indians-oN1cdfuEW02KzOVVyrp7ig/

https://phrases.org.uk/meanings/my-better-half.html,
https://phrases.org.uk/meanings/sam-hill.html

https://prezi.com/3ffi-kv_aelc/dna-doesnt-lie/

https://lonewolf.com/twin-flame/

https://quora.com/Where-did-the-concept-of-twin-flames-originate

https://searchmicroservices.techtarget.com/definition/breadcrumbtrail

https://smallbiztrends.com/2011/03/what-is-an-app.html

https://web.archive.org/web/20120220152124/ \
http://jcs.dtic.mil/j6/cceb/acps/acp125/ACP125F.pdf#

https://writingexplained.org/idiom-dictionary/tough-as-nailshttps://writingexplained.org/idiom-dictionary/brush-up

https://www.atlasobscura.com/articles/origin-bleeding-heart-liberal

https://www.britannica.com/topic/Kuna

https://www.cbsnews.com/news/a-wild-herr/

https://www.dictionary.com/brouse/saddle

https://www.englishforums.com/English/GetInOnTheAction/cmcxw/post.htm

https://www.english.stockexchange.com

https://www.etymonline.com/word/deal;
https://www.etymonline.com/word/fraidy-cat;
https://www.etymonline.com/word/numbskull;
https://www.etymonline.com/word/mothball;
https://www.etomonline.com/word/hard;
https://www.etymonline.com/word/point%20of%20view
https://www.etymonline.com/word/boob%20tube;
https://etymonline.com-saddle
https://etymonline.com/word/hoot

http://www.etymonline.com-word-flip
https://www.etymonline.com/word/zero

https://www.etymonline.com/word/brush
http://www.etomonline.com/word/mealy-mouthed

https://www.grammarphobia.com/blog/2010/03/and-by-the-way.html

https://www.google.com/search?q=who+first+said+nobody+cares+how+much+you+know+until+they+know+how+moch+you+care (https://theodorerrooseveltcenter.org)

https://www.idioms.online/dont-mention-it/

https://www.knowyourphrase.com/scaredy-cat

http:www.mootgame.com/mootlistOut/06_14_05.html

https://www.phrases.org.uk/bulletin_board/30/messages/2049.html
https://www.phrases.org.uk/bulletin_board/60/messages/1021.html
https://www.phrases.org.uk/meanings'a-bad-penny-always-turns-up.htm
https://www.phrases.org.uk/meanings/fish-or-cut-bait.html;
https//www.phrases.org.uk/meanings/hissy-fit
https://www.phrases.org.uk/meanings/nitty-gritty.html
https://www.phrases.org.uk/bulletin_board/60/messages/187.html
http://www.phrases.org.uk/meanings/188800.html
https://www.phrases.org.uk/meanings/ raise-cain
https://phrases.org.uk/bulletin_board/56/messages/430.html
https://phrases.org.uk/bulletin_board/14/messages/695.html
https://www.phrases.org/uk/bulletin_board/61/messages/631.html
https://www.phrases.org.uk/meanings/slush-fund.html
https://www.phrases.org.uk/meanings/out-of-sorts.html

https://www.quora.com/What-does-the-phrase-monkey-on-your-back-mean
https://www.quara.com/How-did-the-slang-term-rad-originate

https://www.solidus.info/en/the-lowdown-on-shoes/expressions/

https://www.songfacts.com/facts/aerosmith/dream-on

https://www.theidioms.com/go-through-channels/; https://www.theidioms.com/cutting-edge/

https://www.urbandictionary.com/define.php?term=hell%20on%20wheels

http://verbmall.blogspot.com/2007/12/coin-of-realm-redux.html

http://www.bbcamerica.com/anglophenia/2011/12/frasers-phrases-spot-on-bang-on-and-wicked-wizards

http://www.ccel.org/ccel/spurgeon/sermons58.x.html

http://www.google.com/amp/ask.metafilter.com/23973/coulda-shoulda-woulda/amp

http://www.mayodanpolice.org/boozeitloseit.html

http://www.philosophybasics.com/philosophers_nietzsche.html

http://www.waywordradio.org/I've-slept-since-then/

http://www.worldwidewords.org/qu-chi4.htm
http://www.worldwidewords.org/qa/qa-doo2.htm
http://www.worldwidewords.org/qa/qa-wor4.htm

Contributors

Major:

Niven Sinclair, Esq., Surry, U.K.; friend, retired entrepreneur (deceased), FSA Scot; contributor of hundreds of British sayings

Kelly Marlowe, McMinnville, TN, U.S.A.; friend, radio host and announcer, contributor- mostly Southern U.S. sayings

Rondo B B Me, Queensland, Australia; friend, author; most Aussie sayings

D. Kent Hesselbein. Manchester, TN, U.S.A.; friend, associate; cover design

Kathy Ann Barney, Greenville, SC, U.S.A.; friend, editor, proofer

Others

Rhonda St. Clair, McMinnville, TN, U.S.A.; devoted wife, contributor

Allison Clark, Cookeville, TN, U.S.A.; friend, Tennessee Tech University basketball coach, author, contributor

Joe Bost, McMinnville, TN, U.S.A.; friend, retired school principle, contributor

Gerald Sinclair, Queensland, Australia; friend, author, contributor, Aussie expressions

Tommy Schultz, Nashville, TN, U.S.A.; friend, political campaign manager, contributor

Bunnie V. Stamps, Jasper, GA, U.S.A.; 1st cousin, State of Georgia DOT Secretary, contributor

Cordell Smith, McMinnville, TN, U.S.A.; contributor

April Geartner, Lascassas, TN, U.S.A.. neice, contributor

Maria Alverez Vint, Corinth, TX, U.S.A., friend, associate, contributor

Made in the USA
Columbia, SC
03 April 2022

58462581R00386